MARKET SHARE REPORTER

ISSN 1052-9578

MARKET SHARE REPORTER

AN ANNUAL COMPILATION

OF REPORTED MARKET SHARE

DATA ON COMPANIES,

PRODUCTS, AND SERVICES

2 0 0 7

Volume 1

ROBERT S. LAZICH, Editor

THOMSON

GALE

Detroit • New York • San Francisco • New Haven, Conn. • Waterville, Maine • London • Munich

Market Share Reporter 2007
Robert S. Lazich

Project Editor
Virgil L. Burton III

Editorial
Joyce P. Simkin, Susan M. Turner

Manufacturing
Rita Wimberley

ISBN 0-7876-8609-3 (2 vol. set)
ISBN 0-7876-9462-2 (Vol. 1)
ISBN 0-7876-9463-0 (Vol. 2)
ISSN 1052-9578

TABLE OF CONTENTS

Indexes

Appendix I - Industrial Classifications

TABLE OF TOPICS

The *Table of Topics* lists all topics used in *Market Share Reporter* in alphabetical order. One or more page references follow each topic; the page references identify the starting point where the topic is shown. The same topic name may be used under different SICs; therefore, in some cases, more than one page reference is provided. Roman numerals indicate volume number.

INTRODUCTION

Market Share Reporter (MSR) is a compilation of market share reports from periodical literature. As shown by reviews of previous editions plus correspondence and telephone contact with many users, this is a unique resource for competitive analysis, diversification planning, marketing research, and other forms of economic and policy analysis.

This is the seventeenth edition of *Market Share Reporter*. In previous editions, *Market Share Reporter* presented market share data on the North American market. In 1997, *World Market Share Reporter* was first published, which provided international coverage -- market shares on global industries or markets in countries other than the United States, Canada and Mexico.

The editorial staff of *Market Share Reporter* decided that the needs of the users would best be served by combining the two titles into one two-volume set. *Market Share Reporter* became a two-volume title with the fifteenth edition. Previously, users would need to consult two separate books to gather research on market shares. The 2007 edition of *MSR* now provides market share information on domestic and international markets in one book. A user seeking market share information on the automobile market, for example, will find entries covering the United States as well as foreign countries and the entire global industry. Having such data together in one chapter should be informative and entertaining to readers.

Market Share Reporter contains many of the same features that it had in recent editions. Frequent users will find that the book is still primarily arranged around the *Standard Industrial Classification* (SIC) code. Features of the 2007 edition include—

- More than 3,600 entries, all new or updated.
- Entries arranged under both SIC and NAICS codes.
- Corporate, brand, product, service and commodity market shares.
- Coverage of private and public sector activities.
- Comprehensive indexes, including products, companies, brands, places, sources, NAICS, ISIC, Harmonized and SIC codes.
- Table of Topics showing topical subdivisions of chapters with page references.
- Graphics.
- Annotated source listing—provides publishers' information for journals cited in this edition of *MSR*.
- *MSR* is a one-of-a-kind resource for ready reference, marketing research, economic analysis, planning, and a host of other disciplines.

Categories of Market Shares

Entries in *Market Share Reporter* fall into four broad categories. Items were included if they showed the relative strengths of participants in a market or provided subdivisions of economic activity in some manner that could assist the analyst.

- *Corporate market shares* show the names of companies that participate in an industry, produce a product, or provide a service. Each company's market share is shown as a percent of total industry or product sales for a defined period, usually a year. In some cases, the company's share represents the share of the sales of the companies shown (group total)—because shares of the total market were not cited in the source or were not relevant. In some corporate share tables, brand information appears behind company names in parentheses. In these cases, the tables can be located using either the company or the brand index.

- *Institutional shares* are like corporate shares but show the shares of other kinds of organizations. The most common institutional entries in *MSR* display the shares of states, provinces, or regions in an activity. The shares of not-for-profit organizations in some economic or service functions fall under this heading.

- *Brand market shares* are similar to corporate shares with the difference that brand names are shown. Brand names include equivalent categories such as the names of television programs, magazines, publishers' imprints, etc. In some cases, the names of corporations appear in parentheses behind the brand name; in these cases, tables can be located using either the brand or the company index.

- *Product, commodity, service, and facility shares* feature a broad category (e.g. household appliances) and show how the category is subdivided into components (e.g. refrigerators, ranges, washing machines, dryers, and dishwashers). Entries under this category cover products (autos, lawnmowers, polyethylene, etc.), commodities (cattle, grains, crops); services (telephone, childcare), and facilities (port berths, hotel suites, etc.). Subdivisions may be products, categories of services (long-distance telephone, residential phone service, 800-service), types of commodities (varieties of grain), size categories (e.g., horsepower ranges), modes (rail, air, barge), types of facilities (categories of hospitals, ports, and the like), or other subdivisions.

- *Other shares.* MSR includes a number of entries that show subdivisions, breakdowns, and shares that do not fit neatly into the above categorizations but properly belong in such a book because they shed light on public policy, foreign trade, and other subjects of general interest. These items include, for instance, subdivisions of governmental expenditures, environmental issues, and the like.

Coverage

MSR reports on *published* market shares rather than attempting exhaustive coverage of the market shares, say, of all major corporations and of all products and services. Despite this limitation, *MSR* holds share information on more than 6,780 companies, more than 3,210 brands, and more than 2,390 product, commodity, service, and facility categories. Several entries are usually available for each industry group in the SIC classification; omitted groups are those that do not play a conventional role in the market, e.g., Private Households (SIC 88).

As pointed out in previous editions, *MSR* tends to reflect the current concerns of the business press. In addition to being a source of market share data, it mirrors journalistic preoccupations, issues in the business community, and events abroad. Important and controversial industries and activities get most of the ink. Heavy coverage is provided in those areas that are—

- large, important, basic (autos, chemicals)
- on the leading edge of technological change (computers, electronics, software)
- very competitive (toiletries, beer, soft drinks)
- in the news because of product recalls, new product introductions, mergers and acquisitions, lawsuits, and for other reasons
- relate to popular issues (environment, crime), or have excellent coverage in their respective trade press.

Variation in coverage from previous editions is due in part to publication cycles of sources and a different mix of brokerage house reports for the period covered (due to shifting interests within the investment community).

How Entries Are Prepared

In many cases, several entries are provided on a subject each citing the same companies. No attempt was made to eliminate such seeming duplication if the publishing and/or original sources were different and the market shares were not identical. Those who work with such data know that market share reports are often little more than the "best guesses" of knowledgeable observers rather than precise measurements. To the planner or analyst, variant reports about an industry's market shares are useful for interpreting the data.

Publications appearing in the January 2005 to July 2006 period were used in preparing *MSR*. Market shares were gathered from newspapers, magazines, newsletters, government reports, market research studies and press releases.

As a rule, material on market share data for 2006 were used by preference; in response to reader requests, we have included historical data when available. In some instances, information for earlier years was included if the category was unique or if the earlier year was necessary for context. In a number of cases, projections for 2007 and later years were also included.

The user may deem some of the entries covering the global marketplace "old". However, it is important to note that when analyzing the international marketplace the most recent data available may indeed be several years old. Such data are kept to a minimum and are used only if the share provides coverage of an unusual market or a popular, competitive one (diapers or toiletries, for example).

Entry titles. Because *Market Share Reporter* now holds entries on domestic and international markets, titles have become more descriptive than in previous editions. Each entry will indicate in the title if it is for a particular country, state, city or region. An entry may address a global market (Top Computer Makers World-

wide). In such entries, the title will feature "worldwide" or "global" so that the reader understands the market being discussed.

Many entries do not feature any geographical reference in the title. In these instances, the entries are referring to the market in the United States. Market data on the United States make up well over half the entries in this book, so such an editorial decision seemed reasonable to the staff of *MSR*.

It is important to note that some sources do not explicitly state whether the market shares they publish are for the domestic or international market. Often, it is obvious by some measure in the article—dollar sales or unit shipments, for example—if the shares describe the United States or some global industry. However, in a handful of entries the staff of *MSR* has had to use their best judgment. As stated earlier, market share data are often best guesses of knowledgeable observers. The staff of *MSR* feels that its own best guesses have been sufficient.

SIC and NAICS

The United States has used the *Standard Industrial Classification* code for roughly 60 years. It became clear, however, that the SIC code had its limitations. It was difficult to address the new technologies and ways of selling that had come to the global marketplace, such as warehouse clubs, office supply stores, and Internet businesses and technology. The *North American Industrial Classification System (NAICS)* is intended to serve as a more comprehensive method to classify industries.

The transition between SIC and NAICS was implemented for the *1997 Economic Census*. The new NAICS coding—which is used in the United States, Canada and Mexico—is a major revamping of the industrial classification system. *NAICS* coding includes new sectors and a more detailed study of the "services" category (industries that would fall under the 5300 and higher section of the SIC code).

Under *NAICS* coding, a 6-digit industry code replaces the old 4-digit SIC code. The first two digits indicate the sector, the third the subsector, the fourth designates the industry group, the fifth the NAICS industry and the sixth the national industry. There are 20 sectors in *NAICS* and 1,170 industries.

Because the SIC code is still the more popular classification system, *Market Share Reporter* is organized around its coding. However, each entry now contains *NAICS* codes appropriate to the industry being discussed. Most entries will have only one *NAICS* code. However, some entries will have more than one code (three is the maximum). As stated, *NAICS* codes are more detailed than *SIC* classifications. Because of this, more than one *NAICS* code was sometimes necessary to provide the most accurate description of the industry being analyzed.

More information about *NAICS* is available through the U.S. Department of Commerce web site at http://www.ntis.gov/naics.

"Unusual" Market Shares

Some reviewers of the first edition questioned—sometimes tongue-in-cheek, sometimes seriously—the inclusion of tables on such topics as computer crime, the pet population, children's allowances, governmental budgets, and weapons system stockpiles. Indeed, some of these categories do not fit the sober meaning of "market share." A few tables on such subjects are present in every edition—because they provide market information, albeit indirectly, or because they are the "market share equivalents" in an industrial classification which is in the public sector or dominated by the public sector's purchasing power.

Organization of Chapters

Market Share Reporter is organized into chapters by 2-digit SIC categories (industry groups). The exception is the first chapter, entitled *General Interest and Broad Topics*; this chapter holds all entries that bridge two or more 2-digit SIC industry codes (e.g. retailing in general, beverage containers, building materials, etc.) and cannot, therefore, be classified using the SIC system without distortion. Please note, however, that a topic in this chapter will often have one or more additional entries later—here the table could be assigned to a detailed industry. Thus, in addition to tables on packaging in the first chapter, numerous tables appear later which deal with glass containers, metal cans, etc.

Within each chapter, entries are shown by 4-digit SIC (industry level). Within blocks of 4-digit SIC entries, entries are sorted alphabetically by topic, then alphabetically by title.

SIC and Topic Assignments

MSR's SIC classifications are based on the coding as defined in the *Standard Industrial Classification Manual* for 1987, issued by the Bureau of the Census, Department of Commerce. This 1987 classification system introduced significant revisions to the 1972 classification (as slightly modified in 1977); the 1972 system is still in widespread use (even by the Federal government); care should be used in comparing data classified in the new and in the old way.

The closest appropriate 4-digit SIC was assigned to each table. In many cases, a 3-digit SIC had to be used because the substance of the table was broader than the nearest 4-digit SIC category. Such SICs always end with a zero. In yet other cases, the closest classification possible was at the 2-digit level; these SICs terminate with double-zero. If the content of the table did not fit the 2-digit level, it was assigned to the first chapter of *MSR* and classified by topic only.

Topic assignments are based on terminology for commodities, products, industries, and services in the SIC Manual; however, in many cases phrasing has been simplified, shortened, or updated; in general, journalistically succinct rather than bureaucratically exhaustive phraseology was used throughout.

Organization of Entries

Entries are organized in a uniform manner. A sample entry is provided below. Explanations for each part of an entry, shown in boxes, are provided below the sample.

★ 753 ★ 1
Pasta 2
SIC: 2098; NAICS: 311823 3

Top Noodle Brands, 2006 4

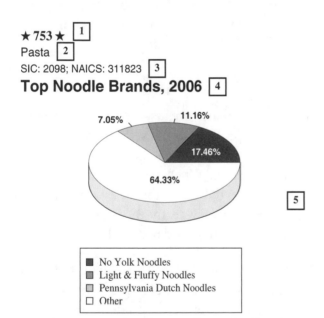

5

■ No Yolk Noodles
■ Light & Fluffy Noodles
■ Pennsylvania Dutch Noodles
□ Other

Brands are ranked by sales in millions of dollars for the 52 weeks ended January 22, 2006. 6

	($ mil.)	Share 7
No Yolk Noodles	$ 20.16	17.46%
Light & Fluffy Noodles	12.88	11.16
Pennsylvania Dutch Noodles	8.14	7.05 8
Other	74.27	64.33

Source: *Food Institute Report,* April 10, 2006, p. 4, from Information Resources Inc. 9

1 *Entry Number.* A numeral between star symbols. Used for locating an entry from the index.

2 *Topic.* Second line, small type. Gives the broad or general product or service category of the entry. The topic for Top Noodle Brands, 2006 is Pasta.

3 *SIC and NAICS Code.* Second line, small type, follows the topic. General entries in the first chapter do not have an SIC code.

4 *Title.* Third line, large type. Describes the entry with a headline.

5 *Graphic.* When a graphic is present, it follows the title. Some entries will be illustrated with a pie or bar chart. The information used to create the graphic is always shown below the pie or bar chart.

6 *Note Block.* When present, follows the title and is in italic type. The note provides contextual information about the entry to make the data more understandable. Special notes about the data, information about time periods covered, market totals, and other comments are provided. Self-explanatory entries do not have a note block.

7 *Column headers.* Follow the note block. Some entries have more than one column or the single column requires a header. In these cases, column headers are used to describe information covered in the column. In most cases, column headers arc years (2006) or indicators of type and magnitude ($ mil.). Column headers are shown only when necessary for clarity of presentation.

8 *Body.* Follows the note block or the column header and shows the actual data in two or more columns. In most cases, individual rows of data in the body are arranged in descending order, with the largest market share holder heading the list. Collective shares, usually labeled "Others" are placed last.

9 *Source.* Follows the body. All entries cite the source of the table, the date of publication, and the page number (if given). In many cases, the publisher obtained the information from another source (primary source); in all such cases, the primary source is also shown.

Continued entries. Entries that extend over two adjacent columns on the same page are not marked to indicate continuation with *continue* in the second column. Entries that extend over two pages are marked *Continued on the next page.* Entries carried over from the previous page repeat the entry number, topic (followed by the word *continued*), title, and column header (if any).

Use of Names

Company Names. The editors reproduced company names as they appeared in the source unless it was clearly evident from the name and the context that a name had been misspelled in the original. Large companies, of course, tend to appear in a large number of entries and in variant renditions. General Electric Corporation may appear as GE, General Electric, General Electric Corp., GE Corp., and other variants. No attempt was made to enforce a uniform rendition of names in the entries. In the Company Index, variant renditions were reduced to a single version or cross-referenced.

Use of Numbers

Throughout *MSR*, tables showing percentage breakdowns may add to less than 100 or fractionally more than 100 due to rounding. In those cases where only a few leading participants in a market are shown, the total of the shares may be substantially less than 100.

Numbers in the note block showing the total size of the market are provided with as many significant digits as possible in order to permit the user to calculate the sales of a particular company by multiplying the market total by the market share.

In a relatively small number of entries, actual unit or dollar information is provided rather than share information in percent. In such cases, the denomination of the unit (tons, gallons, $) and its magnitude (thousands, indicated by 000, millions indicated by mil., and billions indicated by bil.) are mentioned in the note block or are shown in the column header.

Data in some entries are based on different kinds of currencies and different weight and liquid measures. Where necessary, the unit is identified in the note block or in the column header. Examples are long tons, short tons, metric tons or Canadian dollars, etc.

Graphics

Pie and bar charts are used to illustrate some of the entries. The graphics show the names of companies, products, and services when they fit on the charts. When room is insufficient to accommodate the label, the first word of a full name is used followed by three periods (...) to indicate omission of the rest of the label.

Pie charts include a key to indicate the name that corresponds to each "pie slice" in the graphic. Bar charts now include a scale on the bottom axis with a denomination such as "million dollars" or "billion units." The largest share sets the width of the column, and smaller shares are drawn in proportion.

In the case of more than one column of data, the pie or bar graph always represents the most recent year of data.

Sources

The majority of entries were extracted from newspapers and from general purpose, trade, and technical periodicals normally available in larger public, special, or university libraries.

Many World Wide Web sources have also been used. For these sources the citation includes the Web address, the date on which the article was retrieved, and, if possible, the title of the article or report. If the data comes from a report or a press release the source will provide the publication date. While the Internet is a source of wonderful information, it does present a researcher with certain challenges. In many cases Web pages have no title and/or author name. If data are cited, a year may not be included. Furthermore, it is not uncommon for Web pages to be moved or be temporarily out of operation.

In previous editions, *MSR* referred to sources used as primary and original sources. The primary source was the source from which the MSR editors obtained the market share data. This primary source is the one that appeared in the citation following the word "Source." The original source was the source from which the primary source was quoting. This original source could be another publication, brokerage house, market research firm, government agency, etc. The name of the original source appeared after the "from" in the market share entry citation.

After receiving requests from several librarians and other *MSR* users, the editorial staff has decided to change the terms used in referring to sources. Our intention is to more closely mirror the source terminology used by librarians generally.

What we used to call an original source will now be referred to as the *primary source*. What we used to call the primary source will now appear as either the *primary source* (when it refers to the source that has originated the market data) or the *secondary source* (when it refers to a source that is reproducing market data from another source, when it is quoting from the primary source). Not all entries in *MSR* have both a primary and secondary source.

The main reason for this change is recognition that the comments from users on this point make a great deal of sense. This change brings *MSR* into greater alignment with the actual definitions of the terms primary source and secondary source. A primary source stands on its own. It is the source that conducts the market research, originated the data. A secondary source provides commentary on the research published by the primary source.

It is helpful to study the sample book entry shown earlier in this introduction to better understand this distinction. Information Resources Inc. (IRI) is a well-known market research firm that provides data on the packaged goods industry. It is the primary source for the sample entry. *Food Institute Report* is a newsletter that features articles on all facets of the food industry. It quoted IRI's data in an article and it was this article that the editors used in producing the sample entry. In this case, *Food Institute Report* is the secondary source.

There were 2,474 unique primary and secondary sources used in this edition of *Market Share Reporter*.

It is important to note that this editorial change only affects the Source Index. It does not affect the formatting and presentation of the entries themselves.

Indexes

Market Share Reporter features five indexes and two appendices.

- **Source Index**. This index holds 2,474 references in two groupings. *Primary sources* are the original sources for the data. They are the sources that have conducted the survey or done the market research. *Secondary sources* cite the primary sources' data. Each item in the index is followed by one or more entry numbers arranged sequentially, beginning with the first mention of the source.

- **Place Names Index**. This index provides references to cities, states, parks and regions in North America. Five hundred sixty three place name citations are included. References are to entry numbers.

- **Products, Services, Names and Issues Index**. This index holds 2,391 references to products, personal names and services in alphabetical order. The index also lists subject categories that do not fit the definition of a product or service but properly belong in the index. Examples include *aquariums, consumer spending, crime, defense spending, economies, lotteries*, and the like. Some listings are abbreviations for such things as chemical substances and computer software which may not be meaningful to those unfamiliar with the industries. Wherever possible, the full name is also provided for abbreviations commonly in use. Proper names are indexed by both first name and last name. Each listing is followed by one or more references to entry numbers.

- **Company Index**. This index shows references to 6,783 company names by entry number. Companies are arranged in alphabetical order. In some cases, the market share table from which the company name was derived showed the share for a combination of two or more companies; these combinations are reproduced in the index.

- **Brand Index**. The Brand Index shows references to 3,216 brands by entry number. The arrangement is alphabetical. Brands include names of publications, computer software, operating systems, etc., as well as the more conventional brand names (Coca Cola, Maxwell House, Budweiser, etc.)

Appendix I

- **SIC Coverage**. The first appendix shows SICs covered by *Market Share Reporter*. The listing shows major SIC groupings at the 2-digit level as bold-face headings followed by 4-digit SIC numbers, the names of the SIC, and a *page* reference (rather than a reference to an entry number, as in the indexes). The page shows the first occurrence of the SIC in the book. *MSR*'s SIC coverage is quite comprehensive, as shown in the appendix. However, many 4-digit SIC categories are further divided into major product groupings. Not all of these have corresponding entries in the book.

- **NAICS Coverage**. This section of the appendix contains a listing of the *North American Industry Classification System* codes that appear in *Market Share Reporter*. NAICS is a six digit classification system that covers 20 sectors and 1,170 industries.

- **ISIC Coverage**. This section of the appendix provides a listing of the International Standard Industrial Classification (ISIC) codes that appear in *Market Share Reporter*. The ISIC system, like the Harmonized Codes system, is a coding system similar to NAICS. The ISIC features broader classifications and is less widely used than the NAICS. The ISIC listing shows the 4-digit level along with the name of the industry. References to entries are not included.

- **HC Coverage**. This section provides a listing of the Harmonized Commodity classifications that appear in *MSR*. The listing shows industrial groups at the 2-digit or chapter level along with the names of the industries. Reference entries are not included. Both the Harmonized Code and the ISIC sections are included in *MSR* because while they are older classification systems they are still of interest to some readers.

Appendix II

- **Annotated Source List**. The second appendix provides publisher names, addresses, telephone and fax numbers, and publication frequency of primary and secondary sources cited in this 17th edition of *Market Share Reporter*.

What's New

The editorial staff is always looking to add new features to *Market Share Reporter*.

The last edition introduced more sophisticated looking graphics. The book also now features horizontal bar graphs in addition to vertical bar graphs and pie charts. Readers have often called looking for information on sales in a particular market by year. More of these types of entries have been included in this edition.

Also, the editors have redesigned the indexes, from two to three columns. The geographic index has also been better organized. For countries and regions that have a large number of entries, subheadings have now been included. In previous editions, for example, the United States was followed by a long list of entries in which the country appears. Now these entries have been organized by industry subheadings such as "apparel", "building materials", "chemicals".

In this edition, and at the request of *MSR* users, the editors have changed the terminology used in the Source Index. See the paragraph on "Sources" for more information.

Available in Electronic Formats

Licensing. *Market Share Reporter* is available for licensing. The complete database is provided in a fielded format and is deliverable on such media as disk, CD-ROM or tape. For more information, contact Thomson Gale's Business Development Group at (800) 877-GALE or visit us on our web site at www.galegroup.com/bizdev.

Online. *Market Share Reporter* is accessible online as File MKTSHR through LEXIS-NEXIS and as part of the MarkIntel service offered by Thomson Financial Securities Data. For more information, contact LEXIS-NEXIS, P.O. Box 933, Dayton, OH 45401-0933, phone (937) 865-6800, toll-free (800) 227-4908, website: http://www.lexis-nexis.com; or Thomson Financial Securities Data, Two Gateway Center, Newark, NJ 07102, phone: (973) 622-3100, toll-free: (888) 989-8373, website: www.tfsd.com.

Acknowledgements

Market Share Reporter is a collective enterprise which involves not only the editorial team but also many users who share comments, criticisms, and suggestions over the telephone. Their help and encouragement is very much appreciated. In particular, the comments and suggestions from Ms. Judy Growe, Reference Librarian with the Langara College Library in Vancouver, BC Canada, were helpful in making changes in this year's edition. *MSR* could not have been produced without the help of many people in and outside of Thomson Gale. The editors would like to express their special appreciation to Virgil Burton (Coordinating Editor, Thomson Gale) and to the staff of Editorial Code and Data, Inc.

Comments and Suggestions

Comments on *MSR* or suggestions for improvement of its usefulness, format, and coverage are always welcome. Although every effort is made to maintain accuracy, errors may occasionally occur; the editors will be grateful if these are called to their attention. Please contact:

Editors
Market Share Reporter
Thomson Gale
27500 Drake Road
Farmington Hills, MI 48331-3535
Phone: (248) 699-GALE
or (800) 347-GALE
Fax: (248) 699-8069

General Interest and Broad Topics

★1★
Adult Entertainment

Adult Entertainment Market, 2004

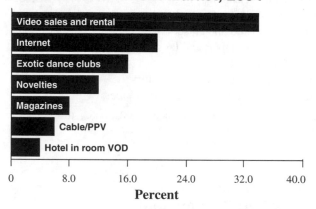

Percent

The industry was valued at $12.6 billion. Video sales led the category with sales of $4.2 billion. The Internet followed with $2.5 billion, up from $1 billion in 2002. The number of unique visitors to adult web sites grew from 23 million in 2001 to 34 million in 2004. Mobile represents less than 1% of the market but it is growing.

Video sales and rental	34.0%
Internet	20.0
Exotic dance clubs	16.0
Novelties	12.0
Magazines	8.0
Cable/PPV	6.0
Hotel in room VOD	4.0

Source: "New Study Finds Adult Revenue Eclipses $12B This Year." [online] from http://www.avnonline.com [Published December 13, 2005] from Kagan Research, *Forbes*, Juniper Research and Free Speech Coalition.

★2★
Auctions

Live Auction Sales, 2005

The value of goods and services sold at live auctions reached $240.2 billion in 2005, a $23 billion increase over 2004. The real estate category was up 8.4%, the largest increase for the year.

	($ mil.)	Share
Automotive	$81.9	32.73%
Real estate	51.2	20.46
Agricultural machinery and equipment	18.2	7.27
Livestock	17.2	6.87
Art, antiques and collectibles	12.1	4.84
Commercial/industrial machinery and equipment	12.0	4.80
Personal property	10.0	4.00
Other	47.6	19.02

Source: "Live Auction Industry Revenues Rise by $23B in 2005." [online] from http://www.auctioneers.org [Press release February 2006] from National Auctioneers Association.

★3★
Beverageware

Beverageware/Barware Sales

Data are for October 2004 - September 2005. The top brands are Libbey, Luminarc, Mikasa, Pacific Market and Inno-Art.

Plastics	55.2%
Glass	28.0
Ceramic	7.2
Stainless steel	6.6
Full-lead crystal	2.4
Other crystal	1.0

Source: *Gourmet Retailer*, February 2006, p. 16, from NPD Group/NPD Houseworld/POS.

★ 4 ★
Beverageware

Beverageware Sales by Shape

The source notes that the category has enjoyed some activity in recent years. The wine market benefited from consumers who have an appreciation for wine and how best to drink and enjoy it. Martinis and margaritas are also popular. Figures come from a survey conducted by the source. It surveyed female adults (ages 18 and over) from December 13 - 22, 2005.

Hiball tumbler	29.2%
Cooler/ice tea	11.0
Coffee mug/cappuccino cup	9.3
DOF/DOR	8.5
Pitcher	6.4
Shot/double shot	4.0
Pitcher/decanter	3.4
Pilsner	3.2
Carafe	1.5
Decanter	1.5

Source: *Gourmet Retailer*, March 2006, p. 32, from NPD Group/NPD Houseworld/POS.

★ 5 ★
Consumer Spending

Back-to-School Spending, 2000-2005

Data show sales in billions of dollars for August - September. Figures for 2005 are placed at between $23.2 and $23.4 billion. The back to school sales period, from late July to mid- to late September, is the largest sales generator for retailers after the November - December holiday season.

2000	$ 20.3
2001	19.9
2002	20.9
2003	21.9
2004	22.1
2005	23.4

Source: *Investor's Business Daily*, August 17, 2005, p. 1, from U.S. Department of Commerce and International Council of Shopping Centers.

★ 6 ★
Consumer Spending

Back-to-School Spending by Product, 2004

Sales are average weekly sales for the 52 weeks ended December 25, 2004.

Pens and pencils	$ 1,652,595
Glue	742,380
Markets	697,460
Personal planners, binders and folders	678,579
Household scissors	315,832
Bags, paper lunch	312,394
Correction fluid and erasers	190,089
Dividers, tabs, labels and tags	163,460
Pencils, colored	135,646
Report covers and sheet protectors	104,697
School and office measurers, sharpeners	91,128

Source: *Progressive Grocer*, June 1, 2005, p. 62, from AC-Nielsen.

★ 7 ★
Consumer Spending

Expedited Bill Payment

Expedited bill payment refers to any method that is faster than mailing paper checks to pay a bill. It can be conducted online or via telephone. There were about 430 million such transactions conducted in 2004. Roughly half were face-to-face payments. ACH stands for automated clearing house, or electronic checks.

ACH debit	43.0%
Cash	32.0
Credit cards	13.0
Check	7.0
PIN-based debit cards	2.0
Signature-based debit cards	2.0

Source: *Electronic Payments International*, November 2005, p. 6, from TowerGroup.

★ 8 ★
Countertops

Bath & Kitchen Countertop Demand, 2004

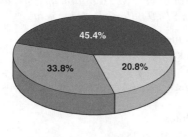

In 2004, U.S. kitchen and bath countertops were a $3 billion industry; demand is expected to reach 467 million square feet in 2007. Sales of the more expensive materials have been increasing. Demand is shown in percent. E-stone stands for engineered stone.

Laminates 45.4%
Natural stone 33.8
Solid surface & e-stone 20.8

Source: *Solid Surface*, July-August 2005, p. 40, from Catalina Research.

★ 9 ★
Coupons

Where Coupons Are Located

Internet coupons represent less than 1% of coupons issued. Manufacturers are issuing fewer because they are concerned about fraud and counterfeiting.

Free-standing insert 79.0%
In-ad 12.0
Instant redeemable 1.5
Other 7.5

Source: *Prepared Foods*, August 2005, p. 32, from Promotional Marketing Association.

★ 10 ★
Entertainment

Leading Media Groups Worldwide, 2004

About half of the top 50 firms are based in the United States. Mergers in the last two decades have created giant media firms. The development of cable and pay services helped to create new powerful firms. Firms are ranked in millions of euros.

Time Warner . . . . € 30,466.4
Walt Disney 18,401.6
Viacom 16,988.2
Comcast 16,245.6
Sony 15,824.8
News Corporation 12,182.6
NBC 10,308.8
Cox Enterprises 9,446.5
DirecTV 9,088.0
EchoStar 8,939.0
Cablevision 6,166.1
Liberty Media 6,145.6

Source: *Screen Digest*, July 2005, p. 198.

★ 11 ★
Flooring

Flooring Industry, 2004

Market shares are shown in percent. Research and Markets reports that the residential market represents 80% of the flooring market. This sector was valued at $17.4 billion.

Carpet and area rugs 62.3%
Ceramic 12.5
Hardwood 10.5
Vinyl 7.9
Laminates 6.2
Rubber 0.6

Source: *Floor Covering Weekly*, July 2005, p. NA, from *Floor Covering Weekly*.

★ 12 ★
Freight Industry

Shipping Transportation Industry, 2004

The industry was valued at $765 billion. The Waterways Council reports that more than 607 million tons of goods were shipped along the nation's inland navigational system. The American Trucking Association reports that the trucking industry saw a record carrying load of 10.7 billion tons and $623 billion in revenue in 2005.

Truck	.87.7%
Rail	4.3
Pipeline	3.9
Air	1.8
Intermodal	1.1
Water	1.1

Source: "Stephens Logistics & Transportation." [online] from http://library. corporate-ir.net/library/19/192/192936/items/183328/BBT_021406.pdf [Published Nov. 2, 2005] from American Trucking Association.

★ 13 ★
Licensed Merchandise

College Licensing Market, 2005

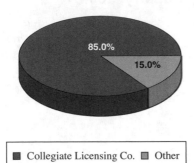

85.0%

15.0%

■ Collegiate Licensing Co. ■ Other

The sporting goods market was worth $55.7 billion in wholesale shipments. This is an increase of 6.8% from the previous year.

Collegiate Licensing Co.	.85.0%
Other	.15.0

Source: *Daily News Record*, January 30, 2006, p. 12.

★ 14 ★
Licensed Merchandise

Leading Art Merchandisers, 2004

Firms are ranked by sales in millions of dollars. Worldwide retail sales were $18.6 billion in 2004, down slightly from $18.9 billion the prior year.

Precious Moments	$ 500
Thomas Kinkade	500
The Flavia Company	142
Susan Winget	100
Wyland	100
Mary Engelbreit	70
The Hautman Brothers	58
Paul Brent Designer Inc.	57
Challis & Roos	41
Rachael Hale	35

Source: *License!*, October 2005, p. 31, from *License!* Research.

★ 15 ★
Luxury Goods

Luxury Goods Market Worldwide

Goldman Sachs predicts that the Chinese will overtake Japan as the world's top consumer of luxury goods within a decade. According to the China Association of Branding Strategy about 13% of China's population can afford luxury goods. This figure should increase dramatically by 2010. China includes Hong Kong residents.

Japan	.41.0%
United States	.17.0
China	.12.0
Other	.30.0

Source: *Asian Chemical News*, October 31, 2005, p. 7, from Goldman Sachs.

★ 16 ★
Mobile Entertainment

Mobile Entertainment Market Worldwide, 2005 and 2010

The global games industry is worth $35.3 billion in 2005, up over 5% from 2004. The mobile games sector is the fastest growing segment. The broadband sector is also performing well. Market value is shown in millions of dollars.

	2005	2010
Console software	$ 13,055	$ 17,164
Mobile	2,572	11,186
Broadband	1,944	6,352
Console hardware	3,894	5,771
Handheld software	4,829	3,113
Interactive TV	786	3,037
PC software	4,313	2,955
Handheld hardware	3,855	1,715

Source: "Report Predicts $58.4B Games Market." [online] from http://www.businessweekonline.com [Published October 2005] from Yankee Group's *U.S. Portable Entertainment Forecast.*

★ 17 ★
Packaging

Cap & Closure Market, 2001, 2005, and 2009

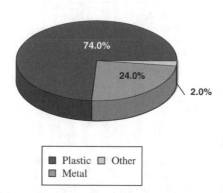

74.0%
24.0%
2.0%

■ Plastic □ Other
■ Metal

Freedonia forecasts demand for caps and closures will increase at an average annual rate of 4.8 percent to $25.9 billion by 2009, partially driven by economic growth and rising personal income. Plastic will take market share from metal closures as well as cork-based types of closures.

	2001	2005	2009
Plastic	63.0%	71.0%	74.0%
Metal	35.0	27.0	24.0
Other	2.0	2.0	2.0

Source: "O-I Investor Day." [online] from http://www.o-i.com/about/investors/InvestorPres11-15.pdf [Published November 15, 2005] from Freedonia Group.

★ 18 ★
Packaging

Container Industry

The industry is shown in percent. Plastic container demand will grow 4.6% annually through 2010, according to the Freedonia Group. Euromonitor estimates the paper and cardboard packaging market to be worth $45.6 billion in 2004. One estimate places the overall packaging market at $104.5 billion.

Paper & related	.35.0%
Plastics	.35.0
Metal	.20.0
Glass	.10.0

Source: *American Ceramic Society Bulletin*, vol 84, no 4, p. 41.

★ 19 ★
Packaging

Flexible Packaging Market

Flexible packaging is the second largest packaging type, according to the Flexible Packaging Association. It takes 17% of the U.S. $124 billion packaging market. BOPP stands for Biaxially Oriented Polypropylene.

Blown polyethylene	.33.0%
BOPP	.22.0
Aluminum	.14.0
Paper	.14.0
Other	.17.0

Source: *Plastics News*, May 1, 2006, p. 22.

★ 20 ★
Packaging

Food Container Market, 2004

The industry is valued at $17.7 billion. Freedonia forecasts this figure to climb to $20.7 billion by 2009. The market will be driven by such things as disposable income, smaller household sizes and consumer demand for convenience.

Pouches and bags	.39.0%
Paperboard	.23.0
Metal	.18.0
Plastic	.15.0
Glass	5.0

Source: *Converting*, November 2005, p. 4, from Freedonia Group.

★ 21 ★

Packaging

Global Packaging Market

Market shares are shown based on sales.

North America	29.0%
Western Europe	27.0
Japan	15.0
Non-Japan Asia	13.0
Other	16.0

Source: *Global Packaging 101v.3*, Credit Suisse First Boston, September 12, 2005, p. 3, from *World Packaging* companies, *Packaging* magazine and CS First Boston.

★ 22 ★

Packaging

Largest Flexible Packaging Makers, 2004

The flexible packaging industry is valued at $21 billion. Firms are ranked by sales in millions of dollars.

Bemis Flexible Packaging	$ 2,250
Sealed Air Corp.	1,500
Alcan Packaging	1,300
Printpack Inc.	1,000
Pliant Corp.	969
Tyco Plastics	965
Pactiv	958
Alcoa Flexible Packaging	850
Dow Chemical	750
Sigma Plastics Group	659

Source: *Flexible Packaging*, June 2005, p. 20, from Flexible Packaging Association.

★ 23 ★

Packaging

Leading Cap & Closure Makers Worldwide, 2004

The industry is forecast to be worth $20.5 billion. Figures include metals, corks, pumps, aerosols and overcaps.

Crown Holdings	6.9%
AptarGroup	5.4
Amcor	3.2
Alcoa	2.5
O-I	2.4
Other	79.6

Source: "O-I Investor Day." [online] from http://www.o-i.com/about/investors/InvestorPres11-15.pdf [Published November 15, 2005] from Freedonia Group.

★ 24 ★

Packaging

Leading Converted Packaging Makers in Europe

Behind Amcor Flexibles and Alcan Packaging are eight or so flex-pack converters with 2-7% share. The bottom 30% of companies serve successful niche markets. Germany leads with a quarter of the flexible packaging market.

Alcan Packaging/Amcor Flexibles	35.0%
Other	65.0

Source: *Paper, Film & Foil Converter (Online Exclusive)*, April 1, 2006, p. NA.

★ 25 ★

Packaging

Top Packaging Firms in Brazil

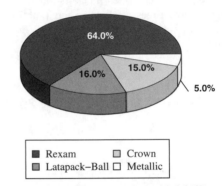

Shares are shown based on a market of 9.9 billion units.

Rexam	64.0%
Latapack-Ball	16.0
Crown	15.0
Metallic	5.0

Source: "First Quarter 2005 Review and Management Briefing." [online] from http://library. corporate-ir.net/./FINAL-1st%20Qtr%202005%20Earnings%20Release%20EN-TIRE%20SCRIPT%20(4-28-05).pdf [Published April 28, 2005].

★ 26 ★
Packaging

Top Packaging Firms in China

Shares are shown based on a market of 8.6 billion units. Data include metal beverage containers and plastic containers (non-food).

Ball Asia	33.0%
Crown	25.0
Great China	15.0
Pacific Can	14.0
Bao Yi Steel	7.0
Other	6.0

Source: "First Quarter 2005 Review and Management Briefing." [online] from http://library. corporate-ir.net/./FINAL-1st%20Qtr%202005%20Earnings%20Release%20ENTIRE%20SCRIPT%20(4-28-05).pdf [Published April 28, 2005].

★ 27 ★
Packaging

Top Packaging Firms in Europe

Shares are shown based on a market of 40 billion units.

Rexam	42.0%
Ball Packaging Europe	29.0
Crown	20.0
Can-Pack	6.0
Other	3.0

Source: "First Quarter 2005 Review and Management Briefing." [online] from http://library. corporate-ir.net/./FINAL-1st%20Qtr%202005%20Earnings%20Release%20ENTIRE%20SCRIPT%20(4-28-05).pdf [Published April 28, 2005].

★ 28 ★
Pipe

Pipe Demand, 2004 and 2009

Overall pipe demand is forecast to increase 2.4% to 16.4 billion feet in 2009. The market is helped by highway and street construction and the replacing of water management and sewer systems. Figures are in millions of feet.

	2004	2009	Share
Plastic	5,777	6,600	40.37%
Copper	5,637	6,370	38.96
Steel	2,411	2,630	16.09
Other	685	750	4.59

Source: *Public Works*, October 2005, p. 11, from Freedonia Group.

★ 29 ★
Private Label

Private Label Industry, 2005

Market shares are shown based on supermarket, drug store and mass merchandiser sales (excluding Wal-Mart) for the 52 weeks ended August 7, 2005. The fastest-growing categories: eyeshadow (+34%), drinkable yogurt (+28%) and chewing gum (+23%).

Refrigerated food	32.0%
Paper, plastic and wraps	31.0
Frozen food	25.0
Pet food	21.0
Shelf-stable food	19.0
Diapers and feminine hygiene	14.0
Health care	14.0
Non-alcoholic beverages	12.0
Home care	10.0
Snacks and confectionery	9.0

Source: *Private Label Buyer*, November 2005, p. 44, from ACNielsen and *Power of Private Label*.

★ 30 ★
Siding

Exterior Siding Market in North America, 2003

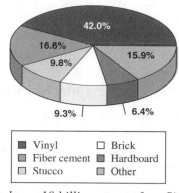

Total demand was 10 billion square feet. Siding and exterior trim has grown into a combined $12 billion market in the building products industry, according to Principia Consulting.

Vinyl	42.0%
Fiber cement	16.6
Stucco	9.8
Brick	9.3
Hardboard	6.4
Other	15.9

Source: "Louisiana Pacific Corporation." [online] from http://media. corporate-ir.net/media_files/NYS/LPX/presentations/UBS0922-041.pdf [Published September 22, 2004] from Freedonia Group, Ciprus, James Hardie and LP Intl.

★ 31 ★
Siding

Residential Repair/Remodeling Market

Market shares are shown in percent. Vinyl takes 30% of new residential construction (brick and stucco follow with 21% each).

Vinyl	63.0%
Wood	19.0
Fiber cement	10.0
Stucco	4.0
Brick	1.0
Other	3.0

Source: *EDGAR Online 8-K Glimpse*, May 18, 2006, p. NA, from Pure Strategy.

★ 32 ★
Soy Products

Soy Product Sales, 2004 and 2009

Demand is expected to increase over 5% annually to $8.7 billion in 2009.

	2004	2009	Share
Soybean oil	$ 3,660	$ 4,195	48.50%
Protein products	1,265	1,685	19.48
Soy milk & other	1,130	1,450	16.76
Chemicals	700	1,320	15.26

Source: *Food Institute Report*, October 3, 2005, p. NA, from Freedonia Group.

★ 33 ★
Water

Global Water Purification Market

The global market was worth $360 billion. Worldwide, 1.2 billion people do not have access to safe, usable water daily, and 5 million people die each year from waterborne diseases.

	($ bil.)	Share
Chemicals	$ 14	28.0%
Equipment	13	26.0
Membranes	10	20.0
International services	8	16.0
Desalination	5	10.0

Source: *Water World*, May 2005, p. 100, from GE Infrastructure Water and Process Technologies.

★ 34 ★
Water

Ultrapure Water Market Worldwide

Semiconductors are one of the leading end markets in ultrapure water. It is used to remove contaminents and particles from wafers as they move through each treatment process. Sales are shown in millions of dollars.

	($ mil.)	Share
Semiconductor	$ 1,300	40.63%
Non-cleanroom	1,247	38.97
Pharmaceutical	231	7.22
Flat panel	222	6.94
Other cleanroom	200	6.25

Source: *CleanRooms*, July 2005, p. 14, from McIlvaine Co.

★ 35 ★
Windows & Doors

Leading Window & Door Makers in North America

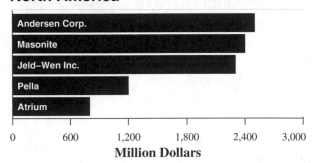

Firms are ranked by estimated sales in millions of dollars. Andersen claims to be the largest wood window and door manufacturer in the world, making more than 6 million windows and doors annually. Masonite is the world's largest door maker. Pella and Masonite's sales figures come from Forbes magazine.

Andersen Corp.	$ 2,500
Masonite	2,400
Jeld-Wen Inc.	2,300
Pella	1,200
Atrium	800

Source: *Window & Door*, February 2006 from *Window & Door's Top 100*.

★ 36 ★
Windows & Doors

Residential Window Demand, 2009 and 2014

The residential market represents about three quarters of window & door demand. The industry is forecast to increase 3.7% annually through 2009. Plastic windows and doors nudge out wood and metal products for replacement applications. Demand is shown in millions of units.

	2009	2014
Vinyl	37.0	49.3
Wood	24.8	25.5
Aluminum	5.9	5.5
Other	1.2	1.2

Source: *Window & Door*, May 2005, p. NA, from Freedonia Group.

★ 37 ★
Windows & Doors

Window Market in Germany, 2004 and 2006

Demand for wooden windows has been falling steadily since 1998, when 5.9 million units were produced. Data are in millions of units.

	2004	2006	Share
Plastic	6.2	5.9	55.66%
Aluminum	2.4	2.1	19.81
Wood	2.4	2.1	19.81
Aluminum + wood	0.7	0.5	4.72

Source: "Germany Solid Wood Products Annual 2005." [online] from http://www.usatrade.gov [Published December 2005] from German Windows Manufacturers Association.

SIC 01 - Agricultural Production - Crops

★ 38 ★
Grain

SIC: 0110; NAICS: 11114, 11115

Leading Grain Handlers in Western Canada, 2005

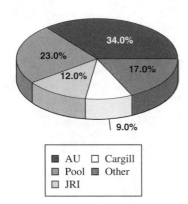

Market shares are estimated in percent.

AU	.34.0%
Pool	.23.0
JRI	.12.0
Cargill	.9.0
Other	.17.0

Source: "New Pool Beyond Tomorrow." [online] from http://www.swp.com/pdf/frantransportNONOTES.pdf [Accessed June 20, 2006].

★ 39 ★
Grain

SIC: 0110; NAICS: 11114, 11115

Top Grain Handlers in Canada, 2003

Market shares are shown based on storage capacity.

Agricore United	.23.0%
Saskatchewan Wheat Pool	.22.9
Pioneer Grain	.10.3
Cargill	.8.2
Other	.35.6

Source: "Market Share Matrix Project." [online] from http://www.marketsharematrix.org [Published January 2005] from Canadian Grains Council's *Statistical Handbook*.

★ 40 ★
Grain

SIC: 0110; NAICS: 11114, 11115

Top States for Farming

Cash receipts in the United States totaled $224.9 billion in 2004.

	($ bil.)	Share
California	$ 32.3	12.9%
Texas	17.6	7.0
Iowa	15.9	6.3
Nebraska	12.5	5.0
Illinois	10.9	4.3
Minnesota	10.5	4.2
Kansas	10.1	4.0
North Carolina	8.4	3.3
Arkansas	7.3	2.9
Other	125.5	50.0

Source: *Business North Carolina*, February 2006, p. 20, from North Carolina Department of Agriculture.

★ 41 ★
Seeds

SIC: 0110; NAICS: 11114, 11115

Leading Seed Firms

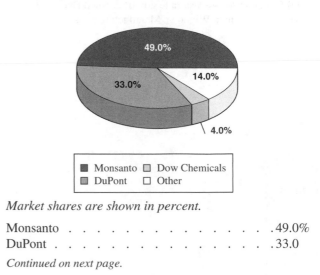

Market shares are shown in percent.

Monsanto	.49.0%
DuPont	.33.0

Continued on next page.

★ 41 ★
[Continued]
Seeds
SIC: 0110; NAICS: 11114, 11115

Leading Seed Firms

Market shares are shown in percent.

Dow Chemicals 4.0%
Other 14.0

Source: "Ethanol Boom Reaches the Chemical Industry."
[online] from http://www.checkbiotech.org/blocks/dsp_
document.cfm?doc_id12793 [Published May 16, 2006].

★ 42 ★
Seeds
SIC: 0110; NAICS: 11114, 11115

Top Seed Companies Worldwide, 2004

*The top 10 firms control about half of worldwide sales.
There were a number of takeovers in 2005. Monsanto
acquired Seminis in January 2005 (company's total
sales were $2,277 million plus $526 million in pro for-
ma sales). This move knocked DuPont's Hi-Bred International out of the number one slot. Firms are ranked
by 2004 sales in millions of dollars.*

	($ mil.)	Share
Monsanto	$ 2,803	13.55%
DuPont	2,600	12.57
Syngenta	1,239	5.99
Groupe Limagrain	1,044	5.05
KWS AG	622	3.01
Land O'Lakes	538	2.60
Sakata	416	2.01
Bayer Crop Science	387	1.87
Taikii	366	1.77
DLF-Trifolium	320	1.55
Other	10,350	50.04

Source: *ETC Communique*, September/October 2005, p. 1.

★ 43 ★
Wheat
SIC: 0111; NAICS: 11114

Wheat Seed Market in the U.K.

Market shares are shown in percent.

Robigus 21.0%
Einstein 14.0
Cordiale 5.0
New Group 4 Alchemy 4.0
Other 56.0

Source: *Arable Farming*, October 17, 2005, p. NA.

★ 44 ★
Corn
SIC: 0115; NAICS: 11115

Corn Seed Market

Monsanto has about half of Pioneer's market share.

Pioneer 35.0%
Monsanto 17.0
Other 48.0

Source: *Philadelphia Inquirer*, August 5, 2005, p. NA, from
Pioneer.

★ 45 ★
Soybeans
SIC: 0116; NAICS: 11111

Leading Soybean Processors

*Companies are ranked by estimated capacity in thou-
sands of barrels per day.*

	(000)	Share
Archer-Daniels-Midland	1,686	29.7%
Bunge	1,327	23.4
Cargill	1,278	22.5
AGP	684	12.0
Honeymeade	100	1.8
Owensboro	100	1.8
Purdue	75	1.3
CGB (Japanese)	70	1.2
South Dakota Soybean Processors . .	70	1.2

Source: *Agribusiness Chartbook*, CS First Boston, December 5, 2005, p. 14, from CS First Boston Equity Research.

★ 46 ★
Soybeans
SIC: 0116; NAICS: 11111

Leading Soybean Producers Worldwide, 2006

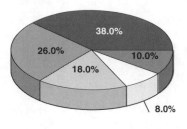

Brazil leads in the export market, with 39% to the 36% held by the United States.

United States	.38.0%
Brazil	.26.0
Argentina	.18.0
China	8.0
Other	.10.0

Source: *Soybeans*, ING Wholesale Banking, May 24, 2006, p. 1, from U.S. Department of Agriculture.

★ 47 ★
Soybeans
SIC: 0116; NAICS: 11111

Leading Soybean Seed Firms, 2004

Market shares are estimated for newly purchased seed.

Regional seed companies	.41.0%
Pioneer	.24.0
Asgrow/DEKALB	.21.0
SGTA/Garst/GH	.13.0
Dow/Mycogen	1.0

Source: "Field of Dreams Tour." [online] from http://www.monsanto.com [Published August 2004] from Monsanto estimates.

★ 48 ★
Potatoes
SIC: 0134; NAICS: 111211

Potato Market in Alberta

Fresh has less than 10% of the market. Seed potatoes market share is estimated also.

Processed	.73.0%
Seeds	.20.0
Fresh	.10.0

Source: *Edmonton Journal*, May 27, 2005, p. NA.

★ 49 ★
Vegetables
SIC: 0160; NAICS: 111219

Prepared Produce Sales, 2005

Fresh cut vegetables and fruit sales totaled $6.6 billion in 2005. They represented 16% of all produce sales in supermarkets.

Salads	.53.0%
Carrots	.13.0
Melons	9.0
Mixed fruit	6.0
Mushrooms	6.0
Mixed vegetables	5.0
Pineapples	3.0
Other	5.0

Source: "Fresh Facts on Fresh Cut." [online] from http://www.fresh-cuts.org/content/Fri_Marketing_1.pdf [Accessed June 1, 2006] from Perishables Group and International Fresh Cut Produce Association.

★ 50 ★
Vegetables
SIC: 0161; NAICS: 111219

Fresh Vegetable Industry by State, 2005

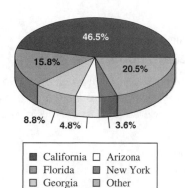

The value of the crop is estimated at $9.82 billion.

California 46.5%
Florida 15.8
Georgia 8.8
Arizona 4.8
New York 3.6
Other 20.5

Source: *Vegetables 2005 Summary*, January 2006, p. 1, from U.S. Department of Agriculture.

★ 51 ★
Vegetables
SIC: 0161; NAICS: 111219

Largest Vegetable Growers in the North

Companies are ranked by acreage devoted to crop production.

R.D. Offutt Co. 65,000
Hartung Brothers Inc. 24,298
Heartland Farms Inc. 12,820
Black Gold Farms 12,810
Paramount Farms Inc. 11,765
L. Walther & Sons Inc. 9,325
Wysocki Produce Farm Inc. 7,992
Okray Family Farms Inc. 7,024
Charles H. West Farms Inc. 6,860
Tri-Campbell Farms 6,800

Source: *American Vegetable Grower*, October 2005, p. NA.

★ 52 ★
Vegetables
SIC: 0161; NAICS: 111219

Largest Vegetable Growers in the Southeast

Companies are ranked by acreage devoted to crop production.

Thomas Produce Co. 17,230
Pacific Tomato Growers Ltd/Triple E.
  Produce Corp. 16,288
Hundley Farms Inc. 16,213
A. Duda & Sons Inc. 14,000
Six L's Packing Co. Inc. 13,000
Pero Family Farms Inc. 10,050
Gargiulo Inc. 9,500
Suwannee Farms/Eagle Island Farms 7,434
Barnes Farming Corp. 5,735
Dimare Homestead 5,250

Source: *American Vegetable Grower*, October 2005, p. NA.

★ 53 ★
Vegetables
SIC: 0161; NAICS: 111219

Largest Vegetable Growers in the Southwest

Companies are ranked by acreage devoted to crop production.

Navajo Agricultural Products Industry 14,896
Martori Farms 11,400
Amigo Farms Inc. 7,398
Pasquinelli Produce Co. 6,725
Del Monte Fresh Produce 6,427
J&D Produce Inc. 6,000
Greer Farms 5,500
Wyatt Hidalgo Farms Inc. 5,426
Rousseau Farming Co. 5,260
Barkley Co. 4,500

Source: *American Vegetable Grower*, October 2005, p. NA.

★ 54 ★
Vegetables
SIC: 0161; NAICS: 111219

Largest Vegetable Growers in the West

Companies are ranked by acreage devoted to crop production.

Grimmway Farms	45,700
Yanimura & Antle	45,307
D'Arrigo Bros. Co. of California	34,130
Mission Ranches	21,463
Ocean Mist Farms/Boutonnet Farms	21,029
Rio Farms	16,950
Nunes Vegetables Inc.	16,503
Betteravia Farms	14,484
Dresick Farms Inc.	14,400
J.G. Boswell Co.	13,952

Source: *American Vegetable Grower*, October 2005, p. NA.

★ 55 ★
Vegetables
SIC: 0161; NAICS: 111219

Lettuce Market Shares, 2004

Lettuce and salad mixes averaged sales of $3,714 each week per store.

Packaged salads	68.0%
Iceberg	14.0
Romaine	10.0
Green leaf	3.0
Red leaf	2.0
Boston	1.0
Other	3.0

Source: *Produce Merchandising*, August 2005, p. 42, from Perishables Group and ACNielsen.

★ 56 ★
Vegetables
SIC: 0161; NAICS: 111219

Monsanto and the Vegetable Seed Market, 2005

Monsanto has a dominant position in the vegetable seed market. Its share of various categories is below.

Cucumbers	38.0%
Hot peppers	34.0
Beans	31.0
Sweet peppers	29.0

Onions	25.0%
Tomatos	23.0

Source: *ETC Communique*, September - October 2005, p. NA.

★ 57 ★
Vegetables
SIC: 0161; NAICS: 111219

Onion Sales, 2005

Onion sales contributed an average of $1,096 per week per store to national produce sales, according to ACNielsen. Sales are shown as of November 2004 - October 2005.

Yellow onions	34.0%
Sweet onions	18.0
Scallions	15.0
Red onions	11.0
White onions	11.0
Vidalia onions	9.0
Other	2.0

Source: *Produce Merchandising*, April 2006, p. 34, from Perishables Group and ACNielsen.

★ 58 ★
Vegetables
SIC: 0161; NAICS: 111219

Pepper Sales, 2004

Peppers were the sixth largest contributor to supermarket produce sales. Pepper sales average $841 per store per week across the country according to ACNielsen.

Sweet peppers	90.0%
Hot peppers	10.0

Source: *Produce Merchandising*, November 2005, p. 90, from Perishables Group and ACNielsen.

★ 59 ★
Vegetables
SIC: 0161; NAICS: 111219

Produce Sales at Supermarkets

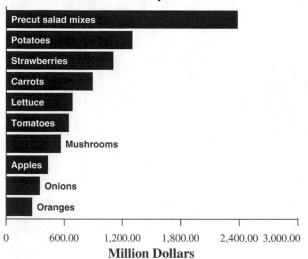

Million Dollars

Supermarket sales are shown in millions of dollars.

Precut salad mixes	$ 2,382.03
Potatoes	1,302.62
Strawberries	1,104.90
Carrots	891.51
Lettuce	682.78
Tomatoes	645.05
Mushrooms	562.12
Apples	432.41
Onions	348.20
Oranges	268.11

Source: *Progressive Grocer*, September 15, 2005, p. 22, from *Progressive Grocer's 26th Annual Consumer Expenditures Study*.

★ 60 ★
Vegetables
SIC: 0161; NAICS: 111219

Tomato Sales by Variety, 2004

Total average weekly sales were $2,414 in 2004 according to ACNielsen. The Eastern part of the United States had the highest sales by region at $3,196 per week.

Hothouse on-the-vine	27.0%
Field	23.0
Cherry/grape	22.0
Hothouse beefsteak	14.0
Roma	13.0
Retailer-assigned	1.0

Source: *Produce Merchandising*, July 2005, p. 42, from Perishables Group and ACNielsen.

★ 61 ★
Fruit
SIC: 0170; NAICS: 111333, 111334, 111336

Fresh Fruit Sales, 2005

Sales are shown for the 52 weeks ended September 2005.

Berries	$ 1,935.44
Apples	1,909.58
Grapes	1,885.43
Bananas	1,610.86
Melons	1,341.51
Oranges	666.01
Avocados	492.64
Cherries	380.23
Peaches	379.77
Pears	314.46

Source: "Retail Grocery Report." [online] from http://www.eatcalifornia-fruit.com/ppn/growers-shippers/pdf/2005RetailTrendsReport. pdf [Published Dec. 22, 2005] from Information Resources Inc. Fresh Look Data.

★ 62 ★
Fruit
SIC: 0170; NAICS: 111333, 111334, 111336

Noncitrus Fruit Production, 2005

Fruits are ranked by production in millions of dollars.

	($ mil.)	Share
Grapes	$ 3,013	32.26%
Apples	1,787	19.13
Strawberries	1,383	14.81
Peaches	510	5.46
Sweet cherries	484	5.18
Pears	315	3.37
Other	1,849	19.79

Source: "Noncitrus Fruits and Nuts." [online] from http:///usda.mannlib.cornell.edu/reports/nassr/fruit/pnf-bb/ [Published January 2006] from U.S. Department of Agriculture.

★ 63 ★
Berries
SIC: 0171; NAICS: 111333

Boysenberry Production by State, 2005

States are ranked by production in thousands of dollars.

	($ 000)	Share
California	$ 3,724	52.03%
Oregon	3,434	47.97

Source: "Noncitrus Fruits and Nuts." [online] from http:/// usda.mannlib.cornell.edu/reports/nassr/fruit/pnf-bb/ [Published January 2006] from U.S. Department of Agriculture.

★ 64 ★
Berries
SIC: 0171; NAICS: 111333

Leading Strawberry Producing Nations, 2004

Data are in thousands of short tons.

	(000)	Share
United States	1,107	28.8%
Spain	316	8.2
Russia	237	6.2
South Korea	231	6.0
Japan	226	5.9
Other	1,732	45.0

Source: *Fruit and Tree Nuts Situation and Outlook Yearbook,* U.S. Department of Agriculture, October 2005, p. 39, from Food and Agriculture Organization, United Nations.

★ 65 ★
Berries
SIC: 0171; NAICS: 111333

Strawberry Industry in California

California produces nearly 2 billion pounds of strawberries annually, representing more than 85% of strawberries in the country.

Fresh	.75.0%
Processed	.25.0

Source: *Sacramento Bee*, May 25, 2006, p. NA.

★ 66 ★
Berries
SIC: 0171; NAICS: 111333

Strawberry Production by State, 2005

States are ranked by production in thousands of dollars.

	($ 000)	Share
California	$ 1,110,174	80.27%
Florida	196,790	14.23
North Carolina	18,525	1.34
Oregon	13,680	0.99
Pennsylvania	12,810	0.93
New York	8,060	0.58
Washington	6,940	0.50
Other	16,085	1.16

Source: "Noncitrus Fruits and Nuts." [online] from http:/// usda.mannlib.cornell.edu/reports/nassr/fruit/pnf-bb/ [Published January 2006] from U.S. Department of Agriculture.

★ 67 ★
Grapes
SIC: 0172; NAICS: 111332

Grape Production by State, 2005

States are ranked by production in thousands of tons.

	(000)	Share
California	940,000	99.22%
New York	3,000	0.32
Michigan	700	0.07
Pennsylvania	500	0.05
North Carolina	200	0.02
Ohio	100	0.01
Missouri	60	0.01
Other	2,810	0.30

Source: "Noncitrus Fruits and Nuts." [online] from http:/// usda.mannlib.cornell.edu/reports/nassr/fruit/pnf-bb/ [Published January 2006] from U.S. Department of Agriculture.

★ 68 ★
Grapes
SIC: 0172; NAICS: 111332
Grape Production by Type

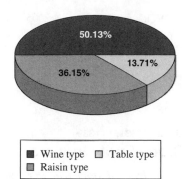

Data are in thousands of short tons.

	(000)	Share
Wine type	2,815	50.13%
Raisin type	2,030	36.15
Table type	770	13.71

Source: *Fruit and Tree Nuts Situation and Outlook Year-book,* U.S. Department of Agriculture, October 2005, p. 39, from National Agricultural Statistics Service, U.S. Department of Agriculture.

★ 69 ★
Nuts
SIC: 0173; NAICS: 111335
Leading Almond Producing Nations, 2004

Data are in thousands of short tons.

	(000)	Share
United States	810	27.71%
Syria	143	4.89
Italy	100	3.42
Spain	95	3.25
Iran	88	3.01
Other	1,687	57.71

Source: *Fruit and Tree Nuts Situation and Outlook Year-book,* U.S. Department of Agriculture, October 2005, p. 39, from Food and Agriculture Organization, United Nations.

★ 70 ★
Nuts
SIC: 0173; NAICS: 111335
Leading Pistachio Producing Nations, 2004

Data are in thousands of short tons.

	(000)	Share
Iran	303	50.00%
United States	174	28.71
Syria	44	7.26
China	33	5.45
Turkey	33	5.45
Other	19	3.14

Source: *Fruit and Tree Nuts Situation and Outlook Year-book,* U.S. Department of Agriculture, October 2005, p. 39, from Food and Agriculture Organization, United Nations.

★ 71 ★
Nuts
SIC: 0173; NAICS: 111335
Leading Walnut Producing Nations, 2004

Data are in thousands of short tons.

	(000)	Share
China	457	28.18%
United States	325	20.04
Iran	165	10.17
Turkey	143	8.82
Ukraine	75	4.62
Other	457	28.18

Source: *Fruit and Tree Nuts Situation and Outlook Year-book,* U.S. Department of Agriculture, October 2005, p. 39, from Food and Agriculture Organization, United Nations.

★ 72 ★

Citrus Fruit

SIC: 0174; NAICS: 11131, 11132

Leading Citrus Producing Nations, 2004

Data are in thousands of short tons. The United States was the top grapefruit and pomelo producer, taking 42% of production. Mexico was the top lemon and lime producer, taking 15% of production. Brazil was the top orange producer with 29% of production.

	(000)	Share
Brazil	22,701	18.97%
United States	16,433	13.74
China	16,154	13.50
Mexico	7,138	5.97
Spain	6,842	5.72
Other	50,372	42.10

Source: *Fruit and Tree Nuts Situation and Outlook Yearbook*, U.S. Department of Agriculture, October 2005, p. 37, from Food and Agriculture Organization, United Nations.

★ 73 ★

Citrus Fruit

SIC: 0174; NAICS: 11131, 11132

Orange Market

Sunkist also has about 75% of the lemon market.

Sunkist	60.0%
Other	40.0

Source: "Reading International." [online] from http://www.sec.edgar-online.com [Accessed June 1, 2006].

★ 74 ★

Fruit

SIC: 0175; NAICS: 111331

Apple Production in Europe, 2005

Data are in thousands of metric tons.

	(000)	Share
Poland	2,200	21.63%
Italy	2,145	21.09
France	1,778	17.48
Germany	915	9.00
Spain	671	6.60
Netherlands	380	3.74
Belgium	325	3.20
Portugal	288	2.83

	(000)	Share
Greece	265	2.61%
U.K.	183	1.80
Austria	169	1.66
Other	850	8.36

Source: "Fresh Deciduous Fruit Annual 2005." [online] from http://www.usatrade.gov [Published September 7, 2005] from German Central Market and Price Reporting Agency.

★ 75 ★

Fruit

SIC: 0175; NAICS: 111331, 111339

Largest Stone Fruit Growers

Farms are ranked by total stone fruit acreage. Stone fruit includes grapes, peaches, prunes and pome fruit.

Gerawan Farming	5,871
Fowler Packing	4,095
ITO Packing	3,586
Sun Valley Packing Co.	3,183
Sunwest Fruit Co.	3,000
Lane Packing	2,800
Taylor Orchards	2,800
Thiara Brothers Orchards	2,680
Titan Peach Farms	2,457
Cherry Ke Inc.	2,193

Source: *American/Western Fruit Grower*, August 2005, p. 12.

★ 76 ★

Fruit

SIC: 0175; NAICS: 111339

Leading Plum Producing Nations, 2004

Data are in thousands of short tons.

	(000)	Share
China	4,888	46.57%
Germany	626	5.96
Serbia and Montenegro	618	5.89
Romania	524	4.99
United States	320	3.05
Other	3,519	33.53

Source: *Fruit and Tree Nuts Situation and Outlook Yearbook*, U.S. Department of Agriculture, October 2005, p. 39, from Food and Agriculture Organization, United Nations.

★ 77 ★
Fruit
SIC: 0175; NAICS: 111339
Peach Production by State, 2005

States are ranked by production in thousands of tons.

	(000)	Share
California	385,000	32.56%
South Carolina	75,000	6.34
Georgia	40,000	3.38
New Jersey	35,000	2.96
Pennsylvania	26,600	2.25
Washington	22,000	1.86
Alabama	12,000	1.01
Colorado	12,000	1.01
Illinois	11,200	0.95
Michigan	11,200	0.95
Other	552,600	46.73

Source: "Noncitrus Fruits and Nuts." [online] from http:/// usda.mannlib.cornell.edu/reports/nassr/fruit/pnf-bb/ [Published January 2006] from U.S. Department of Agriculture.

★ 78 ★
Fruit
SIC: 0175; NAICS: 111339
Pear Production in Europe, 2005

Data are in thousands of metric tons.

	(000)	Share
Italy	842	35.20%
Spain	573	23.95
France	230	9.62
Belgium	212	8.86
Netherlands	200	8.36
Portugal	137	5.73
Greece	56	2.34
Germany	43	1.80
U.K.	27	1.13
Denmark	5	0.21
Other	67	2.80

Source: "Fresh Deciduous Fruit Annual 2005." [online] from http://www.usatrade.gov [Published September 7, 2005] from German Central Market and Price Reporting Agency.

★ 79 ★
Bananas
SIC: 0179; NAICS: 111339
Banana Sales, 2004

Banana sales totaled $1,778 average weekly sales in supermarkets according to ACNielsen. The Eastern United States saw sales of $2,270 a week, followed by the Central region with $2,164, the Southern region with $1,316, and the Western region with $2,170.

Yello	98.0%
Plantains	1.0
Other	1.0

Source: *Produce Merchandising*, October 2005, p. 90, from Perishables Group and ACNielsen.

★ 80 ★
Bananas
SIC: 0179; NAICS: 111339
Leading Banana Producing Nations, 2004

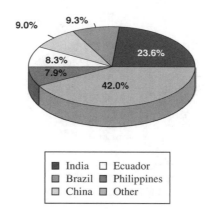

9.0%   9.3%
23.6%
8.3%
7.9%
42.0%

■ India □ Ecuador
■ Brazil ■ Philippines
□ China ■ Other

Data are in thousands of short tons.

	(000)	Share
India	18,541	23.6%
Brazil	7,278	9.3
China	7,077	9.0
Ecuador	6,504	8.3
Philippines	6,215	7.9
Other	33,026	42.0

Source: *Fruit and Tree Nuts Situation and Outlook Yearbook,* U.S. Department of Agriculture, October 2005, p. 39, from Food and Agriculture Organization, United Nations.

★ 81 ★
Bananas
SIC: 0179; NAICS: 111339

Top Banana Firms in Europe, 2003

Market shares are estimated.

Chiquita	.31.0%
Dole	.12.0
Fyffes	.12.0
Del Monte	.10.0
Noboa	.9.0
Other	.26.0

Source: "Chiquita Brands International." [online] from http://www.chiquita.com/bottomline/confcall/Turnaround-andTransformation-121603.ppt [Published Dec. 13, 2003] from Chiquita estimates.

★ 82 ★
Bananas
SIC: 0179; NAICS: 111339

Top Banana Firms in North America, 2003

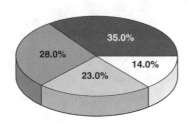

Market shares are estimated.

Dole	.35.0%
Chiquita	.28.0
Del Monte	.23.0
Other	.14.0

Source: "Chiquita Brands International." [online] from http://www.chiquita.com/bottomline/confcall/Turnaround-andTransformation-121603.ppt [Published Dec. 13, 2003] from Chiquita estimates.

★ 83 ★
Bananas
SIC: 0179; NAICS: 111339

Top Banana Firms Worldwide

Market shares are shown in percent.

Chiquita	.25.0%
Dole	.25.0

Del Monte	.15.0%
Noboa	.11.0
Fyffes	.8.0
Other	.16.0

Source: "Bananas." [online] from http://www.fairtrade-toronto.com/products/banana.html [Accessed November 9, 2005].

★ 84 ★
Floriculture
SIC: 0181; NAICS: 111422

Cut Flower Production, 2005

The wholesale value of domestically cut flowers is $397 million. California led with $289 million, or 73% of the total. The number of cut flower growers dropped 8% during the year to 498.

	($ mil.)	Share
Lillies	$ 76.9	18.94%
Tulips	39.7	9.78
Roses	39.0	9.61
Other	250.4	61.67

Source: *Floriculture Crops*, April 2006, p. 4, from U.S. Department of Agriculture.

★ 85 ★
Floriculture
SIC: 0181; NAICS: 111422

Iris Production by State, 2005

The wholesale value of production is $20 million.

	($ 000)	Share
California	$ 17,081	85.37%
Ohio	28	0.14
Michigan	16	0.08
Pennsylvania	14	0.07
Wisconsin	8	0.04
Other	2,861	14.30

Source: *Floriculture Crops*, April 2006, p. 4, from U.S. Department of Agriculture.

★ 86 ★
Floriculture
SIC: 0181; NAICS: 111422
Largest Green Goods Sales, 2005

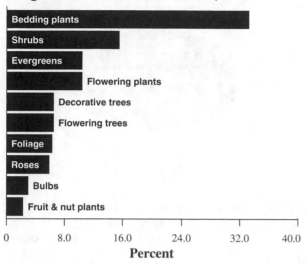

Green goods represent $55 billion of the $108.8 garden retail market.

Bedding plants	.33.2%
Shrubs	.15.5
Evergreens	.10.4
Flowering plants	.10.4
Decorative trees	6.5
Flowering trees	6.5
Foliage	6.3
Roses	5.9
Bulbs	3.0
Fruit & nut plants	2.3

Source: *Nursery Retailer*, January/February 2006, p. 56.

★ 87 ★
Floriculture
SIC: 0181; NAICS: 111422
Lily Production by State

The wholesale value of production is $20 million.

	($ 000)	Share
California	$ 65,478	85.17%
Florida	1,689	2.20
Colorado	938	1.22
New York	749	0.97
Minnesota	469	0.61
Other	7,554	9.83

Source: *Floriculture Crops*, April 2006, p. 4, from U.S. Department of Agriculture.

★ 88 ★
Floriculture
SIC: 0181; NAICS: 111422
Potted Flowering Plant Production, 2005

The wholesale value of domestically potted flowering plants for indoor and patio use was $809 million. Poinsettias were down 2% over the previous year, florist crysanthmum were up 1%, and potted orchids were up 11%.

	($ mil.)	Share
Poinsettias	$ 242.0	29.91%
Potted orchids	144.0	17.80
Florist Crysanthemum	68.9	8.52
Other	354.1	43.77

Source: *Floriculture Crops*, April 2006, p. 4, from U.S. Department of Agriculture.

★ 89 ★
Floriculture
SIC: 0181; NAICS: 111422
Rose Production by State, 2005

The wholesale value of production is $38.9 million.

	($ 000)	Share
California	$ 29,280	75.16%
Minnesota	2,517	6.46
New York	33	0.08
Other	7,126	18.29

Source: *Floriculture Crops*, April 2006, p. 4, from U.S. Department of Agriculture.

★ 90 ★
Floriculture
SIC: 0181; NAICS: 111422
Top States for Floriculture, 2005

The total wholesale value of floriculture crops grown by operations exceeding the $100,000 sales level was $5.05 billion, up 2% from 2004. These operations account for 95% of total value of floricuture crops but represent about 42% of all growers. Bedding and garden plants represent the largest contributor to wholesale production with sales of $2.61 billion.

California	.19.0%
Florida	.19.0
Michigan	.7.0

Continued on next page.

★ 90 ★
[Continued]
Floriculture
SIC: 0181; NAICS: 111422

Top States for Floriculture, 2005

The total wholesale value of floriculture crops grown by operations exceeding the $100,000 sales level was $5.05 billion, up 2% from 2004. These operations account for 95% of total value of floriculture crops but represent about 42% of all growers. Bedding and garden plants represent the largest contributor to wholesale production with sales of $2.61 billion.

Texas	5.0%
New York	3.0
Other	47.0

Source: *Floriculture Crops*, April 2006, p. 4, from U.S. Department of Agriculture.

★ 91 ★
Floriculture
SIC: 0181; NAICS: 111422

Tulip Production by State, 2005

The wholesale value of production is $38.9 million.

	($ 000)	Share
Washington	$ 10,818	27.63%
Oregon	1,911	4.88
Minnesota	706	1.80
Other	25,712	65.68

Source: *Floriculture Crops*, April 2006, p. 4, from U.S. Department of Agriculture.

★ 92 ★
Mushrooms
SIC: 0182; NAICS: 111411

Mushroom Sales by Type

Specialty mushrooms include shittake, oyster, chanterelle.

White	87.0%
Portobello/cremini	11.0
Specialty	2.0

Source: *Winston-Salem Journal*, March 1, 2006, p. E1.

★ 93 ★
Mushrooms
SIC: 0182; NAICS: 111411

Specialty Mushroom Sales, 2004-2005

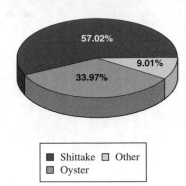

■ Shittake □ Other
■ Oyster

The overall value of sales was $908 million in 2004-2005. Figures are in thousands of pounds.

	(000)	Share
Shittake	9,081	57.02%
Oyster	5,409	33.97
Other	1,435	9.01

Source: "Mushrooms." [online] from http://www.nas.usda.gov [Published August 16, 2005] from U.S. Department of Agriculture.

SIC 02 - Agricultural Production - Livestock

★ 94 ★

Cattle Feedlots

SIC: 0211; NAICS: 112112

Largest Cattle Feeders, 2004

Companies are ranked by one-time capacity. The top 10 firms represent about 30% of the market for finished cattle marketed in the United States.

Cactus Feeders	520,000
ContiBeef	455,000
Smithfield Beef Group	387,000
Caprock Industries	293,000
Friona Industries	275,000
AzTx Cattle Co.	232,000
J.R. Simplot Co.	230,000
Cattico/Liberal Feedyards	195,000
Agri Beef Co.	180,000

Source: *Limousin's Commercial Connection*, Fall 2005, p. 3, from *Cattle Buyer's Weekly*.

★ 95 ★

Hogs and Pigs

SIC: 0213; NAICS: 11221

Hog and Pig Production by State, 2005

Figures include allowance for higher average price of state inshipment and outshipment of feeder pigs.

	($ 000)	Share
Iowa	$ 3,647,975	26.74%
North Carolina	2,088,694	15.31
Minnesota	1,570,302	11.51
Illinois	901,842	6.61
Nebraska	730,035	5.35
Oklahoma	604,390	4.43
Ohio	392,206	2.87
Other	3,708,124	27.18

Source: *Meat Animals Production, Disposition and Income*, April 2006, p. 16, from National Agricultural Statistics Service, U.S. Department of Agriculture.

★ 96 ★

Hogs and Pigs

SIC: 0213; NAICS: 11221

Leading Pork Producers, 2005

Companies are ranked by number of sows produced. Shares are shown based on 2,573,100 sows produced by the top 20 firms.

	Sows	Share
Smithfield Foods	798,000	31.01%
Premium Standard Farms	221,000	8.59
Seaboard Foods	213,600	8.30
Iowa Select Farms	150,000	5.83
Christensen Farms	148,800	5.78
Prestage Farms	140,000	5.44
The Maschhoffs	115,000	4.47
The Pipestone System	110,000	4.27
Cargill	94,000	3.65
Goldsboro Hog Farm	76,000	2.95
The Hanor Company	73,500	2.86
Tyson Foods	70,000	2.72
Other	363,200	14.12

Source: *Successful Farming*, October 2005, p. NA.

★ 97 ★

Sheep and Goats

SIC: 0214; NAICS: 11241, 11242

Sheep and Goats by State, 2006

Figures show total value of population as of January 1, 2006.

	($ 000)	Share
Texas	$ 124,260	14.19%
California	83,850	9.58
Wyoming	66,600	7.61
South Dakota	56,210	6.42
Colorado	53,040	6.06
Virginia	44,240	5.05

Continued on next page.

★ 97 ★
[Continued]
Sheep and Goats
SIC: 0214; NAICS: 11241, 11242

Sheep and Goats by State, 2006

Figures show total value of population as of January 1, 2006.

	($ 000)	Share
Montana	$ 43,365	4.95%
Other	403,915	46.14

Source: *Meat Animals Production, Disposition and Income*, April 2006, p. 16, from National Agricultural Statistics Service, U.S. Department of Agriculture.

★ 98 ★
Wool
SIC: 0214; NAICS: 11241

Wool Production by State, 2005

States are ranked by production in millions of dollars.

	($ mil.)	Share
Texas	$ 5,328	20.42%
Wyoming	3,530	13.53
California	2,450	9.39
Montana	2,440	9.35
Colorado	1,570	6.02
Idaho	1,418	5.43
Other	9,356	35.86

Source: "Sheep and Goats." [online] from http://www.nass.usda.gov [Published January 27, 2006] from U.S. Department of Agriculture.

★ 99 ★
Broilers
SIC: 0251; NAICS: 11232

Broiler Production by State, 2005

States are ranked by value of production in thousands of dollars.

	($ 000)	Share
Georgia	$ 2,897,383	12.85%
Arkansas	2,652,048	11.76
Alabama	2,409,591	10.69
North Carolina	2,231,782	9.90
Mississippi	2,054,970	9.11
Texas	1,436,644	6.37
Delaware	844,100	3.74
Kentucky	704,297	3.12
Other	7,316,095	32.45

Source: *Poultry - Production and Value 2005 Summary*, April 2006, p. 2, from National Agricultural Statistics Service, U.S. Department of Agriculture.

★ 100 ★
Broilers
SIC: 0251; NAICS: 11232

Largest Poultry Processors

Companies are ranked by weekly ready-to-cook production in millions of pounds. The top 3 firms held just 15% of the chicken market in 1978. By 2003 the top 3 held 45% of the market after industry consolidations.

	(mil.)	Share
Tyson Foods Inc.	148.84	22.45%
Pilgrim's Pride	109.06	16.45
Gold Kist Inc.	61.51	9.28
Perdue Farms Inc.	48.15	7.26
Wayne Farms Inc.	29.15	4.40
Sanderson Farms Inc.	25.11	3.79
Mountaire Farms Inc.	19.71	2.97
Cagle's Inc.	16.18	2.44
Foster Farms	15.54	2.34
House of Raeford Farms	13.40	2.02
George's Inc.	13.21	1.99
Fieldale Farms	12.85	1.94
Other	150.40	22.68

Source: *WATT PoultryUSA*, July 2005, p. 17.

★ 101 ★
Broilers
SIC: 0251; NAICS: 11232

Top Chicken Firms in Mexico

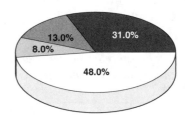

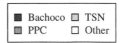

Three players control more than half of the market. The bulk of the Mexican market is unprocessed chicken with live chickens taking 31%, rotisserie 24%, and public markets accounting for 27%.

Bachoco	.31.0%
PPC	.13.0
TSN	. 8.0
Other	.48.0

Source: *US Meat Industry*, North American Equity Research, January 4, 2006, p. 5, from North American Equity Research.

★ 102 ★
Eggs
SIC: 0252; NAICS: 11231

Egg Production by State, 2005

Data are in millions of eggs.

	(000)	Share
Iowa	12,978	14.43%
Ohio	7,506	8.34
Pennsylvania	6,608	7.35
Indiana	6,254	6.95
California	5,082	5.65
Georgia	4,850	5.39
Texas	4,682	5.20
Arizona	3,416	3.80
Nebraska	3,217	3.58
Other	35,367	39.31

Source: *Egg Industry*, April 2006, p. 8, from U.S. Department of Agriculture National Agricultural Statistics Service.

★ 103 ★
Eggs
SIC: 0252; NAICS: 11231

Leading Egg Firms in Russia, 2004

Companies are ranked by annual egg production, in thousands. In 2004, Russia produced a total of 35.6 billion eggs.

GP P/F Reftinckaya	39,000.0
OOO Belgrankorm	22,734.5
PPZ Rus	15,285.0
ZAO PPZ "Etulckii"	15,261.6
ONO PPZ "Smena"	14,621.0
OOO PPZ "Lebiaje"	12,994.0
OOO EPX "Sibnip"	8,385.0
ONO PPZ "Konkursnii"	7,202.0
ONO PPZ "Pachelma"	6,914.0
PPZ Blagovarckii Bachk.	6,800.5

Source: *World Poultry*, no 12, 2005, p. 30, from Russian Poultry Union.

★ 104 ★
Turkeys
SIC: 0253; NAICS: 11233

Fresh Turkey Sales

The fresh turkey category averaged $1,193 in sales weekly per store, according to ACNielsen. About half was processed, about 40% fresh and the balance turkey in a tray.

Ground turkey	26.4%
Bone-in breasts	20.7
Whole ham	20.4
Whole Tom	16.9
Strips	3.1
Boneless roasts	2.5
Wings	2.5
Drums/legs	2.1
Giblets/necks	1.8

Source: *Meat & Seafood Merchandising*, November/December 2005, p. 23, from Perishables Group and ACNielsen.

★ 105 ★
Turkeys
SIC: 0253; NAICS: 11233

Largest Turkey Producers, 2004

Minnesota is the top producing state with a value of light weight placed at $516 million. Producers are ranked by processed weight in thousands of tons.

Jennie-O Turkey Store	514
Cargill	417
ConAgra	342
Carolina Turkey	308
Pilgrim's Pride	196
Bil Mar Foods	124
Kraft Foods	121
Foster Farms	99
Raeford	97
Perdue Farms	94

Source: *World Poultry*, no. 12, 2005, p. 12.

★ 106 ★

Turkeys

SIC: 0253; NAICS: 11233

Turkey Production by State, 2005

States are ranked by value of production in thousands of dollars.

	($ 000)	Share
Minnesota	$ 540,675	16.73%
North Carolina	491,832	15.21
Missouri	289,665	8.96
Arkansas	260,130	8.05
Virginia	242,466	7.50
Indiana	192,960	5.97
Iowa	140,352	4.34
South Carolina	133,472	4.13
Other	941,024	29.11

Source: *Poultry - Production and Value 2005 Summary*, April 2006, p. 2, from National Agricultural Statistics Service, U.S. Department of Agriculture.

★ 107 ★

Duck Meat

SIC: 0259; NAICS: 11239

Leading Duck Meat Producers Worldwide, 2005

A total of 3.3 million tons was produced. France led in per capita consumption.

China	66.36%
France	7.27
Thailand	2.63
Vietnam	2.55
Malaysia	1.76
Other	19.43

Source: *World Poultry*, no. 11, 2005, p. 10, from FAO.

★ 108 ★

Horses

SIC: 0272; NAICS: 11292

Horse Population

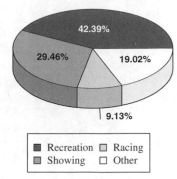

There are an estimated 9.2 million horses in the United States. Distribution is shown by type. By breed, the quarter horse led with 3.38 million. Thoroughbred followed with 1.29 million and other breeds take 4.64 million. The horse industry contributed $39 billion to the national economy, according to the American Horse Council.

	(mil.)	Share
Recreation	3.90	42.39%
Showing	2.71	29.46
Racing	0.84	9.13
Other	1.75	19.02

Source: ''Horse Industry Has $39B Impact on U.S. Economy.'' [online] from http://www.equisearch.com/equiwire_news [Published June 29, 2005] from American Horse Council.

★ 109 ★

Aquaculture

SIC: 0273; NAICS: 112511, 112512, 112519

Fish Production in Germany, 2005

Germany is the fourth largest fish processor in Europe (behind the United Kingdom, France and Spain). Total volume of fish and fishery products produced in Germany amounted to 474,428 metric tons.

Frozen	11.0%
Salted	6.0
Fresh/chilled	2.0
Other	81.0

Source: ''Germany Fishery Products Annual 2005.'' [online] from http://www.usatrade.gov [Published September 2005] from FAO and Association of the German Fish Industry and Fish Wholesalers.

★ 110 ★

Aquaculture

SIC: 0273; NAICS: 112511

Largest Salmon Producers Worldwide, 2006

Farmers are ranked by estimated production in thousand tons wfe. Pan Fish Marine Harvest also has 21% of the salmon market in Europe and 18% in the Asia market. Global production was 1,244,000 tons (wfe). Norway has 40.9% of the global production of Pacific Atlantic salmon, Chile has 35.6% of the total and Canada follows with 8.9% of the total.

	(000)	Share
Pan Fish Marine Harvest	346	20.0%
Cermaq	119	7.0
Aqua Chile	100	6.0
Fjord Seafood	78	5.0
Camanchaca	50	3.0
Los Fjordos	50	3.0
Lerey	42	2.0

Source: *Fish Farming Sector*, Handelsbanken Capital Markets, March 20, 2006, p. 10, from Kontali.

★ 111 ★

Aquaculture

SIC: 0273; NAICS: 112511, 112512, 112519

Leading Animal Aquaculture Firms, 2004

American Seafoods has fish farms in the Northern Pacific and Atlantic oceans. They also have catfish farms in the south. ARM provides feed to farms but also engages in fish farms. Red Chamber is the third largest seafood supplier in North America (after StarKist and ConAgra).

American Seafoods Group	14.2%
Archer Daniels Midland	13.3
Red Chamber Group	4.7
ContiGroupCompanies Inc.	2.9
Other	54.9

Source: "US Animal Aquaculture Industry Research Report." [online] from http://www.ibisworld.com [Accessed June 9, 2006] from IBISWorld.

★ 112 ★

Pets

SIC: 0279; NAICS: 112519, 11299

Small Pet Ownership, 1992 and 2004

There are about 73 million dogs and 90 million cats kept as pets in the United States. There are 18.2 million exotic pets, up from 16.8 million in 2002. The table shows the types of pets kept by small animal households. Households may have more than one type of pet.

	1992	2004
Hamsters	32.0%	36.0%
Rabbits	24.0	43.0
Gerbils	8.0	5.0
Guinea pig	8.0	20.0
Mouse/rat	8.0	8.0
Ferrets	2.0	7.0

Source: *USA TODAY*, July 25, 2005, p. 6D, from *National Pet Owners Survey*, American Pet Products Manufacturers Association.

★ 113 ★

Farming

SIC: 0291; NAICS: 11299

Farms by Region, 2005

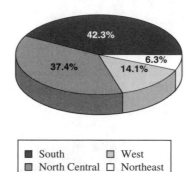

There were 2.1 million farms in the United States in 2005, 0.6 percent fewer than in 2004. Total land in farms, at 933.4 million acres, was down 2.9 million acres, or 0.3 percent, from 2004. The average farm size was 444 acres during 2005. The decline in the number of farms and land in farms reflects a continuing consolidation in farming operations and diversion of agricultural land to nonagricultural uses.

South	42.3%
North Central	37.4
West	14.1
Northeast	6.3

Source: "Charts and Maps." [online] from http://www.nass.usda.gov [Published January 2006], p. NA, from U.S. Department of Agriculture.

SIC 07 - Agricultural Services

★ 114 ★
Cotton Ginning
SIC: 0724; NAICS: 115111

Cotton Ginning by State, 2005

States are ranked by running bales ginned (excluding Linters).

	Bales	Share
Texas	8,333,750	45.65%
Arkansas	2,099,700	11.50
Mississippi	2,089,300	11.45
California	1,590,250	8.71
North Carolina	1,398,300	7.66
Louisiana	1,105,650	6.06
Tennessee	1,083,250	5.93
Other	553,850	3.03

Source: *Cotton Ginnings 2005 Summary*, May 2006, p. 1, from National Agricultural Statistics Service, U.S. Department of Agriculture.

★ 115 ★
Veterinarians
SIC: 0740; NAICS: 54194

Vet Labs

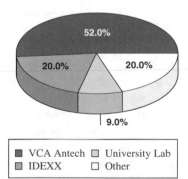

VCA Antech ● University Lab
IDEXX ● Other

VCA has more than 50% market share among vets that use only one reference laboratory. Data are based on 411 respondents.

VCA Antech	.52.0%
IDEXX	.20.0
University Lab	. 9.0%
Other	.20.0

Source: *2006 Veterinarian Survey*, William Blair & Company, February 14, 2006, p. 22, from William Blair & Co.

★ 116 ★
Veterinarians
SIC: 0742; NAICS: 54194

Vets by State, 2005

California had the most veterinarians in 2005. Nevada, Arizona and Idaho were the fastest-growing states.

California	6,975
Texas	5,198
Florida	4,219
New York	3,504
Pennsylvania	3,003
Ohio	2,847
Illinois	2,795
North Carolina	2,593
Michigan	2,583
Virginia	2,348

Source: *DVM News*, March 2006, p. 26, from American Veterinary Medical Association.

★ 117 ★
Lawn & Garden Services
SIC: 0782; NAICS: 56173

Largest Lawn/Garden Maintenance Firms

Firms are ranked by sales in millions of dollars.

TruGreen Cos.	$ 1,030.0
ValleyCrest	675.0
The Brickman Group	420.0
The Davey Tree Expert Co.	415.0
American Civil Constructors	200.0
Scotts Lawnservice	185.0
Gothic Landscape	125.0
Weed Man	105.0

Continued on next page.

★ 117 ★

[Continued]
Lawn & Garden Services
SIC: 0782; NAICS: 56173

Largest Lawn/Garden Maintenance Firms

Firms are ranked by sales in millions of dollars.

Lawn Doctor	$ 85.0
OneSource Landscape & Golf Services	78.0
Landscape Concepts	58.4
Villa & Son	58.4

Source: *Landscape Management*, July 2005, p. 24.

SIC 08 - Forestry

★ 118 ★

Timber

SIC: 0811; NAICS: 11311

Largest Timberland Owners

Firms are ranked by land owned in millions of acres.

International Paper	10.0
Plum Creek	8.1
Weyerhaeuser	7.4
MeadWestvaco	3.5
Hancock Timber	2.6
Boise	2.3
Rayonier	2.1
Temple-Inland	2.1
Potlatch	1.5

Source: *Panel World Magazine*, May 2003, p. NA.

★ 119 ★

Timber

SIC: 0811; NAICS: 11311

Leading Timber Purchasers, 2004

Companies are ranked by timber purchased in thousands of board feet during fiscal year 2004.

D.R. Johnson Lumber	101,856
Viking Lumber	51,332
Sierra-Pacific Industries	47,569
Boise Cascade	46,891
Pope & Talbot	45,660
Franklin Logging	43,396
Travis Lumber	41,540
Tricon Timber	38,480
Crown Pacific	31,948
Neiman Timber	31,234

Source: "Top 25 Purchasers of U.S. National Forest Timber." [online] from http://www.endgame.org/gtt-purchasers-2004.html [Accessed May 1, 2006] from U.S. Forest Service and Endgame.org.

SIC 09 - Fishing, Hunting, and Trapping

★ 120 ★
Fishing
SIC: 0910; NAICS: 114111
Fishing and Seafood Industry

The industry consists of 25,000 commercial fishing vessels, 700 fish processors and 2,800 distributors. It is valued at $14 billion. Annual revenues are shown for each segment. The 20 largest processors have about 40% of the market.

	($ bil.)	Share
Distributors	$ 14	56.0%
Fish processors	7	28.0
Commercial fishers	4	16.0

Source: *Business Wire*, December 5, 2005, p. NA, from Research and Markets.

★ 121 ★
Fishing
SIC: 0912; NAICS: 114111
Leading Fishing Ports, 2004

Landings are ranked by millions of pounds.

Dutch Harbor/Unalaska, Alaska	886.4
Reedville, VA	400.5
Empire-Venice, LA	379.0
Kodiak, AL	312.6
Intracoastal City, LA	301.8
Cameron, LA	243.1
New Bedford, MA	175.1
Pascagolua-Moss Point, MS	162.8
Astoria, OR	135.8
Gloucester, MA	113.3

Source: *National Fisherman*, February 2006, p. 14, from National Marine Manufacturers Association.

★ 122 ★
Fishing
SIC: 0912; NAICS: 114111
Trout Sales, 2005

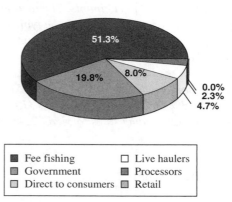

Legend:
- ■ Fee fishing
- □ Live haulers
- ■ Government
- ■ Processors
- □ Direct to consumers
- ■ Retail

The total value of both fish and eggs was $69.1 million in 2005. Distribution is shown based on 6''-12'' by point of first sale.

Fee fishing	.51.3%
Government	.19.8
Direct to consumers	8.0
Live haulers	4.7
Processors	2.3
Retail	0.0

Source: *Trout Production*, February 2006, p. 1, from National Agricultural Statistics Service, U.S. Department of Agriculture.

★ 123 ★
Hunting
SIC: 0971; NAICS: 11421

Hunters and Shooters

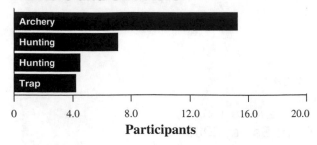

Data show millions of participants. The average number of days spent on these sports by the typical participant: Hunting (bow) 17.5 days, archery 16.9, trap (skeet) 16.8 days, hunting (rifle/shotgun) 15.8 days. The states with the highest 20 year increases in hunting license holders: North Dakota was up 51.7%, Tennessee up 34.3% and South Carolina up 31.4%. Total hunting/shooting product sales totaled $2.9 billion in 2004.

Archery	15.2
Hunting (rifle/shotgun)	7.1
Hunting (bow)	4.5
Trap (skeet)	4.2

Source: *USA TODAY*, December 1, 2005, p. 2B, from National Shooting Sports Foundation.

SIC 10 - Metal Mining

★ 124 ★

Iron

SIC: 1011; NAICS: 21221

Iron Ore Production by Country

Data show mine production in millions of metric tons of usable ore.

	(mil.)	Share
China	370	24.34%
Brazil	300	19.74
Australia	280	18.42
India	140	9.21
Russia	95	6.25
Ukraine	69	4.54
United States	55	3.62
Other	211	13.88

Source: *Mineral Commodities Summaries 2006*, Annual, p. 21, from U.S. Geological Survey, U.S. Department of the Interior.

★ 125 ★

Iron

SIC: 1011; NAICS: 21221

Iron-Ore Seaborne Trade Worldwide

Market shares are shown in percent.

CVRD	.33.0%
Rio Tinto	.24.0
BHP Billiton	.17.0
Other	.26.0

Source: *Wall Street Journal*, August 9, 2005, p. A9, from AME Iron Outlook and Dow Jones.

★ 126 ★

Iron

SIC: 1011; NAICS: 21221

Top Iron Ore Firms, 2005

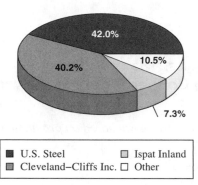

- ■ U.S. Steel
- ■ Cleveland–Cliffs Inc.
- ▢ Ispat Inland
- ▢ Other

Market shares are shown based on revenue.

U.S. Steel	.42.0%
Cleveland-Cliffs Inc.	.40.2
Ispat Inland	.7.3
Other	.10.5

Source: "IBISWorld: If Mining Giants Look to America What Will They Find?" [online] from http://biz.yahoo.com/prnews/060518/clth054.html?.v54 - 14k [Published May 18, 2006] from IBISWorld.

★ 127 ★

Copper

SIC: 1021; NAICS: 212234

Copper Production by Country

Data show mine production in thousands of metric tons.

	(000)	Share
Chile	5,320	35.70%
United States	1,150	7.72
Indonesia	1,050	7.05
Peru	1,000	6.71
Australia	930	6.24
Russia	675	4.53
China	640	4.30

Continued on next page.

★ 127 ★
[Continued]
Copper
SIC: 1021; NAICS: 212234

Copper Production by Country

Data show mine production in thousands of metric tons.

	(000)	Share
Canada	580	3.89%
Other	3,555	23.86

Source: *Mineral Commodities Summaries 2006*, Annual, p. 21, from U.S. Geological Survey, U.S. Department of the Interior.

★ 128 ★
Copper
SIC: 1021; NAICS: 212234

Leading Copper Miners Worldwide, 2004

Market shares are shown based on production.

Codelco	.12.8%
BHP Billiton	7.1
Phelps Dodge	6.9
Rio Tinto	5.2
Grupo Mexico	4.8
Other	.63.2

Source: *Materials/Construction*, Samsung Securities Equity Research, January 20, 2006, p. 3, from WMS and Samsung Securities.

★ 129 ★
Lead
SIC: 1031; NAICS: 212231

Leading Lead Miners Worldwide, 2004

Market shares are shown based on production.

BHP Billiton	9.1%
Doe Run	7.9
Xstrata	4.8
Teck Cominco	3.7
Zinifex	3.4
Other	.71.1

Source: *Materials/Construction*, Samsung Securities Equity Research, January 20, 2006, p. 3, from WMS and Samsung Securities.

★ 130 ★
Zinc
SIC: 1031; NAICS: 212231

How Zinc is Used

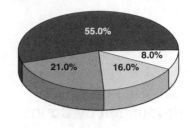

■ Galvanizing	□ Brass and bronze	
▨ Zinc–based alloys	□ Other	

The value of mined zinc was $1.06 billion in 2005. Alaska, Missouri, Montana and Washington represented 99.9% of domestic mine output.

Galvanizing	.55.0%
Zinc-based alloys	.21.0
Brass and bronze	.16.0
Other	8.0

Source: *Mineral Commodities Summaries 2006*, Annual, p. 21, from U.S. Geological Survey, U.S. Department of the Interior.

★ 131 ★
Zinc
SIC: 1031; NAICS: 212231

Largest Zinc Suppliers Worldwide, 2005

Zinc will have a greater deficit in 2006 than in 2005. Pricing will be higher in 2007 than in 2006. Market shares are estimated in percent.

Teck Cominco	.10.0%
Zinifex	9.0
Glencore	7.0
Anglo American	6.0
Hindustan Zinc	6.0
Boliden	4.0
Volcan	4.0
Xstrata (free float)	4.0
Penoles	3.0
Other	.41.0

Source: *Basic Materials*, Morgan Stanley Equity Research, December 14, 2005, p. 38, from CRU.

★ 132 ★
Zinc
SIC: 1031; NAICS: 212231

Leading Zinc Producers

Countries are ranked by mine production in thousands of tons.

	(000)	Share
China	2,300	22.77%
Australia	1,400	13.86
Peru	1,300	12.87
Canada	790	7.82
United States	760	7.52
Other	3,550	35.15

Source: *Mineral Commodities Summaries 2006*, Annual, p. 21, from U.S. Geological Survey, U.S. Department of the Interior.

★ 133 ★
Zinc
SIC: 1031; NAICS: 212231

Leading Zinc Refiners in China, 2004

China was the world's largest producer and consumer of refined zinc in 2004. It overtook the United States in 1999 and now has about 25% of the production market. Companies are ranked by share of the annual capacity of 2,537,000 tons.

Zhouzhou Smelter	11.9%
Huludao Zinc	9.6
Baijin Nonferrous Metal	5.6
Zhongjin Nonferrous Metal	5.6
Yunnan Metallurgical General	3.7
Other	63.6

Source: *Materials/Construction*, Samsung Securities Equity Research, January 20, 2006, p. 3, from Bloomberg.

★ 134 ★
Gold
SIC: 1041; NAICS: 212221

How Gold is Used Worldwide, 2005

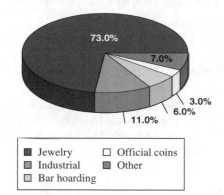

Jewelry ☐ Official coins
Industrial ■ Other
Bar hoarding

Data show top end markets. According to the World Gold Council 3,726.6 tons were consumed in 2005, with nearly three quarters of the total consumed by jewelry manufacturing.

Jewelry	73.0%
Industrial	11.0
Bar hoarding	6.0
Official coins	3.0
Other	7.0

Source: *Financial Times*, November 18, 2005, p. 4, from GEMS Ltd. and World Gold Council.

★ 135 ★
Gold
SIC: 1041; NAICS: 212221

Largest Gold Firms Worldwide, 2004

Total production of ore in 2004 was estimated at 2,461 tons. A further 829 tons was recovered from scrap. Production is shown in tons.

Newmont Mining	212.0
Anglo-Gold Ashanti	188.2
Barrick Gold	154.2
Gold Fields	128.5
Placer Dome	113.6
Harmony	101.5
Navoi Metals & Mining	58.3
De Minas Buenaventura	51.3
Kinross	49.5
Rio Tinto	48.3

Source: *African Business*, January 2006, p. 28, from World Gold Council.

★ 136 ★
Gold
SIC: 1041; NAICS: 212221

Top Gold Firms, 2004

Market shares are shown based on revenue.

Newmont Mining	.30.70%
Barrick Gold	.26.95
Rio Tinto	9.83
Placer Dome	9.33
Other	.23.19

Source: "IBISWorld: If Mining Giants Look to America What Will They Find?" [online] from http://biz.yahoo.com/prnews/060518/clth054.html?.v54 - 14k [Published May 18, 2006] from IBISWorld.

★ 137 ★
Silver
SIC: 1044; NAICS: 212222

Largest Silver Mining Firms Worldwide

Companies are ranked by silver output in millions of ounces. The Carrington mine in Australia is the world's largest silver mine. It produced 45.9 million ounces for BHP Billiton, its owner.

BHP Billiton	49.7
Industrias Penoles	44.5
KGHM Polska Miedz	43.2
Grupo Mexico	19.4
Kazakhmys	17.7
Barrick Gold	17.3
Polymetal	17.3
Rio Tinto	14.8
Coeur d'Alene Mines	14.1

Source: *Silver Sector Review and Outlook*, CIBC World Markets, February 7, 2006, p. 22, from GFMS.

★ 138 ★
Silver
SIC: 1044; NAICS: 212222

Silver Production by Country

Countries are ranked by mine production in thousands of metric tons.

	(000)	Share
Peru	3,060	16.17%
China	2,800	14.80
Mexico	2,700	14.27
Australia	2,250	11.89
Canada	1,330	7.03

	(000)	Share
Poland	1,300	6.87%
United States	1,300	6.87
Other	4,180	22.09

Source: *Mineral Commodities Summaries 2006*, Annual, p. 21, from U.S. Geological Survey, U.S. Department of the Interior.

★ 139 ★
Cobalt
SIC: 1061; NAICS: 212299

Cobalt Production by Country

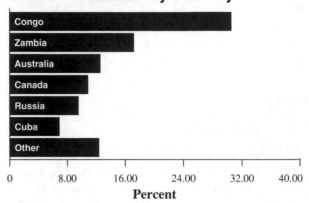

In the United States 43% of cobalt was used in superalloys (gas turbines), 9% for carbide for cutting and wear-resistant applications and 22% of production is used for various metal uses.

	(000)	Share
Congo (Kinshasa)	16,000	30.53%
Zambia	9,000	17.18
Australia	6,600	12.60
Canada	5,700	10.88
Russia	5,000	9.54
Cuba	3,600	6.87
Other	6,500	12.40

Source: *Mineral Commodities Summaries 2006*, Annual, p. 21, from U.S. Geological Survey, U.S. Department of the Interior.

★ 140 ★
Nickel
SIC: 1061; NAICS: 212234

Largest Nickel Suppliers Worldwide

The top 10 hold 73% of the market. Firms six through ten: Cubaniquel, ANTAM, Jinchuan, Sherrit and Murrin Murrin.

Norilsk/Inco/BHP Billiton/Falconbridge/SLN	.56.0%
Other	.44.0

Source: *Basic Materials*, Morgan Stanley Equity Research, December 14, 2005, p. 38, from Morgan Stanley Research and Chemical Marketing Associates Inc.

★ 141 ★
Nickel
SIC: 1061; NAICS: 212234

Nickel Production by Country

Countries are ranked by mine production in thousands of tons.

	(000)	Share
Russia	315,000	22.45%
Australia	210,000	14.97
Canada	196,000	13.97
Indonesia	140,000	9.98
New Caledonia	122,000	8.70
Cuba	75,000	5.35
Colombia	72,500	5.17
China	71,000	5.06
Other	201,500	14.36

Source: *Mineral Commodities Summaries 2006*, Annual, p. 21, from U.S. Geological Survey, U.S. Department of the Interior.

★ 142 ★
Beryllium
SIC: 1099; NAICS: 212299

Beryllium Production by Country, 2005

Data show mine production in thousands of metric tons.

United States	90
China	20
Mozambique	3
Other	1

Source: *Mineral Commodities Summaries 2006*, Annual, p. 21, from U.S. Geological Survey, U.S. Department of the Interior.

★ 143 ★
Platinum
SIC: 1099; NAICS: 212299

Platinum Demand, 2005

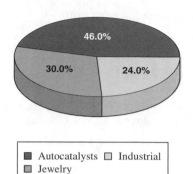

Legend: ■ Autocatalysts □ Industrial ■ Jewelry

South Africa had 78% of the 6.59 million oz. in supply in 2005, while Russia took 13%, North America took 5% and other 4%.

Autocatalysts	.46.0%
Jewelry	.30.0
Industrial	.24.0

Source: "Platinum Charts." [online] from http://www.platinum.matthey.com/market_data/1132069777.html [Accessed November 30, 2005].

★ 144 ★
Platinum
SIC: 1099; NAICS: 212299

Platinum Production by Country

Countries are ranked by mine production in kilograms.

	Kg	Share
South Africa	170,000	78.05%
Russia	27,000	12.40
Canada	9,000	4.13
United States	4,200	1.93
Other	7,600	3.49

Source: *Mineral Commodities Summaries 2006*, Annual, p. 21, from U.S. Geological Survey, U.S. Department of the Interior.

★ 145 ★
Rare Earths
SIC: 1099; NAICS: 212299

How Rare Earths Are Used

Consumption was valued at $1 billion.

Automotive catalytic convertors	.32.0%
Metallurgical additives and alloys	.16.0
Rare earth phosphors	.15.0

Continued on next page.

★ 145 ★
[Continued]
Rare Earths
SIC: 1099; NAICS: 212299

How Rare Earths Are Used

Consumption was valued at $1 billion.

Glass polishing and ceramics 12.0%
Permanent magnets 4.0
Petroleum refining catalysts 4.0
Other 17.0

Source: *Mineral Commodities Summaries 2006*, Annual,
p. 21, from U.S. Geological Survey, U.S. Department of the
Interior.

SIC 12 - Coal Mining

★ 146 ★
Coal

SIC: 1220; NAICS: 212111, 212112

Coal Supply by Region, 2004

Production is shown in millions of tons.

	(mil.)	Share
Power River Basin	420.9	37.20%
Central Appalachia	232.1	20.51
Northern Appalachia	135.0	11.93
Illinois Basin	90.2	7.97
Colorado/Utah	81.6	7.21
Other	171.7	15.17

Source: *Coal Age*, November 2005 from Platts COALdat, Energy Velocity and Energy Information Administration.

★ 147 ★
Coal

SIC: 1220; NAICS: 212111, 212112

Largest Coal Firms in China, 2003

China is the world's largest coal producer, accounting for nearly 28% of the world's annual production. Coal supplies about 70% of energy consumption in the country. Companies are ranked by output in millions of tons.

Shenhua Group	101.97
Datong Coal Mining Group	50.15
Shanxi Coking Coal Group	46.50
Yankuang Coal Mining Group	45.60
China National Coal Group	35.89
Huainan Coal Mining Group	28.31
Pingdingshan Coal Mining Group	26.69
Kailuan Group	25.50
Yangquan Coal Mining Group	22.69

Source: "Coal Mining Equipment Market in China." [online] from http://www.stat-usa.gov [Published July 2005].

★ 148 ★
Coal

SIC: 1220; NAICS: 212111, 212112

Largest Coal Mines, 2004

Mines are ranked by total production in millions of short tons. Nine of the top mines are located in Wyoming. North Rochelle is in North Dakota.

North Antelope Rochelle Complex	82.40
Black Thunder	72.22
Cordero Mine	38.74
Jacobs Ranch Mine	38.54
Antelope Coal Mine	29.68
Carbello Mine	26.48
Eagle Butte Mine	23.00
Buckskin Mine	20.26
Belle Ayr Mine	18.70
North Rochelle	15.23

Source: "Major U.S. Coal Mines." [online] from http://www.eia.doe.gov/cneaf/coal/page/acr/table10.html [Published September 2005] from Energy Information Administration and COALdat.

★ 149 ★
Coal

SIC: 1220; NAICS: 212111, 212112

Largest Coal Producers, 2004

Companies are ranked by share of total production of 1,112,099 thousand short tons. This is an increase of 40.3 million tons over the previous year. Not all sectors saw increases, it should be noted — both the industrial and coking sectors saw minor dips of 1.1% and 2.4% respectively.

Peabody Coal	17.3%
Kennecott Energy & Coal Co.	11.2
Arch Coal	10.4
CONSOL Energy	5.9
Foundation Coal Corp.	5.4
A.T. Massey Coal Co.	3.6
Vulcan Partners	3.2
North American Coal Corp.	2.8
Westmoreland Coal Co.	2.6
Robert Murray	1.9

Continued on next page.

★ 149 ★
[Continued]
Coal
SIC: 1220; NAICS: 212111, 212112

Largest Coal Producers, 2004

Companies are ranked by share of total production of 1,112,099 thousand short tons. This is an increase of 40.3 million tons over the previous year. Not all sectors saw increases, it should be noted — both the industrial and coking sectors saw minor dips of 1.1% and 2.4% respectively.

TXU Corp.	1.9%
Alliance Coal LLC	1.6
Other	32.2

Source: "Major U.S. Coal Producers." [online] from http://www.eia.doe.gov/cneaf/coal/page/acr/table10.html [Published September 2005] from Energy Information Administration and COALdat.

★ 150 ★
Coal
SIC: 1220; NAICS: 212111, 212112

Largest Coking Coal Suppliers Worldwide, 2004

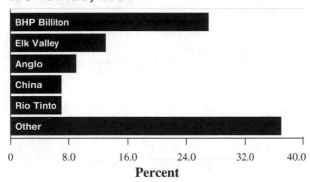

Percent

The total market for seaborne traded coking coal was 213 metric tons per year.

BHP Billiton	27.0%
Elk Valley (Fording)	13.0
Anglo	9.0
China	7.0
Rio Tinto	7.0
Other	37.0

Source: *Basic Materials*, Morgan Stanley Equity Research, December 14, 2005, p. 38, from International Iron and Steel Institute and Morgan Stanley research.

SIC 13 - Oil and Gas Extraction

★ 151 ★

Natural Gas

SIC: 1311; NAICS: 211111

Global Leaders in Natural Gas Reserves, 2004

Companies are ranked by billions of cubic meters.

Gazprom	16,400
ConocoPhillips	7,344
BP	1,275
PetroChina	1,169
Shell	1,067

Source: *Wall Street Journal*, September 29, 2005, p. A16, from United Financial Group.

★ 152 ★

Natural Gas

SIC: 1311; NAICS: 211111

Largest Natural Gas Producers, 2004

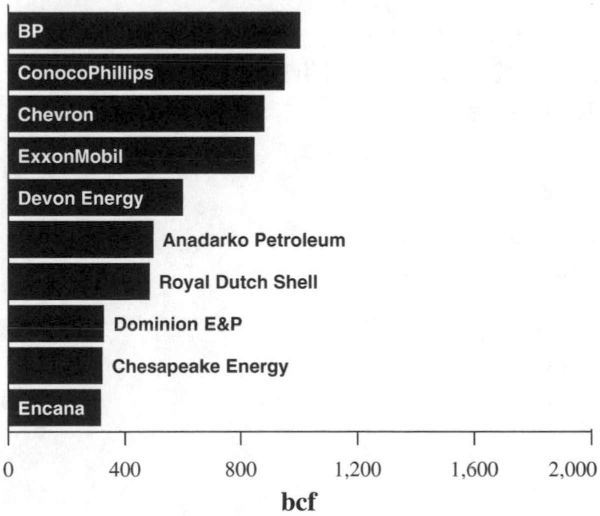

bcf

There are about 8,000 national gas producers in the United States. Companies are ranked by production in billions of cubic feet (bcf). The top ten firms have about a third of the market.

BP	1,003
ConocoPhillips	950
Chevron	880
ExxonMobil	846

Devon Energy	602
Anadarko Petroleum	499
Royal Dutch Shell	486
Dominion E&P	327
Chesapeake Energy	322
Encana	317

Source: *Oil & Gas Journal*, September 19, 2005, p. NA.

★ 153 ★

Natural Gas

SIC: 1311; NAICS: 211111

Leading Natural Gas Producers in Europe, 2004

Market shares are shown in percent.

ExxonMobil	18.0%
Shell	16.0
EBN	13.0
ENI	7.0
Total	7.0
BP	6.0
Centrica	5.0
Other	28.0

Source: "Strategey of Players." [online] from http://www.ifp.fr/IFP/en/events/panorama/IFP-Panorama06_06-StrategieActeurs-VA.pdf [Accessed June 1, 2006] from annual reports.

★ 154 ★

Natural Gas

SIC: 1311; NAICS: 211111

Leading Natural Gas Producers in Spain, 2004

The gas industry in the country is booming. Total sales for the first nine months of the year were placed at 26 billion cubic meters, up 20% from the same period in 2004. Shares are for liberalized firms.

Gas Natural	53.0%
Iberdrola	14.0
BP	9.0

Continued on next page.

★ 154 ★

[Continued]
Natural Gas
SIC: 1311; NAICS: 211111

Leading Natural Gas Producers in Spain, 2004

The gas industry in the country is booming. Total sales for the first nine months of the year were placed at 26 billion cubic meters, up 20% from the same period in 2004. Shares are for liberalized firms.

Endesa	5.0%
Union Fenosa Gas	5.0
Other	14.0

Source: *World Gas Intelligence*, November 9, 2005, p. NA.

★ 155 ★

Natural Gas
SIC: 1311; NAICS: 211111

Natural Gas Demand, 2004

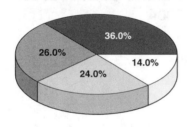

Total consumption was 22 trillion cubic feet. Distribution shows volume delivered.

Industry	36.0%
Power	26.0
Residential	24.0
Commercial	14.0

Source: *New York Times*, November 15, 2005, p. C1, from Energy Information Administration.

★ 156 ★

Natural Gas
SIC: 1311; NAICS: 211111

Natural Gas Reserves Worldwide

Natural gas demand increased in the 1980s, in part as the country recovered from the problems of the oil industry in the 1970s. Natural gas production is forecast to increase to 28.5 Tcf (trillion cubic feet) in 2020. Total demand is forecast to be 33.8 Tcf. This suggests a 5 Tcf gap, while some sources estimate an even larger gap. Countries are ranked by reserves in trillions of cubic feet.

	Tcf	Share
Rusia	1,680.00	27.5%
Iran	971.15	15.9
Qatar	910.52	14.9
Saudi Arabia	241.84	3.9
United Arab Emirates	214.40	3.5
United States	192.51	3.1
Nigeria	184.66	3.0
Algeria	160.50	2.6
Venezuela	151.39	2.5
Iraq	111.90	1.8

Source: *World Oil*, April 2006, p. 113, from U.S. Energy Information Administration.

★ 157 ★

Oil
SIC: 1311; NAICS: 211111

Largest Oil & Gas Firms Worldwide by Reserves

Firms are ranked by gas & oil reserves in billions of barrels.

Gazprom	254.0
Saudi Aramco	250.0
PDVSA	247.9
Qatar Petroleum	199.4
Iraqi Oil Ministry	136.9
Exxon Mobil	71.3
KPC	61.3
BP	56.5
ADNOC	55.8
Royal Dutch Shell	52.7
NIOC	49.3
Total	39.5

Source: *New York Times*, May 6, 2006, p. B9, from PFC Energy and Wood Mackenzie.

★ 158 ★

Oil

SIC: 1311; NAICS: 211111

Largest Oil Producing Nations, 2005

Countries are ranked by millions of barrels a day. Figures are an average for the first six months.

Saudi Arabia	9.5
Russia	8.9
United States	5.5
Iran	4.1
China	3.6
Mexico	3.4
Norway	2.7
Nigeria	2.6
Venezuela	2.6
Kuwait	2.5
United Arab Emirates	2.5

Source: *New York Times*, October 27, 2005, p. C6, from Energy Information Administration.

★ 159 ★

Oil

SIC: 1311; NAICS: 211111

Largest Oil Reserves Worldwide, 2006

At the time of the article, oil was at $75 a barrel, the highest level in nominal terms (not taking in the cost of inflation). Countries are ranked by estimates of proven oil-reserves in billions of barrels as of January 1, 2006. Total reserves were 1,292.5 million barrels in 2006, up from 1,277 million in 2005 and 1,265 million in 2004.

	(bil.)	Share
Saudi Arabia	266.8	20.64%
Canada	178.8	13.83
Iran	132.5	10.25
Iraq	115.0	8.90
Kuwait	104.0	8.05
United Arab Emirates	97.8	7.57
Venezuela	79.7	6.17
Russia	60.0	4.64
Libya	39.1	3.03
Nigeria	35.9	2.78
Other	182.9	14.15

Source: *Wall Street Journal*, April 26, 2006, p. A12, from U.S. Department of Energy.

★ 160 ★

Oil

SIC: 1311; NAICS: 211111

Oil Demand in China, 2008

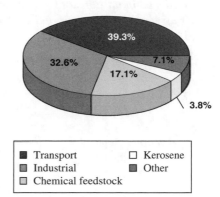

- ■ Transport
- ■ Industrial
- ☐ Chemical feedstock
- ☐ Kerosene
- ■ Other

In 2008, demand is estimated at between 6-8 million barrels a day. By 2030, demand is thought to be at 12-14 million barrels.

Transport	39.3%
Industrial	32.6
Chemical feedstock	17.1
Kerosene	3.8
Other	7.1

Source: *Financial Times*, October 15, 2005, p. 1, from International Energy Association and CS First Boston.

★ 161 ★

Oil

SIC: 1311; NAICS: 211111

Oil Production Worldwide, 2004-2005

Figures show daily production in thousands of barrels.

	2004	2005	Share
Middle East	21,573.3	22,662.1	31.26%
Eastern Europe	11,252.5	11,713.6	16.16
North America	10,904.7	10,005.4	13.80
Africa	8,869.6	9,430.9	13.01
Far East	6,689.4	6,768.9	9.34
South America	6,299.4	6,222.0	8.58
Western Europe	5,462.9	5,113.4	7.05
South Pacific	573.1	582.8	0.80

Source: *World Oil*, February 2006, p. 61, from *World Oil* surveys and third party data.

★ 162 ★
Oil
SIC: 1311; NAICS: 211111
Oil Reserves by Company, 2004

Companies are ranked in millions of barrels. Lukoil is one of Russia´s largest integrated oil and gas companies. It has 1.3% of global oil reserves.

Lukoil	15,972
PetroChina	10,997
Exxon Mobil	10,894
Petrobras	10,757
BP	9,934

Source: *Wall Street Journal*, September 29, 2005, p. A16, from United Financial Group.

★ 163 ★
Oil
SIC: 1311; NAICS: 211111
Top Oil Firms in Denmark's North Sea Region, 2004

North Sea oil was discovered in the early 1960s. The North Sea contains the bulk of Europe's oil reserves and is one of the largest non-OPEC producing regions in the world. Most reserves lie beneath waters belonging to the United Kingdom and Norway. Some of the fields belong to Denmark and other countries. Market shares are shown in percent.

Shell	36.4%
A.P. Meller	30.9
Texaco	11.9
Dong	7.9
Amerada H	5.7
Denerco Oil	3.7

Source: "Danish Oil & Gas Market." [online] from http://www.export.gov [Published July 2005] from Danish Energy Authority.

★ 164 ★
Oil
SIC: 1311; NAICS: 211111
U.S. Oil Imports, 2005

Data show the top U.S. exporting countries to the United States as of May 2005.

Canada	11.0%
Mexico	11.0
Saudi Arabia	9.0
Venezuela	8.0
Nigeria	7.0
Iraq	4.0
Other	66.0

Source: *Time*, August 30, 2005, p. 34, from Energy Information Administration.

★ 165 ★
Liquified Natural Gas
SIC: 1321; NAICS: 211112
LNG Capacity in North America

North America consumes about a third of natural gas consumption worldwide. Interest in importing liquified natural gas to North America has been moved by such things as rising gas prices and increased power plant demand. Data show share of BCF/day (billions of cubic feet) of import capacity.

Filed	18.5%
Approved	13.0
Under construction	8.2
Operational	4.2
Other planned	13.1

Source: *Oil and Gas Investor*, October 2005, p. 69.

★ 166 ★
Oil Rigs
SIC: 1381; NAICS: 213111

Jack-Up Rigs Market in the Gulf of Mexico

According to Schlumberger jack-up rigs are "A self-contained combination drilling rig and floating barge, fitted with long support legs that can be raised or lowered independently of each other. The jackup, as it is known informally, is towed onto location with its legs up and the barge section floating on the water. Upon arrival at the drilling location, the legs are jacked down onto the seafloor, preloaded to securely drive them into the seabottom, and then all three legs are jacked further down. Since the legs have been preloaded and will not penetrate the seafloor further, this jacking down of the legs has the effect of raising the jacking mechanism, which is attached to the barge and drilling package. In this manner, the entire barge and drilling structure are slowly raised above the water to a predetermined height above the water, so that wave, tidal and current loading acts only on the relatively small legs and not the bulky barge and drilling package." Figures show working rigs.

	Units	Share
Rowan	21	21.65%
Ensco	17	17.53
Diamond Offshore Drilling	12	12.37
Todco	12	12.37
Nabors Industries	4	4.12
Other	31	31.96

Source: *Investor's Business Daily*, August 17, 2005, p. A6, from ODS-Petrodata.

★ 167 ★
Oil Rigs
SIC: 1381; NAICS: 213111

Largest Workover Rig Operators

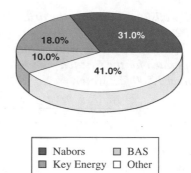

Market shares are shown in percent.

Nabors	.31.0%
Key Energy	.18.0
BAS	.10.0
Other	.41.0

Source: "Basic Energy Services In-Depth Analysis." [online] from http://energystockblog.com/by/symbol/nbr/feed [Published Dec. 1, 2005].

★ 168 ★
Oil Wells
SIC: 1381; NAICS: 213111

Horizontal Directional Drilling, 2005

There were about 2,000 units sold in 2005, meaning roughly 20,177 units have entered the market since 1982. The market has begun to rebound over the last four years. Unit sales by year: 3,990 in 2000, 1,355 in 2001, 535 in 2002, 460 in 2003, 1,045 in 2004 in 2,000 in 2005.

Telecommunications	.21.8%
Gas distribution	.18.6
Water	.13.4
Electric	.12.3
Sewer	.12.3
Oil/gas pipelines	.11.3
Other	.10.3

Source: *Underground Construction*, June 2005, p. 28, from *Underground Construction's 7th Annual HDD Survey.*

★ 169 ★
Oil Wells
SIC: 1381; NAICS: 213111

Largest Well Operators in the Gulf of Mexico, 2005

A total of 837 wells are forecast to be drilled in 2006, up 13% from 2005. About 80% of these wells will be drilled in less than 1,500 feet of water. Data show number of well operated for the first ten months of the year in less than 1,500 feet water.

	Wells	Share
Apache	65	12.52%
Chevron	48	9.25
Remington O&G	24	4.62
Energy Partners	23	4.43
Bois d-Arc	20	3.85
Arena Offshore	20	3.85
LLOG Expl	18	3.47
W&T	16	3.08
Other	285	54.91

Source: *Offshore*, January 2006, p. 34, from James H. Dodson Company.

★ 170 ★
Oil Wells
SIC: 1381; NAICS: 213111

Leading Offshore Drilling Contractors, 2005

Firms are ranked by sales in drilling size as of November 14, 2005. Figures include jackups, semisubmersibles and drillships.

Transocean	81
GlobalSantaFe	61
Noble Drilling	59
ENSCO	46
Pride International	45
Diamond Offshore	43
Todco	24
Rowan	22
China Oilfield Svcs.	16
Nabors International	16

Source: *World Oil*, December 2005, p. R16, from RigLogix mobile offshore rig database.

★ 171 ★
Oil Wells
SIC: 1381; NAICS: 213111

Leading Offshore Well Drilling Firms Worldwide, 2005

ffshore well drilling by region: 31% in North America, 26% in Asia (not including China), 16% in the North Sea, 13% in Latin America and 5% in the Middle East.

Transocean	19.0%
Global Santa Fe	8.0
Pride International	7.0
Diamond Offshore	5.5
ENSCO International	5.5
Other	55.0

Source: "Exploration & Production Activites and Markets." [online] from http://www.ifp.fr/IFP/en/events/panorama/IFP-Panorama06_01-ActiviteExploProd-VA.pdf [Accessed May 1, 2006].

★ 172 ★
Oil Wells
SIC: 1381; NAICS: 213111

Leading Onshore Well Drilling Firms Worldwide, 2005

In 2005, onshore activity accounted for 95% of the world total, with a heavy concentration in North America (88%).

Nabor Industries	17.0%
Ensign Resource Service	11.0
Precision Drilling	10.0
Patterson UTI Energy	8.5
Grey Wolf	5.0
Helmerich & Payne	5.0
Pride International	5.0
Other	38.5

Source: "Exploration & Production Activites and Markets." [online] from http://www.ifp.fr/IFP/en/events/panorama/IFP-Panorama06_01-ActiviteExploProd-VA.pdf [Accessed May 1, 2006].

★ 173 ★

Oil Wells

SIC: 1381; NAICS: 213111

Oil Well Drilling in Canada

Oil traded at C$70/bbl at the start of 2005 and gas was above C$15/GJ (gigajoule) in December 2005. The Canadian Association of Petroleum Producers predicts that spending will hit a record C$39 billion in 2006. About C$30 billion will be spent on oil sand expenditures while the rest will be spent on conventional oil and gas development. Canadian Natural Resources is the top spender with a budget of C$6.8 billion. A total of 12,584 wells were drilled in 2005 and 12,464 wells are forecast for 2006.

	2005	2006	Share
Alberta	10,256	10,493	84.19%
Saskatchewan	1,292	907	7.28
British Columbia	967	937	7.52
Ontario	30	58	0.47
Manitoba	12	42	0.34

Source: *World Oil*, February 2006, p. 73, from Canadian Association of Petroleum Producers.

★ 174 ★

Oil Wells

SIC: 1381; NAICS: 213111

Oil Well Drilling Worldwide, 2005-2006

A total of 54,407 wells are forecast to be drilled in 2006. Drilling is at a level that has not been seen in two decades. The industry is facing all sorts of issues: high prices on oil, high cost of anything related to development or exploration, inadequate rig capacities, and shortages of qualified personnel to run the rigs.

	2005	2006	Share
North America	24,550	25,080	46.40%
Far East	14,914	15,284	28.28
Eastern Union/Former Soviet Union	5,738	5,450	10.08
South America	3,815	3,867	7.15
Middle East	1,603	1,867	3.45
Africa	1,052	1,099	2.03
Western Europe	620	651	1.20
South Pacific	322	334	0.62

Source: *World Oil*, February 2006, p. 61, from *World Oil* survey.

★ 175 ★

Oil Wells

SIC: 1381; NAICS: 213111

Oil Wells by State, 2005

Data show the number of wells drilled.

	Units	Share
Texas	11,938	29.25%
Wyoming	3,650	8.94
Pennsylvania	3,277	8.03
Oklahoma	3,250	7.96
Colorado	2,625	6.43
California	2,206	5.41
Louisiana	2,125	5.21
Kansas	2,055	5.04
New Mexico	1,385	3.39
Other	8,303	20.34

Source: *Oil & Gas Journal*, January 16, 2006, p. 35.

★ 176 ★

Oil Wells

SIC: 1381; NAICS: 213111

Subsea Spending Worldwide, 2004-2008

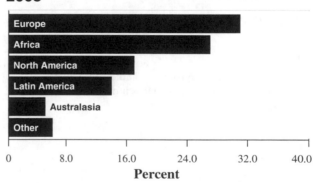

There are 2,121 subsea wells expected to be installed from 2005 - 2009. Market spending is forecast to be $31 billion, up from $18.6 billion from 1998 - 2003.

Europe	31.0%
Africa	27.0
North America	17.0
Latin America	14.0
Australasia	5.0
Other	6.0

Source: "Subsea Market Update to 2009." [online] from http://www.infield.com/subsea_production_market_reports.htm [Published Jan. 25, 2006] from *Subsea Market Update Report*.

★ 177 ★

Offshore Service Vessels

SIC: 1382; NAICS: 213112

OSV Leaders Worldwide, 2004

Offshore service vessels are used for the exploration, development and production of oil and gas at sea. Totals are as of December 31, 2004. Seacor Holdings recently acquired Sebulk International, giving them a total of 324 vessels to Tidewater's 437 vessels.

Tidewater	437
Seacor Holdings	324
Seabulk International	112
Trico Marine	83
Gulfmark Offshore	45
Hornbeck Offshore	24

Source: *Workboat*, May 2005, p. 42, from *Workboat* and company reports.

★ 178 ★

Oil Field Services

SIC: 1389; NAICS: 213112

Corrosion Engineering/Tubular Maintenance in the North Sea

Market shares are shown in percent.

Ramco	80.0%
Other	20.0

Source: "Oil Services Division." [online] from http://www.ramco-plc.com/ops_oilservices.html [Accessed May 15, 2006].

★ 179 ★

Oil Field Services

SIC: 1389; NAICS: 213112

Leading Seismic Contractors, 2004

Market shares are shown in percent. The number of active seismic crews has been falling steadily since 1999. In 2004 it took a sharp drop, falling 16%. During the first nine months of the year the industry rebounded noticeably with activity up 30%. Europe was up 22% and Latin America was up 39%. Chinese firms have recently entered the market. As China's economy develops it will be increasingly looking for oil. Chinese firms are dominant in their home market but they do have a global presence.

WesternGeco	24.0%
CGG	17.0
PGS	14.0

Veritas DCG	11.0%
BGP	6.0
Fugro	6.0
Other	22.0

Source: "Exploration & Production Activites and Markets." [online] from http://www.ifp.fr [Published May 10, 2006].

SIC 14 - Nonmetallic Minerals, Except Fuels

★ 180 ★
Stone
SIC: 1411; NAICS: 212311
How Dimension Stone is Used

Distribution is shown based on value. Rough block represented 45% of dimension stone, including exports (it represents about 61% of the tonnage).

Granite	.39.0%
Limestone	.34.0
Sandstone	.9.0
Misc. stone	.7.0
Marble	.6.0
Slate	.5.0

Source: *Mineral Commodities Summaries 2006*, Annual, p. 21, from U.S. Geological Survey, U.S. Department of the Interior.

★ 181 ★
Stone
SIC: 1420; NAICS: 212312
How Crushed Stone is Used

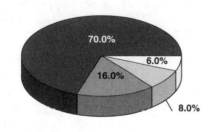

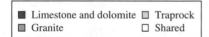

Total crushed stone was $10.2 billion in 2005. Texas, Florida and Pennsylvania were the top producers.

Limestone and dolomite	.70.0%
Granite	.16.0
Traprock	.8.0
Shared	.6.0

Source: *Mineral Commodities Summaries 2006*, Annual, p. 21, from U.S. Geological Survey, U.S. Department of the Interior.

★ 182 ★
Stone
SIC: 1420; NAICS: 212312
Leading Stone Mining Firms, 2005

Vulcan Materials had a 12%-14% share, Martin Marietta a 9%-12% share and Lafarge North America a 3%-5% share.

Vulcan Materials	.14.0%
Martin Marietta Materials	.12.0
Lafarge North America	.5.0
Other	.69.0

Source: ''Stone Mining and Quarrying in the U.S.'' [online] from http://www.ibisworld.com [Published April 13, 2006] from IBISWorld.

★ 183 ★
Sand and Gravel
SIC: 1442; NAICS: 212321
How Sand and Gravel Are Used

A total of $7.2 billion of construction sand and gravel was produced during the year by 3,900 companies.

Concrete aggregates	.45.0%
Road base and coverings for road stabilization	.24.0
Asphaltic concrete products	.13.0
Construction fill	.13.0
Other	.4.0

Source: *Mineral Commodities Summaries 2006*, Annual, p. 21, from U.S. Geological Survey, U.S. Department of the Interior.

★ 184 ★
Sand and Gravel
SIC: 1442; NAICS: 212321

Industrial Sand and Gravel Production by Country, 2005

Countries are ranked by mine production in thousands of metric tons.

	(000)	Share
United States	31,300	26.75%
Slovenia	11,000	9.40
Germany	7,500	6.41
Austria	6,800	5.81
France	6,500	5.56
Spain	6,500	5.56
Australia	4,500	3.85
United Kingdom	4,500	3.85
Other	38,400	32.82

Source: *Mineral Commodities Summaries 2006*, Annual, p. 21, from U.S. Geological Survey, U.S. Department of the Interior.

★ 185 ★
Clays
SIC: 1455; NAICS: 212324

How Ball Clay is Used, 2005

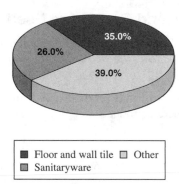

Total production was 1.3 million tons.

Floor and wall tile	.35.0%
Sanitaryware	.26.0
Other	.39.0

Source: *Mineral Commodities Summaries 2006*, Annual, p. 21, from U.S. Geological Survey, U.S. Department of the Interior.

★ 186 ★
Clays
SIC: 1455; NAICS: 212324

How Common Clay is Used, 2005

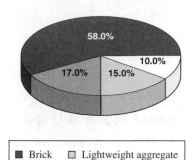

Total production was 25.5 million tons.

Brick	.58.0%
Cement	.17.0
Lightweight aggregate	.15.0
Other	.10.0

Source: *Mineral Commodities Summaries 2006*, Annual, p. 21, from U.S. Geological Survey, U.S. Department of the Interior.

★ 187 ★
Feldspar
SIC: 1459; NAICS: 212325

Feldspar Production by Country, 2005

Data show mine production in thousands of metric tons. Feldspar is mostly used in glass production.

	(000)	Share
Italy	2,500	21.74%
Turkey	2,000	17.39
Thailand	1,000	8.70
United States	760	6.61
France	650	5.65
Czech Republic	450	3.91
Spain	450	3.91
Other	3,690	32.09

Source: *Mineral Commodities Summaries 2006*, Annual, p. 21, from U.S. Geological Survey, U.S. Department of the Interior.

★ 188 ★
Boron
SIC: 1474; NAICS: 212391

Boron Production by Country, 2005

Data show mine production in thousands of metric tons. About half of U.S. production is exported.

	(000)	Share
United States	1,230	23.37%
Chile	600	11.40
Argentina	550	10.45
Russia	500	9.50
China	140	2.66
Other	2,243	42.62

Source: *Mineral Commodities Summaries 2006*, Annual, p. 21, from U.S. Geological Survey, U.S. Department of the Interior.

★ 189 ★
Potash
SIC: 1474; NAICS: 212391

Potash Production by Country, 2005

Countries are ranked by mine production in thousands of metric tons of potash equivalent.

	(000)	Share
Canada	10,700	34.52%
Russia	5,000	16.13
Belarus	4,500	14.52
Germany	3,800	12.26
Israel	2,100	6.77
Jordan	1,200	3.87
United States	1,200	3.87
China	600	1.94
Other	1,900	6.13

Source: *Mineral Commodities Summaries 2006*, Annual, p. 21, from U.S. Geological Survey, U.S. Department of the Interior.

★ 190 ★
Phosphate Rock
SIC: 1475; NAICS: 212392

Phosphate Rock Production by Country, 2005

Countries are ranked by mine production in thousands of tons.

	(000)	Share
United States	38,300	25.88%
Morocco/Western Sahara	28,000	18.92
China	26,000	17.57
Russia	11,000	7.43
Tunisia	8,000	5.41
Jordan	7,000	4.73
Brazil	6,400	4.32
Other	23,300	15.74

Source: *Mineral Commodities Summaries 2006*, Annual, p. 21, from U.S. Geological Survey, U.S. Department of the Interior.

★ 191 ★
Lithium
SIC: 1479; NAICS: 212393

Lithium Production by Country

Countries are ranked by mine production in thousands of tons.

	(000)	Share
Chile	8,000	39.22%
Australia	4,000	19.61
China	2,700	13.24
Russia	2,200	10.78
Argentina	2,000	9.80
Other	1,500	7.35

Source: *Mineral Commodities Summaries 2006*, Annual, p. 21, from U.S. Geological Survey, U.S. Department of the Interior.

★ 192 ★
Diamonds
SIC: 1499; NAICS: 212399
Industrial Diamond Production by Country

Data show mine production in millions of karats. Industrial diamonds are used to coat the edges of saws used in road construction and repair work.

	(mil.)	Share
Australia	22.7	30.68%
Congo (Kinasha)	22.0	29.73
Russia	10.4	14.05
South Africa	9.0	12.16
Botswana	7.5	10.14
Other	2.4	3.24

Source: *Mineral Commodities Summaries 2006*, Annual, p. 21, from U.S. Geological Survey, U.S. Department of the Interior.

★ 193 ★
Diamonds
SIC: 1499; NAICS: 212399
Largest Polished Diamond Exporters in Israel

Companies are ranked by value of exports in millions of dollars. The top 30 firms exported $3.13 billion representing nearly half of all diamond exports.

L.L.D. Diamonds Ltd.	$ 601
Leo Schachter Diamonds Ltd.	418
Moshe Namdar Ltd.	185
Fabrikant & Salant	175
A. Dalumi Diamonds Ltd.	149
Yerushalmi Brothers Dimaonds Ltd.	147
Yahalomei Espeka (Israel) Ltd.	139
M.I.D. House of Diamonds Ltd.	115
Wertheimer-Fruchter Diamonds	111

Source: *Diamond Intelligence Briefs*, January 19, 2006, p. NA, from Israeli Diamond Controller at the Ministry of Industry, Trade and Labor.

★ 194 ★
Diamonds
SIC: 1499; NAICS: 212399
Leading Rough Diamond Producers Worldwide, 2004

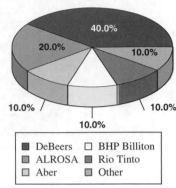

DeBeer's share is above 40% and ALROSA's is above 20%. Rio Tinto, BHP Billiton's and Aber's shares are below 10%. De Beers once controlled about 80% of the world supply of rough stones. As recently as 1998 it accounted for nearly two-thirds of supply. The rough diamond market was worth $12 billion in 2004.

DeBeers	.40.0%
ALROSA	.20.0
Aber	.10.0
BHP Billiton	.10.0
Rio Tinto	.10.0
Other	.10.0

Source: "FAQs on DeBeers." [online] from http://www.diamonds.net [Published February 22, 2006].

★ 195 ★
Diamonds
SIC: 1499; NAICS: 212399
Rough Diamond Industry Worldwide

The industry is valued at $270 billion.

	($ bil.)	Share
Africa	$ 200	74.07%
Russia	48	17.78
Australasia	6	2.22
South America	6	2.22
Canada	5	1.85
Other	5	1.85

Source: *Financial Times*, June 28, 2005, p. 2, from WH Ireland.

★ 196 ★
Diamonds
SIC: 1499; NAICS: 212319

Top Diamond Producing Nations

Countries are ranked by value of production.

	($ bil.)	Share
Botswana	$ 2.50	25.0%
Russia	1.90	18.4
Canada	1.60	16.2
South Africa	1.20	11.7
Angola	0.90	8.7
Namibia	0.65	6.3
Democratic Rep. of Congo	0.60	5.8
Australia	0.28	2.7

Source: *Jewelers Circular Keystone*, November 15, 2005, p. 62, from Minerals Bureau of South Africa's Department of Minerals and Energy.

★ 197 ★
Garnets
SIC: 1499; NAICS: 212399

Garnet Production by Country, 2005

Data show mine production in thousands of metric tons.

	(000)	Share
Australia	155,000	49.65%
India	65,000	20.82
China	29,000	9.29
United States	28,400	9.10
Other	34,800	11.15

Source: *Mineral Commodities Summaries 2006*, Annual, p. 21, from U.S. Geological Survey, U.S. Department of the Interior.

★ 198 ★
Gemstones
SIC: 1499; NAICS: 212399

Gemstone Production by Country, 2005

Data show mine production in millions of dollars.

	($ mil.)	Share
Botswana	23,000	22.77%
Russia	21,400	21.19
Australia	20,600	20.40

	($ mil.)	Share
Canada	11,700	11.58%
Angola	6,300	6.24
South Africa	6,000	5.94
Other	12,000	11.88

Source: *Mineral Commodities Summaries 2006*, Annual, p. 21, from U.S. Geological Survey, U.S. Department of the Interior.

★ 199 ★
Graphite
SIC: 1499; NAICS: 212319

How Graphite is Used, 2005

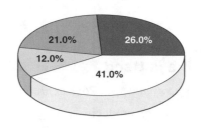

Legend	
■ Refractory applications	□ Brake linings
■ Batteries, foundries, lubricants	□ Other

Market shares are shown in percent.

Refractory applications	.26.0%
Batteries, foundries, lubricants	.21.0
Brake linings	.12.0
Other	.41.0

Source: *Mineral Commodities Summaries 2006*, Annual, p. 21, from U.S. Geological Survey, U.S. Department of the Interior.

★ 200 ★
Gypsum
SIC: 1499; NAICS: 212399

Gypsum Production by Country, 2005

Data show mine production in thousands of metric tons.

	(000)	Share
United States	17,500	15.91%
Iran	11,000	10.00
Canada	9,500	8.64
Thailand	8,000	7.27
Spain	7,500	6.82
Mexico	7,000	6.36
Japan	5,800	5.27

Continued on next page.

★ 200 ★
[Continued]
Gypsum
SIC: 1499; NAICS: 212399

Gypsum Production by Country, 2005

Data show mine production in thousands of metric tons.

	(000)	Share
Australia	4,000	3.64%
Other	39,700	36.09

Source: *Mineral Commodities Summaries 2006*, Annual, p. 21, from U.S. Geological Survey, U.S. Department of the Interior.

★ 201 ★

Perlite
SIC: 1499; NAICS: 212399

How Perlite is Used

The United States leads with 26% of production.

Building construction products	.62.0%
Horticultural aggregate	.14.0
Fillers	.11.0
Other	.13.0

Source: *Mineral Commodities Summaries 2006*, Annual, p. 21, from U.S. Geological Survey, U.S. Department of the Interior.

SIC 15 - General Building Contractors

★ 202 ★
Construction
SIC: 1500; NAICS: 23321, 23331
Largest General Building Firms, 2004

Firms are ranked by revenues in millions of dollars.

Centex	$ 10,077.0
The Turner Corp.	5,861.6
Bovis Lend Lease	2,938.7
Skanska USA Inc.	2,938.7
Clark Construction Group	2,178.0
The Whiting-Turner Contracting . . .	2,005.2
Gilbane Building Co.	1,891.0
Swinerton Inc.	1,684.0
Hensel Phelps Construction	1,651.0
Structure Tone Inc.	1,592.1

Source: *ENR*, May 16, 2005, p. NA.

★ 203 ★
Construction
SIC: 1500; NAICS: 23321, 23331
Top Construction Firms in New York

The top five firms take 64% of New York-area industry revenues.

Turner Construction	$ 2,125.0
Skanska USA	1,810.0
Tishman Construction	1,310.0
Structure Tone	1,258.0
Bovis Lend Lease	1,127.5

Source: *Crain's New York Business*, November 7, 2005, p. 28.

★ 204 ★
Residential Construction
SIC: 1521; NAICS: 23321
Green Housing Starts, 2005 and 2010

The source defines green buildings as "innovative and environmentally sensitive construction techniques and products to reduce energy and water consumption and improve residential comfort and safety". There was a 20% increase in 2005 in green home building and a 30% increase is projected for 2006. Green housing took 2% of housing starts (representing $7.4 billion) in 2005 and may take 5-10% of starts in 2010 (representing $19-38 billion).

	2005	2010
Green buildings	2.0%	10.0%
Other	98.0	90.0

Source: *PR Newswire*, April 27, 2006, p. NA, from McGraw-Hill Construction/National Association of Home Builders.

★ 205 ★
Residential Construction
SIC: 1521; NAICS: 23321
Leading Home Builders in Atlanta, GA

Market shares are shown based on number of closings.

Pulte Homes	2.8%
D.R. Horton/Torrey Dobson Homes	2.6
Bowen Family Homes	2.5
McCar Homes	2.0
John Wieland Homes and Neighborhoods . . .	1.9
The Ryland Group	1.7
KB Home/Colony Homes	1.5
Brayson Homes	1.3
Centex Corp.	1.3
Beazer Homes USA	1.2
Other	81.0

Source: *Builder*, June 2005, p. 126.

★ 206 ★
Residential Construction
SIC: 1521; NAICS: 23321

Leading Home Builders in Baltimore, MD

Market shares are shown based on closings.

NVR/NV Home/Ryan Homes	16.4%
Ryland Homes	11.3
Lennar Corp./Barry Andrews Homes	7.4
Beazer Homes USA	6.0
Technical Olympic/Masonry Homes	5.4
Pulte Homes	5.1
Other	48.4

Source: "75 Hottest Housing Markets in America." [online] from http://marketing.hanleywood.com/web/ahc/PDF/Tom_Flynn_Top_75_Final.pdf [Published Sept. 2005] from Hanley Wood Market Intelligence.

★ 207 ★
Residential Construction
SIC: 1521; NAICS: 23321

Leading Home Builders in Charlotte/Gastonia NC/Rock Hill, SC

Market shares are shown based on number of closings.

NVR/Ryan Homes	6.8%
Beazer Homes USA	4.3
Centex Corp.	3.9
St. Joe Towns & Resorts/Saussy	3.9
Pasquinelli Construction/Portrait Homes	3.2
Mattamy U.S. Group/Mulvaney Homes	2.9
Pulte Homes	2.8
The Ryland Group	2.8
D.R. Horton/Torrey Dobson Homes	2.7
Other	38.1

Source: *Builder*, June 2005, p. 126.

★ 208 ★
Residential Construction
SIC: 1521; NAICS: 23321

Leading Home Builders in Chicago, IL

Market shares are shown based on number of closings.

Pulte Homes/Del Webb	5.8%
Lennar Corp./Concord Homes/Summit Homes	5.1
D.R. Horton/Cambridge Homes	4.9
Lakewood Homes	4.9
Neumann Homes	4.4
The Ryland Group	3.5

American Invesco	3.3%
Centex Corp.	3.2
Hartz Construction Co.	2.5
Town & Country Homes	2.4
Other	58.9

Source: *Builder*, June 2005, p. 126.

★ 209 ★
Residential Construction
SIC: 1521; NAICS: 23321

Leading Home Builders in Columbus, OH

Market shares are shown based on number of closings.

Dominion Homes	23.0%
M/I Homes	21.7
Centex Corp.	6.1
Rockford Homes	4.5
Epmark	3.8
Village Communities	1.9
American Heritage Homes	1.7
Diyanni Homes	1.7
Beazer Homes USA	1.5
Joshua Homes	1.4
Other	32.8

Source: *Builder*, June 2005, p. 126.

★ 210 ★
Residential Construction
SIC: 1521; NAICS: 23321

Leading Home Builders in Dayton-Deltona, FL

Market shares are shown based on 9,119 permits issued in 2004. Figures are for the metropolitan statistical area.

Holiday Builders	7.1%
ICI Homes	5.6
Maronda Homes	4.5
Seagate Homes	4.5
Mercedes Homes	3.2
Other	75.0

Source: *Builder*, October 2005, p. 250.

★ 211 ★
Residential Construction
SIC: 1521; NAICS: 23321

Leading Home Builders in Denver, CO

Market shares are shown based on number of closings.

D.R. Horton/Continental Homes/Trimark USA	.19.7%
M.D.C. Holdings/Richmond American Homes	. 8.2
KB Homes	7.4
Lennar Corp./U.S. Home Corp.	6.8
American West Development/Oakwood Homes	. 5.5
Technical Olympic USA/Engle Homes Shea Homes	4.7
Shea Homes	4.6
The Ryland Group	4.1
Village Homes of Colorado	3.6
Beazer Homes	2.8
Other	.32.7

Source: *Builder*, June 2005, p. 126.

★ 212 ★
Residential Construction
SIC: 1521; NAICS: 23321

Leading Home Builders in Detroit, MI

Market shares are shown based on number of closings.

Pulte Homes	8.9%
MJC Cos.	6.8
Crosswinds Communities	3.8
Neumann Homes	3.3
Ivanhoe-Huntley Homes	2.6
Lombardo Cos.	2.3
Toll Brothers	1.9
Hometown Building Co.	1.7
Centex Corp.	1.6
R. Lockwood Construction	1.5
Other	.65.7

Source: *Builder*, June 2005, p. 126.

★ 213 ★
Residential Construction
SIC: 1521; NAICS: 23321

Leading Home Builders in Fort Worth-Arlington, TX

Market shares are shown based on number of closings.

D.R. Horton/Continental Homes	7.6%
Choice Homes	7.5
Lennar Corp.	5.8
KB Home	5.6

Highland Homes/Horizon Homes	5.3%
Heritage Homes Corp./Legacy Homes/ Hammonds Homes/Monterey Homes	4.7
Centex Corp./Fox & Jacobs Homes	4.0
History Maker Homes	3.5
Other	.56.5

Source: *Builder*, June 2005, p. 126.

★ 214 ★
Residential Construction
SIC: 1521; NAICS: 23321

Leading Home Builders in Greenville/Spartanburg/Anderson, SC

Market shares are shown based on number of closings.

Poinsett Homes	4.4%
McCar Homes	4.0
D.R. Horton/Torrey Homes	3.6
NVR/Ryan Homes	3.0
Southern Homes of the Upstate	2.6
Centex Corp.	2.4
Lennar Corp./Sappala Homes	2.2
Lazarus-Shouse Communities	2.1
Eastwood Homes	2.0
The Ryland Group	1.5
Other	.72.2

Source: *Builder*, June 2005, p. 126.

★ 215 ★
Residential Construction
SIC: 1521; NAICS: 23321

Leading Home Builders in Houston, TX

Market shares are shown based on number of closings.

Lennar Corp./U.S. Home Corp./Village Builders	.10.8%
KB Home	6.8
Perry Homes, a Joint Venture	6.1
D.R. Horton/Emerald/Dietz-Crane	5.8
MHI/McGuyer Homebuilders	4.7
Hovnanian Enterprises/Brighton Homes/ Parkwood Builders/Parkside Homes Royce Homes	4.0
Royce Homes	3.5
David Weekley Homes	3.3
Meritage Homes Corp./Legacy Homes/ Hammonds Homes/Monterey Homes	3.2
Pulte Homes	2.7
Other	.49.0

Source: *Builder*, June 2005, p. 126.

★ 216 ★
Residential Construction
SIC: 1521; NAICS: 23321
Leading Home Builders in Jacksonville, FL

Market shares are shown based on number of closings.

D.R. Horton	9.5%
KB Home	6.1
Maronda Homes	4.8
Mercedes Homes	4.4
Pulte Homes	4.3
Beazer Homes USA	3.4
M.D.C. Holdings/Richmond American Homes/ Crawford Homes	3.1
Mattamy U.S. Group/Atlantic Builders	3.0
SEDA Construction	3.0
Centex Corp.	2.8
Other	55.6

Source: *Builder*, June 2005, p. 126.

★ 217 ★
Residential Construction
SIC: 1521; NAICS: 23321
Leading Home Builders in Las Vegas, NV

Market shares are shown based on number of closings.

KB Home	10.8%
Pulte Homes/Del Webb	9.8
M.D.C. Holdings/Richmond American	7.7
D.R. Horton	4.9
Beazer Homes USA	4.4
Centex Corp.	3.2
Weyerhaeuser Real Estate Co./Pardee Homes	3.1
Lennar Corp./Greystone Homes/U.S. Home Corp.	2.9
American West Homes	2.3
Other	47.6

Source: *Builder*, June 2005, p. 126.

★ 218 ★
Residential Construction
SIC: 1521; NAICS: 23321
Leading Home Builders in McAllen, TX

Market shares are shown based on 6,706 permits issued in 2004.

Landmark Valley Homes	5.3%
Casa Linda Homes	4.3

Obra Homes	3.4%
McAllen Affordable Homes	1.7
KB Home	1.5
Other	83.0

Source: *Builder*, October 2005, p. 250.

★ 219 ★
Residential Construction
SIC: 1521; NAICS: 23321
Leading Home Builders in Miami, FL

Market shares are shown based on number of closings.

Lennar Corp.	8.2%
Century Homebuilders	7.9
Shoma Homes	4.4
Fredrick Builders	2.5
Jal Consultants	2.2
Jose M. Garcia-Montes	2.1
Northstar Homebuilders	1.9
Lucky Start	1.8
Sierra Construction	1.7
Centerline Homes	1.5
Other	65.8

Source: *Builder*, June 2005, p. 126.

★ 220 ★
Residential Construction
SIC: 1521; NAICS: 23321
Leading Home Builders in Nashville, TN

Market shares are shown based on number of closings.

Ole South Properties	6.0%
Beazer Homes USA	5.1
The Jones Co. of Tennessee	3.0
Greenvale Homes	2.2
Centex Corp.	1.8
John Maher Builders	1.3
Pulte Homes	1.3
The Drees Co.	1.3
Capitol Homes	1.2
Technical Olympic USA/Newmark Homes	1.0
Other	75.8

Source: *Builder*, June 2005, p. 126.

★ 221 ★
Residential Construction
SIC: 1521; NAICS: 23321

Leading Home Builders in New Orleans, LA

Market shares are shown based on number of closings.

Willow	3.5%
Landcraft Homes	2.7
Southern Homes	2.7
JBL Homes	1.3
LA Homes	1.2
Reve	0.8
Conbeth	0.7
Habitat for Humanity International	0.5
Landmark Investments & Construction Co.	0.4
Other	85.8

Source: *Builder*, June 2005, p. 126.

★ 222 ★
Residential Construction
SIC: 1521; NAICS: 23321

Leading Home Builders in Orlando, FL

Market shares are shown based on number of closings.

The Villages of Lake-Sumpter	14.4%
Lennar Corp./U.S. Home Corp.	4.8
Avatar Holdings/Brooksman-Fels	4.7
KB Home	4.1
D.R. Horton	3.9
Park Square Homes	3.8
Morrison Homes	3.5
The Ryland Group	3.4
Pulte Homes	3.1
Mercedes Homes	3.0
Other	51.3

Source: *Builder*, June 2005, p. 126.

★ 223 ★
Residential Construction
SIC: 1521; NAICS: 23321

Leading Home Builders in Philadelphia, PA

Market shares are shown based on number of closings.

NVR/Ryan Homes	6.4%
Pulte Homes	6.0
Orleans Homebuilders/Realen Homes	5.0
Toll Brothers	4.8
T.H. Properties	4.1

D.R. Horton/SGS Communities	3.9%
David Cutler Group	3.8
Hovnanian Enterprises	3.5
Beazer Homes USA	3.4
DeLuca Enterprises	2.2
Other	57.0

Source: *Builder*, June 2005, p. 126.

★ 224 ★
Residential Construction
SIC: 1521; NAICS: 23321

Leading Home Builders in Phoenix Mesa, AZ

Market shares are shown based on number of closings.

D.R. Horton/Continental Homes/Dietz-Crane Homes/Schuler Homes	9.6%
Pulte Homes/Sivage-Thomas Homes	9.6
M.D.C. Holdings/Richmond American Homes	4.3
Shea Homes	4.0
KB Home	3.1
Fulton Homes	2.9
Standard Pacific Corp.	2.9
Lennar Corp.	2.8
Meritage Home Corp./Monterey	2.6
Beazer Homes	2.4
Other	55.8

Source: *Builder*, June 2005, p. 126.

★ 225 ★
Residential Construction
SIC: 1521; NAICS: 23321

Leading Home Builders in Portland, OR/Vancouver, WA

Market shares are shown based on number of closings.

Arbor Custom Homes	6.9%
Matrix Development/Legend Homes	4.4
Hayden Homes	4.3
D.R. Horton	4.2
Centex Corp.	2.7
Helmes/New Tradition Homes	2.5
JLS Custom Homes	2.5
Don Morissette Homes	2.4
AHO Construction	2.1
Other	65.4

Source: *Builder*, June 2005, p. 126.

★ 226 ★
Residential Construction
SIC: 1521; NAICS: 23321

Leading Home Builders in Reno, NV

Market shares are shown based on closings.

Reynen & Bardis Communities	.14.2%
Barker-Coleman Communities	. 8.7
Centex Homes	. 8.7
Bailey & Dutton	. 6.3
Lakemont Homes Inc.	. 4.7
Lifestyle Homebuilders	. 4.2
Other	.53.2

Source: "75 Hottest Housing Markets in America." [online] from http://marketing.hanleywood.com/web/ahc/PDF/Tom_Flynn_Top_75_Final.pdf [Published Sept. 2005] from Hanley Wood Market Intelligence.

★ 227 ★
Residential Construction
SIC: 1521; NAICS: 23321

Leading Home Builders in Salt Lake City/Ogden, UT

Market shares are shown based on number of closings.

Ivory Homes	8.5%
M.D.C. Holdings/Richmond American Homes	. 6.7
Woodside Group	. 4.4
Hamlet Homes	. 3.4
D.R. Horton	. 2.5
Fieldstone Communities/Fieldstone Homes of	
Utah	. 2.3
Liberty Homes	. 1.7
Reliance Homes	. 1.7
Mike Schultz Construction	. 1.6
Perry Homes	. 1.5
Other	.65.6

Source: *Builder*, June 2005, p. 126.

★ 228 ★
Residential Construction
SIC: 1521; NAICS: 23321

Leading Home Builders in Seattle/Bellevue/Everett, WA

Market shares are shown based on number of closings.

Weyerhaeuser Real Estate Co./Quadrant Homes	. 9.3%
Polygon Northwest Co.	. 5.6
D.R. Horton Northwest Co.	. 4.9
Burnstead Construction Co.	. 2.8

Harbour Homes	. 2.6%
Pageantry Cos.	. 1.9
Centex Corp.	. 1.8
Conner Homes	. 1.8
Schneider Homes	. 1.7
Shea Homes	. 1.7
Other	.66.0

Source: *Builder*, June 2005, p. 126.

★ 229 ★
Residential Construction
SIC: 1521; NAICS: 23321

Leading Home Builders in the U.K., 2006

Market shares are estimated for the year.

Persimmon	. 9.8%
Barratt	. 8.9
Wimprey	. 7.3
Taylor Woodrow	. 5.0
Bellway	. 4.2
Other	.63.8

Source: *Retail and Communities, U.K.*, May 2006, p. 23, from *UK House Building*, Merrill Lynch February 2006.

★ 230 ★
Residential Construction
SIC: 1521; NAICS: 23321

Top Home Builders

Firms are ranked by housing revenues in billions of dollars.

Pulte Homes	$ 11.09
D.R. Horton Inc.	10.80
Lennar Corporation	9.55
Centex Corporation	8.92
KB Home	6.95
NVR Inc.	4.20
Hovnanian Enterprises Inc.	4.08
Beazer Homes Inc.	4.00
M.D.C. Holdings Inc.	3.93
Toll Brothers Inc.	3.83
The Ryland Group	3.79
Standard Pacific Corp.	3.48

Source: "2005 GIANTS Results." [online] from http://www.housingzone.com/factory.html [Accessed November 21, 2005].

★ 231 ★

Residential Construction

SIC: 1521; NAICS: 23321

Top Home Builders by Market Share, 1992, 2004 and 2016

The top 10 builders took 8% of the market in 1992. In 2004, they took 21% of the market. By 2016, the National Association of Home Builders forecasts the top 10 taking 35-40% of the market.

	1992	2004	2016
Top 10	8.0%	21.0%	40.0%
Other	92.0	79.0	60.0

Source: *Orlando Sentinel*, January 14, 2006, p. NA, from National Association of Home Builders.

★ 232 ★

Residential Construction

SIC: 1521; NAICS: 23321

Top Single-Family Home Makers in Japan, 2004

Market shares are shown based on housing starts of 506,663.

Sekisui House	4.0%
Daiwa House Industry	2.5
Misawa Homes	2.5
Asahi Kasei Homes	2.4
Sekisui Chemical	2.4
Other	86.2

Source: "2004 Market Share Report." [online] from http://www.nikkei.co.jp [Published July 27, 2005] from Nikkei estimates and Ministry of Land, Infrastructure and Transport.

★ 233 ★

Residential Construction

SIC: 1522; NAICS: 23322

Largest Multi-Apartment Builders in Australia, 2003-2004

Firms are ranked by number of starts.

Multiplex Limited	1,734
Meriton Apartments	1,600
Barclay Mowlem Construction	1,344
L.U. Simon Builders	1,030
Mirvac Group	980
Pindan	843

Australand Holdings	777
PFK Construction	751

Source: "Construction Equipment - Australian Industry Report." [online] from http://www.stat-usa.com [Published October 2005].

★ 234 ★

Residential Construction

SIC: 1522; NAICS: 23322

Leading Multifamily Builders, 2005

Companies are ranked by number of starts.

The Related Group of Florida	6,720
Trammell Crow Residential	6,098
Wood Partners	4,545
Tarragon Corp.	4,503
A.G. Spanos Cos.	4,400
Alliance Residential Co.	4,202
Clark Realty	3,932
Lane Co.	3,572
AvalonBay Communities	3,365
Colson & Colson Holiday Retirement	2,979

Source: *Multifamily Executive*, May 2006, p. NA, from *Multifamily Executive's Top 50 Builders*.

★ 235 ★

Residential Construction

SIC: 1522; NAICS: 23322

Leading Single Multi-Family Housing Markets, 2006

Permits are for January - March 2006. Data are unadjusted.

Atlanta-Sandy Springs-Marietta, GA	18,914
Houston-Baytown-Sugar Land, TX	17,713
Dallas-Ft. Worth-Arlington, TX	14,552
New York-Northern New Jersey-Long Island, NY-NJ-PA	14,543
Phoenix-Mesa-Scottsdale, AZ	13,393
Chicago-Naperville-Joliet, IL-IN-WI	12,588
Las Vegas-Paradise, NV	12,550
Riverside-San Bernadino-Ontario, CA	11,738
Miami-Fort Lauderdale-Miami Beach, FL	11,031
Los Angeles-Long Beach-Santa Ana, CA	9,152

Source: "Top 50 U.S. Housing Markets." [online] from http://www.buildingteamforecast.com [Published May 12, 2006] from U.S. Bureau of the Census and Reed Construction Data - CanaData.

★ 236 ★

Residential Construction

SIC: 1531; NAICS: 23321

Top Condominium Makers in Japan, 2004

Market shares are shown based on domestic sales of 159,639 units.

Daikyo	5.7%
Mitsui Fudosan	3.1
Nomura Real Estate	2.9
Sumitomo Realty & Development	2.9
Anabuki Construction	2.7
Other	82.7

Source: "2004 Market Share Report." [online] from http://www.nikkei.co.jp [Published July 27, 2005] from Real Estate Economic Institute.

★ 237 ★

Nonresidential Construction

SIC: 1541; NAICS: 23331, 23332

Nonresidential Construction Spending, 2006

Total nonresidential construction is valued at $343.7 billion in 2006. Spending on lodging grew 11.6% over 2004, the largest jump in the category.

	($ bil.)	Share
Education	$ 88.5	25.73%
Commercial	72.9	21.20
Office	54.8	15.93
Health care	41.8	12.15
Manufacturing	31.7	9.22
Amusement & recreation	21.3	6.19
Lodging	13.8	4.01
Public safety	10.6	3.08
Religious	8.3	2.41
Other	0.2	0.06

Source: *Construction Equipment*, January 1, 2006, p. 4.

★ 238 ★

Nonresidential Construction

SIC: 1542; NAICS: 23332

Largest Retail Construction Starts, 2005

Data are for the first six months of the year.

Chicago, IL	$ 488.3
Los Angeles, CA	413.1
Atlanta, GA	$ 340.1
New York City, NY	305.3
Dallas/Fort Worth, TX	294.5
Phoenix, AZ	278.0
Miami, FL	255.2
Houston, TX	227.6

Source: *Display & Design Ideas*, October 2005, p. 12, from McGraw-Hill.

SIC 16 - Heavy Construction, Except Building

★ 239 ★

Contracting Work

SIC: 1600; NAICS: 23321, 23331, 23332

Leading Specialty Contractors

Firms are ranked by revenue in millions of dollars.

EMCOR	$ 1,848.00
Comfort Systems	819.55
American Residential Services/AMS/ Rescue Rooter	690.50
Lennox Retail/Service Experts	611.70
Kinetic Systems	452.00
Limbach Facility Services	448.80
FirstEnergy Facilities Services Group	398.00
PPL Energy Services	380.44
Residential Services Group	350.00
Southland Industries	342.00

Source: *Contractor*, May 2005, p. 28.

★ 240 ★

Heavy Construction

SIC: 1620; NAICS: 23411, 23412

Heavy Construction Spending, 2006

Figures are in billions of dollars.

	($ bil.)	Share
Highways & streets	$ 70.8	33.91%
Power	41.9	20.07
Water & sewer	34.0	16.28
Transportation	30.3	14.51
Communication	16.1	7.71
Conservation & development	5.7	2.73
Other	10.0	4.79

Source: *Construction Equipment*, January 1, 2006, p. 4.

★ 241 ★

Dredging

SIC: 1629; NAICS: 23499

Dredging Market, 2006

The company had 42% of the bid market for the first quarter of 2006.

Great Lakes Dredge & Dock Corp.	42.0%
Other	58.0

Source: *EDGAR Online-8-K Glimpse*, April 24, 2006, p. NA.

★ 242 ★

Nuclear Plant Construction

SIC: 1629; NAICS: 23493

Nuclear Power Construction Worldwide, 1975-2006

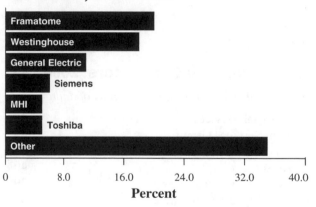

Data show share of power plant construction from 1975 - March 2006. Figures exclude Eastern Europe and the former Soviet Union.

Framatome	20.0%
Westinghouse	18.0
General Electric	11.0
Siemens	6.0
MHI	5.0
Toshiba	5.0
Other	35.0

Source: *Financial Times*, February 7, 2006, p. 17, from Credit Suisse, Goldman Sachs and companies.

SIC 17 - Special Trade Contractors

★ 243 ★
Remodeling
SIC: 1700; NAICS: 23521, 23511

Leading Remodeling Firms

Firms are ranked by volume in millions of dollars.

Champion Windows & Patio Room Co.	$ 280.27
Window World Inc.	136.55
Patio Enclosures	103.56
U.S. Home Systems Inc.	87.49
Thermoview Industries Inc.	68.86
K-Designers	56.80
Archadeck	42.08
Castle "The Window People" Inc.	37.59
Mark Four Enterprises Inc.	36.85
Windowwizard	36.12

Source: *Qualified Remodeler*, November 2005, p. 25.

★ 244 ★
Contracting Work - Painting
SIC: 1721; NAICS: 23521

Largest Painting Contractors, 2004

Firms are ranked by revenue in millions of dollars.

K2 Industrial Services	$ 58.6
Protherm Services Group	51.5
Avalotis Corp.	41.6
The Aulson Co.	40.8
Techno Coatings Inc.	39.3
Fine Painting & Decorating	35.9
Ascher Brothers Co. Inc.	33.9
Swanson & Youngdale Inc.	33.7
Robison-Prezioso Inc.	28.0
Xserv Inc.	24.5

Source: *ENR*, October 17, 2005, p. 40, from *ENR's Top 400 Specialty Contractors*.

★ 245 ★
Contracting Work - Concrete
SIC: 1741; NAICS: 23541

Largest Concrete Contractors, 2004

Firms are ranked by revenue in millions of dollars.

Miller & Long	$ 266.7
Baker Concrete Construction	212.0
Structural Group	210.0
Ceco Construction Group	183.5
United Forming Inc.	137.0
Capform Inc.	120.2
S&F Concrete Contractors Inc.	120.0
Gate Construction Materials Group	117.0
S.B. Ballard Construction Co.	116.0

Source: *ENR*, October 17, 2005, p. 40, from *ENR's Top 400 Specialty Contractors*.

★ 246 ★
Contracting Work - Masonry
SIC: 1741; NAICS: 23541

Leading Masonry Contractors

Firms are ranked by masonry revenue in millions of dollars.

McGee Brothers	$ 85.0
Western Construction Group	56.0
Pyramid Masonry Contractors	48.1
Dee Brown	44.9
Sun Valley Masonry	40.3
Griffin Masonry	29.6
Wasco	27.0
Lucia Group	25.1
Mid-Continental Restoration	24.7
F.A. Wilhelm Construction	23.4
D'Agostino Associates	23.0
Masonry Arts	23.0

Source: *Masonry Construction*, September 2005, p. 30.

★ 247 ★
Contracting Work - Wall/Ceiling
SIC: 1742; NAICS: 23542
Largest Wall/Ceiling Contractors, 2004

Firms are ranked by revenue in millions of dollars.

KHS&S Contractors	$ 357.9
Performance Contracting Group Inc.	328.0
National Construction Enterprises Inc.	156.4
Acousti Engineering Co. of Florida	150.0
Standard Drywall Inc.	135.1
Midwest Drywall Co. Inc.	109.0
Precision Walls Inc.	107.9
E&K Cos. Inc.	99.7
F.L. Crane & Sons Inc.	82.7
Baker Drywall Ltd.	79.3

Source: *ENR*, October 17, 2005, p. 40, from *ENR's Top 400 Specialty Contractors.*

★ 248 ★
Contracting Work - Sheet Metal
SIC: 1761; NAICS: 23561
Largest Sheet Metal Contractors, 2004

Firms are ranked by revenue in millions of dollars.

Limbach Facility Services	$ 88.8
Crown Corr Inc.	81.7
Kirk & Blum	62.8
Hill Mechanical Group	60.6
TDIndustries	49.6
Bonland Industries	47.2
McKinstry Co.	32.6
Dee Cramer Inc.	28.3
Midwest Mechanical Group	25.9
Holaday - Parks Inc.	22.8

Source: *ENR*, October 17, 2005, p. 40, from *ENR's Top 400 Specialty Contractors.*

★ 249 ★
Roofing
SIC: 1761; NAICS: 23561
Popular Types of Roofing

Data show the types of materials used by contractors.

Laminated shingles	48.0%
Fiberglass/asphalt	23.0
Metal	10.0
Clay tile	3.0
Wood shales	3.0
Organic asphalt	2.0%
Other	11.0

Source: *RSI*, December 2005, p. 27.

★ 250 ★
Roofing
SIC: 1761; NAICS: 23561
Residential New Roofing Market in the Western U.S., 2005

The market was valued at $2 billion. New roofs represent 36% of the market (reroofs took 52% and repairs/maintenance took 12%).

Fiberglass shingles	41.1%
Concrete tile	22.2
Clay tile	13.8
Metal/architectural	9.0
Slate	5.5
Wood shingles/shakes	1.7
Other	6.7

Source: *Western Roofing*, September/October 2005, p. NA.

★ 251 ★
Contracting Work - Steel
SIC: 1791; NAICS: 23591
Largest Steel Contractors, 2004

Firms are ranked by revenue in millions of dollars.

Schuff International Inc.	$ 126.9
Midwest Steel Inc.	80.2
The Williams Group	71.8
Area Erectors Inc.	54.0
Ben Hur Construction Co.	39.5
Danny's Construction Co.	39.2
Buckner Cos.	39.0
Sowles Co.	38.0
Century Steel Erectors	36.1
Pittsburgh Tank and Tower Co.	32.4

Source: *ENR*, October 17, 2005, p. 40, from *ENR's Top 400 Specialty Contractors.*

★ 252 ★
Contracting Work - Glazing and Curtain Wall
SIC: 1793; NAICS: 23592

Largest Glazing/Curtain Wall Contractors, 2004

Firms are ranked by sales in millions of dollars.

Harmon Inc.	$ 168.5
Enclos Corp.	131.6
Trainor Glass Co.	75.0
Walters & Wolf	67.5
W&W Glass LLC	54.0
Karas & Karas Glass Co.	37.8
Haley-Greer Inc.	27.4
Architectural Glass & Aluminum Co. Inc.	26.0
Masonry Arts Inc.	23.8
MTH Industries	22.9

Source: *Glass Magazine*, June 2006, p. NA.

★ 253 ★
Contracting Work - Excavation/Foundation
SIC: 1794; NAICS: 23593

Largest Excavation/Foundation Contractors, 2004

Firms are ranked by revenue in millions of dollars.

Hayward Baker Inc.	$ 162.0
American Asphalt & Grading	147.4
Berkel & Co. Contractors	130.0
Malcolm Drilling	123.1
Manafort Brothers Inc.	79.5
Independence Excavating Inc.	76.1
Case Foundation Co.	75.0
Beaver Excavating Co.	70.0
McKinney Drilling Co.	66.0
Condon Johnson & Associates	64.5

Source: *ENR*, October 17, 2005, p. 40, from *ENR's Top 400 Specialty Contractors*.

★ 254 ★
Contracting Work - Swimming Pools
SIC: 1799; NAICS: 23599

Largest Swimming Pool Builders

Firms are ranked by construction revenue in millions of dollars. Shares are shown based on revenue of $1,810.73 million for the top 50 firms.

	($ mil.)	Share
Blue Haven Pools & Spas	$ 254.50	14.06%
Anthony & Sylvan Pools Corp.	205.00	11.32
California Pools & Spas	175.76	9.71
Paddock Pool Construction	103.00	5.69
Shasta Industries	100.60	5.56
Swan Pools	70.20	3.88
Premier Pools & Spas Inc.	61.81	3.41
Aqua Pool & Spa Inc.	47.00	2.60
Pacific Pools and Spas	41.00	2.26
Mission Pools	34.90	1.93
Presidential Pools & Spas	33.50	1.85
The Pool People Inc.	28.40	1.57
Other	655.06	36.18

Source: *Pool & Spa News*, August 22, 2005, p. 58, from *Pool & Spa News Top 50 Builders*.

SIC 20 - Food and Kindred Products

★ 255 ★
Food

SIC: 2000; NAICS: 11231, 311412, 311421

Largest Food Processors, 2004

Firms are ranked by sales in millions of dollars.

Tyson Foods Inc.	$ 24,806
Kraft Foods Inc.	22,060
PepsiCo Inc.	19,399
Nestle	13,775
ConAgra Foods Inc.	11,896
Anheuser-Busch	11,351
Dean Foods	10,822
Sara Lee Corp.	10,743
Mars Inc.	10,600
Smithfield Foods Inc.	10,332
General Mills Inc.	9,519
H.J. Heinz Co.	8,912

Source: *Food Processing*, August 2005, p. 32.

★ 256 ★
Food

SIC: 2000; NAICS: 311511, 311513, 312111

Packaged Food Sales Worldwide, 2005-2008

Sales are shown in billions of dollars.

2005	$ 1,404.7
2006	1,441.5
2007	1,478.8
2008	1,514.9

Source: *ECRM Focus*, September 2005, p. 9, from Euromonitor.

★ 257 ★
Food

SIC: 2000; NAICS: 311513, 311615, 311812

Top Food/Drink Makers in Western Europe

The top companies are ranked by market share. Data refer to products sold for human consumption in retail, catering and artisanal markets. Germany took 23% of the market, followed by United Kingdom with 15% and France 16%.

Artisanal	4.0%
Nestle	3.0
Unilever	2.6
Danish Crown	1.2
Altria Group	1.1
Coca-Cola	1.1
Mars	1.0
Cadbury Schweppes	0.9
Diageo	0.9
Danone	0.8
Other	83.4

Source: "Confectionery Markets." [online] from http://www.fft.com [Published April 2005] from Food for Thought.

★ 258 ★
Food

SIC: 2000; NAICS: 311511, 312111

Top Grocery Brands, 2005

Brands are ranked by supermarket, drug store and mass merchandiser for the 52 weeks ended July 3, 2005.

Coke Classic Regular soft drinks	$ 1,866
Pepsi Regular soft drinks	1,525
Bud Light Domestic beer/ale	1,328
Tropicana Pure Premium ref. Orange juice	1,142
Diet Coke low calorie soft drinks	1,126
Fresh Express fresh cut salad	967
Campbells Condensed wet soup	946
Oscar Mayer ref. sliced lunchmeat	845

Source: *Retail Merchandiser*, September 2005, p. 45, from Information Resources Inc.

★ 259 ★
Food
SIC: 2000; NAICS: 311421, 311511, 311513
Top Supermarket Food Categories

Sales are shown in billions of dollars. Cigarettes actually placed ninth on the list with sales of $4.96 billion.

Carbonated beverages	$ 11.96
Milk	10.88
Fresh bread, buns & rolls	9.34
Beer/ale/alcoholic cider	7.50
Salty snacks	6.61
Natural cheese	5.92
Cold cereal	5.77
Frozen dinners/entrees	5.51
Ice cream/sherbert	4.22
Still wine	3.86
Rfg. Juices/drinks	3.82

Source: *Supermarket News*, August 22, 2005, p. 30, from Information Resources Inc.

★ 260 ★
Specialty Food Industry
SIC: 2000; NAICS: 31123, 31133, 31152
Children's Food Sales in the European Union, 2005

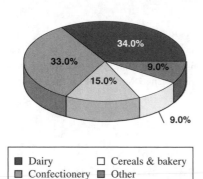

Dairy   Cereals & bakery
Confectionery   Other
Snacks

The source calculates that total sales of food marketed directly or mainly to children was 16 billion euros in 2005. Total food spending in the region was 823 billion euros.

Dairy	34.0%
Confectionery	33.0
Snacks	15.0
Cereals & bakery	9.0
Other	9.0

Source: *International Food Ingredients*, April - May 2006, p. 30, from RTS Resource.

★ 261 ★
Specialty Food Industry
SIC: 2000; NAICS: 11231, 311421, 311511
Leading Prepared Food Importers in Chile

Market shares are shown in percent.

Importadora Café do Brail	14.7%
Chilefood	8.6
Pesquera San Jose	7.1
McCain Chile	6.7
Demaria	4.5
Other	58.4

Source: "HRI Food Service Sector Annual 2006." [online] from http://www.usatrade.gov.com [Published February 2006] from Chilean Customs Service.

★ 262 ★
Specialty Food Industry
SIC: 2000; NAICS: 311421, 311615, 312111
Organic Food Sales Worldwide, 2005

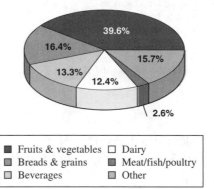

Fruits & vegetables   Dairy
Breads & grains   Meat/fish/poultry
Beverages   Other

The United States takes 46.6% of the industry, followed by Europe with a 35.7% share.

Fruits & vegetables	39.6%
Breads & grains	16.4
Beverages	13.3
Dairy	12.4
Meat/fish/poultry	2.6
Other	15.7

Source: *Datamonitor Industry Market Research*, December 1, 2005, p. NA, from Datamonitor.

★ 263 ★
Specialty Food Industry
SIC: 2000; NAICS: 311612, 311615, 311999

Prepared Food Sales at Supermarkets

Supermarket sales are shown in millions of dollars.

Beans with meat, shelf-stable	$ 434.70
Chili, shelf stable	324.53
Meat, imitation/additives	321.90
Oriental foods, misc.	293.45
Entrees, shelf stable	192.15
Chicken, shelf stable	169.23
Macaroni products, shelf stable	118.15
Corned beef hash, canned	45.82
Corned beef, canned	30.13

Source: *Progressive Grocer*, September 15, 2005, p. 22, from *Progressive Grocer's 26th Annual Consumer Expenditures Study.*

★ 264 ★
Specialty Food Industry
SIC: 2000; NAICS: 311412, 311611, 311615

Ready-to-Eat Meals in North America

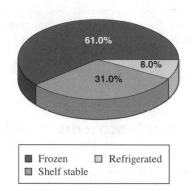

■ Frozen   □ Refrigerated
■ Shelf stable

Consumers spent $15 billion on ready-to-eat meals.

Frozen	61.0%
Shelf stable	31.0
Refrigerated	8.0

Source: *The Record*, May 23, 2006, p. L7, from market research cited by Sealed Air.

★ 265 ★
Specialty Food Industry
SIC: 2000; NAICS: 311412, 311421, 312111

Sugar-Free Food Market, 2004

Data show share of sales of selected sugar-free foods and drinks. Carbonated beverages make up 81% of the total, gum follows with 11% and desserts 4%. During the previous year, 10 new products containing Sweet'N Low (saccharin) were launched, compared to 352 products with Splenda and 130 with NutraSweet (asparteme).

Coca-Cola	36.0%
PepsiCo.	27.0
Cadbury Schweppes	18.0
Wrigley	6.9
Kraft Foods (Jell-O)	3.0
Other	9.2

Source: *Prepared Foods*, January 2006, p. 27, from Information Resources Inc. and Mintel.

★ 266 ★
Meat Packing
SIC: 2011; NAICS: 311611

Leading Beef Packers

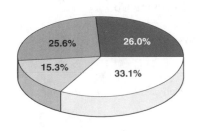

■ Cargill Meat Solutions   □ Swift & Co.
■ Tyson Foods   □ Other

In 1985, the then-top four packers accounted for 39% of all cattle slaughter. In 2004, it was about 71% of the total. The top five firms control 82.5% of the market.

Cargill Meat Solutions	26.0%
Tyson Foods	25.6
Swift & Co.	15.3
Other	33.1

Source: *The Wichita Eagle*, October 29, 2005, p. NA, from *Cattle Buyer's Weekly.*

★ 267 ★
Meat Packing
SIC: 2011; NAICS: 311611

Leading Beef Packers in Canada, 2004

Market shares are shown in percent.

Cargill	.43.9%
Tyson	.29.3
XL Foods	.12.6
Ecolait Ltee	2.4
Other	.11.8

Source: "Market Share Matrix Project." [online] from http://www.marketsharematrix.org [Published January 2005] from *Canfax Annual Report, 2004.*

★ 268 ★
Meat Packing
SIC: 2011; NAICS: 311611

Leading Beef/Poultry Processors

Firms are ranked by sales in millions of dollars.

Tyson Foods	$ 26,000
Cargill Meat Solutions	16,500
Smithfield Foods	10,900
Swift & Co.	9,700
Pilgrim's Pride	5,600
National Beef Packing Co.	4,300
Sara Lee Corp.	4,200
Hormel Foods Corp.	3,900
OSI Group	3,800
ConAgra	3,000

Source: *Refrigerated & Frozen Foods*, March 2006, p. 16.

★ 269 ★
Meat Packing
SIC: 2011; NAICS: 311611

Leading Meat Processors in Australia, 2004

Companies are ranked by metric tons of raw red meat processed. Shares are shown based on the top 25 firms.

	MT	Share
Primo Smallgoods	23,700	11.80%
Australia Meat Holdings	20,330	10.12
The Top Cut/Pacific Foods/Colonial Farm/Caterfare Group	18,500	9.21
Comgroup Supplies	17,250	8.59
Beak and Johnston	14,000	6.97
Somerville Retail Services	14,000	6.97

	MT	Share
OSI International Foods	12,300	6.13%
Australian Country Choice	11,920	5.94
Heinz Wattie's Limited	8,000	3.98
Other	60,806	30.28

Source: *Feedback - Meat & Livestock Industry Journal Supplement*, December 2005, p. 2, from ProAnd Associates Australia.

★ 270 ★
Meat Packing
SIC: 2011; NAICS: 311611

Leading Meat Processors in Denmark, 2005

Market shares are shown in percent.

Danish Crown	.50.8%
Spira Interessenter	7.8
Harboe Farm	3.6
Rose Poultry	2.9
Defco	2.6
Jens O Christiansen	2.6
Other	.20.7

Source: "National Report Denmark." [online] from http://foodqualityschemes.jrc.es/en/documents/NationalreportFR_000.pdf [Published November 2005] from Food for Thought.

★ 271 ★
Meat Packing
SIC: 2011; NAICS: 311611

Leading Meat Processors in Finland, 2005

Market shares are shown in percent.

Investor/EQT	.28.5%
Cloetta Fazer	.13.4
Danone	.13.2
Laihian Mallas	.10.5
Orkla	5.4
Barilla	3.4
Other	.25.6

Source: "National Report Denmark." [online] from http://foodqualityschemes.jrc.es/en/documents/NationalreportFR_000.pdf [Published November 2005] from Food for Thought.

★ 272 ★
Meat Packing
SIC: 2011; NAICS: 311611

Leading Meat Processors in France, 2005

Market shares are shown in percent.

Socopa	8.6%
Alliance Bigard Charal	7.3
Doux	4.9
Cana	4.1
Intermarche	3.4
LDC	3.3
Sara Lee	3.3
Other	65.1

Source: "National Report France." [online] from http://foodqualityschemes.jrc.es/en/documents/NationalreportFR_000.pdf [Published November 2005] from Food for Thought.

★ 273 ★
Meat Packing
SIC: 2011; NAICS: 311611

Leading Meat Processors in the Czech Republic, 2005

Market shares are shown in percent.

Swissholding	13.0%
Milkagro	10.1
Masospol	7.8
Agrofert	7.3
Drubezasky Podnik	6.0
Hanacky M.K.	5.2
Other	50.6

Source: "National Report Denmark." [online] from http://foodqualityschemes.jrc.es/en/documents/NationalreportFR_000.pdf [Published November 2005] from Food for Thought.

★ 274 ★
Meat Packing
SIC: 2011; NAICS: 311611

Top Fresh/Processed Meat Makers in Central/Eastern Europe

The top companies are ranked by market share. Data refer to products sold for human consumption in retail, catering and artisanal markets. Poland took 44% of the market, followed by Hungary with 19% and Romania 18%.

Smithfield Foods	7.1%
Artisanal	6.3

Saturn Nordic	5.1%
Arago	2.5
Mutenia Invest	2.4
LDC	2.1
Rawa Mazow'ka	1.6
Comtorn Tomesti	1.3
Globe Meat Tec.	1.3
Swissholding	1.2
Other	69.1

Source: "Fresh and Processed Meat Markets." [online] from http://www.fft.com [Published October 2005] from Food for Thought.

★ 275 ★
Bacon
SIC: 2013; NAICS: 311612

Top Bacon Brands, 2005

Brands are ranked by supermarket, drug store and mass merchandiser sales (excluding Wal-Mart) for the 52 weeks ended September 4, 2005.

	($ mil.)	Share
Oscar Mayer	$ 392.70	22.10%
Hormel Black label	142.61	8.03
Bar S	69.61	3.92
Farmland	69.02	3.88
Gwaltney	63.77	3.59
Smithfield	61.57	3.47
Wright	61.55	3.46
Louis Rich	57.38	3.23
Hormel	50.66	2.85
Private label	392.70	22.10
Other	415.20	23.37

Source: *Meat & Deli Retailer*, November 2005, p. NA, from Information Resources Inc.

★ 276 ★
Bacon
SIC: 2013; NAICS: 311612

Top Bacon Makers, 2005

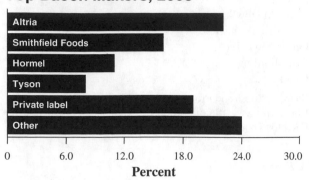

Percent

The industry was worth $2 billion.

Altria	.22.0%
Smithfield Foods	.16.0
Hormel	.11.0
Tyson	8.0
Private label	.19.0
Other	.24.0

Source: "Annual Meat Conference." [online] from http://
www.meatami.com/Education/D%20Rosenthol%20Final%
203-14-06.pdf [Published March 2006] from Information Resources Inc.

★ 277 ★
Cocktail Links
SIC: 2013; NAICS: 311612

Cocktail Link Market

Market shares are shown in percent.

Sara Lee	.74.0%
Other	.26.0

Source: *Food/Agribusiness Beverages Tobacco*, Prudential
Equity Group Research, March 8, 2005, p. 31, from Prudential Equity Group estimates.

★ 278 ★
Hot Dogs
SIC: 2013; NAICS: 311612

Top Hot Dog Brands (Refrigerated), 2005

*Market shares are shown based on supermarket, drug
store and mass merchandiser sales (excluding Wal-
Mart) for the 52 weeks ended May 15, 2005. The industry sold 837 million packages worth $1.8 billion.*

	($ mil.)	Share
Oscar Mayer	$ 308.57	17.14%
Ball Park	251.07	13.95
Bar S	119.59	6.64
Hebrew National	81.96	4.55
Nathan's Famous	67.45	3.75
Gwaltney	36.52	2.03
Bryan	33.24	1.85
Armour	32.16	1.79
Eckrich	28.47	1.58
Private label	98.57	5.48
Other	742.40	41.24

Source: *Meat & Deli Retailer*, July 2005, p. 30, from Information Resources Inc.

★ 279 ★
Hot Dogs
SIC: 2013; NAICS: 311612

Top Hot Dog Makers, 2005

*Market shares are shown based on food store, drug
store and mass merchandiser sales (excluding Wal-
Mart) for the 52 weeks ended January 26, 2006.*

Kraft/Oscar Mayer	.18.9%
Ball Park Brands	.17.5
ConAgra Inc.	8.6
Bar-S Foods Co.	8.5
Private label	6.0
Other	.40.5

Source: *Grocery Headquarters*, April 2006, p. 56, from Information Resources Inc.

★ 280 ★
Lunch Meat
SIC: 2013; NAICS: 311612

Canned Lunch Meat Market

Market shares are shown in percent. Hormel manufactures the SPAM brand.

Hormel 87.0%
Other 13.0

Source: *Food/Agribusiness Beverages Tobacco*, Prudential Equity Group Research, March 8, 2005, p. 31, from Prudential Equity Group.

★ 281 ★
Lunch Meat
SIC: 2013; NAICS: 311612

Top Lunch Meat Brands (Refrigerated, Sliced), 2005

Market shares are shown based on supermarket, drug stores and mass merchandiser sales (excluding Wal-Mart) for the 52 weeks ended May 15, 2005.

Oscar Mayer 26.5%
Hillshire Farm Deli Select 8.3
Buddig 4.3
Butterball 3.6
Land O Frost Premium 2.5
Bar S 2.4
Louis Rich 2.4
Hormel 2.3
Bryan 1.5
Private label 14.3
Other 31.9

Source: *National Provisioner*, August 2005, p. 42, from Information Resources Inc.

★ 282 ★
Lunch Meat
SIC: 2013; NAICS: 311612

Top Lunch Meat Makers (Refrigerated, Sliced), 2005

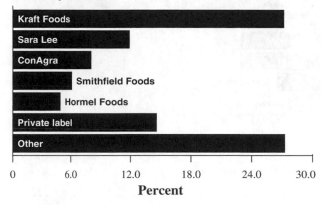

Market shares are shown based on food store, drug store and mass merchandiser sales (excluding Wal-Mart) for the 52 weeks ended January 2006.

Kraft Foods 27.2%
Sara Lee 11.9
ConAgra 8.1
Smithfield Foods 6.1
Hormel Foods 4.8
Private label 14.6
Other 27.3

Source: *US Food Industry*, North American Equity Research, January 17, 2006, p. 100, from ACNielsen and JPMorgan.

★ 283 ★
Meat
SIC: 2013; NAICS: 311612

Fresh Meat Sales, 2005

The Western United States led the nation in fresh beef sales from October - September 2005. Average sales were $9,008 per week per store, according to ACNielsen.

Loin 36.4%
Rib 20.3
Round 18.5
Chuck 13.0
Cubes 4.9
Brisket 2.7

Source: *Meat & Seafood Merchandising*, January/February 2006, p. 11, from Perishables Group and ACNielsen.

★ 284 ★

Meat

SIC: 2013; NAICS: 311612

How Beef is Consumed

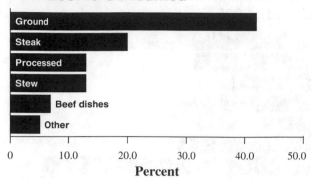

Market shares are shown in percent.

Ground	42.0%
Steak	20.0
Processed	13.0
Stew	13.0
Beef dishes	7.0
Other	5.0

Source: *Feedstuffs*, January 16, 2006, p. 8.

★ 285 ★

Meat

SIC: 2013; NAICS: 311612

Meat Sales by Volume, 2005

The beef cuts segment sold more than 2.2 billion pounds in volume and total sales were $9.8 billion.

Fresh cuts	56.0%
Ground beef	38.6
Beef patties	3.7
Prepared beef	1.7

Source: "Promotion Puzzle: Getting Real Results." [online] from http://www.meatconference.com/2006/AxmanMIPresentation3-14FINAL.pdf [Published May 16, 2006] from Perishables Group FreshFacts powered by ACNielsen.

★ 286 ★

Meat

SIC: 2013; NAICS: 311612

Packaged Meat Sales, 2005

Sales are shown in thousands of dollars for the 52 weeks ended September 19, 2005.

Frankfurters, refrigerated	$ 1,614,002
Bacon, refrigerated	1,063,963
Lunch meat, sliced refrigerated	2,340

Sausage, dinner	$ 1,287
Lunch meat, deli pouches refrigerated	963
Sausage, breakfast	940
Lunch meat, nonsliced refrigerated	292
Bratwurst and knockwurst	256
Franks, cocktail, refrigerated	100
Ham, canned or refrigerated	35
Bacon, beef and canned	5
Ham patties, canned	2

Source: *Progressive Grocer*, November 1, 2005, p. 36, from ACNielsen.

★ 287 ★

Meat

SIC: 2013; NAICS: 311612

Processed Meat Sales, 2005

The industry was worth $11.1 billion.

Sliced lunchmeat	28.0%
Refrigerated bacon	18.0
Dinner sausage	14.0
Frankfurters	14.0
Frozen handheld entrees	10.0
Refrigerated breakfast sausage/ham	8.0
Other	8.0

Source: "Annual Meat Conference." [online] from http://www.meatami.com/Education/D%20Rosenthol%20Final%203-14-06.pdf [Published March 2006] from Information Resources Inc.

★ 288 ★

Pepperoni

SIC: 2013; NAICS: 311612

Pepperoni Market

Market shares are shown for the retail sector.

Hormel	52.0%
Other	48.0

Source: *Food/Agribusiness Beverages Tobacco*, Prudential Equity Group Research, March 8, 2005, p. 31, from Prudential Equity Group.

★ 289 ★
Refrigerated Entrees
SIC: 2013; NAICS: 311612
Top Refrigerated Entree Brands, 2005

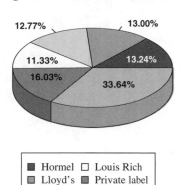

■ Hormel	□ Louis Rich	
■ Lloyd's	■ Private label	
□ Tyson	■ Other	

Market shares are shown based on supermarket, drug store and mass merchandiser sales (excluding Wal-Mart) for the 52 weeks ended April 17, 2005.

	($ mil.)	Share
Hormel	$ 89.2	13.24%
Lloyd's	87.6	13.00
Tyson	86.0	12.77
Louis Rich	76.3	11.33
Private label	108.0	16.03
Other	226.6	33.64

Source: *Refrigerated & Frozen Foods*, June 2005, p. 44, from Information Resources Inc.

★ 290 ★
Sausage
SIC: 2013; NAICS: 311612
Sausage Sales in the U.K., 2004

Brits are expected to consume an estimated 189,000 tons of sausage worth 530 million British pounds.

Standard	55.0%
Premium	32.2
Low-fat	7.4
Economy	4.5
Microwave	0.2

Source: *Meat Process*, September 14, 2005, p. NA, from Mintel.

★ 291 ★
Sausage
SIC: 2013; NAICS: 311612
Top Dinner Sausage Brands, 2005

Market shares are shown based on food store, drug store and mass merchandiser sales (excluding Wal-Mart) for the 52 weeks ended January 26, 2006.

Hillshire Farm	17.3%
Johnsonville	15.7
Eckrich	5.3
Aidells	1.6
Bryan	1.5
Johnsonville Beddar With Cheese . . .	1.4
Bar-S	1.0
John Morrell	1.0
Premio	1.0
Private label	7.8
Other	46.4

Source: *Grocery Headquarters*, April 2006, p. 56, from Information Resources Inc.

★ 292 ★
Sausage
SIC: 2013; NAICS: 311612
Top Dinner Sausage Makers, 2006

Market shares are shown based on food store, drug store and mass merchandiser sales (excluding Wal-Mart) for the 52 weeks ended January 26, 2006.

Hillshire Farm & Kahns	20.0%
Johnsonville Foods Inc.	18.8
ConAgra	8.7
John Morrell & Co.	2.2
Private label	7.8
Other	42.5

Source: *Grocery Headquarters*, April 2006, p. 56, from Information Resources Inc.

★ 293 ★
Sausage
SIC: 2013; NAICS: 311612
Top Ham/Sausage Makers in Japan, 2004

Market shares are shown based on domestic shipments of 536,505 tons.

Nippon Meat Packers	22.8%
Itoham Foods	20.9
Marudai Food	16.7

Continued on next page.

★ 293 ★

[Continued]
Sausage
SIC: 2013; NAICS: 311612

Top Ham/Sausage Makers in Japan, 2004

Market shares are shown based on domestic shipments of 536,505 tons.

Prima Meat Packers	.11.2%
Yonekyu	. 6.0
Other	.23.4

Source: ''2004 Market Share Report.'' [online] from http://www.nikkei.co.jp [Published July 27, 2005] from Nikkei estimates and Ministry of Agriculture.

★ 294 ★

Sausage
SIC: 2013; NAICS: 311612

Top Sausage (Breakfast Sausage/Ham) Makers, 2005

The industry was worth $840 million in 2005.

Sara Lee	.25.0%
Bob Evans	.17.0
Johnsonville Foods Inc.	. 8.0
Smithfield Foods	. 7.0
Private label	. 7.0
Other	.36.0

Source: ''Annual Meat Conference.'' [online] from http://www.meatami.com/Education/D%20Rosenthol%20Final%203-14-06.pdf [Published March 2006] from Information Resources Inc.

★ 295 ★

Liquid Eggs
SIC: 2015; NAICS: 311615

Top Liquid Egg Brands

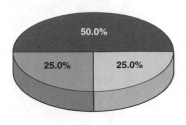

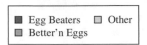

The industry is worth $197.7 million.

Egg Beaters	.50.0%
Better'n Eggs	.25.0
Other	.25.0

Source: *Omaha World-Herald*, May 3, 2006, p. NA, from companies.

★ 296 ★

Poultry
SIC: 2015; NAICS: 311615

Largest Pork Processors

Companies are ranked by daily slaughter capacity.

Smithfield Foods	97,600
Tyson Foods	67,600
Swift & Co.	39,500
Cargill Meat Solutions	35,500
Hormel Foods Corp.	24,500
Premium Standard Farms	17,100
Seaboard Farms	16,000
Indiana Packers	13,000
Hatfield	10,000
Sara Lee Corp.	8,200

Source: *Feedstuffs*, August 1, 2005, p. 2, from Sterling Marketing Inc.

★ 297 ★
Poultry
SIC: 2015; NAICS: 311615
Leading Hog Slaughter Firms

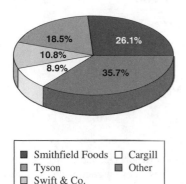

In 1985 the source reports that the then-top four companies claimed half of all steer/heifer slaughter and 39% of all cattle slaughter. Market shares are shown in percent.

Smithfield Foods	.26.1%
Tyson	.18.5
Swift & Co.	.10.8
Cargill	. 8.9
Other	.35.7

Source: "Livestock Marketing and Competition Issues." [online] from http://www.nationalaglawcenter.org/assets/crs/RL33325.pdf [Published March 20, 2006] from *Cattle Buyer's Weekly*.

★ 298 ★
Poultry
SIC: 2015; NAICS: 311615
Top Frozen Poultry Vendors, 2005

Market shares are shown based on supermarkets, drug stores and mass merchandiser sales (excluding Wal-Mart) for the 52 weeks ended April 17, 2005.

Tyson Foods	.30.5%
ConAgra	.25.8
Pilgrim's Pride	. 3.7
Advance Food	. 3.6
Private label	.25.8
Other	.27.0

Source: *Refrigerated & Frozen Foods*, June 2005, p. 56, from Information Resources Inc.

★ 299 ★
Poultry
SIC: 2015; NAICS: 311615
Top Poultry Firms in Brazil

Broiler production is expected to increase by 5% in 2006 to 9.1 million metric tons. Market shares are shown based on total slaughter.

Sadia	.14.0%
Perdigao	.12.0
Seara	. 7.0
Fragosul	. 6.0
Avipal	. 5.0
DaGranja	. 3.0
Other	.53.0

Source: "Poultry and Products Annual Poultry Report." [online] from http://www.export.gov [Published August 19, 2005].

★ 300 ★
Dairy Industry
SIC: 2020; NAICS: 311511, 311513, 311514
Dairy Products Industry Worldwide, 2004

The industry is shown by segment.

Unprocessed cheese	.25.0%
Fresh/pasteurized cheese	.23.0
Long-life/UHT milk	. 7.0
Processed cheese	. 6.0
Fruit yogurt	. 5.0
Cream	. 4.0
Flavored milk drinks	. 4.0
Chilled and shelf-stable desserts	. 3.0
Other	.23.0

Source: *Dairy Field*, August 2005, p. 68, from Euromonitor.

★ 301 ★
Dairy Industry
SIC: 2020; NAICS: 311511, 311513, 311514
Largest Dairy Firms in the Netherlands

Firms are ranked by turnover in millions of euros.

Royal Friesland Foods	4,723
Campina	3,707
Nestle Nederland	355

Continued on next page.

★ 301 ★
[Continued]
Dairy Industry
SIC: 2020; NAICS: 311511, 311513, 311514
Largest Dairy Firms in the Netherlands

Firms are ranked by turnover in millions of euros.

Leerdammer Company	292
D.O.C. Hoogeveen	269

Source: *Dairy Industries International*, September 2005, p. 37, from Productschap Zuivel (Dutch Dairy Board) and annual reports.

★ 302 ★
Dairy Industry
SIC: 2020; NAICS: 311511, 311513, 311514
Largest Dairy Producers, 2004

Firms are ranked by sales in millions of dollars.

Dean Foods	$ 10,146
Kraft Foods North America	4,700
Land O'Lakes Inc.	3,956
Saputo Inc.	3,009
Schreiber Foods Inc.	2,700
HP Hood	2,200
Kroger Co. Dairy Operation	2,100
Dairy Farmers of America	2,092
Leprino Foods Co.	1,950
Parmalat Canada	1,900

Source: *Dairy Foods*, August 2005, p. NA.

★ 303 ★
Dairy Industry
SIC: 2020; NAICS: 311511, 311513, 311514
Leading Dairy Food Makers in Denmark, 2005

Market shares are shown in percent.

Arla Foods	61.4%
Danaeg	8.8
Dansk Ost	6.6
Tholstrup	5.2
Uhrenholt	2.0
Bornholms Andelsmejeri	1.4
Lacatalis	1.1
Other	13.5

Source: "National Report Denmark." [online] from http://foodqualityschemes.jrc.es/en/documents/NationalreportFR_000.pdf [Published November 2005] from Food for Thought.

★ 304 ★
Dairy Industry
SIC: 2020; NAICS: 311511, 311513, 311514
Leading Dairy Processors in the Czech Republic, 2005

Market shares are shown in percent.

Madeta	11.9%
Milkagro	7.1
Bongrain	6.7
Dubrezama Vejprnice	5.0
Danone	4.6
Drubezasky Podnik	4.1
Other	60.6

Source: "National Report Denmark." [online] from http://foodqualityschemes.jrc.es/en/documents/NationalreportFR_000.pdf [Published November 2005] from Food for Thought.

★ 305 ★
Butter
SIC: 2021; NAICS: 311512
Top Butter Brands, 2005

Market shares are shown based on supermarket, drug stores and mass merchandiser sales (excluding Wal-Mart) for the 52 weeks ended March 20, 2005.

	($ mil.)	Share
Land O'Lakes	$ 387.6	29.27%
Challenge	64.2	4.85
Breakstone	34.0	2.57
Tillamook	30.2	2.28
Crystal Farms	25.2	1.90
Keller's	20.6	1.56
Hotel Bar	16.9	1.28
Cabot	15.7	1.19
Darigold	10.4	0.79
Private label	610.1	46.07
Other	109.5	8.27

Source: *Dairy Field*, May 2005, p. 16, from Information Resources Inc.

★ 306 ★
Butter
SIC: 2021; NAICS: 311512

Top Butter Makers, 2006

Market shares are shown based on food store, drug store and mass merchandiser sales (excluding Wal-Mart) for the 52 weeks ended January 26, 2006.

Land O'Lakes Inc. 28.6%
Keller's Creamery 6.4
Challenge Dairy Products 5.4
Tillamook County Creamery 2.1
Private label 46.2
Other 11.3

Source: *Grocery Headquarters*, April 2006, p. 56, from Information Resources Inc.

★ 307 ★
Spreads
SIC: 2021; NAICS: 311512

Top Flavored Spread Brands, 2005

Brands are ranked by sales for the 12 weeks ended October 30, 2005.

	Sales	Share
Athenos	$ 8,515,323	30.51%
Rite Tribe of the Two Sheiks . .	4,719,820	16.91
Cedars	4,612,422	16.53
Sabra	2,719,835	9.75
Rite	1,274,701	4.57
Joseph's	986,905	3.54
Cantare	556,537	1.99
Meza	369,006	1.32
Yorgo	277,574	0.99
Private label	622,827	2.23
Other	3,251,782	11.65

Source: *Frozen Food Age*, December 2005, p. 11, from Information Resources Inc.

★ 308 ★
Spreads
SIC: 2021; NAICS: 311512

Top Margarine/Spread/Butter Blend Brands, 2005

Market shares are shown based on supermarket, drug stores and mass merchandiser sales (excluding Wal-Mart) for the 52 weeks ended March 20, 2005.

	($ mil.)	Share
I Can't Believe It's Not Butter . . .	$ 248.9	20.0%
Shedd's Country Crock	186.2	15.0
Land O'Lakes	98.2	7.9
Parkay	92.5	7.4
Blue Bonnet	88.4	7.1
Imperial	59.3	4.8
Fleischmann's	51.3	4.1
Smart Balance	44.8	3.6
Brummel & Brown	38.2	3.1
Other	335.8	27.0

Source: *Dairy Field*, May 2005, p. 16, from Information Resources Inc.

★ 309 ★
Spreads
SIC: 2021; NAICS: 311512

Top Margarine/Spread/Butter Blend Makers, 2006

Market shares are shown based on supermarket, drug store and mass merchandiser sales (excluding Wal-Mart) for the 52 weeks ended January 26, 2006.

Unilever Bestfoods North America 52.4%
ConAgra Inc. 17.7
Great Foods of America 8.7
Land O'Lakes Inc. 8.4
Private label 7.6
Other 5.2

Source: *Grocery Headquarters*, April 2006, p. 56, from Information Resources Inc.

★ 310 ★
Spreads
SIC: 2021; NAICS: 311512

Top Spread Makers Worldwide, 2002

Data show the market shares of the top multinationals.

Unilever 7.1%
Kraft 2.2

Continued on next page.

★ 310 ★
[Continued]
Spreads
SIC: 2021; NAICS: 311512

Top Spread Makers Worldwide, 2002

Data show the market shares of the top multinationals.

Nestle	0.6%
Mars	0.4
Danone	0.2
Other	89.5

Source: *New Directions in Global Food Markets*, February 2005, p. 66, from Economic Research Service, U.S. Department of Agriculture and Euromonitor.

★ 311 ★
Cheese
SIC: 2022; NAICS: 311513

Bulk Sandwich Cheese Market Shares

According to ACNielsen the Eastern United States led in deli sandwich cheese sales with sales of $3,892 per week per store. It also took 14.1% of industry sales.

American Cheese	40.6%
Swiss	24.0
Provolone	11.7
Cheddar	7.9

Source: *InStore Buyer*, May 2005, p. 98, from Perishables Group and ACNielsen.

★ 312 ★
Cheese
SIC: 2022; NAICS: 311513

Leading Cheese Brands in the U.K., 2005

Sales are shown for the 52 weeks ended October 1, 2005. Figures are in thousands of pounds sterling and for all outlets.

	(000)	Share
Dairylea	£ 116,822	5.24%
Cathedral City	85,855	3.85
Cheestrings	52,717	2.37
Philadelphia	51,504	2.31
McLelland	48,398	2.17
Pilgrims Choice	41,305	1.85
Mini Baby Bel	33,843	1.52
Laughing Cow	22,101	0.99
Primula	14,072	0.63
Wyke	13,909	0.62
Other	1,747,286	78.43

Source: *Grocer*, December 17, 2005, p. 77, from ACNielsen.

★ 313 ★
Cheese
SIC: 2022; NAICS: 311513

Top Cheese Brands in the U.K., 2004

The industry was worth 1.83 billion British pounds in 2004. Sales were up about 16% from 2000, largely because of consumers moving up to specialty cheeses. Continental cheeses, one of the more popular types, grew 26% from 2000 to 2004. Kids' snacks are also booming.

	(mil.)	Share
Dairylea	120	6.56%
Cathedral City	92	5.03
Seriously Strong	52	2.84
Pilgrim's Choice	51	2.79
Cheestrings	49	2.68
Philadelphia	46	2.51
Davidstow	36	1.97
Babybel	34	1.86
The Laughing Cow	33	1.80
Other	1,317	71.97

Source: *Marketing*, September 21, 2005, p. 38, from Mintel.

★ 314 ★
Cheese
SIC: 2022; NAICS: 311513

Top Cheese Brands (Natural Cubed), 2005

Brands are ranked by sales for the 12 weeks ended October 30, 2005.

	Sales	Share
Kraft	$ 6,231,798	24.1%
Sargento Sunbursts	1,253,997	4.8
Hoffman's	770,622	3.0
Sargento Stars and Moons	693,226	2.7
Sorrento Shapesters	616,080	2.4
Sargento	385,690	1.5
Black Bear	195,931	0.8
Rosenborg	194,914	0.8
Private label	2,585,336	10.0
Other	12,927,594	50.0

Source: *Frozen Food Age*, December 2005, p. 11, from Information Resources Inc.

★ 315 ★
Cheese
SIC: 2022; NAICS: 311513

Top Cheese Makers, 2005

Market shares are shown based on food store, drug store and mass merchandiser sales (excluding Wal-Mart) for the 52 weeks ended January 2006.

Kraft Foods	37.2%
Sargento Foods	4.5
Borden	2.4
Groupe Lactalis	2.4
Tillamook County	2.3
Land O'Lakes	1.5
Private label	31.9
Other	17.9

Source: *US Food Industry*, North American Equity Research, January 17, 2006, p. 100, from ACNielsen and JPMorgan.

★ 316 ★
Cheese
SIC: 2022; NAICS: 311513

Top Cheese Processors in Canada

Market shares are shown in percent.

Saputo Inc.	25.54%
Kraft Canada Inc.	23.31
Agropur Cooperative Ltd.	18.87
Parmalat Canada Ltd.	12.30
Gerber Cheese Co Ltd.	1.82
Other	18.16

Source: "Dairy Processing in Canada 2004-2005." [online] from http://www.dairyinfo.gc.ca/pdf_files/dairy_processing_canada_e.pdf [Published August 2005] from Euromonitor's *Packaged Food in Canada*, January 2005.

★ 317 ★
Cheese
SIC: 2022; NAICS: 311513

Top Natural Cheese Brands, 2005

Market shares are shown based on food store, drug store and mass merchandiser sales (excluding Wal-Mart) for the 52 weeks ended August 7, 2005.

	($ mil.)	Share
Kraft	$ 1,342.0	22.51%
Sargento	414.1	6.95
Tillamook	201.1	3.37
Crystal Farms	138.1	2.32
Precious	105.3	1.77

	($ mil.)	Share
Polly O	$ 101.0	1.69%
Sorrento	99.5	1.67
Frigo	96.5	1.62
Borden	79.7	1.34
Private label	2,136.9	35.85
Other	1,246.9	20.92

Source: *Dairy Foods*, September 2005, p. 16, from Information Resources Inc.

★ 318 ★
Cheese
SIC: 2022; NAICS: 311513

Top Natural Cheese Brands (Chunks), 2005

Market shares are shown based on food store, drug store and mass merchandiser sales (excluding Wal-Mart) for the 52 weeks ended August 7, 2005.

	($ mil.)	Share
Kraft	$ 230	10.46%
Tillamook	154	7.01
Kraft Cracker Barrel	103	4.69
Land O'Lakes	50	2.27
Cacique	47	2.14
Helluva Good	44	2.00
Cabot	43	1.96
Polly O	42	1.91
Precious	36	1.64
Private label	815	37.08
Other	634	28.84

Source: *Dairy Foods*, December 2005, p. 46, from Information Resources Inc.

★ 319 ★
Cheese
SIC: 2022; NAICS: 311513

Top Natural Cheese Brands (Processed), 2006

Market shares are shown based on food store, drug store and mass merchandiser sales (excluding Wal-Mart) for the 52 weeks ended February 19, 2006.

	($ mil.)	Share
Kraft Singles	$ 508	38.40%
Kraft Deli Deluxe	124	9.37
Borden	102	7.71
Kraft Velveeta	65	4.91

Continued on next page.

[Continued]
Cheese
SIC: 2022; NAICS: 311513

Top Natural Cheese Brands (Processed), 2006

Market shares are shown based on food store, drug store and mass merchandiser sales (excluding Wal-Mart) for the 52 weeks ended February 19, 2006.

	($ mil.)	Share
Kraft Free	$ 33	2.49%
Land O'Lakes	32	2.42
Crystal Farms	22	1.66
Galaxy Foods Veggie Slices	15	1.13
Kraft Deluxe	10	0.76
Other	412	31.14

Source: *Dairy Foods*, April 2006, p. 16, from Information Resources Inc.

★ 320 ★
Cheese
SIC: 2022; NAICS: 311513

Top Natural Cheese (Sliced) Brands, 2005

Market shares are shown based on supermarket, drug store and mass merchandiser sales (excluding Wal-Mart) for the 52 weeks ended November 27, 2005.

	($ mil.)	Share
Sargento	$ 85	13.49%
Kraft	50	7.94
Tillamook	37	5.87
Alpine Lace	26	4.13
Kraft Cracker Cuts	22	3.49
Kraft Deli Deluxe	22	3.49
Sara Lee	18	2.86
Sargento Deli Style	18	2.86
Kraft Deli Thin	15	2.38
Other	337	53.49

Source: *Dairy Field*, May 2005, p. 16, from Information Resources Inc.

★ 321 ★
Cheese
SIC: 2022; NAICS: 311513

Top Natural Shredded Cheese Brands, 2005

Market shares are shown based on food store, drug store and warehouse sales (excluding Wal-Mart) for the 52 weeks ended May 15, 2005.

	($ mil.)	Share
Kraft	$ 575	28.24%
Sargento	227	11.15
Crystal Farms	81	3.98
Borden	58	2.85
Kraft Classic Melts	31	1.52
Kraft Free	31	1.52
Di Giorno	24	1.18
Stella	13	0.64
Sorrento	12	0.59
Private label	870	42.73
Other	114	5.60

Source: *Dairy Foods*, August 2005, p. 16, from Information Resources Inc.

★ 322 ★
Baby Food
SIC: 2023; NAICS: 311514

Top Baby Food Makers, 2005

Market shares are shown based on food store, drug store and mass merchandiser sales (excluding Wal-Mart) for the 52 weeks ended July 10, 2005.

Gerber Products	81.2%
Beech-Nut Corp.	10.8
Del Monte Foods	5.1
Hain Celestial Group	1.5
Kraft/Nabisco	0.9
Other	1.4

Source: *Grocery Headquarters*, October 2005, p. 20, from Information Resources Inc.

★ 323 ★
Baby Formula
SIC: 2023; NAICS: 311514

Top Baby Formula Brands, 2005

Brands are ranked by sales in millions of dollars at supermarkets, drug stores and discount stores (excluding Wal-Mart) for the 52 weeks ended October 2, 2005.

	($ mil.)	Share
Similac Advance	$ 71.6	14.56%
Enfamil Lipil	40.9	8.32
Isomil Advance	33.1	6.73
Similac Alimentum Advance	25.4	5.17
Similac	14.1	2.87
Enfamil AR Lipil	11.9	2.42
Enfamil Prosobee Lipil	10.6	2.16
Enfamil	9.5	1.93
Nutramigen	8.8	1.79
Carnation Good Start	8.1	1.65
Other	257.6	52.40

Source: *MMR*, November 14, 2005, p. 1, from Information Resources Inc.

★ 324 ★
Creamer
SIC: 2023; NAICS: 311514

Top Cream/Half & Half Brands, 2005

Brands are ranked by sales for the 12 weeks ended October 30, 2005.

	Sales	Share
Land O'Lakes	$ 10,653,099	9.06%
Land O'Lakes Ultra Fresh	8,623,662	7.33
Hood H	5,140,500	4.37
Garelick Farms	3,973,153	3.38
Nestle Coffee Mate	2,938,035	2.50
Dean's	2,652,646	2.26
C.F. Burger	1,678,386	1.43
Darigold	1,592,153	1.35
Hiland	1,433,311	1.22
Private label	53,676,576	45.64
Other	25,246,959	21.47

Source: *Frozen Food Age*, December 2005, p. 11, from Information Resources Inc.

★ 325 ★
Frozen Desserts
SIC: 2024; NAICS: 31152

Top Frozen Novelty Brands, 2005

Brands are ranked by sales in millions of dollars at supermarkets, drug stores and discount stores (excluding Wal-Mart) for the 52 weeks ended September 4, 2005.

	($ mil.)	Share
Nestle Drumstick	$ 131	4.12%
Klondike	129	4.05
Dreyer's Edy's Whole Fruit	101	3.17
Popsicle	98	3.08
Carvel	87	2.73
Silhouette	78	2.45
Haagen Dazs	57	1.79
Weight Watchers	54	1.70
Weight Watchers Smart Ones	49	1.54
Other	2,399	75.37

Source: *Dairy Foods*, November 2005, p. 1, from Information Resources Inc.

★ 326 ★
Frozen Desserts
SIC: 2024; NAICS: 31152

Top Frozen Novelty Makers, 2005

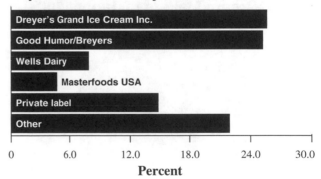

Percent

Market shares are shown based on food store, drug store and mass merchandiser sales (excluding Wal-Mart) for the 52 weeks ended January 26, 2006.

Dreyer's Grand Ice Cream Inc.	25.6%
Good Humor/Breyers	25.2
Wells Dairy	7.9
Masterfoods USA	4.6
Private label	14.8
Other	21.9

Source: *Grocery Headquarters*, April 2006, p. 56, from Information Resources Inc.

★ 327 ★
Ice Cream
SIC: 2024; NAICS: 31152

Leading Ice Cream Makers, 2005

Market shares are shown for the 52 weeks ended August 7, 2005.

Dreyer's Grand	.25.1%
Good Humor/Breyers	.17.1
Blue Bell Creameries	6.2
Ben & Jerry's	5.3
Turkey Hill Dairy	3.0
Wells Dairy	3.0
Friendly Ice Cream	1.8
Marigold Foods	1.6
ConAgra Inc.	1.3
Mayfield Dairy Farms	1.3
Integrated Brands	1.2
Prairie Farms Dairy	1.0
Private label	.20.7
Other	.11.4

Source: *Food Processing*, October 2005, p. 4, from Information Resources Inc.

★ 328 ★
Ice Cream
SIC: 2024; NAICS: 31152

Top Ice Cream Makers in Japan, 2004

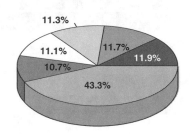

- ■ Ezaki Glico
- ▨ Haagen−Dazs Japan
- ▢ Lotte
- □ Morinaga
- ■ Meiji
- ▨ Other

Market shares are shown based on domestic sales of 355 billion yen.

Ezaki Glico	.11.9%
Haagen-Dazs Japan	.11.7
Lotte	.11.3
Morinaga	.11.1
Meiji	.10.7
Other	.43.3

Source: "2004 Market Share Report." [online] from http://www.nikkei.co.jp [Published July 27, 2005] from Nikkei estimates and Japan Ice Cream Association.

★ 329 ★
Ice Cream
SIC: 2024; NAICS: 31152

Top Ice Cream Makers Worldwide, 2002

Data show the market shares of the top multinationals.

Unilever	.19.3%
Nestle	8.9
Mars	1.9
Danone	0.2
Kraft	0.1
Other	.69.6

Source: *New Directions in Global Food Markets*, February 2005, p. 66, from Economic Research Service, U.S. Department of Agriculture and Euromonitor.

★ 330 ★
Ice Cream
SIC: 2024; NAICS: 31152

Top Ice Cream Processors in Canada

Market shares are shown in percent.

Nestle Canada Inc.	.27.88%
Unilever Canada Ltd.	.22.76
Artisanal	.14.43
David Chapman's Ice Cream Ltd.	4.61
Delicious Alternative Desserts Ltd.	2.60
Cadbury Trebor Allan Inc.	0.87
Yogen Fruz Canada Inc.	0.58
Private label	.11.59
Other	.14.68

Source: "Dairy Processing in Canada 2004-2005." [online] from http://www.dairyinfo.gc.ca/pdf_files/dairy_processing_canada_e.pdf [Published August 2005] from Euromonitor's *Packaged Food in Canada*, January 2005.

★ 331 ★
Ice Cream
SIC: 2024; NAICS: 31152

Top Ice Cream/Sherbert Brands, 2005

Market shares are shown based on supermarket, drug store and mass merchandiser sales (excluding Wal-Mart) for the 52 weeks ended December 25, 2005.

	($ mil.)	Share
Breyers	$ 580	12.98%
Dreyers/Edy's Grand	443	9.91
Haagen Dazs	254	5.68

Continued on next page.

★ 331 ★

[Continued]
Ice Cream
SIC: 2024; NAICS: 31152

Top Ice Cream/Sherbert Brands, 2005

Market shares are shown based on supermarket, drug store and mass merchandiser sales (excluding Wal-Mart) for the 52 weeks ended December 25, 2005.

	($ mil.)	Share
Blue Bell	$ 245	5.48%
Ben & Jerry's	192	4.30
Dreyer's/Edy's Grand Light	127	2.84
Well's Blue Bunny	106	2.37
Turkey Hill	102	2.28
Dreyer's/Edy's	92	2.06
Other	2,329	52.10

Source: *Dairy Foods*, March 2006, p. 32, from Information Resources Inc.

★ 332 ★

Cottage Cheese
SIC: 2026; NAICS: 311514

Top Cottage Cheese Brands, 2005

Brands are ranked by sales in millions of dollars at supermarkets, drug stores and discount stores (excluding Wal-Mart) for the 52 weeks ended September 4, 2005.

	($ mil.)	Share
Breakstone	$ 136.8	15.84%
Knudsen	96.3	11.15
Breakstone Cottage Doubles	33.5	3.88
Dean's	27.8	3.22
Friendship	22.5	2.61
Hood	22.0	2.55
Prairie Farms	19.5	2.26
Light 'n Lively	14.1	1.63
Hiland	13.4	1.55
Private label	309.1	35.80
Other	168.4	19.50

Source: *Dairy Field*, November 2005, p. 16, from Information Resources Inc.

★ 333 ★

Cottage Cheese
SIC: 2026; NAICS: 311514

Top Cottage Cheese Makers, 2005

Market shares are shown based on supermarket, drug store and mass merchandiser sales (excluding Wal-Mart) for the 52 weeks ended April 17, 2005.

Kraft Foods Inc.	15.7%
Kraft/Knudsen Corp.	11.1
Dean Foods Co.	3.8
Friendship Dairies Inc.	3.2
HP Hood	2.6
Crowley Foods Inc.	2.5
Prairie Farms Dairy	2.2
Hiland Dairy	1.7
Marigold Foods Inc.	1.5
Private label	35.9
Other	19.8

Source: *Dairy Foods*, August 2005, p. 46, from Information Resources Inc.

★ 334 ★

Cream
SIC: 2026; NAICS: 311511

Top Fresh Cream Makers, 2005

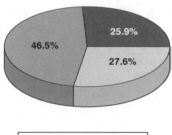

Market shares are shown based on food store, drug store and mass merchandiser sales (excluding Wal-Mart) for the 52 weeks ended January 2006.

Dean Foods	25.9%
Private label	46.5
Other	27.6

Source: *US Food Industry*, North American Equity Research, January 17, 2006, p. 28, from ACNielsen and JPMorgan.

★ 335 ★
Dips
SIC: 2026; NAICS: 311514

Top Dip Brands (Refrigerated), 2005

Market shares are shown based on supermarket, drug store and mass merchandiser sales (excluding Wal-Mart) for the 52 weeks ended August 7, 2005.

	($ mil.)	Share
T. Marzetti	$ 80.9	19.84%
Dean's	47.1	11.55
Heluva Good	29.6	7.26
Kraft	27.0	6.62
Classic Guacamole	16.8	4.12
Litehouse	10.4	2.55
Salads of the Sea	5.0	1.23
Marie's	4.7	1.15
Bison	4.5	1.10
Private label	72.3	17.73
Other	109.5	26.85

Source: *Dairy Field*, October 2005, p. 16, from Information Resources Inc.

★ 336 ★
Dips
SIC: 2026; NAICS: 311514

Top Dip Makers (Refrigerated), 2005

Market shares are shown based on supermarket, drug store and mass merchandiser sales (excluding Wal-Mart) for the 52 weeks ended July 10, 2005.

T. Marzetti Co.	19.8%
Dean Foods Co.	12.0
Heluva Good Cheese Inc.	7.3
Kraft Foods Inc.	6.7
Avomex Inc.	4.6
Litehouse Inc.	2.5
Lakeview Farms Inc.	1.4
Future Food Inc.	1.2
Morningstar Foods Inc.	1.2
Other	25.6

Source: *Dairy Foods*, August 2005, p. 46, from Information Resources Inc.

★ 337 ★
Milk
SIC: 2026; NAICS: 311511

Global Milk Market, 2003

Market shares are shown in percent.

United States	15.3%
India	7.2
Russian Federation	6.5
Germany	5.6
France	4.9
Brazil	4.6
United Kingdom	3.0
China	2.8
New Zealand	2.8
Other	47.3

Source: *Beverage Industry*, September 15, 2005, p. 20, from Beverage Marketing Corp.

★ 338 ★
Milk
SIC: 2026; NAICS: 311511

Leading Milk Firms in Chile, 2005

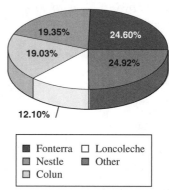

Companies are ranked by milk produced in millions of liters. A total of 15 companies run 28 plants and represent 75% of local milk production.

	(mil.)	Share
Fonterra (Soprole)	380	24.60%
Nestle	299	19.35
Colun	294	19.03
Loncoleche	187	12.10
Other	385	24.92

Source: "Chile Food Processing Ingredients Sector Annual Report 2006." [online] from http://www.usatrade.gov.com [Published February 2006] from Chilean Milk Producers Association.

★ 339 ★

Milk

SIC: 2026; NAICS: 311511

Milk Sales by Type

Convenience store shoppers lean towards milk with higher fat content.

Whole milk	33.5%
Flavored milk	27.7
2% milk	25.8
Skim non-fat	7.5
1% milk	3.9
Other	1.6

Source: *Convenience Store Decisions*, July 2005, p. 28, from *2005 NACS State of the Industry Survey.*

★ 340 ★

Milk

SIC: 2026; NAICS: 311511

Milk Sales in Canada, 2004

Total fluid milk sales were 2,714.2 million liters, including eggnog and buttermilk.

	(mil.)	Share
Milk 2%	1,281.0	47.13%
Milk 1%	571.1	21.01
Milk 3.25%	418.0	15.38
Skim	275.4	10.13
Chocolate	172.4	6.34

Source: *Food in Canada*, April 2005, p. 30, from Dairy Information Section, Agriculture and Agri-Food Canada.

★ 341 ★

Milk

SIC: 2026; NAICS: 311511

Top Flavored Milk Brands, 2006

Market shares are shown based on sales at food stores, drug stores and mass merchandisers (excluding Wal-Mart) for the 52 weeks ended March 19, 2006.

Nestle Nesquik	13.63%
Dean's	4.02
Kemps	2.27
Mayfield	1.90
Prairie Farms	1.84
Borden Milk	1.64

Garelick Farms	1.59%
Land O' Lakes	1.50
Private label	30.08
Other	41.53

Source: *Dairy Foods*, May 2006, p. 38, from Information Resources Inc.

★ 342 ★

Milk

SIC: 2026; NAICS: 311511

Top Lowfat Milk Brands, 2005

Brands are ranked by food store, drug store and mass merchandiser sales (excluding Wal-Mart) for the 52 weeks ended December 25, 2005.

	($ mil.)	Share
Lactaid 100	$ 209	3.10%
Horizon Organic	122	1.81
Kemps	88	1.30
Deans	83	1.23
Garelick Farms	71	1.05
Hood	66	0.98
Mayfield	66	0.98
Prairie Farms	66	0.98
Organic Valley	59	0.87
Private label	4,227	62.62
Other	1,693	25.08

Source: *Dairy Foods*, March 2006, p. 30, from Information Resources Inc.

★ 343 ★

Milk

SIC: 2026; NAICS: 311511

Top Milk Processors in Canada

Market shares are shown in percent.

Agropur Cooperative Ltd.	26.0%
Parmalat Canada Ltd.	25.0
Saputo Inc.	21.0
Neilson Dairy Ltd.	10.0
Other	18.0

Source: "Dairy Processing in Canada 2004-2005." [online] from http://www.dairyinfo.gc.ca/pdf_files/dairy_processing_canada_e.pdf [Published August 2005] from Euromonitor's *Packaged Food in Canada*, January 2005.

★ 344 ★
Milkshakes
SIC: 2026; NAICS: 311511

Top Milkshake Brands, 2005

Market shares are shown based on sales at supermarkets, drug stores and mass merchandisers (excluding Wal-Mart) for the 52 weeks ended August 7, 2005.

Hershey's Morningstar	36.5%
Nestle Nesquik	22.5
Rice Dream	10.5
Libbys Kerns Aguas Frescas	4.2
Deans Choco Riffic	2.6
Marvel Slammers	2.5
Odwalla Future Shake	2.2
Don Jose	1.9
Odwalla Super Protein	1.7
Private label	4.8
Other	10.6

Source: *Beverage Industry*, September 2005, p. 12, from Information Resources Inc.

★ 345 ★
Pudding
SIC: 2026; NAICS: 311511

Top Pudding/Gelatin/Mousse Parfaits, 2005

Brands are ranked by sales for the 12 weeks ended October 30, 2005.

	Sales	Share
Jello	$ 43,741,192	18.3%
Kozy Shack	23,803,576	9.9
Jello Free	11,251,851	4.7
Jello Gelatin Snacks	10,884,184	4.5
Swiss Miss	9,141,696	3.8
Jello Sundae Toppers	5,373,296	2.2
Senior Rico	2,541,338	1.1
Jello Smoothie	1,551,862	0.6
Reser's	1,373,867	0.6
Private label	10,102,150	4.2
Other	119,765,012	50.0

Source: *Frozen Food Age*, December 2005, p. 11, from Information Resources Inc.

★ 346 ★
Sour Cream
SIC: 2026; NAICS: 311514

Top Sour Cream Brands, 2005

Market shares are shown based on supermarket, drug store and mass merchandiser sales (excluding Wal-Mart) for the 52 weeks ended August 7, 2005.

	($ mil.)	Share
Dairy	$ 124.8	18.14%
Breakstone	104.2	15.15
Knudsen Hampshire	51.4	7.47
Friendship	13.2	1.92
Cacique	12.0	1.74
Knudsen	10.8	1.57
Dean's	9.6	1.40
Tillamook	8.8	1.28
Prairie Farms	7.8	1.13
Private label	200.5	29.14
Other	144.9	21.06

Source: *Dairy Field*, October 2005, p. 16, from Information Resources Inc.

★ 347 ★
Sour Cream
SIC: 2026; NAICS: 311514

Top Sour Cream Makers, 2005

Market shares are shown based on supermarket, drug store and mass merchandiser sales (excluding Wal-Mart) for the 52 weeks ended April 17, 2005.

Daisy Brand	18.0%
Kraft Foods Inc.	15.2
Kraft/Knudsen Corp.	9.3
Dean Foods Co.	2.4
Crowley Foods Inc.	2.0
Friendship Dairies Inc.	1.9
Cacique	1.7
Marigold Foods Inc.	1.4
Tillamook County Creamery	1.3
Other	17.6

Source: *Dairy Foods*, August 2005, p. 46, from Information Resources Inc.

★ 348 ★
Whipped Topping
SIC: 2026; NAICS: 311514

Top Whipped Topping Brands, 2005

Brands are ranked by supermarket sales for the 12 weeks ended August 7, 2005.

	Sales	Share
Cool Whip	$ 31,315,752	42.41%
Cool Whip Lite	12,473,842	16.89
Cool Whip Free	9,471,832	12.83
Real Whip	174,677	0.24
Other	20,410,097	27.64

Source: *Frozen Food Age*, September 2005, p. 13, from Information Resources Inc.

★ 349 ★
Yogurt
SIC: 2026; NAICS: 311511

Retail Yogurt Sales, 2004-2008

Sales are shown in millions of dollars at supermarkets, drug stores and mass merchandisers (excluding Wal-Mart). The industry saw only .2% growth over 2003. Products aimed at children have not performed well. Light/no-fat products still do well, as do yogurt drinks.

2004	$ 2,460
2005	2,547
2006	2,630
2007	2,716
2008	2,790

Source: *Prepared Foods*, August 2005, p. 21, from Information Resources Inc.

★ 350 ★
Yogurt
SIC: 2026; NAICS: 311511

Top Yogurt Brands, 2005

Market shares are shown based on supermarket, drug store and mass merchandiser sales (excluding Wal-Mart) for the 52 weeks ended August 7, 2005.

	($ mil.)	Share
Yoplait Original	$ 318	12.52%
Yoplait Light	218	8.59
Dannon Light N Fit	195	7.68
Yoplait Go Gurt	115	4.53
Stonyfield	102	4.02
Toplait Trix	$ 92	3.62%
Yoplait Whips	84	3.31
Dannon Fruit on the Bottom	81	3.19
Yoplait Custard Style	73	2.88
Private label Yogurt	355	13.98
Other	906	35.68

Source: *Dairy Foods*, December 2005, p. 46, from Information Resources Inc.

★ 351 ★
Yogurt
SIC: 2026; NAICS: 311514

Top Yogurt Processors in Canada

Market shares are shown in percent.

Danone Canada Inc.	30.63%
Ultima Foods Ltd.	30.35
Parmalat Canada Ltd.	20.49
Liberty Products Inc.	0.64
Other	17.88

Source: "Dairy Processing in Canada 2004-2005." [online] from http://www.dairyinfo.gc.ca/pdf_files/dairy_processing_canada_e.pdf [Published August 2005] from Euromonitor's *Packaged Food in Canada*, January 2005.

★ 352 ★
Yogurt
SIC: 2026; NAICS: 311511

Top Yogurt/Yogurt Drink Makers, 2005

Market shares are shown based on supermarket, drug store and mass merchandiser sales (excluding Wal-Mart) for the 52 weeks ended April 17, 2005.

Yoplait USA Inc.	34.2%
Dannon Co.	30.7
Stonyfield Farm Inc.	5.7
Kraft Foods Inc.	3.7
Colombo Inc.	1.7
YoFarm Corp.	1.7
Johanna Foods Inc.	1.3
Wells' Dairy	1.3
Meadow Gold Dairy Inc.	1.1
Other	6.7

Source: *Dairy Foods*, August 2005, p. 46, from Information Resources Inc.

★ 353 ★
Baby Food
SIC: 2032; NAICS: 311422

Top Baby Food Brands, 2005

Market shares are shown based on food store, drug store and mass merchandiser sales (excluding Wal-Mart) for the 52 weeks ended July 10, 2005.

Gerber Second Foods 26.0%
Gerber 12.1
Gerber Graduates 11.4
Gerber Third Foods 9.9
Gerber First Foods 6.6
Beech-Nut Stage 2 . . . . 5.1
Del Monte Nature's Goodness 4.8
Gerber Tender Harvest 4.5
Other 19.6

Source: *Grocery Headquarters*, October 2005, p. 20, from Information Resources Inc.

★ 354 ★
Canned Food
SIC: 2032; NAICS: 311422

Baked Beans Market in the U.K.

Market shares are shown in percent.

Heinz 68.0%
Premier Foods 11.2
Other 20.8

Source: *Financial Times*, May 17, 2006, p. 2.

★ 355 ★
Canned Food
SIC: 2032; NAICS: 311422

Canned Bean Sales

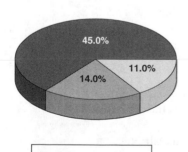

Canned bean sales represent 25% of canned vegetable sales.

Green 45.0%
Kidney/red 14.0
Other 11.0

Source: *ECRM Focus*, September 2005, p. 35, from cannedfood.org and *ACNielsen Strategic Planner*.

★ 356 ★
Canned Food
SIC: 2032; NAICS: 311422

Canned Food Industry in the U.K., 2005

Distribution is shown based on the 52 weeks ended June 19, 2005.

Canned fish incl. Pouches 20.5%
Canned soup 17.7
Baked beans 12.7
Canned hot meats 10.0
Canned fruit 8.7
Cold canned meats 6.2
Canned pasta products 5.8
Other 18.4

Source: *Grocer*, September 10, 2005, p. 1, from TNS Superpanel.

★ 357 ★
Canned Food
SIC: 2032; NAICS: 311422

Canned Fruit Sales at Supermarkets

Supermarket sales are shown in millions of dollars.

Pineapples . . . . $ 219.74
Peaches, cling 208.14
Apple sauce 168.17
Pie and pastry fillings, canned 105.22
Cranberries, shelf stable 95.61
Pears 90.70
Fruit cocktail 86.42
Fruit mixes and salad fruits 68.48
Pumpkins, canned 51.53

Source: *Progressive Grocer*, September 15, 2005, p. 22, from *Progressive Grocer's 26th Annual Consumer Expenditures Study*.

★ 358 ★
Canned Food
SIC: 2032; NAICS: 311422

Canned Pasta Market in the U.K., 2005

Sales are shown for the 52 weeks ended October 1, 2005. Figures are for all outlets in thousands of pounds sterling.

	(000)	Share
Heinz	£ 70,011	65.03%
HP	7,032	6.53

Continued on next page.

★ 358 ★

[Continued]
Canned Food
SIC: 2032; NAICS: 311422

Canned Pasta Market in the U.K., 2005

Sales are shown for the 52 weeks ended October 1, 2005. Figures are for all outlets in thousands of pounds sterling.

	(000)	Share
Weight Watchers	£ 3,432	3.19%
Crosse & Blackwell	1,493	1.39
Princes	138	0.13
Other	25,547	23.73

Source: *Grocer*, December 17, 2005, p. 77, from ACNielsen.

★ 359 ★

Canned Food
SIC: 2032; NAICS: 311422

Canned Vegetable Market in the U.K., 2005

Sales are shown for the 52 weeks ended October 1, 2005. Figures are in thousands of pounds sterling and for all outlets.

	(000)	Share
Green Giant	£ 32,221	8.15%
Princes	28,720	7.26
Batchelors	13,016	3.29
Shesswood	7,574	1.92
Farrow's giant marrowfat processed peas	7,247	1.83
Other	306,637	77.55

Source: *Grocer*, December 17, 2005, p. 77, from ACNielsen.

★ 360 ★

Canned Food
SIC: 2032; NAICS: 311422

Leading Chili Makers, 2005

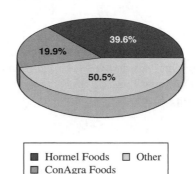

Hormel Foods ☐ **Other**
ConAgra Foods

Market shares are shown based on sales at supermarkets, drug stores and mass merchandisers (excluding Wal-Mart) for the 12 weeks ended June 11, 2005.

Hormel Foods	.39.6%
ConAgra Foods	.19.9
Other	.50.5

Source: *Food/Agribusiness*, Prudential Equity Group Equity Research, June 24, 2005, p. 2, from ACNielsen.

★ 361 ★

Canned Food
SIC: 2032; NAICS: 311422

Mexican Bean Market

Market shares are shown in percent (where distributed).

Rosarita Refried Beans	.50.0%
Other	.50.0

Source: *Food/Agribusiness Beverages Tobacco*, Prudential Equity Group Research, March 8, 2005, p. 31, from Prudential Equity Group.

★ 362 ★

Canned Food
SIC: 2032; NAICS: 311422

Top Canned Food Makers in Western Europe

The top companies are ranked by market share. Data refer to products sold for human consumption in retail, catering and artisanal markets. Germany took 23% of the market, followed by France with 20% and the United Kingdom with 13%.

Mars	8.5%
Nestle	7.9
Heinz	7.8

Continued on next page.

★ 362 ★
[Continued]
Canned Food
SIC: 2032; NAICS: 311422

Top Canned Food Makers in Western Europe

The top companies are ranked by market share. Data refer to products sold for human consumption in retail, catering and artisanal markets. Germany took 23% of the market, followed by France with 20% and the United Kingdom with 13%.

Unilever	3.7%
Bolton	3.6
Bonduelle	3.2
Stockmeyer	3.2
Orkla	2.6
Cirio Del Monte	2.4
Campbell Soup	2.0
Other	55.1

Source: "Canned Product Markets." [online] from http://www.fft.com [Published September 2004] from Food for Thought.

★ 363 ★
Canned Food
SIC: 2032; NAICS: 311422

Top Canned Pasta Makers, 2005

Market shares are shown based on sales (excluding Wal-Mart) for the 52 weeks ended January 2006.

ConAgra	66.4%
Campbell	20.8
Private label	9.1
Other	3.7

Source: *US Food Industry*, North American Equity Research, January 17, 2006, p. 100, from ACNielsen and JPMorgan.

★ 364 ★
Canned Food
SIC: 2032; NAICS: 311422

Top Canned Tomato Makers, 2005

Market shares are shown based on sales (excluding Wal-Mart) for the 52 weeks ended January 2006.

ConAgra	30.0%
Private label	28.5
Other	41.5

Source: *US Food Industry*, North American Equity Research, January 17, 2006, p. 100, from ACNielsen and JPMorgan.

★ 365 ★
Canned Food
SIC: 2032; NAICS: 311422

Top Tinned Pasta Makers in the U.K., 2005

Market shares are shown in percent.

Heinz	68.6%
Premier	11.6
Private label	19.1
Other	0.7

Source: "Sales Data and Market Shares." [online] from http://www.competition-commission.org.uk/rep_pub/reports/2006/fulltext/511ae.pdf [Accessed June 1, 2006] from Competition Commission analysis of IRI data provided by Heinz.

★ 366 ★
Soup
SIC: 2032; NAICS: 311422

Instant Noodle Snack Market in the U.K.

Market shares are shown in percent.

Pot Noodle	88.0%
Other	12.0

Source: *Marketing*, August 24, 2005, p. NA.

★ 367 ★
Soup
SIC: 2032; NAICS: 311422

Largest Ramen Makers

"Other" includes Solafide with a 4% market share.

Nissin Co./Maruchan Inc.	90.0%
Other	10.0

Source: *San Diego Business Journal*, August 15, 2005, p. 30.

★ 368 ★

Soup

SIC: 2032; NAICS: 311422

Top Instant Noodle Makers in Japan, 2004

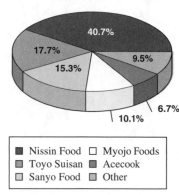

40.7%

17.7%

15.3%

9.5%

10.1%

6.7%

■ Nissin Food □ Myojo Foods
■ Toyo Suisan ■ Acecook
□ Sanyo Food ▨ Other

Market shares are shown based on domestic production of 5.53 billion meals.

Nissin Food	.40.7%
Toyo Suisan	.17.7
Sanyo Food	.15.3
Myojo Foods	.10.1
Acecook	6.7
Other	9.5

Source: "2004 Market Share Report." [online] from http://www.nikkei.co.jp [Published July 27, 2005] from Nikkei estimates and Japan Convenience Foods Industry Association.

★ 369 ★

Soup

SIC: 2032; NAICS: 311422

Top Soup Brands, 2005

Market shares are shown based on supermarket, drug store and mass merchandiser sales (excluding Wal-Mart) for the 52 weeks ended October 2, 2005. R-T-S stands for ready-to-serve.

	($ mil.)	Share
Campbell's condensed	$ 935.5	25.28%
Campbell's Chunky R-T-S	457.1	12.35
Progresso R-T-S	419.6	11.34
Swanson R-T-S	157.2	4.25
Campbell's Select R-T-S	147.4	3.98
Maruchan Ramen	95.7	2.59
Campbell's Healthy	91.8	2.48
Campbell's Soup at Hand R-T-S	91.6	2.48
Maruchan Instant Lunch Ramen	86.4	2.34
Other	1,217.7	32.91

Source: *MMR*, December 12, 2005, p. 38, from Information Resources Inc.

★ 370 ★

Soup

SIC: 2032; NAICS: 311422

Top Soup Brands (Condensed Wet), 2005

Market shares are shown based on food store, drug store and mass merchandiser sales (excluding Wal-Mart) for the 52 weeks ended April 17, 2005.

Campbell's	.77.1%
Campbell's Healthy Request	7.4
Snow's	0.5
College Inn	0.3
Herb Ox	0.3
Bookbinders	0.2
Pacific	0.2
Manischewitz	0.1
Other	.13.9

Source: *Grocery Headquarters*, October 2005, p. NA, from Information Resources Inc.

★ 371 ★

Soup

SIC: 2032; NAICS: 311422

Top Soup Brands (Dry), 2006

Market shares are shown based on food store, drug store and mass merchandiser sales (excluding Wal-Mart) for the 52 weeks ended January 26, 2006.

Lipton Recipe Secrets	.19.9%
Bear Creek	.10.5
Lipton Soup Secrets	.10.1
Knorr	8.0
Lipton Cup A Soup	5.7
Wyler's Soup Starter	4.1
Better Than Bouillon	3.9
Mrs. Grass	3.0
Hurst HamBeens	2.3
Private label	7.8
Other	.22.7

Source: *Grocery Headquarters*, April 2006, p. 56, from Information Resources Inc.

★ 372 ★
Soup
SIC: 2032; NAICS: 311422
Top Soup Brands (RTS), 2006

Market shares are shown based on food store, drug store and mass merchandiser sales (excluding Wal-Mart) for the 52 weeks ended January 26, 2006. RTS stands for ready-to-serve.

Progresso	.24.6%
Campbell's Chunky Soup	.24.2
Swanson	8.9
Campbell's Select	8.1
Campbell's Soup At Hand	5.0
Healthy Choice	3.7
College Inn	3.4
Swanson Natural Goodness	1.9
Wolfgang Puck's	1.7
Private label	7.4
Other	.11.1

Source: *Grocery Headquarters*, April 2006, p. 56, from Information Resources Inc.

★ 373 ★
Soup
SIC: 2032; NAICS: 311422
Top Soup Makers (Condensed Wet), 2005

Market shares are shown based on food store, drug store and mass merchandiser sales (excluding Wal-Mart) for the 52 weeks ended April 17, 2005.

Campbell Soup	.84.5%
Snow's/Doxsee Inc.	0.5
Del Monte Foods	0.3
Hormel Foods	0.3
Bookbinder Foods	0.2
PFC Foods of Oregon	0.2
Manischewitz Co.	0.1
Private label	.13.2
Other	0.7

Source: *Grocery Headquarters*, October 2005, p. NA, from Information Resources Inc.

★ 374 ★
Soup
SIC: 2032; NAICS: 311422
Top Soup Makers (Dry), 2006

Market shares are shown based on food store, drug store and mass merchandiser sales (excluding Wal-Mart) for the 52 weeks ended January 26, 2006.

Unilever Best Foods North America	.46.3%
Bear Creek Country Kitchens	.10.5
H.J. Heinz Co.	4.5
Superior Quality Foods	3.9
Private label	7.8
Other	.27.0

Source: *Grocery Headquarters*, April 2006, p. 56, from Information Resources Inc.

★ 375 ★
Soup
SIC: 2032; NAICS: 311422
Top Soup Makers (RTS), 2005

Market shares are shown based on food store, drug store and mass merchandiser sales (excluding Wal-Mart) for the 52 weeks ended January 2006. RTS stands for ready-to-serve.

Campbell Soup	.51.0%
General Mills	.25.6
ConAgra	3.8
Del Monte	3.5
CountryGourmet	1.7
Hain Celestial	1.4
Private label	7.2
Other	5.9

Source: *US Food Industry*, North American Equity Research, January 17, 2006, p. 86, from ACNielsen and JPMorgan.

★ 376 ★
Soup
SIC: 2032; NAICS: 311422
Top Soup Makers Worldwide, 2002

Data show the market shares of the top multinationals.

Unilever	.17.3%
Nestle	6.9
Kraft	0.2
Other	.75.6

Source: *New Directions in Global Food Markets*, February 2005, p. 66, from Economic Research Service, U.S. Department of Agriculture and Euromonitor.

★ 377 ★
Dried Fruit
SIC: 2033; NAICS: 311421
Top Fig Brands, 2004

Market shares are shown for the 4 weeks ended June 13, 2004. By variety Mission took 33% of the total, and Calimyrna took 20% of the total.

Sun Maid	.40.3%
Blue Ribbon Orchard Voice	.29.5
Nutrafig	.12.8
Jenny	. 5.4
Mariani	. 3.7
Old Orchard	. 1.4
Producers Pride	. 1.2
Other	. 5.7

Source: "Valley Fig Growers." [online] from http://www.valleyfig.com/c_retailers/index.htm [Accessed June 12, 2006].

★ 378 ★
Fruits & Vegetables
SIC: 2033; NAICS: 311421
Leading Fruit & Vegetable Product Makers in France, 2005

Market shares are shown in percent.

Pomona	.11.4%
Bonduelle	. 6.9
Coopagri Bretagne	. 4.7
Dole	. 4.5
Fyffews	. 3.1
Cecab	. 2.4
Other	.67.0

Source: "National Report France." [online] from http://foodqualityschemes.jrc.es/en/documents/NationalreportFR_000.pdf [Published November 2005] from Food for Thought.

★ 379 ★
Jams and Jellies
SIC: 2033; NAICS: 311421
Leading Jam/Jelly Makers, 2005

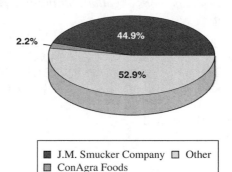

Market shares are shown based on sales at food stores, drug stores and mass merchandisers (excluding Wal-Mart) for the 12 weeks ended June 11, 2005.

J.M. Smucker Company	.44.9%
ConAgra Foods	. 2.2
Other	.52.9

Source: *Food/Agribusiness*, Prudential Equity Group Equity Research, June 24, 2005, p. 2, from ACNielsen.

★ 380 ★
Jams and Jellies
SIC: 2033; NAICS: 311421
Top Jam/Jelly/Fruit Spread Makers, 2004

Companies are ranked by sales in millions of dollars.

	($ mil.)	Share
SJM	$ 276	42.1%
Welch Foods	84	12.8
B&G Foods	32	4.9
Private label	134	20.4
Other	130	19.8

Source: *J.M. Smucker Co.*, Krause Fund Research, November 17, 2005, p. 20, from Mintel's *Sweet Spreads*.

★ 381 ★
Juices
SIC: 2033; NAICS: 311421
Bottled Juice Sales, 2005

Sales are shown in millions of gallons for the first quarter of the year.

	(mil.)	Share
Fruit drinks	403.0	27.20%
Apple juice	331.3	22.36
Cranberry cocktail/drinks	241.2	16.28
Fruit juice blends	91.6	6.18
Tomato/vegetable/cocktail	83.9	5.66
Grape juice	73.2	4.94
Lemonade	65.5	4.42
Cranberry juice/juice blends	49.7	3.35
Cider	23.5	1.59
Grapefruit cocktail	21.1	1.42
Other	97.5	6.58

Source: *Food Institute Report*, July 11, 2005, p. 22, from Beverage Marketing Corporation.

★ 382 ★
Juices
SIC: 2033; NAICS: 311421
Global Cranberry Juice Market

Market shares are shown in percent.

Ocean Spray	.70.0%
Other	.30.0

Source: *Australasian Business Intelligence*, July 26, 2005, p. NA.

★ 383 ★
Juices
SIC: 2033; NAICS: 311421
Grape Juice Market in Canada

Market shares are shown in percent.

Welch's	.60.0%
Other	.40.0

Source: "Welch's International Global Experience." [online] from http://www.welchsinternational.com [Published May 31, 2006].

★ 384 ★
Juices
SIC: 2033; NAICS: 311421
Juice Sales Worldwide, 2004-2005

Sales are in millions of dollars. Figures for 2005 are forecast.

	2004	2005	Share
Fruit/vegetable . . .	$ 93,107.1	$ 96,498.2	50.00%
100% juice	52,084.1	53,323.1	27.63
Juice drinks (up to 24% juice) . . .	24,225.4	25,502.5	13.21
Nectars (25-99% juice)	15,998.1	16,859.5	8.74
Fruit-flavored drinks (no juice content) . .	799.5	813.2	0.42

Source: "Global Juice Drink Sales." [online] from http://www. stagnito.com/charts2005/3globalhotdrink.htm [Accessed March 23, 2006] from Euromonitor.

★ 385 ★
Juices
SIC: 2033; NAICS: 311421
Leading Juice Drink Smoothies, 2006

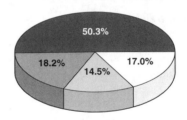

Market shares are shown based on food store, drug store and mass merchandiser sales (excluding Wal-Mart) for the 52 weeks ended February 19, 2006.

V8 Splash Smoothies	.50.3%
Fuze Refresh	.18.2
SoBe	.14.5
Other	.17.0

Source: *Beverage Industry*, April 2006, p. S12, from Information Resources Inc.

★ 386 ★
Juices
SIC: 2033; NAICS: 311421

Leading Smoothie Brands in the U.K., 2004

Sales are shown based on volume sales.

PJ Smoothies 44.0%
Innocent Drinks 16.0
Private label 36.0
Other 4.0

Source: *just-drinks.com*, December 2005, p. 22, from *just-drinks.com* estimates.

★ 387 ★
Juices
SIC: 2033; NAICS: 311421

Orange Juice (Frozen) Sales by Year, 2002-2005

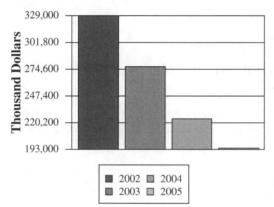

Sales at supermarkets, drug stores and mass merchandisers (excluding Wal-Mart) are shown for the 52 weeks ended September 4, 2005.

2002 . . . . $ 328,356,000
2003   277,325,529
2004   224,900,523
2005   194,015,369

Source: *Corporate Profiles & Industry Statistics - Milling & Baking News Supplement*, November 2005, p. 130, from Information Resources Inc.

★ 388 ★
Juices
SIC: 2033; NAICS: 311421

Premium Juice Market in Thailand

Market shares are shown in percent.

Tipco 26.0%
Malee 23.0
Unif 22.0
UFC 6.0

Nestle 5.0%
Chaba 4.0
Other 14.0

Source: ''Thailand Product Brief Non-Alcoholic Beverage Report 2005.'' [online] from http://www.usatrade.gov [Published November 2005].

★ 389 ★
Juices
SIC: 2033; NAICS: 311421

Top Bottled Juice Brands, 2005

Market shares are shown based on sales at food stores, drug stores and mass merchandisers (excluding Wal-Mart) for the 52 weeks ended June 12, 2005.

Ocean Spray Cranberry cocktail/juice drink . . .   9.1%
Libby's Juicy Juice Fruit Juice Blend 5.3
Welch's Grape Juice 4.0
Private label apple juice 5.8
Private label cranberry cocktail/juice drink . . .   3.7
Other 72.1

Source: *Beverage Industry*, July 2005, p. 12, from Information Resources Inc.

★ 390 ★
Juices
SIC: 2033; NAICS: 311421

Top Bottled Tomato/Vegetable Brands (Shelf-Stable), 2005

Convenience store sales are shown in thousands of dollars for the 52 weeks ended March 20, 2005.

	($ 000)	Share
V8	$ 55,082.7	42.48%
V8 Splash	41,793.1	32.23
Motts Clamato	16,467.4	12.70
Campbells	13,350.3	10.30
Snapple Elements	1,515.7	1.17
Diet V8 Splash	621.8	0.48
Other	830.8	0.64

Source: *Convenience Store Decisions*, July 2005, p. 28, from Information Resources Inc.

★ 391 ★
Juices
SIC: 2033; NAICS: 311421

Top Boxed Juice Brands, 2005

Market shares are shown based on sales at food stores, drug stores and mass merchandisers (excluding Wal-Mart) for the 52 weeks ended June 12, 2005.

Capri Sun	40.5%
Kool Aid Jammers	10.7
Hi C	9.4
Libby's Juicy Juice	8.2
Minute Maid Coolers	5.5
Hi C Blast	3.1
Capri Sun Fruit Waves	2.5
Minute Maid	2.2
Minute Maid Premium	2.2
Other	15.7

Source: *Beverage Industry*, July 2005, p. 12, from Information Resources Inc.

★ 392 ★
Juices
SIC: 2033; NAICS: 311421

Top Fruit-Based Drink Brands in India

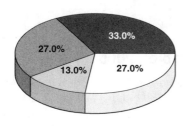

Legend: ■ Maaza □ Slice ■ Frooti □ Other

Market shares are shown in percent.

Maaza (Coca-Cola)	33.0%
Frooti (Parle)	27.0
Slice (PepsiCo.)	13.0
Other	27.0

Source: *The Economic Times*, May 3, 2006, p. NA.

★ 393 ★
Juices
SIC: 2033; NAICS: 311421

Top Fruit/Vegetable Juice Brands in the U.K., 2004

Market shares are shown based on off-trade sales.

Tropicana	17.8%
Ribena	4.5
Ocean Spray	3.5
Robinsons	3.4
Copella	3.2
Del Monte	2.8
Sunny D	2.1
Capri-Sun	1.9
Tropics	1.6
Other	59.2

Source: *Marketing*, November 23, 2005, p. NA, from Euromonitor.

★ 394 ★
Juices
SIC: 2033; NAICS: 311421

Top Juice/Drink Makers (Shelf-Stable), 2006

Market shares are shown based on food store, drug store and mass merchandiser sales (excluding Wal-Mart) for the 52 weeks ended January 2006.

PepsiCo.	22.0%
Cadbury	6.3
Campbell	6.0
Nestle	5.9
Private label	12.2
Other	47.6

Source: *US Food Industry*, North American Equity Research, January 17, 2006, p. 100, from ACNielsen and JPMorgan.

★ 395 ★
Juices
SIC: 2033; NAICS: 311421

Top Lemonade Brands (Bottled, Shelf-Stable), 2005

Convenience store sales are shown in thousands of dollars for the 52 weeks ended March 20, 2005.

	($ 000)	Share
Minute Maid	$ 67,724.0	45.79%
Tropicana	30,021.5	20.30

Continued on next page.

★ 395 ★

[Continued]
Juices
SIC: 2033; NAICS: 311421

Top Lemonade Brands (Bottled, Shelf-Stable), 2005

Convenience store sales are shown in thousands of dollars for the 52 weeks ended March 20, 2005.

	($ 000)	Share
Country Time	$ 15,638.3	10.57%
Tropicana Twister	9,931.6	6.72
Snapple	7,121.8	4.82
Tropicana Light	4,976.7	3.36
Minute Maid Light	2,571.7	1.74
Other	9,910.7	6.70

Source: *Convenience Store Decisions*, July 2005, p. 28, from Information Resources Inc.

★ 396 ★

Juices
SIC: 2033; NAICS: 311421

Top Orange Juice Brands (Bottled, Shelf-Stable), 2005

Brands are ranked by sales at supermarkets, drug stores and mass merchandisers (excluding Wal-Mart) for the 52 weeks ended September 4, 2005.

Minute Maid	$ 12,298,720
Dole	4,628,670
Tropicana	3,762,913
Tropicana Season's Best	2,840,093
Welch's	662,747
Mr. Pure	561,688
Sir Real	459,247
VeryFine	425,775
Everfresh	292,025

Source: *Corporate Profiles & Industry Statistics - Milling & Baking News Supplement*, November 2005, p. 130, from Information Resources Inc.

★ 397 ★

Juices
SIC: 2033; NAICS: 311421

Top Orange Juice Brands (Refrigerated), 2006

Market shares are shown based on food store, drug store and mass merchandiser sales (excluding Wal-Mart) for the 52 weeks ended January 26, 2006.

Tropicana Pure Premium	43.4%
Minute Maid Premium	14.9
Florida's Natural	9.6
Simply Orange	6.5
Minute Maid Premium Heart Wise	1.1
Minute Maid Premium for Kids	0.7
Citrus World Donald Duck	0.6
Indian River Select	0.4
Odwalla	0.4
Private label	15.9
Other	6.5

Source: *Grocery Headquarters*, April 2006, p. 56, from Information Resources Inc.

★ 398 ★

Juices
SIC: 2033; NAICS: 311421

Top Orange Juice (Frozen, Concentrated) Brands, 2005

Brands are ranked by sales at supermarkets, drug stores and mass merchandisers (excluding Wal-Mart) for the 52 weeks ended September 4, 2005. Frozen orange juice sales were $194.05 million.

	($ mil.)	Share
Minute Maid Premium	$ 64.30	33.14%
Minute Maid	21.96	11.32
Old Orchard Premium	6.03	3.11
Old Orchard	4.99	2.57
Tropicana Season's Best	2.60	1.34
Langer's Orange Juice Plus	1.61	0.83
Langer's	1.48	0.76
Citrus World Donald Duck	1.35	0.70
Private label	80.27	41.37
Other	9.42	4.86

Source: *Corporate Profiles & Industry Statistics - Milling & Baking News Supplement*, November 2005, p. 130, from Information Resources Inc.

★ 399 ★
Juices
SIC: 2033; NAICS: 311421

Top Orange Juice Makers, 2006

Market shares are shown based on supermarket, drug store and mass merchandiser sales (excluding Wal-Mart) for the 52 weeks ended January 26, 2006.

Tropicana Dole Beverages 43.8%
The Minute Maid Co. 23.2
Citrus World Inc. 10.6
Dean Foods Co. 0.7
Private label 15.9
Other 5.8

Source: *Grocery Headquarters*, April 2006, p. 56, from Information Resources Inc.

★ 400 ★
Juices
SIC: 2033; NAICS: 311421

Top Powdered Juice Brands in Southeast Asia, 2003

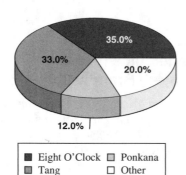

By company, PhilBev took 52% of the total followed by Kraft with 44% . The market is forecast to be worth P8 billion in 2004.

Eight O'Clock 35.0%
Tang 33.0
Ponkana 12.0
Other 20.0

Source: "Powdered Segment of the Fruit Juice Industry." [online] from http://atn-riae.agr.ca/asean/4051_e.htm [Published February 2005] from Key Industry Informant.

★ 401 ★
Juices
SIC: 2033; NAICS: 311421

Top Refrigerated Juices, 2005

Data show supermarket sales for the 52 weeks ended October 2, 2005.

	($ mil.)	Share
Orange juice	$ 1,550.00	40.19%
Fruit drinks	677.90	17.58
Blended fruit juices	206.64	5.36
Lemonade	110.59	2.87
Grapefruit juice	67.00	1.74
Cider	46.05	1.19
Juice and drink smoothies	43.65	1.13
Vegetable juice/cocktails	26.25	0.68
Fruit nectars	14.62	0.38
Pineapple juice	12.59	0.33
Other	1,101.77	28.57

Source: *Progressive Grocer*, December 1, 2005, p. 58, from Information Resources Inc.

★ 402 ★
Ketchup
SIC: 2033; NAICS: 311421

Ketchup Market in Canada

The company also takes 60% of the U.S. market.

Heinz 77.0%
Other 23.0

Source: "Year in Review." [online] from http://www.heinz.com/2004annualreport/year.html [Accessed June 21, 2005].

★ 403 ★
Ketchup
SIC: 2033; NAICS: 311421

Ketchup Market in Switzerland

Market shares are shown in percent.

Heinz 63.0%
Other 37.0

Source: *Heinz Annual Report*, Annual 2005, p. 10.

★ 404 ★
Ketchup
SIC: 2033; NAICS: 311421

Ketchup Market in the Foodservice Industry

Market shares are shown in percent.

Heinz	.80.0%
Other	.20.0

Source: *Heinz Annual Report*, Annual 2005, p. 10.

★ 405 ★
Ketchup
SIC: 2033; NAICS: 311421

Ketchup Market in the U.K.

Market shares are shown in percent.

Heinz	.78.0%
Other	.22.0

Source: *Heinz Annual Report*, Annual 2005, p. 10.

★ 406 ★
Ketchup
SIC: 2033; NAICS: 311421

Leading Ketchup Makers, 2005

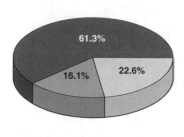

Market shares are shown based on sales at food stores, drug stores and mass merchandisers (excluding Wal-Mart) for the 12 weeks ended June 11, 2005.

H.J. Heinz	.61.3%
ConAgra Foods	.16.1
Other	.22.6

Source: *Food/Agribusiness*, Prudential Equity Group Equity Research, June 24, 2005, p. 2, from ACNielsen.

★ 407 ★
Ketchup
SIC: 2033; NAICS: 311421

Top Ketchup Makers in Japan

Market shares are shown in percent.

Kagome	.52.0%
Kikkoman	.29.0
Nagano Tomato	.10.0
Other	.9.0

Source: *Nikkei Weekly*, July 18, 2005, p. NA.

★ 408 ★
Raisins
SIC: 2033; NAICS: 311421

Top Raisin Brands, 2004

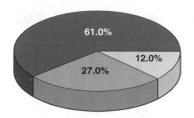

Market shares are shown based on food store sales for the 52 weeks ended April 20, 2004.

Sun-Maid	.61.0%
Private label	.27.0
Other	.12.0

Source: "Sun-Maid." [online] from http://foodqualityschemes.jrc.es/en/documents/NationalreportFR_000.pdf [Accessed May 30, 2006] from Information Resources Inc.

★ 409 ★
Raisins
SIC: 2033; NAICS: 311421

Top Yogurt Raisin Brands, 2004

Market shares are shown based on food store sales for the 52 weeks ended April 20, 2004.

Sun-Maid	.35.0%
Mariani	.24.0
Del Monte	.15.0
Other	.26.0

Source: "Sun-Maid." [online] from http://foodqualityschemes.jrc.es/en/documents/NationalreportFR_000.pdf [Accessed May 30, 2006] from Information Resources Inc.

★ 410 ★
Mayonnaise
SIC: 2035; NAICS: 311941

Top Mayonnaise Makers, 2006

Market shares are shown based on food store, drug store and mass merchandiser sales (excluding Wal-Mart) for the 52 weeks ended January 2006.

Unilever 40.0%
Private label 9.2
Other 50.8

Source: *US Food Industry*, North American Equity Research, January 17, 2006, p. 28, from ACNielsen and JPMorgan.

★ 411 ★
Mustard
SIC: 2035; NAICS: 311941

Leading Mustard Makers, 2005

Market shares are shown based on sales at food stores, drug stores and mass merchandisers (excluding Wal-Mart) for the 12 weeks ended June 11, 2005.

Kraft Foods 14.4%
ConAgra Foods 6.7
Other 78.9

Source: *Food/Agribusiness*, Prudential Equity Group Equity Research, June 24, 2005, p. 2, from ACNielsen.

★ 412 ★
Mustard
SIC: 2035; NAICS: 311941

Top Mustard Brands, 2004

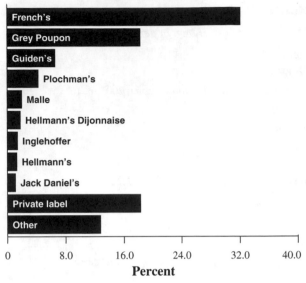

Percent

Market shares are shown based on supermarket sales for the 52 weeks ended June 13, 2004.

French's 32.1%
Grey Poupon 18.3
Guiden's 6.6
Plochman's 4.3
Malle 2.0
Hellmann's Dijonnaise 1.8
Inglehoffer 1.4
Hellmann's 1.3
Jack Daniel's 1.1
Private label 18.3
Other 12.8

Source: *Food Processing*, February 2005, p. 45, from Information Resources Inc.

★ 413 ★
Pickles
SIC: 2035; NAICS: 311941

Private-Label Pickle Market

Market shares are shown in percent.

Treehouse 90.0%
Other 10.0

Source: *Medill News Service*, November 3, 2005, p. NA.

★ 414 ★

Pickles

SIC: 2035; NAICS: 311941

Top Pickle Brands, 2005

Brands are ranked by sales for the 12 weeks ended October 2, 2005.

	Sales	Share
Claussen	$ 24,785,586	87.29%
BA Tampte	1,439,957	5.07
Bubbles	467,902	1.65
Nathan's	332,504	1.17
Boars Head	302,564	1.07
Schorr	124,614	0.44
Vlasic	70,895	0.25
Freestone	66,721	0.23
Flanagan	55,897	0.20
Other	746,420	2.63

Source: *Frozen Food Age*, November 2005, p. 30, from Information Resources Inc.

★ 415 ★

Salad Dressings

SIC: 2035; NAICS: 311941

Salad Dressing Sales at Supermarkets

Supermarket sales are shown in millions of dollars.

Dressing, liquid	$ 1,246.40
Mayonnaise	749.45
Miracle Whip type	301.90
Dressing, reduced low caloric	253.14
Salad & potato toppings dry	101.27
Dressing mixes, dry	88.00
Sandwich spreads, relish type	19.00

Source: *Progressive Grocer*, September 15, 2005, p. 22, from *Progressive Grocer's 26th Annual Consumer Expenditures Study*.

★ 416 ★

Salad Dressings

SIC: 2035; NAICS: 311941

Top Salad Dressing Brands (Pourable), 2005

Brands are ranked by sales at supermarkets, drug stores and mass merchandisers (excluding Wal-Mart) for the 52 weeks ended September 4, 2005.

	($ mil.)	% of Group
Maries	$ 65.32	36.00%
Litehouse	40.20	22.16
T Marzetti	$ 31.69	17.47%
Naturally Fresh	16.17	8.91
Walden Farms	5.89	3.25
Bob's	5.08	2.80
Maries Lite	5.02	2.77
Makoto	4.35	2.40
O'Charley's Secret Recipe	2.55	1.41
Private label	5.17	2.85

Source: *Corporate Profiles & Industry Statistics - Milling & Baking News Supplement*, November 2005, p. 130, from Information Resources Inc.

★ 417 ★

Salad Dressings

SIC: 2035; NAICS: 311941

Top Salad Dressing Makers, 2005

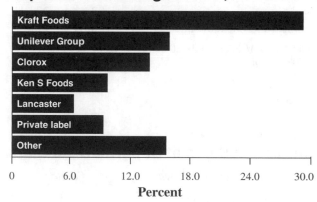

Total sales were $1.5 billion. Sales exclude Wal-Mart and other large format mass retailers.

Kraft Foods	29.2%
Unilever Group	15.9
Clorox	13.9
Ken S Foods	9.7
Lancaster	6.4
Private label	9.3
Other	15.6

Source: *U.S. Personal Care and Household Products Digest*, Citigroup Equity Research, February 24, 2006, p. 238, from ACNielsen.

★ 418 ★
Sauces
SIC: 2035; NAICS: 311941

Condiment and Dressing Sales, 2003 and 2005

Data show sales in millions of dollars for the year-to-date.

	May 17, 2003	May 17, 2005
Salad dressings, liquid	$ 1,235.33	$ 1,239.02
Mexican sauces	1,075.90	1,077.98
Pickles	711.00	669.00
Catsup	474.51	464.14
Olives	415.47	407.15
Barbecue sauces	372.26	361.37
Salad dressings, creamy . . .	321.29	303.18
Mustard	304.42	293.89
Meat sauces	213.47	198.03
Peppers	187.48	200.41
Fish/seafood/cocktail sauces . .	110.04	11.56

Source: *ECRM Focus*, July 2005, p. 50, from *ACNielsen Strategic Planner*.

★ 419 ★
Sauces
SIC: 2035; NAICS: 311941

Condiment Sales at Supermarkets

Supermarket sales are shown in millions of dollars.

Spaghetti/marinara sauce	$ 1,290.14
Mexican sauces	895.82
Catsup	456.69
Barbeque sauces	362.73
Mustard	292.54
Meat sauces	200.96
Gravy, canned	183.36
Gravy mixes, packaged	155.61
Cooking sauces	122.78

Source: *Progressive Grocer*, September 15, 2005, p. 22, from *Progressive Grocer's 26th Annual Consumer Expenditures Study*.

★ 420 ★
Sauces
SIC: 2035; NAICS: 311941

Sauce and Spread Sales, 2003 and 2005

Data show sales in millions of dollars for the year-to-date.

	May 17, 2003	May 14, 2005
Spaghetti/marinara sauce . . .	$ 1,421.53	$ 1,338.17
Peanut butter	839.84	856.67
Table syrup	494.48	480.97
Preserves, marmalade	265.29	268.63
Tomato sauce, canned	247.12	229.49
Marinades/tenderizers/MSG . .	208.52	215.89
Canned gravy	195.88	186.24
Honey	184.65	201.39
Gravy mixes	182.76	170.40

Source: *ECRM Focus*, July 2005, p. 50, from *ACNielsen Strategic Planner*.

★ 421 ★
Sauces
SIC: 2035; NAICS: 311941

Sauce Sales in the U.K., 2005

Distribution of sales is shown for the 52 weeks ended July 17, 2005.

Thick & thin sauces	33.8%
Salad accompaniments	32.9
Condiment sauces	11.8
Pickles & chutneys	11.7
Other	9.8

Source: *Grocer*, October 1, 2005, p. 54.

★ 422 ★
Sauces
SIC: 2035; NAICS: 311941

Steak Sauce Market

Market shares are shown in percent.

A1	63.0%
Other	37.0

Source: *Food/Agribusiness Beverages Tobacco*, Prudential Equity Group Research, March 8, 2005, p. 31, from Prudential Equity Group.

★ 423 ★
Sauces
SIC: 2035; NAICS: 311941

Top Barbeque Sauce Brands, 2005

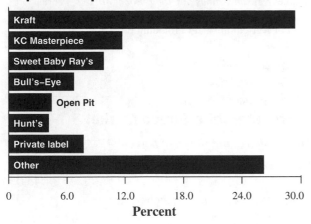

Market shares are shown in percent. Figures exclude Wal-Mart and other large format mass retailers.

Kraft	.29.4%
KC Masterpiece	.11.7
Sweet Baby Ray's	. 9.8
Bull's-Eye	. 6.7
Open Pit	. 4.4
Hunt's	. 4.1
Private label	. 7.7
Other	.26.2

Source: *U.S. Personal Care and Household Products Digest*, Citigroup Equity Research, February 24, 2006, p. 239, from ACNielsen.

★ 424 ★
Sauces
SIC: 2035; NAICS: 311941

Top Barbeque Sauce Makers in the U.K., 2005

Market shares are shown for the 52 weeks ended November 5, 2005.

HP	.21.1%
Own label	.16.4
Heinz	.10.3
Other	.52.2

Source: "Sales Data and Market Shares." [online] from http://www.competition-commission.org.uk/rep_pub/reports/2006/fulltext/511ae.pdf [Accessed June 1, 2006] from Competition Commission analysis of IRI data provided by Heinz.

★ 425 ★
Sauces
SIC: 2035; NAICS: 311941

Top Dressing Makers in Western Europe

The top companies are ranked by market share. Data refer to products sold for human consumption in retail, catering and artisanal markets. Germany took 26% of the market, followed by France and Italy with 11% each.

Unilever	.12.9%
Heinz	. 6.3
McCormick	. 5.1
Hergstenberg	. 4.1
Altria	. 3.8
Fuchs Gruppe	. 3.7
Kuhne	. 3.7
Orkla	. 3.5
Nestle	. 2.8
Develey	. 2.0
Other	.52.1

Source: "Dressing & Condiment Markets." [online] from http://www.fft.com [Published September 2005] from Food for Thought.

★ 426 ★
Sauces
SIC: 2035; NAICS: 311941

Top Mexican Sauce Makers, 2005

Market shares are shown based on food store, drug store and mass merchandiser sales (excluding Wal-Mart) for the 52 weeks ended January 2006.

PepsiCo.	.25.3%
Campbell	.20.1
Ralcorp.	.11.2
Private label	.11.2
Other	.32.2

Source: *US Food Industry*, North American Equity Research, January 17, 2006, p. 100, from ACNielsen and JPMorgan.

★ 427 ★
Sauces
SIC: 2035; NAICS: 311941
Top Pasta Sauce Brands, 2006

Market shares are shown based on food store, drug store and mass merchandiser sales (excluding Wal-Mart) for the 52 weeks ended January 26, 2006.

Prego .	.16.1%
Classico .	.11.3
Ragu Old World Style	.11.0
Hunts	6.4
Ragu Chunky Garden Style	5.9
Barilla .	3.9
Five Brothers Bertolli Lucca	3.8
Ragu	3.6
Ragu Cheese Creations	3.2
Private label	5.6
Other .	.29.2

Source: *Grocery Headquarters*, April 2006, p. 56, from Information Resources Inc.

★ 428 ★
Sauces
SIC: 2035; NAICS: 311941
Top Pasta Sauce Makers, 2006

Market shares are shown based on food store, drug store and mass merchandiser sales (excluding Wal-Mart) for the 52 weeks ended January 26, 2006.

Unilever Bestfoods North America	.34.6%
Campbell Soup Co.	.18.4
H.J. Heinz Co.	.12.2
ConAgra Inc.	6.8
Private label	5.6
Other .	.22.4

Source: *Grocery Headquarters*, April 2006, p. 56, from Information Resources Inc.

★ 429 ★
Sauces
SIC: 2035; NAICS: 311941
Top Sauce/Dressing/Condiment Makers Worldwide, 2002

Data show the market shares of the top multinationals.

Unilever	.10.7%
Kraft .	4.3
Nestle .	3.0
PepsiCo.	0.8

Danone .	0.7%
Mars .	0.7
Other .	.69.8

Source: *New Directions in Global Food Markets*, February 2005, p. 66, from Economic Research Service, U.S. Department of Agriculture and Euromonitor.

★ 430 ★
Sauces
SIC: 2035; NAICS: 311941
Worcestershire Sauce Market

Market shares are shown in percent.

Lea & Perrins	.55.0%
Other .	.45.0

Source: *The Record*, June 21, 2005, p. NA.

★ 431 ★
Frozen Fruit
SIC: 2037; NAICS: 311411
Top Frozen Fruit Brands, 2005

Brands are ranked by sales for the 12 weeks ended August 7, 2005.

	Sales	Share
Dole .	$ 5,543,832	8.76%
Birds Eye .	1,939,064	3.06
Cascadian Farm	1,419,164	2.24
VIP .	1,335,413	2.11
Private label	45,964,188	72.59
Other .	7,116,035	11.24

Source: *Frozen Food Age*, September 2005, p. 13, from Information Resources Inc.

★ 432 ★
Frozen Vegetables
SIC: 2037; NAICS: 311411
Top Corn On The Cob Brands, 2006

Brands are ranked by sales for the 12 weeks ended January 22, 2006.

	Sales	Share
Green Giant Nibblers	$ 5,915,338	26.68%
Birds Eye	3,795,951	17.12
Green Giant	1,193,797	5.38
Westpac .	371,716	1.68
Fresh Frozen	262,383	1.18
Sack O Corn	124,840	0.56

Continued on next page.

★ 432 ★

[Continued]
Frozen Vegetables
SIC: 2037; NAICS: 311411

Top Corn On The Cob Brands, 2006

Brands are ranked by sales for the 12 weeks ended January 22, 2006.

	Sales	Share
Private label	$ 8,222,249	37.08%
Other	2,288,578	10.32

Source: *Frozen Food Age*, February 2006, p. 12, from Information Resources Inc.

★ 433 ★

Frozen Vegetables
SIC: 2037; NAICS: 311411

Top Prepared Vegetable Brands (Sauce/Crumbs), 2006

Brands are ranked by sales for the 12 weeks ended January 22, 2006.

	Sales	Share
Green Giant	$ 43,936,468	75.19%
Birds Eye	3,850,840	6.59
Birds Eye Fresh Frozen Steam and Serve	3,115,320	5.33
Green Giant Le Sueur	2,506,467	4.29
Green Giant Select	1,803,322	3.09
Mckenzie's	167,732	0.29
Other	3,055,355	5.23

Source: *Frozen Food Age*, February 2006, p. 12, from Information Resources Inc.

★ 434 ★

Frozen Dinners and Entrees
SIC: 2038; NAICS: 311412

Top Breakfast Entree Brands, 2005

Brands are ranked by sales for the 12 weeks ended October 30, 2005.

	Sales	Share
Tennessee Pride	$ 1,855,940	9.1%
Bob Evans	1,556,852	7.6
Purnell Old Folks	1,232,432	6.1
Owens	1,225,101	6.0
Rudy's Farm	943,308	4.6
Williams	813,686	4.0

	Sales	Share
Owens Border Breakfasts . . .	$ 673,870	3.3%
Bob Evans Farms Snackwiches .	558,086	2.7
Webber Farms	506,073	2.5
Private label	824,900	4.1
Other	10,190,248	50.0

Source: *Frozen Food Age*, December 2005, p. 11, from Information Resources Inc.

★ 435 ★

Frozen Dinners and Entrees
SIC: 2038; NAICS: 311412

Top Dinner/Entree Brands (Multi-Serve), 2005

Brands are ranked by sales for the 12 weeks ended October 30, 2005.

	Sales	Share
Stouffers Family Style Recipes .	$ 42,090,084	19.44%
Stouffers	24,278,826	11.22
Bertolli	23,319,114	10.77
Souffers Skillet Sensations . .	14,629,118	6.76
Banquet Crock Pot Classsics . .	14,494,252	6.70
Contessa	8,686,099	4.01
Banquet	1,016,600	0.47
Private label	15,296,691	7.07
Other	72,651,648	33.56

Source: *Frozen Food Age*, December 2005, p. 11, from Information Resources Inc.

★ 436 ★

Frozen Dinners and Entrees
SIC: 2038; NAICS: 311412

Top Frozen Dinner Brands (Single-Serve), 2006

Market shares are shown based on food store, drug store and mass merchandiser sales (excluding Wal-Mart) for the 52 weeks ended January 26, 2006.

Stouffer's	.10.9%
Stouffer's Lean Cuisine Café Classics	8.0
Weight Watchers Smart Ones	5.8
Healthy Choice	5.3
Stouffers Lean Cuisine Everyday Favorite . .	5.1
Marie Callender's Complete Dinners	3.9
Stouffer's Homestyle	3.8
Banquet Select Menu	3.7

Continued on next page.

★ 436 ★

[Continued]

Frozen Dinners and Entrees

SIC: 2038; NAICS: 311412

Top Frozen Dinner Brands (Single-Serve), 2006

Market shares are shown based on food store, drug store and mass merchandiser sales (excluding Wal-Mart) for the 52 weeks ended January 26, 2006.

Banquet Value Menu	3.5%
Swanson Hungry-Man	3.5
Other	.46.5

Source: *Grocery Headquarters*, April 2006, p. 56, from Information Resources Inc.

★ 437 ★

Frozen Dinners and Entrees

SIC: 2038; NAICS: 311412

Top Frozen Dinner/Entree Makers, 2005

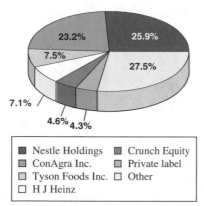

- ■ Nestle Holdings
- ■ ConAgra Inc.
- ■ Tyson Foods Inc.
- □ H J Heinz
- ■ Crunch Equity
- ■ Private label
- □ Other

Market shares are shown based on food store, drug store and mass merchandiser sales (excluding Wal-Mart) for the 52 weeks ended January 2006.

Nestle Holdings	.25.9%
ConAgra Inc.	.23.2
Tyson Foods Inc.	7.5
H J Heinz	7.1
Crunch Equity	4.6
Private label	4.3
Other	.27.5

Source: *US Food Industry*, North American Equity Research, January 17, 2006, p. 100, from ACNielsen and JPMorgan.

★ 438 ★

Frozen Dinners and Entrees

SIC: 2038; NAICS: 311412

Top Frozen Dinner Makers (Single-Serve), 2006

Market shares are shown based on food store, drug store and mass merchandiser sales (excluding Wal-Mart) for the 52 weeks ended January 26, 2006.

Nestle USA Inc.	.35.7%
ConAgra Inc.	.22.9
Weight Watchers Co.	8.7
Luigino's Inc.	6.5
Pinnacle Foods Group	6.5
Other	.19.7

Source: *Grocery Headquarters*, April 2006, p. 56, from Information Resources Inc.

★ 439 ★

Frozen Dinners and Entrees

SIC: 2038; NAICS: 311412

Top Frozen Entrée Vendors, 2005

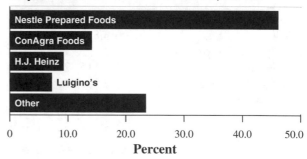

Market shares are shown based on supermarket, drug store and mass merchandiser sales (excluding Wal-Mart) for the 52 weeks ended April 17, 2005.

Nestle Prepared Foods	.46.1%
ConAgra Foods	.14.1
H.J. Heinz	9.2
Luigino's	7.2
Other	.23.4

Source: *Refrigerated & Frozen Foods*, June 2005, p. 56, from Information Resources Inc.

★ 440 ★

Frozen Dinners and Entrees

SIC: 2038; NAICS: 311412

Top Handheld Entrée Brands (Non-Breakfast), 2005

Market shares are shown based on supermarket, drug store and mass merchandiser sales (excluding Wal-Mart) for the 52 weeks ended April 17, 2005.

	($ mil.)	Share
Hot Pockets	$ 283.5	26.83%
Lean Pockets	157.2	14.88
Croissant Pockets	79.6	7.53
El Monterey	70.2	6.64
State Fair	55.6	5.26
Other	410.6	38.86

Source: *Refrigerated & Frozen Foods*, June 2005, p. 56, from Information Resources Inc.

★ 441 ★

Frozen Dinners and Entrees

SIC: 2038; NAICS: 311412

Top Handheld Entrée Makers, 2006

Market shares are shown based on food store, drug store and mass merchandiser sales (excluding Wal-Mart) for the 52 weeks ended January 26, 2006.

Chef America	.50.7%
Ruiz Food Prods.	6.9
State Fair Foods Inc.	5.1
White Castle Sys. Inc.	4.5
Camino Real Foods Inc.	4.3
Other	.28.5

Source: *Grocery Headquarters*, April 2006, p. 56, from Information Resources Inc.

★ 442 ★

Frozen Dinners and Entrees

SIC: 2038; NAICS: 311412

Top Handheld Entree Makers (Breakfast), 2005

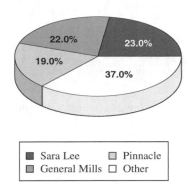

Sara Lee · Pinnacle
General Mills · Other

The industry was worth $0.7 billion. Breakfast items are not included.

Sara Lee	.23.0%
General Mills	.22.0
Pinnacle	.19.0
Other	.37.0

Source: "Annual Meat Conference." [online] from http://www.meatami.com/Education/D%20Rosenthol%20Final%203-14-06.pdf [Published March 2006] from Information Resources Inc.

★ 443 ★

Frozen Dinners and Entrees

SIC: 2038; NAICS: 311412

Top Handheld Entree Makers (Non-Breakfast), 2005

The industry was worth $1.1 billion. Breakfast items are not included.

Nestle	.51.0%
Ruiz Foods	7.0
Sara Lee	6.0
Camino Real	4.0
Other	.32.0

Source: "Annual Meat Conference." [online] from http://www.meatami.com/Education/D%20Rosenthol%20Final%203-14-06.pdf [Published March 2006] from Information Resources Inc.

★ 444 ★

Frozen Foods

SIC: 2038; NAICS: 311412

Frozen Food Market in Canada, 2004

The industry is valued at $4 billion annually.

Dinners & entrees	.27.3%
Seafood	.11.2
Ice cream & related products	.10.4
Frozen & refrigerated pizza	.9.1
Refrigerated pizza confections	.6.7
Other	.35.3

Source: *Quick Frozen Foods International*, April 2006, p. 84, from ACNielsen MarketTrack.

★ 445 ★

Frozen Foods

SIC: 2038; NAICS: 311412

Frozen Food Market in Europe, 2004

Sales are shown in millions of euros. All totals refer to final human consumption, including retail, catering, foodservice and artisanal/craft. Industrial and farm consumption are excluded. Pizza was the leader in 22 categories, up 9.3% in 2004 to 638,000 tons. The overall market was worth 51.109 billion euros.

Germany	€ 15,221.3
United Kingdom	10,132.8
France	8,160.3
Italy	7,198.9
Spain	6,536.5
Belgium/Luxembourg	1,807.4
Norway	1,738.9
Denmark	1,568.2
Austria	1,426.1

Source: *Quick Frozen Foods International*, October 2005, p. 86, from Food for Thought.

★ 446 ★

Frozen Foods

SIC: 2038; NAICS: 311412

Leading French Fry Producers Worldwide

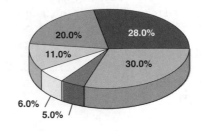

■ McCain		□ Aviko	
■ Lamb Weston/Meijer		■ Farm frites	
■ Simplot		■ Other	

Market shares are shown in percent.

McCain	.28.0%
Lamb Weston/Meijer	.20.0
Simplot	.11.0
Aviko	.6.0
Farm frites	.5.0
Other	.30.0

Source: "Netherlands Frozen Potato Products Annual 2005." [online] from http://www.usatrade.gov [Published December 2005] from *Boerderij* and Akkerbouw.

★ 447 ★

Frozen Foods

SIC: 2038; NAICS: 311412

Leading Side Dish/Appetizer Makers

Firms are ranked by sales in millions of dollars.

H.J. Heinz Co.	$ 900
McCain Foods USA	726
Windsor Foods	650
Reser's Fine Foods	525
Rich-SeaPak Corp.	450
Kraft Foods	375
Orval Kent Foods	300
J&J Snack Foods Corp.	275
Pillsbury USA	260
Kozy Shack Enterprises	200

Source: *Refrigerated & Frozen Foods*, March 2006, p. 16.

★ 448 ★
Frozen Foods
SIC: 2038; NAICS: 311412

Top Frozen Appetizer Brands, 2005

Market shares are shown based on supermarket, drug store and mass merchandiser sales (excluding Wal-Mart) for the 52 weeks ended May 15, 2005.

	($ mil.)	Share
Totino's	$ 173.4	21.10%
TGI Friday's	109.6	13.34
Bagel Bites	52.9	6.44
Jose Ole	38.0	4.62
Private label	41.4	5.04
Other	406.4	49.46

Source: *Refrigerated & Frozen Foods*, June 2005, p. 44, from Information Resources Inc.

★ 449 ★
Frozen Foods
SIC: 2038; NAICS: 311412

Top Frozen Food Categories, 2005

Brands are ranked by sales for the 52 weeks ended December 25, 2005.

	($ mil.)	Share
Ice cream	$ 3,847.72	14.04%
Single-serve entrees	3,609.00	13.17
Pizza	2,525.66	9.22
Frozen novelties	2,144.21	7.83
Chicken/chicken substitutes	1,143.62	4.17
Handheld entrees (non-breakfast)	1,073.82	3.92
IQF chicken/chicken substitutes	883.78	3.23
Potatoes/fries/hash browns	840.22	3.07
Appetizers/snack rolls	814.54	2.97
Meat (no poultry)	705.68	2.58
Other	9,811.75	35.81

Source: *Frozen Food Age*, April 2006, p. 16, from Information Resources Inc.

★ 450 ★
Frozen Foods
SIC: 2038; NAICS: 311412

Top Frozen Food Makers in Japan, 2004

Market shares are shown based on domestic sales of 886.7 billion yen.

Nichirei	20.0%
Katokichi	19.8
Ajinomoto Frozen Foods	11.6
Nichiro	11.2
Nippon Suisan Kaisha	7.5
Other	29.9

Source: "2004 Market Share Report." [online] from http://www.nikkei.co.jp [Published July 27, 2005] from Japan Frozen Food Association.

★ 451 ★
Frozen Foods
SIC: 2038; NAICS: 311412

Top Frozen Food Makers in the U.K.

Market shares are shown for the 52 weeks ended August 6, 2005.

Unilever	15.8%
MacCain	7.3
Heinz	5.4
Youngs/Bluecrest	5.0
Tryton	2.2
Other	64.3

Source: "Retail Market Breakdown by Products." [online] from http://www.bfff.co.uk/RetailMarketBreakdown.pdf [Published October 25, 2005].

★ 452 ★
Frozen Foods
SIC: 2038; NAICS: 311412

Top Frozen Meat Alternative Brands, 2005

Market shares are shown based on supermarket, drug store and mass merchandiser sales (excluding Wal-Mart) for the 52 weeks ended April 17, 2005.

	($ mil.)	Share
Morningstar Farms	$ 106.6	53.01%
Boca Foods	51.6	25.66

Continued on next page.

★ 452 ★
[Continued]
Frozen Foods
SIC: 2038; NAICS: 311412

Top Frozen Meat Alternative Brands, 2005

Market shares are shown based on supermarket, drug store and mass merchandiser sales (excluding Wal-Mart) for the 52 weeks ended April 17, 2005.

	($ mil.)	Share
Gardenburger	$ 25.1	12.48%
Other	17.8	8.85

Source: *Refrigerated & Frozen Foods*, June 2005, p. 44, from Information Resources Inc.

★ 453 ★
Frozen Foods
SIC: 2038; NAICS: 311412

Top Frozen Pizza Brands, 2006

Market shares are shown based on supermarket, drug store and mass merchandiser sales (excluding Wal-Mart) for the 52 weeks ended January 26, 2006.

DiGiorno	18.8%
Red Baron	10.2
Tombstone	10.1
Freschetta	6.2
Totino's Party Pizza	5.7
Tony's	5.2
Stouffer's	3.5
California Pizza Kitchen	3.3
Jack's Original	3.2
Other	33.8

Source: *Grocery Headquarters*, April 2006, p. 56, from Information Resources Inc.

★ 454 ★
Frozen Foods
SIC: 2038; NAICS: 311412

Top Frozen Pizza Makers, 2006

Market shares are shown based on supermarket, drug store and mass merchandiser sales (excluding Wal-Mart) for the 52 weeks ended January 26, 2006.

Kraft Foods Inc.	33.2%
Tony's Pizza Services	26.1
General Mills	7.7
Nestle USA Inc.	7.2
Kraft/Jack's Frozen Pizza Inc.	5.5

Pinnacle Foods Group	2.6%
Home Run Inn	1.3
McCain Ellio's Foods Inc.	1.3
Bud's Pizza	1.0
Private label	7.3
Other	6.8

Source: *Grocery Headquarters*, April 2006, p. 56, from Information Resources Inc.

★ 455 ★
Frozen Foods
SIC: 2038; NAICS: 311412

Top Meat Pie Brands, 2005

Brands are ranked by sales for the 12 weeks ended August 7, 2005.

	Sales	Share
Mrs. Budds	$ 2,030,632	76.73%
Nobrand	69,227	2.62
Morrison	44,087	1.67
Mailhots Best	38,651	1.46
Private label	344,638	13.02
Other	119,205	4.50

Source: *Frozen Food Age*, September 2005, p. 13, from Information Resources Inc.

★ 456 ★
Frozen Foods
SIC: 2038; NAICS: 311412

Top Waffle Brands, 2005

Brands are ranked by sales for the 12 weeks ended October 30, 2005.

	Sales	Share
Kellogg's Eggo	$ 59,324,484	52.77%
Kellogg's Nutri Grain Eggo	7,144,573	6.36
Aunt Jemima	6,267,181	5.57
Pillsbury Hungry Jack	5,830,793	5.19
Kellogg's Eggo Minis	3,205,520	2.85
Vans	2,329,920	2.07
Kellogg's Eggo Flip Flop	2,167,225	1.93
Kellogg's Special K Eggo	2,165,422	1.93
Pillsbury	1,852,047	1.65
Private label	17,229,714	15.33
Other	4,901,553	4.36

Source: *Frozen Food Age*, December 2005, p. 11, from Information Resources Inc.

★ 457 ★
Frozen Foods
SIC: 2038; NAICS: 311412

Top Waffle Makers, 2005

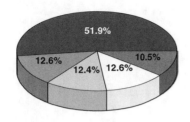

Legend:
- ■ Kellogg
- ■ Crunch Equity Holding
- □ General Mills
- □ Private label
- ■ Other

Market shares are shown based on food store, drug store and mass merchandiser sales (excluding Wal-Mart) for the year ended February 19, 2005.

Kellogg	.51.9%
Crunch Equity Holding	.12.6
General Mills	.12.4
Private label	.12.6
Other	.10.5

Source: *Food/Agribusiness Beverages Tobacco*, Prudential Equity Group Research, March 8, 2005, p. 31, from Prudential Equity Group and LLC estimates.

★ 458 ★
Flour
SIC: 2041; NAICS: 311211

Top Flour Producers in Japan

Market shares are shown in percent.

Nisshin Seifun Group/Nippon Flour Mills Co./ Showa Sangyo Co.	.70.0%
Other	.30.0

Source: *Nihon Keizai Shimbun*, September 13, 2005, p. NA.

★ 459 ★
Flour
SIC: 2041; NAICS: 311211

Top Flour Refiners, 2004

Firms are ranked by daily milling capacity in hundredweights (hundredpounds). The top four firms took 63% of the capacity, up from 44% in 1987.

Cargill/CHS (Horizon Milling)	293,000
Archer Daniels Midland	288,800
ConAgra	250,100
Cereal Food Processors	93,100

Source: "Market Share Matrix Project." [online] from http://www.marketsharematrix.org [Published May 2005] from *Milling and Baking News*.

★ 460 ★
Flour
SIC: 2041; NAICS: 311211

Top Wheat Flour Refiners in Canada, 2004

Market shares are shown in percent.

Archer Daniels Midland Company	.42.247%
Robin Hood (J.M. Smucker Company)	.20.790
Dover Industries (Dover Flour Mills)	. 8.560
Parrish & Heimbecker Limited	. 7.150
Other	.21.250

Source: "Market Share Matrix Project." [online] from http://www.marketsharematrix.org [Published August 2005] from *Grain and Milling Annual, 2005*.

★ 461 ★
Cereal
SIC: 2043; NAICS: 31123

Leading Hot Cereals in the U.K.

Market shares are shown in percent.

Quaker Oatso Simple	.24.0%
Ready Brek	.20.0
Other	.56.0

Source: *Marketing Week*, February 23, 2006, p. 31.

★ 462 ★
Cereal
SIC: 2043; NAICS: 31123

Top Cereal Brands, 2005

Brands are ranked by sales at supermarkets, drug stores and mass merchandisers (excluding Wal-Mart) for the 52 weeks ended September 4, 2005.

	($ mil.)	Share
General Mills Cheerios	$ 289.64	7.62%
General Mills Honey Nut Cheerios	247.85	6.52
Kellogg's Frosted Flakes	247.69	6.51
Post Honey Bunches of the Oats	239.84	6.31
Kellogg's Frosted Mini Wheats	174.75	4.60

Continued on next page.

★ 462 ★

[Continued]
Cereal
SIC: 2043; NAICS: 31123

Top Cereal Brands, 2005

Brands are ranked by sales at supermarkets, drug stores and mass merchandisers (excluding Wal-Mart) for the 52 weeks ended September 4, 2005.

	($ mil.)	Share
General Mills Cinnamon Toast Crunch	$ 154.24	4.06%
General Mills Lucky Charms	148.71	3.91
Kellogg's Froot Loops	139.42	3.67
Quaker Life	128.14	3.37
Private label	548.66	14.43
Other	1,483.33	39.01

Source: *Corporate Profiles & Industry Statistics - Milling & Baking News Supplement*, November 2005, p. 130, from Information Resources Inc.

★ 463 ★

Cereal
SIC: 2043; NAICS: 31123

Top Cereal Makers, 2005

Market shares are shown based on food store, drug store and mass merchandiser sales (excluding Wal-Mart) for the 52 weeks ended January 2006.

Kellogg	33.9%
General Mills	30.6
Kraft Foods	14.8
Pepsico	6.2
Malt O Meal	3.5
Hain Celestial	0.2
Private label	9.3
Other	1.4

Source: *US Food Industry*, North American Equity Research, January 17, 2006, p. 86, from ACNielsen and JPMorgan.

★ 464 ★

Cereal
SIC: 2043; NAICS: 31123

Top Cereal Makers in Australia

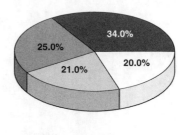

Legend: Kellogg ■ Sanitarium □ Goodman ■ Other □

Market shares are shown in percent.

Kellogg	34.0%
Goodman	25.0
Sanitarium	21.0
Other	20.0

Source: *Australasian Business Intelligence*, July 25, 2005, p. NA.

★ 465 ★

Cereal
SIC: 2043; NAICS: 31123

Top Cereal Makers in India

Market shares are shown for the retail sector.

Kellogg's	75.0%
Other	25.0

Source: *Food/Agribusiness Beverages Tobacco*, Prudential Equity Group Research, March 8, 2005, p. 31, from Prudential Equity Group and LLC estimates.

★ 466 ★

Cereal
SIC: 2043; NAICS: 31123

Top Cereal Makers in Mexico

Market shares are shown for the retail sector.

Kellogg's	70.0%
Other	30.0

Source: *Food/Agribusiness Beverages Tobacco*, Prudential Equity Group Research, March 8, 2005, p. 31, from Prudential Equity Group and LLC estimates.

★ 467 ★
Cereal
SIC: 2043; NAICS: 31123

Top Cereal Makers Worldwide

Market shares are shown in percent.

Kellogg 33.0%
General Mills 14.0
PepsiCo. 10.0
Cereal Partners Worldwide 9.0
Kraft Foods 8.0
Other 26.0

Source: ''Prospects in the Global Breakfast Cereal Market.'' [online] from http://www.ffas.usda.gov [Published June 2005] from U.S. Department of Agriculture.

★ 468 ★
Rice
SIC: 2044; NAICS: 311212

Top Dry Rice Brands, 2004-2005

Prices of traditional rice have fallen from lack of consumer interest. There has been a move towards rice mixes. Brands are ranked by sales in millions of dollars.

	($ mil.)	Share
Mahatma Dry Rice	$ 114.71	10.39%
Kraft Minute Rice	59.93	5.43
Uncle Ben's Converted Rice	58.91	5.34
Success Dry Rice	39.10	3.54
Private label dry rice	544.06	49.28
Other	287.24	26.02

Source: *Food Institute Report*, April 10, 2006, p. 4, from Information Resources Inc.

★ 469 ★
Rice
SIC: 2044; NAICS: 311212

Top Dry Rice Mix Brands, 2004-2005

Industry sales were $488.76 million.

	($ mil.)	Share
Rice-A-Roni Dry Rice Mixes . . .	$ 114.93	23.51%
Zatarain's Dry Rice Mixes	65.06	13.31
Lipton's Rice Sides Dry Rice Mixes	41.54	8.50
Uncle Ben's Dry Rice Mixes	35.56	7.28
Other	231.67	47.40

Source: *Food Institute Report*, April 10, 2006, p. 4, from Information Resources Inc.

★ 470 ★
Rice
SIC: 2044; NAICS: 311212

Top Rice Brands in the U.K.

Market shares are shown for the 52 weeks ended October 2005.

Tilda 33.0%
Kohinoor 5.0
Natco 4.0
Uncle Ben's 2.0
Private label 52.0
Other 4.0

Source: *Grocer*, November 26, 2005, p. NA, from ACNielsen.

★ 471 ★
Baking Mixes
SIC: 2045; NAICS: 311822

Baking and Gelatin/Pudding Mix Sales

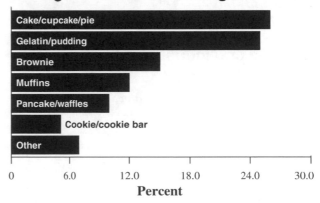

Sales of dessert and pudding mixes have been falling steadily in recent years and are expected to continue to do so. Sales were $1,963 million in 2005 and are expected to fall to $1,678 million by 2009.

Cake/cupcake/pie 26.0%
Gelatin/pudding 25.0
Brownie 15.0
Muffins 12.0
Pancake/waffles 10.0
Cookie/cookie bar 5.0
Other 7.0

Source: *Prepared Foods*, May 2006, p. 23, from Mintel.

★ 472 ★
Baking Mixes
SIC: 2045; NAICS: 311822

Baking Mix Sales at Supermarkets

Supermarket sales are shown in millions of dollars.

Cake/layer over 10 ounces	$ 311.32
Brownies	227.73
Pancakes	176.36
Muffins	174.25
Rolls and biscuits	107.96
Bread	80.49
Cookies	64.53
Cake/specialty over 10 ounces	33.34
Gingerbread	4.97
Hush puppies	3.75

Source: *Progressive Grocer*, September 15, 2005, p. 22, from *Progressive Grocer's 26th Annual Consumer Expenditures Study*.

★ 473 ★
Baking Mixes
SIC: 2045; NAICS: 311822

Home Baking Industry in the U.K., 2005

The home baking industry was valued at 36.5 million pounds sterling in 2004. The fruit sector represents much of the growth in the category, with snacking fruits up 22% and baking fruits up 17% for the 52 weeks ended May 22, 2005.

Snacking fruits	.33.5%
Baking fruits	.23.7
Culinary nuts	.15.5
Flour mixes	.12.5
Cake coverings	9.2
Cherries and peel	5.4
Snacking fruits and nuts	0.2

Source: *Grocer*, August 6, 2005, p. 44, from TNS Superpanel.

★ 474 ★
Baking Mixes
SIC: 2045; NAICS: 311822

Leading Baking Mix Makers, 2005

Market shares are shown based on sales at food stores, drug stores and mass merchandisers (excluding Wal-Mart) for the 12 weeks ended June 11, 2005.

General Mills	.35.0%
J.M. Smucker Company	.15.0
Other	.50.0

Source: *Food/Agribusiness*, Prudential Equity Group Equity Research, June 24, 2005, p. 2, from ACNielsen.

★ 475 ★
Baking Mixes
SIC: 2045; NAICS: 311822

Top Cake Mix Brands, 2005

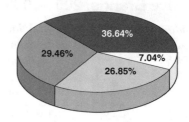

Betty Crocker ■   Duncan Hines □
Pillsbury ■   Other □

Market shares are shown in percent.

Betty Crocker	.36.64%
Pillsbury	.29.46
Duncan Hines	.26.85
Other	7.04

Source: "Empirical Analysis of Competitive Pricing Strategies." [online] from www.fcee.lisboa.ucp.pt/resources/documents/seminario/CompPricing-Dec-2005.pdf [Published Dec. 2005].

★ 476 ★
Dough
SIC: 2045; NAICS: 311822

Top Refrigerated Dough Makers, 2005

Market shares are shown based on food store, drug store and mass merchandiser sales (excluding Wal-Mart) for the 52 weeks ended January 2006.

General Mills	.68.1%
Nestle	.13.4

Continued on next page.

★ 476 ★

[Continued]

Dough

SIC: 2045; NAICS: 311822

Top Refrigerated Dough Makers, 2005

Market shares are shown based on food store, drug store and mass merchandiser sales (excluding Wal-Mart) for the 52 weeks ended January 2006.

Private label 17.1%
Other 1.4

Source: *US Food Industry*, North American Equity Research, January 17, 2006, p. 28, from ACNielsen and JPMorgan.

★ 477 ★

Pet Food

SIC: 2047; NAICS: 311111

Top Cat/Dog Food Makers, 2004

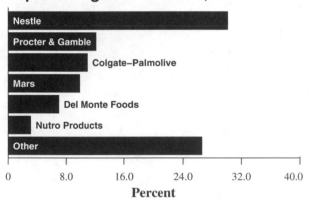

Percent

Some of the brands manufactured by each company: Nestle - Friskies, Purina. Procter & Gamble - Iams. Colgate-Palmolive - Hill's Science Diet. Mars - Pedigree, Whiskas, Sheba. Del Monte Foods - Kibbles 'n Bits, 9Lives, Nutro Products - Max, Natural Choice, Ultra.

Nestle 30.2%
Procter & Gamble 12.2
Colgate-Palmolive 11.0
Mars 9.9
Del Monte Foods 7.0
Nutro Products 3.1
Other 26.6

Source: *Financial Times*, March 27, 2006, p. 19, from Euromonitor.

★ 478 ★

Pet Food

SIC: 2047; NAICS: 311111

Top Cat Food Brands, 2005

Total sales were $1.94 billion. Sales exclude Wal-Mart and other large format mass retailers.

Friskies 21.0%
Iams 9.7
9 Lives 7.9
Cat Chow 7.0
Meow Mix 7.0
Whiskas 6.6
Purina One 6.1
Kit'n Kaboodle 2.1
Private label 7.7
Other 24.9

Source: *U.S. Personal Care and Household Products Digest*, Citigroup Equity Research, February 24, 2006, p. 232, from ACNielsen.

★ 479 ★

Pet Food

SIC: 2047; NAICS: 311111

Top Cat Food Brands in the U.K., 2004

A Sainsbury Bank survey found that cat owners spend 475.7 pounds sterling a year on their pets. Most of the spending is on food, but some spending is devoted to treats and grooming.

Whiskas 23.8%
Felix 19.3
Friskies Go-Cat 7.8
Kitekat 7.3
Iams 6.2
Friskies Gourmet 3.1
Sheba 2.2
Arthur's 1.6
Hill's 1.5
Other 27.2

Source: *Marketing*, October 12, 2005, p. 36, from Euromonitor.

★ 480 ★

Pet Food

SIC: 2047; NAICS: 311111

Top Cat Food Brands (Wet), 2006

Brands are ranked by sales for the 52 weeks ended March 19, 2006.

	($ mil.)	Share
Friskies Fancy	$ 297.4	33.13%
Friskies Wet	162.1	18.06
9 Lives	96.4	10.74
Whiskas Choice	34.6	3.85
Private label	62.7	6.99
Other	244.4	27.23

Source: *Pet Aisle*, June 2006, p. 28, from Information Resources Inc.

★ 481 ★

Pet Food

SIC: 2047; NAICS: 311111

Top Dog/Cat Treats, 2005

Market shares are shown in percent. Figures exclude Wal-Mart and other large format mass retailers.

Milk-Bone	19.7%
Pup-Peroni	7.8
Beggin' Strips	7.5
Pedigree	4.9
Whiskas	4.4
Whisker Lickins	4.2
Meaty Bone	4.0
Snausages	3.7
Pounce	3.0
Private label	9.7
Other	31.1

Source: *U.S. Personal Care and Household Products Digest*, Citigroup Equity Research, February 24, 2006, p. 233, from ACNielsen.

★ 482 ★

Pet Food

SIC: 2047; NAICS: 311111

Top Dog Food Brands, 2005

Total sales were $2.28 billion. Figures exclude Wal-Mart and other large format mass retailers.

Purina	40.1%
Pedigree	19.0
Iams	13.3
Kibbles 'N Bit	6.3

Cesar Select Dinners	3.6%
Dad's	1.2
Gravy Train	1.2
Private label	9.5
Other	5.8

Source: *U.S. Personal Care and Household Products Digest*, Citigroup Equity Research, February 24, 2006, p. 231, from ACNielsen.

★ 483 ★

Pet Food

SIC: 2047; NAICS: 311111

Top Dog Food Brands (Dry), 2006

Market shares are shown based on sales at food stores, drug stores and mass merchandisers (excluding Wal-Mart) for the 52 weeks ended January 26, 2006.

Iams	16.6%
Purina One	9.8
Beneful	9.2
Pedigree Mealtime	7.6
Purina Dog Chow	7.2
Ken-L Ration Kibbles N Bits 3X	3.3
Purina Dog Chow	2.9
Pedigree	2.5
Friskies Come & Get It	2.1
Private label	8.7
Other	30.1

Source: *Grocery Headquarters*, April 2006, p. 56, from Information Resources Inc.

★ 484 ★

Pet Food

SIC: 2047; NAICS: 311111

Top Dog Food Brands in the U.K., 2004

A Sainsbury Bank survey found that dog owners spend 981.31 pounds sterling a year on their pets. Most of the spending is on food, but some spending is devoted to treats and grooming.

Pedigree	20.2%
Winalot	15.0
Butcher's	5.7
Baker's	4.6
Schmackos	3.2
Cesar	3.1
Chappie	2.7
Pal	2.6

Continued on next page.

★ 484 ★

[Continued]
Pet Food

SIC: 2047; NAICS: 311111

Top Dog Food Brands in the U.K., 2004

A Sainsbury Bank survey found that dog owners spend 981.31 pounds sterling a year on their pets. Most of the spending is on food, but some spending is devoted to treats and grooming.

Iams	2.3%
Other	40.6

Source: *Marketing*, October 12, 2005, p. 36, from Euromonitor.

★ 485 ★

Pet Food

SIC: 2047; NAICS: 311111

Top Dog Food Brands (Wet), 2006

Brands are ranked by sales for the 52 weeks ended March 19, 2006.

	($ mil.)	Share
Cesar Select	$ 74.0	12.12%
Pedigree Wet	71.4	11.70
Alpo	69.1	11.32
Mighty Dog	64.1	10.50
Pedigree Choice	53.5	8.76
Other	278.3	45.59

Source: *Pet Aisle*, June 2006, p. 28, from Information Resources Inc.

★ 486 ★

Pet Food

SIC: 2047; NAICS: 311111

Top Dog Food Makers (Dry), 2005

Companies are ranked by supermarket, drug store and mass merchandiser sales (excluding Wal-Mart) for the 52 weeks ended May 15, 2005.

	($ mil.)	Share
Nestle Purina	$ 700.0	43.75%
Iams Company	275.0	17.19
Masterfoods USA	254.0	15.88
Del Monte Foods	148.0	9.25
Dad's Products Co.	32.0	2.00
Sunshine Mills Inc.	17.0	1.06
Nunn Milling Co. Inc.	11.0	0.69

	($ mil.)	Share
American Nutrition Inc.	$ 8.7	0.54%
Other	154.3	9.64

Source: *Petfood Industry*, July 19, 2005, p. NA, from Information Resources Inc.

★ 487 ★

Pet Food

SIC: 2047; NAICS: 311111

Top Dog Treats, 2006

Brands are ranked by sales in millions of dollars for the 52 weeks ended February 19, 2006.

	($ mil.)	Share
Milk-Bone Dog Biscuits	$ 69.9	13.98%
Purina Beggin' Strips	43.1	8.62
Ken-L Ration Pupperoni	25.5	5.10
Milk-Bone Flavor Snacks	20.5	4.10
Private label biscuits	60.4	12.08
Other	280.6	56.12

Source: *Grocery Headquarters*, May 2006, p. 76, from Information Resources Inc.

★ 488 ★

Pet Food

SIC: 2047; NAICS: 311111

Top Pet Food Firms Worldwide, 2004-2005

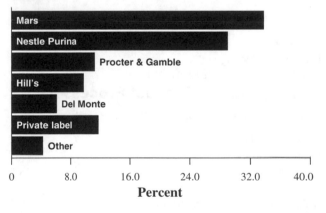

Market shares are shown in percent.

	2004	2005
Mars	33.5%	33.8%
Nestle Purina	28.7	29.0
Procter & Gamble	11.1	11.3
Hill's	9.6	9.8

Continued on next page.

★ 488 ★
[Continued]
Pet Food
SIC: 2047; NAICS: 311111

Top Pet Food Firms Worldwide, 2004-2005

Market shares are shown in percent.

	2004	2005
Del Monte	6.4%	6.0%
Private label	11.9	11.8
Other	4.1	4.2

Source: *Convenience Store Decisions*, July 2005, p. 50, from Morgan Stanley estimates.

★ 489 ★
Livestock Feed
SIC: 2048; NAICS: 311119

Top Livestock Feed Makers, 2003

Firms are ranked by annual capacity. The top 4 firms took 34% of the market.

Land O'Lakes	12.5
Cargill Animal Nutrition	9.0
Archer Daniels Midland	3.2
J.D. Heiskell & Co.	2.8

Source: "Market Share Matrix Project." [online] from http://www.marketsharematrix.org [Accessed January 20, 2006] from M+M Planet Retail Ltd. and *Feedstuffs Reference Issue*.

★ 490 ★
Bakery Products
SIC: 2050; NAICS: 311812, 311821

Leading Bakery Product Processors

Firms are ranked by sales in millions of dollars.

General Mills	$ 2,700
Rich Products Corp.	1,500
Sara Lee Corp.	900
Schwan's Bakery	550
Ralcorp Frozen Bakery Products	475
Dawn Food Products	450
Otis Spunkmeyer	425
Maple Leaf Frozen Bakery	300
Maplehurst Bakeries	285
Harlan Bakeries	225
The Bama Cos. Inc.	225

Source: *Refrigerated & Frozen Foods*, March 2006, p. 16.

★ 491 ★
Bakery Products
SIC: 2050; NAICS: 311812, 311821

Top Bakery Product Makers Worldwide, 2002

Data show the market shares of the top five multinationals.

Kraft	3.0%
Danone	1.7
PepsiCo.	1.2
Unilever	1.0
Nestle	0.5
Other	92.6

Source: *New Directions in Global Food Markets*, February 2005, p. 66, from Economic Research Service, U.S. Department of Agriculture and Euromonitor.

★ 492 ★
Bagels
SIC: 2051; NAICS: 311812

Top Fresh Bagel/Bialys Brands, 2004

Market shares are shown based on supermarket, drug store and mass merchandiser sales (excluding Wal-Mart) for the 52 weeks ended December 26, 2004.

Thomas	36.3%
Sara Lee	16.0
Pepperidge Farm	6.6
Lenders Bagel Shop	4.2
Earth Grains	3.1
Oroweat	2.1
Atkins	1.4
The Alternative Bagel	1.4
Natural Ovens	1.3
Other	27.6

Source: *Snack Food & Wholesale Bakery*, June 2005, p. 31, from Information Resources Inc.

★ 493 ★
Bakery Products
SIC: 2051; NAICS: 311812

Bakery Goods Sales, 2005

Shares are shown based on supermarket sales for the 52 weeks ended August 13, 2005.

	($ mil.)	Share
Bread	$ 5,893.0	46.61%
Cakes	1,531.5	12.11

Continued on next page.

★ 493 ★
[Continued]
Bakery Products
SIC: 2051; NAICS: 311812
Bakery Goods Sales, 2005

Shares are shown based on supermarket sales for the 52 weeks ended August 13, 2005.

	($ mil.)	Share
Buns	$ 1,121.6	8.87%
Donuts	706.1	5.59
Rolls	680.2	5.38
Muffins	663.9	5.25
Bagels	499.6	3.95
Pies	293.7	2.32
Other	1,253.1	9.91

Source: *Progressive Grocer*, October 1, 2005, p. 6, from AC-Nielsen.

★ 494 ★
Bakery Products
SIC: 2051; NAICS: 311812
Cake Sales by Type

Cakes represent 27.6% of instore bakery department store sales per week per store. Average cake sales are $1,883 per week per store.

Quarter sheet	19.2%
Half sheet	8.7
8-inch round cakes	8.0

Source: *InStore Buyer*, April 2005, p. 58, from Perishables Group.

★ 495 ★
Bakery Products
SIC: 2051; NAICS: 311812
Donut Sales by Type, 2005

Donuts represent 8.9% of bakery department store sales per week per store. This translates into sales of $656 per week per store, according to ACNielsen.

Yeast	37.9%
Non-specific	35.6
Cake	8.0
Donut holes	7.0
Fritters	3.2
Other	2.1

Source: *InStore Buyer*, May/June 2006, p. 66, from Perishables Group and ACNielsen.

★ 496 ★
Bakery Products
SIC: 2051; NAICS: 311812
Leading Bakery Product Makers in Poland, 2005

Market shares are shown in percent.

PSS Spolem	10.3%
Danone	9.1
Svenska Lantmannen Riksforbund	2.9
GS	2.8
Bahlsen SuBwaren	2.2
Lubella	1.6
Other	71.1

Source: "National Report Denmark." [online] from http://foodqualityschemes.jrc.es/en/documents/NationalreportFR_000.pdf [Published November 2005] from Food for Thought.

★ 497 ★
Bakery Products
SIC: 2051; NAICS: 311812
Leading Cake Brands in the U.K., 2005

Sales are shown for the 52 weeks ended October 1, 2005. Figures are in thousands of pounds sterling and for all outlets.

	(000)	Share
Cadbury Mini Rolls	£ 34,861	3.32%
Mr. Kipling Fruit Pies	17,504	1.67
Soreen Malt Loaf	9,844	0.94
Mr. Kipling Bakewell Tarts	9,362	0.89
McVitie's Jamaica Ginger Cake	8,406	0.80
Mr. Kipling Lemon Slices	8,148	0.78
Mr. Kipling Viennese Whirls	7,212	0.69
Mr. Kipling Mini Classics	6,968	0.66
Mr. Kipling French Fancies	1,015	0.10
Other	945,981	90.15

Source: *Grocer*, December 17, 2005, p. 77, from ACNielsen.

★ 498 ★
Bakery Products
SIC: 2051; NAICS: 311812
Leading Flour/Bakery Product Makers in Denmark, 2005

Market shares are shown in percent.

Svenska Lantmannen Riksforbund	25.2%
Barilla	12.4

Continued on next page.

★ 498 ★

[Continued]
Bakery Products
SIC: 2051; NAICS: 311812

Leading Flour/Bakery Product Makers in Denmark, 2005

Market shares are shown in percent.

Dansk Biscuit Co.	.12.1%
Kohberg	6.4
Danone	3.2
Coronet Cake	3.0
Other	.37.7

Source: ''National Report Denmark.'' [online] from http://foodqualityschemes.jrc.es/en/documents/NationalreportFR_000.pdf [Published November 2005] from Food for Thought.

★ 499 ★

Bakery Products
SIC: 2051; NAICS: 311812

Leading Flour/Bakery Product Makers in France, 2005

Market shares are shown in percent.

Danone	.10.1%
Barilla	7.4
Limagrain	4.0
Ebro Puleva	2.7
Norac	2.2
Saveurs de France	2.2
Other	.41.4

Source: ''National Report France.'' [online] from http://foodqualityschemes.jrc.es/en/documents/NationalreportFR_000.pdf [Published November 2005] from Food for Thought.

★ 500 ★

Bakery Products
SIC: 2051; NAICS: 311812

Top Donut Brands, 2005

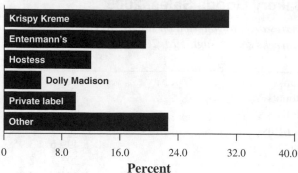

Market shares are shown based on supermarket sales for the 52 weeks ended August 7, 2005.

Krispy Kreme	.30.9%
Entenmann's	.19.5
Hostess	.12.0
Dolly Madison	5.1
Private label	9.9
Other	.22.6

Source: *Snack Food & Wholesale Bakery*, September 2005, p. 44, from Information Resources Inc.

★ 501 ★

Bread
SIC: 2051; NAICS: 311812

Bread Sales, 2005

Bread sales contributed an average of $2,156 per week per store nationwide, according to ACNielsen.

Hot/hearth breads	.24.8%
Sandwich rolls/breakfast buns	.21.0
Hamburger/hot dogs	.11.5
Artisan/crusty/specialty	7.7
Dinner rolls	5.1
Other	.29.9

Source: *InStore Buyer*, April 2006, p. 34, from Perishables Group and ACNielsen.

★ 502 ★

Bread

SIC: 2051; NAICS: 311812

Top Bread Makers (Fresh), 2006

Market shares are shown based on supermarket, drug store and mass merchandiser sales (excluding Wal-Mart) for the 52 weeks ended January 26, 2006.

Interstate Brands Corp.	12.4%
Sara Lee Bakery	9.8
George Weston Inc.	9.6
Flower Foods Bakeries Group	8.3
Bimbo Bakeries	7.6
Pepperidge Farm	5.9
Stroehmann Bakeries Inc.	2.3
Perfection Bakers Inc.	1.3
United States Bakeries	1.2
La Brea	1.1
Schwebel Baking Co.	0.8
Lewis Bakeries	0.7
Roush Prods. Co.	0.7
Private label	26.3
Other	12.0

Source: *Grocery Headquarters*, April 2006, p. 56, from Information Resources Inc.

★ 503 ★

Bread

SIC: 2051; NAICS: 311812

Top Fresh Bread/Rolls/Biscuit Brands, 2005

Brands are ranked by sales for the 12 weeks ended October 30, 2005.

	Sales	Share
New York	$ 20,147,538	19.17%
Pepperidge Farm	17,655,266	16.80
Pillsbury Home Baked Classics	16,096,770	15.32
Cole's	11,589,733	11.03
Sister Schubert's	5,233,828	4.98
Mamma Bella	4,017,676	3.82
Pillsbury	3,859,870	3.67
Pillsbury Microwave	1,997,802	1.90
Joseph Campione	1,599,154	1.52
Private label	11,715,546	11.15
Other	11,184,601	10.64

Source: *Frozen Food Age*, December 2005, p. 11, from Information Resources Inc.

★ 504 ★

Buns and Rolls

SIC: 2051; NAICS: 311812

Top English Muffin Brands, 2004

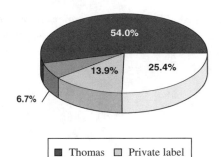

Market shares are shown based on supermarket, drug store and mass merchandiser sales (excluding Wal-Mart) for the 52 weeks ended December 26, 2004.

Thomas	54.0%
Oroweat	6.7
Private label	13.9
Other	25.4

Source: *Snack Food & Wholesale Bakery*, June 2005, p. 31, from Information Resources Inc.

★ 505 ★

Buns and Rolls

SIC: 2051; NAICS: 311812

Top Fresh Hamburger/Hot Dog Bun Brands, 2004

Market shares are shown based on supermarket, drug store and mass merchandiser sales (excluding Wal-Mart) for the 52 weeks ended December 26, 2004.

Wonder	5.2%
Sara Lee	2.9
Sunbeam	2.7
Oroweat Super Premium	2.5
Private label	47.4
Other	39.3

Source: *Snack Food & Wholesale Bakery*, June 2005, p. 31, from Information Resources Inc.

★ 506 ★
Buns and Rolls
SIC: 2051; NAICS: 311812

Top Fresh Roll/Bun/Croissant Brands, 2004

Market shares are shown based on supermarket, drug store and mass merchandiser sales (excluding Wal-Mart) for the 52 weeks ended December 26, 2004.

Martin's	4.9%
Wonder	3.5
King's Hawaiian	2.5
Oroweat	2.3
Pepperidge Farm	2.2
Sara Lee	2.2
Sunbeam	2.1
Francisco	1.7
Rainbo	1.7
Private label	37.2
Other	39.7

Source: *Snack Food & Wholesale Bakery*, June 2005, p. 31, from Information Resources Inc.

★ 507 ★
Snack Cakes
SIC: 2051; NAICS: 311812

Snack Cake Market in the U.K.

Distribution is shown based on 358 million pounds sterling for the MAT June 2005.

Tea cakes	14.0%
Crumpets	12.0
Croissants	11.0
Pancakes	9.0
Scones	8.0
Sweet muffins	8.0
Hot cross buns	7.0
Other	31.0

Source: *Grocer*, September 3, 2005, p. S1, from ACNielsen.

★ 508 ★
Snack Cakes
SIC: 2051; NAICS: 311812

Top Snack Cake Brands, 2005

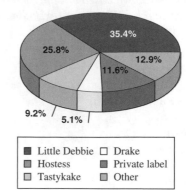

■ Little Debbie	□ Drake
■ Hostess	■ Private label
□ Tastykake	■ Other

Market shares are shown based on supermarket sales for the 52 weeks ended August 7, 2005.

Little Debbie	35.4%
Hostess	25.8
Tastykake	9.2
Drake	5.1
Private label	11.6
Other	12.9

Source: *Snack Food & Wholesale Bakery*, September 2005, p. 44, from Information Resources Inc.

★ 509 ★
Cookies
SIC: 2052; NAICS: 311821

Top Cookie Brands, 2005

Market shares are shown based on supermarket, drug store and mass merchandiser sales (excluding Wal-Mart) for the 52 weeks ended April 17, 2005.

Nabisco Oreo	5.3%
Nabisco Chips Ahoy	3.3
Nabisco Oreo Double Stuff	2.9
Pepperidge Farm Distinctive Milano	2.2
Nabisco Chips Ahoy! Chewy	2.1
Little Debbie Nutty Bar	1.8
Little Debbie Oatmeal Cream Pies	1.8
Nabisco Nilla Wafers	1.7
Private label chocolate chip	1.9
Private label Sanwich all other	1.6
Other	77.4

Source: *Snack Food & Wholesale Bakery*, June 2005, p. 31, from Information Resources Inc.

★ 510 ★
Cookies
SIC: 2052; NAICS: 311821

Top Cookie Vendors, 2005

Market shares are shown based on supermarket sales for the 52 weeks ended September 4, 2005.

Nabisco 37.5%
Keebler 10.6
Pepperidge Farm 8.0
Little Debbie 6.0
Murray Biscuit Co. 4.5
Archway 3.0
Mothers/Bakery Wagon 2.4
Voortman 1.6
Masterfoods/Mars 1.1
Other 25.3

Source: *Food Processing*, November 2005, p. 31, from Information Resources Inc.

★ 511 ★
Crackers
SIC: 2052; NAICS: 311821

Top Cracker Brands, 2005

Market shares are shown based on sales at supermarkets, drug stores and mass merchandisers (excluding Wal-Mart) for the 52 weeks December 25, 2005.

Nabisco Ritz 7.3%
Pepperidge Farm Goldfish 5.4
Nabisco Premium Saltines 4.9
Sunshine Cheez-It 4.8
Nabisco Wheat Thins 4.6
Nabisco Triscuits 4.2
Nabisco Honey Maid Grahams 3.2
Keebler Club 3.1
Nabisco Wheat Thins, Reduced Fat 2.8
Private label saltines 1.9
Other 57.8

Source: *Snack Food & Wholesale Bakery*, April 2006, p. 11, from Information Resources Inc.

★ 512 ★
Crackers
SIC: 2052; NAICS: 311821

Top Cracker Makers, 2006

Market shares are shown based on food store, drug store and mass merchandiser sales (excluding Wal-Mart) for the 52 weeks ended January 2006.

Kraft Foods Inc. 47.9%
Kellogg 27.7
Campbell Soup Co. 8.8
Wind Point 1.3
Dare Foods 1.0
Private label 7.4
Other 5.9

Source: *US Food Industry*, North American Equity Research, January 17, 2006, p. 100, from ACNielsen and JPMorgan.

★ 513 ★
Frozen Bakery Products
SIC: 2053; NAICS: 311813

Top Bagel Brands (Frozen), 2005

Brands are ranked by sales for the 12 weeks ended October 30, 2005.

	Sales	Share
Lenders	$ 5,844,232	47.47%
Lenders Big 'N Crusty	2,562,905	20.82
Ray's Bagels	793,447	6.44
Bagels Forever	480,532	3.90
Ray's New York Bagels	156,887	1.27
Sara Lee	113,406	0.92
Glutino	14,515	0.12
Myer's Bagels	12,948	0.11
Hartan Bakeries	11,895	0.10
Private label	2,277,639	18.50
Other	44,240	0.36

Source: *Frozen Food Age*, December 2005, p. 11, from Information Resources Inc.

★ 514 ★

Frozen Bakery Products

SIC: 2053; NAICS: 311813

Top Cheesecake Brands, 2005

Brands are ranked by sales for the 12 weeks ended October 30, 2005.

	Sales	Share
Sara Lee	$ 9,185,333	54.78%
Edwards	1,598,250	9.53
Jon Donaire	1,300,162	7.75
The Fathers Table	1,054,772	6.29
Weight Watchers Smart Ones	749,489	4.47
Nobrand	400,063	2.39
Cheesecake Factory	286,420	1.71
Eli's	266,228	1.59
Adams Matthews	181,404	1.08
Private label	860,993	5.14
Other	883,962	5.27

Source: *Frozen Food Age*, December 2005, p. 11, from Information Resources Inc.

★ 515 ★

Frozen Bakery Products

SIC: 2053; NAICS: 311813

Top Cheesecake Makers

Cheesecake sales were $96 million.

Polzella Foods	19.0%
Private label	34.0
Other	47.0

Source: *Wisconsin Journal Sentinel*, May 20, 2005, p. NA.

★ 516 ★

Frozen Bakery Products

SIC: 2053; NAICS: 311813

Top Frozen Bakery Product Brands, 2005

Brands are ranked by sales at supermarkets and mass merchandisers (excluding Wal-Mart) in millions of dollars. Figures exclude cheesecakes.

	($ mil.)	Share
Sara Lee	$ 41.60	19.8%
Pepperidge Farm Three Layer Cake	37.65	18.0
Mrs. Smith's	26.75	12.8
Delizza	18.99	9.1
Pepperidge Farm	15.60	7.4
Kellogg's Eggo Toaster Swirlz	10.38	5.0

	($ mil.)	Share
Hot Pockets	$ 9.57	4.6%
Weight Watchers Smart Ones	6.69	3.2
Marie Callenders	5.89	2.8
Sister Schuberts	2.93	1.4
Pepperidge Farm Dessert Classics	2.62	1.3
Marie Callenders	2.49	1.2

Source: *Quick Frozen Foods International*, January 2006, p. 92, from Information Resources Inc.

★ 517 ★

Frozen Bakery Products

SIC: 2053; NAICS: 311813

Top Frozen Pie Brands, 2006

Market shares are shown based on sales at supermarkets, drug stores and mass merchandisers (excluding Wal-Mart) for the 52 weeks ended March 19, 2006.

Mrs. Smith's	36.5%
Edward's Baking Co.	23.4
Sara Lee Bakery Group	18.2
American Pie	16.8
Weight Watchers Co.	1.5
Bonert's Inc.	0.6
Quality Baker	0.5
Wick's Pies Inc.	0.3
Fruit & Vegetable Warehouse	0.2
Other	2.0

Source: *Snack Food & Wholesale Bakery*, May 2006, p. 11, from Information Resources Inc.

★ 518 ★

Taco Kits

SIC: 2053; NAICS: 311813

Top Hard/Soft Tortilla and Taco Kit Brands, 2006

Brands are ranked by sales at supermarkets, drug stores and mass merchandisers (excluding Wal-Mart) for the 52 weeks February 19, 2006.

	($ mil.)	Share
Guerrero	$ 185.5	19.47%
Mission	156.3	16.40
Old El Paso	128.8	13.52
Tia Rosa	41.0	4.30
Private label	81.4	8.54

Source: *Snack Food & Wholesale Bakery*, April 2006, p. 11, from Information Resources Inc.

★ 519 ★
Sugar
SIC: 2061; NAICS: 311311
Largest Sugar Producers Worldwide

Countries are ranked by production in millions of tons.

Brazil	26.0
India	21.7
EU-15	16.6
China	11.4
United States	8.0
Thailand	7.7
Mexico	5.4
Australia	5.3
Pakistan	4.1
Colombia	3.6

Source: *Business India*, February 14, 2005, p. 60.

★ 520 ★
Sugar
SIC: 2061; NAICS: 311311
Leading Sugar Substitutes, 2006

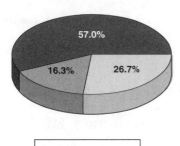

Market shares are shown based on sales at food stores, drug stores and mass market outlets (excluding Wal-Mart) for the 52 weeks ended March 19, 2006.

Splenda	57.0%
Equal	16.3
Other	26.7

Source: *Promo*, April 5, 2006, p. NA, from Information Resources Inc.

★ 521 ★
Sugar
SIC: 2061; NAICS: 311311
Sugar Sales at Supermarkets

Supermarket sales are shown in millions of dollars.

	($ mil.)	Share
Sugar, granulated	$ 808.10	60.74%
Sugar substitutes	332.80	25.02
Sugar, brown	109.12	8.20
Sugar, powdered	61.98	4.66
Sugar, remaining	18.37	1.38

Source: *Progressive Grocer*, September 15, 2005, p. 22, from *Progressive Grocer's 26th Annual Consumer Expenditures Study*.

★ 522 ★
Sugar
SIC: 2062; NAICS: 311312
Leading Sugar Refiners, 2006

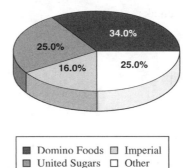

The United States is the fifth largest producer of sugar worldwide. It ranks fourth in the consumption and import of sugar. Prices were low in the late 1990s, which helped to drive some consolidation. Amalgamated, Cargill, Western and Michigan have market shares from 4%-9%.

Domino Foods	34.0%
United Sugars	25.0
Imperial	16.0
Other	25.0

Source: "U.S. Sugar Industry Consolidation." [online] from http://www.mckeanyflavell.com [Published November 11, 2005].

★ 523 ★
Sugar
SIC: 2062; NAICS: 311312

Leading Sugar Refiners in Saudi Arabia

The company produced 941,000 tons in 2004.

United Sugar Company 92.0%
Other 8.0

Source: *Gulf Magazine*, October 2005, p. NA.

★ 524 ★
Breath Fresheners
SIC: 2064; NAICS: 31134

Top Breath Freshener Brands, 2005

Market shares are shown based on sales at supermarkets, drug stores and mass merchandisers (not Wal-Mart) for the 52 weeks ended October 2, 2005.

Altoids 21.4%
Tic Tac 18.4
Listerine Pocketpaks 16.5
Icebreakers 12.4
Ice Breakers Liquid Ice 7.8
Breathsavers 7.3
Wrigley's Eclipse 6.9
Aqua Drops 1.6
Certs Cool Mint Drops 1.3
Private label 1.0
Other 5.4

Source: *The Manufacturing Confectioner*, January 2006, p. 16, from Information Resources Inc. InfoScan.

★ 525 ★
Breath Fresheners
SIC: 2064; NAICS: 31134

Top Breath Freshener Brands (Sprays/Drops), 2005

Market shares are shown based on drug store sales for the 52 weeks ended October 30, 2005.

Sweet Breath 25.3%
MintAsure 23.8
Binaca 22.3
Therabreath 6.0
Puretek Breath Relief 5.4
Dentek Breath Remedy 5.1

Crystal Breath 3.1%
Sweet Breath Lil Squirt 1.1
Private label 5.4
Other 2.5

Source: *Chain Drug Review*, January 2, 2006, p. 94.

★ 526 ★
Breath Fresheners
SIC: 2064; NAICS: 31134

Top Breath Freshener Makers, 2005

Market shares are shown based on sales at supermarkets, drug stores and mass merchandisers (not Wal-Mart) for the 52 weeks ended October 2, 2005.

Hershey Company 27.6%
Kraft/Callard & Bowser-Suchard 21.4
Ferrero USA Inc. 18.4
Pfizer Inc. 16.5
Wm. Wrigley Jr. Co. 8.0
Cadbury Adams USA 2.9
Masterfoods USA 1.6
Private label 1.0
Other 2.6

Source: *The Manufacturing Confectioner*, January 2006, p. 16, from Information Resources Inc. InfoScan.

★ 527 ★
Breath Fresheners
SIC: 2064; NAICS: 31134

Top Plain Mint Brands, 2005

Market shares are shown based on sales at supermarkets, drug stores and mass merchandisers (not Wal-Mart) for the 52 weeks ended October 2, 2005.

Lifesavers 35.7%
Van Melles Mentos 20.0
Brach's Star Brites 5.9
Red Bird 2.8
Sathers 2.2
Bob's Sweet Stripes 2.0
Brach's 2.0
Richardson Mints 1.8
Tic Tac Silvers 1.0
Other 26.6

Source: *The Manufacturing Confectioner*, January 2006, p. 16, from Information Resources Inc. InfoScan.

★ 528 ★
Breath Fresheners
SIC: 2064; NAICS: 31134

Top Plain Mint Makers, 2005

Market shares are shown based on sales at supermarkets, drug stores and mass merchandisers (not Wal-Mart) for the 52 weeks ended October 2, 2005.

Kraft/Nabisco	35.7%
Perfetti Van Melle	20.0
Brach's Confections	7.8
Farley's & Sathers Candy	3.2
Piedmont Candy Co. Inc.	2.8
Bob's Candies Inc.	2.4
Richardson Co.	1.8
Necco	1.1
Ferrero USA Inc.	1.0
Private label	16.2
Other	8.0

Source: *The Manufacturing Confectioner*, January 2006, p. 16, from Information Resources Inc. InfoScan.

★ 529 ★
Confectionery Products
SIC: 2064; NAICS: 31133, 31134

Best-Selling Easter Candies, 2005

Brands are ranked by sales of non-chocolate Easter candies at supermarkets, drug stores and mass merchandisers (excluding Wal-Mart) for the 52 weeks ended February 20, 2005.

	($ mil.)	Share
Reese's	$ 48.79	12.49%
M&M's	34.95	8.95
Russell Stover	29.62	7.58
Hershey's	29.22	7.48
Palmer	23.72	6.07
Hershey's Kisses	19.47	4.98
Cadbury Crème Egg	16.38	4.19
Cadbury Mini Eggs	16.25	4.16
Dove	12.86	3.29
Robin Eggs	12.64	3.24
Other	146.76	37.57

Source: *Professional Candy Buyer*, July - August 2005, p. 4, from Information Resources Inc.

★ 530 ★
Confectionery Products
SIC: 2064; NAICS: 31133, 31134

Best-Selling Lollipops

Brands are ranked by food stores, drug stores and mass merchandisers (excluding Wal-Mart) for the 52 weeks ended July 10, 2005.

Jolly Rancher	$ 42.6
Tootsie Roll Pops	20.8
Charms Blow Pop	14.9
Spangler Dum Dum Pops	9.0
Starburst Fruit Chew Pops	3.3
Tootsie Bunch Pops	3.3
Tootsie Roll Caramel Apple Pops	3.2

Source: *Candy Industry*, August 2005, p. 40, from Information Resources Inc.

★ 531 ★
Confectionery Products
SIC: 2064; NAICS: 31133, 31134

Candy Sales, 2005

Sales are shown for the 52 weeks ended November 5, 2005.

Candy, chocolate	$ 2,440,183.00
Candy, nonchocolate	1,403,777.00
Candy, chocolate, special	538,178.10
Candy, chocolate, miniatures	403,906.30
Breath sweeteners	166,734.20
Candy, lollipops	140,793.00
Marshmallows	112,344.30
Candy, dietetic, chocolate	96,386.20
Candy, dietetic, nonchocolate	63,030.20
Candy, hard rolled	61,430.90
Candy, nonchocolate, miniatures	42,744.20
Candy, kits	4,270.60

Source: *ECRM Focus*, January 2006, p. 32, from ACNielsen.

★ 532 ★
Confectionery Products
SIC: 2064; NAICS: 31133, 31134

Confectionery Industry Worldwide (Tonnage), 2004

Data are in thousands of metric tons.

	(000)	Share
Western Europe	2,412	38.19%
North America	1,798	28.47
Eastern Europe	960	15.20
Asia Pacifica	470	7.44
Latin America	378	5.98
Africa and Middle East	165	2.61
Australasia	133	2.11

Source: *Professional Candy Buyer*, May - June 2005, p. S17, from Euromonitor.

★ 533 ★
Confectionery Products
SIC: 2064; NAICS: 31133, 31134

Confectionery Product Sales Worldwide, 2005 and 2009

Sales are in billions of dollars.

	2005	2009
Chocolate countlines	$ 18.4	$ 19.7
Chocolate tablets (bars)	15.4	17.2
Chewing gum	14.0	16.0
Chocolate boxed assortments	12.7	13.8
Chocolate bagged seelines/softlines	10.1	11.0
Pastilles, gums, jellies and chews	9.8	10.6
Boiled sweets	8.2	8.7
Seasonal chocolate	6.9	7.3
Mints	5.3	5.6
Chocolate with toys	1.8	1.9

Source: *Candy Industry*, August 2005, p. 31, from Euromonitor.

★ 534 ★
Confectionery Products
SIC: 2064; NAICS: 31133, 31134

Confectionery Sales Worldwide, 2005 and 2009

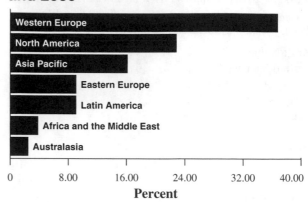

Sales are in billions of dollars.

	2005	2009	Share
Western Europe	$ 46.7	$ 48.8	36.72%
North America	29.2	30.3	22.80
Asia Pacific	18.7	21.4	16.10
Eastern Europe	10.3	12.0	9.03
Latin America	10.2	12.0	9.03
Africa and the Middle East	4.2	5.1	3.84
Australasia	2.9	3.3	2.48

Source: *Candy Industry*, August 2005, p. 31, from Euromonitor.

★ 535 ★
Confectionery Products
SIC: 2064; NAICS: 31133, 31134

Gourmet Candy Sales, 2001-2006

Gourmet candy represents about 10% of both the chocolate and non-chocolate market. Annual growth in the overall gourmet chocolate market has been 20% since 2001. Sales in the organic niche were 30% annually.

Year	Sales
2001	$ 1,436
2002	1,630
2003	1,850
2004	2,100
2005	2,384
2006	2,706

Source: *ECRM Focus*, October 2005, p. NA, from Packaged Facts.

★ 536 ★
Confectionery Products
SIC: 2064; NAICS: 31133, 31134

Largest Kashi Suppliers in Japan

Companies are ranked by sales in millions of yen. Total candy sales were 173 billion yen, chocolate sales were 297.8 billion yen and chewing gum sales were 13.7 billion yen.

Meiji Seika	¥ 2,719
Lotte Shoji	1,610
Morinaga & Co.	1,495
Ezaki Glico	1,346
Calbee	939
Borbon	841
Fujiya	790
Kameda Seika	629
Kanebo Foods	465
Yamazaki Nabisco	343

Source: *The Manufacturing Confectioner*, March 2006, p. 37.

★ 537 ★
Confectionery Products
SIC: 2064; NAICS: 31133, 31134

Leading Non-Chocolate Confectionery Makers, 2006

Market shares are shown for the 52 weeks ended February 19, 2006.

Hershey's	13.9%
M&M/Mars	10.3
Wrigley	9.6
Nestle	9.1
Tootsie Roll	6.2
Brach's	4.0
Other	46.9

Source: ''Hershey's Filling the New Product Funnel.'' [online] from http://www.cals.vt.edu/ee/images/uploads/podcasts/IA_3_06/azzara_032806.pdf [Accessed June 1, 2006] from ACNielsen.

★ 538 ★
Confectionery Products
SIC: 2064; NAICS: 31133, 31134

Leading Sugar Confectionery Brands in the U.K.

Sales are shown for the 52 weeks ended October 1, 2005. Figures are in thousands of pounds sterling and for all outlets.

	(000)	Share
Wrigley's Extra	£ 164,572	9.69%
Haribo gums & jellies	68,075	4.01
Rowntree	50,304	2.96
Maynards	46,639	2.75
Wrigley's Airwaves	39,791	2.34
Wrigley's Orbit	36,382	2.14
Bassett's	34,935	2.06
Polo	29,803	1.76
Trebor Extra Strong Mints	29,772	1.75
Other	1,197,299	70.53

Source: *Grocer*, December 17, 2005, p. 77, from ACNielsen.

★ 539 ★
Confectionery Products
SIC: 2064; NAICS: 31133, 31134

Top Candy Brands (Sugarfree/ Sugarless), 2005

Market shares are shown based on sales at supermarkets, drug stores and mass merchandisers (not Wal-Mart) for the 52 weeks ended October 2, 2005.

Lifesavers	17.5%
Crème Savers	9.9
Pearson Nips	7.4
Sweet N Low	6.4
Altoids	4.4
Russell Stover	4.4
Lifesavers Delites	3.8
Werthers	3.8
Jolly Rancher	3.7
Private label	9.0
Other	29.7

Source: *The Manufacturing Confectioner*, January 2006, p. 16, from Information Resources Inc. InfoScan.

★ 540 ★
Confectionery Products
SIC: 2064; NAICS: 31133, 31134

Top Candy Makers (Sugarfree/ Sugarless), 2005

Market shares are shown based on sales at supermarkets, drug stores and mass merchandisers (not Wal-Mart) for the 52 weeks ended October 2, 2005.

Kraft/Nabisco	.31.2%
Nestle USA Inc.	7.4
Simply Lite	6.6
Russell Stover Candies Inc.	4.6
Kraft/Callard & Bowser-Suchard	4.4
Hershey Company	4.3
Storck USA	3.8
American Licorice	3.6
Bestsweet Inc.	3.6
Private label	9.0
Other	.21.5

Source: *The Manufacturing Confectioner*, January 2006, p. 16, from Information Resources Inc. InfoScan.

★ 541 ★
Confectionery Products
SIC: 2064; NAICS: 31133, 31134

Top Chewy Candy Brands (Nonchocolate), 2005

Market shares are shown based on sales at supermarkets, drug stores and mass merchandisers (not Wal-Mart) for the 52 weeks ended October 2, 2005.

Starburst	.12.2%
Skittles	8.9
Lifesavers Gummisavers	3.9
Tootsie Roll	3.8
Jelly Belly	3.1
Reese's Pieces	3.1
Jaret Swedish Fish	2.6
Just Born Mike & Ike	2.4
Kraft	2.4
Private label	9.9
Other	.47.7

Source: *The Manufacturing Confectioner*, January 2006, p. 16, from Information Resources Inc. InfoScan.

★ 542 ★
Confectionery Products
SIC: 2064; NAICS: 31133, 31134

Top Chewy Candy Makers (Nonchocolate), 2005

Market shares are shown based on sales at supermarkets, drug stores and mass merchandisers (not Wal-Mart) for the 52 weeks ended October 2, 2005.

Masterfoods USA	.22.0%
Kraft/Nabisco	9.8
Hershey Company	7.6
Tootsie Roll Industries	6.1
Cadbury Adams	5.3
Just Born Inc.	4.9
Farleys & Sathers Candy	4.4
Other	.39.9

Source: *The Manufacturing Confectioner*, January 2006, p. 16, from Information Resources Inc. InfoScan.

★ 543 ★
Confectionery Products
SIC: 2064; NAICS: 31133, 31134

Top Confectionery Firms in EMEA, 2004

Market shares are shown in percent. EMEA stands for Europe, Middle East and Africa.

Cadbury Schweppes	.11.0%
Nestle	.10.1
Mars	8.0
Ferrero	7.3
Kraft	7.0
Wrigley	4.7
Other	.51.9

Source: "Cadbury Schweppes." [online] from http://www.cadbury-schweppes.com [Accessed January 20, 2006] from Euromonitor.

★ 544 ★
Confectionery Products
SIC: 2064; NAICS: 31133, 31134

Top Confectionery Firms in Latin America, 2004

Market shares are shown in percent.

Cadbury Schweppes	.17.4%
Nestle	8.3
Kraft	6.1
Mars	2.6

Continued on next page.

★ 544 ★

[Continued]
Confectionery Products
SIC: 2064; NAICS: 31133, 31134

Top Confectionery Firms in Latin America, 2004

Market shares are shown in percent.

Hershey	2.1%
Wrigley	1.6
Other	.61.9

Source: "Cadbury Schweppes." [online] from http://www. cadbury-schweppes.com [Accessed January 20, 2006] from Euromonitor.

★ 545 ★

Confectionery Products
SIC: 2064; NAICS: 31133, 31134

Top Confectionery Firms in North America, 2004

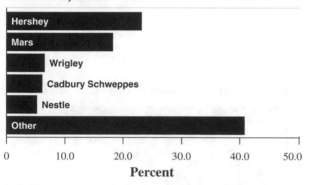

Percent

Market shares are shown in percent.

Hershey	.23.2%
Mars	.18.2
Wrigley	6.5
Cadbury Schweppes	6.1
Nestle	5.2
Other	.40.8

Source: "Cadbury Schweppes." [online] from http://www. cadbury-schweppes.com [Accessed January 20, 2006] from Euromonitor.

★ 546 ★

Confectionery Products
SIC: 2064; NAICS: 31133, 31134

Top Confectionery Makers in Western Europe

The top companies are ranked by market share. Data refer to products sold for human consumption in retail, catering and artisanal markets. Germany took 26% of the market, followed by United Kingdom with 22% and France with 14%.

Nestle	.11.1%
Cadbury Schweppes	.10.8
Altria	.10.6
Mars	9.5
Ferrero	8.1
Wrigley	4.3
CSM	4.0
Lindt & Sprungli	3.0
Haribo	2.7
Ritter	2.5
Other	.33.4

Source: "Confectionery Markets." [online] from http:// www.fft.com [Published September 2005] from Food for Thought.

★ 547 ★

Confectionery Products
SIC: 2064; NAICS: 31133, 31134

Top Confectionery Makers Worldwide, 2004

Market shares are shown in percent.

Cadbury	.10.0%
Nestle	7.8
Hershey	5.8
Kraft	4.9
Wrigley	4.8
Mars	0.3
Other	.66.4

Source: *Wall Street Journal*, February 16, 2006, p. C3, from Thomson Datastream and Euromonitor.

★ 548 ★
Confectionery Products
SIC: 2064; NAICS: 31133, 31134

Top Easter Candy Makers, 2005

Companies are ranked by sales of non-chocolate East-er candies at supermarkets, drug stores and mass mer-chandisers (excluding Wal-Mart) for the 52 weeks ended May 15, 2005.

	($ mil.)	Share
Just Born Inc.	$ 21.05	21.17%
Brach's Confections	16.35	16.44
Nestle USA Inc.	7.74	7.78
Masterfoods USA	6.39	6.43
Kraft/Nabisco	6.28	6.32
Hershey Co.	4.28	4.30
Frankford Candy & Chocolate	3.99	4.01
Tootsie Roll Industries	3.17	3.19
Galerie Au Chocolate	2.84	2.86
Other	27.35	27.50

Source: *Professional Candy Buyer*, September - October 2005, p. 4, from Information Resources Inc.

★ 549 ★
Confectionery Products
SIC: 2064; NAICS: 31134

Top Fruit Snack Brands, 2005

Market shares are shown based on sales at supermar-kets, drug stores and mass merchandisers (excluding Wal-Mart) for the 52 weeks ended September 4, 2005.

Fruit Gushers	12.2%
Fruit by the Foot	10.4
Fruit Roll Ups	10.3
Kelloggfruit Twistables	4.4
Betty Crocker Scooby Doo	3.4
Betty Crocker Fruit Smoothie Blitz	3.1
Air Heads Fruit Spinners	2.4
Kelloggs Fruit Streamers	2.2
Betty Crocker Shrek	2.1
Other	49.5

Source: *Professional Candy Buyer*, November - December 2005, p. 24, from Information Resources Inc. InfoScan.

★ 550 ★
Confectionery Products
SIC: 2064; NAICS: 31134

Top Hard Sugar Candy Brands, 2005

Market shares are shown based on sales at supermar-kets, drug stores and mass merchandisers (excluding Wal-Mart) for the 52 weeks ended October 2, 2005.

Jolly Rancher	15.8%
Altoids	13.2
Lifesavers Crème Savers	9.3
Werthers	8.2
Lifesavers	8.0
Tootsie Roll Pops	7.8
Pearson Nips	6.8
Charms Blow Pop	5.4
Spangler Dum Dum Pops	3.4
Private label	4.8
Other	17.3

Source: *The Manufacturing Confectioner*, January 2006, p. 16, from Information Resources Inc. InfoScan.

★ 551 ★
Confectionery Products
SIC: 2064; NAICS: 31134

Top Hard Sugar Candy Makers, 2005

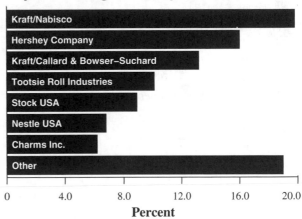

Market shares are shown based on sales at supermar-kets, drug stores and mass merchandisers (excluding Wal-Mart) for the 52 weeks ended October 2, 2005.

Kraft/Nabisco	19.8%
Hershey Company	16.0
Kraft/Callard & Bowser-Suchard	13.2
Tootsie Roll Industries	10.1
Stock USA	8.9
Nestle USA	6.8
Charms Inc.	6.2
Other	19.0

Source: *The Manufacturing Confectioner*, January 2006, p. 16, from Information Resources Inc. InfoScan.

★ 552 ★

Confectionery Products

SIC: 2064; NAICS: 31134

Top Licorice Box/Bag Brands > 3.5 oz, 2006

Market shares are shown based on sales at supermarkets, drug stores and mass merchandisers (excluding Wal-Mart) for the 52 weeks ended March 19, 2006.

	($ mil.)	Share
Twizzler	$ 99.90	61.21%
Red Vines	29.77	18.24
Good & Plenty	12.68	7.77
Twizzler Sourz	2.88	1.76
Twizzler Twerpz	2.82	1.73
Bassetts	2.77	1.70
Snaps	2.66	1.63
Nibs	2.27	1.39
Lucky Country	2.00	1.23
Panda	1.59	0.97
Other	3.87	2.37

Source: *Professional Candy Buyer*, May - June 2006, p. 46, from Information Resources Inc.

★ 553 ★

Confectionery Products

SIC: 2064; NAICS: 31134

Top Licorice Box/Bag Makers > 3.5 oz, 2005

Market shares are shown based on sales at supermarkets, drug stores and mass merchandisers (excluding Wal-Mart) for the 52 weeks ended October 2, 2005.

Hershey Company	70.7%
American Licorice Co.	21.3
Trebor Bassett Ltd.	1.6
Cal Marketing Pty. Ltd.	1.4
Private label	1.0
Other	4.0

Source: *The Manufacturing Confectioner*, January 2006, p. 16, from Information Resources Inc. InfoScan.

★ 554 ★

Confectionery Products

SIC: 2064; NAICS: 31134

Top Novelty Candy Brands (Nonchocolate), 2005

Market shares are shown based on sales at supermarkets, drug stores and mass merchandisers (excluding Wal-Mart) for the 52 weeks ended October 2, 2005.

Wonka Nerds	7.9%
Tootsie Roll Childs' Play	7.8
Sweetarts	7.3
Topps Baby Bottle Pop	5.6
Pez	4.4
Ce De Smarties	3.9
Topps Ring Pop	3.0
Spree	2.8
Topps Push Pop	2.8
Private label	4.0
Other	50.5

Source: *The Manufacturing Confectioner*, January 2006, p. 16, from Information Resources Inc. InfoScan.

★ 555 ★

Confectionery Products

SIC: 2064; NAICS: 31134

Top Novelty Candy Makers (Nonchocolate), 2005

Market shares are shown based on sales at supermarkets, drug stores and mass merchandisers (excluding Wal-Mart) for the 52 weeks ended October 2, 2005.

Nestle USA Inc.	29.9%
Topps Company Inc.	13.9
Tootsie Roll Industries	8.9
Pez Candy	4.6
De De Candy Inc.	3.9
Impact Confections Inc.	3.5
Frankford Candy & Chocolate	2.7
Necco	2.5
The Hammer Corporation	2.0
Private label	3.9
Other	24.2

Source: *The Manufacturing Confectioner*, January 2006, p. 16, from Information Resources Inc. InfoScan.

★ 556 ★
Confectionery Products
SIC: 2064; NAICS: 31134

Top Specialty Nut/Coconut Candy Brands, 2005

Market shares are shown based on sales at supermarkets, drug stores and mass merchandisers (excluding Wal-Mart) for the 52 weeks ended October 2, 2005.

Leaf Pay Day	26.3%
Pearsons Salted Nut Roll	6.4
Sophia Mae	4.3
Brach's Maple Nut Goodies	3.9
Lance	3.3
Confetteria Raffaello	3.2
Ferrera Pan Boston Baked Beans	3.0
Brach's	2.7
Annabelle Big Hunk	2.2
Other	44.7

Source: *The Manufacturing Confectioner*, January 2006, p. 16, from Information Resources Inc. InfoScan.

★ 557 ★
Confectionery Products
SIC: 2064; NAICS: 31134

Top Specialty Nut/Coconut Candy Makers, 2005

Market shares are shown based on sales at supermarkets, drug stores and mass merchandisers (excluding Wal-Mart) for the 52 weeks ended October 2, 2005.

Hershey Company	26.8%
Brach's Confections	6.6
Pearson Candy Co.	6.4
Sophie Mae Candy Corp.	4.3
Lance Inc.	3.3
Ferrero USA Inc.	3.2
Ferrara Pan Candy Co Inc.	3.0
Annabelle Candy Co Inc.	2.2
Private label	8.3
Other	35.9

Source: *The Manufacturing Confectioner*, January 2006, p. 16, from Information Resources Inc. InfoScan.

★ 558 ★
Confectionery Products
SIC: 2064; NAICS: 31133, 31134

Top Valentine's Day Candy Makers, 2005

Companies are ranked by sales of non-chocolate Valentine's Day candies at supermarkets, drug stores and mass merchandisers (excluding Wal-Mart) for the 52 weeks ended February 20, 2005.

	($ mil.)	Share
Necco	$ 13.48	17.98%
Nestle USA Inc.	11.59	15.46
Brach's Confections	7.66	10.22
Masterfoods	4.05	5.40
Frankford Candy & Chocolate	4.04	5.39
Kraft/Nabisco	3.75	5.00
Tootsie Roll Industries	2.64	3.52
Hershey Foods	2.30	3.07
Tzetzo Bros.	1.71	2.28
Charms Inc.	1.69	2.25
Other	22.06	29.43

Source: *Professional Candy Buyer*, July - August 2005, p. 4, from Information Resources Inc.

★ 559 ★
Cough Drops
SIC: 2064; NAICS: 31134

Top Cough Drop/Square Brands, 2005

Market shares are shown based on sales at grocery stores, drug stores and mass merchandisers (excluding Wal-Mart) for the 52 weeks ended October 2, 2005.

Halls	26.6%
Ricola	9.7
Cold Eeze	8.4
Halls Fruit Breezers	6.7
Halls Defense	6.0
Ludens	5.4
Cepacol	4.4
Halls Plus	2.9
Chloraseptic	2.8
Other	27.1

Source: *The Manufacturing Confectioner*, January 2006, p. 16, from Information Resources Inc. InfoScan.

★ 560 ★
Cough Drops
SIC: 2064; NAICS: 31134

Top Cough Drop/Square Makers, 2005

Market shares are shown based on sales at grocery stores, drug stores and mass merchandisers (excluding Wal-Mart) for the 52 weeks ended October 2, 2005.

Cadbury Adams USA	.43.6%
Ricola Inc.	.10.7
Quigley Corporation	8.6
Pfizer Inc.	5.4
Prestige Brands International	4.5
Wyeth Labs Inc.	4.5
Combe Inc.	4.4
Heritage Products	2.7
Amerifit Nutrition Inc.	0.9
Other	.14.7

Source: *The Manufacturing Confectioner*, January 2006, p. 16, from Information Resources Inc. InfoScan.

★ 561 ★
Snack Bars
SIC: 2064; NAICS: 31134

Granola/Yogurt Bar Sales, 2002-2005

Brands are ranked by sales at supermarkets, drug stores and mass merchandisers (excluding Wal-Mart) for the 52 weeks ended September 4, 2005.

2002	$ 718.89
2003	839.38
2004	861.81
2005	933.44

Source: *Corporate Profiles & Industry Statistics - Milling & Baking News Supplement*, November 2005, p. 130, from Information Resources Inc.

★ 562 ★
Snack Bars
SIC: 2064; NAICS: 31134

Leading Food Bar Makers

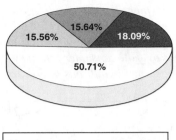

In 2005, granola bars are expected to take 33.35% of the market, with nutritional bars second with a 29.92% share.

Kellogg Co.	.18.09%
General Mills	.15.64
Quaker Oats	.15.56
Other	.50.71

Source: "Health is Key to Growing Food Bar Market." [online] from http://www.nutraingredients-usa.com/news/printNewsBis.asp?id63738 [Accessed June 1, 2006] from Packaged Facts.

★ 563 ★
Snack Bars
SIC: 2064; NAICS: 31134

Nutrition Bar Sales by Type

Market shares are shown for the first quarter of 2005.

High protein	.33.7%
Healthy snack	.23.8
Energy	.23.3
Low-carb lifestyle	.19.2

Source: *Convenience Store News*, July 18, 2005, p. 53, from McLane Mpulse.

★ 564 ★

Snack Bars

SIC: 2064; NAICS: 31134

Snack Bar Sales Worldwide, 2004

The United States experienced a decline in nutrition and meal replacement bars for the first time in 2004. The source cites some explanations for this: the low-carb diet has become less popular, the saturation of the market and overall consumer fatigue with the product. Sales are shown in millions of dollars.

	($ mil.)	Share
North America	$ 4,219.17	64.88%
Western Europe	1,211.36	18.63
Asia Pacific	486.09	7.47
Australasia	289.76	4.46
Latin America	201.72	3.10
Africa & Middle East	74.52	1.15
Eastern Europe	20.85	0.32

Source: *Functional Foods & Nutraceuticals*, November 2005, p. NA, from Euromonitor.

★ 565 ★

Snack Bars

SIC: 2064; NAICS: 31134

Top Breakfast Bar Makers, 2005

Market shares are shown based on sales at supermarkets, drug stores and mass merchandisers (not Wal-Mart) for the 52 weeks ended October 2, 2005.

Kellogg Co.	.42.5%
Quaker Oats	.15.7
Kraft Foods	.13.5
General Mills	9.6
Slim Fast Foods Co.	4.5
Atkins Nutritional	3.1
Private label	5.1
Other	6.0

Source: *The Manufacturing Confectioner*, January 2006, p. 16, from Information Resources Inc. InfoScan.

★ 566 ★

Snack Bars

SIC: 2064; NAICS: 31133

Top Granola Bar Brands, 2005

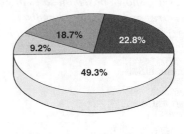

Quaker Chewy ■ □ Private label
Nature Valley ■ □ Other

Market shares are shown based on supermarket, drug store and mass merchandiser sales (excluding Wal-Mart) for the 52 weeks ended November 27, 2005.

Quaker Chewy	.22.8%
Nature Valley	.18.7
Private label	9.2
Other	.49.3

Source: *Snack Food & Wholesale Bakery*, January 2006, p. 31, from Information Resources Inc.

★ 567 ★

Snack Bars

SIC: 2064; NAICS: 31134

Top Granola Bar Makers, 2006

Market shares are shown based on supermarket, drug store and mass merchandiser sales (excluding Wal-Mart) for the 52 weeks ended January 26, 2006.

General Mills	.38.5%
Quaker Oats Co.	.30.3
McKee Foods Corp.	7.2
Masterfoods USA	5.1
Kellogg Co.	3.8
Unilever Bestfoods North America	3.3
Atkins Nutritionals	0.8
Small Planet Foods	0.6
Health Valley Natural Foods	0.4
Private label	9.5
Other	0.5

Source: *Grocery Headquarters*, April 2006, p. 56, from Information Resources Inc.

★ 568 ★
Snack Bars
SIC: 2064; NAICS: 31134

Top Nutritional Health Bar Makers, 2005

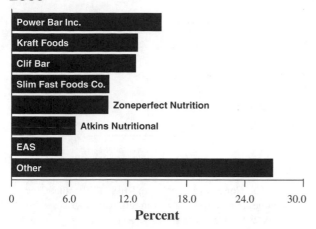

Percent

Market shares are shown based on sales at supermarkets, drug stores and mass merchandisers (not Wal-Mart) for the 52 weeks ended October 2, 2005.

Power Bar Inc.	15.4%
Kraft Foods	13.0
Clif Bar	12.8
Slim Fast Foods Co.	10.1
Zoneperfect Nutrition	10.0
Atkins Nutritional	6.6
EAS	5.2
Other	26.9

Source: *The Manufacturing Confectioner*, January 2006, p. 16, from Information Resources Inc. InfoScan.

★ 569 ★
Snack Bars
SIC: 2064; NAICS: 31134

Top Nutritional/Intrinsic Brands, 2005

Market shares are shown based on supermarket, drug store and mass merchandiser sales (excluding Wal-Mart) for the 52 weeks ended November 27, 2005.

Zone Perfect	10.2%
Clif Luna	6.5
Atkins Advantage	5.8
Slim Fat Optima	5.5
Clif	5.4
Other	66.6

Source: *Snack Food & Wholesale Bakery*, January 2006, p. 31, from Information Resources Inc.

★ 570 ★
Snack Bars
SIC: 2064; NAICS: 31133

Top Snack Bar Makers Worldwide, 2002

Data show the market shares of the top multinationals.

PepsiCo.	9.9%
Unilever	5.7
Kraft	4.0
Nestle	3.1
Mars	1.7
Danone	1.3
Other	74.3

Source: *New Directions in Global Food Markets*, February 2005, p. 66, from Economic Research Service, U.S. Department of Agriculture and Euromonitor.

★ 571 ★
Chocolate
SIC: 2066; NAICS: 31132, 31133

Dark Chocolate Market

Data show Hershey's share of the $700 million market.

Hershey	45.0%
Other	55.0

Source: *Patriot-News*, October 21, 2005, p. NA.

★ 572 ★
Chocolate
SIC: 2066; NAICS: 31132, 31133

Largest Chocolate Candy Makers, 2005

Companies are ranked by sales at supermarkets, drug stores and mass merchandisers (excluding Wal-Mart) for the 52 weeks ended September 4, 2005.

	($ mil.)	Share
Hershey	$ 1,900	43.50%
Masterfoods	1,000	22.89
Nestle	368	8.42
Other	1,100	25.18

Source: *Advertising Age*, October 3, 2005, p. 3, from Information Resources Inc.

★ 573 ★
Chocolate
SIC: 2066; NAICS: 31132, 31133

Largest Chocolate Markets Worldwide, 2004-2005

Countries are ranked by retail sales in millions of dollars. Shares are shown based on the top 40 firms.

	2004	2005	Share
United States	$ 14,056	$ 14,237	22.03%
United Kingdom	7,083	7,668	11.86
Germany	6,750	7,226	11.18
France	4,056	4,471	6.92
Russia	3,641	3,896	6.03
Japan	2,933	3,196	4.94
Italy	2,482	2,816	4.36
Australia	1,531	1,662	2.57
Canada	1,372	1,551	2.40
Brazil	1,284	1,594	2.47

Source: *The Manufacturing Confectioner*, March 2006, p. 29, from *World Confectionery Report & Export Handbook* and National Confectioners Association.

★ 574 ★
Chocolate
SIC: 2066; NAICS: 31132, 31133

Leading Chocolate Confectionery Brands in the U.K., 2005

Sales are shown for the 52 weeks ended October 1, 2005. Figures are in thousands of pounds sterling and for all outlets.

	(000)	Share
Cadbury Dairy Milk	£ 317,466	8.39%
Galaxy	137,482	3.63
Maltesers	127,404	3.37
Mars	96,953	2.56
Cadbury Flake	70,252	1.86
Kit Kat	69,853	1.85
Celebrations	69,387	1.83
Cadbury Roses	68,760	1.82
Quality Street	68,402	1.81
Other	2,759,260	72.90

Source: *Grocer*, December 17, 2005, p. 77, from ACNielsen.

★ 575 ★
Chocolate
SIC: 2066; NAICS: 31132, 31133

Leading Chocolate Firms in Russia, 2004

The chocolate market is forecast to grow 30% up to 2010.

Nestle	.22.0%
Kraft Foods	. 9.5
Mars	. 9.5
Krasnyi Okteabri	. 6.6
SladCo	. 5.3
Babayevski	. 5.2
Rot Front	. 5.2
Other	.36.7

Source: ''Top Concerns Revealed in Russian Chocolate Sector.'' [online] from http://www.confectionerynews.com [Accessed June 30, 2005] from *Business Analytika*.

★ 576 ★
Chocolate
SIC: 2066; NAICS: 31132, 31133

Top Chocolate Candy Box/Bag Brands > 3.5 oz, 2005

Market shares are shown based on sales at supermarkets, drug stores and mass merchandisers (excluding Wal-Mart) for the 52 weeks ended October 30, 2005.

	($ mil.)	Share
Hershey's	$ 211.1	23.60%
M&Ms	209.2	23.39
Hershey's Kisses	113.0	12.63
Reese's	96.8	10.82
Hershey's Nuggets	67.3	7.52
Snickers	47.6	5.32
Dove	36.0	4.02
York Peppermint Patty	34.2	3.82
Cadbury	0.4	0.04
Private label	40.0	4.47
Other	38.9	4.35

Source: *Retail Merchandiser*, January 2006, p. 16, from Information Resources Inc. InfoScan.

★ 577 ★
Chocolate
SIC: 2066; NAICS: 31132, 31133

Top Chocolate Candy Box/Bag Makers < 3.5 oz, 2005

Market shares are shown based on sales at supermarkets, drug stores and mass merchandisers (excluding Wal-Mart) for the 52 weeks ended October 2, 2005.

Hershey Company	.46.7%
Masterfoods	.31.7
Nestle USA	.12.5
Ferrero USA Inc.	1.3
Other	8.7

Source: *The Manufacturing Confectioner*, January 2006, p. 16, from Information Resources Inc. InfoScan.

★ 578 ★
Chocolate
SIC: 2066; NAICS: 31132, 31133

Top Chocolate Candy Box/Bag Makers > 3.5 oz, 2005

Market shares are shown based on sales at supermarkets, drug stores and mass merchandisers (excluding Wal-Mart) for the 52 weeks ended October 2, 2005.

Hershey Company	.49.5%
Masterfoods USA	.24.0
Nestle USA Inc.	6.3
Lindt & Sprungli A.G.	2.7
Ferrero USA Inc.	2.0
Brach's Confections	1.2
Ghiradelli Chocolate Co.	1.2
Storck USA	1.0
Tootsie Roll Industries	1.0
Private label	2.6
Other	.10.5

Source: *The Manufacturing Confectioner*, January 2006, p. 16, from Information Resources Inc. InfoScan.

★ 579 ★
Chocolate
SIC: 2066; NAICS: 31132, 31133

Top Chocolate Candy Brands (Sugarfree/Sugarless), 2005

Market shares are shown based on sales at supermarkets, drug stores and mass merchandisers (excluding Wal-Mart) for the 52 weeks ended October 2, 2005.

Russell Stover	.44.3%
Atkins Indulge	.11.1
Hershey's	9.8
Reese's	5.8
Whitman's Sampler	4.3
York Peppermint Patty	3.1
Carborite	2.9
Nestle Turtles	2.7
Russell Stover Net Carb	1.5
Other	.14.5

Source: *The Manufacturing Confectioner*, January 2006, p. 16, from Information Resources Inc. InfoScan.

★ 580 ★
Chocolate
SIC: 2066; NAICS: 31132, 31133

Top Chocolate Candy Makers (Sugarfree/Sugarless), 2005

Market shares are shown based on sales at supermarkets, drug stores and mass merchandisers (excluding Wal-Mart) for the 52 weeks ended October 2, 2005.

Russell Stover Candies	.46.2%
Hershey Company	.20.2
Atkins Nutritional	.11.1
Whitman's Chocolates	5.2
Nestle USA Inc.	3.8
Carbolite Food Inc.	3.1
Richardson Labs	1.1
Carblite	0.8
Simply Lite	0.8
Private label	1.0
Other	6.7

Source: *The Manufacturing Confectioner*, January 2006, p. 16, from Information Resources Inc. InfoScan.

★ 581 ★
Chocolate
SIC: 2066; NAICS: 31132, 31133

Top Chocolate Candy Snack/Fun Size Brands, 2005

Market shares are shown based on sales at supermarkets, drug stores and mass merchandisers (excluding Wal-Mart) for the 52 weeks ended October 2, 2005.

Snickers	.14.0%
Reese's	.12.7
Kit Kat	. 9.2
M&M's	. 7.0
Hershey's	. 6.8
Nestle Butterfinger	. 6.6
Milky Way	. 6.4
Three Musketeers	. 5.2
Nestle Crunch	. 4.5
Nestle Baby Ruth	. 3.5
Other	.24.1

Source: *The Manufacturing Confectioner*, January 2006, p. 16, from Information Resources Inc. InfoScan.

★ 582 ★
Chocolate
SIC: 2066; NAICS: 31132, 31133

Top Chocolate Candy Snack/Fun Size Makers, 2005

Market shares are shown based on sales at supermarkets, drug stores and mass merchandisers (excluding Wal-Mart) for the 52 weeks ended October 2, 2005.

Hershey Company	.42.4%
Masterfoods USA	.40.0
Nestle USA Inc.	.16.6
Other	. 1.0

Source: *The Manufacturing Confectioner*, January 2006, p. 16, from Information Resources Inc. InfoScan.

★ 583 ★
Chocolate
SIC: 2066; NAICS: 31132, 31133

Top Chocolate Confectionery Makers in Australia, 2002

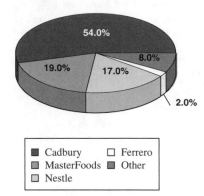

The chocolate confectionery industry is valued at $1,550 million. The overall confectionery market was valued at A$2.72 billion.

Cadbury	.54.0%
MasterFoods	.19.0
Nestle	.17.0
Ferrero	. 2.0
Other	. 8.0

Source: "Australian Confectionery Industry Profile 2004." [online] from http://www.candy.net.au [Published September 2004].

★ 584 ★
Chocolate
SIC: 2066; NAICS: 31132, 31133

Top Chocolate Firms in Convenience Stores

Market shares are shown in percent.

Hershey	.29.0%
Masterfoods	.19.0
Nestle	. 8.0
Other	.54.0

Source: *Confectioner*, October 2005, p. 22, from *McLane Category Management Handbook*.

★ 585 ★
Chocolate
SIC: 2066; NAICS: 31132, 31133

Top Gift Box Chocolate Makers, 2005

Market shares are shown based on sales at grocery stores, drug stores and mass merchandisers (excluding Wal-Mart) for the 52 weeks ended October 2, 2005.

Russell Stover Candies Inc.	.40.0%
Whitman's Chocolates	.19.7
Hershey Company	.18.2
Gray & Co.	6.7
Fannic May Candy	3.9
Maxfield Candy Co.	1.7
Esther Price Candies	1.5
Other	8.3

Source: *The Manufacturing Confectioner*, January 2006, p. 16, from Information Resources Inc. InfoScan.

★ 586 ★
Chocolate
SIC: 2066; NAICS: 31132, 31133

Top Gift Box Chocolates, 2005

Market shares are shown based on sales at supermarkets, drug stores and mass merchandisers (excluding Wal-Mart) for the 52 weeks ended October 2, 2005.

Russell Stover	.39.9%
Hershey's Pot of Gold	.18.2
Whitman's Sampler	.18.0
Queen Anne	6.7
Fannie May	3.9
Whitman's	1.7
Esther Price	1.5
Celebrations	1.2
Maxfields	1.1
Nestle Turtles	0.7
Other	7.4

Source: *The Manufacturing Confectioner*, January 2006, p. 16, from Information Resources Inc. InfoScan.

★ 587 ★
Chocolate Syrup
SIC: 2066; NAICS: 31132, 31133

Top Chocolate Syrup Makers, 2006

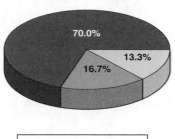

Market shares are shown based on food store, drug store and mass merchandiser sales (excluding Wal-Mart) for the 52 weeks ended January 2006.

Hershey	.70.0%
Private label	.16.7
Other	.13.3

Source: *US Food Industry*, North American Equity Research, January 17, 2006, p. 28, from ACNielsen and JPMorgan.

★ 588 ★
Cocoa
SIC: 2066; NAICS: 31132, 31133

Global Cocoa Market, 2003-2005

World cocoa production hit its peak in the 2003-2004 seaason with 3,396 MT. West Africa takes 69% of the total. Weather has had an effect on production in that the crop could not mature. Data are in thousands of tons.

	2003-04	2004-05	Share
Ivory Coast	1,500	1,275	41.14%
Ghana	605	530	17.10
Indonesia	420	415	13.39
Nigeria	165	170	5.49
Cameroon	150	150	4.84

Source: *Candy Business*, May - June 2005, p. S11, from LMC International, International Cocoa Organization, Reuters and United States Department of Agriculture.

★ 589 ★
Gum
SIC: 2067; NAICS: 31134

Gum Sales in the U.K., 2005

Market shares are shown in percent.

Wrigley	.52.5%
Cadbury Trebor Bassett	.20.8
Nestle Polo	5.8
Big Bear	2.7
Other	.18.2

Source: *Marketing*, February 8, 2006, p. 32, from Mintel.

★ 590 ★
Gum
SIC: 2067; NAICS: 31134

Top Antismoking Gum Brands, 2005

Market shares are shown based on drug store sales for the 52 weeks ended October 30, 2005.

Nicorette	.56.2%
Rugby	0.1
Private label	.21.6
Other	.22.1

Source: *Chain Drug Review*, January 2, 2006, p. 94.

★ 591 ★
Gum
SIC: 2067; NAICS: 31134

Top Bubble Gum Makers, 2006

Market shares are shown based on food store, drug store and mass merchandiser sales (excluding Wal-Mart) for the 52 weeks ended January 2006.

Wrigley	.30.3%
Cadbury	.20.4
Hershey	.13.0
Private label	2.8
Other	.33.5

Source: *US Food Industry*, North American Equity Research, January 17, 2006, p. 28, from ACNielsen and JPMorgan.

★ 592 ★
Gum
SIC: 2067; NAICS: 31134

Top Gum Brands in Spain

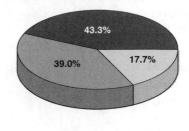

Market shares are shown in percent.

Trident	.43.3%
Orbit	.39.0
Other	.17.7

Source: *just-food.com*, May 3, 2006, p. NA, from ACNielsen.

★ 593 ★
Gum
SIC: 2067; NAICS: 31134

Top Gum Brands (Sugarfree/Sugarless), 2005

Market shares are shown based on sales at grocery stores, drug stores and mass merchandisers (not Wal-Mart) for the 52 weeks ended October 2, 2005.

Wrigley's Extra	.20.6%
Orbit	.18.0
Trident	.12.8
Wrigley's Eclipse	.12.7
Dentyne Ice	9.6
Trident White	7.8
Altoids	3.8
Orbit White	3.2
Ice Breakers	2.7
Other	8.8

Source: *The Manufacturing Confectioner*, January 2006, p. 16, from Information Resources Inc. InfoScan.

★ 594 ★
Gum
SIC: 2067; NAICS: 31134

Top Gum Makers, 2005

Market shares are shown based on sales at grocery stores, drug stores and mass merchandisers (excluding Wal-Mart) for the 52 weeks ended October 2, 2005.

Wm. Wrigley Jr. Co.	.74.0%
Cadbury Adams USA	6.9
Hershey Company	4.4
Farleys & Sathers Candy	3.5
Masterfoods USA	2.5
Concord Confections Inc.	2.1
Topps Company Inc.	1.5
Private label	1.4
Other	3.7

Source: *The Manufacturing Confectioner*, January 2006, p. 16, from Information Resources Inc. InfoScan.

★ 595 ★
Gum
SIC: 2067; NAICS: 31134

Top Gum Makers in Latin America

Market shares are shown in percent.

Cadbury Schweppes	.69.7%
Chicles Canel's	5.7
Wrigley	5.7
Perfetti	4.8
Other	14.1

Source: *Financial Times*, October 19, 2005, p. 18, from Euromonitor.

★ 596 ★
Gum
SIC: 2067; NAICS: 31134

Top Gum Makers in the Asia Pacific Region

Market shares are shown in percent.

Lotte	.43.3%
Wrigley	.17.8
Cadbury Schweppes	8.2
Meiji Seika Kaisha	5.6
Ezaki Glico	5.1
Other	.20.0

Source: *Financial Times*, October 19, 2005, p. 18, from Euromonitor.

★ 597 ★
Gum
SIC: 2067; NAICS: 31134

Top Gum Makers in Western Europe

Market shares are shown in percent.

Wrigley	.43.2%
Cadbury Schweppes	.21.4
Perfetti	.16.1
Other	.19.3

Source: *Financial Times*, October 19, 2005, p. 18, from Euromonitor.

★ 598 ★
Gum
SIC: 2067; NAICS: 31134

Top Gum Makers (Sugarfree/ Sugarless), 2005

Market shares are shown based on sales at grocery stores, drug stores and mass merchandisers (excluding Wal-Mart) for the 52 weeks ended October 2, 2005.

Wm. Wrigley Jr. Co.	.54.6%
Cadbury Adams USA	.34.4
Hershey Company	6.0
Kraft/Callard & Bowser-Suchard	3.8
Other	1.2

Source: *The Manufacturing Confectioner*, January 2006, p. 16, from Information Resources Inc. InfoScan.

★ 599 ★
Gum
SIC: 2067; NAICS: 31134

Top Gum Makers Worldwide, 2004

Market shares are shown in percent.

Wrigley	.35.4%
Cadbury	.26.3
Hershey	1.7
Kraft	0.5

Continued on next page.

★ 599 ★

[Continued]

Gum

SIC: 2067; NAICS: 31134

Top Gum Makers Worldwide, 2004

Market shares are shown in percent.

Mars 0.2%
Other 35.9

Source: *Wall Street Journal*, February 16, 2006, p. C3, from Thomson Datastream and Euromonitor.

★ 600 ★

Gum

SIC: 2067; NAICS: 31134

Top Gum Markets Worldwide, 2004-2005

Countries are ranked by retail sales in millions of dollars. Shares are shown based on the top 40 countries.

	2004	2005	Share
United States	$ 3,326	$ 3,502	22.34%
Japan	1,782	1,970	12.57
Mexico	799	834	5.32
United Kingdom	710	758	4.84
Italy	709	828	5.28
Germany	689	733	4.68
France	683	798	5.09
Brazil	648	774	4.94
China	610	648	4.13
Russia	447	461	2.94

Source: *The Manufacturing Confectioner*, March 2006, p. 29, from *World Confectionery Report & Export Handbook* and National Confectioners Association.

★ 601 ★

Gum

SIC: 2067; NAICS: 31134

Top Sugarfree Gum Brands in Australia, 2004

Shares are for the year ended April 18, 2004.

Extra 88.0%
Other 12.0

Source: ''Australian Confectionery Industry Profile 2004.'' [online] from http://www.candy.net.au [Published September 2004] from ACNielsen.

★ 602 ★

Nuts

SIC: 2068; NAICS: 311911

Culinary/In-Shell Nut Market, 2006

Market shares are for the 52 weeks ended April 16, 2006.

Diamond 38.9%
Planters 9.0
Sanfilippo 2.5
Azar 1.5
Private label 16.8
Other 31.3

Source: ''Form 8-K.'' [online] from http://library. corporate-ir.net/library/18/189/189398/items/199175/DiamondFoods-Inc8K.pdf [Published May 22, 2006] from Information Resources Inc.

★ 603 ★

Nuts

SIC: 2068; NAICS: 311911

Snack Nut Market, 2006

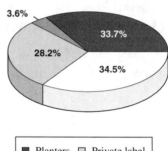

Market shares are for the 52 weeks ended April 16, 2006.

Planters 33.7%
Emerald 3.6
Private label 28.2
Other 34.5

Source: ''Form 8-K.'' [online] from http://library. corporate-ir.net/library/18/189/189398/items/199175/DiamondFoods-Inc8K.pdf [Published May 22, 2006] from Information Resources Inc.

★ 604 ★
Nuts
SIC: 2068; NAICS: 311911
Top Snack Walnut Brands, 2005

Market shares are shown for the 52 weeks ended Feburary 20, 2005.

Diamond	.51.0%
Planters	7.0
Suntree	2.0
Private label	.11.0
Other	.29.0

Source: ''Building Sustainable Brand Value.'' [online] from http://aic.ucdavis.edu/events/CAS_05/mendes_partA.pdf [Accessed June 4, 2006] from Information Resources Inc.

★ 605 ★
Fats and Oils
SIC: 2079; NAICS: 311225
Fish Oil Supplement Market in the U.K.

Total sales in the market were 35 million (excluding sales at Boots and Superdrug).

Seven Seas Cod Liver Oil	.48.3%
Own label fish oils	.18.7
Haliborange DHA	.11.6

Source: *Community Pharmacy*, December 8, 2005, p. 22, from IMS Health.

★ 606 ★
Fats and Oils
SIC: 2079; NAICS: 311225
Olive Oil Sales

Retail sales rose to $553.3 million in 2005. Olive oil is projected to take half of the pourable oil market in 2007.

Major	.83.6%
Private label	.16.4

Source: *Research Alert*, April 21, 2006, p. 12, from ACNielsen and *Facts, Figures & the Future*.

★ 607 ★
Fats and Oils
SIC: 2079; NAICS: 311225
Olive Oil Sales, 2005

Market shares are shown in percent.

Extra virgin	.58.0%
Pure	.27.0
Extra light	.15.0

Source: ''North American Retail Olive Oil Market.'' [online] from http://www.mytradeassociation.org/naooa/chairmansreportjan06.ppt [Published Jan. 20, 2006] from Information Resources Inc.

★ 608 ★
Fats and Oils
SIC: 2079; NAICS: 311225
Pourable Oil Sales, 2005

Total sales were $1.5 billion for the 52 weeks ended December 11, 2005.

Olive	.35.0%
Vegetable	.25.0
Canola	.13.0
Corn	.10.0
Peanut	2.0
Other	.15.0

Source: ''North American Retail Olive Oil Market.'' [online] from http://www.mytradeassociation.org/naooa/chairmansreportjan06.ppt [Published Jan. 20, 2006] from Information Resources Inc.

★ 609 ★
Fats and Oils
SIC: 2079; NAICS: 311225
Salad/Cooking Oil Sales at Supermarkets

Supermarket sales are shown in millions of dollars.

Salad and cooking oils	$ 890.61
Olive oil	491.14
Cooking sprays	239.55
Shortening	126.17
Lard	24.19

Source: *Progressive Grocer*, September 15, 2005, p. 22, from *Progressive Grocer's 26th Annual Consumer Expenditures Study*.

★ 610 ★
Fats and Oils
SIC: 2079; NAICS: 311225

Shortening Market

Market shares are shown in percent.

J.M. Smucker 63.5%
Other 36.5

Source: "J.M. Smucker Company." [online] from http://library. corporate-ir.net/library/77/779/77952/items/164508/SeptemberIRPre-sentation.pdf [Published Sept. 2005].

★ 611 ★
Fats and Oils
SIC: 2079; NAICS: 311225

Top Cooking Oil Brands, 2004

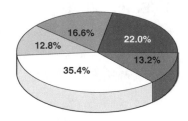

Market shares are shown for the 52 weeks ended February 22, 2004.

Crisco 22.0%
Wesson 16.6
Mazzola 12.8
Private label 35.4
Other 13.2

Source: "J.M. Smucker Company." [online] from http://media. corporate-ir.net/media_files/NYS/SJM/reports/proxy-2005.pdf [Published March 23, 2004] from Information Resources Inc.

★ 612 ★
Fats and Oils
SIC: 2079; NAICS: 311225

Top Cooking Oil Makers, 2005

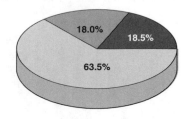

Market shares are shown based on sales at food stores, drug stores and mass merchandisers (excluding Wal-Mart) for the 12 weeks ended June 11, 2005.

J.M. Smucker Company 18.5%
ConAgra Foods 18.0
Other 63.5

Source: *Food/Agribusiness*, Prudential Equity Group Equity Research, June 24, 2005, p. 2, from ACNielsen.

★ 613 ★
Fats and Oils
SIC: 2079; NAICS: 311225

Top Edible Fat/Oil Makers, 2004

Companies are ranked by sales in thousands of dollars.

	($ 000)	Share
Unilever	$ 555,019	20.4%
Kraft Foods	495,052	18.2
JM Smucker	278,080	10.2
ConAgra	267,110	9.8

Source: *J.M. Smucker Co.*, Krause Fund Research, November 17, 2005, p. 20, from Mintel's *Sweet Spreads*.

★ 614 ★
Fats and Oils
SIC: 2079; NAICS: 311225

Top Edible Oil Brands in India, 2005

The packaged edible oil market has grown 12% by volume making it the fastest sector in the fast moving consumer goods industry. Market shares are for the year ended March 31, 2005.

Fortune (Adani Wilmar) 22.0%
Gemini (Cargill) 12.5

Continued on next page.

★ 614 ★
[Continued]
Fats and Oils
SIC: 2079; NAICS: 311225

Top Edible Oil Brands in India, 2005

The packaged edible oil market has grown 12% by volume making it the fastest sector in the fast moving consumer goods industry. Market shares are for the year ended March 31, 2005.

Agrotech	.11.0%
Gold Winner (Tamil Nadu)	.10.0
Other	.44.5

Source: ''Going for the Heart is a Darn Good Sales Pitch.'' [online] from http://dnaindia.com/report.asp?NewsID6384 [Published October 19, 2005] from ACNielsen.

★ 615 ★
Fats and Oils
SIC: 2079; NAICS: 311225

Top Fats and Oils Makers in Indonesia, 2004

Market shares are shown in percent.

Indofood Sukses Makmur Tbk PY	.38.2%
Sinar Mas Group	.17.1
Bina Karya Prima PT	.15.2
Unilever Group	.15.2
San Agrotama Persada	5.1
Pabrik Minyak Goreng Barco Ltd.	2.0
Other	7.2

Source: *Oil & Fats International*, January 2006, p. 19, from Euromonitor.

★ 616 ★
Fats and Oils
SIC: 2079; NAICS: 311225

Top Fats and Oils Makers Worldwide, 2002

Data show the market shares of the top multinationals.

Unilever	.13.4%
Danone	0.6
Kraft	0.4
Nestle	0.3
Other	.85.3

Source: *New Directions in Global Food Markets*, February 2005, p. 66, from Economic Research Service, U.S. Department of Agriculture and Euromonitor.

★ 617 ★
Fats and Oils
SIC: 2079; NAICS: 311225

Top Olive Oil Makers, 2006

Market shares are shown based on sales (excluding Wal-Mart) for the 52 weeks ended January 2006.

Unilever	.19.4%
Private label	5.8
Other	.74.8

Source: *US Food Industry*, North American Equity Research, January 17, 2006, p. 28, from ACNielsen and JPMorgan.

★ 618 ★
Beverages
SIC: 2080; NAICS: 31212, 31213, 31214

Alcohol Consumption, 2004

Market shares are shown in percent.

Beer	.86.1%
Wine	8.6
Distilled spirits	5.3

Source: *Beer Handbook*, Annual 2005, p. 50, from Institute for Brewing Studies.

★ 619 ★
Beverages
SIC: 2080; NAICS: 312111, 312112

Largest Beverage Marketers in North America

Firms are ranked by sales in millions of dollars.

Coca-Cola Company	$ 21,962.0
Coca-Cola Enterprises	18,158.0
Anheuser-Busch	14,934.2
PepsiCo Inc.	11,000.0
Pepsi Bottling Group	10,906.0
FEMSA	6,348.4
Southern Wine & Spirits	5,500.0
Diageo North America	4,805.9
Miller Brewing Co.	4,778.0
Adolph Coors Co.	4,305.8
Constellation Brands	4,090.0
Grupo Modelo	4,017.8

Source: *Beverage World*, July 15, 2005, p. 48.

★ 620 ★
Beverages
SIC: 2080; NAICS: 312111, 312112

Largest Beverage Marketers Worldwide

Firms are ranked by sales in millions of dollars.

Nestle	$ 25,010.3
Coca-Cola Company	21,962.0
Coca-Cola Enterprises	18,158.0
Diageo	16,163.0
Anheuser-Busch	14,934.2
Heineken	13,646.8
Suntory	12,270.7
SABMiller	11,366.0
Asahi	11,360.6
PepsiCo.	11,000.0

Source: *Beverage World*, October 15, 2005, p. 48.

★ 621 ★
Beverages
SIC: 2080; NAICS: 312111, 312112

Largest Bottlers

Companies are ranked by sales in millions of dollars.

Coca-Cola Enterprises	$ 18,158.0
Pepsi Bottling Group	10,906.0
PepsiAmericas Inc.	3,300.0
Dr. Pepper/Seven Up Bottling Group	1,900.0
Coca-Cola Bottling Company Consolidated	1,256.5
Honickman Affiliates	1,100.0
Coca-Cola Bottling Company	535.4
Pepsi Bottling Ventures	524.0
Philadelphia Coca-Cola Bottling Company	510.0
Buffalo Rock Company	480.0

Source: *Beverage World*, September 15, 2005, p. 34.

★ 622 ★
Beer
SIC: 2082; NAICS: 31212

Beer Sales by Category, 2005

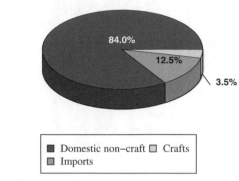

Market shares are shown in percent.

Domestic non-craft	84.0%
Imports	12.5
Crafts	3.5

Source: *Advertising Age*, June 19, 2006, p. 4, from Brewers Association.

★ 623 ★
Beer
SIC: 2082; NAICS: 31212

Global Beer Sales, 2004-2005

Sales are shown in millions of dollars.

	2004	2005	Share
Lager	$ 371,614.0	$ 380,411.2	90.19%
Dark beer	26,015.8	26,201.5	6.21
Stout	8,990.0	9,119.5	2.16
Non-/low-alcohol	5,996.8	6,076.2	1.44

Source: *Beverage Industry*, July 2005, p. 20, from Information Resources Inc.

★ 624 ★
Beer
SIC: 2082; NAICS: 31212

Largest Beer Brands (Imported), 2005

Market shares are shown based on the import category.

Corona Extra	29.0%
Heineken	18.7
Tecate	4.6
Modelo Expecial	4.2
Labatt Blue	3.8
Guinness	3.5

Continued on next page.

★ 624 ★

[Continued]

Beer

SIC: 2082; NAICS: 31212

Largest Beer Brands (Imported), 2005

Market shares are shown based on the import category.

Amstel Light	2.9%
Corona Light	2.8
Beck's	2.4
Other	28.1

Source: *Beverage World*, April 15, 2006, p. 52, from Beverage Marketing Corporation.

★ 625 ★

Beer

SIC: 2082; NAICS: 31212

Largest Beer Brands (Light/Low Calorie), 2005

Market shares are shown based on the light category.

Bud Light	39.9%
Miller Lite	18.2
Coors Light	14.4
Natural Light	8.3
Busch Light Draft	5.4
Michelob Ultra	3.1
Budweiser Select	2.6
Michelob Light	1.7
Amstel Light	0.7
Corona Light	0.7
Other	5.0

Source: *Beverage World*, April 15, 2006, p. 52, from Beverage Marketing Corporation.

★ 626 ★

Beer

SIC: 2082; NAICS: 31212

Largest Beer Import Markets, 2003

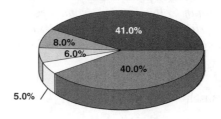

United States ☐ France

United Kingdom ■ Other

☐ Italy

The market size was $6.6 billion.

United States	41.0%
United Kingdom	8.0
Italy	6.0
France	5.0
Other	40.0

Source: ''Prospects in the Global Beer Market.'' [online] from http://www.ffas.usda.gov [Published December 2004] from U.S. Department of Agriculture.

★ 627 ★

Beer

SIC: 2082; NAICS: 31212

Largest Beer Wholesalers

Firms are ranked by millions of cases.

The Reyes Family	40.4
Ben E. Keith Beers	34.1
Goldring/Moffett Family Holdings	32.2
Manhattan Beer Distributors	26.1
Silver Eagle Distributors	25.9
Topa Equities	23.9
JJ Taylor Companies Inc.	23.3
Hensley	22.6
The Sheehan Family	22.5
Gold Coast Beverage Distributors	20.7

Source: *Beverage World*, August 15, 2005, p. 34.

★ 628 ★

Beer

SIC: 2082; NAICS: 31212

Largest Brewers Worldwide

SABMiller announced plans to buy Grupo Empresarial Bavaria of Colombia, the second largest brewer in South America, in July 2005. Companies are ranked by beer production in billions of gallons.

InBev	4.85
SABMiller	4.01
Anheuser-Busch	3.81
Heineken	3.81
Carlsberg	1.77
Maine Coast Brewing	1.52
Scottish & Newcastle	1.36
Modelo	1.13
Tsingtao	0.98
Kirin	0.95

Source: *New York Times*, July 19, 2005, p. C5, from Plato Logic and company reports.

★ 629 ★

Beer

SIC: 2082; NAICS: 31212

Top Beer Brands, 2006

Market shares are shown based on supermarket, drug store and mass merchandiser sales (excluding Wal-Mart) for the 52 weeks ended February 19, 2006.

Bud Light	15.4%
Budweiser	9.2
Miller Lite	8.2
Coors Light	6.9
Natural Light	3.3
Michelob Ultra Light	2.5
Busch	2.3
Miller Genuine Draft	2.1
Busch	2.0
Miller High Life	2.0
Other	46.1

Source: *Beverage Industry*, April 2006, p. 17, from Information Resources Inc.

★ 630 ★

Beer

SIC: 2082; NAICS: 31212

Top Beer Brands in Panama

Market shares are shown in percent.

Bavaria	93.0%
Other	7.0

Source: *Sunday Business*, July 24, 2005, p. NA.

★ 631 ★

Beer

SIC: 2082; NAICS: 31212

Top Beer Makers in Canada

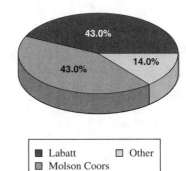

■ Labatt	□ Other
■ Molson Coors	

Market shares are shown based on units.

Labatt	43.0%
Molson Coors	43.0
Other	14.0

Source: *U.S. Beverages Beverage Bulletin*, Credit Suisse First Boston, January 9, 2006, p. 18, from CS First Boston and company data.

★ 632 ★

Beer

SIC: 2082; NAICS: 31212

Top Beer Makers in Greece

Market shares are shown in percent.

Heineken	83.0%
Other	17.0

Source: *just-drinks.com*, March 2006, p. 19.

★ 633 ★
Beer
SIC: 2082; NAICS: 31212
Top Beer Makers in Israel

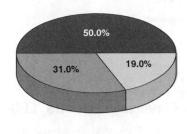

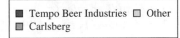

Market shares are shown in percent.

Tempo Beer Industries 50.0%
Carlsberg 31.0
Other 19.0

Source: *just-drinks.com (Management Briefing)*, February 2006, p. 16, from ACNielsen.

★ 634 ★
Beer
SIC: 2082; NAICS: 31212
Top Beer Makers in Japan, 2005

Beer and quasi-beer shipments fell 3.1% to 501 million cases in 2005, a record low. Quasi beer is described in the source as third-segment beverages with little or no malt content.

Asahi Breweries 38.8%
Kirin Brewery 35.7
Sapporo Breweries 14.2
Suntory 10.5
Other 0.8

Source: *Jiji*, January 17, 2006, p. NA, from Brewer Association of Japan.

★ 635 ★
Beer
SIC: 2082; NAICS: 31212
Top Beer Makers in Nigeria

Market shares are shown in percent.

Heineken 60.0%
Other 40.0

Source: *just-drinks.com*, March 2006, p. 19.

★ 636 ★
Beer
SIC: 2082; NAICS: 31212
Top Beer Makers in Poland, 2005

Poland is the fifth largest beer market in Europe.

Kompania Piwowarska 37.1%
Zywiec 36.0
Carlsberg Okocim 14.1
Other 12.8

Source: *Poland Business News*, February 1, 2006, p. NA.

★ 637 ★
Beer
SIC: 2082; NAICS: 31212
Top Brewers in Russia

Baltika was the top brand with 13% of the market, followed by Klinksoe with 6%. Arsenalnoye, Story Melnik and Ochkovo each held 4% of the market.

BBH 36.0%
Sun Interbrew 15.8
Etes 6.5
Heineken 6.5
Other 35.2

Source: *Financial Times*, August 29, 2005, p. 14, from Aton Capital and Carlsberg.

★ 638 ★
Beer
SIC: 2082; NAICS: 31212
Top Craft Brewers, 2004

Market shares are shown in percent.

Boston Beer Company 19.2%
Sierra Nevada Brewing Company 9.0
New Belgium Brewing Company 5.0
Spoetzl Brewing Company 4.6
F.X. Matt Brewing Company 3.5
Redhook Ale Brewery 3.3
Widmer Brothers Brewing Company 3.0
Pyramid Breweries 2.2
Deschutes Brewery 2.0
Alaskan Brewing Company 1.4
Boulevard Brewing Company 1.4
Other 45.4

Source: *Beer Handbook*, Annual 2005, p. 50, from Institute for Brewing Studies.

★ 639 ★

Beer

SIC: 2082; NAICS: 31212

Top Micro/Craft Beer Brands, 2006

Brands are ranked by supermarket, drug store and mass merchandiser sales for the year-to-date ended January 1, 2006.

	(mil.)	Share
Sierra Nevada Pale Ale	49.1	11.9%
Samuel Adams Lager	43.6	10.4
Samuel Adams Seasonal	20.4	4.9
Fat Tire Amber Ale	19.0	4.6
Samuel Adams Light	18.2	4.4
Widmer Hefeweizen	15.4	3.7
Shiner Bock	15.2	3.6
Redhook ESB	11.9	1.7
Pyramid Hefeweizen Ale	7.3	1.7
Deschutes Mirror Pond PA	7.1	1.6

Source: *Modern Brewery Age*, Spring 2006, p. 17, from Information Resources Inc.

★ 640 ★

Beer

SIC: 2082; NAICS: 31212

Top Premium Brands, 2004

Market shares are shown in percent.

Budweiser	80.8%
Miller Genuine Draft	11.3
Coors	4.1
Other	1.3

Source: *Beer Handbook*, Annual 2005, p. 50.

★ 641 ★

Beer

SIC: 2082; NAICS: 31212

Top Regions for Premium Beer, 2004

The top metropolitan statistical areas are ranked by sales of thousands of 2.25 gallon cases.

	(000)	Share
Chicago, IL	12,493	2.6%
Los Angeles-Long Beach, CA	12,056	2.5
New York, NY	9,859	2.1
Phoenix-Mesa, AZ	10,059	2.1
Houston, TX	9,274	1.9
Washington D.C.	8,164	1.7

	(000)	Share
Atlanta, GA	7,859	1.6%
Detroit, MI	7,767	1.6
Dallas, TX	7,747	1.6
Philadelphia, PA	7,598	1.6

Source: *Beer Handbook*, Annual 2005, p. 50.

★ 642 ★

Malt Beverages

SIC: 2082; NAICS: 31212

Top Malt Beverage Brands, 2006

Market shares are shown based on supermarket, drug store and mass merchandiser sales (excluding Wal-Mart) for the 52 weeks ended February 19, 2006.

	($ mil.)	Share
Smirnoff Ice	$ 46.64	13.86%
Mike's Hard Lemonade	35.83	10.65
Smirnoff Twisted V Green Apple	23.84	7.09
Smirnoff Ice Triple Black	20.85	6.20
Mike's Hard Cranberry Lemonade	20.78	6.18
Sminoff Twisted V Raspberry	20.62	6.13
Smirnoff Twisted V Watermelon	16.42	4.88
Mike's Hard Lime	13.74	4.08
Smirnoff Twisted V Black Cherry	13.74	4.08
Other	123.97	36.85

Source: *Beverage Industry*, April 2006, p. 17, from Information Resources Inc.

★ 643 ★

Malt Beverages

SIC: 2082; NAICS: 31212

Top Malt Liquor Brands, 2004

Market shares are shown in percent.

Colt 45	20.9%
King Cobra	20.4
Old English 800	18.0
Schlitz Malt Liquor	12.9
Magnum	7.4
Other	20.4

Source: *Beer Handbook*, Annual 2005, p. 50.

★ 644 ★
Malt Beverages
SIC: 2084; NAICS: 31212

Top Malt Beverage/Wine Cooler Brands, 2004

Brands are ranked by sales in thousands of 9-liter cases.

	(000)	Share
Smirnoff Ice	10,940	18.05%
Smirnoff Twisted V	8,550	14.10
Mike's Hard Lemonade	8,050	13.28
Bartles & Jaymes	6,440	10.62
Seagram's Coolers	5,130	8.46
Smirnoff's Ice Triple Black . . .	4,590	7.57
Skyy Blue	3,125	5.15
Bacardi Silver	2,370	3.91
Other	11,430	18.85

Source: *Wine Handbook*, Annual 2005, p. 32.

★ 645 ★
Wine
SIC: 2084; NAICS: 31213

Best-Selling Varietals in Supermarkets

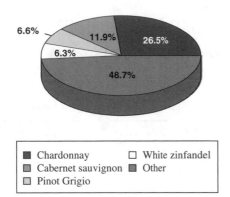

- ■ Chardonnay
- □ White zinfandel
- ■ Cabernet sauvignon
- ■ Other
- □ Pinot Grigio

Shares are shown based on dollar sales.

Chardonnay	.26.5%
Cabernet sauvignon	.11.9
Pinot Grigio	. 6.6
White zinfandel	. 6.3
Other	.48.7

Source: *Wine Business Monthly*, January 24, 2006, p. NA, from ACNielsen.

★ 646 ★
Wine
SIC: 2084; NAICS: 31213

Largest Wine Companies Worldwide, 2004

Companies are ranked by sales in millions of dollars.

Diageo	$ 14,396
Allied Domecq	3,904
E&J Gallo Winery	1,800
Brown-Forman	1,795
Pernod Ricard	1,694
Constellation Wines	1,674
LVMH	1,512
Beringer Blass	1,275
Castel Freres	1,073
Southcorp	806

Source: *just-drinks.com*, May 2005, p. 34, from Canadean.

★ 647 ★
Wine
SIC: 2084; NAICS: 31213

Leading Wine Makers in Canada

Market shares are shown based on volume.

Vincor	.21.0%
Andres	. 7.0
Maxxium	. 7.0
Maison de Futailles	. 6.0
Gallo	. 3.0
Other	.56.0

Source: "Vincor International Investor Presentation." [online] from http://www.vincorinternational.com/download/VN_FallSept30-2005.pdf [Published Sept 30, 2005].

★ 648 ★
Wine
SIC: 2084; NAICS: 31213

Leading Wine Makers in France, 2005

Market shares are shown in percent.

Societe des Investissements d'Aquitaine	. 9.2%
Allied Domecq	. 7.6
Pitters	. 5.6
Duke Street	. 4.5
La Languedocienne	. 4.3
Other	.68.8

Source: "National Report France." [online] from http://foodqualityschemes.jrc.es/en/documents/NationalreportFR_000.pdf [Published November 2005] from Food for Thought.

★ 649 ★
Wine
SIC: 2084; NAICS: 31213

Top Cities for Wine Sales

Cities are ranked by sales of wine at food stores in millions of dollars. Portland, Oregon was the top city for Pinot Noir, taking 5.9% of table wine dollar sales. New Orleans/Mobile was the top market for Merlot, taking 18.3% of sales.

Los Angeles, CA	$ 274.2
San Francisco, CA	251.5
Miami, FL	203.3
Tampa, FL	158.3
Seattle, WA	154.5
Chicago, IL	139.0

Source: *Wine Business Monthly*, October 15, 2005, p. NA, from ACNielsen.

★ 650 ★
Wine
SIC: 2084; NAICS: 31213

Top Dessert/Fortified Wine Brands, 2004

Brands are ranked by thousands of 9 liter cases.

	(000)	Share
Richard's Wild Irish Rose	2,296	25.01%
MD 20/20	1,715	18.68
Fairbanks	900	9.80
Taylor Dessert	701	7.64
Thunderbird	600	6.54
Takara Sake	530	5.77
Cisco	456	4.97
Sheffield Cellars	320	3.49
Gekkeikan Sake	295	3.21
Other	1,367	14.89

Source: *Wine Handbook*, Annual 2005, p. 32.

★ 651 ★
Wine
SIC: 2084; NAICS: 31213

Top Dessert Wine Makers, 2004

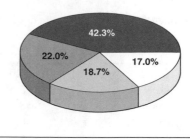

■ Constellation Brands   □ The Wine Group
■ E&J Gallo Winery   □ Other

Market shares are shown in percent. Dessert fortified wine declined for the eighth consecutive year.

Constellation Brands	42.3%
E&J Gallo Winery	22.0
The Wine Group	18.7
Other	17.0

Source: *Wine Handbook*, Annual 2005, p. 32.

★ 652 ★
Wine
SIC: 2084; NAICS: 31213

Top Table Wine Brands, 2004

Brands are ranked by sales in thousands of 9-liter cases.

	(000)	Share
Franzia Winetaps	23,630	12.56%
Carlo Rossi	13,200	7.02
Twin Valley	9,700	5.16
Almaden	9,634	5.12
Beringer	7,720	4.10
Sutter Home	7,229	3.84
Livingston Cellars	7,200	3.83
Woodbridge	7,075	3.76
Charles Shaw	5,000	2.66
Other	97,752	51.96

Source: *Wine Handbook*, Annual 2005, p. 32.

★ 653 ★
Wine
SIC: 2084; NAICS: 31213

Top Wine Companies, 2005

Companies are ranked by sales in millions of cases.

E&J Gallo Winery	75.0
Constellation Brands	54.0
The Wine Group	42.0
Bronco Wine Company	20.0
Foster's Wine Estates	17.0
Trinchero Family Estates	9.3
Brown-Forman Wines	6.4
Diageo Chateau & Estate Wines	5.0
Kendall-Jackson	5.0
Ste. Michelle Wine Estates	4.0
Beam Wine Estates	3.0
Delicato Vineyards	1.6

Source: *Wine Business Monthly*, February 15, 2006, p. NA.

★ 654 ★
Wine
SIC: 2084; NAICS: 31213

Wine Distribution in Chile, 2005

Market shares are shown in percent.

Supermarkets	40.0%
Wholesalers	33.0
Restaurants, bars, hotels	8.0
Other	19.0

Source: "HRI Food Service Sector Annual 2006." [online] from http://www.usatrade.gov.com [Published February 2006] from company interviews.

★ 655 ★
Wine
SIC: 2084; NAICS: 31213

Wine Sales at Supermarkets

Supermarket sales are shown in millions of dollars.

Domestic dry table	$ 2,595.56
Imported dry table	906.55
Sparkling	266.69
Flavored (noncooler)	130.90
Sweet desserted-domestic	43.77
Sangria	27.53

Kosher table	$ 25.61
Vermouth	20.22
Sweet dessert-imported	18.35
Sake	6.31
Aperitifs	1.24

Source: *Progressive Grocer*, September 15, 2005, p. 22, from *Progressive Grocer's 26th Annual Consumer Expenditures Study*.

★ 656 ★
Wine
SIC: 2084; NAICS: 31213

Wine Sales by Price Range

By case volume, the low-priced segment still makes up the majority of wine and champagne sales. The premium category ($7-$9.99) increased 13.8% in sales and 10.4% in case volume. The luxury category ($25-$59) added 20.7% in dollar volume and 17.3% in case volume.

Under $6.99	55.0%
$10-$15	21.9
$7-$9.99	12.7
Other	10.4

Source: *Wine Business Monthly*, December 2005, p. NA, from ACNielsen.

★ 657 ★
Liquor
SIC: 2085; NAICS: 31214

Distilled Spirit Sales

Market shares are shown in percent.

Vodka	26.6%
Rum	12.6
Cordials & liqueurs	12.3
Canadian	9.5
Straights	8.4
Gin	6.6
Brandy & cognac	6.1
Scotch	5.4
Tequila	5.0
Prepared cocktails	4.1
Other	3.5

Source: *Wine & Spirit Industry Marketing*, Annual 2005, p. 10.

★ 658 ★
Liquor
SIC: 2085; NAICS: 31214

Leading Liquor Firms, 2005

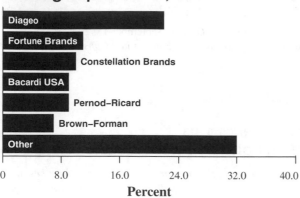

Percent

Market shares are estimated in percent.

Diageo	22.0%
Fortune Brands	11.0
Constellation Brands	10.0
Bacardi USA	9.0
Pernod-Ricard	9.0
Brown-Forman	7.0
Other	32.0

Source: *U.S. Beverages Beverage Bulletin*, Credit Suisse First Boston, January 9, 2006, p. 18, from CS First Boston, Impact Marketing Consultants and *Adams Handbook*.

★ 659 ★
Liquor
SIC: 2085; NAICS: 31214

Leading Liquor Firms in Australia

Market shares are shown in percent.

Constellation	25.0%
Fosters	22.0
Pernod Ricard	14.0
Other	39.0

Source: "Constellation Brands Takeover Bid for Vincor." [online] from http://www.cbrands.com/news/pdf/offer% 20presentation.pdf [Published October 18, 2005] from AC-Nielsen.

★ 660 ★
Liquor
SIC: 2085; NAICS: 31214

Leading Liquor Firms in New Zealand

Market shares are shown in percent.

Pernod Ricard	49.0%
Constellation	12.0

Fosters	7.0%
Other	32.0

Source: "Constellation Brands Takeover Bid for Vincor." [online] from http://www.cbrands.com/news/pdf/offer% 20presentation.pdf [Published October 18, 2005] from AC-Nielsen.

★ 661 ★
Liquor
SIC: 2085; NAICS: 31214

Leading Liquor Firms Worldwide, 2004

Firms are ranked by sales in millions of dollars. From 2002 - 2004 the industry recorded growth over 10%. Whiskey was up 11%, liquers and cordials was up 11%, vodka was up 18% and gin was up 17%. The European Union is a major exporter of spirits. By value it is three times the level of beer. The spirits market grew 40% from 1999 - 2004.

Diageo	$ 16,161.00
Suntory	12,770.70
Allied Domecq	5,823.00
Pernod Ricard	4,407.85
Bacardi	3,300.00
Brown-Forman	2,213.00
Takara Holdings	1,863.80
V&S Vin & Spirit	1,400.80
The Glenmorangie	1,254.00
Remy Cointreau	1,081.30

Source: *just-drinks.com*, March 2006, p. 19.

★ 662 ★
Liquor
SIC: 2085; NAICS: 31214

Liquor Sales Worldwide, 2004-2005

Sales are in millions of dollars. Figures for 2005 are forecast.

	2004	2005	Share
Whiskey	$ 60,900.0	$ 61,764.4	23.46%
White spirits	49,474.8	51,506.8	19.56
Liquers	28,659.7	29,769.8	11.31
Brandy and cognac	25,148.4	25,889.6	9.83
Rum	20,550.6	21,757.5	8.26
Tequila (and mezcal)	8,230.5	8,824.8	3.35
Other spirits	61,190.4	63,797.8	24.23

Source: "Global Spirits Sales." [online] from http://www. stagnito.com/charts2005/3globalhotdrink.htm [Accessed March 23, 2006] from Euromonitor.

★ 663 ★
Liquor
SIC: 2085; NAICS: 31214

Pre-Mixed Drink Market in Australia

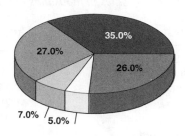

Market shares are shown in percent.

Diageo	.35.0%
Independent	.27.0
Fosters	7.0
Lion Nathan	5.0
Other	.26.0

Source: *International Herald Tribune*, May 30, 2006, p. 16.

★ 664 ★
Liquor
SIC: 2085; NAICS: 31214

Top Bottled Scotch Brands, 2005

Brands are ranked by sales in thousands of 9-liter cases.

Clan MacGregor	715
Scoresby	387
Cluny	285
Inver House	218
Old Smuggler	193

Source: *Beverage Dynamics*, March - April 2006, p. 52, from Adams Beverage Group Database.

★ 665 ★
Liquor
SIC: 2085; NAICS: 31214

Top Bottled Scotch Brands (Foreign), 2005

Brands are ranked by sales in thousands of 9-liter cases.

Dewar's	1,375
Johnnie Walker Black	730
Johnnie Walker Red	675

Chivas Regal	484
J&B	355

Source: *Beverage Dynamics*, March - April 2006, p. 52, from Adams Beverage Group Database.

★ 666 ★
Liquor
SIC: 2085; NAICS: 31214

Top Champagne Brands, 2004

Market shares are shown based on 1.69 million cases sold.

Moet & Chandon	.37.0%
Veuve Clicquot	.18.0
Perrier-Jouet	6.0
Mumm	5.0
Piper Heidsieck	4.0
Other	.30.0

Source: *Beverages: Champagne Play Premium Brands and Solid Financials*, Societe Generale, April 2006 from Societe Generale Cross Asset Research.

★ 667 ★
Liquor
SIC: 2085; NAICS: 31214

Top Champagne Groups Worldwide, 2005

Market shares are shown based on cases sold. By brand Moet & Chandon led the market with a 10.6% share (in 2004). Veuve Clicquot followed with a 4.9% share.

Moet-Hennessy	.17.0%
Marne et Champagne	7.8
Vranken	5.8
Laurent-Perrier	4.1
Remy-Cointreau	3.3
GH Martel	2.6
Cooperatif Alliance Champagne	2.4
Other	.56.9

Source: *Beverages: Champagne Play Premium Brands and Solid Financials*, Societe Generale, April 2006 from Societe Generale Cross Asset Research.

★ 668 ★

Liquor

SIC: 2085; NAICS: 31214

Top Champagne/Sparkling Wine Brands, 2004

Brands are ranked by sales in thousands of 9-liter cases.

	(000)	Share
Andre/Wycliff	2,000	24.10%
Cook's	1,435	17.29
Korbel	1,194	14.39
J. Roget	601	7.24
Ballatore	600	7.23
Domaine Chardon	314	3.78
Domaine Ste. Michelle	247	2.98
Mumm Cuvee Napa	155	1.87
Tott's	155	1.87
Gloria Ferrer	113	1.36
Other	1,486	17.90

Source: *Wine Handbook*, Annual 2005, p. 32.

★ 669 ★

Liquor

SIC: 2085; NAICS: 31214

Top Cordial/Liquer Brands, 2004

Brands are ranked by sales in thousands of 9-liter cases.

	(000)	Share
DeKuyper	2,790	13.84%
Jagermeister	1,800	8.93
Southern Comfort	1,393	6.91
Kahlua	1,310	6.50
Baileys	1,285	6.38
Hiram Walker Cordials	1,060	5.26
Hpnotiq	630	3.13
Alize	530	2.63
Other	9,357	46.43

Source: *Beverage Dynamics*, September - October 2005, p. 21, from Adams Beverage Group.

★ 670 ★

Liquor

SIC: 2085; NAICS: 31214

Top Liquer Brands, 2005

Brands are ranked by sales in thousands of 9-liter cases.

	(000)	Share
DeKuyper	2,779	13.41%
Jagermeister	2,300	11.10
Southern Comfort	1,448	6.99
Baileys	1,283	6.19
Kahlua	1,255	6.06
Hiram Walker Cordials	1,015	4.90
Hpnotiq	600	2.90
Grand Marnier	547	2.64
Other	9,498	45.83

Source: *Beverage Dynamics*, May - June 2006, p. 36, from Adams Beverage Group.

★ 671 ★

Liquor

SIC: 2085; NAICS: 31214

Top Non-Alcohol/Cider Brands, 2004

Brands are ranked by sales in thousands of 2.25 gallon cases.

	(000)	Share
O'Doul's	8,300	48.65%
Sharp's NA	1,600	9.38
Busch	1,500	8.79
Old Milwaukee	1,500	8.79
Malta Goya	800	4.69
Coors	545	3.19
Other	2,815	16.50

Source: *Beer Handbook*, Annual 2005, p. 50.

★ 672 ★

Liquor

SIC: 2085; NAICS: 31214

Top Rum Brands

Brands are ranked by sales in thousands of 9-liter cases.

	(000)	Share
Bacardi	8,450	41.00%
Captain Morgan	4,759	23.09

Continued on next page.

★ 672 ★

[Continued]

Liquor

SIC: 2085; NAICS: 31214

Top Rum Brands

Brands are ranked by sales in thousands of 9-liter cases.

	(000)	Share
Malibu	1,300	6.31%
Castillo	1,200	5.82
Ronrico	535	2.60
Cruzan Rum	435	2.11
Myer's	300	1.46
Barton Rum	195	0.95
Monarch Rum	178	0.86
Other	3,258	15.81

Source: *Beverage Dynamics*, July - August 2005, p. 40.

★ 673 ★

Liquor

SIC: 2085; NAICS: 31214

Top Tequila Brands, 2005

Brands are ranked by sales in thousands of 9-liter cases.

	(000)	Share
Jose Cuervo	3,558	39.53%
Sauza	1,350	15.00
Patron	615	6.83
Montezuma Tequila	567	6.30
Juarez Luxco	440	4.89
1800	395	4.39
Margaritaville	220	2.44
House of Cazadores	215	2.39
El Jimador	160	1.78
Rio Grande Tequila	149	1.66
Other	1,331	14.79

Source: *Beverage Dynamics*, March - April 2006, p. 52, from Adams Beverage Group Database.

★ 674 ★

Liquor

SIC: 2085; NAICS: 31214

Top Vodka Brands, 2005

Brands are ranked by sales in thousands of 9-liter cases.

	(000)	Share
Smirnoff	8,149	17.63%
Absolut	4,636	10.03
Grey Goose	2,075	4.49
Skyy	2,065	4.47
Stolichnaya	1,985	4.29
McCormick Vodka	1,900	4.11
Popov Vodka	1,780	3.85
Ketel One	1,593	3.45
Barton Vodka	1,546	3.34
Other	20,492	44.33

Source: *Beverage Dynamics*, May - June 2006, p. 14, from Adams Beverage Group.

★ 675 ★

Liquor

SIC: 2085; NAICS: 31213

Top Vodka Brands in Poland

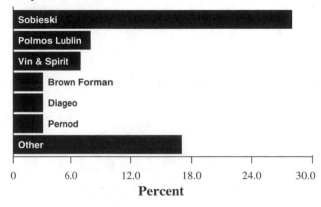

Market shares are shown in percent.

Sobieski	28.0%
Polmos Lublin	8.0
Vin & Spirit	7.0
Brown Forman	3.0
Diageo	3.0
Pernod	3.0
Other	17.0

Source: *EDGAR Online 8-K Glimpse*, May 19, 2006, p. NA, from ACNielsen.

★ 676 ★

Liquor
SIC: 2085; NAICS: 31214

Top Vodka Brands Worldwide

Market shares are shown in percent.

Smirnoff	5.0%
Absolut	2.0
Other	93.0

Source: *Business Week Online*, January 17, 2006, p. NA, from Euromonitor.

★ 677 ★

Bottled Water
SIC: 2086; NAICS: 312112

Bottled Water Market in Jordan

Market shares are shown in percent.

Nestle	48.0%
Marwa	12.4
Atheb	6.2
Hada	3.0
Other	30.4

Source: *just-drinks.com (Management Briefing)*, February 2006, p. 16, from ACNielsen.

★ 678 ★

Bottled Water
SIC: 2086; NAICS: 312112

Bottled Water Market in Thailand

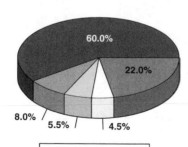

Market shares are shown in percent.

Singha	60.0%
Crystal	8.0
Namthip	5.5
Siam	4.5
Other	22.0

Source: "Thailand Product Brief Non-Alcoholic Beverage Report 2005." [online] from http://www.usatrade.gov [Published November 2005].

★ 679 ★

Bottled Water
SIC: 2086; NAICS: 312112

Bottled Water Sales, 2004 - 2005

The total market is forecast to grow from $9.16 billion in 2004 to $10.01 billion in 2005. PET stands for poly-ethylene terephthalate.

	2004	2005
PET	58.0%	61.2%
Direct delivery	17.9	16.7
1-2.5 gallon	9.0	8.3
Imports	8.6	7.2
Domestic sparkling	4.3	4.5
Vending	2.1	2.0

Source: *Beverage World*, April 15, 2006, p. 47, from Beverage Marketing Corporation.

★ 680 ★

Bottled Water
SIC: 2086; NAICS: 312112

Global Bottled Water Sales, 2004

Sales are shown in millions of dollars.

	($ mil.)	Share
Still	$ 73,958.5	68.18%
Carbonated	28,438.9	26.22
Flavored	3,075.9	2.84
Functional	2,997.4	2.76

Source: *Beverage Industry*, July 2005, p. 20, from Euromonitor.

★ 681 ★

Bottled Water
SIC: 2086; NAICS: 312112

Largest Bottled Water Markets, 2005

Market shares are shown in percent.

United States	17.1%
Mexico	11.5
China (incl. Taiwan)	7.8
Brazil	7.4
Italy	6.8
Germany	6.4
France	5.1
Indonesia	4.6
India	3.8
Spain	3.6
Other	25.9

Source: *Beverage World*, April 15, 2006, p. 51, from Beverage Marketing Corporation.

★ 682 ★
Bottled Water
SIC: 2086; NAICS: 312112

Top Bottled Water Brands (PET), 2006

Market shares are shown based on supermarket, drug store and mass merchandiser sales (excluding Wal-Mart). PET stands for polyethylene terephthalate.

Aquafina	.14.5%
Dasani	.11.8
Poland Spring	6.8
Propel	6.3
Dannon	5.4
Arrowhead	4.9
Deer Park	3.7
Crystal Geyser	2.8
Ozarka	2.7
Private label	.13.2
Other	.27.9

Source: *Beverage World*, April 2006, p. 41, from Beverage Marketing Corporation.

★ 683 ★
Bottled Water
SIC: 2086; NAICS: 312112

Top Convenience/Still Water Makers, 2006

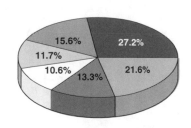

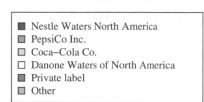

■ Nestle Waters North America
■ PepsiCo Inc.
□ Coca–Cola Co.
□ Danone Waters of North America
■ Private label
■ Other

Market shares are shown based on supermarket, drug store and mass merchandiser sales (excluding Wal-Mart) for the 52 weeks ended January 26, 2006.

Nestle Waters North America	.27.2%
PepsiCo Inc.	.15.6
Coca-Cola Co.	.11.7
Danone Waters of North America	.10.6
Private label	.13.3
Other	.21.6

Source: *Grocery Headquarters*, April 2006, p. 56, from Information Resources Inc.

★ 684 ★
Bottled Water
SIC: 2086; NAICS: 312112

Top Jug/Bulk Still Water Brands, 2006

Market shares are shown based on supermarket, drug store and mass merchandiser sales (excluding Wal-Mart).

Poland Spring	8.3%
Arrowhead	7.8
Crystal Geyser	4.5
Deer Park	4.1
Zephyrhills	3.9
Ozarka	3.2
Sparkletts	2.7
Ice Mountain	2.2
Nursery	1.9
Private label	.42.7
Other	.18.7

Source: *Beverage World*, April 15, 2006, p. 41, from Beverage Marketing Corporation.

★ 685 ★
Bottled Water
SIC: 2086; NAICS: 312112

Top Seltzer/Tonic Water/Club Brands, 2005

Convenience store sales are shown in thousands of dollars for the 52 weeks ended March 20, 2005.

	($ 000)	Share
Canada Dry	$ 8,067.8	38.33%
Schweppes	6,028.3	28.64
Polar	1,966.1	9.34
Seagrams	1,939.3	9.21
Ritz	880.7	4.18
Canada Dry Seltzer	779.0	3.70
Diet Schweppes	504.0	2.39
White Rock	286.7	1.36
Other	598.9	2.85

Source: *Convenience Store Decisions*, July 2005, p. 28, from Information Resources Inc.

★ 686 ★
Energy Drinks
SIC: 2086; NAICS: 312111

Energy Drink Market in Thailand

Market shares are shown in percent.

TC Pharma 54.0%
Osotspa 34.0
Carabao Dang 12.0

Source: "Thailand Product Brief Non-Alcoholic Beverage Report 2005." [online] from http://www.usatrade.gov [Published November 2005].

★ 687 ★
Energy Drinks
SIC: 2086; NAICS: 312111

Energy Drink Sales by Country, 2004, 2006 and 2008

Sales in selected markets are shown based on off-trade volume sales. Market research firm Canadean estimates the global market will exceed 11 billion liters at the end of 2005.

	2004	2006
United States	$ 1,100.0	$ 1,250.0
United Kingdom	274.9	352.6
China	114.4	131.4
France	28.2	26.0
Canada	6.4	7.0

Source: *just-drinks.com*, December 2005, p. 22, from *just-drinks.com* estimates.

★ 688 ★
Energy Drinks
SIC: 2086; NAICS: 312111

Energy Drink Sales Worldwide, 2000-2004

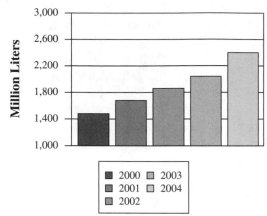

Energy drinks make up a small section of the soft drink market, but are a large contributor to growth. Red Bull is the market leader but other companies are jumping into the market with ginseng and green tea additives to help boost energy. Data are in millions of liters.

2000 1,470
2001 1,680
2002 1,860
2003 2,050
2004 2,410

Source: *International Food Ingredients*, February - March 2006, p. 14, from Zenith International.

★ 689 ★
Energy Drinks
SIC: 2086; NAICS: 312111

Top Energy Drinks, 2005

Market shares are shown based on supermarket, drug store and mass merchandiser sales (excluding Wal-Mart) for the 52 weeks ended June 12, 2005.

Red Bull 57.7%
Rockstar 9.1
Monster Energy 7.8
Sobe Adrenaline Rush 5.5
AMP 5.1
SoBe No Fear 4.0
Full Throttle 2.7
Hansen's Energy 0.7
Hansen's Lost Energy 0.7
Other 6.7

Source: *Beverage Industry*, July 2005, p. 20, from Information Resources Inc.

★ 690 ★
Soft Drinks
SIC: 2086; NAICS: 312111

Carbonated Drink Market in Mexico

Market shares are shown in percent.

Coca-Cola 70.0%
Other 30.0

Source: *Food/Agribusiness Beverages Tobacco*, Prudential Equity Group Research, March 8, 2005, p. 31, from Prudential Equity Group and LLC estimates.

★ 691 ★
Soft Drinks
SIC: 2086; NAICS: 312111

Carbonated Drink Market in Philippines

Market shares are shown in percent.

Coca-Cola 85.0%
Other 15.0

Source: *Food/Agribusiness Beverages Tobacco*, Prudential Equity Group Research, March 8, 2005, p. 31, from Prudential Equity Group and LLC estimates.

★ 692 ★
Soft Drinks
SIC: 2086; NAICS: 312111

Flavored Carbonated Drink Market in Thailand

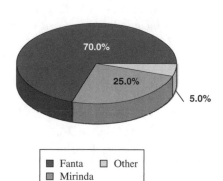

| ■ Fanta | □ Other |
| ■ Mirinda | |

Market shares are shown in percent.

Fanta 70.0%
Mirinda 25.0
Other 5.0

Source: "Thailand Product Brief Non-Alcoholic Beverage Report 2005." [online] from http://www.usatrade.gov [Published November 2005].

★ 693 ★
Soft Drinks
SIC: 2086; NAICS: 312111

Health Drink Market in India

Market shares are shown in percent.

GSK Consumer Healthcare 70.0%
Other 30.0

Source: *The Economic Times*, February 7, 2006, p. NA.

★ 694 ★
Soft Drinks
SIC: 2086; NAICS: 312111

Leading Bottlers in Peru, 2004

Market shares are shown in percent.

J.R. Lindley ELSA 70.0%
AjeGroup 19.0
AmBev Peru 8.0
Other 3.0

Source: "Food Processing and Packaging Equipment." [online] from http://www. buyusainfo.net [Published February 2006] from *2004 Banco Wiese Sector Report*.

★ 695 ★
Soft Drinks
SIC: 2086; NAICS: 312111

Leading Soft Drink Firms in Chile, 2005

Non-alcoholic beverages represent the third largest food and beverage category in the country. The industry is valued at $1.05 billion.

Coca-Cola 65.6%
Ecusa (CCU-Pepsi) 21.5
Other 12.9

Source: "Chile Food Processing Ingredients Sector Annual Report 2006." [online] from http://www.usatrade.gov.com [Published February 2006] from Chilean Milk Producers Association.

★ 696 ★
Soft Drinks
SIC: 2086; NAICS: 312111

New Age Beverage Sales, 2004

Shares are shown based on $16,463.2 million in whole-sale sales. Pet stands for polyethylene terephthalate. RTD stands for ready-to-drink.

Retail PET waters 34.7%
Sports beverages 18.5
Single-serve fruit beverages 15.2
RTD tea 9.1
Energy drinks 6.0
Enhanced water 2.6
Other 13.9

Source: *Beverage World*, January 15, 2006, p. 16, from Beverage Marketing Corporation.

★ 697 ★
Soft Drinks
SIC: 2086; NAICS: 312111

Soft Drink Market in Jordan, 2004

The market was worth $115 million in 2004.

Pepsi 77.0%
Coca-Cola 22.0
Other 1.0

Source: *just-drinks.com (Management Briefing)*, February 2006, p. 16.

★ 698 ★
Soft Drinks
SIC: 2086; NAICS: 312111

Soft Drink Market in Libya

The company is a Pepsi franchise.

One Nine Trading International 75.0%
Other 25.0

Source: *just-drinks.com (Management Briefing)*, February 2006, p. 11.

★ 699 ★
Soft Drinks
SIC: 2086; NAICS: 312111

Soft Drink Market in Syria

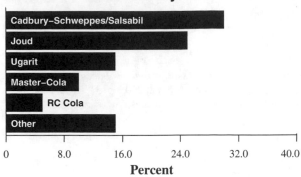

Joud Company is run by Pepsi and takes 20-25% of the market.

Cadbury-Schweppes/Salsabil 30.0%
Joud 25.0
Ugarit 15.0
Master-Cola 10.0
RC Cola 5.0
Other 15.0

Source: *just-drinks.com (Management Briefing)*, February 2006, p. 11.

★ 700 ★
Soft Drinks
SIC: 2086; NAICS: 312111

Soft Drink Sales, 2005

Data are based on a total of 28,882 million gallons. Top trademarks include Pepsico, Coca-Cola and Dr. Pepper/Seven Up.

	(mil.)	Share
Carbonated soft drinks	15,271.6	52.87%
Bottled water	7,537.2	26.10
Fruit beverages	4,119.0	14.26
Sports drinks	1,207.5	4.18
Ready-to-drink tea	555.9	1.92
Energy drinks	152.5	0.53
Ready-to-drink coffee	38.9	0.13

Source: *Research Alert*, May 5, 2006, p. 3, from Beverage Marketing Corporation.

★ 701 ★
Soft Drinks
SIC: 2086; NAICS: 312111
Soft Drink Sales Worldwide, 2004

Distribution is shown based on 480 billion liters.

North America	25.0%
Asia/Australasia	22.0
Latin America	19.0
Africa Middle East	8.0
Eastern Europe	6.0
Western Europe	6.0
Other	14.0

Source: *International Food Ingredients*, February - March 2006, p. 14, from globaldrinks.com.

★ 702 ★
Soft Drinks
SIC: 2086; NAICS: 312111
Top Diet Soft Drinks, 2006

Market shares are shown based on 4,749.7 million cases.

	Market Share	Diet Share
Diet Coke	9.9%	31.8%
Diet Pepsi	5.8	18.5
Caffeine-Free Diet Coke	1.6	5.1
Diet Dr. Pepper	1.4	4.4
Diet Mountain Dew	1.3	4.3
Caffeine Free Diet Pepsi	1.0	3.1
Diet Sprite	0.6	2.0
Diet 7Up	0.4	1.3
Coke Zero	0.3	1.0
Fresca	0.2	1.1

Source: *Beverage World*, April 2006, p. 41, from Beverage Marketing Corporation.

★ 703 ★
Soft Drinks
SIC: 2086; NAICS: 312111
Top Functional Drink Brands in Japan, 2004

The sports drink market may reach $3.5 billion by 2010. Market shares are shown based on off-trade volume sales.

Pocari Sweat	33.0%
Aquarius	26.0
Liptovitan	10.0
Dakara	8.0
Oronamin C	5.0
Other	18.0

Source: *just-drinks.com*, December 2005, p. 22, from *just-drinks.com* estimates.

★ 704 ★
Soft Drinks
SIC: 2086; NAICS: 312111
Top Ready-to-Drink Tea Brands, 2005

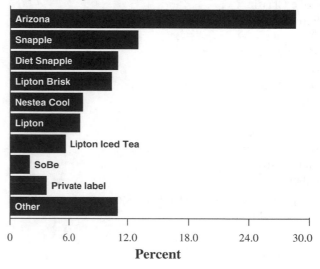

Market shares are shown based on sales at supermarkets, drug stores and mass merchandisers (excluding Wal-Mart) for the 52 weeks ended December 25, 2005.

Arizona	28.6%
Snapple	13.0
Diet Snapple	11.0
Lipton Brisk	10.4
Nestea Cool	7.5
Lipton	7.2
Lipton Iced Tea	5.6
SoBe	2.0

Continued on next page.

★ 704 ★

[Continued]
Soft Drinks
SIC: 2086; NAICS: 312111

Top Ready-to-Drink Tea Brands, 2005

Market shares are shown based on sales at supermarkets, drug stores and mass merchandisers (excluding Wal-Mart) for the 52 weeks ended December 25, 2005.

Private label	3.7%
Other	11.0

Source: *Beverage Industry*, February 2006, p. 14, from Information Resources Inc.

★ 705 ★

Soft Drinks
SIC: 2086; NAICS: 312111

Top Soft Drink (Carbonated) Brands, 2005

Market shares are shown based on 10,223.6 million cases.

Coke Classic	17.6%
Pepsi-Cola	11.2
Diet Coke	9.8
Mountain Dew	6.5
Diet Pepsi	6.0
Dr. Pepper	5.7
Sprite	5.7
Fanta	1.6
CF Diet Coke	1.5
Diet Mountain Dew	1.4
Sierra Mist	1.4
Other	31.6

Source: *Beverage Digest*, March 8, 2006, p. NA, from Beverage Digest/Maxwell.

★ 706 ★

Soft Drinks
SIC: 2086; NAICS: 312111

Top Soft Drink (Carbonated) Firms, 2005

Market shares are shown based on 10,223.6 million cases. In 2005, the carbonated soft drink industry posted an all-channel volume decline of 0.2%. This is the first decline since Beverage Digest/Maxwell began tracing the industry in 1985. The decline would have been worse (0.7%) were it not for the performance of energy drinks.

Coca-Cola Co.	43.1%
Pepsi-Cola Co.	31.4
Cadbury Schweppes	14.6
Cott Corp.	5.4
National Beverage	2.4
Big Red	0.4
Red Bull	0.4
Hansen Natural	0.3
Rockstar	0.2
Monarch Co.	0.1
Other	1.7

Source: *Beverage Digest*, March 8, 2006, p. NA, from Beverage Digest/Maxwell.

★ 707 ★

Soft Drinks
SIC: 2086; NAICS: 312111

Top Soft Drink Firms in Japan, 2004

Market shares are shown based on domestic sales of 1,670 million cases.

Coca-Cola	30.7%
Suntory	18.9
Kirin Beverage	10.6
Ito En	7.4
Asahi Soft Drinks	6.4
Other	26.0

Source: "2004 Market Share Report." [online] from http://www.nikkei.co.jp [Published July 27, 2005] from Nikkei estimates.

★ 708 ★
Soft Drinks
SIC: 2086; NAICS: 312111

Top Soft Drink/Juice Makers in Western Europe

The top companies are ranked by market share. Data refer to products sold for human consumption in retail, catering and artisanal markets. Germany took 26% of the market, followed by United Kingdom with 24% and Italy 11%.

Coca-Cola	.21.1%
PepsiCo.	. 7.1
Nestle	. 5.0
Cadbury Schweppes	. 3.9
Danone	. 3.5
Britvic	. 2.5
Eckes	. 2.1
GSK	. 1.9
Cott	. 1.7
Other	.51.2

Source: "Soft Drinks and Juice Markets." [online] from http://www.fft.com [Published November 2004] from Food for Thought.

★ 709 ★
Sports Drinks
SIC: 2086; NAICS: 312111

Sports Drink Sales Worldwide, 2005

The global sports drinks market raced ahead by 10% in 2005 to 9,700 million. Markets in Eastern Europe and the Middle East increased 17% and 19% respectively. Japan and China represent the bulk of Asia-Pacific sales.

North America	.49.0%
Asia Pacific	.38.0
Other	.13.0

Source: *M2 Presswire*, February 27, 2006, p. NA, from Zenith International.

★ 710 ★
Sports Drinks
SIC: 2086; NAICS: 312111

Top Energy/Sports Drink Brands in China, 2004

Market shares are shown based on off-trade volume sales.

Jianlibao	.40.0%
Gatorade	.11.0
Red Bull	.10.0
Suntory	. 4.0
Kirin	. 2.0
Other	.33.0

Source: *just-drinks.com*, December 2005, p. 22, from *just-drinks.com* estimates.

★ 711 ★
Sports Drinks
SIC: 2086; NAICS: 312111

Top Energy/Sports Drink Brands in France, 2004

Market shares are shown based on off-trade volume sales. By 2010, the energy drinks market will be valued at 33 million euros and the sports drinks market will be valued at 13.9 million euros.

Hype	.26.0%
Dark Dog	.22.0
Black Booster	.14.0
Extreme Energy	.13.0
Isostar	.10.0
Other	.15.0

Source: *just-drinks.com*, December 2005, p. 22, from *just-drinks.com* estimates.

★ 712 ★
Sports Drinks
SIC: 2086; NAICS: 312111

Top Sports Drink Brands, 2006

Market shares are shown based on supermarket, drug store and mass merchandiser sales (excluding Wal-Mart).

Gatorade	.49.0%
Powerade	.14.4
Gatorade Frost	. 9.9
Gatorade Fierce	. 7.7
Gatorade X Factor	. 7.0
Gatorade All Stars	. 6.6

Continued on next page.

★ 712 ★

[Continued]
Sports Drinks
SIC: 2086; NAICS: 312111

Top Sports Drink Brands, 2006

Market shares are shown based on supermarket, drug store and mass merchandiser sales (excluding Wal-Mart).

Gatorade Xtremo	1.7%
Gatorade Ice	1.4
Gatorade Endurance	1.0
Private label	0.5
Other	0.8

Source: *Beverage World*, April 2006, p. 41, from Beverage Marketing Corporation.

★ 713 ★

Sports Drinks
SIC: 2086; NAICS: 312111

Top Sports Drink Brands in Canada, 2004

Market shares are shown based on off-trade volume sales.

Gatorade	75.0%
Powerade	20.0
All Sport	3.0
Other	2.0

Source: *just-drinks.com*, December 2005, p. 22, from *just-drinks.com* estimates.

★ 714 ★

Flavoring Syrups
SIC: 2087; NAICS: 31193

Leading Flavoring Syrup Makers, 2004

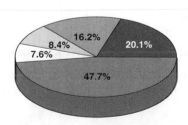

- Archer Daniels Midland
- Cargill
- Tate & Lyle
- Corn Products International
- Other

Market shares are shown in percent.

Archer Daniels Midland	20.1%
Cargill	16.2

Tate & Lyle	8.4%
Corn Products International	7.6
Other	47.7

Source: "Flavoring Syrup and Concentrate in the U.S." [online] from http://www.ibisworld.com [Published March 31, 2006] from IBISWorld.

★ 715 ★

Seafood
SIC: 2091; NAICS: 311711

Salmon Consumption in France

Household consumption of 41,000 metric tons for a value of 565.8 million euros.

Smoked	54.0%
Fresh cut	27.0
Frozen cut	9.0
Fresh prepacked	7.0
Fresh whole	3.0

Source: "Fishery Products Annual 2005." [online] from http://www.ffas.usda.gov [Published October 3, 2005] from OFIMER and SECODIP.

★ 716 ★

Seafood
SIC: 2091; NAICS: 311711

Top Canned Tuna Brands, 2005

Brands are ranked by sales at supermarkets, drug stores and mass merchandisers (excluding Wal-Mart) for the 52 weeks ended September 4, 2005.

	($ mil.)	Share
StarKist	$ 349.39	34.77%
Bumble Bee	302.95	30.15
Chicken of the Sea	157.86	15.71
StarKist Tuna Creations	22.07	2.20
Three Diamond	16.19	1.61
Geisha	13.80	1.37
StarKist Charles Lunch Kit	11.20	1.11
StarKist Lunch to Go	4.80	0.48
Genova Tonno	3.26	0.32
Private label	97.19	9.67
Other	26.15	2.60

Source: *Corporate Profiles & Industry Statistics - Milling & Baking News Supplement*, November 2005, p. 130, from Information Resources Inc.

★ 717 ★
Seafood
SIC: 2091; NAICS: 311711
Top Seafood Brands, 2006

Brands are ranked by sales for the 12 weeks ended January 22, 2006.

	Sales	Share
Sail	$ 39,992,644	9.45%
Aqua Star	14,951,254	3.53
Tastee Choice	11,232,776	2.65
Seamazz	8,764,945	2.07
Contessa	6,260,278	1.48
Censea	5,323,336	1.26
Singleton	4,675,982	1.10
Northern Chef	3,332,849	0.79
Private label	143,795,936	33.98
Other	184,845,680	43.68

Source: *Frozen Food Age*, February 2006, p. 12, from Information Resources Inc.

★ 718 ★
Seafood
SIC: 2092; NAICS: 311712
Fresh Seafood Sales, 2005

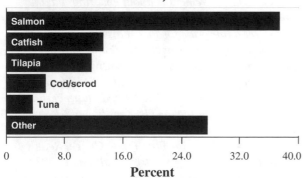

Total seafood department sales per week per store averaged $4,993 in 2005, up 7.4% from 2004, according to ACNielsen.

Salmon	37.4%
Catfish	13.3
Tilapia	11.7
Cod/scrod	5.4
Tuna	3.6
Other	27.6

Source: *Progressive Grocer*, April 15, 2006, p. 98, from Perishables Group and ACNielsen.

★ 719 ★
Seafood
SIC: 2092; NAICS: 311712
Leading Seafood Processors in Denmark, 2005

Market shares are shown in percent.

Royal Greenland	16.8%
Gilde Buy-Out Fund	16.6
Aker RGI	14.8
Orkla	10.5
Sorensen	3.2
Investor/EQT	2.7
Dat-Schaub	2.4
Other	33.0

Source: "National Report Denmark." [online] from http://foodqualityschemes.jrc.es/en/documents/NationalreportFR_000.pdf [Published November 2005] from Food for Thought.

★ 720 ★
Seafood
SIC: 2092; NAICS: 311712
Leading Seafood Suppliers in North America, 2005

Firms are ranked by sales in millions of dollars.

Pacific Seafood Group	$ 874
Red Chamber Co.	828
Trident Seafoods Corp.	800
Connor Bros. (Bumble Bee Foods)	714
Thai Union International (Chicken of the Sea)	708
Tri Marine	700
Fishery Products International	688
Nippon Suisan	630

Source: *Seafood Business*, May 2006, p. 1.

★ 721 ★
Seafood
SIC: 2092; NAICS: 311712
Top Frozen Seafood Brands, 2006

Market shares are shown based on food store, drug store and mass merchandiser sales (excluding Wal-Mart) for the 52 weeks ended January 26, 2006.

Gorton's	22.2%
Van de Kamp's	9.5
Mrs. Paul's	5.0
Gorton's Grilled Fillets	2.9
Great Fish Company	2.8
Sea Best	2.1

Continued on next page.

★ 721 ★
[Continued]
Seafood
SIC: 2092; NAICS: 311712

Top Frozen Seafood Brands, 2006

Market shares are shown based on food store, drug store and mass merchandiser sales (excluding Wal-Mart) for the 52 weeks ended January 26, 2006.

Aqua Star	1.9%
Phillips	1.6
Mrs. Paul's Select Cuts	1.5
Private label	19.9
Other	30.6

Source: *Grocery Headquarters*, April 2006, p. 56, from Information Resources Inc.

★ 722 ★
Seafood
SIC: 2092; NAICS: 311712

Top Frozen Seafood Makers, 2006

Market shares are shown based on food store, drug store and mass merchandiser sales (excluding Wal-Mart) for the 52 weeks ended January 26, 2006.

Gorton's Corp.	25.4%
Pinnacle Foods Corp.	16.8
Colorado Boxed Beef Co.	2.8
Sea-Est Inc.	2.1
Private label	19.9
Other	33.0

Source: *Grocery Headquarters*, April 2006, p. 56, from Information Resources Inc.

★ 723 ★
Coffee
SIC: 2095; NAICS: 31192

Coffee Market in Germany

Coffee was the most consumed beverage in the country in 2004, with 151 litres per head, compared to water (123) and beer (114).

Roasted caffeinated	52.0%
Mildly treated varieties	20.0
Natural milds	18.0
Roasted decaf	10.0

Source: *Tea & Coffee Trade Journal*, November 20, 2005, p. 60.

★ 724 ★
Coffee
SIC: 2095; NAICS: 31192

Coffee Sales by Type, 2005

More than half (50.5%) of all adults used ground coffee in their homes in 2005, up from 47.9% in 2003. Supermarkets account for 56.6% of retail sales of packaged coffee, followed by mass merchants with 15.7% and club stores with 6.7%.

Ground	60.7%
Instant	11.6
Whole bean	9.9
Ready-to-drink packaged coffee beverages	8.8
Specialty instant coffee mix	4.5
Filter packs	2.4
Pods and bags	2.4

Source: *Research Alert*, February 17, 2006, p. 8, from Packaged Facts.

★ 725 ★
Coffee
SIC: 2095; NAICS: 31192

Fair Trade Coffee Market, 2002-2004

The Fair Trade movement is about ensuring that the majority of the world's coffee farmers (who are small holders) get a fair price for their harvests in order to achieve a decent living wage. Fair Trade guarantees to poor farmers organized in cooperatives around the world a living wage (minimum price of $1.26/pound regardless of market prices). The United States certifies 31% of all coffee worldwide (18.3 million of 61.3 million pounds). It recently surpassed the Netherlands as the largest destination for Fair Trade Coffee. Retail value of Fair Trade Coffee: $109.6 million in 2002, $208.1 million in 2003 and $369 million in 2003. Market shares show Fair Trade's percent of sales of each category.

	2002	2003
Specialty	1.3%	2.3%
All coffee	0.6	1.0

Source: "2005 Fair Trade Coffee Facts and Figures." [online] from http://www.transfairusa.org [Published July 13, 2005].

★ 726 ★
Coffee
SIC: 2095; NAICS: 31192

Foodservice Sales of Coffee, 2005

Foodservice takes 87.9% of the $34.5 billion spent each year on coffee. In foodservice, restaurants took the top share of sales, followed by coffee houses that have seating (20.1%), convenience stores (17%) and office coffee services (11.7%).

Regular, brewed	$ 50.5
Specialty, brewed	42.4
Instant cappuccino	3.6
Regular, made from liquid concentrate	3.3
Ready-to-drink packaged coffee beverages	0.2

Source: *Research Alert*, February 17, 2006, p. 8, from Packaged Facts.

★ 727 ★
Coffee
SIC: 2095; NAICS: 31192

Largest Coffee Consumers Worldwide

Market shares are shown in percent.

United States	17.8%
Germany	8.3
Japan	6.3
Italy	4.8
France	4.4
Other	58.4

Source: *US Food Industry*, North American Equity Research, March 29, 2005, p. 3, from International Cocoa Organization and JPMorgan estimates.

★ 728 ★
Coffee
SIC: 2095; NAICS: 31192

Soluble Coffee Market in Vietnam

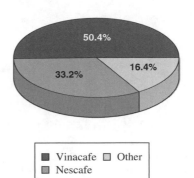

While only a few companies dominate the industry there are more than 20 brands on the market.

Vinacafe	50.4%
Nescafe	33.2
Other	16.4

Source: *FWN Financial News*, May 24, 2006, p. NA.

★ 729 ★
Coffee
SIC: 2095; NAICS: 31192

Top Coffee Brands, 2005

Brands are ranked by sales at supermarkets, drug stores and mass merchandisers (excluding Wal-Mart) for the 52 weeks ended September 4, 2005.

	($ mil.)	Share
Folgers Ground	$ 398.7	14.14%
Maxwell House Ground	255.5	9.06
Starbucks Ground	168.1	5.96
Folgers Ground House Ground	99.5	3.53
Folgers Instant	91.3	3.24
Starbucks Whole Beans	90.4	3.21
Maxwell House Master Blend Ground	80.1	2.84
Eight O'Clock Whole Beans	77.9	2.76
General Foods Intl. Instant	77.4	2.74
Folgers Decaffeinated Ground	71.1	2.52
Private label	132.4	4.70
Other	1,277.6	45.30

Source: *MMR*, December 12, 2005, p. 37, from Information Resources Inc.

★ 730 ★
Coffee
SIC: 2095; NAICS: 31192
Top Ground Coffee Makers, 2006

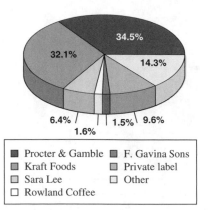

Market shares are shown based on food store, drug store and mass merchandiser sales (excluding Wal-Mart) for the 52 weeks ended January 2006.

Procter & Gamble	.34.5%
Kraft Foods	.32.1
Sara Lee	6.4
Rowland Coffee	1.6
F. Gavina Sons	1.5
Private label	9.6
Other	.14.3

Source: *US Food Industry*, North American Equity Research, January 17, 2006, p. 100, from ACNielsen and JPMorgan.

★ 731 ★
Coffee Drinks
SIC: 2095; NAICS: 31192
Leading Coffee Drink Brands, 2005

Brands are ranked by sales in millions of dollars for the 52 weeks ended October 30, 2005. Folgers Jakada had 48% of the market.

Folgers Jakada	$ 1,174.0
Arizona	500.0
Autocrat	497.0
Upstate Farms	368.0
Royal Kona	236.0
Starbucks	136.0
Havana	28.0
Mr. Brown	23.0
XTZ Kaffe	9.7
Ito EN	6.7

Source: *Dairy Foods*, January 2006, p. 50, from Information Resources Inc.

★ 732 ★
Coffee Drinks
SIC: 2095; NAICS: 31192
Top Ready-to-Drink Coffee Drinks, 2005

Market shares are shown based on sales at supermarkets, drug stores and mass merchandisers (excluding Wal-Mart) for the 52 weeks ended December 25, 2005.

Frappuccino	.82.8%
Starbucks Doubleshot	.12.8
Wolfgang Puck	2.6
Starbucks	0.8
Kahlua	0.4
Havana	0.2
Caffe D Vita	0.1
Main St. Café	0.1
Mr. Brown	0.1
Royal Kona	0.1

Source: *Beverage Industry*, February 2006, p. 14, from Information Resources Inc.

★ 733 ★
Snacks
SIC: 2096; NAICS: 311919
Healthy Snack Market, 2004

Healthy snack sales were $14.6 billion based on sales at supermarkets, drug stores and mass merchandisers.

Crackers	$ 3,355
Cheese	2,223
Yogurt	1,708
Nuts and seeds	1,524
Energy, cereal, diet and snack bars	1,271
Cereal	1,219
Dried fruit and fruit snacks	1,010
Popcorn	847

Source: *Prepared Foods*, February 2006, p. 11, from Mintel.

★ 734 ★
Snacks
SIC: 2096; NAICS: 311919
Rice Snack Market in Thailand

Market shares are shown in percent.

Dozo	.66.0%
Osen	.23.0
Shinmai	5.0

Source: *Bangkok Post*, October 10, 2005, p. NA.

★ 735 ★
Snacks
SIC: 2096; NAICS: 311919
Snack Market Worldwide, 2004

Sales are in billions of dollars.

	($ bil.)	Share
United States	$ 24.3	43.63%
Western Europe	14.0	25.13
Asia-Pacific	13.9	24.96
Eastern Europe	2.0	3.59
Africa/Middle East	1.5	2.69

Source: *just-food.com*, August 2005, p. p1, from Snack Food Association.

★ 736 ★
Snacks
SIC: 2096; NAICS: 311919
Snack Sales, 2003 and 2005

Sales are shown in thousands of dollars at supermarkets, drug stores and mass merchandisers (excluding Wal-Mart) for the 52 week period listed.

	May 17, 2003	May 15, 2005	Share
Potato chips	$ 2,709,674	$ 2,776,110	28.26%
Tortilla chips . . .	1,861,457	1,868,548	19.02
Popcorn, unpopped .	716,792	691,478	7.04
Puffed cheese . . .	537,312	576,054	5.86
Pretzels	611,597	566,618	5.77
Corn chips	323,373	324,247	3.30
Dips, shelf stable . .	282,894	282,194	2.87
Caramel corn/ popped popcorn .	216,394	199,263	2.03
Rice cakes	170,450	137,199	1.40
Other	2,331,608	2,400,984	24.44

Source: *ECRM Focus*, July 2005, p. 48, from *ACNielsen Strategic Planner*.

★ 737 ★
Snacks
SIC: 2096; NAICS: 311919
Top Chocolate-Covered Salted Snack Brands, 2005

Brands are ranked by convenience store sales in thousands of dollars for the 52 weeks ended March 20, 2005.

	($ 000)	Share
Hersheys Take Five	$ 5,418.2	57.99%
Nestle Flips	1,970.5	21.09
Hershey Bites	760.9	8.14
Utz	296.4	3.17
Beny Bigalos	269.8	2.89
Herrs	226.7	2.43
Tastykake	100.7	1.08
Flipz	74.8	0.80
Branch Popz	39.6	0.42
Martin	38.2	0.41
Other	147.9	1.58

Source: *Convenience Store Decisions*, July 2005, p. 40, from Information Resources Inc.

★ 738 ★
Snacks
SIC: 2096; NAICS: 311919
Top Meat Snack Brands, 2005

Market shares are shown based on supermarket, drug store and mass merchandiser sales (excluding Wal-Mart) for the 52 weeks ended October 2, 2005.

Oh Boy! Oberto	21.9%
Slim Jim	16.9
Jack Links	14.9
Bridgford	7.1
Private label	6.8
Other	32.4

Source: *Snack Food & Wholesale Bakery*, December 2005, p. 31, from Information Resources Inc.

★ 739 ★
Snacks
SIC: 2096; NAICS: 311919

Top Popcorn Brands, 2006

Americans eat 17 billion quarts of popped popcorn an-nually or 54 quarts per person, according to the Pop-corn Board. Some 30 percent of popcorn is eaten out-side the home, including movie theatres, which leaves 70 percent eaten in the home. Market shares are shown based on supermarket sales for the 52 weeks ended Feburary 19, 2006.

Orville Redenbacher	.26.0%
Pop Secret	.17.0
Act II	.10.0
Orville Redenbacker Smart Pop	.10.0
Pop Secret Homestyle	.5.0
Jolly Time Healthy Pop	.3.0
Act II Butter Lovers	.2.0
Jolly Time Blast O Butter	.2.0
Pop Secret Jumbo Pop	.2.0
Smart Balance	.2.0
Private label	.11.0
Other	.10.0

Source: *Food Processing*, September 3, 2006, p. NA, from In-formation Resources Inc.

★ 740 ★
Snacks
SIC: 2096; NAICS: 311919

Top Popcorn Brands (SS Microwave), 2005

Brands are ranked by convenience store sales in thou-sands of dollars for the 52 weeks ended March 20, 2005. SS stands for shelf stable.

	($ 000)	Share
Act II	$ 8,598.3	49.99%
Pop Secret	2,457.1	14.28
Orville Redenbacher	1,150.4	6.69
Pop Secret Jumbo Pop	1,090.6	6.34
Act II 2000	721.9	4.20
Act II Corn on the Cob	503.5	2.93
Popz	218.3	1.27
Orville Redenbacher Smart Pop . .	214.1	1.24
Other	2,246.6	13.06

Source: *Convenience Store Decisions*, July 2005, p. 40, from Information Resources Inc.

★ 741 ★
Snacks
SIC: 2096; NAICS: 311919

Top Popcorn Makers, 2006

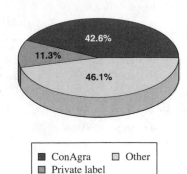

Market shares are shown based on food store, drug store and mass merchandiser sales (excluding Wal-Mart) for the 52 weeks ended January 2006.

ConAgra	.42.6%
Private label	.11.3
Other	.46.1

Source: *US Food Industry*, North American Equity Re-search, January 17, 2006, p. 100, from ACNielsen and JPMorgan.

★ 742 ★
Snacks
SIC: 2096; NAICS: 311919

Top Pork Rind Brands, 2005

Brands are ranked by convenience store sales in thou-sands of dollars for the 52 weeks ended March 20, 2005.

	($ 000)	Share
Baken Ets	$ 42,414.5	42.75%
Toms	12,332.7	12.43
Turkey Creek Snacks	6,317.8	6.37
Brims Old South	3,658.9	3.69
Utz	3,579.0	3.61
Golden Flake	3,143.1	3.17
Lance	2,965.0	2.99
Carolina Country Snacks	2,693.6	2.71
Lees	1,742.8	1.76
Andys	1,401.6	1.41
Other	18,964.9	19.12

Source: *Convenience Store Decisions*, July 2005, p. 40, from Information Resources Inc.

★ 743 ★
Snacks
SIC: 2096; NAICS: 311919

Top Potato Chip Brands, 2005

Brands are ranked by sales at supermarkets, drug stores and mass merchandisers (excluding Wal-Mart) for the 52 weeks ended September 4, 2005.

	($ mil.)	Share
Lay's	$ 760.0	28.90%
Wavy Lay's	279.9	10.64
Ruffles	257.6	9.79
Pringles	243.1	9.24
Utz	80.8	3.07
Lay's Stax	74.9	2.85
Cape Cod	59.2	2.25
Herr's	47.9	1.82
Ruffles Light	46.3	1.76
Wise	46.2	1.76
Private label	126.4	4.81
Other	607.7	23.11

Source: *MMR*, December 12, 2005, p. 37, from Information Resources Inc.

★ 744 ★
Snacks
SIC: 2096; NAICS: 311919

Top Potato Chip Makers, 2006

Market shares are shown based on food store, drug store and mass merchandiser sales (excluding Wal-Mart) for the 52 weeks ended January 26, 2006.

Frito-Lay	58.8%
Procter & Gamble	12.6
Utz Quality Foods	3.5
Wise Foods	2.6
Private label	4.8
Other	17.7

Source: *Grocery Headquarters*, April 2006, p. 56, from Information Resources Inc.

★ 745 ★
Snacks
SIC: 2096; NAICS: 311919

Top Potato Chip Makers in Southeast Michigan

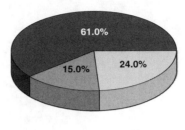

Market shares are shown in percent.

Frito-Lay	61.0%
Better Made	15.0
Other	24.0

Source: *Crain's Detroit Business*, October 3, 2005, p. 1, from ACNielsen.

★ 746 ★
Snacks
SIC: 2096; NAICS: 311919

Top Salty Snack Brands, 2006

Market shares are shown based at sales at supermarkets, drug stores and mass merchandisers (excluding Wal-Mart) for the 52 weeks ended March 19, 2006.

Pringles potato chips	10.9%
Lay's potato chips	10.6
Doritos tortilla chips	10.5
Cheetos cheese snacks	7.9
General Mills Chex Mix	4.6
Poppycock popcorn	3.4
Tostitos tortilla chips	2.9
Fritos corn snacks	2.8
Ruffles potato chips	2.7
Houston Harvest popcorn	2.5
Other	41.2

Source: *Chain Drug Review*, May 22, 2006, p. 47, from Information Resources Inc.

★ 747 ★
Snacks
SIC: 2096; NAICS: 311919

Top Snack Makers, 2006

Market shares are shown for the 52 weeks ended February 19, 2006.

PepsiCo.	18.7%
Kraft	12.2
Hershey	9.6
Kelloggs	7.1
Mars	5.8
Wrigley	4.3
General Mills	2.6
Other	39.9

Source: "Hershey's Filling the New Product Funnel." [online] from http://www.cals.vt.edu/ee/images/uploads/podcasts/IA_3_06/azzara_032806.pdf [Accessed June 1, 2006] from ACNielsen.

★ 748 ★
Snacks
SIC: 2096; NAICS: 311919

Top Snack Makers Worldwide, 2002

Data show the market shares of the top multinationals.

PepsiCo.	32.4%
Kraft	3.0
Danone	0.3
Mars	0.3
Nestle	0.1
Other	63.9

Source: *New Directions in Global Food Markets*, February 2005, p. 66, from Economic Research Service, U.S. Department of Agriculture and Euromonitor.

★ 749 ★
Snacks
SIC: 2096; NAICS: 311919

Top Tortilla/Tostada Chip Brands, 2005

Market shares are shown based on supermarket, drug store and mass merchandiser sales (excluding Wal-Mart) for the 52 weeks ended June 12, 2005.

Doritos	35.7%
Tostitos	22.6
Tostitos Scoops	8.6
Santitas	3.9
Mission	2.7
Tostitos Gold	2.1
Baked Doritos	1.5
Tostitos Natural	1.0

Old Dutch	0.9%
Other	16.7

Source: *Snack Food & Wholesale Bakery*, June 2005, p. 31, from Information Resources Inc.

★ 750 ★
Snacks
SIC: 2096; NAICS: 311919

Top Tortilla/Tostada Chip Makers, 2006

Market shares are shown based on supermarket, drug store and mass merchandisers (excluding Wal-Mart) for the 52 weeks ended January 26, 2006.

Frito-Lay	79.1%
Mission Foods Inc.	2.9
The Hain Celestial Group Inc.	2.0
Old Dutch Foods Inc.	0.9
Private label	4.5
Other	10.6

Source: *Grocery Headquarters*, April 2006, p. 56, from Information Resources Inc.

★ 751 ★
Ice
SIC: 2097; NAICS: 312113

Ice Shipments by Year, 1999-2001

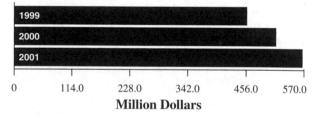

Million Dollars

Shipments are shown in millions of dollars. Reddy Ice Holdings claims to be the largest manufacturer and distributor of packaged ice in the United States, serving approximately 82,000 customer locations in 31 states and the District of Columbia. They estimate the wholesale market to be worth $1.8 billion. The industy is highly fragmented with many local and regional producers. Most claim annual revenue of less than $1 million.

1999	$ 457.3
2000	515.0
2001	566.7

Source: "Ice." [online] from http://www.referenceforbusiness.com/industries/Food-Kindred-Products [Accessed November 14, 2005] from U.S. Bureau of the Census.

★ 752 ★
Pasta
SIC: 2098; NAICS: 311823

Pasta Sales by Year, 2002-2005

Sales are shown in thousands of dollars at supermarkets, drug stores and mass merchandisers (excluding Wal-Mart) for the 52 weeks ended September 4, 2005.

2002	$ 1,259,679
2003	1,237,364
2004	1,174,212
2005	1,208,026

Source: *Corporate Profiles & Industry Statistics - Milling & Baking News Supplement*, November 2005, p. 130, from ACNielsen.

★ 753 ★
Pasta
SIC: 2098; NAICS: 311823

Top Noodle Brands, 2006

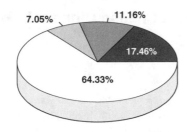

Brands are ranked by sales in millions of dollars for the 52 weeks ended January 22, 2006.

	($ mil.)	Share
No Yolk Noodles	$ 20.16	17.46%
Light & Fluffy Noodles	12.88	11.16
Pennsylvania Dutch Noodles	8.14	7.05
Other	74.27	64.33

Source: *Food Institute Report*, April 10, 2006, p. 4, from Information Resources Inc.

★ 754 ★
Pasta
SIC: 2098; NAICS: 311823

Top Pasta Brands, 2005

Brands are ranked by sales at supermarkets, drug stores and mass merchandisers (excluding Wal-Mart) for the 52 weeks ended September 4, 2005.

	($ mil.)	Share
Barilla	$ 199.95	19.4%
Ronzoni	69.18	6.7
Muellers	60.49	5.9
Creamette	55.63	5.4
San Giorgio	44.70	4.3
American Beauty	40.46	3.9
De Cecco	22.30	2.2
Skinner	21.72	2.1
Other	514.53	50.0

Source: *Corporate Profiles & Industry Statistics - Milling & Baking News Supplement*, November 2005, p. 130, from Information Resources Inc.

★ 755 ★
Pasta
SIC: 2098; NAICS: 311823

Top Pasta Makers in Japan, 2004

Market shares are shown based on domestic shipments of 262,000 tons.

Nisshin Foods	30.2%
Nippon Flour Mills	23.1
Showa Sangyo	6.9
Hagoromo Foods	6.6
Okumoto Flour Mills	2.8
Other	30.4

Source: "2004 Market Share Report." [online] from http://www.nikkei.co.jp [Published July 27, 2005] from Nikkei estimates and Japan-Pasta Association.

★ 756 ★
Pasta
SIC: 2098; NAICS: 311823

Top Pasta Makers Worldwide, 2002

Data show the market shares of the top multinationals.

Nestle	4.6%
Kraft	3.1
PepsiCo	0.4

Continued on next page.

★ 756 ★
[Continued]
Pasta
SIC: 2098; NAICS: 311823

Top Pasta Makers Worldwide, 2002

Data show the market shares of the top multinationals.

Unilever	0.1%
Other	91.8

Source: *New Directions in Global Food Markets*, February 2005, p. 66, from Economic Research Service, U.S. Department of Agriculture and Euromonitor.

★ 757 ★
Pasta
SIC: 2098; NAICS: 311823

Top Pasta/Sauce Makers in Western Europe

The top companies are ranked by market share. Data refer to products sold for human consumption in retail, catering and artisanal markets. Italy took 32% of the market, followed by Germany with 17% and France 14%.

Barilla	14.4%
Nestle	7.2
Ebro Puleva	5.1
Rana	4.7
Artisanal	3.4
Unilever	3.4
Mars	3.3
Birkel	2.9
Heinz	2.9
De Cecco	2.4
Other	50.3

Source: "Pasta & Pasta Sauce Markets." [online] from http://www.fft.com [Published June 2005] from Food for Thought.

★ 758 ★
Baking Powder
SIC: 2099; NAICS: 311999

Top Baking Powder/Soda Makers, 2005

Market shares are shown based on dollar sales for the 12 weeks ended November 27, 2005.

Church & Dwight	47.8%
Hulman & Co.	21.0
Altria Group	9.5
Rumford Co.	5.3

Private label	15.8%
Other	0.6

Source: *High Yield Consumer Products*, Deutsche Bank, December 15, 2005, p. 13, from Information Resources Inc.

★ 759 ★
Dry Desserts
SIC: 2099; NAICS: 311423

Packaged Dry Dessert Market

Market shares are shown in percent.

Kraft	83.0%
Other	17.0

Source: *Food/Agribusiness Beverages Tobacco*, Prudential Equity Group Research, March 8, 2005, p. 31, from Prudential Equity Group and LLC estimates.

★ 760 ★
Dry Dinners
SIC: 2099; NAICS: 311823

Macaroni & Cheese Dinner Market

Market shares are shown in percent.

Kraft	82.0%
Other	18.0

Source: *Food/Agribusiness Beverages Tobacco*, Prudential Equity Group Research, March 8, 2005, p. 31, from Prudential Equity Group and LLC estimates.

★ 761 ★
Dry Dinners
SIC: 2099; NAICS: 311823

Top Dry Dinner Brands, 2005

Brands are ranked by sales at supermarkets, drug stores and mass merchandisers (excluding Wal-Mart) for the 52 weeks ended September 4, 2005.

	($ mil.)	Share
Betty Crocker Hamburger Helper	$ 217.4	14.37%
Kraft Macaroni & Cheese	172.0	11.37
Kraft Velveeta Macaroni & Cheese	127.6	8.43
Rice A Roni Pasta Roni	82.4	5.44
Lipton Pasta Sides	75.8	5.01
Kraft Deluxe	69.8	4.61
Kraft Easy Mac Macaroni & Cheese	67.5	4.46

Continued on next page.

★ 761 ★

[Continued]
Dry Dinners
SIC: 2099; NAICS: 311823

Top Dry Dinner Brands, 2005

Brands are ranked by sales at supermarkets, drug stores and mass merchandisers (excluding Wal-Mart) for the 52 weeks ended September 4, 2005.

	($ mil.)	Share
Banquet Homestyle Bakes	$ 50.8	3.36%
Betty Crocker Tuna Helper . . .	40.6	2.68
Campbell's Supper Bakes	35.1	2.32
Private label	103.4	6.83
Other	471.0	31.12

Source: *MMR*, December 12, 2005, p. 37, from Information Resources Inc.

★ 762 ★

Dry Dinners
SIC: 2099; NAICS: 311823

Top Dry Dinner Makers, 2006

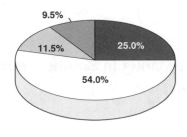

Market shares are shown based on sales (excluding Wal-Mart) for the 52 weeks ended January 2006.

General Mills 25.0%
Unilever 9.5
Private label 11.5
Other 54.0

Source: *US Food Industry*, North American Equity Research, January 17, 2006, p. 28, from ACNielsen and JPMorgan.

★ 763 ★

Frosting
SIC: 2099; NAICS: 311999

Frosting Market

Market shares are shown in percent (where distributed).

General Mills (Betty Crocker) 50.0%
Other 50.0

Source: *Food/Agribusiness Beverages Tobacco*, Prudential Equity Group Research, March 8, 2005, p. 31, from Prudential Equity Group and LLC estimates.

★ 764 ★

Frosting
SIC: 2099; NAICS: 311999

Top Frosting Brands, 2005

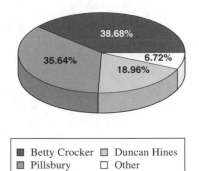

Market shares are shown in percent.

Betty Crocker 38.68%
Pillsbury 35.64
Duncan Hines 18.96
Other 6.72

Source: "Empirical Analysis of Competitive Pricing Strategies." [online] from www.fcee.lisboa.ucp.pt/resources/documents/seminario/CompPricing-Dec-2005.pdf [Published Dec. 2005].

★ 765 ★

Gelatin
SIC: 2099; NAICS: 311423

Leading Gelatin Mix Makers, 2005

Market shares are shown based on supermarket, drug store and mass merchandiser sales (excluding Wal-Mart) for the 12 weeks ended June 11, 2005.

Kraft 78.7%
Other 21.3

Source: *Food/Agribusiness*, Prudential Equity Group Equity Research, June 24, 2005, p. 2, from ACNielsen.

★ 766 ★
Honey
SIC: 2099; NAICS: 311999
Honey Market in Ireland

Market shares are shown in percent.

Boyne Valley 61.0%
Other 39.0

Source: *Checkout*, March 2006, p. NA.

★ 767 ★
Hot Drinks
SIC: 2099; NAICS: 31192
Hot Drink Sales Worldwide, 2004-2005

Data show sales at supermarkets, drug stores and mass merchandisers (excluding Wal-Mart) in millions of dollars. Figures for 2005 are forecast.

	2004	2005	Share
Coffee	$ 21,533.6	$ 21,889.5	28.96%
Coffee, instant . . .	14,637.1	15,305.8	20.25
Black standard tea . .	8,011.9	8,114.2	10.73
Flavored powdered drinks	5,522.6	5,709.4	7.55
Green tea	4,470.3	4,624.7	6.12
Fruit/herbal tea . . .	3,387.1	3,559.7	4.71
Black specialty tea . .	3,165.2	3,279.9	4.34
Instant tea	215.3	212.8	0.28
Other hot drinks . . .	8,600.0	9,012.4	11.92
Other plant-based hot drinks	3,078.1	3,303.0	4.37
Other	554.4	585.0	0.77

Source: "Global Hot Drink Sales." [online] from http://www. stagnito.com/charts2005/3globalhotdrink.htm [Accessed March 23, 2006] from Euromonitor.

★ 768 ★
Hot Drinks
SIC: 2099; NAICS: 31192
Hot Drinks Industry in Asia/Pacific

Asia-Pacific was the fastest growing market for hot drinks between 2000 and 2004. The market will grow over 41% to 4.4 million tons by 2011. The region will also increase its share of the global market by 6.4% to 40.4% by 2011. China tends to be a large market for green tea consumption, but as wealth increases among its urban residents, they have developed a taste for other types of tea and even coffee.

China 53.3%
India 11.5
Japan 8.9
Indonesia 7.7
Malaysia 3.9
Other 14.7

Source: *just-drinks.com*, October 18, 2005, p. NA, from *just-drinks.com's Global Market Review of Retail Hot Drinks - Forecasts to 2011*.

★ 769 ★
Hummus
SIC: 2099; NAICS: 311999
Hummus Market in Southeastern MI

Market shares are shown in percent.

Basha 68.0%
Other 32.0

Source: *Crain's Detroit Business*, May 8, 2006, p. 1.

★ 770 ★
Ice Cream Toppings
SIC: 2099; NAICS: 31134
Ice Cream Toppings Market

Market shares are shown in percent.

J.M. Smucker 62.2%
Other 37.8

Source: "J.M. Smucker Company." [online] from http://library. corporate-ir.net/library/77/779/77952/items/164508/SeptemberIRPre-sentation.pdf [Published Sep. 2005].

★ 771 ★
Ingredients
SIC: 2099; NAICS: 311942, 311991, 311999
Global Ingredient Sales, 2005

The term "ingredients" in the source is defined as a term "used to include those products which are added to the main constituents of a food or drink in order to add or enhance colour, flavour, stability (both physical and microbiological) and 'healthiness'." The industry is valued at $30.3 billion. Growth is driven by population increases and increased urbanization.

United States	25.0%
China	9.0
Germany	6.0
Japan	6.0
United Kingdom	6.0
Russia	5.0
France	4.0
Other	38.0

Source: *International Food Ingredients*, February - March 2005, p. 16, from RTS Resource.

★ 772 ★
Lunch Kits
SIC: 2099; NAICS: 311991, 311999
Top Lunch Kits, 2006

Brands are ranked by sales for the 52 weeks ended February 19, 2006.

	($ mil.)	Share
Oscar Mayer Lunchables	$ 511.67	76.59%
Kraft South Beach Diet	32.68	4.89
Armour Lunch Makers	29.85	4.47
Hormel	26.77	4.01
Oscar Mayer Lunchables Fun Fuel	25.38	3.80
Armour Lunch Makers Cracker Crunchables	8.74	1.31
Other	33.01	4.94

Source: *Frozen Food Age*, March 2006, p. 31, from Information Resources Inc.

★ 773 ★
Oat Fiber
SIC: 2099; NAICS: 311999
Oat Fiber Market

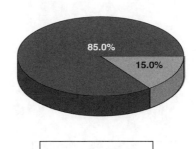

Market shares are shown in percent.

SunOpta	85.0%
Other	15.0

Source: "SunOpta Investor Presentation."[online] from http://library. corporate-ir.net/library/82/827/82712/items/134554/October-2005SunOptaPresentation.pdf [Published Oct. 2005].

★ 774 ★
Peanut Butter
SIC: 2099; NAICS: 311911
Natural Peanut Butter Market

Market shares are shown in percent. Brands include Smucker's, Laura Scudder's and Adams.

J.M. Smucker	66.0%
Other	34.0

Source: *Food/Agribusiness Beverages Tobacco*, Prudential Equity Group Research, March 8, 2005, p. 31, from Prudential Equity Group and LLC estimates.

★ 775 ★
Peanut Butter
SIC: 2099; NAICS: 311911
Top Peanut Butter Brands, 2004

Market shares are shown for the 52 weeks ended February 22, 2004.

Jif	33.6%
Skippy	19.7
Peter Pan	14.6
Smucker Natural	7.4
Private label	18.9
Other	5.8

Source: "J.M. Smucker Company." [online] from http://media. corporate-ir.net/media_files/NYS/SJM/reports/proxy-2005.pdf [Published March 23, 2004] from Information Resources Inc.

Market Share Reporter - 2007

★ 776 ★
Peanut Butter
SIC: 2099; NAICS: 311911

Top Peanut Butter Makers, 2004

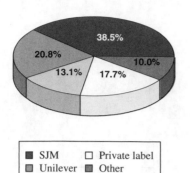

Companies are ranked by sales in millions of dollars.

	($ mil.)	Share
SJM	$ 339	38.5%
Unilever	183	20.8
ConAgra	115	13.1
Private label	156	17.7
Other	88	10.0

Source: *J.M. Smucker Co.*, Krause Fund Research, November 17, 2005, p. 20, from Mintel's *Sweet Spreads*.

★ 777 ★
Powdered Drinks
SIC: 2099; NAICS: 311999

Powdered Drink Market

Market shares are shown in percent. Brands include Kool-Aid, Crystal Light and Country Time.

Kraft	85.0%
Other	15.0

Source: *Food/Agribusiness Beverages Tobacco*, Prudential Equity Group Research, March 8, 2005, p. 31, from Prudential Equity Group and LLC estimates.

★ 778 ★
Rice Cakes
SIC: 2099; NAICS: 311999

Top Rice Cake Makers, 2006

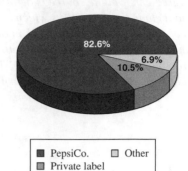

Market shares are shown based on food store, drug store and mass merchandiser sales (excluding Wal-Mart) for the 52 weeks ended January 2006.

PepsiCo.	82.6%
Private label	10.5
Other	6.9

Source: *US Food Industry*, North American Equity Research, January 17, 2006, p. 28, from ACNielsen and JPMorgan.

★ 779 ★
Salad
SIC: 2099; NAICS: 311991

Lettuce and Packaged Salad Sales, 2005

Lettuce and packaged sales contributed an average of $3,694 per week per store to national produce sales, according to ACNielsen.

Salad blends	38.3%
Iceberg lettuce	13.5
Romaine lettuce	11.0
Garden salads	7.5
Salad kits	5.8
Organic salad blends	3.6
Premium garden	3.2
Shredded lettuce	2.7
Spinach	2.6
Coleslaw	2.5
Green leaf lettuce	2.5
Other	6.7

Source: *Produce Merchandising*, April 2006, p. 34, from Perishables Group and ACNielsen.

★ 780 ★
Salad
SIC: 2099; NAICS: 311991

Organic Salad Market

The company has more than 70% of the market.

Earthbound Farms	70.0%
Other	30.0

Source: *Global Logistics & Supply Chain Strategies*, November 2005, p. NA.

★ 781 ★
Salad
SIC: 2099; NAICS: 311991

Pre-Cut Salad Sales

Sales of pre-cut fresh salads totaled $2.44 billion in 2005. Organic sales were $175 million and non-organic sales were $2,263.4 million.

	($ mil.)	Share
Salad mix	$ 2,209.5	90.62%
Salad kits	228.8	9.38

Source: *Research Alert*, April 7, 2006, p. 12, from ACNielsen and *Facts, Figures & the Future*.

★ 782 ★
Salad
SIC: 2099; NAICS: 311991

Top Bagged Salad Makers

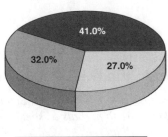

Market shares are shown in percent.

Fresh Express	41.0%
Dole	32.0
Other	27.0

Source: "Chiquita Acquires Fresh Express." [online] from http://www.thepacker.com/icms/_dtaa2/content/print.asp?alink200 [Published July 11, 2005].

★ 783 ★
Salad
SIC: 2099; NAICS: 311991

Top Fresh-Cut Salad Brands, 2005

Brands are ranked by sales at supermarkets, drug stores and mass merchandisers (excluding Wal-Mart) for the 52 weeks ended September 4, 2005.

	($ mil.)	Share
Fresh Express	$ 977.63	37.97%
Dole	791.09	30.72
Ready Pac	215.70	8.38
Earthbound Farm	127.96	4.97
Dole Greener	97.54	3.79
Salad Time	17.59	0.68
Noreast	12.91	0.50
New Star Young and Tender	7.28	0.28
Garden Cuts	6.47	0.25
Private label	320.68	12.45

Source: *Corporate Profiles & Industry Statistics - Milling & Baking News Supplement*, November 2005, p. 130, from Information Resources Inc.

★ 784 ★
Sandwiches
SIC: 2099; NAICS: 311999

Cold Sandwich Sales, 2005

The cold sandwich market was worth $747.08 million for the 52 weeks ended May 29, 2005. Sub sales increased nearly 130% over 2004 (sales were $93.17 million). The source cites possible reasons for the increase are convenience, taste and consumers looking for alternatives to fried foods. The entire sandwich market was worth $820.64 million.

	Sales	Share
Subs	$ 213,969,134	30.58%
Turkey	82,573,935	11.80
Ham	56,924,584	8.13
Beef	41,414,156	5.92
Chicken breast	18,289,353	2.61
Wraps	16,717,203	2.39
Hoagies	13,805,032	1.97
Tuna	8,750,472	1.25
Bologna	799,022	0.11
Other cold	246,532,210	35.23

Source: *Meat & Deli Retailer*, September 2005, p. NA, from FreshLook Marketing Group LLC.

★ 785 ★
Sandwiches
SIC: 2099; NAICS: 311999

Deli Sandwich Meat Shares

Bulk turkey breast represented 35.6% of sales, followed by bulk ham with a 31.4% and bulk beef with a 14% share.

Bulk, regular sandwich meat	83.5%
Pre-sliced, regular sandwich meat	9.5
Bulk, lite sandwich meats	6.1
Pre-sliced, lite sandwich meats	0.9

Source: *InStore Buyer*, May 2005, p. 97, from ACNielsen.

★ 786 ★
Seasonings
SIC: 2099; NAICS: 311942

Seasonings Market in the U.K.

Salt sales have fallen 13% since 2000. Sales of fresh herbs are expected to double (124%). Pepper is estimated to have increased by as much as 55%. Shares are esimated.

Drieds herbs, seasonings, spices	41.0%
Fresh herbs	22.0
Pepper	18.0
Salt	13.0
Curry	12.0

Source: *just-food.com*, October 6, 2005, p. NA, from Mintel.

★ 787 ★
Seasonings
SIC: 2099; NAICS: 311942

Top Seasoning Brands, 2005

Market shares are shown for the 12 months ended December 2005.

McCormick Spices & Extracts	31.9%
McCormick Dry Seasonings Mix	11.3
McCormick Private label	6.3
Lawry's	4.6
ACH	4.3
Other private label	6.7
Other	34.9

Source: "McCormick & Company." [online] http://www. library. corporate-ir.net/library/65/654/65454/items/184758/ MKC_022206.pdf [Published Feb. 22, 2006] from Information Resources Inc. Custom S&E databases and Wal-Mart Retail Link company estimates.

★ 788 ★
Seasonings
SIC: 2099; NAICS: 311942

Top Seasoning Brands in the U.K., 2005

Spending stood at 69 million pounds in 2005, up from 62 million in 2001.

	(mil.)	Share
Schwartz	£ 31	44.29%
Own label	28	40.00
Bart	5	7.14
Lion	1	1.43
Other	5	7.14

Source: *Marketing*, November 16, 2005, p. 36, from Mintel.

★ 789 ★
Syrup
SIC: 2099; NAICS: 31134

Table Syrup Market, 2005

Market shares are as of September 25, 2005. Log Cabin and Mrs. Butterworth's, owned by Pinnacle Foods, are number two and three in the $483 million market. Aunt Jemima is the leader.

Log Cabin	9.6%
Mrs. Butterworth's	9.4
Other	80.9

Source: "Pinnacle Foods." [online] from http://sec.edgar-online.com [Published December 20, 20005].

★ 790 ★
Tea
SIC: 2099; NAICS: 31192

Tea Market in the U.K., 2006 and 2008

Sales are shown based on dollar sales. Standard bags will lose market share to herbals as special bags and decaffeinated tea will increase.

	2006	2008
Standard bags	62.7%	58.3%
Specialty bags	14.7	16.4
Herbal/fruit	12.7	15.5
Loose	4.0	3.8
Decaffeinated	3.1	3.4

Continued on next page.

★ **790** ★
[Continued]
Tea
SIC: 2099; NAICS: 31192
Tea Market in the U.K., 2006 and 2008

Sales are shown based on dollar sales. Standard bags will lose market share to herbals as special bags and decaffeinated tea will increase.

	2006	2008
Instant	1.6%	1.5%
One cup	1.2	1.1

Source: *just-drinks.com*, December 2005, p. 22, from *just-drinks.com* estimates.

★ **791** ★
Tea
SIC: 2099; NAICS: 31192
Top Instant Tea Mixes, 2005

Brands are ranked by sales at supermarkets, drug stores and mass merchandisers (excluding Wal-Mart) for the 52 weeks ended September 4, 2005.

Lipton	$ 68.84
Crystal Light Teas	56.43
Nestea	27.77
4C	16.91
Oregon Chai	9.92
General Foods International	6.48
Wyler's Light	4.05
Tazo	3.96

Source: *Corporate Profiles & Industry Statistics - Milling & Baking News Supplement*, November 2005, p. 130, from Information Resources Inc.

★ **792** ★
Tea
SIC: 2099; NAICS: 31192
Top Tea Makers in India

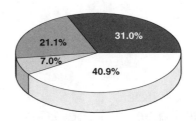

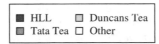

India is the largest producer of tea in the world (9.25 million kilograms). Most of their tea is consumed domestically also. The branded packet tea industry is worth 5,500 crore.

HLL	31.0%
Tata Tea	21.1
Duncans Tea	7.0
Other	40.9

Source: *Financial Express*, February 24, 2006, p. NA.

SIC 21 - Tobacco Products

★ 793 ★
Cigarettes
SIC: 2111; NAICS: 312221
Cigarette Sales by Type, 2004

Cigarettes remain one of the top sellers in convenience stores. They represented 34.7% of in-store sales in 2004, up .2% from 2003. Sales of full price cigarettes have been declining since selling 312 billion units in 1999 (274 billion were sold in 2004). Savings brands increased from 115 billion in 1999 to 133 billion in 2002 then fell to 119 billion in 2004. Figures refer to convenience stores.

Premium	.82.65%
Branded discount	.10.16
Fourth tier	. 2.28
Import	. 0.04

Source: *Convenience Store Decisions*, July 2005, p. 28, from *2005 NACS State of the Industry Survey*.

★ 794 ★
Cigarettes
SIC: 2111; NAICS: 312221
Top Cigarette Brands in Drug Stores, 2005

Market shares are shown based on drug store stores for the 52 weeks ended February 20, 2005.

Marlboro Lights single pack	.16.8%
Marlboro single pack	.10.0
Marlboro Lights multi pack/cart	. 6.1
Newport single pack	. 5.7
Marlboro Ultra Lights single pack	. 4.5
Marlboro multi pack/cart	. 3.5
Parliament Light single pack	. 3.0
Kool single pack	. 1.6
Marlboro Medium single pack	. 1.6
Other	.47.2

Source: *Chain Drug Review*, May 23, 2006, p. 79, from Information Resources Inc.

★ 795 ★
Cigarettes
SIC: 2111; NAICS: 312221
Top Cigarette Brands in Russia

Russia is the world's fourth largest cigarette market. An estimated two-thirds of Russian men and one-third of Russian women smoke.

L&M	.19.3%
Winston	.16.8
Bond	.13.7
Yava Zolotaya	.11.4
Parliament	.11.0
LD	.10.9
Kent	.10.3
Pyotr	.10.3
Prima	.10.2
Yava	. 9.9

Source: *World Tobacco*, May 2005, p. 29, from Komkon.

★ 796 ★
Cigarettes
SIC: 2111; NAICS: 312221
Top Cigarette Brands in the U.K., 2005

Sales are shown for the 52 weeks ended October 1, 2005. Figures are in thousands of pounds sterling and for all outlets.

	(000)	Share
Lambert & Butler	£ 1,268,032	13.56%
Richmond	865,832	9.26
Benson & Hedges Gold	726,001	7.76
Mayfair	707,119	7.56
Marlboro Gold	630,889	6.75
Royals Red	371,811	3.98
Silk Cut Purple	353,303	3.78
Superkings	335,026	3.58
Regal	326,354	3.49
Embassy No 1	291,120	3.11

Continued on next page.

★ 796 ★

[Continued]
Cigarettes
SIC: 2111; NAICS: 312221

Top Cigarette Brands in the U.K., 2005

Sales are shown for the 52 weeks ended October 1, 2005. Figures are in thousands of pounds sterling and for all outlets.

	(000)	Share
Mayfair Smooth	£ 261,731	2.80%
Other	3,215,774	34.38

Source: *Grocer*, December 17, 2005, p. 77, from ACNielsen.

★ 797 ★

Cigarettes
SIC: 2111; NAICS: 312221

Top Cigarette Firms, 2005

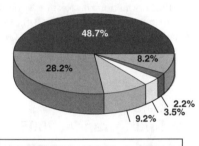

■ Phillip Morris	□ Commonwealth
■ RJ Reynolds	■ Liggett & Meyers
□ Lorillard	■ Other

Annual sales were 381 billion cigarettes. An estimated 44.5 million adults smoke.

Phillip Morris	.48.7%
RJ Reynolds	.28.2
Lorillard	9.2
Commonwealth	3.5
Liggett & Meyers	2.2
Other	8.2

Source: "Tobacco and Cigarette Industry." [online] from http://www.secinfo.com/d15EX7v4g.htm [Accessed June 7, 2006].

★ 798 ★

Cigarettes
SIC: 2111; NAICS: 312221

Top Cigarette Firms in France, 2005

Market shares are shown for MAT (moving annual total) to September 17, 2005.

PMI	.39.3%
Altadis	.28.1

BAT	.16.3%
JTI	. 9.6
Imperial Tobacco	3.4
Gallaher	3.0
Other	0.3

Source: *ACNielsen Trends in Europe*, Citigroup Global Markets, October 18, 2005, p. 7, from ACNielsen.

★ 799 ★

Cigarettes
SIC: 2111; NAICS: 312221

Top Cigarette Firms in Germany, 2005

Market shares are shown for MAT (moving annual total) to September 17, 2005. Data covers only 22 billion out of 101 billion cigarettes.

PMI	.33.3%
BAT	.19.9
Imperial Tobacco	.18.4
JTI	. 2.4
Private label	.25.2
Other	0.8

Source: *ACNielsen Trends in Europe*, Citigroup Global Markets, October 18, 2005, p. 7, from ACNielsen.

★ 800 ★

Cigarettes
SIC: 2111; NAICS: 312221

Top Cigarette Firms in Korea

Foreign brands represent about 25% of the domestic market. Companies are ranked by sales of cigarettes.

	(bil.)	Share
KT&G	60.1	73.0%
BAT	12.8	15.6
Phillip Morris	6.9	8.4
JTI	2.5	3.0

Source: *Digital Chosun*, January 26, 2006, p. NA.

★ 801 ★
Cigarettes
SIC: 2111; NAICS: 312221

Top Cigarette Firms in the U.K., 2005

Market shares are shown for MAT (moving annual total) to September 17, 2005.

Imperial Tobacco	.45.1%
Gallaher	.37.2
PMI	. 7.8
BAT	. 6.3
Private label	. 1.1
Other	. 2.5

Source: *ACNielsen Trends in Europe*, Citigroup Global Markets, October 18, 2005, p. 7, from ACNielsen.

★ 802 ★
Pipe Tobacco
SIC: 2111; NAICS: 312221

Top Pipe/Cigarette Tobacco Brands, 2005

Brands are ranked by convenience store sales in thousands of dollars for the last 25 months ended March 2005.

	($ 000)	Share
Top Tobacco 12 Pouch	$ 3,526.2	26.14%
Bugler Tobacco 12 Pouch	2,491.4	18.47
Top Tobacco SS 1 Pouch	1,512.7	11.21
Bugler Tobacco 1 Pouch	1,327.9	9.84
Top Tobacco 1 Pouch	708.5	5.25
Other	3,924.8	29.09

Source: *Convenience Store Decisions*, July 2005, p. 40, from McLane Co.

★ 803 ★
Cigars
SIC: 2121; NAICS: 312229

Top Cigar Brands, 2005

Market shares are shown based on sales at convenience stores for the 52 weeks ended December 3, 2005.

Middleton's Black & Mild Small Tip, 5-ct.	.11.4%
Swisher Sweets Mild Small Non-Tip, 5-ct.	. 5.9
Middleton's Black & Mild Small Tip, 1-ct.	. 3.4
Phillies Large Non-Tip 1-ct.	. 2.4

Backwoods Mild Small Non-Tip, 8-ct.	. 2.1%
Other	.74.8

Source: *Convenience Store News*, May 29, 2006, p. 80, from ACNielsen, courtesy of Smokeless Tobacco Co.

★ 804 ★
Cigars
SIC: 2121; NAICS: 312229

Top Cigar Makers in North America, 2005

Market shares are shown based on mass market volume sales for the year ended December 31, 2005.

Swisher International	.34.8%
Altadis	.31.1
John Middleton	.14.5
Swedish Match North America	. 6.8
Other	.12.8

Source: "Investor Information and Results." [online] from http://www.swedishmatch.com/Archive/Pdf/SMQ42005-InterimPresentation.pdf [Accessed April 21, 2006].

★ 805 ★
Smokeless Tobacco
SIC: 2131; NAICS: 312229

Top Moist Snuff Brands, 2005

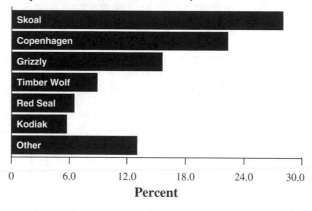

Market shares are shown for the 52 weeks ended December 31, 2005.

Skoal	.28.0%
Copenhagen	.22.3
Grizzly	.15.6
Timber Wolf	. 8.9
Red Seal	. 6.5

Continued on next page.

★ 805 ★

[Continued]
Smokeless Tobacco
SIC: 2131; NAICS: 312229

Top Moist Snuff Brands, 2005

Market shares are shown for the 52 weeks ended December 31, 2005.

Kodiak 5.7%
Other 13.0

Source: ''Reynolds American.'' [online] from http://
www.reynolds-american.com/common/ViewDoc.asp?
postID1147&DocTypePDF [Report dated May 11, 2006],
p. 40, from ACNielsen.

★ 806 ★

Smokeless Tobacco
SIC: 2131; NAICS: 312229

Top Smokeless Tobacco Brands, 2005

Brands are ranked by convenience store sales in thousands of dollars for the 25 months ended March 2005.

	($ 000)	Share
Copenhagen Full Cut	$ 184,482.4	15.18%
Copenhagen Long Cut	71,564.8	5.89
Kodiak Wintergreen	60,212.5	4.95
Skoal LC Wintergreen . . .	50,964.7	4.19
Skoal FC Wintergreen . . .	45,595.3	3.75
Skoal LC Straight	45,086.6	3.71
Skoal LC Mint	42,520.0	3.50
Other	715,095.2	58.83

Source: *Convenience Store Decisions*, July 2005, p. 40,
from Information Resources Inc.

★ 807 ★

Smokeless Tobacco
SIC: 2131; NAICS: 312229

Top Smokeless Tobacco Makers, 2005

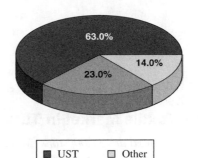

Market shares are shown in percent.

UST 63.0%
Conwood 23.0
Other 14.0

Source: *Winston-Salem Journal*, April 26, 2006, p. A1.

SIC 22 - Textile Mill Products

★ 808 ★
Textiles
SIC: 2200; NAICS: 313312

Technical Textile Market in Turkey

The market was valued at 131,000 tons. Mobiltech includes autos, ships and aircraft. Clothtech includes apparel. Agrotech includes agriculture. Hometech includes furniture and carpets.

Mobiltech	.30.0%
Clothtech	.20.0
Agrotech	.12.0
Hometech	.10.0
Other	.28.0

Source: *just-style.com (Management Briefing)*, February 2006, p. 9, from David Rigby Associates.

★ 809 ★
Fabric Mills
SIC: 2241; NAICS: 313221

Leading Broadwoven Fabric Mills, 2005

International Textile Group had 9.9%-10.2%, Milliken & Company 8.4%-8.8%, Avondale Incorporated 4.4%-4.6% and Guiford Mills Inc. 2.5%- 2.7%.

International Textile Group	.10.2%
Milliken & Company	8.8
Avondale Incorporated	4.6
Guiford Mills Inc.	2.7
Other	.73.7

Source: "US Broadwoven Fabric Mills Industry Research." [online] from http://www.ibisworld.com [Accessed May 2, 2006] from IBISWorld.

★ 810 ★
Fabric Mills
SIC: 2241; NAICS: 313221

Leading Narrow Fabric Mills/Schiffli Machine Mills

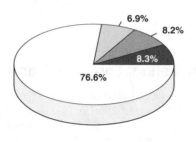

Legend: ■ Unific Inc. □ QST Industries Inc. ■ Worldtex Inc. □ Other

Unifi had an 8.2%-8.3% market share, Worldtex Inc. had an 8.1%-8.2% share and QST Industries a 6.7%-6.9% share.

Unific Inc.	8.3%
Worldtex Inc.	8.2
QST Industries Inc.	6.9
Other	.76.6

Source: "Narrow Fabric Mills and Schiffli Machine Embroidery." [online] from http://www.ibisworld.com [Accessed May 2, 2006] from IBISWorld.

★ 811 ★
Hosiery
SIC: 2251; NAICS: 315111

Pantyhose and Tights Sales

Data show department store sales in millions of dollars.

	($ mil.)	Share
Sheer pantyhose	$ 695	46.33%
Tights	53	3.53
Other	752	50.13

Source: *Seattle Times*, January 4, 2006, p. F6, from NPD Group.

★ 812 ★
Hosiery
SIC: 2251; NAICS: 315111
Top Hosiery Brands, 2005

Market shares are shown based on supermarket, drug store and mass merchandiser sales (excluding Wal-Mart) for the 52 weeks ended June 12, 2005.

Leggs Sheer Energy	.16.2%
No Nonsense	.11.0
Leggs Silken Mist	9.5
Everyday by Leggs	5.7
Just My Size	4.1
No Nonsense Grt	3.6
On the Go	3.1
No Nonsense Sheer Endurance	3.0
Leggs Sheer Comfort	2.9
Private label	.14.2
Other	.26.7

Source: *Grocery Headquarters*, August 2005, p. S6, from Information Resources Inc.

★ 813 ★
Hosiery
SIC: 2251; NAICS: 315111
Top Hosiery Makers, 2005

Market shares are shown based on supermarket, drug store and mass merchandiser sales (excluding Wal-Mart) for the 52 weeks ended June 12, 2005.

Leggs Products	.56.1%
Kayser-Roth Corp.	.22.1
Smith Hosiery Inc.	3.1
Americal Corp.	1.5
Private label	.14.2

Source: *Grocery Headquarters*, August 2005, p. S6, from Information Resources Inc.

★ 814 ★
Knitted Apparel
SIC: 2253; NAICS: 315191
Flat Knitted Tops Sales for Women in Europe

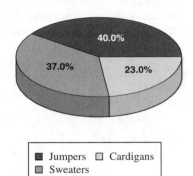

Distribution is shown based on sales of 800 million flat knitted tops. Germany is the largest market but the United Kingdom is seeing the fastest growth.

Jumpers	.40.0%
Sweaters	.37.0
Cardigans	.23.0

Source: *Market Europe*, August 1, 2005, p. NA.

★ 815 ★
Knitted Apparel
SIC: 2253; NAICS: 315191
Leading Knit Apparel Makers, 2004

Russell Holdings had 6.1%-6.2% of the market and Russell had 12.1%-2.3% of the market.

Russell Corporation	.12.3%
Anvil Holdings	6.2
Other	.81.5

Source: ''Other Apparel Knitting Mills in the US.'' [online] from http://www.ibisworld.com [Published February 28, 2006] from IBISWorld.

★ 816 ★
Screen Printing
SIC: 2261; NAICS: 313311
Screen Printing Revenues

There were 18,000 apparel decorators who identified their primary business as screen printing. Sales amounted to $18.8 billion, of which 68% was derived from screen printing.

	($ bil.)	Share
Screen printing	$ 12.7	66.84%
Embroidery	3.2	16.84

Continued on next page.

★ 816 ★
[Continued]
Screen Printing
SIC: 2261; NAICS: 313311

Screen Printing Revenues

There were 18,000 apparel decorators who identified their primary business as screen printing. Sales amounted to $18.8 billion, of which 68% was derived from screen printing.

	($ bil.)	Share
Outsourced services	$ 1.6	8.42%
Promotional products	0.6	3.16
Other	0.9	4.74

Source: *Impressions*, August 2005, p. NA, from *Impressions 2005 Decorated Apparel Universe Study.*

★ 817 ★
Carpet Backing
SIC: 2273; NAICS: 31411

Leading Carpet Backing Makers

Market shares are estimated.

Propex Fabrics	80.0%
Other	20.0

Source: *Chattanooga Times/Free Press*, May 7, 2006, p. NA.

★ 818 ★
Rugs
SIC: 2273; NAICS: 31411

Leading Bath Rug Makers, 2005

Firms are ranked by sales in millions of dollars.

Mohawk Home	$ 190
Springs Industries	130
Maples Industries	110
Shaw Rugs	54
Bacova Guild	25

Source: *Home Textiles Today*, January 9, 2006, p. 24, from *Home Textiles Today Supplier Giants.*

★ 819 ★
Rugs
SIC: 2273; NAICS: 31411

Leading Rug Makers, 2005

Firms are ranked by sales in millions of dollars.

Mohawk Home	$ 323
Shaw Living	220
Maples Rugs	150
Oriental Weavers USA	147
Springs Industries	85

Source: *Home Textiles Today*, January 9, 2006, p. 24, from *Home Textiles Today* market research.

★ 820 ★
Thread
SIC: 2284; NAICS: 313113

Largest Thread Firms, 2003

Sales declined in the late 1990s and early 2000s. In 2001, estimated shipments were $410 million. Companies are ranked by sales in millions of dollars.

Coats North America Consolidated	$ 334
American & Efird	293

Source: "Thread Mills." [online] from http://www.referenceforbusiness.com/industries/Textile-Mill/Thread [Accessed November 14, 2005].

★ 821 ★
Coated Fabric
SIC: 2295; NAICS: 31332

Coated Fabric Demand, 2004

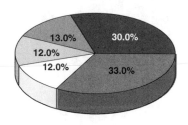

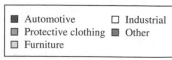

The total market was placed at 580 million square yards in 2004.

Automotive	30.0%
Protective clothing	13.0
Furniture	12.0

Continued on next page.

★ 821 ★
[Continued]
Coated Fabric
SIC: 2295; NAICS: 31332

Coated Fabric Demand, 2004

The total market was placed at 580 million square yards in 2004.

Industrial 12.0%
Other 33.0

Source: *Urethanes Technology*, June/July 2005, p. 37, from Freedonia Group.

★ 822 ★
Rope
SIC: 2298; NAICS: 314991

Fishing Rope Market in India

Market shares are shown in percent.

GWRL 85.0%
Other 15.0

Source: *India Business Insight*, January 8, 2006, p. NA.

SIC 23 - Apparel and Other Textile Products

★ 823 ★

Apparel

SIC: 2300; NAICS: 315211, 315212, 315223

Apparel Sales, 2005

Total U.S. apparel sales reached $181 billion in 2005, a 4 percent increase over 2004. Men's apparel led the industry's growth with an increase of five percent, reaching nearly $53 billion in 2005. Strong sales in T-shirts, jeans, tailored clothing and pajamas helped fuel overall industry growth.

	($ bil.)	Share
Women's	$ 101	55.80%
Men's	53	29.28
Children's	27	14.92

Source: "Young Men Discover the Suit." [online] from http://blogs.mediapost.com/research_brief/?p1140 [Published March 20, 2006] from NPD Group.

★ 824 ★

Apparel

SIC: 2300; NAICS: 315211, 315212, 315223

Leading Apparel Firms

Firms are ranked by most recent year sales in millions of dollars.

Gap Inc.	$ 16,267.0
Nike	12,253.1
VF Corp.	6,054.5
Jones Apparel Group	4,649.7
Liz Clairborne	4,632.8
Reebok International	3,785.3
Polo Ralph Lauren	3,305.4
Cintas	2,814.1
Kellwood Co.	2,555.7
Charming Shoppes	2,332.3
Abercrombie & Fitch	2,021.3

Source: *Apparel Magazine*, November 2005, p. NA.

★ 825 ★

Apparel

SIC: 2300; NAICS: 315211, 315212, 315223

Leading Apparel Firms in China

Firms are ranked by revenue in millions of dollars. Sales of clothing and footwear totaled $93 billion in 2005. Clothing takes about 79% of this total, with footwear taking the balance. Women's clothing takes 35% of the market, with men's outerwear taking 22% of the total. Knitwear was 15.8% in 2005.

Jiangsu Zongyi Co. Ltd.	$ 478
Hongdou Group Company	380
Qingdao Jifa Group Co. Ltd.	289
Gingbo Shenzhou Weaving	234
Group Co. Ltd. Youngor Group Ltd.	224
Guangdong Esquel Textiles	176
Chengde Dixam Knitwear	155

Source: *just-style.com (Management Briefing)*, May 2006, p. 5.

★ 826 ★

Apparel

SIC: 2300; NAICS: 315211, 315212, 315239

Leading Children's Apparel Brands

Data show brand preferences based on a survey.

Hanes	16.0%
Levi's	12.0
Carter's	9.0
Nike	8.0
Fruit of the Loom	6.0
Oshkosh B'Gosh Inc.	6.0
The Gap	6.0
Lee	4.0
Wrangler	4.0

Source: *DSN Retailing Today*, October 24, 2005, p. 38, from Leo J. Shapiro & Associates.

★ 827 ★
Apparel
SIC: 2300; NAICS: 315211, 315212, 315223

Leading Children's Apparel Makers

Firms are ranked by turnover in millions of dollars.

Sara Lee	$ 19,600.0
VF Corp.	6,050.0
Carter's	823.0
Oshkosh B'Gosh Inc.	398.7
Berkshire Hathaway	74.4

Source: "Childrenswear in the USA." [online] from http://www.euromonitor.com/Childrenswear_in_USA [Published September 2005] from Euromonitor.

★ 828 ★
Apparel
SIC: 2300; NAICS: 315211, 315212, 315223

Leading Decorated T-Shirt Makers

Market shares are shown in percent.

Gildan	38.0%
Fruit of the Loom	19.0
Hanes	19.0
Russell	15.0
Other	9.0

Source: *Impressions*, May 8, 2006, p. NA, from *ACNielsen S.T.A.R.S. Report*.

★ 829 ★
Apparel
SIC: 2300; NAICS: 315211, 315228, 315239

Leading Fleece Makers, 2004

Market shares are shown in percent.

Russell	39.0%
Hanes	19.0
Gildan	13.0
Fruit of the Loom	8.0
Other	21.0

Source: "Russell Corp. Equipped to Win." [online] from http://www.sec.edgar-online.com [Published May 12, 2005].

★ 830 ★
Apparel
SIC: 2300; NAICS: 315211, 315212, 315223

Leading Sportshirt Makers, 2004

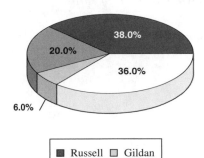

Market shares are shown in percent.

Russell	38.0%
Hanes	20.0
Gildan	6.0
Other	36.0

Source: "Russell Corp. Equipped to Win." [online] from http://www.sec.edgar-online.com [Published May 12, 2005].

★ 831 ★
Apparel
SIC: 2300; NAICS: 315211, 315212, 315223

Leading T-Shirt Makers, 2004

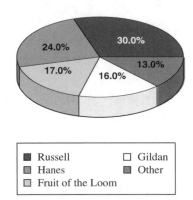

Market shares are shown in percent.

Russell	30.0%
Hanes	24.0
Fruit of the Loom	17.0
Gildan	16.0
Other	13.0

Source: "Russell Corp. Equipped to Win." [online] from http://www.sec.edgar-online.com [Published May 12, 2005].

★ 832 ★
Apparel
SIC: 2300; NAICS: 315228, 315239

Outerwear Apparel Market in Europe

Sales are shown in millions of euros.

Germany	€ 48,301
United Kingdom	43,641
Italy	34,802
France	26,639
Spain	18,630
Netherlands	8,791
Belgium	6,665
Austria	5,550
Sweden	5,045
Greece	4,719

Source: "Outerwear including Leather Garments." [online] http://www.cbi.nl/show.php?fileshow_summary.html& id2612 [Published June 2005] from Euromonitor and Retail Intelligence.

★ 833 ★
Apparel
SIC: 2300; NAICS: 315211, 315212, 315228

Top Cotton Trouser Exporters to the United States

Market shares are volume of dozens year ending July 2005.

Mexico	31.0%
Guatemala	20.0
Cambodia	7.0
Honduras	7.0
Nicaragua	7.0
Other	28.0

Source: *Apparel Magazine*, November 2005, p. 16.

★ 834 ★
Apparel
SIC: 2300; NAICS: 315211, 315223

Top Men's Apparel Firms in Japan, 2004

Market shares are shown based on domestic sales of 2.76 trillion yen.

Onward Kashiyama	3.1%
Sanyo Shokai	2.4
Five Foxes	1.4
World	1.1
D'Urban	0.8

Source: "2004 Market Share Report." [online] from http://www.nikkei.co.jp [Published July 27, 2005] from Nikkei estimates.

★ 835 ★
Sportswear
SIC: 2300; NAICS: 315228, 315239

Compression Apparel Market

Market shares are shown in percent.

Under Armour	76.0%
Other	24.0

Source: *Baltimore Sun*, January 15, 2006, p. NA.

★ 836 ★
Sportswear
SIC: 2300; NAICS: 315211, 315239

Golf Apparel Sales in Germany

The market for golf apparel and equipment stood at $150 million in 2003. Steady growth is anticipated for the next five years.

Shoes	33.0%
Shirts	18.0
Gloves	17.0
Pants	12.0
Caps	9.0
Other	11.0

Source: "German Market for Golf Apparel and Shoes." [online] from http://www.export.gov [Published September 2005].

★ 837 ★
Sportswear
SIC: 2300; NAICS: 315228, 315239

Heated Apparel Market

Market shares are shown in percent.

Gerbing's Heated Clothing	70.0%
Other	30.0

Source: *Powersports Business*, March 13, 2006, p. 57.

★ 838 ★
Sportswear
SIC: 2300; NAICS: 315211, 315239

Leading Athletic Apparel Makers in India

The branded sportswear industry is valued at Rs 375-400 crore.

Reebok	45.0%
Adidas	30.0
Nike	25.0

Source: "Global Winners, Indian Losers." [online] from http://us.rediff.com/2004/nov/09spec.htm [Published November 9, 2004].

★ 839 ★
Sportswear
SIC: 2300; NAICS: 315211, 315239

Leading Athletic Apparel Makers Worldwide, 2003

Market shares are shown based on $43,903 million in wholesale sales.

Nike 7.5%
Adidas-Salomon 5.4
Reebok 2.9
Russell 2.7
Quiksilver 2.2
VF Knitwear 2.0
Columbia 1.8
Champion 1.5
Puma 1.5
Other 25.5

Source: *Apparel & Footwear Yearbook*, JPMorgan North American Equity Research, January 8, 2005, p. 37, from Sporting Goods Intelligence.

★ 840 ★
Sportswear
SIC: 2300; NAICS: 315211, 315239

Leading Sports Apparel Makers

Market shares are shown in percent.

Nike 8.0%
Russell Athletics 6.0
Reebok 3.0
Other 83.0

Source: *Baltimore Sun*, August 27, 2005, p. NA, from Sporting Goods Intelligence.

★ 841 ★
Sportswear
SIC: 2300; NAICS: 315211, 315239

Performance Glove Market

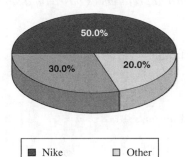

Market shares are shown in percent.

Nike 50.0%
Under Armour 30.0
Other 20.0

Source: "Under Armour Going Public." [online] from http://www.oregonlive.com/weblogs/playbooksandprofits [Published August 30, 2005].

★ 842 ★
Sportswear
SIC: 2300; NAICS: 315211, 315239

Top Athletic Swimwear Makers

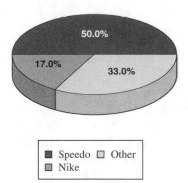

Market shares are shown in percent.

Speedo 50.0%
Nike 17.0
Other 33.0

Source: *WWD*, February 14, 2006, p. 10, from Sportscan.

★ 843 ★

Apparel

SIC: 2311; NAICS: 315211

Top Men's Apparel Brands

Data show brand preferences based on a survey.

Hanes	.32.0%
Levi's	.16.0
Fruit of the Loom	.12.0
Wrangler	.11.0
Docker's	. 6.0
Nike	. 4.0
Polo/Ralph Lauren	. 4.0
Jockey	. 3.0
Lee	. 3.0

Source: *DSN Retailing Today*, October 24, 2005, p. 38, from Leo J. Shapiro & Associates.

★ 844 ★

Apparel

SIC: 2325; NAICS: 315224

Men's Dress Pants Sales, 2005

Sales are in thousands of dollars for October 2004 - September 2005. Those 25-34 years old spent the most ($289.7 million) on men's dress pants. Other age groups: 45-54 ($257.9 million), 35-44 ($230.5 million), 12 and under ($3.2 milllion), 13-17 ($100 million), 18-24 ($188.6 million), 55-64 ($ 150.4 million), 65+ ($64.8 million).

$20-$29.99	$ 360,604
$10-$19.99	259,306
$30-$39.99	235,968
$40-$49.99	155,001
$70+	90,037
$60-$69.99	83,823
$50-$59.99	78,500
Under $10	22,124

Source: *DNR*, December 5, 2005, p. 19, from NPD Group/ NPD Fashionworld Consumer Data estimates.

★ 845 ★

Apparel

SIC: 2330; NAICS: 315212

Long Top Market, 2006

Long tops are the thin strap taps with built-in foundations (bras) for women. Market shares are shown for the week ended February 19, 2006.

Nike	.70.0%
Other	.30.0

Source: "Sportscaninfo." [online] from http:// www.sportscaninfo.com/pdf/SportScanINFO%20Weekly% 20Index.pdf [Accessed May 15, 2006] from Sportscaninfo.

★ 846 ★

Apparel

SIC: 2330; NAICS: 315231

Top Women's Apparel Firms in Japan, 2004

Market shares are shown based on domestic sales of 6.55 trillion yen.

World	2.5%
Onward Kashiyama	2.3
Itokin	1.8
Sanyo Shokai	1.6
Sanei International	1.5
Other	.90.3

Source: "2004 Market Share Report." [online] from http:// www.nikkei.co.jp [Published July 27, 2005] from Nikkei estimates.

★ 847 ★
Lingerie
SIC: 2341; NAICS: 315231
Global Lingerie Market, 2004

According to the source, the world lingerie market will grow 8% from 2004 to 2012, from $29.15 billion to $31.6 billion. The fastest growing segment in this period will be the bodywear/daywear/shapewear (corsets) segment. The developed world took 82% of the market in 2004 with the rest of the world representing only 18% of the market.

	($ bil.)	Share
Bras	$ 16.20	56.0%
Briefs	9.25	32.0
Bodywear/daywear/shapewear	3.70	12.0

Source: *just-style.com*, January 18, 2006, p. NA, from *just-style.com*.

★ 848 ★
Lingerie
SIC: 2341; NAICS: 315231
Top Lingerie Firms in Japan, 2004

Market shares are shown based on domestic sales of 408 billion yen.

Wacoal	23.3%
Triumph International (Japan)	12.5
Gunze	5.2
Charle	5.1
Cecile	3.8
Other	50.1

Source: "2004 Market Share Report." [online] from http://www.nikkei.co.jp [Published July 27, 2005] from Nikkei estimates.

★ 849 ★
Hats
SIC: 2353; NAICS: 315991
Leading Hat Makers Worldwide

Market shares are shown in percent.

Young An/Dada/Yupong Inc.	40.0%
Other	60.0

Source: *KSA Newsletter*, August 2004, p. 6.

★ 850 ★
Fur
SIC: 2371; NAICS: 315292
Fur Sales, 2004

Sales of fur and fur-trimmed apparel and accessories were $1.81 billion in 2004. The industry was up only 1.1% but analysts consider this good news in light of price increases and a warm winter. Men's products represent just under 8% of sales.

Regular mink	42.5%
Shearling	7.5
Other	50.0

Source: "U.S. Fur Retail Sales Still Edging Higher." [online] from http://www.furcommission.com/news/newsF)-*z.htm [Published September 15, 2005] from Fur Information Council of America.

★ 851 ★
Fur
SIC: 2371; NAICS: 315292
Fur Sales by Year, 1999-2003

According to a recent survey, 55% of those who purchase fur are under 44 years of age. One in five women own a fur coat. Men's furs represent about 5% of sales. Figures are in billions of dollars.

1999	$ 1.40
2000	1.69
2001	1.53
2002	1.70
2003	1.80

Source: "FICA." [online] from http://www.fur.org/poen_faqs.cfm?sectfact [Accessed November 3, 2005] from Fur Information Council of America.

★ 852 ★
Fur
SIC: 2371; NAICS: 315292
Global Fur Sales, 2000-2004

Figures are in billions of dollars.

2000-2001	$ 9.838
2001-2002	10.900
2002-2003	11.300
2003-2004	11.700

Source: "6th Consecutive Year for Growth." [online] from http://www.furcommission.com/news/newsF08i.htm [Published September 15, 2005] from International Fur Trade Federation.

★ 853 ★
Gloves
SIC: 2381; NAICS: 315992

Glove and Mitten Sales, 1998-2001

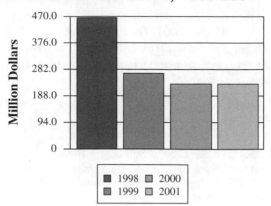

Shipments are shown in millions of dollars.

1998	$ 467.0
1999	268.4
2000	230.2
2001	228.8

Source: "Dress and Work Gloves." [online] from http://www.referenceforbusiness.com/industries/Apparel [Accessed November 14, 2005].

★ 854 ★
Robes and Gowns
SIC: 2384; NAICS: 315211, 315212

Leading Robe/Dressing Gown Firms, 2003

In 2001 shipments of men's and boy's robes totaled $9.3 million. Women's and girl's robes and dressing gowns totaled $112.6 million. Companies are ranked by sales in millions of dollars.

Lillian Vernon of Rye	$ 238.0
NAP Inc.	90.0
Movie Star Inc.	64.9

Source: "Robes and Dressing Gowns." [online] from http://www.referenceforbusiness.com/industries/Apparel [Accessed November 14, 2005].

★ 855 ★
Outerwear
SIC: 2385; NAICS: 315222, 315234

Largest Waterproofed Outerwear Firms

Companies are ranked by estimated sales in millions of dollars. Londontown manufactures London Fog. Shipments fell from $333 million in 1987 to $95 million in the late 1990s. Raincoats make up the major share of the category.

Londontown Corp.	$ 350
Galleon	145
Whaling Manufacturing	55

Source: "Waterproof Outerwear." [online] from http://www.referenceforbusiness.com/industries/Textile-Mill/Apparel [Accessed November 14, 2005].

★ 856 ★
Lined Apparel
SIC: 2386; NAICS: 315292

Leading Leather/Sheep-Lined Apparel Firms, 1999-2001

Shipments are shown in millions of dollars. Leaders in the industry: L.L. Bean, DeLong Sportswear Inc. and Avirex Inc.

1999	$ 128.8
2000	135.8
2001	128.2

Source: "Leather and Sheep-Lined Clothing." [online] from http://www.referenceforbusiness.com/industries/Apparel [Accessed November 14, 2005] from U.S. Bureau of the Census.

★ 857 ★
Belts
SIC: 2387; NAICS: 315999

Leather Belt Shipments, 1999-2001

Shipments are shown in millions of dollars. Leaders in the industry: St. John Knits Inc., Lillian Vernon and Tandy Brands.

1999	$ 371.9
2000	396.8
2001	395.8

Source: "Apparel Belts." [online] from http://www.referenceforbusiness.com/industries/Apparel [Accessed November 14, 2005] from U.S. Bureau of the Census.

★ 858 ★
Cleanroom Apparel
SIC: 2389; NAICS: 315999

Cleanroom Apparel Sales Worldwide, 2008

Much of the 8% increase in demand comes from Asian countries.

United States	$ 141
Japan	109
South Korea	60
Taiwan	59
China	39
United Kingdom	29
Germany	25
Thailand	25
Malaysia	24
France	23

Source: "Asia Drives the Cleanroom Market." [online] from http://www.mcilvainecompany.com/newsreleases/ NR1097.htm [Published May 9, 2005] from McIlvaine Company.

★ 859 ★
Cleanroom Apparel
SIC: 2389; NAICS: 315299

Disposable Cleanroom Clothing Sales Worldwide, 2002-2006

Sales of disposable garments are larger than sales of reusable garments. The annual cost of reusable clothing (including processing) is higher than the annual cost of disposables. Figures are in millions of dollars.

2002	$ 461.95
2003	528.51
2004	561.71
2005	609.75
2006	675.90

Source: "Disposable Cleanroom Garmet Use." [online] from http://cr.pennet.com/articles/article_display.cfm?article_ID [Accessed Jan. 18, 2006] from McIlvaine Company.

★ 860 ★
Cleanroom Apparel
SIC: 2389; NAICS: 315299

Reusable Apparel Market Worldwide, 2009

Sales are in millions of dollars. Shares are shown for the top 25 markets. China has the fastest-growing reusable apparel market.

	($ mil.)	Share
Japan	$ 136	18.11%
United States	113	15.05
South Korea	102	13.58
Taiwan	102	13.58
Malaysia	42	5.59
Thailand	42	5.59
China	41	5.46
United Kingdom	28	3.73
Philippines	21	2.80
Other	124	16.51

Source: *CleanRooms*, March 2006, p. 16, from McIlvaine Company.

★ 861 ★
Curtains and Draperies
SIC: 2391; NAICS: 314121

Leading Curtain/Drapery Makers, 2005

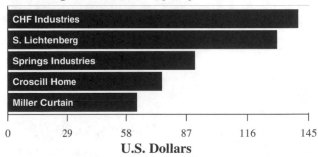

Firms are ranked by sales in millions of dollars.

CHF Industries	$ 140
S. Lichtenberg	130
Springs Industries	91
Croscill Home	75
Miller Curtain	63

Source: *Home Textiles Today*, January 9, 2006, p. 24, from *Home Textiles Today* market research.

★ 862 ★
Curtains and Draperies
SIC: 2391; NAICS: 314121

Window Coverings Market in the U.K., 2003

The window coverings market was placed at 1.2 billion pounds. Curtains are the largest sector but being challenged by blinds.

Curtains	.56.0%
Blinds	.27.0
Curtain suspension	.11.0
Other	. 6.0

Source: ''Domestic Window Coverings Market - UK 2004.'' [online] from http://www.the-infoshop.com [Published November 2004].

★ 863 ★
Curtains and Draperies
SIC: 2391; NAICS: 314121

Window Treatments by Pattern, 2004

Synthetics represent 75% of fabrics, cotton-dominant blends follow with 11% of the market.

Sheers	.34.0%
Solids	.30.0
Jacquards	.21.0
Prints	.11.0
Lace	. 4.0

Source: *Home Textiles Today*, June 13, 2005, p. 12.

★ 864 ★
Homefurnishings
SIC: 2392; NAICS: 314129

Leading Bath Towel Makers, 2005

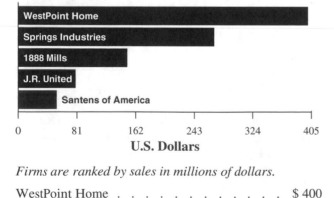

Firms are ranked by sales in millions of dollars.

WestPoint Home	$ 400
Springs Industries	270
1888 Mills	150

J.R. United	$ 79
Santens of America	54

Source: *Home Textiles Today*, January 9, 2006, p. 24, from *Home Textiles Today* market research.

★ 865 ★
Homefurnishings
SIC: 2392; NAICS: 314129

Leading Blanket Makers, 2005

Firms are ranked by sales in millions of dollars.

Sunbeam	$ 127
WestPoint Home	110
Charles D. Owen, div of	101
Berkshire Blankets	55
Pendleton Woolen Mills	18

Source: *Home Textiles Today*, January 9, 2006, p. 24, from *Home Textiles Today* market research.

★ 866 ★
Homefurnishings
SIC: 2392; NAICS: 314129

Leading Comforter Makers, 2005

Firms are ranked by sales in millions of dollars.

Springs Industries	$ 410
WestPoint Home	200
American Pacific	190
Dan River	116
Croscill Home	110

Source: *Home Textiles Today*, January 9, 2006, p. 24, from *Home Textiles Today* market research.

★ 867 ★
Homefurnishings
SIC: 2392; NAICS: 314129

Leading Comforter Makers (Down & Down Alt.), 2005

Firms are ranked by sales in millions of dollars.

Pacific Coast Feather	$ 106
Down Lite International	71
Phoenix Down	68
Hollander Home Fashions	47
WestPoint Home	40

Source: *Home Textiles Today*, January 9, 2006, p. 24, from *Home Textiles Today* market research.

★ 868 ★
Homefurnishings
SIC: 2392; NAICS: 314129

Leading Decorative Pillow Makers, 2005

Firms are ranked by sales in millions of dollars.

Brentwood Originals	$ 144
Arlee Home Fashions	64
Mohawk Home	27
Newport/Layton Home	24
Fashion Industries	22

Source: *Home Textiles Today*, January 9, 2006, p. 24, from *Home Textiles Today* market research.

★ 869 ★
Homefurnishings
SIC: 2392; NAICS: 314129

Leading Foam Pillows/Toppers, 2005

Firms are ranked by sales in millions of dollars.

Sleep Innovations	$ 250
Carpenter	80
Sleep Comfort Systems	43
Louisville Bedding	31
Hudson Industries	27

Source: *Home Textiles Today*, January 9, 2006, p. 24, from *Home Textiles Today* market research.

★ 870 ★
Homefurnishings
SIC: 2392; NAICS: 314129

Leading Kitchen Textile Makers, 2005

Firms are ranked by sales in millions of dollars.

Franco Manufacturing	$ 68
The John Ritzenthaler Co.	60
Town and Country Living	52
Elrene Home Fashions	17
Avonhome	15

Source: *Home Textiles Today*, January 9, 2006, p. 24, from *Home Textiles Today* market research.

★ 871 ★
Homefurnishings
SIC: 2392; NAICS: 314129

Leading Mattress Pad Makers, 2005

Firms are ranked by sales in millions of dollars.

Louisville Bedding	$ 100
Perfect Fit	48
Pacific Coast Feather	46
Springs Industries	35
Hollander Home Fashions	34

Source: *Home Textiles Today*, January 9, 2006, p. 24, from *Home Textiles Today* market research.

★ 872 ★
Homefurnishings
SIC: 2392; NAICS: 314129

Leading Quilt Makers, 2005

Firms are ranked by sales in millions of dollars.

PHI	$ 79
Sunham Home Fashions	65
Keeco	62
American Pacific	52
Britannica Home Fashions	48

Source: *Home Textiles Today*, January 9, 2006, p. 24, from *Home Textiles Today* market research.

★ 873 ★
Homefurnishings
SIC: 2392; NAICS: 314129

Leading Sheet/Pillowcase Makers, 2005

Firms are ranked by sales in millions of dollars.

Springs Industries	$ 690
WestPoint Home	400
Divatex Home Fashions	140

Continued on next page.

★ 873 ★
[Continued]
Homefurnishings
SIC: 2392; NAICS: 314129

Leading Sheet/Pillowcase Makers, 2005

Firms are ranked by sales in millions of dollars.

Dan River	$ 136
Franco Manufacturing	108

Source: *Home Textiles Today*, January 9, 2006, p. 24, from *Home Textiles Today* market research.

★ 874 ★
Homefurnishings
SIC: 2392; NAICS: 314129

Leading Shower Curtain Makers, 2005

Firms are ranked by sales in millions of dollars.

Allure Home Creation	$ 75
Ex-Cell Home Fashions	75
Springs Industries	57
Maytex Mills	52
Creative Bath Products	31

Source: *Home Textiles Today*, January 9, 2006, p. 24, from *Home Textiles Today* market research.

★ 875 ★
Homefurnishings
SIC: 2392; NAICS: 314129

Leading Sleep Pillow Makers, 2005

Firms are ranked by sales in millions of dollars.

Hollander Home Fashions	$ 170
Pacific Coast Feather	129
Springs Industries	105
WestPoint Home	60
Louisville Bedding	44

Source: *Home Textiles Today*, January 9, 2006, p. 24, from *Home Textiles Today* market research.

★ 876 ★
Homefurnishings
SIC: 2392; NAICS: 314129

Leading Table Linen Makers, 2005

Firms are ranked by sales in millions of dollars.

Town and Country	$ 151
Elrene Home Fashions	63

Bardwil Linens	$ 57
Avonhome	55
Ex-Cell Home Fashions	23

Source: *Home Textiles Today*, January 9, 2006, p. 24, from *Home Textiles Today* market research.

★ 877 ★
Homefurnishings
SIC: 2392; NAICS: 314129

Leading Throw Makers, 2005

Firms are ranked by sales in millions of dollars.

The Northwest Company	80.0%
Manual Woodworkers	70.0
Mohawk Home	61.0
Biederlack of America	40.0
Phoenix Down	18.0

Source: *Home Textiles Today*, January 9, 2006, p. 24, from *Home Textiles Today* market research.

★ 878 ★
Homefurnishings
SIC: 2392; NAICS: 314129

Placemat and Tea Tray Production Worldwide

Pimpernel makes one million mats and trays a week.

Pimpernel	80.0%
Other	20.0

Source: *The Journal (Newcastle, England)*, October 24, 2005, p. NA.

★ 879 ★
Homefurnishings
SIC: 2392; NAICS: 314129

Sleep Pillow Composition, 2004

Retail sales were $725 million.

Synthetic fill	68.0%
Natural fill	19.0
Memory foam	13.0

Source: *Home Textiles Today*, September 26, 2005, p. 1.

★ 880 ★
Textile Bags
SIC: 2393; NAICS: 314911

Leading Textile Bag Makers, 2004

Royal Ten Café's share was estimated at 3.3%-3.5% in 2004. Industry revenues were placed at $2.49 billion.

Royal Ten Café 3.5%
Taylor Made Group 1.3
Other 95.2

Source: "US Textile Bag & Canvas Mills Industry Research." [online] from http://www.ibisworld.com [Accessed May 2, 2006] from IBISWorld.

★ 881 ★
Embroidery Shops
SIC: 2395; NAICS: 315211, 315212

Embroidery Revenues, 2004

The embroidery industry consists of an estimated 20,000 shops whose primary business is embroidery and another 5,000 shops whose secondary business is embroidery. The industry had gross sales of $8.5 billion in 2004. Figures show sources of embroidery revenues by primary and secondary business.

	($ bil.)	Share
Embroidery/monogramming . . .	$ 4,000	47.33%
Textile screen printing	2,900	34.32
Ad specialty/promotional products . .	1,000	11.83
Other	551	6.52

Source: *Embroidery Monogram Business*, August 2005, p. 14, from *2005 Impressions Decorated Apparel Universe Study.*

★ 882 ★
Embroidery Shops
SIC: 2395; NAICS: 315211, 315212

Leading Embroidery Shops, 2004

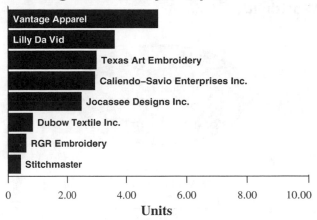

Companies are ranked by millions of pieces stitched.

Vantage Apparel 5.05
Lilly Da Vid 3.60
Texas Art Embroidery 3.00
Caliendo-Savio Enterprises Inc. 2.95
Jocassee Designs Inc. 2.50
Dubow Textile Inc. 0.82
RGR Embroidery 0.60
Stitchmaster 0.41

Source: *Stitches*, July 2006, p. NA.

★ 883 ★
Pleating and Stitching
SIC: 2395; NAICS: 314999

Pleating and Decorative Stitching Shipments, 1999-2001

Shipments are shown in millions of dollars. Leaders in the industry during this period: Morning Sun, Caliendo-Savio and Embroideries Inc.

1999 . . . . $ 632
2000 663
2001 561

Source: "Apparel Belts." [online] from http://www.referenceforbusiness.com/industries/Apparel [Accessed November 14, 2005].

★ 884 ★
Automotive Restraints
SIC: 2399; NAICS: 33636

Automotive Restraint Market Worldwide

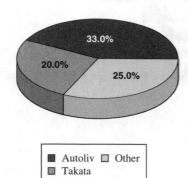

"Other" includes Toyoda Gosei and Key Safety Systems.

Autoliv	.33.0%
Takata	.20.0
Other	.25.0

Source: "Autoliv Annual Report 2005." [online] from http://autoliv2005.halvarsson.se/index.aspx?p212 [Accessed April 20, 2006].

★ 885 ★
Body Armor
SIC: 2399; NAICS: 314999

Body Armor Industry

DHB's market share is shown for the military market. It has 60% of the federal agency and 40% of the law enforcement market.

DHB Industries	.80.0%
Other	.20.0

Source: "DHB Industries Leadership, Quality & Innovations." [online] from http://www.dhbindustries.com/pdf/DHB_Investor_Book.pdf [Accessed June 1, 2006].

SIC 24 - Lumber and Wood Products

★ 886 ★
Lumber
SIC: 2421; NAICS: 321113
Largest Lumber Firms

Companies are ranked by production in billions of board feet.

Weyerhaeuser	7.2
Canfor	5.2
West Fraser Timber	4.0

Source: *Wood Markets*, March 2005, p. 3.

★ 887 ★
Lumber
SIC: 2421; NAICS: 321113
Largest Lumber Makers

Firms are ranked by sales in billions of dollars. New residential construction took 38% of the market, followed by repair & remodeling with 31%, nonresidential purposes 14% and other 17%.

Weyerhaeuser	$ 17.27
Louisiana-Pacific	2.02
Nexfor Inc.	1.36
Rayonier Inc.	1.10
Crown Pacific Partners	0.50

Source: *U.S. Industry Quarterly Review*, First Quarter 2005, p. NA.

★ 888 ★
Lumber
SIC: 2421; NAICS: 321113
Lumber Production by State, 2004

Western mills saw their highest production level in 14 years. Total production was $7,9588.6 million (18,762 million board fleet).

	($ mil.)	Share
Oregon	$ 2,951.2	36.94%
Washington	2,308.1	28.89
California	$ 1,287.4	16.12%
Idaho	869.4	10.88
Montana	393.1	4.92
South Dakota	71.6	0.90
Wyoming	42.5	0.53
Other	65.3	0.82

Source: *America's Intelligence Wire*, August 19, 2005, p. NA, from Western Wood Products Association.

★ 889 ★
Flooring
SIC: 2426; NAICS: 321918
Leading Wood Floor Makers, 2002

Shares are shown based on a $1.9 billion market.

Armstrong	32.1%
Domco Tarkett	6.2
Andersen Corp.	3.1
Mannington	2.3
Memphis Hardwood	2.3
Other	54.0

Source: "U.S. Market for Floor Coverings." [online] from http://www.osec.ch [Published December 2004] from Freedonia Group.

★ 890 ★

Flooring

SIC: 2426; NAICS: 321918

Wood Flooring Market in the U.K., 2006-2008

Figures are in millions of pounds sterling. Wood flooring covers 6% of the overall flooring market. In 2008, beech accounts for about 29.4%, oak 24.2% and maple 12.8% of the total market.

	2006	2007	2008
Beech	£ 60.5	£ 56.5	£ 52.1
Oak	32.2	37.8	42.9
Maple	22.1	22.5	22.8
Other	48.0	54.2	59.1

Source: *Contract Flooring Journal*, August 2005, p. 38, from trade and MSI forecasts.

★ 891 ★

Millwork

SIC: 2431; NAICS: 321918

Leading Millwork Firms, 2004

Market shares are shown in percent.

Andersen Corporation	4.23%
Masonite International Corporation	4.20
Georgia-Pacific	3.80
Pella Corporation	3.74
Other	84.03

Source: "US Millwork Industry Research." [online] from http://www.ibisworld.com [Accessed May 2, 2006] from IBISWorld.

★ 892 ★

Wood Trim

SIC: 2431; NAICS: 321918

Top Wood Trim Makers in North America

BIC has 70% of the market for center consoles, instrument panels, side door panels and other wood components.

BIC	70.0%
Other	30.0

Source: *just-auto.com*, December 2005, p. NA.

★ 893 ★

Cabinets

SIC: 2434; NAICS: 33711

Leading Cabinet Makers, 2005

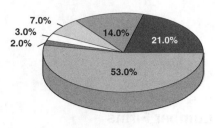

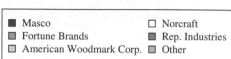

■ Masco	□ Norcraft
■ Fortune Brands	■ Rep. Industries
■ American Woodmark Corp.	■ Other

Cabinet sales are estimated to increase from $14.7 billion in 2005 to $15.3 billion in 2006.

Masco	21.0%
Fortune Brands	14.0
American Woodmark Corp.	7.0
Norcraft	3.0
Rep. Industries	2.0
Other	53.0

Source: *Homebuilding June 2006 Monthly*, Credit Suisse, June 2006 from Census Bureau, company reports and Credit Suisse analysis and estimates.

★ 894 ★

Cabinets

SIC: 2434; NAICS: 33711

Leading Kitchen Cabinet Makers, 2005

Market shares are shown in percent.

Masco Corporation	12.98%
Fortune Brands	5.61
American Woodmark Corp.	4.42
Other	76.99

Source: "US Wood Kitchen Cabinet & Countertop Manufacturing." [online] from http://www.ibisworld.com [Accessed May 2, 2006] from IBISWorld.

★ 895 ★
Softwood
SIC: 2436; NAICS: 321212

Largest Softwood Lumber Firms in North America

Companies are ranked by production in millions of board feet. Shares for the United States and Canada are based on a total of 73,705 million board feet.

	(mil.)	Share
Weyerhaeuser	6,992	9.49%
Canfor (Slocan)	4,612	6.26
West Fraser Timber (Weldwood)	4,021	5.46
International Paper	2,406	3.26
Abitibi-Consolidated	2,148	2.91
Tolko (Riverside-Lignum)	2,074	2.81
Georgia-Pacific	1,749	2.37
Sierra-Pacific Industries	1,731	2.35
Tembec	1,524	2.07
Hampton Affiliates	1,387	1.88
Simpson Timber	1,175	1.59
Stimson Timber	1,145	1.55
Other	42,741	57.99

Source: *Wood Markets*, April 2005, p. 1, from *Wood Markets* research.

★ 896 ★
Oriented Strand Board
SIC: 2439; NAICS: 321213

Leading OSB Makers in North America, 2004

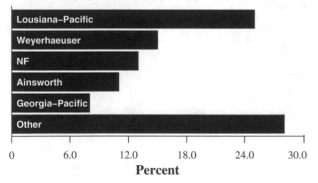

Market shares are shown in percent.

Lousiana-Pacific	25.0%
Weyerhaeuser	15.0
NF	13.0
Ainsworth	11.0

Georgia-Pacific	8.0%
Other	28.0

Source: "Louisiana Pacific Corporation." [online] from http://media.cor-porate-ir.net/media_files/NYS/LPX/presentations/UBS0922-041.pdf [Published September 22, 2004] from Resource Information Systems Inc.

★ 897 ★
Structural Panel
SIC: 2439; NAICS: 321213

Leading Structural Panel Makers in North America, 2004

Market shares are shown in percent.

Georgia Pacific	18.0%
Louisiana Pacific	15.0
Weyerhaeuser	14.0
NBD	8.0
Ainsworth	7.0
Other	38.0

Source: "Louisiana Pacific Corporation." [online] from http://media.cor-porate-ir.net/media_files/NYS/LPX/presentations/UBS0922-041.pdf [Published September 22, 2004] from Resource Information Systems Inc.

★ 898 ★
Pallets and Skids
SIC: 2448; NAICS: 32192

Pallet Industry in Japan, 2003-2004

Data are in 10,000 sheets. The total was 6,024 in 2004, up from 4,938 in 2000.

	2003	2004	Share
Wood	3,350	4,750	78.85%
Plastic	770	900	14.94
Metal	387	374	6.21

Source: "Solid Wood Products Annual Report 2005." [online] from http://www.fas.usda.gov [Published August 31, 2005] from Japan Pallet Trade Association.

★ 899 ★

Pallets and Skids

SIC: 2448; NAICS: 32192

Wood Box/Pallet Shipments by Year, 1998-2001

Shipments are in millions of dollars. Top firms are IFCO Systems, Love Box Company and TRAK International.

1998	$ 4.5
1999	4.6
2000	4.8
2001	4.4

Source: "Wood Pallets and Skids." [online] from http://www.referenceforbusiness.com/industries/Lumber-Wood [Accessed November 14, 2005] from U.S. Bureau of the Census.

★ 900 ★

Manufactured Homes

SIC: 2451; NAICS: 321991

Largest Manufactured Home Makers (Multi-Section), 2004

Market shares are shown in percent.

Clayton	18.4%
Fleetwood	18.3
Champion	15.8
Palm Harbor	6.4
Skyline	5.9
Other	35.2

Source: "Fleetwood Enterprises Annual Report 2005." [online] from http://ir.fleetwood.com/phoenix.zhtml?c63938&pirol-reports [Accessed June 1, 2006] from Statistical Surveys Inc.

★ 901 ★

Manufactured Homes

SIC: 2451; NAICS: 321991

Leading Factory Built Home Makers

Firms are ranked by revenues in millions of dollars.

Champion Enterprises	$ 1,002.16
Clayton Homes	951.00
Fleetwood Enterprises	854.94
Homes Inc.	557.11
Skyline Corporation	311.35
Cavalier Homes	229.87
All American Homes	220.00
Wausau Homes	207.60

Southern Homes Inc.	$ 154.10
Patriot Homes	147.99

Source: "2005 Factory Built Results." [online] from http://www.housingzone.com/factory.html [Accessed November 21, 2005].

★ 902 ★

Manufactured Homes

SIC: 2451; NAICS: 321991

Top Manufactured Home Makers, 2005

Market shares are year-to-date through November 2005.

Clayton	21.3%
Fleetwood	19.0
Champion	13.8
Skyline	5.4
Palm Harbor	5.2
Cavalier	4.1
Other	31.2

Source: "Fleetwood Emerald Asset Management." [online] from http://library. corporate-ir.net/library/63/639/63938/items/181969/road-show2_06Emerald.pdf [Published Feb 2, 2006] from Statistical Surveys Inc.

★ 903 ★

Decking

SIC: 2493; NAICS: 321219

Composite Decking Market, 2005

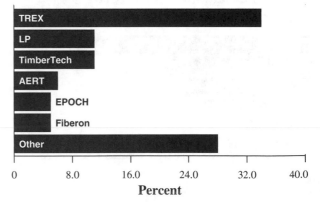

The market is seeing double digit growth.

TREX	34.0%
LP	11.0
TimberTech	11.0
AERT	6.0
EPOCH	5.0

Continued on next page.

★ 903 ★
[Continued]
Decking
SIC: 2493; NAICS: 321219
Composite Decking Market, 2005

The market is seeing double digit growth.

Fiberon 5.0%
Other 28.0

Source: ''Louisiana Investor Presentation [online] from http://library.corporate-ir.net/library/73/730/73030/items/184491/InvestorPresentation022006.pdf [Published Feb. 2006].

★ 904 ★
Decking
SIC: 2493; NAICS: 321219
Decking/Railing Market, 2000 and 2004

The market is estimated to be worth $3.75 billion in 2004. WPC stands for wood/plastic composites.

	2000	2004
Lumber	89.0%	79.0%
WPC	8.0	15.0
Plastic	2.0	2.0
Imported	1.0	4.0

Source: ''Wood Plastic Composites.'' [online] from http://www.woodsymposium.edu [Accessed October 1, 2005] from International Wood Composites Symposium and Washington State University.

★ 905 ★
Engineered Wood
SIC: 2493; NAICS: 321219
Engineered Wood Product Sales

There are about 1,500 companies in the engineered wood products industry. The value of production has increased from $21.3 billion in 2000 to $29.5 billion in 2004.

Reconstituted wood products 27.0%
Softwood veneer & plywood 25.0
Trusses 23.0
Engineered wood 16.0
Hardwood veneer & plywood 16.0

Source: ''Veneer, Plywood and Engineered Wood Product Manufacturing.'' [online] from http://www.globalwood.org [Published May 2005] from Global Wood Trade Network.

★ 906 ★
Wood Composites
SIC: 2493; NAICS: 321219
Wood/Plastic Composite Market, 2005

The wood plastic composite lumber market is estimated to be worth $11 billion in 2005.

Residential trucking and railings 66.0%
Window and door frames 11.0
Other 23.0

Source: *Forest Product Journal*, March 2006, p. 5.

★ 907 ★
Railroad Ties
SIC: 2499; NAICS: 321999
Class 1 Railroad Tie Market, 2003-2004

Class 1 track is the lowest class of operation for passenger trains. Freight train speeds are still limited to 10 mph, and passenger trains are restricted to 15 mph.

	2003	2004
Class 1	94.9%	95.5%
Other	5.1	4.5

Source: *Railway Track and Structures*, August 2005, p. 21, from Railroad Tie Association.

SIC 25 - Furniture and Fixtures

★ 908 ★

Furniture

SIC: 2500; NAICS: 337122, 337124, 337211

Furniture Sales by Segment, 2005

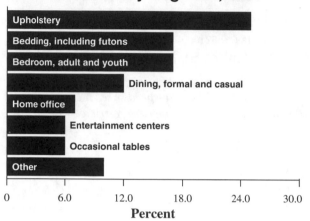

Percent

The industry is shown by segment.

Upholstery	.25.0%
Bedding, including futons	.17.0
Bedroom, adult and youth	.17.0
Dining, formal and casual	.12.0
Home office	7.0
Entertainment centers	6.0
Occasional tables	6.0
Other	.10.0

Source: *Homebuilding June 2006 Monthly*, Credit Suisse, June 2006 from *Furniture Today*.

★ 909 ★

Furniture

SIC: 2500; NAICS: 337122, 337124, 337211

Furniture Shipments by Type, 2000, 2003 and 2005

Shipments are in billions of dollars. Wood takes about 49% of the market in 2005, upholstery 44% with the balance held by metal and other types of furniture.

	2000	2003	2005
Wood	.$ 13.0	$ 12.2	$ 13.1
Upholstery	9.6	10.7	11.7
Metal & other	3.4	2.3	2.0

Source: *Homebuilding June 2006 Monthly*, Credit Suisse, June 2006 from Census Bureau, company reports and Credit Suisse analysis and estimates.

★ 910 ★

Furniture

SIC: 2500; NAICS: 337122, 337124, 337211

Infant Furniture Sales, 2005 and 2010

Furniture sales are shown in millions of dollars.

	2005	2010	Share
California	$ 140.4	$ 177.9	11.86%
Texas	86.4	111.4	7.43
New York	79.9	96.0	6.40
Illinois	51.9	63.5	4.23
Pennsylvania	50.6	60.6	4.04
Ohio	46.8	56.1	3.74
Michigan	41.5	50.5	3.37
New Jersey	37.3	46.2	3.08
North Carolina	35.1	44.2	2.95

Source: *Kids Today*, January 1, 2006, p. 6, from Easy Analytic Software Inc.

★ 911 ★
Furniture
SIC: 2500; NAICS: 337122, 337124, 337211
Leading Furniture Makers in Canada

The market grew by about 15% in 2004, but its growth will be much smaller in 2005. The import/export markets are about equal. Firms are ranked by sales in millions of Canadian dollars.

Dorel Industries	703.6
Palliser Furniture	399.3
Shermag Inc.	218.1
Canadel Furniture	165.0
La-Z-Boy Canada Ltd.	132.5
Magnussen Home Furnishings	130.0
Primo International	115.0
Gusdorf Canada	104.0
South Shore Industries	100.0
Dutalier	65.0

Source: "Canadian Household Furniture Market." [online] from http://www. buyusainfo.net [Published January 2006].

★ 912 ★
Bedding
SIC: 2515; NAICS: 337121, 33791
Top Bedding Makers, 2004

Market shares are shown based on $5.6 billion in wholesale bedding shipments. Sealy's brands include Sealy, Stearns & Foster, Bassett Bedding. Serta brands are Serta and Masterpiece. Spring Air includes Spring Air and Chattem & Wells.

Sealy	21.26%
Simmons	15.42
Serta	13.94
Spring Air	6.73
Tempur-Pedic	5.70
Select Comfort	4.68
King Koil	2.45
Therapedic	2.13
Kingsdown	1.89
Englander	1.76
IBC	1.72
Symbol	1.37
Other	20.95

Source: *Furniture Today*, May 30, 2005, p. NA, from *Furniture Today* market research.

★ 913 ★
Mattresses
SIC: 2515; NAICS: 33791
Visco-Elastic Mattress Market

Tempur-Pedic has 80%-90% of the market.

Tempur-Pedic	90.0%
Other	10.0

Source: "Restive Slumber." [online] from http://www. smartmoney.com [Published July 18, 2005].

★ 914 ★
Office Furniture
SIC: 2520; NAICS: 337214
Leading Office Furniture Makers, 2004

Steelcase Inc's share was 4.19%-5.23%, Herman Miller Inc.'s share was 4.19%-4.68%, HNI Corporation's was 3.73%-3.86% and Kimball International's was 1.06%-1.23%.

Steelcase Inc.	5.2%
Herman Miller Inc.	4.7
HNI Corporation	3.9
Kimball International inc.	1.2
Other	85.0

Source: "US Office Furniture Industry Research." [online] from http://www.ibisworld.com [Accessed May 2, 2006] from IBISWorld.

★ 915 ★
Office Furniture
SIC: 2520; NAICS: 337214
Leading Office Furniture Makers in North America

Market shares are shown based on shipments.

HNI	17.6%
Steelcase Inc.	15.3
HermanMiller	12.9
Knoll	7.2
Other	47.0

Source: "Knoll Good Design is Good Business." [online] http://library.corporate-ir.net/library/66/661/66169/items/176194/InvestorPresentation_12.05.pdf [Accessed June 6, 2006] from Business and Institutional Furniture Manufacturers Association.

★ 916 ★

Automotive Seating

SIC: 2531; NAICS: 33636

Leading Auto Seat Suppliers in Europe, 2005

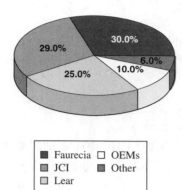

■ Faurecia   □ OEMs
■ JCI   ■ Other
□ Lear

Market shares are shown for the first half of the year.

Faurecia	.30.0%
JCI	.29.0
Lear	.25.0
OEMs	.10.0
Other	.6.0

Source: "First Half 2005 Results." [online] from http://www.faurecia.com/data/en/download/presentation/2005/faurecia_pres210705en.ppt [Published July 21, 2005].

★ 917 ★

Automotive Seating

SIC: 2531; NAICS: 33636

Leading Auto Seat Suppliers in North America, 2005

Market shares are shown for the first half of the year.

JCI	.38.0%
Lear	.33.0
Magna	.10.0
Faurecia	.3.0
Other	.16.0

Source: "First Half 2005 Results." [online] from http://www.faurecia.com/data/en/download/presentation/2005/faurecia_pres210705en.ppt [Published July 21, 2005].

★ 918 ★

Automotive Seating

SIC: 2531; NAICS: 33636

Leading Auto Seat Suppliers Worldwide, 2005

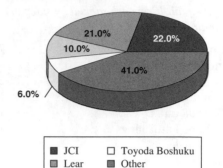

■ JCI   □ Toyoda Boshuku
■ Lear   ■ Other
□ Faurecia

Market shares are shown for the first half of the year.

JCI	.22.0%
Lear	.21.0
Faurecia	.10.0
Toyoda Boshuku	.6.0
Other	.41.0

Source: "First Half 2005 Results." [online] from http://www.faurecia.com/data/en/download/presentation/2005/faurecia_pres210705en.ppt [Published July 21, 2005].

★ 919 ★

Fixtures

SIC: 2541; NAICS: 337127

Lighting Fixture Demand Worldwide, 2008

Total demand is expected to increase 6.2% annually to reach $85 billion in 2008.

Asia/Pacific	.35.0%
North America	.29.0
Western Europe	.22.0
Other	.14.0

Source: *World Lighting Fixtures*, Freedonia Group, December 2004, p. 1, from Freedonia Group.

★ 920 ★
Fixtures
SIC: 2541; NAICS: 337215

Office Furniture Panel Market

Market shares are shown in percent.

Interface Fabrics 50.0%
Other 50.0

Source: "Interface." [online] from http://www.pharmaceuticalbusinessonline.com [Accessed October 31, 2005].

★ 921 ★
Blinds and Shades
SIC: 2591; NAICS: 33792

Leading Curtain/Shade Makers, 2005

Newell Rubbermaid had 19%-21% of the market and Springs Industries 15%-17.8% of the market.

Newell Rubbermaid 21.0%
Springs Industries 17.8
Other 62.2

Source: "US Blind and Shade Manufacturing." [online] from http://www.ibisworld.com [Accessed May 2, 2006] from IBISWorld.

★ 922 ★
Hospital Beds
SIC: 2599; NAICS: 337127

Hospital Bed Market

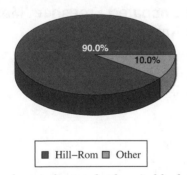

■ Hill–Rom ■ Other

Hill-Rom's share is for regular hospital beds. It holds 55% of the market for specialty beds, such as bariatric beds for obese patients.

Hill-Rom 90.0%
Other 10.0

Source: *Post and Courier*, November 17, 2005, p. B7.

★ 923 ★
Hospital Beds
SIC: 2599; NAICS: 337127

Premium Hospital Bed Market in Germany

Volker sells about 800 high-end beds a year, giving them over 60% of the market.

Volker 60.0%
Other 40.0

Source: *PTI - The Press Trust of India Ltd.*, May 14, 2006, p. NA.

SIC 26 - Paper and Allied Products

★ 924 ★
Pulp
SIC: 2611; NAICS: 32211

Top Bleached Paperboard Makers in North America, 2005

Market shares are shown based on total North American capacity of 19.6 million tons (2004 figure).

Weyerhaeuser	.13.5%
Tembec	8.1
Canfor	6.7
Koch Cellulose	6.7
Bowater	6.4
International Paper	6.3
West Fraser	5.9
Domtar	5.3
Parsons & Whittemore	4.6
Pope & Talbot	4.0
Other	.32.5

Source: *Pulp & Paper*, August 2005, p. 10, from American Forest & Paper Association.

★ 925 ★
Paper
SIC: 2621; NAICS: 322121

Global Writing/Printing Demand, 2006 and 2009

Data are in thousands of metric tons.

	2006	2009	Share
North America	30,720	31,749	27.32%
Europe	29,820	31,989	27.53
China	14,578	16,712	14.38
Japan	12,190	12,526	10.78
Asia (ex Japan, China)	9,378	10,188	8.77
Middle East	6,259	7,360	6.33
Latin America	5,147	5,678	4.89

Source: *Publishing Handbook*, North American Equity Research, January 2006, p. 83, from Resource Information Systems Inc., American Forest & Paper Association, *Pulp & Paper International* and company reports.

★ 926 ★
Paper
SIC: 2621; NAICS: 322121

Imported Paper and Cardboard Market in Russia

The annual value of imports is placed at $1 billion; 380,000 tons were imported in 2003. About 337,000 tons were imported during the first three quarters of 2004.

Books and magazines	.50.0%
Packaging	.30.0
Advertising and printing materials	.17.0
Special technical papers	3.0

Source: "Russia's Market for Coated Paper and Cardboard." [online] from http://www.stat-usa.gov [Published October 2005] from Russian Association of Pulp and Paper Mills and Institutions.

★ 927 ★
Paper
SIC: 2621; NAICS: 322121

Leading Uncoated Freesheet Makers in North America

Market shares are shown based on capacity.

International Paper	.24.9%
Weyerhaeuser	.18.5
Domtar	.15.0
Boise-Cascade	9.9
Georgia-Pacific	6.9
Nexfor	3.4
Glatfelter	2.6
Mead Westvaco	2.6
Blue Ridge Paper	1.7
Other	.14.5

Source: "Investor Presentation." [online] from http://www.newswire.ca/en/webcast/pages/en/5690/cascades_cibc.pdf [Published Oct. 7, 2005] from *Pulp & Paper Global Fact & Price Book*.

★ 928 ★
Paper
SIC: 2621; NAICS: 322121

Tissue Industry in Asia, 2004

Demand is shown in millions of tons.

	(mil.)	Share
China	3.44	50.22%
Japan	1.79	26.13
Korea	0.42	6.13
Taiwan	0.34	4.96
Other	0.86	12.55

Source: *Tissue World*, October/November 2005, p. NA.

★ 929 ★
Paper
SIC: 2621; NAICS: 322121

Top Kraft Paper Makers in North America, 2005

Market shares are shown based on total North American capacity of 2.15 million tons. Grocery and retail bags represent 40% of total shipments, multiwall bags and shipping sacks took 20% and wrapping/converting papers took 20% of the market.

Longview Fibre	16.3%
Intertnational Paper	13.2
Smurfit-Stone	12.3
Georgia-Pacific	11.1
Delta Natural Kraft	7.4
MeadWestvaco	7.2
Tolko Industries	7.0
Canfor	6.6
West Fraser Timber	5.5
Cascades	4.3
Other	9.7

Source: *Pulp & Paper*, November 2005, p. 10, from American Forest & Paper Association and Pulp & Paper Products Council.

★ 930 ★
Paper
SIC: 2621; NAICS: 322121

Top Newsprint Makers in North America, 2005

Market shares are shown based on total North American capacity of 13.35 million tons.

Abitibi-Consolidated	29.6%
Bowater Inc.	20.6
Kruger Inc.	8.7
SP Newsprint Co.	7.2
White Birch	6.7
Catalyst Paper	5.8
North Pacific Paper Co.	5.1
Tembec Inc.	3.7
Boise Cascade	3.0
Blue Heron	2.2
Other	7.5

Source: *Pulp & Paper*, December 2005, p. 10, from *Pulp & Paper Week*, Pulp & Paper Products Council and Canadian Paper analyst.

★ 931 ★
Paper
SIC: 2621; NAICS: 322121

Top Printing Paper Makers in Japan, 2004

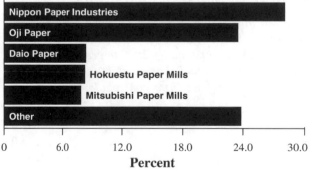

Market shares are shown based on domestic production of 11.38 million tons.

Nippon Paper Industries	28.1%
Oji Paper	23.5
Daio Paper	8.4
Hokuestu Paper Mills	8.3
Mitsubishi Paper Mills	7.9
Other	23.8

Source: "2004 Market Share Report." [online] from http://www.nikkei.co.jp [Published July 27, 2005] from Nikkei estimates and Japan Paper Association.

★ 932 ★

Paper

SIC: 2621; NAICS: 322121

Top Tissue Makers in North America, 2005

Market shares are shown based on total North American capacity of 8.95 million tons. Retail and away-from-home markets took 95% of dometic production. Toilet tissue took 47% toweling 36%, napkins 11% and facial 7%.

Georgia-Pacific	.32.4%
Kimberly-Clark	.17.1
Procter & Gamble	.15.2
Cascades	. 6.6
SCA	. 6.4
Kruger	. 4.2
Potlatch	. 2.4
Irving Tissue	. 2.3
Cellu Tissue	. 2.1
Marcal Paper	. 1.9
Other	. 9.3

Source: *Pulp & Paper*, February 2006, p. 10, from Pulp & Paper Products Council and *Global Fact & Price Book*.

★ 933 ★

Paperboard

SIC: 2631; NAICS: 32213

Cardboard Market in Australia

The Australian Competition & Consumer Commission are looking into charges Amcor and Visy struck an illegal agreement in January 2000 to cease a price war, maintain minimum charges and not compete for customers. The top two firms control almost the entire market.

Amcor/Visy	.97.0%
Other	. 3.0

Source: *Sydney Morning Herald*, December 21, 2005, p. NA.

★ 934 ★

Paperboard

SIC: 2631; NAICS: 322213

Cartonboard Market Worldwide, 2004

The industry was placed at 29.8 million tons. Asia took 43% of the market, North America 28% and Western Europe was third with 17% share.

Whitelined chipboard	.61.0%
Folding boxboard	.15.0
Solid bleached board	.15.0%
Coated unbleached kraft	. 9.0

Source: "ECMA Carton News Annual Review 2005." [online] from http://www.ecma.org/download/ECMACartonNewsWinter-Edition2005.pdf [Accessed June 1, 2006] from European Carton Manufacturers Association.

★ 935 ★

Paperboard

SIC: 2631; NAICS: 32213

Corrugated Board Market in Europe, 2004

Market shares are shown in percent.

Industry packaging	.32.0%
Food products, processed	.17.0
Consumer durables	.15.0
Fresh food products	.15.0
Other	.21.0

Source: "SCA Annual Report 2004." [online] from http://www.sca.com/Pdf/2004ENG.pdf [Accessed June 1, 2006] from SCA.

★ 936 ★

Paperboard

SIC: 2631; NAICS: 32213

Leading Paperboard Makers (Coated, Recycled) in North America

Market shares are shown based on capacity.

Rock-Tenn	.23.2%
Smurfit-Stone	.23.0
Cascades	.15.6
Graphic Packaging/Riverwood	.14.0
Caraustar	.12.7
Other	.11.5

Source: "Investor Presentation." [online] from http://www.newswire.ca/en/webcast/pages/en/5690/cascades_cibc.pdf [Published Oct. 7, 2005] from Goldman Sachs.

★ 937 ★
Paperboard
SIC: 2631; NAICS: 32213

Leading Paperboard Makers (Virgin) in North America

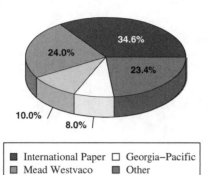

Market shares are shown based on capacity.

International Paper 34.6%
Mead Westvaco 24.0
Potlatch 10.0
Georgia-Pacific 8.0
Other 23.4

Source: "Investor Presentation." [online] from http://www.newswire.ca/en/webcast/pages/en/5690/cascades_cibc.pdf [Published Oct. 7, 2005] from Goldman Sachs.

★ 938 ★
Paperboard
SIC: 2631; NAICS: 32213

Leading Virgin Boxboard in Europe

Market shares are shown based on capacity.

Stora Enso 44.8%
M-Real 23.6
Holman 18.4
Mayr-Melnhof 6.8
Cascades 6.4

Source: "Investor Presentation." [online] from http://www.newswire.ca/en/webcast/pages/en/5690/cascades_cibc.pdf [Published Oct. 7, 2005] from Goldman Sachs.

★ 939 ★
Paperboard
SIC: 2631; NAICS: 32213

Top Bleached Paperboard Makers in North America, 2005

Market shares are shown based on total North American capacity of 6.1 million tons.

International Paper 29.1%
MeadWestvaco 28.0
Potlatch 11.1
Georgia-Pacific 9.7
Rock-Tenn 5.3
Smurfit-Stone 4.8
Blue Ridge Paper 4.7
Weyerhaeuser 4.0
Tembec 2.6
Other 0.7

Source: *Pulp & Paper*, October 2005, p. 10, from American Forest & Paper Association.

★ 940 ★
Paperboard
SIC: 2631; NAICS: 32213

Top Linerboard Makers in North America, 2005

Market shares are shown based on total North American capacity of 27,184 million tons.

Smurfit-Stone 17.4%
Weyerhaeuser 17.4
International Paper 14.1
Temple-Island 11.0
Georgia-Pacific 10.3
Packaging Corp. of America 5.2
Green Bay Packaging 2.4
Longview Fibre 2.2
Boise Cascade 2.0
Norampac 2.0
Other 16.0

Source: *Pulp & Paper*, January 2006, p. 10, from source.

★ 941 ★
Boxes
SIC: 2652; NAICS: 322213

Corrugated Sales Worldwide

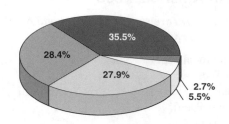

Market shares are shown in percent.

Asia	.35.5%
North America	.28.4
Europe	.27.9
Central/South America	5.5
Africa/Oceania	2.7

Source: *Paperboard Packaging*, August 2005, p. 24, from International Corrugated Case Association.

★ 942 ★
Boxes
SIC: 2652; NAICS: 322213

Largtest Bleached Boxboard Makers

Folding cartons took 41% of the end usemarket, followed by food containers with 14% of the market.

International Paper	2,675
Westvaco	1,635
Potlatch	625
Georgia-Pacific	545
Smurfit-Stone	320
Blue Ridge Paper	270
Gulf States Paper	265
Fort James	225
Weyerhaeuser	220
Durango-Georgia	200

Source: *U.S. Industry Quarterly Review*, First Quarter 2005, p. NA.

★ 943 ★
Boxes
SIC: 2657; NAICS: 322212

Folding Carton Sales

Distribution is shown in percent.

Beverages	.17.0%
Dry food	.13.0
Frozen foods	9.0
Pharmaceuticals & OTC	6.0
Retail carryout	6.0
Hardware	5.0
Paper products	5.0
Other	.39.0

Source: *Paperboard Packaging*, August 2005, p. 24, from Paperboard Packaging Council.

★ 944 ★
Boxes
SIC: 2657; NAICS: 322212

Top Folding Boxboard Makers in North America, 2005

Market shares are shown based on total North American capacity.

MeadWestvaco	.17.1%
International Paper	.11.2
Graphic Packaging	9.3
Rock-Tenn	7.8
Sonoco Products	6.6
Caraustar	6.3
Smurfit-Stone	5.9
Newark Group	5.5
Georgia-Pacific	4.7
Potlatch	3.9
U.S. Gypsum	3.7
Other	.17.6

Source: *Pulp & Paper*, June 2005, p. 10, from Resource Information Systems Inc., American Forest & Paper Association and U.S. Bureau of the Census.

★ 945 ★
Coated Paper
SIC: 2671; NAICS: 322221

Leading Coated Groundwood Makers in North America

Market shares are shown based on capacity.

International Paper	.19.2%
Stora Enso North America	.14.6

Continued on next page.

★ 945 ★

[Continued]
Coated Paper
SIC: 2671; NAICS: 322221

Leading Coated Groundwood Makers in North America

Market shares are shown based on capacity.

UPM Kymmene 14.0%
Bowater 13.2
MeadWestvaco 12.5
Kruger 6.1
Tembec 6.1
Norske Canada 3.8
Weyerhaeuser 3.8
Other 5.7

Source: "Investor Presentation." [online] from http://www.newswire.ca/en/webcast/pages/en/5690/cascades_cibc.pdf [Published Oct. 7, 2005] from *Pulp & Paper Global Fact & Price Book.*

★ 946 ★

Coated Paper
SIC: 2671; NAICS: 322221

Leading Coated Mechanical Paper Makers in North America

Market shares are shown in percent.

International Paper 19.0%
Stora Enso North America 15.5
Bowater 14.7
UPM 13.9
MeadWestvaco 12.4
Kruger 6.4
Tembec 6.0
Norske Canada 3.8
Weyerhaeuser 3.8
Other 4.4

Source: *Pulp & Paper*, May 2005, p. NA, from Resource Information Systems Inc., American Forest & Paper Association and Pulp & Paper Products Council.

★ 947 ★

Tape
SIC: 2672; NAICS: 322222

Top Tape Brands, 2005

Brands are ranked by sales in millions of dollars at supermarkets, drug stores and discount stores (excluding Wal-Mart) for the 52 weeks ended August 7, 2005.

	($ mil.)	Share
Scotch	$ 126.2	54.94%
Scotch Magic	49.0	21.33
Manco	7.7	3.35
Scotch Long Mask	2.8	1.22
Quickstik	2.7	1.18
3M	2.3	1.00
Tartan	2.0	0.87
Le Pages	1.5	0.65
Action	1.0	0.44
Dymo	0.7	0.30
Private label	23.9	10.40
Other	9.9	4.31

Source: *MMR*, September 19, 2005, p. 1, from Information Resources Inc.

★ 948 ★

Tape
SIC: 2672; NAICS: 322222

Top Tape Makers, 2005

Market shares are shown based on supermarkets, drug stores and mass merchandiser sales (excluding Wal-Mart) for the 52 weeks ended June 12, 2005.

3M 80.2%
Manco Inc. 3.8
Le Pages, Inc. Div. 2.0
Tri-Pak Inds. 1.5
Private label 10.5

Source: *Grocery Headquarters*, August 2005, p. S6, from Information Resources Inc.

★ 949 ★
Plastic Bags
SIC: 2673; NAICS: 322223, 326111

Top Cooking/Storage Bag Brands, 2005

Market shares are shown in percent. Figures exclude Wal-Mart and other large format mass retailers.

Ziploc	.32.9%
Hefty	.14.0
Glad	.10.1
Reynolds	4.2
Food Saver	0.3
Private label	.37.2
Other	1.3

Source: *U.S. Personal Care and Household Products Digest*, Citigroup Equity Research, February 24, 2006, p. 198, from ACNielsen.

★ 950 ★
Plastic Bags
SIC: 2673; NAICS: 322223, 326111

Top Garbage/Lawn Bag Brands, 2005

Market shares are shown in percent. Figures exclude Wal-Mart and other large format mass retailers.

Glad	.34.7%
Hefty	.25.2
Ruffies	2.6
Good Sense	1.1
Husky	0.6
Private label	.32.0
Other	3.8

Source: *U.S. Personal Care and Household Products Digest*, Citigroup Equity Research, February 24, 2006, p. 196, from ACNielsen.

★ 951 ★
Plastic Bags
SIC: 2673; NAICS: 322223, 326111

Top Garbage/Lawn Bag Makers, 2005

Market shares are shown in percent. Figures exclude Wal-Mart and other large format mass retailers.

Clorox	.34.7%
Pactiv	.25.2
Tyco International	2.7
CI Holdings Corp.	1.2
Poly America Corp.	0.6

Private label	.32.0%
Other	3.6

Source: *U.S. Personal Care and Household Products Digest*, Citigroup Equity Research, February 24, 2006, p. 196, from ACNielsen.

★ 952 ★
Plastic Bags
SIC: 2673; NAICS: 322223, 326111

Top Plastic Bag Brands, 2005

Market shares are shown based on supermarket, drug store and mass merchandiser sales (excluding Wal-Mart) for the 52 weeks ended August 7, 2005.

Ziploc Sandwich/Freezer/Food storage bags	.13.4%
Glad Garbage/Trash/Lawn & Leaf	9.5
Hefty Cinch Sak Garbage/Trash/Lawn & Leaf Bags	8.2
Private label Garbage/Trash/Lawn & Leaf Bags	.17.2
Private label Sandwich/Freezer/Food Storage Bags	.14.6
Other	.37.1

Source: *Private Label Buyer*, November 2005, p. 44, from Information Resources Inc.

★ 953 ★
Diapers
SIC: 2676; NAICS: 322291

Diaper Market in Ecuador, 2004

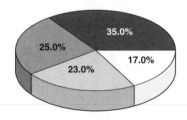

An estimated 480 million diapers are consumed annually, representing $84 million.

Kimberly-Clark	.35.0%
Zaimella	.25.0
Telo	.23.0
Familia and others	.17.0

Source: "Diaper Market in Ecuador." [online] from http://www.export.gov [Published September 2005].

★ 954 ★
Diapers
SIC: 2676; NAICS: 322291
Diaper Market in Ireland

Market shares are shown based on value of sales for the previous 12 months.

Pampers 72.1%
Other .27.9

Source: *Brand Strategy*, May 10, 2005, p. 20, from Pampers.

★ 955 ★
Diapers
SIC: 2676; NAICS: 322291
Diaper Market in Portugal

Market shares are shown based on value of sales for the previous 12 months.

Pampers 74.5%
Other 25.5

Source: *Brand Strategy*, May 10, 2005, p. 20, from Pampers.

★ 956 ★
Diapers
SIC: 2676; NAICS: 322291
Diaper Market in South Korea

Market shares are shown in percent.

Yuhan-Kimberly 70.0%
Other 30.0

Source: *Yonhap*, December 20, 2005, p. NA.

★ 957 ★
Diapers
SIC: 2676; NAICS: 322291
Top Adult Diaper Makers in Thailand

Market shares are shown in percent.

DSG International 75.0%
Other 25.0

Source: *Bangkok Post*, April 1, 2005, p. NA.

★ 958 ★
Diapers
SIC: 2676; NAICS: 322291
Top Adult Incontinence Brands, 2006

Brands are ranked by supermarket and drug store sales in millions of dollars.

	($ mil.)	Share
Depend	$ 180.3	32.45%
Depend Poise	130.9	23.56
Serenity	40.2	7.23
Serenity Night & Day	12.2	2.20
Serenity Dri Active Plus	3.7	0.67
Entrust Plus	2.6	0.47
Prevail	2.6	0.47
Serenity Dri Active	1.6	0.29
Sure Care	1.5	0.27
Sure Care Slip On	1.1	0.20
Private label	175.1	31.51
Other	3.9	0.70

Source: *MMR*, April 24, 2006, p. 30, from Information Resources Inc.

★ 959 ★
Diapers
SIC: 2676; NAICS: 322291
Top Adult Incontinence Product Makers, 2005

Market shares are shown in percent. Sales exclude Wal-Mart and other large-format mass retailers.

Kimberly-Clark 56.5%
Svenska Celluloka Aktiebolaget 10.3
First Quality Enterprises 1.2
Tyco International 0.7
Private label 30.5
Other 0.8

Source: *U.S. Personal Care and Household Products Digest*, Citigroup Equity Research, February 24, 2006, p. 132, from ACNielsen.

★ 960 ★

Diapers

SIC: 2676; NAICS: 322291

Top Diaper Brands, 2005

Brands are ranked by sales in millions of dollars at supermarkets, drug stores and discount stores (excluding Wal-Mart) for the 52 weeks ended August 7, 2005.

	($ mil.)	Share
Huggies	$ 336.5	19.45%
Pampers Baby Dry	316.7	18.31
Pampers Cruisers	252.4	14.59
Luvs Ultra Leakguards	158.4	9.16
Huggies Supreme	117.0	6.76
Pampers Swaddlers	77.9	4.50
Huggies Supreme Baby Shaped . . .	57.8	3.34
Huggies Ultratrim	56.0	3.24
Luvs	55.5	3.21
Private label	245.0	14.16
Other	56.8	3.28

Source: *MMR*, November 14, 2005, p. S14, from Information Resources Inc.

★ 961 ★

Diapers

SIC: 2676; NAICS: 322291

Top Diaper Makers, 2005

Market shares are shown based on supermarket, drug store and mass merchandiser sales (excluding Wal-Mart) for the 52 weeks ended June 12, 2005.

Procter & Gamble	.49.9%
Kimberly-Clark	.35.2
Assc. Hygienic Prods.	0.7
Private label	.14.1

Source: *Grocery Headquarters*, August 2005, p. S6, from Information Resources Inc.

★ 962 ★

Diapers

SIC: 2676; NAICS: 322291

Top Incontinence Product Makers Worldwide

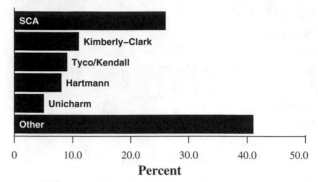

Market shares are shown in percent.

SCA	.26.0%
Kimberly-Clark	.11.0
Tyco/Kendall	9.0
Hartmann	8.0
Unicharm	5.0
Other	.41.0

Source: "SCA Annual Report 2004." [online] from http://www.sca.com/Pdf/2004ENG.pdf [Accessed June 1, 2006] from SCA.

★ 963 ★

Diapers

SIC: 2676; NAICS: 322291

Top Training Pants Brands, 2005

Market shares are shown based on food store, drug store and mass merchandiser sales (excluding Wal-Mart) for the 52 weeks ended June 12, 2005.

Huggies Pull Ups	.41.9%
Huggies Pull Ups Goodnites	.17.5
Pampers Easy Ups	.12.1
Pampers Feel N Learn	5.5
Huggies Little Swimmers	4.9
Huggies Convertibles	1.5
Pampers	0.3
Fitti	0.2
Snuggems	0.2
Private label	.15.8

Source: *Grocery Headquarters*, August 2005, p. S6, from Information Resources Inc.

★ 964 ★
Diapers
SIC: 2676; NAICS: 322291

Top Training Pants Makers, 2006

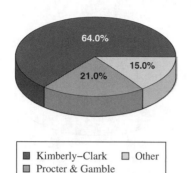

Market shares are shown for the first quarter ended January 22, 2006.

Kimberly-Clark	64.0%
Procter & Gamble	21.0
Other	15.0

Source: *Household & Personal Care*, Morgan Stanley Equity Research, February 2, 2006, p. 7, from Information Resources Inc. and Morgan Stanley.

★ 965 ★
Feminine Hygiene Products
SIC: 2676; NAICS: 322291

Feminine Hygiene Market in Europe

The industry is shown based on 42 billion units. Western Europe represents about three quarters of the market (73%) with Eastern Europe representing the balance.

Pantyliners	40.0%
Standard towels	21.0
Ultra-thin towels	20.0
Tampons	15.0
Other	4.0

Source: *Nonwovens Industry*, November 2005, p. 44.

★ 966 ★
Feminine Hygiene Products
SIC: 2676; NAICS: 322291

Top Feminine Hygiene Brands in the U.K.

The industry was worth 291 million pounds in 2005, with towels taking 108.8 million, tampons 97 million, pantyliners 43.7 million and incontinence products 42 million.

Tampax	19.7%
Always Ultra	13.6

Lil-lets	11.1%
Always Alldays	5.5
Bodyform Ultra Fit	5.5
Kotex Ultra	4.8
Bodyform	4.6
Carefree	4.4
Other	30.8

Source: *Marketing*, March 1, 2006, p. 32, from Euromonitor.

★ 967 ★
Feminine Hygiene Products
SIC: 2676; NAICS: 322291

Top Sanitary Napkin Makers, 2005

Sales fell slightly in the category to $836.7 million. Sales exclude Wal-Mart and other large-format mass retailers. Improved products mean that products function better and are not replaced as often (they can be worn overnight).

Procter & Gamble	44.7%
Johnson & Johnson	22.9
Kimberly Clark	22.9
Private label	9.3
Other	0.2

Source: *U.S. Personal Care and Household Products Digest*, Citigroup Equity Research, February 24, 2006, p. 148, from ACNielsen.

★ 968 ★
Feminine Hygiene Products
SIC: 2676; NAICS: 322291

Top Sanitary Napkins/Liners, 2006

Brands are ranked by supermarket and drug store sales in millions of dollars.

	($ mil.)	Share
Always	$ 319.5	39.72%
Kotex	110.3	13.71
Stayfree	105.0	13.05
Kotex Lightdays	54.8	6.81
Always Cleanweave	32.3	4.02
Carefree To Go	25.5	3.17
Carefree	25.2	3.13
Private label	74.7	9.29
Other	57.0	7.09

Source: *MMR*, April 24, 2006, p. 30, from Information Resources Inc.

★ 969 ★
Feminine Hygiene Products
SIC: 2676; NAICS: 322291

Top Tampon Makers, 2005

Market shares are shown based on dollar sales for the 12 weeks ended November 27, 2005.

Procter & Gamble	.49.6%
Playtex	.25.2
Kimberly-Clark	.10.7
Johnson & Johnson	8.3
Private label	6.0
Other	0.2

Source: *High Yield Consumer Products*, Deutsche Bank, December 15, 2005, p. 13, from Information Resources Inc.

★ 970 ★
Plastic Cups and Plates
SIC: 2676; NAICS: 322291

Top Disposable Tableware Makers in North America

Market shares are shown for all outlets including Wal-Mart for the last 52 weeks ended April 2, 2005. Figures include cups, plates and cutlery.

Georgia-Pacific	.23.0%
Pactiv	.12.0
Solo	.10.0
Chinet	6.0
Private label	.41.0
Other	9.0

Source: "Georgia-Pacific." [online] from http://www.gp.com [Published May 4, 2005] from ACNielsen.

★ 971 ★
Sanitary Paper Products
SIC: 2676; NAICS: 322291

Leading AFH Product Makers in North America, 2004

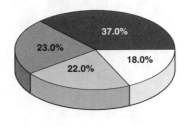

Market shares are shown in percent. AFH stands for away-from-home.

Georgia-Pacific	.37.0%
Kimberly-Clark	.23.0
SCA	.22.0
Other	.18.0

Source: "SCA Annual Report 2004." [online] from http://www.sca.com/Pdf/2004ENG.pdf [Accessed June 1, 2006] from SCA.

★ 972 ★
Sanitary Paper Products
SIC: 2676; NAICS: 322291

Leading Consumer Tissue Firms in Europe

Market shares are shown in percent.

SCA	.22.0%
Kimberly-Clark	.16.0
Georgia-Pacific	.13.0
Sofidel	6.0
Metsa Tissue	5.0
Procter & Gamble	4.0
Other	.34.0

Source: "SCA Annual Report 2004." [online] from http://www.sca.com/Pdf/2004ENG.pdf [Accessed June 1, 2006] from SCA.

★ 973 ★
Sanitary Paper Products
SIC: 2676; NAICS: 322291

Leading Facial Tissue Brands in the U.K., 2005

Sales are shown for the 52 weeks ended October 1, 2005. Figures are in thousands of pounds sterling and for all outlets.

	(000)	Share
Kleenex	£ 80,366	30.90%
Mellow Dairy	2,864	1.10
Tempo	2,828	1.09
Gould	1,257	0.48
Hany Andies	1,150	0.44
Other	171,593	65.98

Source: *Grocer*, December 17, 2005, p. 77, from ACNielsen.

★ 974 ★
Sanitary Paper Products
SIC: 2676; NAICS: 322291

Leading Toilet Tissue Brands in the U.K., 2005

Sales are shown for the 52 weeks ended October 1, 2005. Figures are in thousands of pounds sterling and for all outlets.

	(000)	Share
Andrex	£ 290,494	21.54%
Velvet	101,278	7.51
Charmin	57,760	4.28
Nouvelle	30,993	2.30
Other	868,018	64.37

Source: *Grocer*, December 17, 2005, p. 77, from ACNielsen.

★ 975 ★
Sanitary Paper Products
SIC: 2676; NAICS: 322291

Paper Product Industry, 2003-2005

The market for household paper products was worth $13.7 billion in 2005.

	2003	2004	2005
Toilet tissue	41.5%	41.3%	40.0%
Paper towels	26.6	27.2	27.1
Cups and plates	13.7	13.8	13.6
Facial tissue	12.5	12.0	12.0
Paper napkins	5.8	5.7	5.1

Source: *Research Alert*, February 3, 2006, p. 8, from Information Resources Inc. and Packaged Facts.

★ 976 ★
Sanitary Paper Products
SIC: 2676; NAICS: 322291

Sanitary Paper Sales Worldwide

More than half of all hygiene product retail sales take place in developed markets. The industry is also being driven by low growth rates in the number of women 18-54 years old and declining birth rates. Retail sales are projected in millions of dollars.

	2007	2008	2009
Nappies/diapers/ pants	$ 22,993.7	$ 23,571.2	$ 24,210.2
Sanitary protection	17,500.3	17,981.8	18,414.3
Wipes	6,622.5	6,776.4	6,936.9
Incontinence products	3,304.9	3,451.5	3,780.7

Source: *Tissue World*, August/September 2005, p. NA, from Euromonitor.

★ 977 ★
Sanitary Paper Products
SIC: 2676; NAICS: 322291

Top Facial Tissue Makers, 2005

Total sales were $1 billion. Sales exclude Wal-Mart and other large-format mass retailers.

Kimberly Clark	51.0%
Procter & Gamble	24.0
Irving Tissue	7.0
Private label	17.0
Other	1.0

Source: *U.S. Personal Care and Household Products Digest*, Citigroup Equity Research, February 24, 2006, p. 65, from ACNielsen.

★ 978 ★
Sanitary Paper Products
SIC: 2676; NAICS: 322291

Top Moist Towelette Makers, 2005

Market shares are based on sales at food stores, drug stores and discount stores (excluding Wal-Mart) for the 52 weeks ended June 12, 2005.

Kimberly-Clark Corp.	49.1%
Playtex Products	25.0
Procter & Gamble	6.9
Nice-Pak Products	2.2
Other	16.8

Source: *Grocery Headquarters*, September 21, 2005, p. S14, from Information Resources Inc.

★ 979 ★

Sanitary Paper Products

SIC: 2676; NAICS: 322291

Top Moist Towelettes, 2005

Market shares are based on sales at supermarkets, drug stores and mass merchandisers (excluding Wal-Mart) for the 52 weeks ended July 10, 2005.

Wet Ones	24.8%
Cottonelle Fresh	24.4
Cottonelle	13.3
Pull-Ups Just/Kids	5.1
Scott	3.9
Charmin Fresh Mates	3.8
Splash N Go	2.7
Pampers Tidy Tykes	2.3
Nice N Clean	2.2
Private label	13.3
Other	4.2

Source: *Household & Personal Products Industry*, October 2005, p. 63, from Information Resources Inc.

★ 980 ★

Sanitary Paper Products

SIC: 2676; NAICS: 322291

Top Napkin (Paper) Makers, 2005

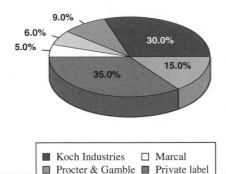

Koch Industries   ☐ Marcal
☐ Procter & Gamble   ■ Private label
☐ Kimberly–Clark   ■ Other

Total sales were $456 million in 2005. Sales exclude Wal-Mart and other large-format mass retailers.

Koch Industries	30.0%
Procter & Gamble	9.0
Kimberly-Clark	6.0
Marcal	5.0
Private label	35.0
Other	15.0

Source: *U.S. Personal Care and Household Products Digest*, Citigroup Equity Research, February 24, 2006, p. 65, from ACNielsen.

★ 981 ★

Sanitary Paper Products

SIC: 2676; NAICS: 322291

Top Paper Towel Brands, 2006

Market shares are shown based on supermarkets, drug stores and mass merchandiser sales (excluding Wal-Mart) for the 52 weeks ended January 22, 2006.

	($ mil.)	Share
Bounty	$ 866.9	36.44%
Brawny	249.9	10.50
Scott	213.3	8.97
Kleenex Viva	178.5	7.50
Sparkle	142.1	5.97
Marcal	42.0	1.77
Bountry Basic	33.4	1.40
Mardi Gras	12.8	0.54
So Dri	12.2	0.51
Jubilee	3.2	0.13
Private label	395.0	16.60
Other	229.8	9.66

Source: *MMR*, March 6, 2006, p. 30, from Information Resources Inc.

★ 982 ★

Sanitary Paper Products

SIC: 2676; NAICS: 322291

Top Paper Towel Makers, 2005

Total sales were $2.28 billion. Sales exclude Wal-Mart and other large-format mass retailers.

Procter & Gamble	41.0%
Koch	19.0
Kimberly-Clark	18.0
Marcal	2.0
Private label	20.0

Source: *U.S. Personal Care and Household Products Digest*, Citigroup Equity Research, February 24, 2006, p. 138, from ACNielsen.

★ 983 ★
Sanitary Paper Products
SIC: 2676; NAICS: 322291

Top Sanitary Paper Makers in Japan, 2004

Market shares are shown based on domestic production of 1.7 million tons.

Daio Paper	14.5%
Crecia	11.7
Oji Nepia	10.7
Tokai Pulp & Paper	1.9
Mitsubishi Paper Mills	0.6
Other	61.6

Source: ''2004 Market Share Report.'' [online] from http://www.nikkei.co.jp [Published July 27, 2005] from Nikkei estimates and Japan Paper Association.

★ 984 ★
Sanitary Paper Products
SIC: 2676; NAICS: 322291

Top Toilet Tissue Brands, 2006

Market shares are shown based on supermarket, drug store and mass merchandiser sales (excluding Wal-Mart) for the 52 weeks ended January 26, 2006.

Scott	16.0%
Kleenex Cottonelle	14.0
Charmin	13.1
Quilted Northern	11.9
Angel Soft	11.0
Charmin Ultra	10.7
Quilted Northern Ultra	3.2
Marcal	1.2
Soft N Gentle	1.2
Private label	13.6
Other	4.1

Source: *Grocery Headquarters*, April 2006, p. 56, from Information Resources Inc.

★ 985 ★
Sanitary Paper Products
SIC: 2676; NAICS: 322291

Top Toilet Tissue Makers, 2005

Market shares are shown in percent. Sales exclude Wal-Mart and other large-format mass retailers.

Kimberly-Clark	31.0%
Koch	28.0
Procter & Gamble	26.0

Private label	14.0%
Other	1.0

Source: *U.S. Personal Care and Household Products Digest*, Citigroup Equity Research, February 24, 2006, p. 136, from ACNielsen.

★ 986 ★
Wipes
SIC: 2676; NAICS: 322291

Global Wipes Market by Segment, 2004 and 2009

Sales are shown in millions of dollars. Unless specified, data refer to impregnated wet wipes.

	2004	2009	Share
Starter kits/sweepers/sticks (dry electro-static)	$ 897.0	$ 878.6	22.85%
Wet floor	522.8	723.4	18.81
Wipes & refills (dry electro-static)	519.2	547.1	14.23
All purpose cleaning	460.4	498.3	12.96
Wipes & refills	311.9	391.0	10.17
Starter kits	210.9	332.4	8.64
Toilet care	167.7	189.6	4.93
Furniture polish	110.6	146.6	3.81
Window/glass	98.5	109.6	2.85
Other	30.1	29.3	0.76

Source: *Household & Personal Products Industry*, October 2005, p. 63, from Euromonitor.

★ 987 ★
Wipes
SIC: 2676; NAICS: 322291

Personal Wipe Market Worldwide, 2005 and 2009

The total market grew from $3,939.6 million in 2005 to $4,351.6 million in 2009.

	2005	2009	Share
Baby	$ 2,593.4	$ 2,817.8	52.15%
Cosmetic	930.1	1,051.9	19.47
Facial cleansing	861.3	974.8	18.04
Adult	416.1	481.8	8.92
Deodorant	68.8	77.1	1.43

Source: *Nonwovens Industry*, June 2005, p. 36, from Euromonitor.

★ 988 ★
Wipes
SIC: 2676; NAICS: 322291
Top Baby Wipe Brands, 2006

*Brands are ranked by supermarket and drug store
sales in millions of dollars.*

	($ mil.)	Share
Huggies Natural Care	$ 92.7	21.33%
Pampers Natural Aloe Touch	63.0	14.50
Huggies	23.2	5.34
Pampers Sensitive	16.5	3.80
Huggies Supreme Care	16.4	3.77
Pampers Kandoo	14.2	3.27
Pampers Original Cotton Care . . .	13.2	3.04
Huggies Newborn	9.5	2.19
Huggies Pull Ups	9.5	2.19
Private label	125.8	28.95
Other	50.6	11.64

Source: *MMR*, April 24, 2006, p. 30, from Information Resources Inc.

★ 989 ★
Wipes
SIC: 2676; NAICS: 322291
Wipes Market Worldwide

Sales are shown in millions of dollars.

	2003	2004	Share
Western Europe	$ 2,374.2	$ 2,776.3	45.67%
North America	1,890.0	1,871.1	30.78
Asia Pacific	909.9	1,000.4	16.46
Latin America	129.5	143.9	2.37
Australasia	115.9	142.3	2.34
Africa/Middle East . . .	70.0	80.2	1.32
North America	49.4	64.3	1.06

Source: *Nonwovens Industry*, September 2005, p. S12, from Euromonitor.

★ 990 ★
Envelopes
SIC: 2678; NAICS: 322233
Envelope Shipments by Year

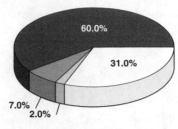

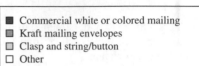

Distribution is shown for shipments.

Commercial white or colored mailing	.60.0%
Kraft mailing envelopes	7.0
Clasp and string/button	2.0
Other	.31.0

Source: "Envelopes." [online] from http://www.reference-forbusiness.com/industries/Paper-Allied/Envelopes [Accessed November 14, 2005] from U.S. Bureau of the Census.

SIC 27 - Printing and Publishing

★ 991 ★
Publishing
SIC: 2700; NAICS: 51111, 51112, 51113
Top Publishing Firms in Japan, 2004

Market shares are shown based on domestic sales of 2.82 trillion yen.

Recruit	14.5%
Benesse	7.9
Kodansha	5.7
Shogakukan	5.5
Shueisha	4.9
Other	61.5

Source: "2004 Market Share Report." [online] from http://www.nikkei.co.jp [Published July 27, 2005] from Research Institute for Publications and Dentsu.

★ 992 ★
Newspapers
SIC: 2711; NAICS: 51111
Free Newspaper Industry Worldwide

There are free newspapers in 35 countries. The newspapers have enjoyed a 33% surge in circulation in Europe during the first nine months of 2005. Circulation is up 98% to 3.6 million in Spain, up 77% in Iceland and more than 20% in France. They rely on advertising for all their revenues and have been stealing market share from traditional newspapers, which are losing market share to online newspapers. There were 14.5 million readers as of September 2005. Metro International distributes 7 million copies daily. The market share for free newspapers is shown in selected countries.

Iceland	76.0%
Spain	46.0
Portugal	31.0
Italy	30.0
Greece	27.0
Denmark	20.0
Sweden	20.0
Netherlands	19.0

Source: *Sunday Business*, October 30, 2005, p. NA, from Piet Bakker, University of Amsterdam.

★ 993 ★
Newspapers
SIC: 2711; NAICS: 51111
Largest Newspaper Markets Worldwide

Global sales and advertising revenues increased in the industry after emerging from a 3 year recession. China, India and Japan represent expanding markets. Data show millions of copied sold daily. Newspaper readership on the Internet rose 32% in 2004.

China	93.5
India	78.8
Japan	70.4
United States	48.3
Germany	22.1

Source: *International Herald Tribune*, May 30, 2005, p. 10, from World Association of Newspapers.

★ 994 ★

Newspapers

SIC: 2711; NAICS: 51111

Top Newspaper Publishers, 2004

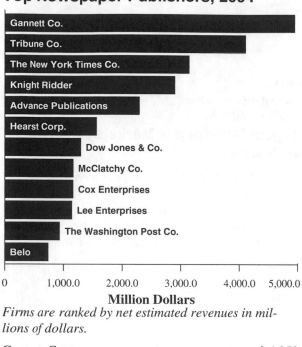

Million Dollars

Firms are ranked by net estimated revenues in millions of dollars.

Gannett Co.	$ 4,950.7
Tribune Co.	4,108.8
The New York Times Co.	3,142.6
Knight Ridder	2,899.5
Advance Publications	2,295.2
Hearst Corp.	1,564.0
Dow Jones & Co.	1,293.3
McClatchy Co.	1,163.4
Cox Enterprises	1,160.2
Lee Enterprises	1,140.0
The Washington Post Co.	938.1
Belo	752.9

Source: *Advertising Age*, August 22, 2005, p. S-10, from BIA Financial Network, public documents and *Advertising Age's 100 Leading Media Companies.*

★ 995 ★

Newspapers

SIC: 2711; NAICS: 51111

Top Newspapers, 2005

Average weekday circulation fell 2.6% during six months ended September 2005. Of those shown, only Star-Ledger saw an increase in figures.

USA TODAY	2,296,335
The Wall Street Journal	2,083,660
The New York Times	1,126,190
Los Angeles Times	843,432

Daily News - New York	688,584
The Washington Post	678,779
New York Post	662,681
Chicago Tribune	586,122
Houston Chronicle	521,419
The Boston Globe	414,225
The Arizona Republic	411,043
The Star-Ledger	400,092

Source: *USA TODAY*, November 8, 2005, p. 7B, from Audit Bureau of Circulations.

★ 996 ★

Comic Books

SIC: 2721; NAICS: 51112

Leading Comic Book Publishers, 2005

Publishers are ranked by share of dollar sales. Top-selling comics for the year: All Star Batman & Robin #1, House of M #1 (of 8), and Infinite Crisis #1 (of 7).

Marvel Comics	.36.97%
DC Comics	.32.96
Dark Horse Comics	5.59
Image Comics	3.56
Tokyopop	3.11
Viz LLC	2.15
Wizard Entertainment	1.99
IDW Publishing	1.33
Devil's Due Publishing	0.83
Avatar Press Inc.	0.74
Dynamic Forces	0.61
Fantagraphics Books/Eros Comix	0.60
A.D. Vision	0.52
Aspen MLT	0.45
Diamond UK	0.42
Random House	0.36
Archie Comic Publications	0.33
Other	6.51

Source: "2005 Year-End Sales Charts." [online] from http://www.newsarama.com/marketreport/05Year_end.html [Published February 3, 2006] from Diamond Comic Distributors.

★ 997 ★
Magazines
SIC: 2721; NAICS: 51112
Leading Building/Construction Magazines, 2005

Titles are ranked by ad pages for January - October 2005. Top publishers are Hanley Wood, McGraw-Hill, Cygnus and Randall Publishing.

	Pages	Share
Builder	1,826.43	20.04%
ENR	1,402.01	15.39
Equipment World	904.18	9.92
Kitchen & Bath Design News	786.50	8.63
Custom Home	687.04	7.54
ProSales	611.04	6.71
Concrete Construction	523.74	5.75
Professional Remodeler	495.29	5.44
Building Products	483.08	5.30
Other	1,393.16	15.29

Source: *Min's B to B*, December 19, 2005, p. NA, from IMS Health's *The Auditor*.

★ 998 ★
Magazines
SIC: 2721; NAICS: 51112
Leading Magazine Publishers in Germany

Shares are shown based on circulation.

Axel Springer	22.0%
Bauer	8.0
WAZ	6.0
Burda	4.0
Holtzbrinck	4.0
G+J	3.0
Other	53.0

Source: "Axel Springer Company Presentation." [online] from http://www.axelspringer.de [Published November 2005].

★ 999 ★
Magazines
SIC: 2721; NAICS: 51112
Most-Read Magazines in Canada

There are about 2,500 Canadian titles, although they represent only about 18% of shelf space. The United States has the balance.

Reader's Digest	7,432,000
Canadian Living	4,449,000
Chatelaine	4,310,000

Source: *Globe & Mail*, October 29, 2005, p. R6, from Print Measurement Bureau.

★ 1000 ★
Magazines
SIC: 2721; NAICS: 51112
Puzzle Magazine Market in the U.K.

Market shares are shown in percent.

Puzzler Media	50.0%
Other	50.0

Source: *Reuters*, December 11, 2005, p. NA.

★ 1001 ★
Magazines
SIC: 2721; NAICS: 51112
Top Magazine Companies, 2004

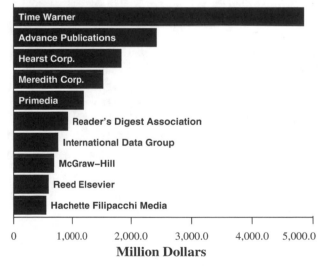

Firms are ranked by magazine net revenues in millions of dollars.

Time Warner	$ 4,851.0
Advance Publications	2,419.8
Hearst Corp.	1,837.0
Meredith Corp.	1,534.4

Continued on next page.

★ 1001 ★
[Continued]
Magazines
SIC: 2721; NAICS: 51112
Top Magazine Companies, 2004

Firms are ranked by magazine net revenues in millions of dollars.

Primedia	$ 1,206.2
Reader's Digest Association	917.3
International Data Group	755.0
McGraw-Hill	686.8
Reed Elsevier	594.0
Hachette Filipacchi Media	552.0

Source: *Advertising Age*, August 22, 2005, p. S-10, from Publishers Information Bureau, *Advertising Age's 100 Leading Media Companies* and TNS Media Intelligence.

★ 1002 ★
Magazines
SIC: 2721; NAICS: 51112
Top Magazines by Ad Revenue

Magazines are ranked by ad revenue in millions of dollars.

People	$ 850.4
Better Homes and Gardens	800.0
Time	631.9
Parade	626.0
Sports Illustrated	623.5
Good Housekeeping	477.7
Newsweek	473.1
USA Weekend	431.4
Woman's Day	408.4
In Style	391.1
New York Times Magazine	373.8

Source: *Adweek*, March 6, 2006, p. S19, from Publishers Information Bureau/TNS Media Intelligence.

★ 1003 ★
Magazines
SIC: 2721; NAICS: 51112
Top Magazines by Circulation, 2005

Magazines are ranked by average circulation for the second half of 2005. The industry saw 35 titles boost their subscription figures, among them Teen Vogue (+694,000), US Weekly (+187,000), Blender (+158,000) and In Touch (+158,000). Leaders among those losing subscribers: Fit Pregnancy (-363,000), National Enquirer (-315,000), 0, The Oprah Magazine (-247,000) and Game Informer (-213,000).

AARP The Magazine	22,791,354
Reader's Digest	10,094,602
Better Homes and Gardens	7,607,694
TV Guide	7,349,619
National Geographic	5,376,750
Good Housekeeping	4,662,725
Family Circle	4,294,841
Ladies' Home Journal	4,112,010
Woman's Day	4,086,381
Time	4,026,891
People	3,691,167
Prevention	3,345,214
Sports Illustrated	3,238,101
Newsweek	3,117,562
Cosmopolitan	3,007,349

Source: *Adweek*, March 6, 2006, p. S19, from Audit Bureau of Circulations.

★ 1004 ★
Magazines
SIC: 2721; NAICS: 51112
Top Magazines in the U.K., 2005

Titles are ranked by circulation as of January - June 2005. FHM is the leader in the men's lifestyle segment. Glamour is the leader in the women's lifestyle market. More is the leader of the teen category.

Sky the Magazine	6,783,581
Asda Magazine	2,631,293
Boots Health & Beauty	1,765,387
What's on TV	1,673,790
U Magazine for Unison Members . . .	1,465,833
Saga Magazine	1,245,006
Take A Break	1,200,397
TV Choice	1,157,622
The Somerfield Magazine	1,134,364
Radio Times	1,080,199

Source: *Campaign*, August 25, 2005, p. 30, from Audit Bureau of Circulations.

★ 1005 ★
Magazines
SIC: 2721; NAICS: 51112

Top Personal Finance Magazines

Magazines are ranked by circulation.

Money	1,900,000
Kiplinger's	1,000,000
Smart Money	819,844
Barron's	300,635
Worth	125,000

Source: *USA TODAY*, November 14, 2005, p. 4B, from Magazine Publishers Association.

★ 1006 ★
Magazines
SIC: 2721; NAICS: 51112

Women's Lifestyle Magazines in Australia

ACP's Woman's Day has become the most read magazine in the country with 2.7 million readers. ACP dominates the woman's lifestyle category.

ACP	63.0%
Other	37.0

Source: *B&T Weekly*, February 24, 2006, p. 12, from Camille Alarcon.

★ 1007 ★
Books
SIC: 2731; NAICS: 51113

Best-Selling Book Categories, 2005 - 2006

Industry sales are expected to reach $38.26 billion. The biggest gains are expected to come in the juvenile paperback segment, where a 10.1% increase is projected, and in the religious book segment, where sales are forecast to increase 6.5%. For the first time, the BISG numbers include results from a survey of small presses with sales under $50 million.

	2005	2006
Trade	$ 14,010.0	$ 14,496.9
Professional	8,618.9	8,906.4
Adult hardcover	5,364.0	5,530.2
Elhi	4,700.5	4,866.2
College	4,504.7	4,584.2
Adult paperback	3,474.4	3,565.0
Standardized tests	2,349.9	2,490.5

	2005	2006
Religious	$ 2,293.6	$ 2,443.5
Mass market paperback . . .	1,835.9	1,884.6
Juvenile paperback	1,698.0	1,868.7
Juvenile hardcover	1,637.9	1,675.4
University Press	465.8	474.8

Source: *Publishers Weekly*, May 22, 2006, p. NA, from Book Industry Study Group.

★ 1008 ★
Books
SIC: 2731; NAICS: 51113

Best-Selling Books, 2005

The book industry grew 9.3% over the previous year to 709.8 million scans as of January 1, 2006. The top 200 best-selling titles generated 74.7 million units, or 10.5% of total sales. But the source points out that the top 200 did not keep up with the industry's overall growth. In 2004, 5 titles sold 2 millon or more copies. Only the most recent Harry Potter book by J.K. Rowling did that this year. In 2004, 10 books sold over 1 million copies; in 2005, only 6 did. Books are shown by millions of copies sold.

Harry Potter and the Half-Blood Prince, J.K. Rowling	7.02
A Million Little Pieces, James Frey	1.77
The Kite Runner, Khaled Hosseini	1.60
1776, David McCullough	1.20
The Da Vinci Code, Dan Brown	1.09
The World is Flat, Thomas Friedman	1.07

Source: *Book Standard*, January 9, 2006, p. B2, from Nielsen BookScan.

★ 1009 ★
Books
SIC: 2731; NAICS: 51113

Best-Selling Books in Australia, 2005

Harry Potter and the Half-Blood Prince was the top-selling book in the country, with sales of 805,575 copies in both the children's and adults' editions. Books are shown by copies sold and value of sales. Data are based on a survey of 1,000 book retailers from January 2 - December 31, 2005.

	Copies	($ mil.)
Harry Potter and the Half-Blood Prince	805,075	$ 22.6
The CSIRO Total Wellbeing Diet, Noakes & Clifton	457,527	10.8

Continued on next page.

★ 1009 ★
[Continued]
Books
SIC: 2731; NAICS: 51113

Best-Selling Books in Australia, 2005

Harry Potter and the Half-Blood Prince was the top-selling book in the country, with sales of 805,575 copies in both the children's and adults' editions. Books are shown by copies sold and value of sales. Data are based on a survey of 1,000 book retailers from January 2 - December 31, 2005.

	Copies	($ mil.)
The Da Vinci Code, Dan Brown . .	425,253	$ 8.3
Angels & Demons, Dan Brown . .	212,794	3.3
Whitethorn, Bryce Courtenay . . .	185,970	5.3
Out of My Comfort Zone, Steve Waugh	155,249	4.7
Guinness World Records, 2006 . .	152,755	3.9

Source: *The Age*, January 9, 2006, p. NA, from Nielsen BookScan.

★ 1010 ★
Books
SIC: 2731; NAICS: 51113

Best-Selling Children's Books, 2005

The Polar Express was the best-selling backlist title with 898,187 copies sold, followed by Goodnight Moon with 627,169 copies.

Harry Potter and the Half-Blood Prince, J.K. Rowling	13,500,000
The Penultimate Peril (A Series of Unfortunate Events), Lemony Snicket .	1,765,315
Eldest, Christopher Paolini	1,752,753
Girl in Pants: The Third Summer of the Sisterhood, Ann Brahares	776,839
If You Give a Pig a Party, Laura Numeroff	479,589
Runny Babitt, Shel Silverstein	469,373
Artemis Fowl: The Opal Deception, Eoin Colfer	450,000
10 Little Rubber Ducks, Eric Carle . . .	373,862
Snowmen at Christmas, Caralyn Buehner	309,373
Jingle Bells, Batman Smells, Barbara Park	307,232

Source: *Publishers Weekly*, March 27, 2006, p. 37.

★ 1011 ★
Books
SIC: 2731; NAICS: 51113

Best-Selling Harry Potter Titles

There are over 100 million copies in print of the first five books. Initial print runs have increased as the series grew more popular. The books have sold 270 million copies worldwide and been translated into over 60 languages. Data show millions of copies in print.

Harry Potter and the Sorcerer's Stone	26.0
Harry Potter and the Chamber of Secrets . . .	24.0
Harry Potter and the Prisoner of Azkaban . . .	19.0
Harry Potter and the Goblet of Fire	17.0
Harry Potter and the Order of the Phoenix . . .	16.0
Harry Potter and the Half-Blood Prince	10.8

Source: *USA TODAY*, July 11, 2005, p. 2D, from Scholastic.

★ 1012 ★
Books
SIC: 2731; NAICS: 51113

Best-Selling Science Fiction Sales in the U.K.

Nearly a fifth of all copies were in adult editions. A total of 6 of the 11 top spots in children's fantasy fiction went to J.K. Rowling. Data show unit sales for the 26 weeks ended November 19, 2005.

Jonathan Strange & Mr. Norrell	125,020
Going Postal	116,133
The Algebraist	66,769
The War of the Worlds	19,513
Gene	19,261
The Magician's Guild	18,164
Haunted	16,154
The Runes of the Earth	14,825
The High Lord	14,660
The Novice	14,570

Source: *The Bookseller*, December 9, 2005, p. 29, from Nielsen BookScan Total Consumer Market.

★ 1013 ★
Books
SIC: 2731; NAICS: 51113
Bible Sales by Type

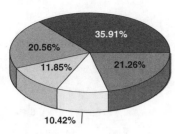

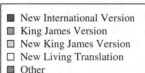

- ■ New International Version
- ■ King James Version
- ■ New King James Version
- □ New Living Translation
- ■ Other

Lifeway Christian Resources released the Holdman Christian Standard Bible in April 2004. It is among only about 10 translations of the Bible, although there are about 15 revisions. The New International Version is published exclusively by Zonderman. Thomson Nelson Inc. is the largest bible publisher. There are 180 million copies of the New King James Version in print.

New International Version	.35.91%
King James Version	.20.56
New King James Version	.11.85
New Living Translation	.10.42
Other	.21.26

Source: "Lifeway Hopes Bible Will Find Audience." [online] from http://www.nashvillecitypaper.com [Accessed November 11, 2005] from Evangelical Christian Publishing Association.

★ 1014 ★
Books
SIC: 2731; NAICS: 51113
Book Sales in Germany

Over 80,000 new and reprinted titles enter the German market every year. The book trade generated total sales of $11.3 billion.

Fiction	.22.0%
Non-fiction	.12.0
School and learning	.11.0
Professional sciences	.11.0
Children's and teen literature	.10.0
Theology/religion	.6.0
Travel	.5.0
Secondhand	.3.0%
Audio books	.3.0
Magazines & other press publications	.7.0
Other	.10.0

Source: "Educational Book Market in Germany." [online] from http://www. buyusainfo.net [Published January 2006] from German Publishers and Booksellers Association.

★ 1015 ★
Books
SIC: 2731; NAICS: 51113
Children's Reference Book Market

Market shares are shown in percent.

World Almanac	.78.0%
Other	.22.0

Source: "World Almanac and Book of Facts." [online] from http://www.store.worldstart.com/product.php?productid110 [Accessed January 4, 2006].

★ 1016 ★
Books
SIC: 2731; NAICS: 51113
Christian Fiction Market

Tyndale is the leader in the market. It has doubled its staff since the success of the "Left Behind" series, which generated $650 million for Tyndale. The source notes that according to the Book Industry Study Group report, sales and books in the religion category are expected to increase by 6 percent a year until 2009. Most of these titles are Christian-based, although some are inspirational titles such as "A Purpose Driven Life".

Tyndale	.39.0%
Other	.61.0

Source: "Christian Fiction Finds a Booming Audience." [online] from http://jscms.jm.columbia.edu/cns/2006-01-10/steele-christianfiction/story_syndication [Accessed June 1, 2006].

★ 1017 ★
Books
SIC: 2731; NAICS: 51113

English-Language Book Publication

There were 375,000 English-language books published in 2004.

United States	.52.0%
United Kingdom	.35.0
Canada	.9.0
Australia	.3.0
New Zealand	.1.0

Source: *Publishers Weekly*, October 17, 2005, p. 3, from Bowker.

★ 1018 ★
Books
SIC: 2731; NAICS: 51113

Leading Book Publishers in the U.K., 2005

Shares are shown based on value of sales through the year ended June 2005. Sales were placed at 1.6 billion pounds sterling for this period (excluding Harry Potter and the Half-blood Prince).

Random House	.14.95%
Hachette Livre	.13.02
Pearson	.12.42
HarperCollins	.8.02
Macmillan	.4.16
Time Warner	.3.57
Bloomsbury	.2.11
OUP	.1.90
BBC	.1.83
Simon & Schuster	.1.75
Other	.36.27

Source: *The Bookseller*, November 25, 2005, p. NA, from Nielsen BookScan Total Consumer Market.

★ 1019 ★
Books
SIC: 2731; NAICS: 51113

Romance Novel Market

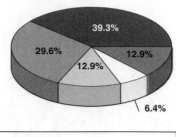

- ■ Romance
- ■ Mystery/thriller
- □ General fiction
- □ Science fiction
- ■ Other fiction

About 29% of Midwesterners read romance novels, while 13% of Northeasterners, 29% of Southerners, and 27% of Westerners do. Torstar (which publishes the Harlequin Romance, Mills & Boon, Mira, Red Dress, Silhouette and Steeple Hill imprints) released 1,141 titles in 2003.

Romance	.39.3%
Mystery/thriller	.29.6
General fiction	.12.9
Science fiction	.6.4
Other fiction	.12.9

Source: *Publishers Weekly*, November 21, 2005, p. 16, from Corona Research study.

★ 1020 ★
Books
SIC: 2731; NAICS: 51113

Top Book Publishers (Hardcover), 2005

Companies are ranked by share of 1,530 hardcover positions on the best-seller list.

Random House	.22.5%
HarperCollins	.17.9
Time Warner	.16.6
Penguin USA	.13.7
Simon & Schuster	.11.2
Von Holtzbrinck	.6.9
Hyperion	.3.7
Rodale	.2.4
Harlequin	.0.8
Houghton Mifflin	.0.8
Other	.3.5

Source: *Publishers Weekly*, January 9, 2006, p. NA.

★ 1021 ★
Books
SIC: 2731; NAICS: 51113
Top Book Publishers in France

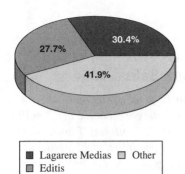

The book market in France is worth 2,593 million euros.

Lagarere Medias	.30.4%
Editis	.27.7
Other	.41.9

Source: ''Books in France.'' [online] from http://www.majormarketprofiles.com [Accessed June 1, 2006] from Euromonitor.

★ 1022 ★
Books
SIC: 2731; NAICS: 51113
Top Book Publishers in the U.K., 2005

The best-selling 100 titles of the year sold 34 million copies, representing 15.7% of the market, up from 13.1% in 2004 and 12.8% in 2003. Much of this comes from the last Harry Potter novel, which sold 3.5 million copies and all of Dan Brown's books (Writer of the Da Vinci Code) which sold a total of 5.6 million copies. Market shares by genre: non-fiction 59.9%, fiction 25.4% and children's 14.8%.

Bertelsmann	.14.0%
Pearson	.12.6
Hachette	.12.5
News Corp.	8.2
Bloomsbury	3.8
Holtzbrinck	3.7
Time Warner	3.6
OUP	1.9
BBC	1.8
Viacom	1.5
Other	.36.5

Source: *The Bookseller*, January 27, 2006, p. 26.

★ 1023 ★
Books
SIC: 2731; NAICS: 51113
Top Book Publishers (Paperback), 2005

Companies are ranked by share of 1,530 paperback positions on the best-seller list.

Random House	.24.8%
Penguin USA	.17.4
Simon & Schuster	.15.3
Time Warner	.13.4
HarperCollins	6.7
Von Holtzbrinck	6.2
Harlequin	3.6
Rodale	0.7
Hyperion	0.5
Other	.11.4

Source: *Publishers Weekly*, January 9, 2006, p. NA.

★ 1024 ★
Books
SIC: 2731; NAICS: 51113
Top Children's Book Publishers in the U.K.

The top selling hardback for the 24 weeks ended June 16, 2005 was Poppy Cat Loves Rainbows. The top paperback was Horrid Henry's Bedtime. The top non-fiction title was Dinosaurs and Prehistoric Life.

Penguin	.17.2%
Egmont	.10.6
Hachette Livre	.10.4
Random House	9.7
Harper Collins	7.6
Pan Macmillan	6.6
Scholastic	6.2
Paragon	4.7
Walker	4.7
Other	.22.0

Source: *The Bookseller*, August 19, 2005, p. 16, from Nielsen BookScan.

★ 1025 ★
Books
SIC: 2731; NAICS: 51113

Top Computer Book Publishers, 2005

Market shares are shown for the top 750 titles in the computer/tech category for the week ended December 4, 2005.

Pearson/Penguin	.29.0%
Wiley	.29.0
O'Reilly	.19.0
Microsoft Press	.10.0
Osborne/McGraw-Hill	4.0
Other	9.0

Source: "Joe Wikert's Book Publisher Blog." [online] from http://jwikert.typepad.com/the_average_joe/ [Accessed January 11, 2005] from Nielsen BookScan.

★ 1026 ★
Books
SIC: 2731; NAICS: 51113

Top STM Publishers Worldwide, 2003

Market shares are shown in percent. STM stands for scientific, technical and medical publishing.

Reed Elsevier	.28.2%
Thomson	9.5
Wolters Kluwer	9.4
Springer	4.7
John Wiley	3.9
American Chemical Society	3.6
Blackwell Publishing	3.6
Taylor & Francis	3.6
Other	.33.6

Source: "Digital Broadband Content: Scientific Publishing." [online] from http://www.oecd.org/dataoecd/42/12/35393145.pdf [Published September 2005].

★ 1027 ★
Books
SIC: 2731; NAICS: 51113

Top Trade Publishers

Firms are ranked by North American/U.S estimated sales in millions of dollars. The top five firms represent 67% of all trade (adult, children's, mass market paperbacks) sales in 2004 according to the American Association of Publishers. According to the Book Industry Study Group the top five firms represent 50% of the market.

Random House	$ 1,330
HarperCollins	965
Penguin Group	$ 900
Simon & Schuster	700
Time Warner Book Group	385

Source: *Publishers Weekly*, April 25, 2005, p. 2.

★ 1028 ★
Books
SIC: 2731; NAICS: 51113

Used Book Sales, 2004

There was an 11 percent increase over 2003 in the used book market, representing 111.2 million used books (valued at $2.2 billion). Figures come from sales in independent bookstores, online and through alternative markets like yard sales and thrift stores. Analysts interviewed in the article point out that the growth is coming from online channels. Of the $2.2 billion, $609 million came from online sales. That segment saw a 33.3 percent increase over the last year.

	(mil.)	Share
Education	38.6	34.71%
Nonfiction	28.7	25.81
Fiction	18.7	16.82
Professional	9.4	8.45
Children	5.8	5.22
Religion	5.0	4.50
Antiquarian & collectible	4.0	3.60
Other	1.0	0.90

Source: *Publishers Weekly*, October 3, 2005, p. 6, from Book Industry Study Group.

★ 1029 ★
Educational Publishing
SIC: 2731; NAICS: 51113

Education Publishing Industry, 2000-2004

The market includes K-12 market and higher education publishing.

2000	$ 6.3
2001	6.9
2002	7.0
2003	7.3
2004	7.6

Source: "Pearson Merrill Lynch TMT Conference." [online] from http://www.pearson.com [Published June 7, 2005] from American Association of Publishers, Management Practice Data and Pearson estimates.

★ 1030 ★

Educational Publishing

SIC: 2731; NAICS: 51113

Education Testing Industry, 2001-2004

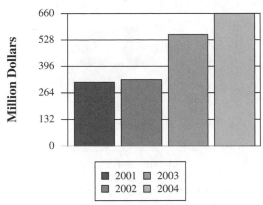

■ 2001	■ 2003
■ 2002	■ 2004

The market includes school and testing sales. Data are in millions of dollars.

2001	$ 320
2002	332
2003	557
2004	657

Source: "Pearson Merrill Lynch TMT Conference." [online] from http://www.pearson.com [Published June 7, 2005] from American Association of Publishers, Management Practice Data and Pearson estimates.

★ 1031 ★

Educational Publishing

SIC: 2731; NAICS: 51113

Top Educational Publishers in Germany

Publishers are ranked by sales in millions of euros.

Cornelsen	€ 339.0
Ernst Klett	330.0
Westermann	214.4
Langenscheidt	85.5

Source: "Educational Book Market in Germany." [online] from http://www.buyusainfo.net [Published January 2006] from *Buchreport*.

★ 1032 ★

Graphic Novels

SIC: 2731; NAICS: 51113

Leading Trade Paperback Publishers, 2005

Market shares are shown based on the top 300 trade paperback final orders. Data are for October 2005.

DC	41.32%
Marvel	38.49

Image	4.95%
Dark Horse	4.65
Devil's Due	1.34
Aspen	1.21
Tokyopop	1.02
IDW	0.95
Gemstone	0.85
Other	5.22

Source: *Comics & Games Retailer*, January 2006, p. 10, from Diamond Comic Distributors.

★ 1033 ★

Manga

SIC: 2731; NAICS: 51113

Manga Industry

Manga refers to Japanese comics (in Japan mange also includes print cartoons). Manga is sometimes adapted into anime (animation). Manga is sometimes referred to as anime, although these terms are not interchangable. Tokyopop has nearly 25 million manga novels in print and is the leading U.S. publisher. Manga accounts for 75% of all graphic novel sales at bookstores. In Japan, manga represents 40% of all publishing sales.

Tokyopop	38.0%
Other	62.0

Source: *Palm Beach Post*, January 7, 2006, p. 1D, from Nielsen BookScan, iCV2 and Manga News Service.

★ 1034 ★

Manga

SIC: 2731; NAICS: 51113

Manga Market Size

Manga refers to Japanese comics (in Japan mange also includes print cartoons). Manga is sometimes adapted into anime (animation). Manga is sometimes referred to as anime, although these terms are not interchangable. The market in the United States and Canada was estimated at $90 - 110 million in 2003 and $110 - 140 million in 2004. Top manga properties for fourth quarter 2004: Rurouni Kenshin, Frutis Basket and Naruto.

2003	$ 110
2004	140

Source: "Manga Market Continues Robust Growth in 2004." [online] from http://www.icv2.com/articles/home/6430.html [Accessed January 20, 2005] from *iCV2 Retailers Guide to Anime*.

★ 1035 ★
Textbooks
SIC: 2731; NAICS: 51113
College Textbook Sales, 2003-2004

Total sales were $10.92 billion

	($ bil.)	Share
New texts	$4.956	45.4%
Used texts	1.751	16.0
Course	0.219	2.0

Source: "Higher Education Retail Market Facts and Figures 2005." [online] from http://www.nacs.org [Retrieved January 2, 2006] from *NACS 2004 College Store Industry Financial Report.*

★ 1036 ★
Textbooks
SIC: 2731; NAICS: 51113
Leading College Publishers

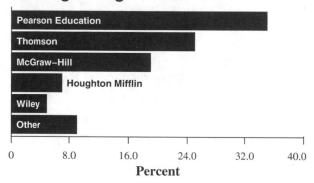

Percent

Shares are shown based on college bookstore sales. Figures exclude trade and reference titles.

Pearson Education	.35.0%
Thomson	.25.0
McGraw-Hill	.19.0
Houghton Mifflin	.7.0
Wiley	.5.0
Other	.9.0

Source: "Pearson Lehman Brothers." [online] from http://www.pearson.com [Published June 15, 2005] from Monument Information Services.

★ 1037 ★
Textbooks
SIC: 2731; NAICS: 51113
Leading ELHI Publishers, 2005

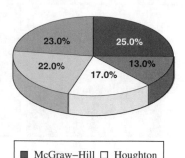

■ McGraw–Hill □ Houghton
■ Pearson   ■ Other
□ Reed Elsevier

Market shares are estimated in percent. Figures include testing. ELHI stands for elementary/high school.

McGraw-Hill	.25.0%
Pearson	.23.0
Reed Elsevier	.22.0
Houghton	.17.0
Other	.13.0

Source: "Making the Grade Economic Outlook for the Educational Publishing." [online] from http://www.publishers.org/SchoolDiv/documents/PeterAppert2006.pdf from Goldman Sachs.

★ 1038 ★
Textbooks
SIC: 2731; NAICS: 51113
Math Textbook Market in Texas

Market shares are shown in percent.

Houghton Mifflin	.70.0%
Other	.30.0

Source: *Educational Marketer*, May 16, 2005, p. 4.

★ 1039 ★
Textbooks
SIC: 2731; NAICS: 51113

Textbook Market in the U.K., 2005

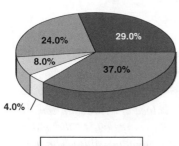

Market shares are shown for school textbooks TCM periods 1-5.

Letts 29.0%
CGP 24.0
Collins 8.0
BBC 4.0
Other 37.0

Source: "Letts Back to School." [online] from http://www.letts-successzone. com/content/letts_success_zone/media/pdfs/bookseller.pdf [Accessed Jan. 20, 2006] from Nielsen BookScan.

★ 1040 ★
Video Game Manuals
SIC: 2731; NAICS: 51113

Strategy Guide Industry

Prima has roughly half of the market for strategy guides in the $7.3 billion video and computer game industry. BradyGames is number two in the market.

Prima 50.0%
Other 50.0

Source: *Sacramento Bee*, December 15, 2005, p. NA.

★ 1041 ★
Book Printing
SIC: 2732; NAICS: 323117

Leading Book Printers

Firms are ranked by book printing sales in millions of dollars. R.R. Donelley and Quebecor World are two of the many large printers that have developed offshore printing relationships or have purchased foreign facilities. As with all outsourcing, it is the small firms that can not afford to develop such relationships and risk being left behind.

Quebecor World . . . . $ 660
Visant Corp. 638
Banta Corp. 371
Bertelsmann Arvato 243
Courier Corp. 211
Taylor Publishing 114
Phoenix Color 98
Walsworth Publishing 92
Maple-Vail Book Mfg. 77
Webcrafters Inc. 77

Source: *Printing Impressions*, December 2005, p. NA, from *Printing Impressions Top 100*.

★ 1042 ★
Health Care Publishing
SIC: 2741; NAICS: 51112, 51113, 51114

Leading Health Care Publishers

The industry is valued at $5.3 billion.

Reed 17.0%
Wolters Kluwer 13.0
Thomson 9.0
McGraw-Hill 1.0
Pearson 1.0
Other 59.0

Source: "Delivering Value from Leading Positions." [online] from http:www.wolterskluwer.com/./UBSConferenceNYFINAL.pps [Published January 2004] from company reports, Outsell, *Pharmaceutical Executive*, Verispan and Wolters Kluwer.

★ 1043 ★
Legal Publishing
SIC: 2741; NAICS: 51112, 51113, 51114
Case Law Interpretation and Indexing

Market shares are shown in percent.

Thomson West	.55.0%
Other	.45.0

Source: *Star Tribune*, November 15, 2005, p. 1D.

★ 1044 ★
Legal Publishing
SIC: 2741; NAICS: 51112, 51113, 51114
Leading Legal Publishers Worldwide

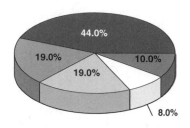

The market is valued at $1,542 million. The figure refers to what the source calls ''the addressable market'' (widest definition possible) and includes specialized legal content and the law school market.

Thomson West	.44.0%
ASPEN/CCH Legal	.19.0
Reed	.19.0
BNA	.8.0
Other	.10.0

Source: ''Delivering Value from Leading Positions.'' [online] from http:www.wolterskluwer.com/./UBSConferenceNYFINAL.pps [Published January 2004] from company reports, UBS Warburg, YE company, Lehman Brothers and MSDW.

★ 1045 ★
Legal Publishing
SIC: 2741; NAICS: 51112, 51113, 51114
Legal Publishing Market

The legal publishing and information market was thought to be worth $5.57 billion in 2003.

Books	.42.9%
Online	.27.3
Newsletters/looseleafs	.15.8
Directories	.6.7

Journals	.2.3%
Other	.4.7

Source: ''Trends in Legal Publishing.'' [online] www. aallnet.org/committee/criv/news/TLP.ppt [Published July 2004] from Simba.

★ 1046 ★
Tax Publishing
SIC: 2741; NAICS: 51112, 51113, 51114
Tax Publishing Market

The market is valued at $1,081 million. The figure refers to what the source calls ''the addressable market'' (widest definition possible). The figure does exclude the accounting market.

Wolters Kluwer	.32.0%
Thomson	.24.0
Intuit	.17.0
BNA	.5.0
Other	.22.0

Source: ''Delivering Value from Leading Positions.'' [online] from http:www.wolterskluwer.com/./UBSConferenceNYFINAL.pps [Published January 2004] from company reports.

★ 1047 ★
Trading Cards
SIC: 2741; NAICS: 511199
Leading Sports Card Makers

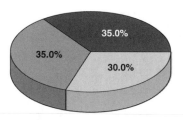

The sports card wholesale market reached its high point with 1991 at $1.1 billion. Sales in 2005 were thought to be about $250 million.

Topps	.35.0%
Upper Deck	.35.0
Other	.30.0

Source: *San Diego Tribune*, July 11, 2005, p. NA.

★ 1048 ★
Trading Cards
SIC: 2741; NAICS: 511199
Trading Card Market, 1991 and 2005

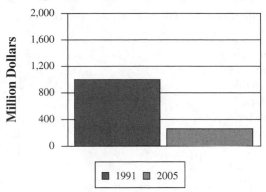

Data show the size of the wholesale market in millions of dollars. Baseball cards represent about a quarter of the market.

1991 . . . . $ 1,000
2005   260

Source: *Beaumont Enterprise*, August 8, 2005, p. NA, from *Card Trade*.

★ 1049 ★
Yearbooks
SIC: 2741; NAICS: 51223
Leading Yearbook Publishers

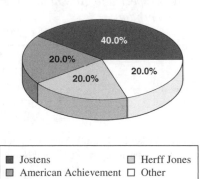

The North American high school and college yearbook market is worth $685 million.

Jostens 40.0%
American Achievement 20.0
Herff Jones 20.0
Other 20.0

Source: ''Text-S&P Assigns Affirms American Achievement Ratings.'' [online] from http://www/forbes.com [Accessed January 10, 2006].

★ 1050 ★
Printing
SIC: 2750; NAICS: 323110
Commercial Printing Revenues, 2005 and 2010

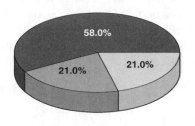
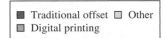

Industry revenues declined from $86.8 billion in 2000 to $78.9 billion in 2003. The number of printers has fallen from around 42,000 in 1998 to 37,000 currently. By 2010 another 5,000 are expected to vanish.

	2005	2010
Traditional offset	77.0%	58.0%
Digital printing	7.4	21.0
Other	15.6	21.0

Source: *Wall Street Journal*, December 19, 2005, p. R12, from National Association of Printing Leadership.

★ 1051 ★
Printing
SIC: 2750; NAICS: 323110
Largest Printers in Canada, 2004

Firms are ranked by sales in millions of dollars.

Quebecor World Inc.	$ 8,596.50
Transcontinental Pipe Line Corp.	1,623.00
CCL Label	505.40
St. Joseph Corporation	285.70
Davis + Henderson	275.58
Data Group of Companies	210.00
Pollard Banknote Ltd.	171.94
PLM Group	117.26
Datamark Systems Group Inc.	115.91
Imprimerie Solisco Inc.	89.00

Source: *Canadian Printer*, June 2005, p. TP6.

★ 1052 ★
Printing
SIC: 2750; NAICS: 323110

Leading Direct Mail Printers

Firms are ranked by direct mail printing sales in millions of dollars. More than $161 billion was spent on direct marketing in the United States. According to the Direct Marketing Association $49.8 billion was spent on printed direct mail, followed by telephone marketing with $47 billion.

Quebecor World	$ 594
Visant Corp.	245
Banta Corp.	212
IWCO Direct	141
Clondalkin Group	135
Japs-Olson Co.	101
Consolidated Graphics	77
Taylor Corp.	50
Holden Communications	45
Valassis Communications	41

Source: *Printing Impressions*, December 2005, p. NA, from *Printing Impressions Top 100*.

★ 1053 ★
Printing
SIC: 2750; NAICS: 323110

Leading In-Plant Printers

Firms are ranked by sales in millions of dollars.

Allstate Print Communication Center	$ 110.00
California Office of State Publishing	52.30
Washington State Department of Printing	31.00
Wal-Mart	30.00
Target	22.08
CVS	20.00
ING Americas	20.00
Papa Johns Support Services	20.00
Spartan Stores	19.39
Blue Cross-Blue Shield of Minnesota	18.20
Best Buy	17.28
Progressive Corp.	17.00

Source: *In-Plant Graphics*, July 2005, p. NA.

★ 1054 ★
Printing
SIC: 2750; NAICS: 323110

Leading Printers in North America

Companies are ranked by annual sales in millions of dollars.

RR Donnelley	$ 7,156
Quebec World	6,600
FedEx Kinko's	2,000
Quad/Graphics	1,800
Cenveo Inc.	1,743
Transcontinental	1,638
Vertis	1,600
Deluxe Corp.	1,567
Banta Corp.	1,520
Visant Corp.	1,462
Valassis	1,044
Bowne & Co.	899
Standard Register	890

Source: *Graphic Arts Monthly*, May 2005, p. 37, from *Graphic Arts Monthly 101, 23rd Edition*.

★ 1055 ★
Printing
SIC: 2750; NAICS: 323110

Printing Industry in Gemany, 2005 and 2010

Digital printing is expected to grow at the expense of offset and desktop printing.

	2005	2010
Offset	58.0%	57.0%
Gravure	21.0	19.0
Digital	10.0	16.0
Desktop	5.0	4.0
Other	6.0	4.0

Source: "German Market for Digital Printing Systems." [online] from http://www.stat-usa.gov [Published September 2005].

★ **1056** ★
Printing
SIC: 2750; NAICS: 323110
Wide-Format Inkjet Market Worldwide

The worldwide value of digitally printed wide format graphics output is forecast to climb from $26 billion in 2004 and $37 billion in 2009.

	2004	2009
Aqueous	73.0%	46.0%
Solvent-based	25.0	47.0
Flatbed	2.0	6.0

Source: *American Printer*, July 27, 2005, p. NA, from I.T. Strategies.

★ **1057** ★
Check Printing
SIC: 2761; NAICS: 323116
Check Printing Market

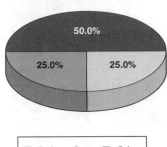

Consumers are writing fewer checks. Checks were used to pay for 44% of all transactions in 2003, down from 57% in 2000. Credit and debit cards represent growing methods of payment (debit cards grew from 11% to 20% in the same period). Some analysts believe this will mean the eventual end of the $1.8 billion check printing industry. Deluxe Corp. has more than half the market. Harland's share is also estimated.

Deluxe Corp.	.50.0%
Harland	.25.0
Other	.25.0

Source: *Atlanta Journal-Constitution*, January 2, 2005, p. B1.

★ **1058** ★
Labels
SIC: 2761; NAICS: 323116
Leading Pressure-Sensitive Material Makers in North America

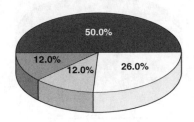

Market shares are shown based on unit production.

Avery Dennison	.50.0%
Bemis	.12.0
UPM-Kymmene (Raflatac)	.12.0
Other	.26.0

Source: *Global Packaging 101v.3*, Credit Suisse First Boston, September 12, 2005, p. 3, from U.S. Department of Justice and CS First Boston.

★ **1059** ★
Greeting Cards
SIC: 2771; NAICS: 511191
Everyday Greeting Cards

Best selling cards by season: Christmas 60%, Valentine's Day 25% and Mother's Day 4%. Americans purchase $7 billion in greeting cards annually.

Birthday	.60.0%
Anniversaries	8.0
Get well	7.0
Friendship	6.0
Sympathy cards	6.0

Source: *Souvenirs, Gifts and Novelties*, May 2005, p. 100.

★ 1060 ★
Greeting Cards
SIC: 2771; NAICS: 511191

Top Greeting Card Makers

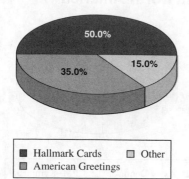

Hallmark has over half of the market.

Hallmark Cards	.50.0%
American Greetings	.35.0
Other	.15.0

Source: *Business Week*, December 5, 2005, p. NA.

★ 1061 ★
Blankbooks and Binders
SIC: 2782; NAICS: 323118

Blankbook and Looseleaf Binder Shipments, 1999-2001

Shipments are in millions of dollars.

1999	$ 2.31
2000	2.30
2001	2.12

Source: "Blankbooks, Looseleaf Binders." [online] from http://www.referenceforbusiness.com/industries/Printing-Publishing [Accessed November 14, 2005].

SIC 28 - Chemicals and Allied Products

★ 1062 ★
Chemicals
SIC: 2800; NAICS: 325131, 325132, 325181
Largest Chemical Firms in Asia

Firms are ranked by sales in millions of dollars.

Sinopec	$ 15,961
Mitsubishi Chemical	14,459
Mitsui Chemicals	11,869
Formosa Plastics Group	11,864
Sumitomo Chemicals	10,334
Dainippon Ink	9,373
Torya Industries	8,254
Sin-Etsu Chemical	7,999
Reliance Industries	6,807
Asahi Kasei	6,184

Source: *Chemical Week*, February 8, 2006, p. 18.

★ 1063 ★
Chemicals
SIC: 2800; NAICS: 325131, 325132, 325181
Leading Chemical Firms

The top firms are ranked by chemicals sales in millions of dollars.

Dow Chemical	$ 46,307.0
ExxonMobil	31,186.0
DuPont	28,114.0
Lyondell Chemical	18,606.0
Huntsman Corp.	12,961.6
Chevron Phillips	10,707.0
PPG Industries	7,964.0
Air Products	7,742.5
Praxair	7,656.0
Rohm and Haas	7,064.0

Source: *C&EN*, May 15, 2006, p. 25.

★ 1064 ★
Chemicals
SIC: 2800; NAICS: 325131, 325132, 325181
Leading Diversified Chemical Makers

Firms are ranked by sales in millions of dollars.

Sinopec	$ 21,039
DuPont	7,454
Sunoco	6,606
ICI	2,603
PPG Industries	2,493
Ashland	2,080
Goodrich	1,282

Source: *Chemical Week*, July 20, 2005, p. 38.

★ 1065 ★
Alkalies and Chlorine
SIC: 2812; NAICS: 325181
Chlorine Market in Europe, 2004

Production is shown by country.

Germany	42.0%
Belgium/Netherlands	13.0
U.K./Austria/Switzerland/Finland	13.0
Spain	6.0
Italy	5.0
Other	7.0

Source: *European Chemical News*, September 19, 2005, p. 10, from Euro Chlor.

★ 1066 ★
Alkalies and Chlorine
SIC: 2812; NAICS: 325181
Largest Chloralkali Suppliers Worldwide, 2005

Market shares are shown based on 113 million tons annually.

Dow Chemical	11.1%
Occidental Chemical	4.4
Formosa Plastics	3.5

Continued on next page.

★ 1066 ★

[Continued]
Alkalies and Chlorine
SIC: 2812; NAICS: 325181

Largest Chloralkali Suppliers Worldwide, 2005

Market shares are shown based on 113 million tons annually.

PPG	2.9%
Bayer	2.6
Solvay	2.2
Akzo Nobel	2.0
Tosch Corporation	1.9
Arkema	1.8
Olin	1.7
Other	.65.8

Source: *Basic Materials*, Morgan Stanley Equity Research, December 14, 2005, p. 7, from Morgan Stanley Research and Chemical Marketing Associates Inc.

★ 1067 ★

Alkalies and Chlorine
SIC: 2812; NAICS: 325181

Leading Canpotex Producers Worldwide

Market shares are shown in percent.

Belaruskali (Belarus) & Russia (Uralkali, Silvinit)	.42.0%
Canpotex/PotashCorp.	.29.0
ICL (Israel, U.K., Spain)	.10.0
K&S (Germany)	8.0
APC (Jordan)	6.0
Other	5.0

Source: "Overview of Potash Corp." [online] from http://www.potashcorp.com [Accessed June 10, 2006], p. 27, from Canpotex, International Fertilizer Association and Potash-Corp.

★ 1068 ★

Alkalies and Chlorine
SIC: 2812; NAICS: 325181

Leading Feed Phosphate Supplement Producers Worldwide, 2004

Market shares are shown based on capacity (Monocal/Dical/DFP).

PotashCorp.	.16.0%
Mosaic	.13.0

Tessenderlo	.11.0%
Other	.60.0

Source: "Overview of Potash Corp." [online] from http://www.potashcorp.com [Accessed June 10, 2006], p. 27, from TFI, SRI and PotashCorp.

★ 1069 ★

Alkalies and Chlorine
SIC: 2812; NAICS: 325181

Soda Ash End Markets

Data show the top markets for soda ash. Total demand is projected to increase from 6,930 thousand short tons in 2004 to 7,155 thousand short tons in 2008. Soda ash was virtually sold out in the first half of 2005.

Glass	.49.0%
Chemicals	.28.0
Soap & detergents	.11.0
Flue gas desulfurization	2.0
Pulp & paper	2.0
Other	8.0

Source: *CMR*, June 3, 2005, p. 34.

★ 1070 ★

Industrial Gases
SIC: 2813; NAICS: 32512

How Helium is Used, 2005

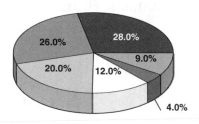

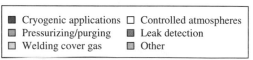

Consumption is shown based on 85 million cubic meters.

Cryogenic applications	.28.0%
Pressurizing/purging	.26.0
Welding cover gas	.20.0
Controlled atmospheres	.12.0
Leak detection	4.0
Other	9.0

Source: *Mineral Commodities Summaries 2006*, Annual, p. 21, from U.S. Geological Survey, U.S. Department of the Interior.

★ 1071 ★
Industrial Gases
SIC: 2813; NAICS: 32512

Leading Industrial Gas Makers in China

The industrial gas market was worth $1.4 billion in 2004.

BOC 9.0%
Air Liquide 8.0
Air Product 7.0
Praxair 7.0
Messer 4.0
Linde 2.0
Other 63.0

Source: ''China Industrial Gas Business Grows Constantly.'' [online] from http://http://china-gases.com/record1_en.php?Primary1&Logic1&ID3471 [Published May 16, 2006].

★ 1072 ★
Industrial Gases
SIC: 2813; NAICS: 32512

Leading Industrial Gas Makers Worldwide, 2004

The industry is valued at $45 billion.

Air Liquide 21.0%
Plaxair 12.8
BOC 12.6
Linde 11.0
Air Products 10.1
Talyo Nippon Sanso 5.2
Other 27.3

Source: *Chemical Week*, February 1, 2006, p. 8, from David Ingles, independent consultant.

★ 1073 ★
Catalysts
SIC: 2819; NAICS: 325188

Global Catalyst Market, 2005

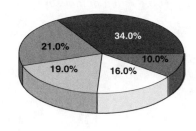

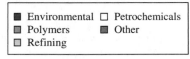

There are several important changes at work in the $14.5 billion industry. The source reports that BASF is trying to acquire Engelhard, a major producer of automotive, fluid catalytic cracking and chemical catalysts. This could possibly lead to more companies buying a catalyst firm rather than buying or leasing from them. Also, demand is shifting to developing markets such as China and the Middle East. This is stimulating demand for local catalyst firms.

Environmental 34.0%
Polymers 21.0
Refining 19.0
Petrochemicals 16.0
Other 10.0

Source: *Chemical Week*, April 12, 2006, p. 22, from The Catalyst Group.

★ 1074 ★
Catalysts
SIC: 2819; NAICS: 325188

Leading FCC Makers

The industry is valued at $1.1 billion each year. FCC stands at fluid cracking catalysts.

Grace 35.0%
Albemarle 27.0
Engelhard 20.0
Other 18.0

Source: *Chemical Week*, January 26, 2005, p. 32, from producers.

★ 1075 ★
Inorganic Chemicals
SIC: 2819; NAICS: 325131

Bauxite Production by Country, 2005

Data show mine production in thousands of metric tons.

	(000)	Share
Australia	58,000	35.15%
Brazil	18,000	10.91
China	17,000	10.30
Guinea	16,000	9.70
India	14,000	8.48
Jamaica	14,000	8.48
Other	28,000	16.97

Source: *Mineral Commodities Summaries 2006*, Annual, p. 21, from U.S. Geological Survey, U.S. Department of the Interior.

★ 1076 ★
Inorganic Chemicals
SIC: 2819; NAICS: 325998

Hydrofluoric Acid Market

Top producers by capacity: Honeywell, DuPont, Quimica Fluor, Solvay Fluor Mexico.

Fluorocarbons	58.0%
Aluminum	13.0
Alkylation catalysts	3.0
Metal etching	3.0
Other	23.0

Source: *Chemical Market Reporter*, November 7, 2005, p. 38.

★ 1077 ★
Inorganic Chemicals
SIC: 2819; NAICS: 325188

Hydrogen Peroxide Industry Worldwide, 2006

The industry is estimated to produce 1.77 million metric tons.

Pulp & paper	60.0%
Chemical & laundry	22.0
Environmental applications	5.0
Textiles	4.0
Other	9.0

Source: *Chemical Week*, August 17, 2005, p. 36.

★ 1078 ★
Inorganic Chemicals
SIC: 2819; NAICS: 325998

Sucralose Consumption

Demand for sucralose has recently outpaced demand for more established high intensity sweeteners such as asparteme and saccharin.

	2002	2007	Share
Beverages	105	160	59.26%
Tabletop sweeteners	50	80	29.63
Food	20	30	11.11

Source: *Chemical Market Reporter*, January 24, 2005, p. 8, from CEH estimates.

★ 1079 ★
Plastics
SIC: 2821; NAICS: 325211

Largest Polypropylene Makers in North America

Firms are ranked by capacity in millions of metric pounds annually.

Equistar	11,375
Dow Chemical	10,915
ExxonMobil	8,600
Chevron Phillips Chemical	7,600
Shell	5,500
Formosa Plastics	3,400
BP Chemicals	2,900
Hunstman	2,830
Westlake Petrochemical	2,650

Source: *U.S. Industry Quarterly Review*, First Quarter 2005, p. NA.

★ 1080 ★
Plastics
SIC: 2821; NAICS: 325211

Largest PVC Producers in China

Firms are ranked by output in thousands of tons. The industry produced 5.03 million tons in 2004. There is short supply in the domestic market.

Tianjin LG Dagu Chemical	344.6
Shanghai Chlor-Alkali Chemical	341.9
Tianjin Dagu Chemical	317.1
Hebei Cangzhou Chemical Industrial	269.7
Sinopec Qilu Petrochemical	229.3

Continued on next page.

★ 1080 ★

[Continued]

Plastics

SIC: 2821; NAICS: 325211

Largest PVC Producers in China

Firms are ranked by output in thousands of tons. The industry produced 5.03 million tons in 2004. There is short supply in the domestic market.

Yibin Tianyuan Co.	195.0
Suzhou Huasu Chemical Plastic Co.	183.9
Sichuan Jinlu Group Co.	172.4
Beijing Huaer Co.	160.0

Source: *China Chemical Reporter*, August 16, 2005, p. 16.

★ 1081 ★

Plastics

SIC: 2821; NAICS: 325211

Leading Polypropylene Makers Worldwide, 2010

Market shares are shown in percent.

Bassell	13.78%
Sinopec	7.59
Sabic	6.17
Reliance/IPCL	4.70
Ineos	4.29
PeroChina	3.97
Borealis	3.79
Total PC	3.70
ExxonMobil	3.59
Formosa Plastics	3.10
Other	45.32

Source: *Chemical Market Reporter*, April 24, 2006, p. 21, from Chemical Marketing Associates Inc.

★ 1082 ★

Plastics

SIC: 2821; NAICS: 325211

Leading Polystyrene Makers in China

Companies are ranked by production in thousands of metric tons.

	(000)	Share
Chi Mei	300	13.97%
Dow Chemical	280	13.04
Sinopec	279	12.99
Guangdong Economy Commission	250	11.64
SK Group	155	7.22
Chevron Texaco	100	4.66

	(000)	Share
Conoco Phillips	100	4.66%
Total Petrochemicals	100	4.66
Other	584	27.19

Source: *Chemical Week*, September 7, 2005, p. 25, from SRI Consulting.

★ 1083 ★

Plastics

SIC: 2821; NAICS: 325211

Leading Polystyrene Makers in North America

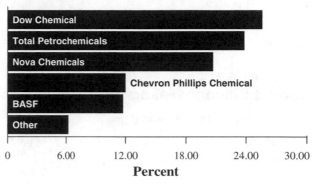

Companies are ranked by production in thousands of metric tons.

	(000)	Share
Dow Chemical	746	25.59%
Total Petrochemicals	694	23.81
Nova Chemicals	603	20.69
Chevron Phillips Chemical	349	11.97
BASF	342	11.73
Other	181	6.21

Source: *Chemical Week*, September 7, 2005, p. 25, from SRI Consulting.

★ 1084 ★

Plastics

SIC: 2821; NAICS: 325211

Leading PVP Makers Worldwide, 2004

Market shares are shown in percent. PVP stands for polyvinyl propylene.

ISP	40.0%
BASF	38.0
Hangzhou Nanhang	3.0
Dai-Ichi Kogyo	2.0
Henan Boai	2.0

Continued on next page.

★ 1084 ★
[Continued]
Plastics
SIC: 2821; NAICS: 325211

Leading PVP Makers Worldwide, 2004

Market shares are shown in percent. PVP stands for polyvinyl propylene.

Meida Fine Chemical	2.0%
Nippon Shokubai	2.0
Showa Denko	2.0
Other	9.0

Source: *European Chemical News*, November 28, 2005, p. 42, from Tran Tech.

★ 1085 ★
Plastics
SIC: 2821; NAICS: 325211

Leading Silicone Makers Worldwide

The industry is worth $7 billion.

Dow Corning	40.0%
GE Silicones	20.0
Other	40.0

Source: *CMR*, March 19, 2006, p. 22, from Wacker Chemie.

★ 1086 ★
Plastics
SIC: 2821; NAICS: 325211

Polycarbonate Demand

Total demand was 650,000 metric tons.

Automotive	20.0%
Optical media	20.0
Window gazing	20.0
Business equipment	15.0

Source: *Chemical Week*, February 22, 2006, p. 27, from Kline & Co.

★ 1087 ★
Plastics
SIC: 2821; NAICS: 325211

Top ABS Resin Firms in Japan, 2004

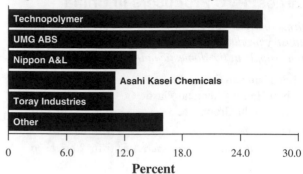

Percent

Market shares are shown based on domestic shipments of 365,000 tons. ABS stands for acrylonitrile butadiene styrene.

Technopolymer	26.3%
UMG ABS	22.7
Nippon A&L	13.2
Asahi Kasei Chemicals	11.0
Toray Industries	10.8
Other	16.0

Source: "2004 Market Share Report." [online] from http://www.nikkei.co.jp [Published July 27, 2005] from Nikkei estimates.

★ 1088 ★
Plastics
SIC: 2821; NAICS: 325211

Top End Markets for Plastics Worldwide

Market shares are shown in percent.

Packaging	37.2%
Consumer products	20.1
Building and construction	18.5
Electrical and electronic	8.5
Automotive	8.0
Industrial	5.8
Agriculture	1.9

Source: *European Chemical News*, August 8, 2005, p. 10, from Frost & Sullivan.

★ 1089 ★

Plastics

SIC: 2821; NAICS: 325211

Top LDPE Firms in Japan, 2004

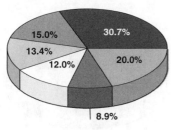

Market shares are shown based on domestic production of 1.6 million tons. LDPE stands for low density polyethylene.

Japan Polyethylene	.30.7%
Sumitomo Chemical	.15.0
Mitsui Chemicals	.13.4
Nippon Unicar	.12.0
Tosoh	. 8.9
Other	.20.0

Source: "2004 Market Share Report." [online] from http://www.nikkei.co.jp [Published July 27, 2005] from Nikkei estimates and Japan Petrochemical Industry Association.

★ 1090 ★

Plastics

SIC: 2821; NAICS: 325211

TPU Industry in China, 2004

TPU stands for thermoplastic elastomers.

Shoes	.41.0%
Adhesives	.15.0
Tube	.12.0
Film	. 8.0
Spandex	. 7.0
Synthetic leather	. 7.0
Other	.10.0

Source: *China Chemical Reporter*, October 26, 2005, p. 37, from CNCIC Chemdata.

★ 1091 ★

Plastics

SIC: 2821; NAICS: 325211

TPU Market Worldwide

TPU stands for thermoplastic polyurethane.

Injection	.48.0%
Extrusion	.34.0
Adhesives	.10.0
Coatings	.10.0

Source: *Chemical Week*, May 4, 2005, p. 29, from IAL Consultants.

★ 1092 ★

Rubber

SIC: 2822; NAICS: 325212

Butyl Rubber Market

Market shares are shown in percent.

Tires, tubes and pneumatic products	.80.0%
Automotive mechanical goods	. 9.0
Adhesives, caulks, sealants	. 6.0
Other	. 5.0

Source: *Chemical Market Reporter*, June 12, 2005, p. 31.

★ 1093 ★

Rubber

SIC: 2822; NAICS: 325212

Global Rubber Consumption, 2005

More than 40 companies in 20 countries produce nearly 12 million metric tons of synthetic rubber annually. Demand is shown in millions of tons.

	(mil.)	Share
Asia/Africa	5,289	44.65%
European Union	2,547	21.50
North America	2,181	18.41
Latin America	774	6.53
Africa	104	0.88
Other European countries	950	8.02

Source: *Rubber & Plastics News*, May 1, 2006, p. 10, from International Rubber Study Group.

★ 1094 ★
Rubber
SIC: 2822; NAICS: 325212

Leading Rubber Makers Worldwide

Firms are ranked by non-tire rubber sales in billions of dollars.

Hutchinson	$ 3,000
Freudenberg	2,870
Bridgestone	2,750
Trelleborg	2,710
Tomkins PLC	2,350
Continental	2,160

Source: *European Rubber Journal*, September 1, 2005, p. 34.

★ 1095 ★
Rubber
SIC: 2822; NAICS: 325212

Top Nitrile Rubber End Markets in North America

Total demand is projected to increase from 91,000 metric tons in 2004 to 99,000 metric tons in 2008. Top producers in North America include Zeon Chemicals, Lanxess and Nitrio SA de CV.

Hoses, belts & cable	27.0%
O-rings and seals	20.0
Latex applications	14.0
Molded and extruded products	14.0

Source: *CMR*, June 13, 2005, p. 34.

★ 1096 ★
Rubber
SIC: 2823; NAICS: 325221

Top Synthetic Rubber Makers in Japan, 2004

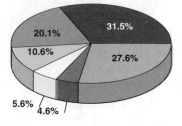

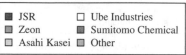

Market shares are shown based on domestic shipments of 1.2 million tons.

JSR	31.5%
Zeon	20.1
Asahi Kasei	10.6
Ube Industries	5.6
Sumitomo Chemical	4.6
Other	27.6

Source: "2004 Market Share Report." [online] from http://www.nikkei.co.jp [Published July 27, 2005] from Japan Rubber Manufactuers Association.

★ 1097 ★
Fibers
SIC: 2824; NAICS: 325222

Top Polyester Filament Makers in Japan, 2004

Market shares are shown based on 298,000 tons.

Toray Industries	32.2%
Teijin	21.8
Toyobo	16.4
Unitikaq Fibers	11.7
Kanebo Gohsen	7.0
Other	10.9

Source: "2004 Market Share Report." [online] from http://www.nikkei.co.jp [Published July 27, 2005] from Nikkei estimates.

★ 1098 ★
Supplements
SIC: 2833; NAICS: 325414

Top Antioxidant Makers in Brazil, 2003

Market shares are shown in percent.

DMS - Nutricional Products 29.5%
Danisco + Rhodia 18.8
M. Cassab 8.2
BASF 7.4
Wenda 6.6
Sunset 5.7
Eastman 4.9
Other 18.9

Source: "Market Share Matrix Project." [online] from http://www.marketsharematrix.org [Published May 2005] from SEAE (Economic Monitoring Secretary) and Ato de Concentracao.

★ 1099 ★
Supplements
SIC: 2833; NAICS: 325411

Top Mineral Supplement Makers, 2005

Market shares are shown based on dollar sales for the 12 weeks ended November 27, 2005.

US Nutrition 20.1%
Pharmavite 12.0
Wyeth Labs 4.1
Glaxosmithkline 3.4
Chattem 0.9
Private label 30.7
Other 28.8

Source: *High Yield Consumer Products*, Deutsche Bank, December 15, 2005, p. 13, from Information Resources Inc.

★ 1100 ★
Vitamins
SIC: 2833; NAICS: 325411

Top Multivitamin Makers, 2005

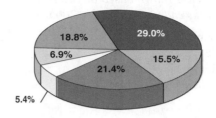
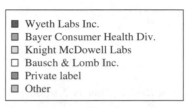

- ■ Wyeth Labs Inc.
- ■ Bayer Consumer Health Div.
- □ Knight McDowell Labs
- □ Bausch & Lomb Inc.
- ■ Private label
- ■ Other

Market shares are shown based on supermarket, drug store and discount store sales (excluding Wal-Mart) for the 52 weeks ended June 12, 2005.

Wyeth Labs Inc. 29.0%
Bayer Consumer Health Div. 18.8
Knight McDowell Labs 6.9
Bausch & Lomb Inc. 5.4
Private label 21.4
Other 15.5

Source: *Grocery Headquarters*, September 21, 2005, p. S14, from Information Resources Inc.

★ 1101 ★
Vitamins
SIC: 2833; NAICS: 325411

Top Vitamin Brands (1 & 2 Letters), 2005

Market shares are shown based on drug store sales for the 52 weeks ended October 30, 2005.

Nature Made 27.3%
Nature's Bounty 9.0
Sundown 4.0
Slo-Niacin 2.1
Windmill 1.1
Lipoflavionoid 1.0
Private label 42.9
Other 12.5

Source: *Chain Drug Review*, January 2, 2006, p. 94.

★ 1102 ★
Vitamins
SIC: 2833; NAICS: 325411
Top Vitamin Brands (Minerals), 2005

Market shares are shown based on drug store sales for the 52 weeks ended October 30, 2005.

Nature's Bounty 7.0%
Nature Made 6.7
Osteo-Bi-Flex 4.7
Nature's Resource 3.2
Natrol 2.5
Os-Cal 2.2
Sundown 2.1
Viactiv 1.8
Flex-A-Min 1.7
Estroven 1.5
Other 66.6

Source: *Chain Drug Review*, January 2, 2006, p. 94.

★ 1103 ★
Vitamins
SIC: 2833; NAICS: 325411
Top Vitamin Brands (Multivitamin), 2005

Market shares are shown based on drug store sales for the 52 weeks ended October 30, 2005.

CentrumSilver 12.8%
Airborne 12.1
Centrum 9.1
One-A-Day 4.0
Ocuvite PreserVision 2.8
Ocuvite 2.4
One-A-Day Weight Smart 2.4
Centrum Performance 2.3
Flintstones 2.1
One-A-Day Men's Health Formula 2.0
Other 47.0

Source: *Chain Drug Review*, January 2, 2006, p. 94.

★ 1104 ★
Vitamins
SIC: 2833; NAICS: 325411
Top Vitamin/Mineral Brands (Liquid), 2005

Brands are ranked by sales in millions of dollars at supermarkets, drug stores and discount stores (excluding Wal-Mart) for the 52 weeks ended October 2, 2005.

	($ mil.)	Share
Alacer Emergen C	$ 10.4	9.60%
Poly VI Sol	9.0	8.31
Nature's Bounty	4.2	3.88
Centrum	3.3	3.05
Knox Nutrajoint Plus	2.4	2.22
Tri VI Sol	2.3	2.12
Geritol	2.2	2.03
Lipovitan	1.9	1.75
Knox Nutrajoint	1.8	1.66
Private label	4.3	3.97
Other	66.5	61.40

Source: *MMR*, September 19, 2005, p. 1, from Information Resources Inc.

★ 1105 ★
Analgesics
SIC: 2834; NAICS: 325412
Cough Medication Market in the U.K., 2005

The industry is shown for the 52 weeks ended July 17, 2005.

Cough liquids 29.9%
Cold treatments 25.5
Cough/throat lozenges 23.8
Decongestants 20.8

Source: *Grocer*, October 22, 2005, p. 49, from TNS Superpanel.

★ 1106 ★
Analgesics
SIC: 2834; NAICS: 325412
Top Acne Treatments, 2005

Market shares are shown based on drug store sales for the 52 weeks ended October 30, 2005.

Clearasil 8.0%
Neutrogena Oil-Free 6.2
Clearasil Ultra 5.8

Continued on next page.

★ 1106 ★
[Continued]
Analgesics
SIC: 2834; NAICS: 325412

Top Acne Treatments, 2005

Market shares are shown based on drug store sales for the 52 weeks ended October 30, 2005.

Biore Pore Perfect	4.9%
Clean & Clear	4.5
Oxy	4.3
Aveeno Clear Complexion	4.1
Neutrogena Advanced Solutions	4.1
AcneFree	3.9
Clean & Clear Clear Advantage	3.8
Other	.50.4

Source: *Chain Drug Review*, January 2, 2006, p. 94.

★ 1107 ★
Analgesics
SIC: 2834; NAICS: 325412

Top Analgesic Brands (External), 2006

Brands are ranked by supermarket and drug store sales in millions of dollars.

	($ mil.)	Share
Icy Hot	$ 56.1	20.26%
Bengay	47.7	17.23
Aspercreme	17.6	6.36
Salonpas	12.5	4.51
Well Patch	8.6	3.11
Absorbine Jr.	7.1	2.56
Capsasin HP	7.0	2.53
Joint Ritis	7.0	2.53
Tiger Balm	6.3	2.28
Mineral Ice	5.5	1.99
Private label	17.6	6.36
Other	83.9	30.30

Source: *MMR*, April 24, 2006, p. 30, from Information Resources Inc.

★ 1108 ★
Analgesics
SIC: 2834; NAICS: 325412

Top Analgesic Brands (Internal/ Liquid), 2006

Brands are ranked by supermarket and drug store sales in millions of dollars.

	($ mil.)	Share
Children's Motrin	$ 55.1	24.70%
Tylenol	49.1	22.01
Children's Tylenol	40.5	18.15
Infants' Motrin	22.8	10.22
Children's Advil	7.3	3.27
Private label	42.1	18.87
Other	6.2	2.78

Source: *MMR*, April 24, 2006, p. 30, from Information Resources Inc.

★ 1109 ★
Analgesics
SIC: 2834; NAICS: 325412

Top Analgesic Brands (Internal/ Tablet), 2006

Brands are ranked by supermarket and drug store sales in millions of dollars.

	($ mil.)	Share
Advil	$ 281.0	14.95%
Tylenol	274.7	14.61
Aleve	128.0	6.81
Bayer	103.6	5.51
Tylenol PM	100.7	5.36
Motrin IB	73.6	3.91
Excedrin	57.9	3.08
Tylenol Arthritis	57.0	3.03
Excedrin Migraine	40.5	2.15
St. Joseph	40.0	2.13
Private label	436.0	23.19
Other	287.0	15.27

Source: *MMR*, April 24, 2006, p. 30, from Information Resources Inc.

★ 1110 ★

Analgesics

SIC: 2834; NAICS: 325412

Top Analgesic Makers (Internal), 2005

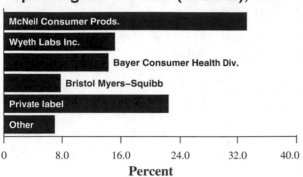

Market shares are based on supermarket, drug store and discount store sales (excluding Wal-Mart) for the 52 weeks ended June 12, 2005.

McNeil Consumer Prods. 33.3%
Wyeth Labs Inc.. . . . . .15.2
Bayer Consumer Health Div. 14.3
Bristol Myers-Squibb 7.8
Private label 22.4
Other 7.0

Source: *Grocery Headquarters*, September 21, 2005, p. S14, from Information Resources Inc.

★ 1111 ★

Analgesics

SIC: 2834; NAICS: 325412

Top Antacid Makers, 2005

Market shares are shown in percent. Sales exclude Wal-Mart and other large-format mass retailers.

Procter & Gamble 32.0%
J J Merck 16.4
GlaxoSmithKline 15.8
Pfizer 12.4
Novartis AG 8.6
Private label 12.6
Other 2.2

Source: *U.S. Personal Care and Household Products Digest*, Citigroup Equity Research, February 24, 2006, p. 65, from ACNielsen.

★ 1112 ★

Analgesics

SIC: 2834; NAICS: 325412

Top Antacid Makers (Tablet), 2005

Market shares are shown based on on supermarket, drug store and discount store sales (excluding Wal-Mart) for the 52 weeks ended June 12, 2005.

Procter & Gamble 27.4%
GlaxoSmithKline 18.9
Johnson & Johnson-Merck 15.4
Pfizer 13.2
Private label 13.7
Other 11.4

Source: *Grocery Headquarters*, September 21, 2005, p. S14, from Information Resources Inc.

★ 1113 ★

Analgesics

SIC: 2834; NAICS: 325412

Top Antacids (Liquid/Powder), 2005

Market shares are shown based on drug store sales for the 52 weeks ended October 30, 2005.

Mylanta 24.8%
Mylicon 17.5
Maalox Max 15.4
Mylanta Supreme 5.3
Gaviscon 5.0
Maalox 4.3
Gerber 3.2
Little Tummys 2.6
Beano 1.4
Brioschi 1.1
Private label 16.5
Other 2.9

Source: *Chain Drug Review*, January 2, 2006, p. 94.

★ 1114 ★

Analgesics

SIC: 2834; NAICS: 325412

Top Anti-itch Treatment Brands, 2005

Market shares are shown based on drug store sales for the 52 weeks ended October 30, 2005.

Benadryl 7.8%
Cortizone 10 . . . . 7.3
Aveeno 5.8
Cortaid 5.6
Zanfel 3.5

Continued on next page.

★ **1114** ★

[Continued]
Analgesics
SIC: 2834; NAICS: 325412

Top Anti-itch Treatment Brands, 2005

Market shares are shown based on drug store sales for the 52 weeks ended October 30, 2005.

Cortizone 10 Plus	3.2%
Lamisil AT	3.2
Lotrimin AF	3.2
Sarna	2.8
Lanacome	2.4
Other	55.2

Source: *Chain Drug Review*, January 2, 2006, p. 94.

★ **1115** ★

Analgesics
SIC: 2834; NAICS: 325412

Top Chest Rub Brands, 2005

Market shares are shown based on drug store sales for the 52 weeks ended October 30, 2005.

Vick's Vaporub	57.9%
Triaminic Vapor Patch	16.8
Mentholatum	6.8
Vicks Baby Rub	6.3
Johnson's Baby	1.3
Private label	10.7

Source: *Chain Drug Review*, January 2, 2006, p. 94.

★ **1116** ★

Analgesics
SIC: 2834; NAICS: 325412

Top Cold/Allergy/Sinus Relievers (Tablet/Packet), 2006

Brands are ranked by supermarket and drug store sales in millions of dollars.

	($ mil.)	Share
Claritin D	$ 129.6	6.72%
Mucinex	117.1	6.07
Benadryl	114.6	5.94
Claritin	110.2	5.71
Mucinex DM	59.9	3.10
Theraflu	58.5	3.03
Vicks DayQuil	53.8	2.79
Alka Seltzer Plus	52.8	2.74
Tylenol Sinus	52.8	2.74
Tylenol Cold	49.8	2.58

	($ mil.)	Share
Private label	$ 459.5	23.81%
Other	671.4	34.79

Source: *MMR*, April 24, 2006, p. 30, from Information Resources Inc.

★ **1117** ★

Analgesics
SIC: 2834; NAICS: 325412

Top Cold/Allergy/Sinus Remedy Makers, 2005

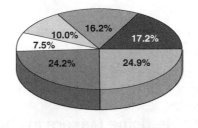

Market shares are based on supermarket, drug store and discount store sales (excluding Wal-Mart) for the 52 weeks ended June 12, 2005.

Schering-Plough	17.2%
Pfizer Inc.	16.2
McNeil Consumer Prods.	10.0
Wyeth Labs Inc.	7.5
Private label	24.2
Other	24.9

Source: *Grocery Headquarters*, September 21, 2005, p. S14, from Information Resources Inc.

★ **1118** ★

Analgesics
SIC: 2834; NAICS: 325412

Top Cold/Allergy/Sinus Treatments (Liquids/Powders), 2005

Market shares are shown based on drug store sales for the 52 weeks ended October 30, 2005.

Vicks Nyquil	12.1%
Tylenol Plus	8.1
Triaminic	5.6
Robitussin CF	4.9
Dimetapp	4.8
Benadryl	4.7

Continued on next page.

★ 1118 ★

[Continued]
Analgesics
SIC: 2834; NAICS: 325412

Top Cold/Allergy/Sinus Treatments (Liquids/Powders), 2005

Market shares are shown based on drug store sales for the 52 weeks ended October 30, 2005.

Tylenol	4.5%
Robitussin	4.1
Pediacare	4.0
Motrin	3.4
Private label	21.9
Other	21.9

Source: *Chain Drug Review*, January 2, 2006, p. 94.

★ 1119 ★

Analgesics
SIC: 2834; NAICS: 325412

Top Cold Medicine Makers in Japan, 2004

Market shares are shown based on domestic shipments of 63.2 billion yen.

Taisho Pharmaceutical	33.5%
Sankyo	11.8
Takeda Pharmaceutical	9.0
SSP	8.5
Zepharma	7.5
Other	29.7

Source: "2004 Market Share Report." [online] from http://www.nikkei.co.jp [Published July 27, 2005] from Nikkei estimates.

★ 1120 ★

Analgesics
SIC: 2834; NAICS: 325412

Top Cough/Cold Remedy Makers, 2005

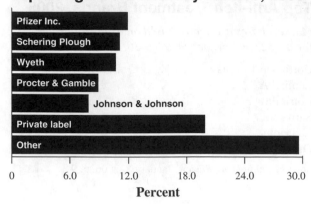

Market shares are shown in percent. Sales exclude Wal-Mart and other large-format mass retailers.

Pfizer Inc.	11.9%
Schering Plough	11.1
Wyeth	10.7
Procter & Gamble	8.9
Johnson & Johnson	7.9
Private label	19.9
Other	29.6

Source: *U.S. Personal Care and Household Products Digest*, Citigroup Equity Research, February 24, 2006, p. 113, from ACNielsen.

★ 1121 ★

Analgesics
SIC: 2834; NAICS: 325412

Top Cough Medicine Brands, 2006

Brands are ranked by supermarket and drug store sales in millions of dollars.

	($ mil.)	Share
Robitussin DM	$ 69.0	25.49%
Delsym	40.0	14.78
Robitussin	34.8	12.86
Viks NyQuil	18.4	6.80
Vicks Formula 44	7.2	2.66
Vicks Formula 44E	5.9	2.18
Robitussin Pediatric	4.7	1.74
Diabetic Tussin	4.5	1.66
Zicam Cough Mist	4.5	1.66
Triaminic	3.9	1.44
Private label	61.4	22.68
Other	16.4	6.06

Source: *MMR*, April 24, 2006, p. 30, from Information Resources Inc.

★ 1122 ★
Analgesics
SIC: 2834; NAICS: 325412

Top Cough/Sore Throat Drops, 2005

Market shares are shown based on drug store sales for the 52 weeks ended October 30, 2005.

Halls .23.3%
Ricola 10.1
Cold Eeze 9.3
Halls Defense 5.5
Ludens 5.3
Cepacol 5.2
Halls Fruit Breezers 5.2
Halls Plus 3.3
Chloraseptic 2.6
Sucrets 2.0
Private label 14.0
Other 14.2

Source: *Chain Drug Review*, January 2, 2006, p. 94.

★ 1123 ★
Analgesics
SIC: 2834; NAICS: 325412

Top Cough Syrup Brands, 2005

Market shares are shown based on drug store sales for the 52 weeks ended October 30, 2005.

Robitussin DM 25.3%
Delsym 16.2
Robitussin 11.6
Vicks NyQuil Cough 5.0
Diabetic Tussin 2.3
Vicks Formula 44 . . . . 2.0
Zicam Cough Mist 2.0
Vicks Formula 44e 1.8
Robitussin Pediatric 1.5
Robitussin Honey Cough 1.4
Private label 25.4
Other 5.5

Source: *Chain Drug Review*, January 2, 2006, p. 94.

★ 1124 ★
Analgesics
SIC: 2834; NAICS: 325412

Top Diarrhea Tablets, 2005

Market shares are shown based on drug store sales for the 52 weeks ended October 30, 2005.

Imodium AD 35.8%
Imodium Advanced 35.3
Kaopectate 2.0
Private label 26.9

Source: *Chain Drug Review*, January 2, 2006, p. 94.

★ 1125 ★
Analgesics
SIC: 2834; NAICS: 325412

Top Digestive Aids (Antacid/ Analgesic), 2006

Brands are ranked by supermarket and drug store sales in millions of dollars.

	($ mil.)	Share
Alka Seltzer	$ 36.5	87.95%
Alka Seltzer PM	0.7	1.69
Private label	3.9	9.40
Other	0.4	0.96

Source: *MMR*, April 24, 2006, p. 30, from Information Resources Inc.

★ 1126 ★
Analgesics
SIC: 2834; NAICS: 325412

Top Digestive Aids (Tablets), 2006

Brands are ranked by supermarket and drug store sales in millions of dollars.

	($ mil.)	Share
Prilosec OTC	$ 284.0	30.14%
Pepcid AC	75.2	7.98
Tums EX	56.8	6.03
Zantac 150	51.8	5.50
Pepcid Complete	47.6	5.05
Rolaids	41.8	4.44
Gas X	39.5	4.19
Zantac 75	39.2	4.16
Tums Ultra	26.8	2.84

Continued on next page.

★ 1126 ★
[Continued]
Analgesics
SIC: 2834; NAICS: 325412

Top Digestive Aids (Tablets), 2006

Brands are ranked by supermarket and drug store sales in millions of dollars.

	($ mil.)	Share
Private label	$ 120.6	12.80%
Other	159.1	16.88

Source: *MMR*, April 24, 2006, p. 30, from Information Resources Inc.

★ 1127 ★
Analgesics
SIC: 2834; NAICS: 325412

Top Douche Brands, 2006

Brands are ranked by supermarket and drug store sales in millions of dollars.

	($ mil.)	Share
Summer's Eve	$ 16.8	46.28%
Massengill	7.9	21.76
Summer's Eve Ultra	2.0	5.51
Vagi-Guard	1.3	3.58
Private label	7.7	21.21
Other	0.6	1.65

Source: *MMR*, April 24, 2006, p. 30, from Information Resources Inc.

★ 1128 ★
Analgesics
SIC: 2834; NAICS: 325412

Top Ear Drop/Treatment Brands, 2005

Market shares are shown based on drug store sales for the 52 weeks ended October 30, 2005.

Similasan	25.9%
Debrox	14.8
Murine	8.5
Swim Ear	6.7
Physicians Choice	5.0
Auro Ori	4.2
Hyland's	3.7
Otix	2.8
Ototek Loop	2.1
Flents	1.6

Private label	18.9%
Other	5.8

Source: *Chain Drug Review*, January 2, 2006, p. 94.

★ 1129 ★
Analgesics
SIC: 2834; NAICS: 325412

Top Ear Drop/Treatment Makers, 2005

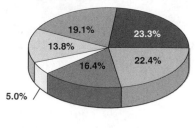

Legend:
- Similasan
- S.C. Johnson
- Prestige Brands
- Del Labs
- Private label
- Other

Market shares are shown based on dollar sales for the 12 weeks ended November 27, 2005.

Similasan	23.3%
S.C. Johnson	19.1
Prestige Brands	13.8
Del Labs	5.0
Private label	16.4
Other	22.4

Source: *High Yield Consumer Products*, Deutsche Bank, December 15, 2005, p. 13, from Information Resources Inc.

★ 1130 ★
Analgesics
SIC: 2834; NAICS: 325412

Top External Analgesic Rub Makers, 2005

Market shares are shown based on dollar sales for the 12 weeks ended November 27, 2005.

Chattem	35.9%
Pfizer	18.6
Hisamitsu Pharm	5.2
Rohot Pharm	3.5
Naturopathic Laboratories	2.4
Private label	7.0
Other	27.4

Source: *High Yield Consumer Products*, Deutsche Bank, December 15, 2005, p. 13, from Information Resources Inc.

★ 1131 ★
Analgesics
SIC: 2834; NAICS: 325412

Top Female Pain Reliever Makers, 2005

Brands are ranked by sales in millions of dollars at supermarkets, drug stores and discount stores (excluding Wal-Mart) for the 52 weeks ended August 7, 2005.

	($ mil.)	Share
Midol	$ 31.8	61.75%
Pamprin	9.8	19.03
Premsyn PMS	2.6	5.05
Women's Tylenol	2.3	4.47
Other	5.0	9.71

Source: *MMR*, September 19, 2005, p. S14, from Information Resources Inc.

★ 1132 ★
Analgesics
SIC: 2834; NAICS: 325412

Top Feminine Pain Relievers, 2005

Market shares are shown based on drug store sales for the 52 weeks ended October 30, 2005.

Midol	58.0%
Pamprin	14.7
Premsyn PMS	6.3
Women's Tylenol	4.4
Diurex PMS	0.4
Humphreys	0.2
Diurex	0.1
Private label	16.1

Source: *Chain Drug Review*, January 2, 2006, p. 94.

★ 1133 ★
Analgesics
SIC: 2834; NAICS: 325412

Top Feminine Pain Relievers, 2006

Brands are ranked by supermarket and drug store sales in millions of dollars.

	($ mil.)	Share
Midol	$ 32.0	61.90%
Pamprin Feminine	9.9	19.15
Premsyn PMS	2.5	4.84
Women's Tylenol	2.0	3.87
Private label	5.1	9.86
Other	0.2	0.39

Source: *MMR*, April 24, 2006, p. 30, from Information Resources Inc.

★ 1134 ★
Analgesics
SIC: 2834; NAICS: 325412

Top Foot Care/Athlete's Foot Medications, 2005

Market shares are shown based on drug store sales for the 52 weeks ended October 30, 2005.

Lamisil AT	14.7%
Lotrimin AF	10.0
Tinactin	7.7
Dr. Scholl's	4.1
Lotrimin Ultra	3.7
Miracle of Aloe	2.8
Reclaim AF	2.8
Flexitol	2.5
Gold Bond	2.5
Desenex	2.4
Private label	15.7
Other	31.1

Source: *Chain Drug Review*, January 2, 2006, p. 94.

★ 1135 ★
Analgesics
SIC: 2834; NAICS: 325412

Top Hair Growth Tonic Makers in Japan, 2004

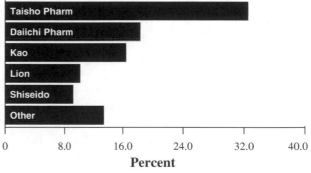

Market shares are shown based on domestic shipments of 39.5 billion yen.

Taisho Pharm	32.5%
Daiichi Pharm	18.3
Kao	16.4
Lion	10.2
Shiseido	9.2
Other	13.4

Source: "2004 Market Share Report." [online] from http://www.nikkei.co.jp [Published July 27, 2005] from Nikkei estimates.

★ 1136 ★
Analgesics
SIC: 2834; NAICS: 325412
Top Hemorrhoidal Creams, 2006

Brands are ranked by supermarket and drug store sales in millions of dollars.

	($ mil.)	Share
Preparation H	$ 46.9	66.34%
Anusol Tucks	4.6	6.51
Nupercainal	2.8	3.96
Tronolane	1.3	1.84
Balneol	1.2	1.70
Private label	10.5	14.85
Other	3.4	4.81

Source: *MMR*, April 24, 2006, p. 30, from Information Resources Inc.

★ 1137 ★
Analgesics
SIC: 2834; NAICS: 325412
Top Laxative Brands (Tablet), 2005

Market shares are shown based on drug store sales for the 52 weeks ended August 7, 2005.

Dulcolax	11.9%
Metamucil	6.5
Colace	6.1
Ex-Lax	5.9
Fibercon	3.4
Fleet	3.2
Senokot S	3.2
Senokot	3.0
Correctol	2.8
Citrucel	2.7
Other	51.3

Source: *Chain Drug Review*, October 10, 2005, p. 44, from ACNielsen.

★ 1138 ★
Analgesics
SIC: 2834; NAICS: 325412
Top Laxatives/Stimulants (Liquid/ Powder), 2005

Market shares are shown based on drug store sales for the 52 weeks ended October 30, 2005.

Metamucil	23.9%
Fleet	11.6

Citrucel	10.1%
Benefiber	7.8
Fleet Phospho Soda	6.5
Konsyl	2.9
Fletcher's Castoria	1.9
Fleet Babylax	1.8
Lactinex	0.8
Little Tummy's	0.8
Other	31.9

Source: *Chain Drug Review*, January 2, 2006, p. 94.

★ 1139 ★
Analgesics
SIC: 2834; NAICS: 325412
Top Lice Remedies, 2006

Brands are ranked by sales in millions of dollars at supermarkets, drug stores and discount stores (excluding Wal-Mart) for the 52 weeks ended January 22, 2006.

	($ mil.)	Share
Rid	$ 25.5	37.72%
Nix	9.9	14.64
Pronto Plus	3.5	5.18
Lice Freee	1.9	2.81
Pronto	1.3	1.92
Lice Guard Robi Comb	1.0	1.48
Acu Life	0.8	1.18
Lice Guard	0.5	0.74
Reese's	0.5	0.74
Mata Piojos	0.3	0.44
Private label	21.2	31.36
Other	1.2	1.78

Source: *MMR*, March 20, 2006, p. 29, from Information Resources Inc.

★ 1140 ★
Analgesics
SIC: 2834; NAICS: 325412
Top Lip Balm/Cold Sore Treatment Makers, 2005

Market shares are ranked by sales in millions of dollars at supermarkets, drug stores and discount stores (excluding Wal-Mart) for the 52 weeks ended June 12, 2005.

Wyeth Labs Inc.	28.3%
GlaxoSmithKline	18.4
Blistex Inc.	18.3

Continued on next page.

★ 1140 ★

[Continued]
Analgesics
SIC: 2834; NAICS: 325412

Top Lip Balm/Cold Sore Treatment Makers, 2005

Market shares are ranked by sales in millions of dollars at supermarkets, drug stores and discount stores (excluding Wal-Mart) for the 52 weeks ended June 12, 2005.

Carma Labs Inc.	5.9%
Private label	3.8
Other	25.3

Source: *Grocery Headquarters*, September 21, 2005, p. S14, from Information Resources Inc.

★ 1141 ★

Analgesics
SIC: 2834; NAICS: 325412

Top Oral Pain Reliever Makers, 2005

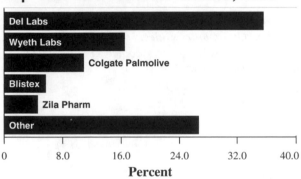

Percent

Market shares are shown based on dollar sales for the 12 weeks ended November 27, 2005.

Del Labs	35.6%
Wyeth Labs	16.5
Colgate Palmolive	10.9
Blistex	5.7
Zila Pharm	4.6
Other	26.7

Source: *High Yield Consumer Products*, Deutsche Bank, December 15, 2005, p. 13, from Information Resources Inc.

★ 1142 ★

Analgesics
SIC: 2834; NAICS: 325412

Top Prickly Heat Powders in Thailand

The British Dispensary Co. is hoping to raise its share for its popular prickly-heat brand Snake from 22% to 25% in the coming year, bringing it even with market leader Protec, made by Colgate Palmolive. The cooling talcum powder market is worth 1.4 billion baht, according to ACNielsen.

British Dispensary Co.	25.0%
Colgate Palmolive	25.0
Other	50.0

Source: *Bangkok Post*, February 24, 2006, p. NA, from company estimates.

★ 1143 ★

Analgesics
SIC: 2834; NAICS: 325412

Top Sleeping Aid Tablets, 2006

Brands are ranked by supermarket and drug store sales in millions of dollars.

	($ mil.)	Share
Simply Sleep	$ 20.7	19.94%
Unisom Sleepgels	16.1	15.51
Unisom	11.6	11.18
Sominex	5.4	5.20
Sleepinal	3.2	3.08
Nytol	1.9	1.83
Sominex 2	1.9	1.83
Private label	33.6	32.37
Other	9.4	9.06

Source: *MMR*, April 24, 2006, p. 30, from Information Resources Inc.

★ 1144 ★

Analgesics
SIC: 2834; NAICS: 325412

Top Stomach Remedies, 2006

Brands are ranked by supermarket and drug store sales in millions of dollars.

	($ mil.)	Share
Pepto Bismol	$ 59.0	38.87%
Phillips	33.9	22.33
Maalox Total Stomach Relief	6.0	3.95

Continued on next page.

★ 1144 ★
[Continued]
Analgesics
SIC: 2834; NAICS: 325412
Top Stomach Remedies, 2006

Brands are ranked by supermarket and drug store sales in millions of dollars.

	($ mil.)	Share
Ex-Lax	$ 1.1	0.72%
Private label	25.4	16.73
Other	26.4	17.39

Source: *MMR*, April 24, 2006, p. 30, from Information Resources Inc.

★ 1145 ★
Analgesics
SIC: 2834; NAICS: 325412
Top Vaginal Treatments, 2006

Brands are ranked by supermarket and drug store sales in millions of dollars.

	($ mil.)	Share
Monistat 1	$ 50.8	22.97%
Monistat 3	44.8	20.25
Monistat 7	23.4	10.58
Monistat 1 Day	12.7	5.74
Vagistat 1	8.0	3.62
Replens	5.6	2.53
KY Silk E	4.5	2.03
Summer's Eve	3.5	1.58
Vagi-Guard	2.1	0.95
Private label	54.4	24.59
Other	11.4	5.15

Source: *MMR*, April 24, 2006, p. 30, from Information Resources Inc.

★ 1146 ★
Analgesics
SIC: 2834; NAICS: 325412
Top Wart Remover Makers, 2005

Market shares are shown based on dollar sales for the 12 weeks ended November 27, 2005.

Schering-Plough	.43.3%
Prestige Brands	.34.5
Lil Drug Store	.12.5
Stiefel Labs	2.4
Pedifix	1.2

Private label	3.8%
Other	2.3

Source: *High Yield Consumer Products*, Deutsche Bank, December 15, 2005, p. 13, from Information Resources Inc.

★ 1147 ★
Drugs
SIC: 2834; NAICS: 325412
Bone Density Drug Market

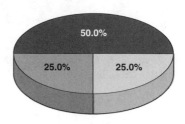

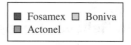

The market for building bone density is worth about $3 billion. Osteopororsis affects about 10 million people annually, mostly women. Another 34 million people suffer from bone weakness.

Fosamex	.50.0%
Actonel	.25.0
Boniva	.25.0

Source: *Contra Costa Times*, June 21, 2006, p. NA.

★ 1148 ★
Drugs
SIC: 2834; NAICS: 325412
Drug Delivery Market, 2004

Market shares are shown in percent.

Oral	.24.7%
Pulmonary	.21.7
Injectable	8.6
Other	4.5

Source: *Datamonitor Industry Market Research*, October 31, 2005, p. NA, from Datamonitor.

★ 1149 ★
Drugs

SIC: 2834; NAICS: 325412

Drug Sales Worldwide, 2005

Total sales were $602 billion in 2005. The top 10 markets grew 5.7%. In 2004 there was 7.2% growth among the top 10 markets. Emerging markets China, Korea, Mexico, Russia and Turkey all saw double-digit growth.

	($ bil.)	Share
North America	$ 265.7	46.95%
Europe	169.5	29.95
Japan	60.3	10.66
Africa	46.4	8.20
Latin America	24.0	4.24

Source: *Asia Pulse*, March 22, 2006, p. NA, from IMS Health.

★ 1150 ★
Drugs

SIC: 2834; NAICS: 325412

ED Drug Market

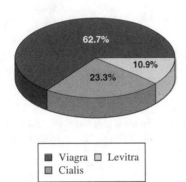

Viagra has been losing market share as other competitors entered the erectile dysfunction market. It had a 90% market share in 2003 and a 73.4% hare in 2004.

Viagra	.62.7%
Cialis	.23.3
Levitra	.10.9

Source: *Advertising Age*, March 27, 2006, p. 48.

★ 1151 ★
Drugs

SIC: 2834; NAICS: 325412

Equine Health Care Industry

Market shares are shown in percent.

Farnam	.60.0%
Other	.40.0

Source: *Pet Product News*, March 2006, p. 1.

★ 1152 ★
Drugs

SIC: 2834; NAICS: 325412

Flu Vaccine Market in Canada

GlaxoSmithKline, which has about a quarter of the world's total vaccine market, placed a bid for ID Biomedical in September 2005.

ID Biomedical	.75.0%
Other	.25.0

Source: *Financial Times*, September 8, 2005, p. 17.

★ 1153 ★
Drugs

SIC: 2834; NAICS: 325412

Leading Animal Health Care Firms, 2004

Firms are ranked by sales in millions of dollars. Total sales of animal drugs and nutrition (including vet drugs, vaccines and food additives) worldwide were $20,225 million.

	($ mil.)	Share
Pfizer	$ 1,953	9.19%
Merial	1,836	8.64
Intervet	1,272	5.98
DSM	1,068	5.02
Bayer	976	4.59
BASF	901	4.24
Fort Dodge	837	3.94
Elanco	799	3.76
Schering-Plough	770	3.62
Novartis	756	3.56
Other	10,087	47.46

Source: *ETC Communique*, November/December 2005, p. 4, from *Animal Pharm Reports, 2005*.

★ 1154 ★
Drugs

SIC: 2834; NAICS: 325412

Leading Antipsychotics, 2004

Market shares are shown based on $9.6 billion in wholesale purchases for class.

Zyprexa	.32.0%
Risperdal	.23.0
Seroquel	.22.0
Abilify	.11.0

Continued on next page.

★ 1154 ★
[Continued]
Drugs
SIC: 2834; NAICS: 325412

Leading Antipsychotics, 2004

Market shares are shown based on $9.6 billion in wholesale purchases for class.

Geodon 5.0%
Other 6.0

Source: *Clinical Psychiatry News*, July 2005, p. 1, from IMS Health.

★ 1155 ★
Drugs
SIC: 2834; NAICS: 325412

Leading Insomnia Treatments, 2005

The prescription anti-insomnia market was valued at $2 billion in 2004, up 20% from 2003. An estimated 70 million Americans suffer from insomnia.

	July	Aug.	Share
Ambien	$ 161.6	$ 164.5	77.34%
Lunesta	26.0	31.6	14.86
Sonata	8.5	8.5	4.00
Other	8.0	8.1	3.81

Source: *Medical Marketing & Media*, November 2005, p. 58, from IMS Health and IMS National Sales Perspectives.

★ 1156 ★
Drugs
SIC: 2834; NAICS: 325412

Ophthalmology Drug Market Worldwide, 2006-2008

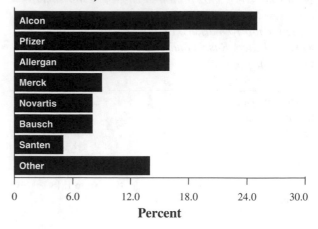

The market is forecast to increase from $9 billion in 2006 to $10.2 billion in 2007 to $11.3 billion in 2008.

	2006	2007	2008
Alcon	23.0%	23.0%	25.0%
Pfizer	18.0	18.0	16.0
Allergan	16.0	15.0	16.0
Merck	10.0	10.0	9.0
Novartis	10.0	9.0	8.0
Bausch	8.0	8.0	8.0
Santen	6.0	5.0	5.0
Other	10.0	13.0	14.0

Source: *Medical Supplies & Technology*, Citigroup Equity Research, October 14, 2005, p. 12, from Citigroup Investment Research.

★ 1157 ★
Drugs
SIC: 2834; NAICS: 325412

SSRI/SNRI Drug Market, 2004

Data show share of total wholesale purchases for the selective serotonin reuptake inhibitor/selective norepinenphrine reuptake inhibitor market.

Zoloft 28.0%
Effexor XR 23.0
Lexapro 16.0
Celexa 9.0
Paxil CR 8.0
Other 16.0

Source: *Family Practice News*, November 1, 2005, p. 41, from IMS Health.

★ 1158 ★
Drugs
SIC: 2834; NAICS: 325412
Top ADHD Drugs, 2006

Market shares are shown based on new prescriptions for the four weeks ended February 24, 2006. ADHD stands for attention deficit hyperactivity disorder.

Adderall	.25.8%
Concerta	.22.2
Strattera	.11.7
Ritalin	.4.0
Other	.36.3

Source: *U.S. Specialty Pharmaceuticals*, Credit Suisse, March 6, 2006, p. 5, from Credit Suisse estimates, IMS Health and company data.

★ 1159 ★
Drugs
SIC: 2834; NAICS: 325412
Top Alzheimer Drugs, 2006

Market shares are shown for the four weeks ended January 20, 2006.

Aricept	.53.3%
Namenda	.29.6
Razadyne	.8.9
Other	.8.2

Source: *Weekly Prescription Report*, Rodman & Renshaw, January 30, 2006, p. 2, from IMS Health's Weekly National Prescription Audit.

★ 1160 ★
Drugs
SIC: 2834; NAICS: 325412
Top Anticholesterol Drugs, 2006

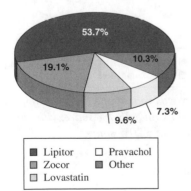

Market shares are shown for the four weeks ended January 20, 2006.

Lipitor	.53.7%
Zocor	.19.1

Lovastatin	.9.6%
Pravachol	.7.3
Other	.10.3

Source: *Weekly Prescription Report*, Rodman & Renshaw, January 30, 2006, p. 2, from IMS Health's Weekly National Prescription Audit.

★ 1161 ★
Drugs
SIC: 2834; NAICS: 325412
Top Antidepressant Markets, 2004

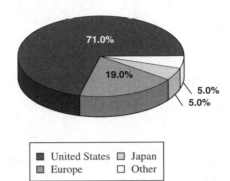

According to the source, The World Health Organization (WHO) predicts that by 2020 depression will be the second-largest cause of the global health burden. There are about 40 million diagnosed cases in the United States, France, Germany, Italy, Spain, United Kingdom, and Japan. The United States has about 15 million of these cases. In 2004, global sales of antidepressant agents topped $15 billion. Effexor and Zoloft led the global market, each generating sales of $3.3 billion.

United States	.71.0%
Europe	.19.0
Japan	.5.0
Other	.5.0

Source: *Business Wire*, March 23, 2006, p. NA, from Research and Markets.

★ 1162 ★
Drugs
SIC: 2834; NAICS: 325412
Top Antidepressants, 2005

Total sales for the first six months of the year were $5.11 billion.

	($ bil.)	Share
Zoloft	$ 1.55	30.33%
Effexor XR	1.29	25.24
Lexapro	1.03	20.16

Continued on next page.

★ 1162 ★

[Continued]
Drugs
SIC: 2834; NAICS: 325412

Top Antidepressants, 2005

Total sales for the first six months of the year were $5.11 billion.

	($ bil.)	Share
Cymbatta	$ 0.27	5.28%
Other	0.97	18.98

Source: *Wall Street Journal*, August 24, 2005, p. A6, from IMS Health.

★ 1163 ★

Drugs
SIC: 2834; NAICS: 325412

Top Arthritis-Cox II Drugs, 2006

Market shares are shown for the four weeks ended February 10, 2006.

	Prescriptions	Share
Ibuprofen (generic)	1,926,013	28.91%
Naproxen (generic)	1,098,416	16.49
PFE Cox-2	967,562	14.52
Total Cox-2	967,562	14.52
Celebrex	967,496	14.52
Other	734,645	11.03

Source: *Prescription Trends*, IMS Health, February 21, 2006, p. 4, from IMS Health and AGE Analysis.

★ 1164 ★

Drugs
SIC: 2834; NAICS: 325412

Top Drug Classes, 2005

Sales include pharmaceutical purchases at wholesale prices by retail, food stores and chains, mass merchandisers, independent pharmacies, mail services, non-federal and federal hospitals, clinics, closed-wall HMOs, long-term pharmacies, home health care and prisons/universities. Excludes co-marketing agreements. Joint-ventures assigned to product owner. Data run by custom redesign to include mergers & acquisitions.

HMG - COA reductase inhibitors (statins)	6.4%
Proton pump inhibitors	5.1
Antipsychotics	4.2
Erythropoietins	3.5
Seizure disorders	3.2
SSRI	2.7
Angiotensin II Antag	2.0
Calcium blockers	1.8

Insulin sensitizer	1.6%
Monoclonal antibodies	1.6
Other	67.9

Source: "Top-Line Industry Data." [online] from http://www.imshealth.com [Published January 2006] from IMS Health, IMS National Health Sales Perspectives.

★ 1165 ★

Drugs
SIC: 2834; NAICS: 325412

Top Drug Firms in Brazil

Market shares are shown based on total billings of $5.5 billion in 2004.

Laboratorios Ache	6.28%
Aventis Pharma	5.76
EMS Sigma Pharma	5.47
Novartis	4.72
Roche	4.48
Boehringer	4.32
Schering do Brasil	3.88
Schering Plough	3.53
Other	61.56

Source: *Pharmaceutical Engineering*, January/February 2005, p. 3.

★ 1166 ★

Drugs
SIC: 2834; NAICS: 325412

Top Drug Firms in Sweden, 2004

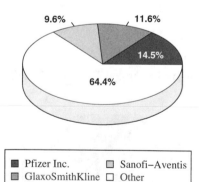

The industry was valued at $29.95 million. Analgesics led the market with a 28.7% share, vitamins and minerals followed with a 20% share.

Pfizer Inc.	14.5%
GlaxoSmithKline	11.6
Sanofi-Aventis	9.6
Other	64.4

Source: *Datamonitor Industry Market Research*, November 18, 2005, p. NA, from Datamonitor.

★ 1167 ★
Drugs
SIC: 2834; NAICS: 325412

Top Drug Firms Worldwide, 2004

Firms are ranked by revenue in billions of dollars. IMS Health reports one of the most striking development in the drug industry worldwide in 2004 was the growth of the pharmaceutical drug market in China. It saw sales increase 28% year-over-year to $9.5 billion.

Pfizer	$ 52.5
GlaxoSmithKline	37.2
Sanofi-Aventis	32.8
Novartis	28.2
Roche	26.1
Merck	22.9
Johnson & Johnson	22.1
AstraZeneca	21.4
Bristol-Myers Squibb	19.4

Source: *Business Travel World*, May 2005, p. 23, from company reports.

★ 1168 ★
Drugs
SIC: 2834; NAICS: 325412

Top Drug Makers, 2005

Sales include pharmaceutical purchases at wholesale prices by retail, food stores and chains, mass merchandisers, independent pharmacies, mail services, non-federal and federal hospitals, clinics, closed-wall HMOs, long-term pharmacies, home health care and prisons/ universities. Excludes co-marketing agreements. Joint-ventures assigned to product owner. Data run by custom redesign to include mergers & acquisitions.

	($ bil.)	Share
Pfizer	$ 27.2	10.8%
GlaxoSmithKline	19.9	7.9
Johnson & Johnson	16.0	6.3
Merck & Co.	15.2	6.0
AstraZeneca	12.9	5.1
Novartis	12.3	4.9
Sanofi-Aventis	11.0	4.4
Lilly	8.7	3.4
Bristol-Myers Squibb	8.4	3.3

Source: "Top-Line Industry Data." [online] from http:// www.imshealth.com [Published January 2006] from IMS Health, IMS National Health Sales Perspectives.

★ 1169 ★
Drugs
SIC: 2834; NAICS: 325412

Top Drug Products, 2005

Sales include pharmaceutical purchases at wholesale prices by retail, food stores and chains, mass merchandisers, independent pharmacies, mail services, non-federal and federal hospitals, clinics, closed-wall HMOs, long-term pharmacies, home health care and prisons/ universities.

	($ bil.)	Share
Lipitor	$ 8.4	3.3%
Nexium	4.4	1.7
Zocor	4.4	1.7
Prevacid	3.8	1.5
Advair Diskus	3.6	1.4
Plavix	3.5	1.4
Zoloft	3.1	1.2
Epogen	3.0	1.2
Procrit	3.0	1.2
Aranesp	2.8	1.1

Source: "Top-Line Industry Data." [online] from http:// www.imshealth.com [Published January 2006] from IMS Health, IMS National Health Sales Perspectives.

★ 1170 ★
Drugs
SIC: 2834; NAICS: 325412

Top Drugs Firms in Japan, 2004

Market shares are shown based on domestic sales of 7.34 trillion yen.

Takeda Pharmaceutical	7.5%
Yamanouchi Pharmaceutical	4.7
Chugai Pharmaceutical	4.5
Pfizer Japan	4.3
Novartis Pharma	3.9
Other	75.1

Source: "2004 Market Share Report." [online] from http:// www.nikkei.co.jp [Published July 27, 2005] from Nikkei estimates and IMS Japan.

★ 1171 ★
Drugs
SIC: 2834; NAICS: 325412
Top Flu Antiviral Drugs, 2006

Market shares are shown for the four weeks ended January 20, 2006.

Tamiflu 99.8%
Relenza 0.2

Source: *Weekly Prescription Report*, Rodman & Renshaw, January 30, 2006, p. 2, from IMS Health's Weekly National Prescription Audit.

★ 1172 ★
Drugs
SIC: 2834; NAICS: 325412
Top Generic Drug Firms

Market shares are shown based on 1,967 million prescriptions dispensed for the 12 months ended June 2005. A total of $23 billion in drugs are coming off patent in 2006. Overall, $56 billion in branded drug will be facing generic competition in the next two years. Amoxicillin clavulanate was the best-selling generic.

Teva 11.9%
Mylan 11.2
Watson 9.1
Novartis 8.1
Ivax 5.0
Mallinckrodt 4.2
Barr 4.0
Alpharma 3.9
Qualitest 3.9
Other 38.7

Source: *Drug Store News*, September 26, 2005, p. 55, from IMS Health's Weekly National Prescription Audit.

★ 1173 ★
Drugs
SIC: 2834; NAICS: 325412
Top Glaucoma Drugs, 2006

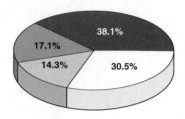

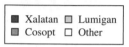

Market shares are shown based on new prescriptions for the four weeks ended February 24, 2006.

Xalatan 38.1%
Cosopt 17.1
Lumigan 14.3
Other 30.5

Source: *U.S. Specialty Pharmaceuticals*, Credit Suisse, March 6, 2006, p. 5, from Credit Suisse estimates, IMS Health and company data.

★ 1174 ★
Drugs
SIC: 2834; NAICS: 325412
Top Hepatitis B Drugs, 2006

Market shares are shown for the four weeks ended February 10, 2006.

	Prescriptions	Share
Hepsera	10,326	53.20%
Epivir HBV	6,183	31.86
Baraclude	2,899	14.94

Source: *Prescription Trends*, IMS Health, February 21, 2006, p. 4, from IMS Health and AGE Analysis.

★ 1175 ★
Drugs
SIC: 2834; NAICS: 325412
Top Oral Diabetes Drugs, 2006

Market shares are shown for the four weeks ended January 20, 2006.

Actos 38.2%
Avandia 38.1

Continued on next page.

★ 1175 ★

[Continued]
Drugs
SIC: 2834; NAICS: 325412

Top Oral Diabetes Drugs, 2006

Market shares are shown for the four weeks ended January 20, 2006.

Flyb/Met 14.3%
Other 9.4

Source: *Weekly Prescription Report*, Rodman & Renshaw, January 30, 2006, p. 2, from IMS Health's Weekly National Prescription Audit.

★ 1176 ★

Drugs
SIC: 2834; NAICS: 325412

Top Osteoporosis Drugs, 2006

Market shares are shown for the four weeks ended February 10, 2006.

	Prescriptions	Share
Fosamax	1,566,855	46.67%
Actonel	843,594	25.13
Evista	453,289	13.50
Other	493,676	14.70

Source: *Prescription Trends*, IMS Health, February 21, 2006, p. 4, from IMS Health and AGE Analysis.

★ 1177 ★

Drugs
SIC: 2834; NAICS: 325412

Top Seizure Disorder Drugs, 2006

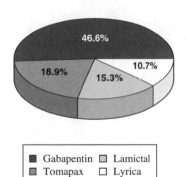

Market shares are shown for the four weeks ended January 20, 2006.

Gabapentin 46.6%
Tomapax 18.9

Lamictal 15.3%
Lyrica 10.7

Source: *Weekly Prescription Report*, Rodman & Renshaw, January 30, 2006, p. 2, from IMS Health's Weekly National Prescription Audit.

★ 1178 ★

Drugs
SIC: 2834; NAICS: 325412

Top Thyroid Drugs, 2006

Market shares are shown based on new prescriptions for the four weeks ended February 24, 2006.

Synthroid 34.2%
Levoxyl 11.7
Levothroid 3.8
Other 50.3

Source: *U.S. Specialty Pharmaceuticals*, Credit Suisse, March 6, 2006, p. 5, from Credit Suisse estimates, IMS Health and company data.

★ 1179 ★

Drugs
SIC: 2834; NAICS: 325412

Top Urinary Incontinence Drugs, 2006

Market shares are shown for the four weeks ended February 10, 2006.

	Prescriptions	Share
Detrol	491,091	46.09%
Ditropan	209,919	19.70
VESIcare	66,355	6.23
Other	298,248	27.99

Source: *Prescription Trends*, IMS Health, February 21, 2006, p. 4, from IMS Health and AGE Analysis.

★ 1180 ★
Smoking Cessation Products
SIC: 2834; NAICS: 325412

Top Smoking Cessation Patches, 2006

Brands are ranked by supermarket and drug store sales in millions of dollars.

	($ mil.)	Share
Nicoderm CQ	$82.7	58.99%
Nicotrol	0.6	0.43
Private label	56.9	40.58

Source: *MMR*, April 24, 2006, p. 30, from Information Resources Inc.

★ 1181 ★
Smoking Cessation Products
SIC: 2834; NAICS: 325412

Top Smoking Cessation Tablets, 2006

Brands are ranked by supermarket and drug store sales in millions of dollars.

	($ mil.)	Share
Commit	$64.9	92.85%
Smoke Away	4.6	6.58
Nicodrops	0.3	0.43
Other	0.1	0.14

Source: *MMR*, April 24, 2006, p. 30, from Information Resources Inc.

★ 1182 ★
Pregnancy Test Kits
SIC: 2835; NAICS: 325413

Top Ovulation Test Kit Brands, 2006

Brands are ranked by supermarket and drug store sales in millions of dollars.

	($ mil.)	Share
Clearblue Easy	$10.7	26.49%
Clearplan Easy	6.0	14.85
First Response	3.3	8.17
Answer Quick & Simple	2.1	5.20
Answer Dot	1.3	3.22
Private label	7.5	18.56
Other	9.5	23.51

Source: *MMR*, April 24, 2006, p. 30, from Information Resources Inc.

★ 1183 ★
Pregnancy Test Kits
SIC: 2835; NAICS: 325413

Top Pregnancy Test Kit Brands, 2005

Brands are ranked by drug store sales in millions of dollars for the 52 weeks ended October 3, 2005.

	($ mil.)	Share
First Response	$29.3	19.53%
e.p.t.	25.3	16.87
Clearblue Easy	17.2	11.47
e.p.t. Certainty	14.9	9.93
Accu Clear	10.9	7.27
Answer Quick & Simple	7.2	4.80
Fact Plus One-Step	5.7	3.80
Answer	2.0	1.33
Clear Choice	0.5	0.33
Private label	36.2	24.13
Other	0.8	0.53

Source: *Drug Store News*, November 21, 2005, p. 29, from Information Resources Inc.

★ 1184 ★
Pregnancy Test Kits
SIC: 2835; NAICS: 325413

Top Pregnancy Test Kit Makers, 2005

Market shares are shown based on dollar sales for the 12 weeks ended November 27, 2005.

Church & Dwight	28.1%
Pfizer	26.1
Inverness	16.7
Abbott Labs	3.7
Private label	24.7
Other	0.7

Source: *High Yield Consumer Products*, Deutsche Bank, December 15, 2005, p. 13, from Information Resources Inc.

★ 1185 ★
Biotechnology
SIC: 2836; NAICS: 325414

Leading Biotech Care Firms Worldwide, 2004

Firms are ranked by revenues in millions of dollars as of June 2005. The source defines biotech firms as "those companies whose primary commercial activity depends on the application of biological organisms, systems or processes, or on providing special service that draw on biological systems."

	($ mil.)	Share
Amgen	$ 10,550	22.67%
Monsanto	5,457	11.73
Genentech	4,621	9.93
Serono	2,458	5.28
Biogen	2,212	4.75
Genzyme	2,201	4.73
Applied Biosystems	1,741	3.74
Chiron	1,723	3.70
Gilead Sciences	1,325	2.85
Medimmune	1,141	2.45
Other	13,104	28.16

Source: *ETC Communique*, November/December 2005, p. 4, from *Nature Biotechnology*.

★ 1186 ★
Blood
SIC: 2836; NAICS: 325414

Blood Market, 2005 and 2010

Driving forces in this industry include the cost of collection and processing, technological advances and the needs of an aging population.

	2005	2010
Blood and blood components	$ 3,192.16	$ 5,451.65
Plasma derived products . . .	3,404.10	4,447.00

Source: *Research Studies - Business Communications Co.*, September 21, 2005, p. NA, from BCC Inc.

★ 1187 ★
Coagulants
SIC: 2836; NAICS: 325414

Leading Coagulant Chemicals in Europe

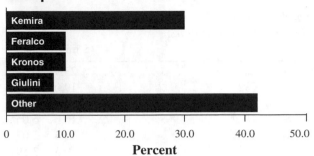

Kemira is the largest maker of cogulant chemicals used in waterworks.

Kemira	.30.0%
Feralco	.10.0
Kronos	.10.0
Giulini	. 8.0
Other	.42.0

Source: "Kemwater Capital Market Day." [online] from http://www.kemira.com [Published September 13, 2005].

★ 1188 ★
Coagulants
SIC: 2836; NAICS: 325414

Leading Coagulant Chemicals in North America

Kemira is the largest maker of cogulant chemicals used in waterworks.

Kemiron	.30.0%
General Chemicals	.26.0
GEO	.12.0
PVS	. 5.0
Other	.27.0

Source: "Kemwater Capital Market Day." [online] from http://www.kemira.com [Published September 13, 2005].

★ 1189 ★
Weight Control Products
SIC: 2836; NAICS: 325414

Top Diet Aid Brands (Candy/Tablet), 2006

Brands are ranked by supermarket and drug store sales in millions of dollars.

	($ mil.)	Share
Relacore	$ 23.9	9.04%
Trim Spa X32	19.0	7.19
Cortislim	17.9	6.77
Zantrex 3	16.0	6.05
Hydroxycut	13.4	5.07
Private label	9.5	3.59
Other	164.6	62.28

Source: *MMR*, April 24, 2006, p. 30, from Information Resources Inc.

★ 1190 ★
Weight Control Products
SIC: 2836; NAICS: 325414

Top Diet Aid Brands (Liquid/Powder), 2006

Brands are ranked by supermarket and drug store sales in millions of dollars.

	($ mil.)	Share
Ensure	$ 150.9	19.61%
Slim Fast Optima	132.0	17.15
Pedia Sure	101.9	13.24
Boost	60.0	7.80
Ensure Plus	58.0	7.54
Ensure Glucerna	41.4	5.38
Atkins Advantage	24.1	3.13
Private label	52.9	6.87
Other	148.5	19.29

Source: *MMR*, April 24, 2006, p. 30, from Information Resources Inc.

★ 1191 ★
Weight Control Products
SIC: 2836; NAICS: 325414

Top Weight Control Candy/Tablet Makers, 2005

Market shares are shown by supermarket, drug store and discount store sales (excluding Wal-Mart) sales for the 52 weeks ended June 12, 2005.

Nutramerica Corporation	12.3%
Metabolife International	10.5
Window Rock Enterprises Inc.	8.9
Zoller Laboratories	7.2
The Carter Reed Company	0.8
Other	60.3

Source: *Grocery Headquarters*, September 21, 2005, p. S14, from Information Resources Inc.

★ 1192 ★
Weight Control Products
SIC: 2836; NAICS: 325414

Top Weight Control Liquids/Powders, 2005

Market shares are shown based on drug store sales for the 52 weeks ended October 30, 2005.

Ensure	18.2%
Slim-Fast Optima	10.0
Boost	9.9
Ensure Plus	9.1
Ensure Glucerna	6.7
PediaSure	6.7
Boost Plus	4.8
Atkins Advantage	2.7
Celebrity Low Carb Diet	1.7
Hollywood Celebrity Diet	1.7
Other	28.8

Source: *Chain Drug Review*, January 2, 2006, p. 94.

★ 1193 ★

Detergents

SIC: 2841; NAICS: 325611

Best-Selling Laundry Detergents (Liquid), 3005

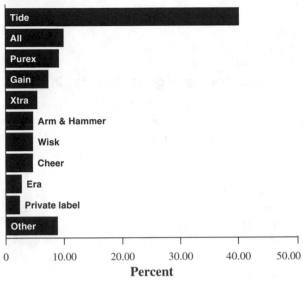

Brands are ranked by sales at supermarkets, drug
stores and mass merchandisers (excluding Wal-Mart)
for the 52 weeks ended October 30, 3005.

	($ mil.)	Share
Tide	$ 1,030.0	40.23%
All	256.1	10.00
Purex	234.8	9.17
Gain	187.6	7.33
Xtra	138.2	5.40
Arm & Hammer	119.7	4.68
Wisk	118.9	4.64
Cheer	117.9	4.61
Era	69.2	2.70
Private label	60.9	2.38
Other	226.7	8.86

Source: *Household & Personal Products Industry*, January
2006, p. 66, from Information Resources Inc.

★ 1194 ★

Detergents

SIC: 2841; NAICS: 325611

Best-Selling Laundry Detergents (Powder), 2005

*Brands are ranked by sales at supermarkets, drug
stores and mass merchandisers (excluding Wal-Mart)
for the 52 weeks ended October 30, 3005.*

	($ mil.)	Share
Tide	$ 368.9	46.99%
Gain	118.3	15.07
Arm & Hammer	44.7	5.69
Cheer	42.3	5.39
Surf	38.6	4.92
Ariel	16.8	2.14
Sun	16.6	2.11
All	11.1	1.41
Dreft	10.1	1.29
Private label	17.6	2.24
Other	100.0	12.74

Source: *Household & Personal Products Industry*, January
2006, p. 66, from Information Resources Inc.

★ 1195 ★

Detergents

SIC: 2841; NAICS: 325611

Global Laundry Detergent Market, 2004

*The industry is valued at $35.8 billion. Procter & Gam-
ble is the leader in the U.S. market. Henkel and Unilever dominate the European market. There was little
growth in these markets, however, as saturation levels
reach 100 percent. Studies by the source show that consumers are just reluctant to spend more on their
laundry needs.*

Western Europe	.29.0%
Asia/Pacific	.25.0
North America	.18.0
Latin America	.15.0
Eastern Europe	7.0
Africa & Middle East	5.0
Australia	1.0

Source: *Chemical Week*, February 1, 2006, p. 26, from Euromonitor.

★ 1196 ★
Detergents
SIC: 2841; NAICS: 325611

Top Detergent Brands in Germany

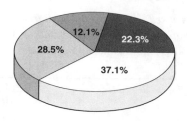

Market shares are shown in percent.

Persil	.22.3%
Ariel	.12.1
Private label	.28.5
Other	.37.1

Source: *Advertising Age*, December 5, 2005, p. 19.

★ 1197 ★
Detergents
SIC: 2841; NAICS: 325611

Top Detergent Makers in India

The detergent market is valued at Rs 5,000 crore.

HLL	.38.5%
P&G	.11.5
Other	.50.0

Source: *Economic Times*, September 16, 2005, p. NA.

★ 1198 ★
Detergents
SIC: 2841; NAICS: 325611

Top Laundry Detergent Brands, 2005

Brands are ranked by sales in millions of dollars.

	($ mil.)	Share
Tide Liquid	$ 1,039.83	31.36%
All Liquid	256.11	7.72
Purex	234.84	7.08
Gain Liquid	187.67	5.66
Etra Liquid	138.27	4.17
Arm & Hammer Liquid	119.47	3.60
Wisk Liquid	118.92	3.59
Cheer Liquid	117.93	3.56
Era Liquid	69.25	2.09

	($ mil.)	Share
Dynamo Liquid	$ 40.67	1.23%
Other	993.04	29.95

Source: *Purchasing*, January 12, 2006, p. 40C9, from Information Resources Inc.

★ 1199 ★
Detergents
SIC: 2841; NAICS: 325611

Top Laundry Detergent Makers, 2005

Total sales were $3.9 billion. Sales exclude Wal-Mart and other large-format mass retailers. Liquid detergent has been increasing its share over powder in recent years: 71% in 2003, 74% in 2004 and 78% in 2005.

Procter & Gamble	.60.0%
Unilever	.14.0
Church & Dwight	.10.0
Henkel	8.0
Colgate	3.0
Private label	2.0
Other	3.0

Source: *U.S. Personal Care and Household Products Digest*, Citigroup Equity Research, February 24, 2006, p. 156, from ACNielsen.

★ 1200 ★
Detergents
SIC: 2841; NAICS: 325611

Top Laundry Detergent Makers in Japan, 2004

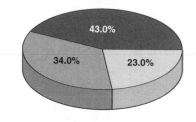

Market shares are shown in percent.

Kao	.43.0%
Lion	.34.0
Other	.23.0

Source: *Cosmetics & Toiletries Household Products Marketing News in Japan*, November 25, 2005, p. NA.

★ 1201 ★
Detergents
SIC: 2841; NAICS: 325611

Top Laundry Detergent Makers (Liquid), 2005

Total sales were $2.6 billion. Sales exclude Wal-Mart and other large-format mass retailers.

Procter & Gamble	.57.2%
Unilever	.15.4
Church & Dwight	.10.3
Henkel	.9.5
Lehman Brothers	.2.7
Private label	.2.5
Other	.2.4

Source: *U.S. Personal Care and Household Products Digest*, Citigroup Equity Research, February 24, 2006, p. 65, from ACNielsen.

★ 1202 ★
Detergents
SIC: 2841; NAICS: 325611

Top Laundry Detergent Makers (Powder), 2005

Market shares are shown in percent. Sales exclude Wal-Mart and other large-format mass retailers.

Procter & Gamble	.75.0%
Church & Dwight	.7.2
Unilever	.6.9
Farbica de Jabon La Corona	.2.9
Private label	.2.4
Other	.5.6

Source: *U.S. Personal Care and Household Products Digest*, Citigroup Equity Research, February 24, 2006, p. 159, from ACNielsen.

★ 1203 ★
Dishwashing Detergents
SIC: 2841; NAICS: 325611

Leading Dishwasher Detergent Additive Makers, 2005

Market shares are shown for the fourth quarter of 2005.

Procter & Gamble	.60.3%
Colgate	.6.7
Other	.33.0

Source: *Household Market Share*, Deutsche Bank, January 6, 2006, p. 12, from Deutsche Bank and Information Resources Inc.

★ 1204 ★
Dishwashing Detergents
SIC: 2841; NAICS: 325611

Top Dishwashing Detergent Brands (Liquid), 2005

Total sales were $565.6 million. Sales exclude Wal-Mart and other large-format mass retailers.

Dawn	.36.6%
Palmolive	.25.2
Ajax	.12.1
Joy	.8.8
Ivory	.4.9
Sunlight	.2.7
Private label	.4.5
Other	.5.2

Source: *U.S. Personal Care and Household Products Digest*, Citigroup Equity Research, February 24, 2006, p. 65, from ACNielsen.

★ 1205 ★
Dishwashing Detergents
SIC: 2841; NAICS: 325611

Top Dishwashing Detergent Makers, 2005

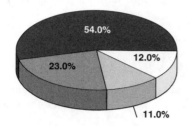

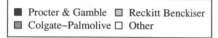

- ■ Procter & Gamble ☐ Reckitt Benckiser
- ▨ Colgate–Palmolive ☐ Other

Industry sales were flat at $1.1 billion. Figures include liquid, automatic and dishwasher rinsing aids.

Procter & Gamble	.54.0%
Colgate-Palmolive	.23.0
Reckitt Benckiser	.11.0
Other	.12.0

Source: *Chemical Market Reporter*, March 20, 2006, p. 46, from ACNielsen.

★ 1206 ★
Dishwashing Detergents
SIC: 2841; NAICS: 325611

Top Dishwashing Detergent Makers (Automatic), 2005

Market shares are shown in percent. Sales exclude Wal-Mart and other large-format mass retailers.

Procter & Gamble	.61.2%
Reckitt Benckiser	.18.4
Colgate Palmolive	.7.6
Lehman Brothers	.5.2
Seventh Generation	.0.2
Private label	.6.7
Other	.0.7

Source: *U.S. Personal Care and Household Products Digest*, Citigroup Equity Research, February 24, 2006, p. 65, from ACNielsen.

★ 1207 ★
Dishwashing Detergents
SIC: 2841; NAICS: 325611

Top Kitchen Detergent Firms in Japan, 2004

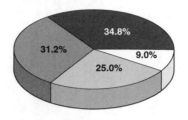

- ■ Procter & Gamble ☐ Lion
- ▨ Kao ☐ Other

Market shares are shown based on domestic shipments of 48.14 billion yen.

Procter & Gamble	.34.8%
Kao	.31.2
Lion	.25.0
Other	.9.0

Source: "2004 Market Share Report." [online] from http://www.nikkei.co.jp [Published July 27, 2005] from Nikkei estimates.

★ 1208 ★
Laundry Aids
SIC: 2841; NAICS: 325611

Leading Fabric Softener Makers (Liquid), 2005

Market shares are shown for the fourth quarter of 2005.

Procter & Gamble	.65.7%
Unilever	.10.2
Dial	.1.0
Other	.23.1

Source: *Household Market Share*, Deutsche Bank, January 6, 2006, p. 12, from Deutsche Bank and Information Resources Inc.

★ 1209 ★
Laundry Aids
SIC: 2841; NAICS: 325611

Top Detergent Boosters, 2005

Market shares are shown in percent. Sales exclude Wal-Mart and other large-format mass retailers.

20 Mule Team Borax	.71.1%
Febreze	.19.8

Continued on next page.

★ 1209 ★
[Continued]
Laundry Aids
SIC: 2841; NAICS: 325611
Top Detergent Boosters, 2005

Market shares are shown in percent. Sales exclude Wal-Mart and other large-format mass retailers.

Miracle White	1.2%
Other	7.9

Source: *U.S. Personal Care and Household Products Digest*, Citigroup Equity Research, February 24, 2006, p. 165, from ACNielsen.

★ 1210 ★
Laundry Aids
SIC: 2841; NAICS: 325611
Top Fabric Washes, 2005

Total sales were $69.5 million. Sales exclude Wal-Mart and other large-format mass retailers.

Woolite	65.3%
Cheer Dark	20.1
Delicare	2.1
Vel Rosita	0.1
Private label	5.4
Other	7.0

Source: *U.S. Personal Care and Household Products Digest*, Citigroup Equity Research, February 24, 2006, p. 163, from ACNielsen.

★ 1211 ★
Laundry Aids
SIC: 2841; NAICS: 325611
Top Liquid Fabric Softeners, 2005

Market shares are shown in percent. Sales exclude Wal-Mart and other large-format mass retailers.

Downy	60.7%
Suavitel	9.9
Snuggle	9.3
Gain	4.6
All	0.9
Arm & Hammer	0.5
Private label	5.4
Other	8.7

Source: *U.S. Personal Care and Household Products Digest*, Citigroup Equity Research, February 24, 2006, p. 162, from ACNielsen.

★ 1212 ★
Soap
SIC: 2841; NAICS: 325611
Global Soap Market

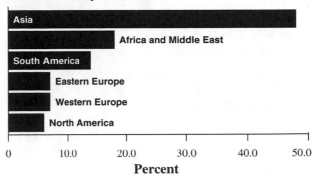

The global market size for soaps and detergents was estimated to be 31 million tons in 2004 and 33 million tons in 2008.

Asia	48.0%
Africa and Middle East	18.0
South America	14.0
Eastern Europe	7.0
Western Europe	7.0
North America	6.0

Source: *Oil & Fats International*, July 2005, p. NA.

★ 1213 ★
Soap
SIC: 2841; NAICS: 325611
Top Bar Soap Makers, 2005

Sales exclude Wal-Mart and other large-format mass retailers. Bar soap took 55% of the market in 2003, 52% in 2004 and 49% in 2005. Sales fell 4% in 2005 to $780 million.

Unilever	43.4%
Procter & Gamble	19.5
Henkel	15.7
Colgate Palmolive	11.7
Johnson & Johnson	3.1
Private label	1.7
Other	4.9

Source: *U.S. Personal Care and Household Products Digest*, Citigroup Equity Research, February 24, 2006, p. 102, from ACNielsen.

★ 1214 ★
Soap
SIC: 2841; NAICS: 325611

Top Bath/Bubble Bath/Fragrance Brands, 2006

Brands are ranked by supermarket and drug store sales in millions of dollars.

	($ mil.)	Share
Mr. Bubbles	$ 6.0	7.33%
Vaseline Intensive Care	5.2	6.36
Batherapy	4.8	5.87
Calgon	3.7	4.52
Village Naturals	3.6	4.40
Aveeno	2.8	3.42
Sesame Street	2.5	3.06
Coty Healing Garden	2.2	2.69
Lander	2.0	2.44
Village Naturals Spa	2.0	2.44
Private label	14.4	17.60
Other	32.6	39.85

Source: *MMR*, April 24, 2006, p. 30, from Information Resources Inc.

★ 1215 ★
Soap
SIC: 2841; NAICS: 325611

Top Bath/Shower Brands in the U.K.

Volume sales of body wash and shower gel grew by 27%. Liquid soap rose 18%.

Radox	13.7%
Imperial Leather	10.1
Dove	8.0
Johnson's pH 5.5	5.5
Oil of Olay	5.5
Carex	5.1
Boots	4.0
Avon	3.5
Palmolive	3.5
Lynx	3.2
Other	37.9

Source: *Marketing*, November 30, 2005, p. 38, from Euromonitor.

★ 1216 ★
Soap
SIC: 2841; NAICS: 325611

Top Bath/Shower Brands Worldwide, 2004

The industry was valued at $21,789.8 million in 2004. Bar soap took $9.27 billion or 42.5% of the total. Body washes and shower gel took $6 billion or 27.5% of the total.

Dove	7.5%
Lux	5.6
Palmolive	3.5
Nivea Bath Care	2.0
Bath & Body Works	1.9
Fa	1.7
Avon	1.5
Safeguard	1.5
Dial	1.4
Zest	1.4
Private label	4.8
Other	67.2

Source: *Soap, Perfumery & Cosmetics*, February 2006, p. 18, from Euromonitor.

★ 1217 ★
Soap
SIC: 2841; NAICS: 325611

Top Hand Sanitizers, 2006

Brands are ranked by supermarket and drug store sales in millions of dollars.

	($ mil.)	Share
Purell	$ 41.2	60.41%
Germ X	3.0	4.40
Dial	2.0	2.93
Private label	21.1	30.94
Other	0.9	1.32

Source: *MMR*, April 24, 2006, p. 30, from Information Resources Inc.

★ 1218 ★

Soap

SIC: 2841; NAICS: 325611

Top Soap Brands (Bar), 2005

Brands are ranked by sales in millions of dollars at supermarkets, drug stores and discount stores (excluding Wal-Mart) for the 52 weeks ended September 4, 2005.

	($ mil.)	Share
Lever 2000	$ 47.91	16.70%
Dial	46.60	16.24
Irish Spring	41.41	14.43
Zest	33.25	11.59
Irish Spring Aloe	15.74	5.49
Coast	13.08	4.56
Safeguard	12.57	4.38
Dial Spring Water	10.05	3.50
Dial Mountain Fresh	8.72	3.04
Zest Whitewater Fresh	7.05	2.46
Other	50.50	17.60

Source: *Household & Personal Products Industry*, November 2005, p. 16, from Information Resources Inc.

★ 1219 ★

Soap

SIC: 2841; NAICS: 325611

Top Soap (Liquid) Brands, 2005

Market shares are shown in percent. Sales exclude Wal-Mart and other large-format mass retailers.

Softsoap	47.1%
Dial	26.7
Ivory Liquid	3.0
Clean & Smooth Liquid	2.8
Jergens	0.5
Private label	14.0
Other	5.9

Source: *U.S. Personal Care and Household Products Digest*, Citigroup Equity Research, February 24, 2006, p. 106, from ACNielsen.

★ 1220 ★

Soap

SIC: 2841; NAICS: 325611

Top Soap (Specialty) Brands, 2005

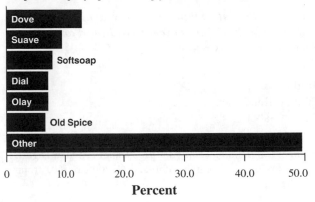

Market shares are shown in percent. Sales exclude Wal-Mart and other large-format mass retailers. The industry includes primarily body washes.

Dove	12.9%
Suave	9.4
Softsoap	7.7
Dial	7.0
Olay	7.0
Old Spice	6.5
Other	49.5

Source: *U.S. Personal Care and Household Products Digest*, Citigroup Equity Research, February 24, 2006, p. 104, from ACNielsen.

★ 1221 ★

Bleach

SIC: 2842; NAICS: 325612

Top Bleach Brands, 2005

Market shares are shown in percent. Sales exclude Wal-Mart and other large-format mass retailers.

Clorox	69.5%
Biz	3.1
Vivid	1.2
Snowy	0.4
Private label	24.1
Other	1.7

Source: *U.S. Personal Care and Household Products Digest*, Citigroup Equity Research, February 24, 2006, p. 161, from ACNielsen.

★ 1222 ★
Bleach
SIC: 2842; NAICS: 325612
Top Bleach Makers, 2005

Sales stood at $469 million in 2005 and have been falling since 2002. Sales exclude Wal-Mart and other large-format mass retailers.

Clorox	.69.5%
Redox	3.1
Reckitt Benckiser	1.6
Private label	.24.1
Other	1.7

Source: *U.S. Personal Care and Household Products Digest,* Citigroup Equity Research, February 24, 2006, p. 160, from ACNielsen.

★ 1223 ★
Cleaning Products
SIC: 2842; NAICS: 325612
Cleaning Product Sales Worldwide, 2004

Sales are shown in billions of dollars.

Household care	$ 90.5
Laundry care	46.5
Surface care	13.9
Dishwashing products	9.3
Air care	6.1
Insecticides	5.1
Chlorine bleach	3.2
Toilet care products	3.2
Polishes	3.0

Source: *Brand Strategy,* December 5, 2005, p. 48, from Euromonitor.

★ 1224 ★
Cleaning Products
SIC: 2842; NAICS: 325612
Laundry Aid Sales at Supermarkets

Supermarket sales are shown in millions of dollars.

Fabric softeners, liquid	$ 409.14
Bleach, liquid	355.43
Fabric softeners, dry	259.13
Laundry treatment aids	104.31
Spot and stain removers	97.01
Laundry and ironing accessories	62.38
Fabric washes, special	40.89
Bleach, dry	27.63

Starch, aerosol and spray	$ 22.94
Dye/dye removers	15.22

Source: *Progressive Grocer,* September 15, 2005, p. 22, from *Progressive Grocer's 26th Annual Consumer Expenditures Study.*

★ 1225 ★
Cleaning Products
SIC: 2842; NAICS: 325612
Leading Cleaning Brands in the U.K., 2005

Sales are shown for the 52 weeks ended October 1, 2005. Figures are in thousands of pounds sterling and for all outlets.

	(000)	Share
Finish auto dishwash	£ 109,935	9.31%
Fairy hand dishwash	102,662	8.69
Airwick aircare	90,445	7.66
Glade aircare	71,697	6.07
Flash hand surface cleaners	67,329	5.70
Domestos bleach	34,997	2.96
Mr. Muscle hard surface cleaners	31,640	2.68
Cif hard surface cleaners	27,043	2.29
Other	645,157	54.63

Source: *Grocer,* December 17, 2005, p. 77, from ACNielsen.

★ 1226 ★
Cleaning Products
SIC: 2842; NAICS: 325612
Leading Oven/Appliance Cleaner Degreasers Makers, 2005

Market shares are shown for the fourth quarter of 2005.

Reckitt Benckiser	.68.0%
Other	.32.0

Source: *Household Market Share,* Deutsche Bank, January 6, 2006, p. 12, from Deutsche Bank and Information Resources Inc.

★ 1227 ★
Cleaning Products
SIC: 2842; NAICS: 325612

Top Abrasive Cleansers, 2005

Total sales were $104 million. Figures exclude Wal-Mart and other large format mass retailers.

Soft Scrub 44.8%
Comet 30.0
Ajax 10.3
Bar Keepers Friend 5.3
Bon Ami 3.0
Private label 4.2
Other 2.4

Source: *U.S. Personal Care and Household Products Digest,* Citigroup Equity Research, February 24, 2006, p. 65, from ACNielsen.

★ 1228 ★
Cleaning Products
SIC: 2842; NAICS: 325612

Top Abrasive Tub/Tile Cleaner Makers, 2005

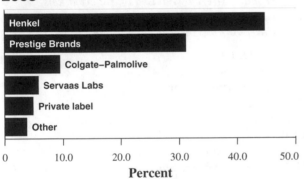

Percent

Market shares are shown based on dollar sales for the 12 weeks ended November 27, 2005.

Henkel 44.8%
Prestige Brands 31.2
Colgate-Palmolive 9.5
Servaas Labs 5.8
Private label 4.9
Other 3.8

Source: *High Yield Consumer Products,* Deutsche Bank, December 15, 2005, p. 13, from Information Resources Inc.

★ 1229 ★
Cleaning Products
SIC: 2842; NAICS: 325612

Top Auto Cleaner Makers, 2005

Market shares are shown in percent. Figures exclude Wal-Mart and other large format mass retailers.

Clorox 34.3%
Turtle Wax 11.9
Meguiars Inc.. . . . . 8.2
Fox Packaging 6.2
Procter & Gamble 3.3
Private label 4.2
Other 11.9

Source: *U.S. Personal Care and Household Products Digest,* Citigroup Equity Research, February 24, 2006, p. 188, from ACNielsen.

★ 1230 ★
Cleaning Products
SIC: 2842; NAICS: 325612

Top Bathroom Cleaner Makers, 2005

Market shares are shown in percent. Figures exclude Wal-Mart and other large format mass retailers.

S.C. Johnson Son Inc. 25.6%
Clorox 19.0
Reckitt Benckiser 15.2
Church & Dwight 11.1
Orange Glo International 6.2
Prestige Brands 5.6
Private label 3.8
Other 13.5

Source: *U.S. Personal Care and Household Products Digest,* Citigroup Equity Research, February 24, 2006, p. 182, from ACNielsen.

★ 1231 ★
Cleaning Products
SIC: 2842; NAICS: 325612

Top Drain Cleaner Brands, 2005

Market shares are shown in percent. Figures exclude Wal-Mart and other large format mass retailers.

Drano 43.3%
Liquid-Plumr 41.1
Lewis Red Devil 3.3
The Works 2.5
Xtra 0.9

Continued on next page.

★ 1231 ★

[Continued]
Cleaning Products
SIC: 2842; NAICS: 325612

Top Drain Cleaner Brands, 2005

Market shares are shown in percent. Figures exclude Wal-Mart and other large format mass retailers.

Private label 5.7%
Other 3.2

Source: *U.S. Personal Care and Household Products Digest,* Citigroup Equity Research, February 24, 2006, p. 183, from ACNielsen.

★ 1232 ★

Cleaning Products
SIC: 2842; NAICS: 325612

Top Drain Cleaner Makers, 2005

Market shares are shown in percent. Figures exclude Wal-Mart and other large format mass retailers.

S.C. Johnson Son Inc. 43.3%
Clorox 41.1
Reckitt Benckiser 3.4
Great Lakes Chemical Corp. 2.5
Alen Del Norte S.A. DE C.V. 0.9
Private label 5.7
Other 3.1

Source: *U.S. Personal Care and Household Products Digest,* Citigroup Equity Research, February 24, 2006, p. 187, from ACNielsen.

★ 1233 ★

Cleaning Products
SIC: 2842; NAICS: 325612

Top Floor Cleaner/Wax Remover Brands, 2005

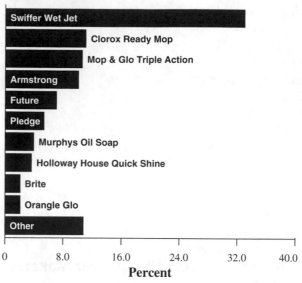

Market shares are shown based on supermarkets, drug stores and mass merchandiser sales (excluding Wal-Mart) for the 52 weeks ended June 12, 2005.

Swiffer Wet Jet 33.0%
Clorox Ready Mop 11.1
Mop & Glo Triple Action 10.6
Armstrong 10.1
Future 7.1
Pledge 5.4
Murphys Oil Soap 4.0
Holloway House Quick Shine 3.7
Brite 2.1
Orangle Glo 2.1
Other 10.8

Source: *Grocery Headquarters,* August 2005, p. S6, from Information Resources Inc.

★ 1234 ★

Cleaning Products
SIC: 2842; NAICS: 325612

Top Floor Cleaner/Wax Remover Makers, 2005

Market shares are shown based on supermarket, drug store and mass merchandiser sales (excluding Wal-Mart) for the 52 weeks ended June 12, 2005.

Procter & Gamble 33.0%
S.C. Johnson Son 27.3
Reckitt Benckiser 12.3
Clorox Company 11.5

Continued on next page.

★ 1234 ★

[Continued]
Cleaning Products
SIC: 2842; NAICS: 325612

Top Floor Cleaner/Wax Remover Makers, 2005

Market shares are shown based on supermarket, drug store and mass merchandiser sales (excluding Wal-Mart) for the 52 weeks ended June 12, 2005.

Holloway House-Chemical	5.0%
Other	10.9

Source: *Grocery Headquarters*, August 2005, p. S6, from Information Resources Inc.

★ 1235 ★

Cleaning Products
SIC: 2842; NAICS: 325612

Top Household Product Makers in Germany

Market shares are shown in percent.

Henkel Wasch-und Reinigungsmittel GmbH	27.1%
Procter & Gamble	12.8
Reckitt Benckiser	9.7
Lever Faberge	6.5
Johnson Wax	4.8
Other	39.1

Source: "German Market for Household Care Products." [online] from http://www.export.gov [Published February 2006].

★ 1236 ★

Cleaning Products
SIC: 2842; NAICS: 325612

Top Liquid Cleaners, 2005

Market shares are shown in percent. Figures exclude Wal-Mart and other large format mass retailers.

Clorox	19.6%
Pine-Sol	10.2
Lysol	9.5
Mr. Clean	7.3
Windex	7.3
Fantastik	5.9
Formula 409	5.8
Fabuloso	3.0
Murphy	2.5
Glass Plus	2.2

Private label	4.3%
Other	22.4

Source: *U.S. Personal Care and Household Products Digest*, Citigroup Equity Research, February 24, 2006, p. 178, from ACNielsen.

★ 1237 ★

Cleaning Products
SIC: 2842; NAICS: 325612

Top Rug/Upholstery Cleaner Brands, 2005

Market shares are shown in percent. Figures exclude Wal-Mart and other large format mass retailers.

Rug Doctor	36.4%
Resolve	25.0
Bissell	9.4
Woolite	7.6
Hoover	4.8
Formula 409	2.9
Armor All	0.2
Private label	1.5
Other	12.2

Source: *U.S. Personal Care and Household Products Digest*, Citigroup Equity Research, February 24, 2006, p. 188, from ACNielsen.

★ 1238 ★

Cleaning Products
SIC: 2842; NAICS: 325612

Top Rug/Upholstery Cleaner/ Deodorizer Makers, 2005

Market shares are shown for the fourth quarter of 2005.

Procter & Gamble	23.8%
Church & Dwight	5.7
Playtex	3.0
Clorox	1.5
Other	66.0

Source: *Household Market Share*, Deutsche Bank, January 6, 2006, p. 12, from Deutsche Bank and Information Resources Inc.

★ 1239 ★
Cleaning Products
SIC: 2842; NAICS: 325612

Top Stain Remover Brands, 2005

Total sales were $297 million. Figures exclude Wal-Mart and other large format mass retailers.

Shout	20.9%
Oxi Clean	19.7
Spray 'N Wash	15.8
Resolve	6.2
Woolite	6.1
Clorox	4.1
Zout	4.1
Bissell Brand	3.1
Other	20.0

Source: *U.S. Personal Care and Household Products Digest,* Citigroup Equity Research, February 24, 2006, p. 182, from ACNielsen.

★ 1240 ★
Cleaning Products
SIC: 2842; NAICS: 325612

Top Stain Remover Makers, 2005

Market shares are shown in percent. Figures exclude Wal-Mart and other large format mass retailers.

Reckitt Benckiser	22.0%
S.C. Johnson Son Inc.	20.9
Bissell Inc.	9.2
Clorox	4.6
Henkel	4.1
Private label	0.9
Other	38.3

Source: *U.S. Personal Care and Household Products Digest,* Citigroup Equity Research, February 24, 2006, p. 180, from ACNielsen.

★ 1241 ★
Cleaning Products
SIC: 2842; NAICS: 325612

Top Toilet Bowl Cleaner Makers, 2005

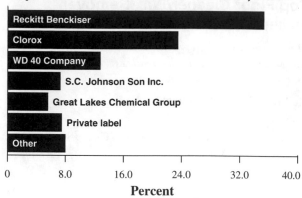

Market shares are shown in percent. Figures exclude Wal-Mart and other large format mass retailers.

Reckitt Benckiser	35.3%
Clorox	23.5
WD 40 Company	12.8
S.C. Johnson Son Inc.	7.3
Great Lakes Chemical Group	5.6
Private label	7.5
Other	8.0

Source: *U.S. Personal Care and Household Products Digest,* Citigroup Equity Research, February 24, 2006, p. 65, from ACNielsen.

★ 1242 ★
Cleaning Products
SIC: 2842; NAICS: 325612

Top Toilet Cleaning Systems, 2005

Market shares are shown in percent. Figures exclude Wal-Mart and other large format mass retailers.

Toilet Wand	41.1%
Scrubbing Bubbles Fresh Brush	35.4
Ready Brush	14.0
Scotch Brite	8.6
Comet Clean and Flush	0.5
Spotless Scrub 'n Flush	0.4

Source: *U.S. Personal Care and Household Products Digest,* Citigroup Equity Research, February 24, 2006, p. 65, from ACNielsen.

★ 1243 ★
Waxes and Polishes
SIC: 2842; NAICS: 325612

Top Auto Cleaner Brands, 2005

Market shares are shown in percent. Figures exclude Wal-Mart and other large format mass retailers.

Armor All	.33.7%
Turtle Wax	.11.9
Meguiars	. 8.2
Splash	. 6.2
Black Magic	. 4.3
Rain-X	. 3.4
Private label	. 4.2
Other	.28.1

Source: *U.S. Personal Care and Household Products Digest*, Citigroup Equity Research, February 24, 2006, p. 189, from ACNielsen.

★ 1244 ★
Waxes and Polishes
SIC: 2842; NAICS: 325612

Wax Polish Market in India

Market shares are shown in percent.

Cherry Blossom	.75.0%
Other	.25.0

Source: *India Business Insight*, February 6, 2006, p. NA.

★ 1245 ★
Baby Care
SIC: 2844; NAICS: 32562

Leading Baby Care Firms Worldwide, 2004

The market for baby's and children's toiletries is valued at $3.9 billion.

Johnson & Johnson	.35.6%
L'Oreal Groupe	. 5.7
Beiersdorf AG	. 3.8
Colgate-Palmolive Co.	. 2.7
Playtex Products Inc.	. 2.3
Sara Lee Corp.	. 2.3
Nestle SA	. 1.7
Pigeon Corp.	. 1.7
Schering-Plough Corp.	. 1.5
Avon Products	. 1.2

Private label	. 3.9%
Other	.37.6

Source: *Soap, Perfumery & Cosmetics*, March 2006, p. 20, from Euromonitor.

★ 1246 ★
Baby Care
SIC: 2844; NAICS: 32562

Top Baby Lotion Brands, 2005

Market shares are shown based on drug store sales for the 52 weeks ended October 30, 2005.

Johnson's	.41.8%
Aveeno	.22.3
Johnson's Bedtime Lotion	.11.2
Baby Magic	. 9.0
Huggies	. 2.7
Gerber Grins & Giggles	. 2.5
Burt's Bees	. 2.4
Gerber Teeny Faces	. 1.2
Gerber Teeny Bodies	. 0.1
Johnson's Baby	. 0.1
Private label	. 6.2
Other	. 0.4

Source: *Chain Drug Review*, January 2, 2006, p. 94.

★ 1247 ★
Baby Care
SIC: 2844; NAICS: 32562

Top Baby Oil Brands, 2006

Brands are ranked by supermarket and drug store sales in millions of dollars.

	($ mil.)	Share
Johnson's	$ 22.2	64.16%
Playtex Baby Magic	0.9	2.60
Lander	0.7	2.02
Burt's Bees	0.4	1.16
Johnson's Baby	0.4	1.16
Other	10.0	28.90

Source: *MMR*, April 24, 2006, p. 30, from Information Resources Inc.

★ 1248 ★
Baby Care
SIC: 2844; NAICS: 32562

Top Baby Ointment/Cream Brands, 2005

Market shares are shown based on drug store sales for the 52 weeks ended October 30, 2005.

Desitin	.28.1%
A and D	.22.2
Balmex	.12.5
Aquaphor Baby	. 5.6
Triple Paste	. 5.5
Boudreaux's Butt Paste	. 4.7
A and D Medicated	. 4.1
Dr. Smith's	. 3.6
Aveeno	. 2.7
Johnson's Bedtime Cream	. 0.7
Private label	. 4.5
Other	. 5.8

Source: *Chain Drug Review*, January 2, 2006, p. 94.

★ 1249 ★
Baby Care
SIC: 2844; NAICS: 32562

Top Baby Powder Brands, 2006

Brands are ranked by supermarket and drug store sales in millions of dollars.

	($ mil.)	Share
Johnson's	$ 36.5	64.37%
Caldesene	1.7	3.00
Johnson & Johnson	1.6	2.82
Gold Bond	1.3	2.29
Huggies	1.0	1.76
Private label	12.2	21.52
Other	2.4	4.23

Source: *MMR*, April 24, 2006, p. 30, from Information Resources Inc.

★ 1250 ★
Cosmetics
SIC: 2844; NAICS: 32562

Cosmetics Sales in Hungary

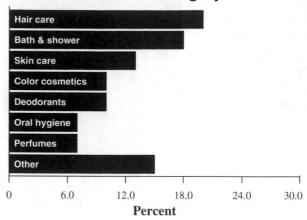

Market shares are shown in percent.

Hair care	.20.0%
Bath & shower	.18.0
Skin care	.13.0
Color cosmetics	.10.0
Deodorants	.10.0
Oral hygiene	. 7.0
Perfumes	. 7.0
Other	.15.0

Source: "Hungary: Cosmetics and Natural Cosmetics Market." [online] from http://www.export.gov [Published March 2006] from Hungarian Cosmetics and Home Care Association, CS Hungary estimates.

★ 1251 ★
Cosmetics
SIC: 2844; NAICS: 32562

Leading Cosmetics Markets Worldwide, 2005

Western Europe overtook North America for the first time. Developing markets in Latin America and Eastern Europe benefited from women working outside the home. Russia's and Brazil's economies have also begun to recover. Data are in billions of dollars.

	($ mil.)	Share
Western Europe	$ 9,319	26.97%
Asia Pacific	9,189	26.60
North America	8,886	25.72
Latin America	2,787	8.07
Eastern Europe	2,478	7.17
Other	1,889	5.47

Source: *Global Cosmetic Industry*, May 2006, p. 48, from Euromonitor.

★ 1252 ★
Cosmetics
SIC: 2844; NAICS: 32562

Top Cosmetic Remover Implement Brands, 2006

Brands are ranked by supermarket and drug store sales in millions of dollars.

	($ mil.)	Share
Almay	$ 11.9	44.07%
Andrea Eye Q's	2.1	7.78
Body Image	1.2	4.44
Buf Puf	1.0	3.70
Body Benefits	0.8	2.96
Almay Gently Clean	0.6	2.22
Compac	0.3	1.11
Calico Face Off	0.2	0.74
Studio Basics	0.2	0.74
Swab Plus	0.2	0.74
Private label	7.2	26.67
Other	1.3	4.81

Source: *MMR*, April 24, 2006, p. 30, from Information Resources Inc.

★ 1253 ★
Cosmetics
SIC: 2844; NAICS: 32562

Top Cosmetic Removers (Lotions/Gels), 2006

Brands are ranked by supermarket and drug store sales in millions of dollars.

	($ mil.)	Share
Maybelline Expert Eyes	$ 7.9	27.34%
L'Oreal Plenitude	5.6	19.38
Neutrogena	4.2	14.53
Almay	2.3	7.96
L'Oreal	1.9	6.57
Almay Dual Phase	1.7	5.88
Nivea Visage	1.2	4.15
Cover Girl Clean	0.9	3.11
Revlon ColorStay	0.6	2.08
Rimmel	0.5	1.73
Private label	1.0	3.46
Other	1.1	3.81

Source: *MMR*, April 24, 2006, p. 30, from Information Resources Inc.

★ 1254 ★
Cosmetics
SIC: 2844; NAICS: 32562

Top Cosmetics Brands Worldwide, 2004

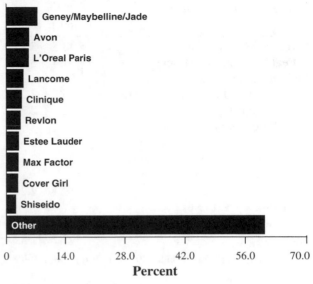

Market shares are shown in percent.

Geney/Maybelline/Jade	7.4%
Avon	5.4
L'Oreal Paris	5.3
Lancome	4.0
Clinique	3.6
Revlon	3.3
Estee Lauder	2.9
Max Factor	2.8
Cover Girl	2.7
Shiseido	2.2
Other	60.4

Source: *Global Cosmetic Industry*, November 2005, p. 38, from Euromonitor.

★ 1255 ★
Cosmetics
SIC: 2844; NAICS: 32562

Top Cosmetics Makers, 2005

Market shares are shown based on dollar sales for the 12 weeks ended November 27, 2005.

L'Oreal	34.5%
Revlon	21.1
Procter & Gamble	20.4
Johnson & Johnson	3.1
Other	20.9

Source: *High Yield Consumer Products*, Deutsche Bank, December 15, 2005, p. 13, from Information Resources Inc.

★ 1256 ★
Cosmetics
SIC: 2844; NAICS: 32562
Top Eye Makeup Brands, 2006

Brands are ranked by supermarket and drug store sales in millions of dollars.

	($ mil.)	Share
Maybelline Great Lash	$ 48.5	5.81%
L'Oreal Voluminous Mascara . . .	31.4	3.76
Maybelline XXL mascara	28.3	3.39
Cover Girl Eye Enhancers mascara .	26.9	3.22
Revlon ColorStay eye liner	22.7	2.72
Maybelline Volume Express mascara	21.8	2.61
L'Oreal Wear Infinite eye shadow . .	21.1	2.53
Cover Girl Perfect Point Plus eye liner	19.1	2.29
Maybelline Expert Eyes eye shadow	18.0	2.16
Other	597.2	71.52

Source: *MMR*, April 24, 2006, p. 30, from Information Resources Inc.

★ 1257 ★
Cosmetics
SIC: 2844; NAICS: 32562
Top Eye Makeup Makers, 2005

Market shares are shown based on dollar sales for the 12 weeks ended November 27, 2005.

L'Oreal	.47.6%
Revlon	.20.0
Procter & Gamble	.18.5
Del Labs	2.0
Johnson & Johnson	0.8
Other	.11.1

Source: *High Yield Consumer Products*, Deutsche Bank, December 15, 2005, p. 13, from Information Resources Inc.

★ 1258 ★
Cosmetics
SIC: 2844; NAICS: 32562
Top Face Makeup Brands, 2006

Brands are ranked by supermarket, drug store and discount store sales (excluding Wal-Mart) for the 52 weeks ended January 22, 2006.

	($ mil.)	Share
Revlon Age Defying foundation . .	$ 34.8	3.85%
CoverGirl Clean powder	26.0	2.88
CoverGirl Clean foundation	21.4	2.37
L'Oreal Tru Match foundation . . .	19.6	2.17
Maybelline Dream Matte foundation	18.6	2.06
L'Oreal Tru Match powder	18.4	2.04
Revlon ColorStay foundation . . .	17.8	1.97
CoverGirl Trublend foundation . . .	16.7	1.85
L'Oreal Visible Life foundation . . .	15.2	1.68
Maybelline Expert Wear blush . . .	13.7	1.52
Other	701.6	77.63

Source: *MMR*, May 8, 2006, p. 97, from Information Resources Inc.

★ 1259 ★
Cosmetics
SIC: 2844; NAICS: 32562
Top Face Makeup/Foundation Makers, 2005

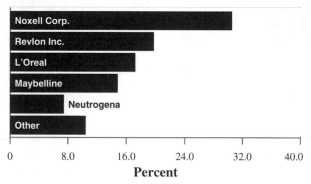

Market shares are shown based on supermarket, drug store and discount store stores (excluding Wal-Mart) for the 52 weeks ended June 12, 2005.

Noxell Corp.	.30.5%
Revlon Inc.	.19.7
L'Oreal	.17.2
Maybelline	.14.8
Neutrogena	7.4
Other	.10.4

Source: *Grocery Headquarters*, September 21, 2005, p. S14, from Information Resources Inc.

★ 1260 ★
Cosmetics
SIC: 2844; NAICS: 32562
Top Lipstick Brands, 2006

Brands are ranked by supermarket and drug store sales in millions of dollars.

	($ mil.)	Share
Revlon Super Lustrous	$ 37.6	10.39%
Cover Girl Outlast	25.2	6.96
L'Oreal Colour Riche	24.1	6.66
Revlon Color Stay Overtime	20.1	5.55
Cover Girl Continuous Color	18.2	5.03
L'Oreal Endless	17.8	4.92
Revlon Moon Drops	13.1	3.62
Cover Girl Outlast Smoothwear	12.8	3.54
Max Factor Lipfinity	10.6	2.93
Other	182.5	50.41

Source: *MMR*, April 24, 2006, p. 30, from Information Resources Inc.

★ 1261 ★
Cosmetics
SIC: 2844; NAICS: 32562
Top Lipstick Makers, 2005

Market shares are shown in percent. Sales exclude Wal-Mart and other large-format mass retailers.

L'Oreal SA	26.5%
Revlon	24.5
Procter & Gamble	18.7
Bonne Bell	8.3
Markwins International Corp.	4.0
Private label	0.8
Other	17.2

Source: *U.S. Personal Care and Household Products Digest,* Citigroup Equity Research, February 24, 2006, p. 55, from ACNielsen.

★ 1262 ★
Denture Care
SIC: 2844; NAICS: 32562
Top Denture Adhesives, 2006

Brands are ranked by supermarket and drug store sales in millions of dollars.

	($ mil.)	Share
Fixodent	$ 60.6	39.43%
Super Poligrip	29.4	19.13
Sea Bond	14.8	9.63
Fixodent Free	11.2	7.29
Fixodent Complete	11.0	7.16
Poligrip Free	8.8	5.73
Poligrip Ultra	5.5	3.58
Fixodent Fresh	2.9	1.89
Super Wernets	1.9	1.24
Rigident	1.8	1.17
Private label	2.7	1.76
Other	3.1	2.02

Source: *MMR*, April 24, 2006, p. 30, from Information Resources Inc.

★ 1263 ★
Denture Care
SIC: 2844; NAICS: 32562
Top Denture Cleansers (Paste/ Powder), 2006

Brands are ranked by supermarket and drug store sales in millions of dollars.

	($ mil.)	Share
Dentu Cream	$ 5.3	54.08%
Stain Away Plus	2.9	29.59
Kleenite	0.7	7.14
Dentu Gel	0.4	4.08
Fresh 'N Brite	0.4	4.08
Other	0.1	1.02

Source: *MMR*, April 24, 2006, p. 30, from Information Resources Inc.

★ 1264 ★
Denture Care
SIC: 2844; NAICS: 32562

Top Denture Cleansers (Tablet), 2006

*Brands are ranked by supermarket and drug store
sales in millions of dollars.*

	($ mil.)	Share
Polident	$ 19.9	24.81%
Efferdent	18.2	22.69
Efferdent Plus	11.8	14.71
Polident Overnight	10.9	13.59
Smoker's Polident	3.2	3.99
Polident for Partials	1.4	1.75
Private label	14.6	18.20
Other	0.2	0.25

Source: *MMR*, April 24, 2006, p. 30, from Information Resources Inc.

★ 1265 ★
Deodorants
SIC: 2844; NAICS: 32562

Deodorant Market in Germany, 2004

Sales are shown in millions of euros.

	(mil.)	Share
Aerosols	251.92	49.03%
Roll-ons	109.29	21.27
Pump sprays	86.38	16.81
Sticks	51.10	9.94
Cream/gel	15.01	2.92
Crystals	0.08	0.02
Wipes	0.05	0.01

Source: *European Cosmetic Markets*, July 2005, p. 252,
from Information Resources Inc.

★ 1266 ★
Deodorants
SIC: 2844; NAICS: 32562

Deodorant Sales by Type

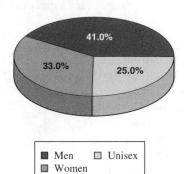

The market was valued at $1.4 billion in 2004.

Men	.41.0%
Women	.33.0
Unisex	.25.0

Source: *Business Wire*, November 10, 2005, p. NA.

★ 1267 ★
Deodorants
SIC: 2844; NAICS: 32562

Leading Men's Deodorant Makers

Market shares are shown in percent.

Procter & Gamble	.47.0%
Unilever	.18.0
Colgate Palmolive	.16.0
Other	.19.0

Source: *Boston Globe*, September 24, 2005, p. NA, from
A.G. Edwards & Sons.

★ 1268 ★
Deodorants
SIC: 2844; NAICS: 32562

Top Deodorant Brands, 2006

*Brands are ranked by supermarket and drug store
sales in millions of dollars.*

	($ mil.)	Share
Degree	$ 81.2	6.88%
Secret	73.5	6.23
Old Spice High Endurance	62.3	5.28
Right Guard Sport	59.6	5.05
Dove	57.8	4.90
Mennen Speed Stick	54.0	4.58
Secret	49.2	4.17
Ban	39.2	3.32

Continued on next page.

★ 1268 ★

[Continued]

Deodorants

SIC: 2844; NAICS: 32562

Top Deodorant Brands, 2006

Brands are ranked by supermarket and drug store sales in millions of dollars.

	($ mil.)	Share
Mitchum	$ 36.4	3.09%
Sure	35.9	3.04
Other	630.5	53.45

Source: *MMR*, April 24, 2006, p. 30, from Information Resources Inc.

★ 1269 ★

Deodorants

SIC: 2844; NAICS: 32562

Top Deodorant Brands in France, 2004

La Scad (L'Oreal) is the top company with a 28.6% share followed by Lever Faberge with 27.4%. Total deodorant and antiperspirant sales were 588.14 million euros. Products for women represented 58% of the total. Market shares are shown by value.

Narta	12.2%
Nivea	9.4
Axe	8.8
Rexona	8.8
Mennen	6.5
Dove	5.2
Ushuala	5.2
Adidas	5.0
Brut	4.9
Other	34.9

Source: *European Cosmetic Markets*, July 2005, p. 252, from *European Cosmetic Markets* based on FIP data.

★ 1270 ★

Deodorants

SIC: 2844; NAICS: 32562

Top Deodorant Brands in Italy, 2004

Market shares are shown based on supermarket and hypermarket sales. Sales at hyper/supermarkets totaled 163.51 million euros as of May 2005.

Borotalco	13.6%
Infasil	13.2
Nivea	12.3
Dove	11.3

Neutro Roberts	11.1%
Other	38.5

Source: *European Cosmetic Markets*, July 2005, p. 252, from Information Resources Inc.

★ 1271 ★

Deodorants

SIC: 2844; NAICS: 32562

Top Deodorant Brands in Spain, 2004

The deodorant market was valued at 100.5 million units worth 246 million euros in 2004. Aerosols represent 61% of sales, with roll-ons taking 25%.

Sanex	14.2%
Axe	13.6
Rexona	9.7
Nivea	8.1
Own label	7.0
Dove	6.8
Byly	4.0
Kinesia	2.3
Other	34.3

Source: *European Cosmetic Markets*, July 2005, p. 252, from Fragrancias y Cosmetica.

★ 1272 ★

Deodorants

SIC: 2844; NAICS: 32562

Top Deodorant Makers, 2005

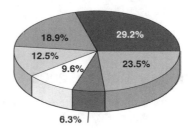

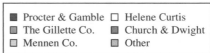

Market shares are ranked by sales in millions of dollars at supermarkets, drug stores and discount stores (excluding Wal-Mart) for the 52 weeks ended June 12, 2005.

Procter & Gamble	29.2%
The Gillette Co.	18.9
Mennen Co.	12.5
Helene Curtis	9.6

Continued on next page.

★ 1272 ★
[Continued]
Deodorants
SIC: 2844; NAICS: 32562

Top Deodorant Makers, 2005

Market shares are ranked by sales in millions of dollars at supermarkets, drug stores and discount stores (excluding Wal-Mart) for the 52 weeks ended June 12, 2005.

Church & Dwight 6.3%
Other 23.5

Source: *Grocery Headquarters*, September 21, 2005, p. S14, from Information Resources Inc.

★ 1273 ★
Deodorants
SIC: 2844; NAICS: 32562

Top Deodorant Makers in Russia, 2004

The deodorant market was valued at $350.9 million. Sprays represented $147.6 million and roll-ons represented $141.6 million. Roll-ons, however, saw stronger growth (7.7% compared to 6.2%). Rexona is the top brand with a 18.8% share.

Unilever 20.0%
Henkel 17.6
Beiersdorf 16.5
Other 45.9

Source: *European Cosmetic Markets*, July 2005, p. 265, from Euromonitor.

★ 1274 ★
Depilatories
SIC: 2844; NAICS: 32562

Top Depilatory Makers, 2005

Market shares are shown based on dollar sales for the 12 weeks ended November 27, 2005.

Del Labs 30.4%
Church & Dwight 28.6
Reckitt Benckiser 14.4
CCA Industries 6.4
Aussie Nads 5.8
Other 14.4

Source: *High Yield Consumer Products*, Deutsche Bank, December 15, 2005, p. 13, from Information Resources Inc.

★ 1275 ★
Eye Care
SIC: 2844; NAICS: 32562

Top Eye Care/Lens Care Solutions, 2006

Brands are ranked by supermarket and drug store sales in millions of dollars.

	($ mil.)	Share
Alcon Opti-Free Express	$ 72.6	9.09%
Bausch & Lomb ReNu MultiPlus . .	66.6	8.34
Amo Complete	24.3	3.04
Allergan Refresh Tears	23.8	2.98
Alcon Systane	23.4	2.93
Bausch & Lomb Renu with Moisture	21.0	2.63
Visine	20.5	2.57
Clear Eyes	20.1	2.52
Ciba Vision Clear Care	18.8	2.35
Visine Advanced Relief	18.3	2.29
Private label	89.4	11.19
Other	400.0	50.08

Source: *MMR*, April 24, 2006, p. 30, from Information Resources Inc.

★ 1276 ★
Eye Care
SIC: 2844; NAICS: 32562

Top Eye Care/Lens Care (Tablets/ Accessories), 2006

Brands are ranked by supermarket and drug store sales in millions of dollars.

	($ mil.)	Share
Ciba Vision Aosept	$ 3.6	7.96%
Ocusoft	2.5	5.53
Amo Ultrazyme	2.3	5.09
Magnivision	2.3	5.09
Bausch & Lomb ReNu	2.0	4.42
Alcon Opti-Free	1.8	3.98
Ciba Vision Eye Scrub	1.6	3.54
Pro Optics Optic Shop	1.6	3.54
Alcon Opti-Zyme	1.5	3.32
Lami	1.5	3.32
Private label	7.8	17.26
Other	16.7	36.95

Source: *MMR*, April 24, 2006, p. 30, from Information Resources Inc.

★ 1277 ★
Foot Care
SIC: 2844; NAICS: 32562

Anti-Fungal Sales in the U.K., 2005

Sales are shown for the 52 weeks ended May 14, 2005.

	Sales	Share
Athlete's foot	$ 6,109,374	53.50%
Anti-thrush	2,719,180	23.81
Other anti-fungals	2,590,885	22.69

Source: *Chemist & Druggist*, July 9, 2005, p. 26, from Analyser Report.

★ 1278 ★
Foot Care
SIC: 2844; NAICS: 32562

Top Foot Care Device Brands, 2006

Brands are ranked by supermarket and drug store sales in millions of dollars.

	($ mil.)	Share
Dr. Scholl's	$ 91.4	34.66%
Dr. Scholl's Tri Comfort	16.2	6.14
Dr. Scholl's Advantage	14.7	5.57
Profoot	10.9	4.13
Airplus	8.3	3.15
Dr. Scholl's Double Air Pillo	5.8	2.20
Profoot Triad	5.8	2.20
Dr. Scholl's Air Pillo	5.4	2.05
Dr. Scholl's One Step	5.1	1.93
Private label	30.3	11.49
Other	69.8	26.47

Source: *MMR*, April 24, 2006, p. 30, from Information Resources Inc.

★ 1279 ★
Fragrances
SIC: 2844; NAICS: 32562

Home Fragrance Market Worldwide, 2004

Top brands were Glade/Brise, Air Wick and Ami Pur. The industry had sales of $6.12 billion in 2004.

	($ mil.)	Share
Western Europe	$ 2,299.5	37.55%
North America	2,159.6	35.26
Asia Pacific	980.4	16.01
Latin America	$ 224.6	3.67%
Eastern Europe	202.0	3.30
Africa & Middle East	146.1	2.39
Australasia	112.2	1.83

Source: *Soap Perfumery & Cosmetics*, April 2006, p. 33, from Euromonitor.

★ 1280 ★
Fragrances
SIC: 2844; NAICS: 32562

Largest Fragrance Markets Worldwide, 2004

Countries are ranked by value of fragrance market in millions of dollars.

United States	$ 5,825.0
France	2,159.5
Germany	1,618.9
Spain	1,425.7
Russia	1,207.6
United Kingdom	1,158.7
Italy	1,047.9

Source: *Soap Perfumery & Cosmetics*, October 2005, p. 52, from Euromonitor.

★ 1281 ★
Fragrances
SIC: 2844; NAICS: 32562

Top Fragrance Firms in Spain

The cosmetics & toiletries industry has expanded dramatically since 1998, when the overall economy grew as well. Fragrances represent about 23.5% of the cosmetics & toiletries industry. Market shares are shown in percent.

Myrurgia	.25.4%
Puig	.25.1
Coty Group	.15.9
Gai	7.4
L'Oreal	6.5
Odeasa	0.7
Other	.19.0

Source: *Soap, Perfumery & Cosmetics*, June 2005, p. 22, from Fragrancias y Cosmetica and ACNielsen.

★ 1282 ★
Fragrances
SIC: 2844; NAICS: 32562

Top Fragrances in the Asia Pacific Region, 2004

The top brands are shown in the $1,094.5 million premium fragrance market.

Chanel No 5	2.8%
Eternity	2.6
Escada Ibiza Hippie	2.4
Chance	1.9
Escada Island Kiss	1.9
L'Eau par Kenzo	1.9
Allure	1.6
Gucci Envy	1.6
Other	83.3

Source: *Soap Perfumery & Cosmetics Asia*, October 2005, p. 26, from Euromonitor.

★ 1283 ★
Fragrances
SIC: 2844; NAICS: 32562

Top Fragrances Worldwide, 2004

Market shares are shown in percent.

Avon	6.0%
Natura	2.4
O Boticario	1.6
Chanel No 5	1.2
Jafra	0.9
Adidas	0.8
J'adore	0.8
Allure	0.7
Eternity	0.7
Pleasures	0.7
Other	84.2

Source: *Global Cosmetic Industry*, June 2005, p. 52, from Euromonitor.

★ 1284 ★
Fragrances
SIC: 2844; NAICS: 32562

Top Men's Fragrance Makers, 2005

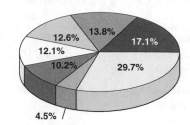

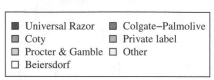

Market shares are shown in percent. Sales exclude Wal-Mart and other large-format mass retailers.

Universal Razor	17.1%
Coty	13.8
Procter & Gamble	12.6
Beiersdorf	12.1
Colgate-Palmolive	10.2
Private label	4.5
Other	29.7

Source: *U.S. Personal Care and Household Products Digest*, Citigroup Equity Research, February 24, 2006, p. 65, from ACNielsen.

★ 1285 ★
Fragrances
SIC: 2844; NAICS: 32562

Top Women's Fragrance Makers, 2005

Market shares are shown in percent. Sales exclude Wal-Mart and other large-format mass retailers.

Coty	36.3%
Elizabeth Arden	12.6
Parfums De Couer	6.4
Revlon	5.9
L'Oreal SA	4.7
Private label	0.7
Other	33.4

Source: *U.S. Personal Care and Household Products Digest*, Citigroup Equity Research, February 24, 2006, p. 65, from ACNielsen.

★ 1286 ★
Fragrances
SIC: 2844; NAICS: 32562

Top Women's Fragrances in Italy, 2004

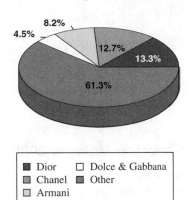

Market shares are shown in percent.

Dior	.13.3%
Chanel	.12.7
Armani	. 8.2
Dolce & Gabbana	. 4.5
Other	.61.3

Source: *European Cosmetic Markets*, May 2006, p. 179.

★ 1287 ★
Hair Care
SIC: 2844; NAICS: 32562

African American Hair Care Sales, 2004

Sales are in million of dollars and exclude Wal-Mart.

Chemical products	$ 41.2
Styling products	35.5
Hair dressing	25.6
Conditioners	21.2
Hair color	20.4
Shampoo	9.9
Curl/wave maintenance	8.1
Men's styling products	4.6
Children's hair care	2.4

Source: *Beauty Biz*, August 1, 2005, p. 12, from Information Resources Inc.

★ 1288 ★
Hair Care
SIC: 2844; NAICS: 32562

Largest Hair Care Brands Worldwide, 2004

The industry was valued at $46.9 billion in 2004. Shampoos led the market with sales of $13.2 billion, colorants followed with $9 billion and conditioners were third with $8.2 billion. The top markets were the United States, Japan and Brazil. Market shares are shown in percent.

Pantene Pro-V	. 6.1%
Elsbve/Elvive	. 2.8
Sunsilk	. 2.7
Gamier Fructis	. 2.5
Head & Shoulders	. 2.5
Clairol Herbal Essences	. 2.0
Dove	. 1.9
Studio Line	. 1.5
Excellence	. 1.4
Other	.76.6

Source: *Soap Perfumery & Cosmetics*, October 2005, p. 46, from Euromonitor.

★ 1289 ★
Hair Care
SIC: 2844; NAICS: 32562

Largest Hair Care Firms Worldwide, 2004

Market shares are shown in percent.

Procter & Gamble	.21.2%
L'Oreal Groupe	.20.2
Unilever	.11.7
Henkel	. 5.1
Kao Corp.	. 3.3
Shiseido Co.	. 2.2
Alberto-Culver	. 1.7
Colgate-Palmolive	. 1.7
John Paul Mitchell	. 1.2
Mandom Corp.	. 1.0
Private label	. 1.7
Other	.29.0

Source: *Global Cosmetic Industry*, October 2005, p. 46, from Euromonitor.

★ 1290 ★
Hair Care
SIC: 2844; NAICS: 32562

Top Baby Shampoo Brands, 2006

Brands are ranked by supermarket and drug store sales in millions of dollars.

	($ mil.)	Share
Johnson's Baby	$ 20.5	64.26%
Huggies	1.7	5.33
Johnson's Softwash	0.9	2.82
Gerber Grins and Giggles	0.8	2.51
Playtex Baby Magic	0.8	2.51
Johnson's Buddies	0.7	2.19
Private label	4.7	14.73
Other	1.8	5.64

Source: *MMR*, April 24, 2006, p. 30, from Information Resources Inc.

★ 1291 ★
Hair Care
SIC: 2844; NAICS: 32562

Top Dandruff Shampoo Makers, 2005

Market shares are shown based on dollar sales for the 12 weeks ended November 27, 2005.

Procter & Gamble	.55.4%
Johnson & Johnson	.17.1
Chattem	.10.2
Private label	6.3
Other	.10.0

Source: *High Yield Consumer Products*, Deutsche Bank, December 15, 2005, p. 13, from Information Resources Inc.

★ 1292 ★
Hair Care
SIC: 2844; NAICS: 32562

Top Hair Coloring Brands, 2006

Brands are ranked by supermarket and drug store sales in millions of dollars.

	($ mil.)	Share
L'Oreal Preference	$ 125.3	12.41%
L'Oreal Excellence	95.2	9.43
Clairol Nice 'n Easy	87.6	8.67
Just for Men	78.0	7.72
Clairol Natural Instincts	74.8	7.41
L'Oreal Feria	73.7	7.30

	($ mil.)	Share
Garnier Nutrisse	$ 55.6	5.50%
Revlon ColorSilk	50.8	5.03
L'Oreal Couleur Experte	44.1	4.37
Clairol Hydrience	31.2	3.09
Other	293.7	29.08

Source: *MMR*, April 24, 2006, p. 30, from Information Resources Inc.

★ 1293 ★
Hair Care
SIC: 2844; NAICS: 32562

Top Hair Coloring Makers, 2005

Market shares are shown based on sales at supermarkets, drug stores and discount stores (excluding Wal-Mart) for the 52 weeks ended June 12, 2005.

L'Oreal USA	.41.7%
Clairol Inc.	.31.3
Combe Inc.	9.6
Revlon Inc.	7.9
Garnier Inc.	7.4
Other	2.1

Source: *Grocery Headquarters*, September 21, 2005, p. S14, from Information Resources Inc.

★ 1294 ★
Hair Care
SIC: 2844; NAICS: 32562

Top Hair Conditioner Brands, 2006

Brands are ranked by supermarket and drug store sales in millions of dollars.

	($ mil.)	Share
Garnier Fructis	$ 57.5	7.01%
Dove	30.8	3.76
Clairol Herbal Essences	25.5	3.11
L'Oreal Vive	24.7	3.01
Alberto VO5	24.4	2.98
Pantene Smooth & Sleek	24.3	2.96
Pantene ProV	23.7	2.89
Infusium 23	23.3	2.84
Tresemme	23.1	2.82
Pantene Daily Moisture	21.8	2.66
Other	540.7	65.96

Source: *MMR*, April 24, 2006, p. 30, from Information Resources Inc.

★ 1295 ★
Hair Care
SIC: 2844; NAICS: 32562
Top Hair Conditioner Makers, 2005

Market shares are shown based on supermarket, drug store and discount store sales (excluding Wal-Mart) for the 52 weeks ended June 12, 2005.

Procter & Gamble	21.2%
Clairol Inc.	11.7
Helene Curtis	10.7
Alberto Culver	9.6
Garnier Inc.	6.4
Other	40.4

Source: *Grocery Headquarters*, September 21, 2005, p. S14, from Information Resources Inc.

★ 1296 ★
Hair Care
SIC: 2844; NAICS: 32562
Top Hair Growth Brands, 2006

Brands are ranked by supermarket and drug store sales in millions of dollars.

	($ mil.)	Share
Rogaine	$ 29.20	11.07%
Barre	0.30	0.11
Alpharma	0.07	0.03
Private label	24.10	9.14
Other	210.03	79.65

Source: *MMR*, April 24, 2006, p. 30, from Information Resources Inc.

★ 1297 ★
Hair Care
SIC: 2844; NAICS: 32562
Top Hair Permanent Brands, 2005

Market shares are shown in percent. Sales exclude Wal-Mart and other large-format mass retailers.

L'Oreal	7.7%
Pantene	7.0
Garnier Frustis Style	6.8
Got2B	5.7
Tresemme	5.1
Clairol	4.4
Frizz-Ease	4.3
Other	59.0

Source: *U.S. Personal Care and Household Products Digest*, Citigroup Equity Research, February 24, 2006, p. 65, from ACNielsen.

★ 1298 ★
Hair Care
SIC: 2844; NAICS: 32562
Top Hair Permanent Makers, 2005

Market shares are shown in percent. Sales exclude Wal-Mart and other large-format mass retailers.

Procter & Gamble	18.9%
L'Oreal SA	18.8
Henkel	14.4
Unilever	8.4
Alberto-Culver	7.4
Kao Corp.	6.0
Private label	0.6
Other	74.5

Source: *U.S. Personal Care and Household Products Digest*, Citigroup Equity Research, February 24, 2006, p. 65, from ACNielsen.

★ 1299 ★
Hair Care
SIC: 2844; NAICS: 32562
Top Hair Relaxer Kit Brands, 2006

Brands are ranked by supermarket and drug store sales in millions of dollars.

	($ mil.)	Share
Soft Sheen Optimum Care	$ 5.0	10.99%
Dark & Lovely	3.6	7.91
Just for Me	3.1	6.81
Proline Soft & Beautiful	3.0	6.59
Organic Root & Stimulator	2.3	5.05
Other	28.5	62.64

Source: *MMR*, April 24, 2006, p. 30, from Information Resources Inc.

★ 1300 ★
Hair Care
SIC: 2844; NAICS: 32562
Top Hair Spray/Spritz Brands, 2006

Brands are ranked by supermarket and drug store sales in millions of dollars.

	($ mil.)	Share
Suave	$ 20.4	5.00%
Pantene Pro-V	20.1	4.93
Tresemme Tres Two	19.8	4.85
Pantene Classic Care	18.0	4.41

Continued on next page.

★ 1300 ★
[Continued]
Hair Care
SIC: 2844; NAICS: 32562

Top Hair Spray/Spritz Brands, 2006

Brands are ranked by supermarket and drug store sales in millions of dollars.

	($ mil.)	Share
Rave	$ 16.6	4.07%
Sebastian Shaper	16.4	4.02
Clairol Herbal Essences	13.1	3.21
Aquanet	12.2	2.99
White Rain Classic	12.0	2.94
Garnier Fructis Style	11.7	2.87
Other	247.6	60.70

Source: *MMR*, April 24, 2006, p. 30, from Information Resources Inc.

★ 1301 ★
Hair Care
SIC: 2844; NAICS: 32562

Top Shampoo Brands, 2006

Brands are ranked by supermarket and drug store sales in millions of dollars.

	($ mil.)	Share
Garnier Fructis	$ 62.0	6.20%
Dove	48.9	4.89
Clairol Herbal Essences	46.3	4.63
Suave Naturals	39.7	3.97
Pantene Smooth and Sleek	34.3	3.43
L'Oreal Vive	32.6	3.26
Pantene Classically Clean	32.4	3.24
Pantene Daily Moisture Renewal . .	29.3	2.93
Pantene Sheer Volume	28.1	2.81
Other	646.4	64.64

Source: *MMR*, April 24, 2006, p. 30, from Information Resources Inc.

★ 1302 ★
Hair Care
SIC: 2844; NAICS: 32562

Top Shampoo Makers, 2005

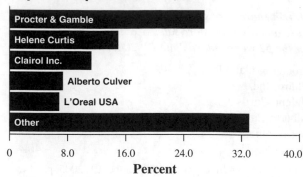

Market shares are ranked by supermarket, drug store and discount stores (excluding Wal-Mart) for the 52 weeks ended June 12, 2005.

Procter & Gamble	.26.8%
Helene Curtis	.14.9
Clairol Inc.	.11.2
Alberto Culver	7.3
L'Oreal USA	6.8
Other	.33.0

Source: *Grocery Headquarters*, September 21, 2005, p. S14, from Information Resources Inc.

★ 1303 ★
Lip Care
SIC: 2844; NAICS: 32562

Top Lip Care Brands, 2005

Market shares are shown based on drug store sales for the 52 weeks ended October 30, 2005.

Abreva	.21.7%
Chap Stick	9.1
Blistex	7.3
Carmax	6.4
Vira Medx Releev	3.9
Chap Stick Lip Moisturizer	3.7
Neosporin	2.6
Campho-Phenique	2.5
Burt's Bees Lip Shimmer	2.4
Burt's Beeswax	2.3
Other	.38.1

Source: *Chain Drug Review*, January 2, 2006, p. 94.

★ 1304 ★

Nail Care

SIC: 2844; NAICS: 32562

Top Artificial Nail/Accessory Brands, 2006

Brands are ranked by supermarket and drug store sales in millions of dollars.

	($ mil.)	Share
Broadway Nails	$ 9.8	12.00%
Kiss	9.3	11.38
Fing'rs	7.2	8.81
Kiss Custom Fit	6.5	7.96
Broadway Nails Natural Deceptions	5.9	7.22
Nailene	4.3	5.26
Broadway Nails Fast French	4.1	5.02
Kiss 1 Easy Step	3.9	4.77
Other	30.7	37.58

Source: *MMR*, April 24, 2006, p. 30, from Information Resources Inc.

★ 1305 ★

Nail Care

SIC: 2844; NAICS: 32562

Top Nail Care Makers, 2005

Market shares are shown in percent. Sales exclude Wal-Mart and other large-format mass retailers.

Kelso Company	38.7%
L'Oreal SA	18.8
Revlon	17.2
Markwins International Corp.	5.2
Procter & Gamble	4.2
Private label	1.0
Other	14.9

Source: *U.S. Personal Care and Household Products Digest*, Citigroup Equity Research, February 24, 2006, p. 56, from ACNielsen.

★ 1306 ★

Nail Care

SIC: 2844; NAICS: 32562

Top Nail Polish Brands, 2006

Brands are ranked by supermarket and drug store sales in millions of dollars.

	($ mil.)	Share
Revlon	$ 22.6	9.52%
Sally Hansen Diamond Strength	15.7	6.62
Sally Hansen Hard as Nails	13.4	5.65
Sally Hansen Maximum Growth	10.5	4.42
Maybelline Express Finish	10.4	4.38
Sally Hansen Advanced Hard as Nails	10.2	4.30
New York Color	10.0	4.21
Cover Girl Continuous Color	8.6	3.62
Milani	8.2	3.46
L'Oreal Jet Set	6.5	2.74
Other	121.2	51.07

Source: *MMR*, April 24, 2006, p. 30, from Information Resources Inc.

★ 1307 ★

Nail Care

SIC: 2844; NAICS: 32562

Top Nail Polish Makers, 2005

Market shares are shown based on dollar sales for the 12 weeks ended November 27, 2005.

Del Labs	42.8%
Revlon	16.1
L'Oreal	16.0
Markwins	4.2
Procter & Gamble	3.6
Other	17.3

Source: *High Yield Consumer Products*, Deutsche Bank, December 15, 2005, p. 13, from Information Resources Inc.

★ 1308 ★
Nail Care
SIC: 2844; NAICS: 32562

Top Nail Polish Remover Makers, 2005

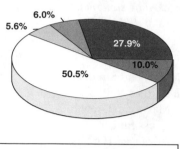

Market shares are shown based on dollar sales for the 12 weeks ended November 27, 2005.

Prestige Brands 27.9%
Del Labs 6.0
J. Stephen Scherer 5.6
Private label 50.5
Other 10.0

Source: *High Yield Consumer Products*, Deutsche Bank, December 15, 2005, p. 13, from Information Resources Inc.

★ 1309 ★
Nail Care
SIC: 2844; NAICS: 32562

Top Nail Polish Removers, 2006

Brands are ranked by supermarket and drug store sales in millions of dollars.

	($ mil.)	Share
Cutex Quick & Gentle	$ 9.5	19.35%
Cutex Essential Care	3.1	6.31
Pretty Nails	2.7	5.50
Sally Hansen	2.4	4.89
Calico Polish Off	2.0	4.07
Revlon	1.1	2.24
Cutex Twister	0.9	1.83
Onyx Professional	0.5	1.02
Cutex	0.4	0.81
Sally Hansen Kwik Off	0.4	0.81
Private label	24.4	49.69
Other	1.7	3.46

Source: *MMR*, April 24, 2006, p. 30, from Information Resources Inc.

★ 1310 ★
Nail Care
SIC: 2844; NAICS: 32562

Top Nail Treatment Brands, 2006

Brands are ranked by supermarket and drug store sales in millions of dollars.

	($ bil.)	Share
Woodwards Mycocid NS	$ 2.6	15.20%
Burt's Bees	1.5	8.77
Nailtiques	1.5	8.77
Sally Hansen	1.2	7.02
Nutra Nail	1.1	6.43
Sally Hansen Cuticle Massage Cream	1.1	6.43
Sally Hansen Insta Dri	1.1	6.43
Other	7.0	40.94

Source: *MMR*, April 24, 2006, p. 30, from Information Resources Inc.

★ 1311 ★
Nasal Care
SIC: 2844; NAICS: 32562

Top Nasal Aspirators, 2005

Market shares are shown based on drug store sales for the 52 weeks ended October 30, 2005.

Luv N Care 34.1%
First Years 31.8
Safety 1st 8.1
Little Noses 7.8
Ross 1.9
Sunmark 1.4
Cara 1.3
Acu Life 0.1
Private label 12.5
Other 1.0

Source: *Chain Drug Review*, January 2, 2006, p. 94.

★ 1312 ★
Nasal Care
SIC: 2844; NAICS: 32562

Top Nasal Sprays/Drops/Inhalers, 2005

Market shares are shown based on drug store sales for the 52 weeks ended October 30, 2005.

Zicam 12.6%
Primatene Mist 10.6
Afrin 9.6

Continued on next page.

★ 1312 ★
[Continued]
Nasal Care
SIC: 2844; NAICS: 32562
Top Nasal Sprays/Drops/Inhalers, 2005

Market shares are shown based on drug store sales for the 52 weeks ended October 30, 2005.

Afrin No Drip	5.3%
Vicks Sinex	4.8
Sudacare	3.8
Nasalcrom	2.9
Vicks	2.8
Blairex Simply Saline	2.7
Neo-Synephrine	2.6
Private label	20.1
Other	22.2

Source: *Chain Drug Review*, January 2, 2006, p. 94.

★ 1313 ★
Nasal Care
SIC: 2844; NAICS: 32562
Top Nasal Strips, 2006

Brands are ranked by supermarket and drug store sales in millions of dollars.

	($ mil.)	Share
Breathe Right	$ 53.70	92.43%
Breathe Free	1.10	1.89
Clear Passage	0.06	0.10
Breathe Right Near Clear	0.01	0.02
Other	3.23	5.56

Source: *MMR*, April 24, 2006, p. 30, from Information Resources Inc.

★ 1314 ★
Oral Care
SIC: 2844; NAICS: 32562
Oral Care Market Worldwide, 2005

Market shares are shown by segment.

Toothpaste	58.9%
Toothbrushes	22.9
Mouthwashes & fresheners	7.4
Denture care	6.2
Tooth whiteners	2.4
Dental floss	2.2

Source: *Datamonitor Industry Market Research*, December 1, 2005, p. NA, from Datamonitor.

★ 1315 ★
Oral Care
SIC: 2844; NAICS: 32562
Top Dental Floss Brands, 2006

Brands are ranked by supermarket and drug store sales in millions of dollars.

	($ mil.)	Share
J&J Reach	$ 22.9	19.57%
Crest Glide	22.0	18.80
Glide Comfort Plus	8.2	7.01
J&J Reach Easy Slide	5.7	4.87
J&J Reach Clean Burst	5.6	4.79
Oral B Satinfloss	5.4	4.62
J&J Reach Dentotape	5.2	4.44
J&J Reach Gentle Gum Care	4.2	3.59
Oral B Satintape	3.4	2.91
Oral B Ultra Floss	3.3	2.82
Private label	20.6	17.61
Other	10.5	8.97

Source: *MMR*, April 24, 2006, p. 30, from Information Resources Inc.

★ 1316 ★
Oral Care
SIC: 2844; NAICS: 32562
Top Dental Floss Makers, 2005

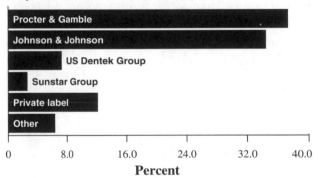

Market shares are shown in percent. Sales exclude Wal-Mart and other large-format mass retailers.

Procter & Gamble	37.3%
Johnson & Johnson	34.4
US Dentek Group	7.2
Sunstar Group	2.6
Private label	12.2
Other	6.3

Source: *U.S. Personal Care and Household Products Digest*, Citigroup Equity Research, February 24, 2006, p. 100, from ACNielsen.

★ 1317 ★
Oral Care
SIC: 2844; NAICS: 32562

Top Mouthwash/Dental Rinse, 2005

Market shares are shown based on drug store sales for the 52 weeks ended October 30, 2005.

Listerine	.44.60%
Scope	. 8.60
Advanced Listerine	. 7.30
Crest	. 5.10
Biatene	. 2.90
Act	. 2.80
Plax	. 1.80
Cepacol	. 1.60
TheraBreath	. 1.50
Colgate Phos-flur	. 1.00
Other	. 2.28

Source: *Chain Drug Review*, January 2, 2006, p. 94.

★ 1318 ★
Oral Care
SIC: 2844; NAICS: 32562

Top Mouthwash/Dental Rinse Makers, 2005

Market shares are shown based on sales at supermarkets, drug stores and discount stores (excluding Wal-Mart) for the 52 weeks ended June 12, 2005.

Pfizer Inc.	.58.1%
Procter & Gamble	.13.2
Johnson & Johnson	. 5.7
Leclede Prof Prods.	. 1.9
Private label	.15.0
Other	. 6.1

Source: *Grocery Headquarters*, September 21, 2005, p. S14, from Information Resources Inc.

★ 1319 ★
Oral Care
SIC: 2844; NAICS: 32562

Top Oral Pain Relievers, 2005

Market shares are shown based on drug store sales for the 52 weeks ended October 30, 2005.

Orajel	.15.6%
Anbesol	.14.3
Baby Orajel	. 8.0
Colgate Peroxyl	. 5.7
Oentek Temparin	. 3.6

Zilactin	. 3.5%
Glyoxide	. 3.4
Dentemp	. 3.1
Kanka	. 3.0
Private label	. 6.8
Other	.33.0

Source: *Chain Drug Review*, January 2, 2006, p. 94.

★ 1320 ★
Oral Care
SIC: 2844; NAICS: 32562

Top Portable Oral Care Brands, 2005

Market shares are shown based on drug store sales for the 52 weeks ended October 30, 2005.

Oral B Brush Ups	.50.0%
Listerine Pocketmist	.19.1
Biotene Oral Balance	.18.0
Orajel	. 6.0
Salivart	. 3.2
Other	. 3.7

Source: *Chain Drug Review*, January 2, 2006, p. 94.

★ 1321 ★
Oral Care
SIC: 2844; NAICS: 32562

Top Teeth Whitening Brands, 2005

Market shares are shown based on drug store sales for the 52 weeks ended October 30, 2005.

Crest Whitestrips Premium	.25.7%
Crest Whitestrips	.19.2
Crest Whitestrips Premium Plus	.11.0
Oral B Rembrandt Whitening Strips	. 5.4
Rembrandt	. 4.6
Crest Night Effects	. 3.7
Colgate Simply White Night	. 2.4
Plus + White	. 2.4
Colgate Simply White	. 2.2

Continued on next page.

★ 1321 ★

[Continued]

Oral Care

SIC: 2844; NAICS: 32562

Top Teeth Whitening Brands, 2005

*Market shares are shown based on drug store sales
for the 52 weeks ended October 30, 2005.*

Rembrandt Plus	2.1%
Other	20.6

Source: *Chain Drug Review*, January 2, 2006, p. 94.

★ 1322 ★

Oral Care

SIC: 2844; NAICS: 32562

Top Tooth Whitener Makers, 2005

*Sales declined 15% to $231 million. Sales exclude Wal-
Mart and other large-format mass retailers. Part of
the decrease may be attributed to new teeth whitener
properties in toothpastes, meaning consumers don't
buy specific teeth whitener products.*

Procter & Gamble	72.8%
Colgate Palmolive	5.4
CCA Industries	2.0
Lorna Mead Brands	0.5
Private label	8.0
Other	13.3

Source: *U.S. Personal Care and Household Products Digest*,
Citigroup Equity Research, February 24, 2006, p. 97, from
ACNielsen.

★ 1323 ★

Oral Care

SIC: 2844; NAICS: 325412

Top Tooth Whitening Brands, 2005

*Market shares are shown based on drug store sales
for the 52 weeks ended October 30, 2005.*

Crest Whitestrips Premium	25.7%
Crest Whitestrips	19.2
Crest Whitestrips Premium Plus	11.0
Oral B Rembrandt Whitening Strips	5.4
Rembrandt	4.6
Crest Night Effects	3.7
Colgate Simply White Night	3.1
Plus +White	2.4
Colgate Simply White	2.2
Rembrandt Plus	2.1

Private label	9.4%
Other	11.2

Source: *Chain Drug Review*, January 2, 2006, p. 94.

★ 1324 ★

Oral Care

SIC: 2844; NAICS: 32562

Top Toothpaste Brands, 2005

*Brands are ranked by sales in millions of dollars at su-
permarkets, drug stores and discount stores (excluding Wal-Mart) for the 52 weeks ended August 7, 2005.*

	($ mil.)	Share
Crest	$ 159.7	8.66%
Colgate Total	101.0	5.48
Colgate	98.0	5.32
Crest Whitening Expressions	70.7	3.84
Sensodyne	57.3	3.11
Crest Plus Scope	38.7	2.10
Colgate Max Fresh	38.4	2.08
Aquafresh Extreme Clean	36.8	2.00
Crest Multicare	32.8	1.78
Colgate 2 in 1	29.7	1.61
Other	1,180.0	64.02

Source: *MMR*, October 3, 2005, p. 47, from Information Resources Inc.

★ 1325 ★

Oral Care

SIC: 2844; NAICS: 32562

Top Toothpaste Brands in India

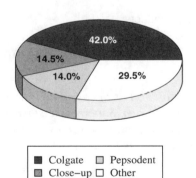

■ Colgate   □ Pepsodent
■ Close–up   □ Other

Market shares are for November 2005.

Colgate	42.0%
Close-up	14.5
Pepsodent	14.0
Other	29.5

Source: *India Consumer Monthly*, Morgan Stanley, February
3, 2006, p. 22, from Morgan Stanley.

★ 1326 ★
Oral Care
SIC: 2844; NAICS: 32562

Top Toothpaste Firms in Japan, 2004

Market shares are shown based on domestic shipments of 62.6 billion yen.

Lion	.43.0%
Kao	.18.1
Sunstar Group	.17.7
Other	.21.2

Source: "2004 Market Share Report." [online] from http://www.nikkei.co.jp [Published July 27, 2005] from Nikkei estimates.

★ 1327 ★
Oral Care
SIC: 2844; NAICS: 32562

Top Toothpaste Makers, 2005

Market shares are shown based on sales at supermarkets, drug stores and discount stores (excluding Wal-Mart) for the 52 weeks ended June 12, 2005.

Colgate Oral Pharmaceuticals	.36.4%
Procter & Gamble	.30.4
GlaxoSmithKline	.14.5
Church & Dwight	9.9
Oral-B Laboratories	1.9
Other	6.9

Source: *Grocery Headquarters*, September 21, 2005, p. S14, from Information Resources Inc.

★ 1328 ★
Personal Care Products
SIC: 2844; NAICS: 325611, 32562

Leading C&T Brands in Latin America, 2004

Data show the top brands of cosmetics & toiletries (C&T) in Latin America. Supermarkets/hypermarkets represent 39.2% of sales, followed by direct sales with 25.9% and specialists with 12%.

Avon	8.9%
Natura	5.3
Colgate	3.2
Sunsilk	2.7
O Boticario	2.5
Gillette Foamy	2.4
Jafra	2.0

Dove	1.6%
Other	.71.4

Source: *Soap Perfumery & Cosmetics*, August 2005, p. 20, from Euromonitor.

★ 1329 ★
Personal Care Products
SIC: 2844; NAICS: 325611, 32562

Leading C&T Makers in Australia, 2004

The cosmetics & toiletries market was valued at $3,604.6 million in Australian dollars. It is the sixteenth largest market worldwide. Supermarkets took 44% of sales followed by department stores taking 13.9%. Top brands were Colgate, Pantene Pro-V, Avon and Dove.

Procter & Gamble	.11.4%
Unilever Australia	.11.4
L'Oreal Australia	9.5
Colgate-Palmolive	9.3
Gillette Australia	5.0
Estee Lauder	4.8
Revlon Australia	4.1
Schwarzkopf & Henkel Cosmetics	3.7
Avon Products	2.7
Other	.38.1

Source: *Global Cosmetic Industry*, May 2005, p. 38, from Euromonitor.

★ 1330 ★
Personal Care Products
SIC: 2844; NAICS: 325611, 32562

Leading C&T Makers in China, 2004

The top category in the cosmetics & toiletries market (C&T) was skin care with sales of $3,027.1 million, oral hygiene with sales of $1,028.5 million, hair care with $1,602.6 million and color cosmetics with $929.9 million in sales.

Procter & Gamble	.14.5%
L'Oreal Groupe	7.7
Unilever Group	6.8
Alticor Inc.	5.7
Avon Products Inc.	3.8
Colgate-Palmolive Co.	3.2
Shiseido Co.	3.0
Beijing San Lu Factory	1.8
Juangsu Longliqi Group	1.8

Continued on next page.

★ 1330 ★

[Continued]
Personal Care Products
SIC: 2844; NAICS: 325611, 32562

Leading C&T Makers in China, 2004

The top category in the cosmetics & toiletries market (C&T) was skin care with sales of $3,027.1 million, oral hygiene with sales of $1,028.5 million, hair care with $1,602.6 million and color cosmetics with $929.9 million in sales.

Mary Kay	1.6%
Other	50.1

Source: *Soap Perfumery & Cosmetics Asia*, September 2005, p. 26, from Euromonitor.

★ 1331 ★

Personal Care Products
SIC: 2844; NAICS: 325611, 32562

Leading C&T Makers in Eastern Europe, 2004

The cosmetics & toiletries market (C&T) is shown by company.

Procter & Gamble	9.3%
Avon Products	8.1
L'Oreal Groupe	6.3
Unilever Group	5.5
Beiersdorf AG	5.1
Henkel KGaA	4.9
Oriflame International	4.2
Gillette	3.2
Other	53.4

Source: *Soap Perfumery & Cosmetics*, November 2005, p. 27, from Euromonitor.

★ 1332 ★

Personal Care Products
SIC: 2844; NAICS: 325611, 32562

Leading C&T Makers in France, 2004

France has been experiencing an economic downturn. Recent trends show consumers have no interest in spending more on toiletries. The industry was worth 11.3 billion euros. Market shares are shown in percent.

L'Oreal	27.9%
Unilever	5.6
Beiersdorf	5.5
LVMH	5.4
Yves Rocher	4.8
Henkel	4.4

Pierre Fabre	3.6%
Colgate-Palmolive	3.4
Fillette	3.1
Chanel	2.9
Private label	3.3
Other	30.1

Source: *Soap Perfumery & Cosmetics*, December 2005, p. 27, from Euromonitor.

★ 1333 ★

Personal Care Products
SIC: 2844; NAICS: 325611, 32562

Leading C&T Makers in Korea, 2005

The cosmetics industry was valued at $42 billion in 2005. Skin care took $17.6 billion, color cosmetic took $6.3 billion, followed by hair care with $6.05 billion. Outdoor markets take 27.45% in 2005, specialists 25.02% and supermarkets/hypermarkets 18.88%.

Amore Pacific Corp.	26.43%
LG Household & Health Care Ltd.	17.10
Aekyung Industrial Co. Ltd.	4.00
Procter & Gamble Korea	2.90
Coreana Cosmetics	2.53
Unilever Korea	2.47
Elca Korea Co.	2.29
Hanbul Cosmetics	1.96
Other	40.32

Source: *Soap Perfumery & Cosmetics Asia*, March 2006, p. 26, from Euromonitor.

★ 1334 ★

Personal Care Products
SIC: 2844; NAICS: 325611, 32562

Leading C&T Makers in Latin America, 2004

Brazil has 42%, Mexico 23% and Argentina 6.4% have in the $23.2 billion cosmetics & toiletries market.

Unilever	12.2%
Colgate-Palmolive	10.2
Avon Products	8.9
L'Oreal Groupe	6.8
Procter & Gamble	6.7
Gillettte	5.7
Natura Cosmeticos	5.5
O Boticario	2.5
Other	41.5

Source: *Soap Perfumery & Cosmetics*, August 2005, p. 20, from Euromonitor.

★ 1335 ★
Personal Care Products
SIC: 2844; NAICS: 325611, 32562

Leading C&T Makers Worldwide, 2005

The global market for cosmetics & toiletries (C&T) reached $253.3 billion in retail value in 2005. Western Europe took $76.3 billion (+2.6%) in 2004, North America took $53.9 billion (+.8%) and Asia/Pacific $63.1 billion (up 5%). Latin America, with $28.8 billion, grew 11.3% over 2004, the highest increase.

Procter & Gamble	12.8%
L'Oreal Groupe	10.2
Unilever	7.5
Colgate-Palmolive	4.1
Estee Lauder	4.0
Beiersdorf	3.1
Shiseido	3.0
Johnson & Johnson	2.2
Private label	2.2
Other	45.7

Source: *Global Cosmetic Industry*, June 2006, p. 41, from Euromonitor.

★ 1336 ★
Personal Care Products
SIC: 2844; NAICS: 325611, 32562

Leading C&T Markets Worldwide, 2005

The global market for cosmetics and toiletries reached $253.3 billion in retail value in 2005. Skin care took $56 billion of the total, followed by hair care with $506 billion, color cosmetics with $34.5 billion and fragrances with $27.6 billion.

	($ bil.)	Share
Western Europe	$ 76.3	30.11%
Asia Pacific	63.1	24.90
North America	53.9	21.27
Latin America	28.8	11.37
Eastern Europe	17.4	6.87
Africa and Middle East	10.4	4.10
Australasia	3.5	1.38

Source: *Global Cosmetic Industry*, June 2006, p. 15, from Euromonitor.

★ 1337 ★
Personal Care Products
SIC: 2844; NAICS: 325611, 32562

Leading Men's Toiletries Firms Worldwide, 2004

Sales of men's grooming products totaled $18.16 billion in 2004. Razors and blades took $7.66 billion of this total followed by deodorants with $4.04 billion. The top brand was Gillette Mach3 with an 8.4% share, followed by Schick-Wilkinson Sword with a 6% share.

The Gillette Co.	35.0%
Unilever Group	7.9
Energizer Holdings	6.9
Beiersdorf	4.0
Colgate-Palmolive	2.5
Procter & Gamble	2.5
Shiseido	2.3
L'Oreal	2.1
Mandom Corp.	2.1
Bic	2.0
Other	32.8

Source: *Soap Perfumery & Cosmetics*, December 2005, p. 27, from Euromonitor.

★ 1338 ★
Personal Care Products
SIC: 2844; NAICS: 325611, 32562

Leading Men's Toiletries in Thailand

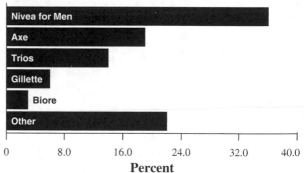

The industry is valued at 1.18 billion baht.

Nivea for Men	36.0%
Axe	19.0
Trios	14.0
Gillette	6.0
Biore	3.0
Other	22.0

Source: *Bangkok Post*, November 16, 2005, p. NA, from AC-Nielsen.

★ 1339 ★
Personal Care Products
SIC: 2844; NAICS: 325611, 32562

Men's Personal Care Sales in Europe/ U.S., 2003 and 2008

Sales are shown in millions of dollars.

	2003	2008
Personal care hygiene	$ 21,545	$ 25,586
Hair care	6,405	7,722
Fragrances	2,172	2,568
Skin care	1,434	1,725

Source: *Chemist & Druggist*, September 3, 2005, p. 27, from Datamonitor.

★ 1340 ★
Personal Care Products
SIC: 2844; NAICS: 325611, 32562

Men's Toiletries Market in the U.K.

Total sales were 542,238 million pounds sterling for the 52 weeks ended May 22, 2005.

Deodorants	41.8%
Fragrances	20.1
Shaving soaps	11.4
Shower products	10.6
Skin care	9.3
Hairdressing	4.8
Hairsprays	1.1
Other	0.9

Source: *Grocer*, August 13, 2005, p. 44, from TNS Super-panel.

★ 1341 ★
Personal Care Products
SIC: 2844; NAICS: 325611, 32562

Personal Care Market Segments Worldwide, 2004

Market shares are shown in percent. The market was valued at $4.8 billion in 2004, $5.11 billion in 2006 and $5.56 billion in 2009.

Hair care	24.8%
Skin care	17.5
Personal hygiene	16.3
Oral care	14.8
Fragrances	13.6
Make up	13.1

Source: *Datamonitor Industry Market Research*, October 31, 2005, p. NA, from Datamonitor.

★ 1342 ★
Personal Care Products
SIC: 2844; NAICS: 325611, 32562

Personal Care Market Worldwide, 2004

Market shares are shown in percent.

Europe	43.2%
Asia-Pacific	23.8
United States	2.2
Other	1.1

Source: *Datamonitor Industry Market Research*, October 31, 2005, p. NA, from Datamonitor.

★ 1343 ★
Personal Care Products
SIC: 2844; NAICS: 32562

Top Personal Lubricant Brands, 2006

Brands are ranked by supermarket and drug store sales in millions of dollars.

	($ mil.)	Share
KY Warming Liquid	$ 14.7	15.15%
Astroglide	11.0	11.34
KY	10.8	11.13
KY Liquid	9.4	9.69
KY Warming Jelly	8.9	9.18
KY Warming Ultragel	8.6	8.87
KY Touch Massage	7.7	7.94
KY Ultragel	6.0	6.19
Vagisil Intimate Moisturizer	1.6	1.65
Astroglide Gel	1.2	1.24
Private label	11.4	11.75
Other	5.7	5.88

Source: *MMR*, April 24, 2006, p. 30, from Information Resources Inc.

★ 1344 ★
Personal Care Products
SIC: 2844; NAICS: 32562

Top Petroleum Jelly Brands, 2006

Brands are ranked by supermarket and drug store sales in millions of dollars.

	($ mil.)	Share
Vaseline	$ 25.1	57.70%
Lander	0.3	0.69
Soft and Precious	0.2	0.46
Eboline	0.1	0.23

Continued on next page.

★ 1344 ★
[Continued]
Personal Care Products
SIC: 2844; NAICS: 32562

Top Petroleum Jelly Brands, 2006

Brands are ranked by supermarket and drug store sales in millions of dollars.

	($ mil.)	Share
Private label	$ 17.4	40.00%
Other	0.4	0.92

Source: *MMR*, April 24, 2006, p. 30, from Information Resources Inc.

★ 1345 ★
Shaving Preparations
SIC: 2844; NAICS: 32562

Shaving Preparation Sales, 2004

Sales are shown in millions of euros.

	(mil.)	Share
Foam	42.56	45.94%
Gel	33.82	36.50
Cream	13.35	14.41
Soap	2.88	3.11
Other	0.04	0.04

Source: *Soap Perfumery & Cosmetics*, October 2005, p. 26, from Information Resources Inc.

★ 1346 ★
Shaving Preparations
SIC: 2844; NAICS: 32562

Top Shaving Cream Brands, 2005

Market shares are shown in percent. Sales exclude Wal-Mart and other large-format mass retailers.

S.C. Johnson Son	41.4%
Procter & Gamble	29.3
Johnson & Johnson	6.5
Colgate Palmolive	4.9
Perio	4.8
Private label	4.8
Other	8.3

Source: *U.S. Personal Care and Household Products Digest*, Citigroup Equity Research, February 24, 2006, p. 65, from ACNielsen.

★ 1347 ★
Shaving Preparations
SIC: 2844; NAICS: 32562

Top Shaving Lotion/Cologne/Talc Brands, 2005

Brands are ranked by sales in millions of dollars at supermarkets, drug stores and discount stores (excluding Wal-Mart) for the 52 weeks ended August 7, 2005.

	($ mil.)	Share
Axe	$ 72.0	20.16%
Old Spice	16.7	4.68
Tag	12.6	3.53
Brut	10.7	3.00
Nivea for Men	10.4	2.91
Old Spice Red Zone	10.0	2.80
Coty Stetson	9.7	2.72
Gillette Series	9.1	2.55
Drakkar Noir	8.3	2.32
Curve for Men	7.6	2.13
Other	190.0	53.21

Source: *MMR*, November 14, 2005, p. S14, from Information Resources Inc.

★ 1348 ★
Skin Care
SIC: 2844; NAICS: 32562

Largest Skin Care Markets Worldwide, 2004

The $31 billion industry is moving in new areas such as resurfaces, peels and pen-like lasers. Sales are shown in billions of dollars.

Japan	$ 13.2
United States	7.1
France	3.6
China	3.0
Germany	2.7
Italy	2.1
South Korea	2.0
United Kingdom	1.7
Brazil	1.1
Spain	1.0

Source: *Soap, Perfumery & Cosmetics*, June 2005, p. 24, from Euromonitor.

★ 1349 ★
Skin Care
SIC: 2844; NAICS: 32562

Professional Skin Care Market Worldwide, 2004

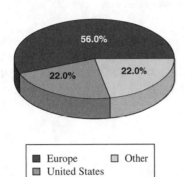

The industry is estimated to be worth $3.1 billion.

Europe	.56.0%
United States	.22.0
Other	.22.0

Source: *Chemical Market Reporter*, September 12, 2005, p. 27, from Kline & Co.

★ 1350 ★
Skin Care
SIC: 2844; NAICS: 32562

Top Depilatory Brands, 2006

Brands are ranked by supermarket and drug store sales in millions of dollars.

	($ mil.)	Share
Sally Hansen	$ 27.9	26.88%
Nair	20.6	19.85
Veet	17.8	17.15
Nad's	6.4	6.17
Magic	5.1	4.91
Bikini Zone	3.7	3.56
Nair Lasting Effects	3.5	3.37
Hair Off	2.9	2.79
Nair for Men	2.9	2.79
Nair Smoothing Effects	2.9	2.79
Other	10.1	9.73

Source: *MMR*, April 24, 2006, p. 30, from Information Resources Inc.

★ 1351 ★
Skin Care
SIC: 2844; NAICS: 32562

Top Facial Cleanser/Cream/Lotion Makers, 2005

Market shares are shown in percent. Sales exclude Wal-Mart and other large-format mass retailers.

Procter & Gamble	.30.5%
Johnson & Johnson	.28.1
L'Oreal SA	.12.3
Unilever	7.1
Beiersdorf AG	5.6
Private label	2.1
Other	.14.3

Source: *U.S. Personal Care and Household Products Digest*, Citigroup Equity Research, February 24, 2006, p. 56, from ACNielsen.

★ 1352 ★
Skin Care
SIC: 2844; NAICS: 32562

Top Facial Cleansers, 2006

Brands are ranked by supermarket and drug store sales in millions of dollars.

	($ mil.)	Share
Olay Daily Facials	$ 42.7	7.81%
Pond's	39.8	7.28
Cetaphil	30.0	5.48
Biore Pore Perfect	29.9	5.47
Neutrogena Deep Clean	28.2	5.16
Johnson's Clean & Clear	25.3	4.63
Olay	24.9	4.55
Neutrogena	21.1	3.86
St. Ives Swiss Formula	18.4	3.36
Noxzema	17.4	3.18
Private label	21.0	3.84
Other	248.3	45.39

Source: *MMR*, April 24, 2006, p. 30, from Information Resources Inc.

★ 1353 ★

Skin Care

SIC: 2844; NAICS: 32562

Top Facial Moisturizers, 2006

Brands are ranked by supermarket and drug store sales in millions of dollars.

	($ mil.)	Share
Olay	$ 42.2	14.94%
Olay Complete	36.8	13.03
Neutrogena Moisture	16.4	5.81
Pond's	16.2	5.74
Olay Regenerist	15.5	5.49
Aveeno	13.7	4.85
Eucerin	11.2	3.97
Neutrogena Healthy Skin	10.4	3.68
Neutrogena Healthy Defense	10.2	3.61
Olay Complete Defense	7.0	2.48
Private label	6.7	2.37
Other	96.1	34.03

Source: *MMR*, April 24, 2006, p. 30, from Information Resources Inc.

★ 1354 ★

Skin Care

SIC: 2844; NAICS: 32562

Top Fade/Age/Bleach Creams, 2006

Brands are ranked by supermarket and drug store sales in millions of dollars.

	($ mil.)	Share
Sally Hansen	$ 6.8	16.55%
Vita K Solutions	5.0	12.17
Jolen	4.7	11.44
Palmer's Coca Butter Fomula . . .	4.7	11.44
Sudden Change Scar Zone	4.6	11.19
Esoterica	2.8	6.81
Porcelana	2.4	5.84
Palmer's Skin Success	1.9	4.62
Albi	1.6	3.89
Private label	1.4	3.41
Other	5.2	12.65

Source: *MMR*, April 24, 2006, p. 30, from Information Resources Inc.

★ 1355 ★

Skin Care

SIC: 2844; NAICS: 32562

Top Hand/Body Creams, 2006

Brands are ranked by supermarket and drug store sales in millions of dollars.

	($ mil.)	Share
Vaseline Intensive Care	$ 555.7	63.4%
Aveeno	48.5	5.5
Jergens Natual Glow	39.2	4.5
Olay Body Quench	34.8	4.0
Eucerin	31.7	3.6
Cetaphil	29.0	3.3
Nivea Body	28.0	3.2
Jergens	22.8	2.6
Jergens Ultra Healing	22.5	2.6
Nivea	20.0	2.3
Private label	43.8	5.0

Source: *MMR*, April 24, 2006, p. 30, from Information Resources Inc.

★ 1356 ★

Skin Care

SIC: 2844; NAICS: 32562

Top Hand/Body Lotion Makers, 2005

Market shares are based on supermarket, drug store and discount store sales (excluding Wal-Mart) for the 52 weeks ended June 12, 2005.

Kao Brands	13.6%
Beiersdorf	13.5
Johnson & Johnson	9.5
Chesebrough Pond's	9.4
Pfizer Inc.	7.5
Other	46.5

Source: *Grocery Headquarters*, September 21, 2005, p. S14, from Information Resources Inc.

★ 1357 ★

Skin Care

SIC: 2844; NAICS: 32562

Top Hand/Care Firms in Asia-Pacific, 2003

The market is growing more slowly than in Europe and the United States. It was valued at $2.2 billion in 2003.

Shiseido	8.0%
Unilever	4.5
Beiersdorf	4.3
Private label	1.7
Other	81.7

Source: *Datamonitor Industry Market Research*, November 18, 2005, p. NA, from Datamonitor.

★ 1358 ★

Skin Care

SIC: 2844; NAICS: 32562

Top Hand/Lotion Makers, 2005

Market shares are shown in percent. Sales exclude Wal-Mart and other large-format mass retailers.

Kao Corp.	27.0%
Johnson & Johnson	15.0
Unilever	14.8
Beiersdorf	8.2
Pfizer	7.7
Private label	5.4
Other	31.9

Source: *U.S. Personal Care and Household Products Digest*, Citigroup Equity Research, February 24, 2006, p. 64, from ACNielsen.

★ 1359 ★

Skin Care

SIC: 2844; NAICS: 32562

Top Skin Care Brands in China

Market shares are shown based on sales at department stores at the top 15 large cities.

Olay	15.24%
Aupres	12.91
L'Oreal	7.48
Maybelline	6.73
Yue-Sai	5.30
Lancome	2.12
SKII	2.04
Avon China	1.99
Kose China	1.75%
Kanebo China	1.63
Other	42.81

Source: *Cosmetics International*, May 20, 2005, p. 5, from Euromonitor.

★ 1360 ★

Skin Care

SIC: 2844; NAICS: 32562

Top Skin Care Brands Worldwide, 2004

The industry was valued at $50.16 billion. Facial care took $39.8 billion.

Avon	4.3%
Nivea Visage/Vital	3.6
L'Oreal Dermo-Expertise	3.2
Olay	3.1
Shiseido	2.5
Nivea Body	2.4
Estee Lauder	2.3
Lancome	2.2
Clinique	2.0
Pond's	1.6
Other	72.8

Source: *Global Cosmetic Industry*, September 2005, p. 34, from Euromonitor.

★ 1361 ★

Skin Care

SIC: 2844; NAICS: 32562

Top Skin Care Makers Worldwide, 2004

The largest markets are Japan with a $13.2 billion market, the United States with $7.1 billion and France $3.6 billion. The overall market is valued at $31 billion.

L'Oreal Groupe	9.6%
Beiersdorf	7.6
Shiseido	6.4
Estee Lauder Cos.	5.6
Avon Products	4.6
Procter & Gamble	4.4
Unilever	4.4
Kao Corp.	2.8
Kanebo Cosmetics	2.6

Continued on next page.

★ 1361 ★
[Continued]
Skin Care
SIC: 2844; NAICS: 32562

Top Skin Care Makers Worldwide, 2004

The largest markets are Japan with a $13.2 billion market, the United States with $7.1 billion and France $3.6 billion. The overall market is valued at $31 billion.

Private label	2.0%
Other	.46.8

Source: *Soap Perfumery & Cosmetics*, June 2005, p. 24, from Euromonitor.

★ 1362 ★
Sun Care
SIC: 2844; NAICS: 32562

Largest Sun Care Brands in Western Europe, 2005

Market shares are shown in percent.

Nivea Sun	.20.0%
Garnier Ambre Solaire	.14.4
Delial	4.1
Soltan	4.1
Piz Buin	3.5
Solar Expertise	2.4
Bilboa	2.3
Clarins	2.2
Lancome	2.1
Isdin	1.9
Private label	6.2
Other	.36.8

Source: *Soap Perfumery & Cosmetics*, April 2006, p. 38, from Euromonitor.

★ 1363 ★
Sun Care
SIC: 2844; NAICS: 32562

Largest Sun Care Markets Worldwide, 2005

Countries are ranked by value in millions of dollars.

United States	$ 1,156.0
United Kingdom	512.8
Spain	421.7
Italy	409.5

France	$ 365.2
Germany	165.7

Source: *Soap Perfumery & Cosmetics*, April 2006, p. 38, from Euromonitor.

★ 1364 ★
Sun Care
SIC: 2844; NAICS: 32562

Sun Care Market in Germany

Data are in millions of euros.

	(mil.)	Share
Sun protection	89.10	62.29%
Self-tanner	33.32	23.30
Aftersun	19.65	13.74
Other	0.96	0.67

Source: *Soap Perfumery & Cosmetics*, October 2005, p. 26.

★ 1365 ★
Sun Care
SIC: 2844; NAICS: 32562

Sun Care Market Worldwide, 2004

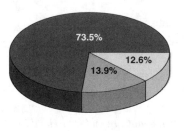

The sun care market was valued at $3.08 billion.

Sun protection	.73.5%
Self-tan	.13.9
After-sun	.12.6

Source: *Datamonitor Industry Market Research*, October 31, 2005, p. NA, from Datamonitor.

★ 1366 ★
Sun Care
SIC: 2844; NAICS: 32562

Top Sun Care Product Makers, 2005

Market shares are shown in percent. Sales exclude Wal-Mart and other large-format mass retailers.

Schering Plough	.30.8%
Playtex	.20.6
Johnson & Johnson	.17.8
Tanning Research	9.0
L'Oreal	5.2
Solar Cosmetics Labs	2.0
Private label	7.5
Other	7.1

Source: *U.S. Personal Care and Household Products Digest*, Citigroup Equity Research, February 24, 2006, p. 56, from ACNielsen.

★ 1367 ★
Sun Care
SIC: 2844; NAICS: 32562

Top Sun Tan/Lotion Brands, 2005

Brands are ranked by sales in millions of dollars for the 52 weeks ended December 25, 2005.

	($ mil.)	Share
Banana Boat	$ 63.86	7.79%
Coppertone	43.90	5.36
Coppertone Sport	34.93	4.26
Hawaiian Tropic	32.82	4.00
Neutrogena	32.64	3.98
Coppertone Water Babies	16.42	2.00
Coppertone Endless Summer	13.98	1.71
L'Oreal	13.33	1.63
Banana Boat Sport	13.05	1.59
Private label	38.34	4.68
Other	516.23	62.99

Source: *Household & Personal Products Industry*, March 2006, p. 90, from Information Resources Inc.

★ 1368 ★
Paints and Coatings
SIC: 2851; NAICS: 32551

Architectural Paint Sales Worldwide, 2004 and 2009

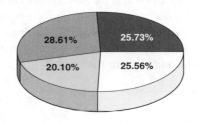

North America ■   Western Europe □
Asia Pacific ■   Other □

Sales are shown in thousands of metric tons.

	2004	2009	Share
North America	4,625	5,095	25.73%
Asia Pacific	4,290	5,665	28.61
Western Europe	3,570	3,980	20.10
Other	4,065	5,060	25.56

Source: *Research Studies - Freedonia Group*, March 15, 2006, p. NA, from Freedonia Group.

★ 1369 ★
Paints and Coatings
SIC: 2851; NAICS: 32551

Auto Coatings Market in Asia, 2003

Figures are based on estimates for passenger cars. The total market was worth 586 kilo metric tons.

Japan	.41.0%
China	.17.0
Southeast Asia	.14.0
South Korea	.13.0
India	.11.0
Other	4.0

Source: *Asia Pacific Coatings Journal*, August 2005, p. 145.

★ 1370 ★
Paints and Coatings
SIC: 2851; NAICS: 32551

Automotive Coatings Markets Worldwide

Data show the market size for automotive OEM coatings. North America and Western Europe represent about two-thirds of the global market, although growth has been relatively flat. South America includes Mexico and Central America.

	($ mil.)	Share
North America	$ 2,500	30.49%
Western Europe	2,300	28.05
Japan	2,000	24.39
South America	400	4.88
China	350	4.27
Eastern Europe	300	3.66
India	200	2.44
Australia	150	1.83

Source: *Coatings World*, March 2006, p. 26, from Chemark Consulting Group.

★ 1371 ★
Paints and Coatings
SIC: 2851; NAICS: 32551

Largest Powder Coating Firms Worldwide

Powder coating revenues will grow 5-6% a year. Firms are ranked by sales in millions of dollars.

Akzo Nobel	$ 700
DuPont	475
Rohm and Haas	342
Jotun	115
PPG Industries	100

Source: *Chemical Week*, June 15, 2005, p. 28, from ChemQuest Group.

★ 1372 ★
Paints and Coatings
SIC: 2851; NAICS: 32551

Paint Additive Market in China, 2004

The industry is valued at $401.7 million in 2004 and $954.8 million in 2011. The additives industry has benefited from an overall blossoming economy. It also benefits from the overall trends in the coatings industry.

Rheology modifiers	.20.9%
Dispersants & wetting agents	.20.6
Foam control agents	.11.0
Driers	9.4
Flatting agents	8.8
Other	.29.3

Source: *CMR*, February 27, 2006, p. 18, from Frost & Sullivan.

★ 1373 ★
Paints and Coatings
SIC: 2851; NAICS: 32551

Paint Additive Sales

The market was worth $940 million in 2004. Distribution is shown based on revenues.

Surfactants	.40.4%
Rheology modifiers	.32.4
Biocides	.12.2
Foam control agents	.10.1
Driers	4.8

Source: *Coatings World*, January 2006, p. 36, from Frost & Sullivan.

★ 1374 ★
Paints and Coatings
SIC: 2851; NAICS: 32551

Paint Industry in Russia, 2004

The country consumes nearly 1,000 kiltons of paint annually. The most popular types of paint are cheap, mid and lower quality coating materials in both the industrial and decorative sectors. Demand is increasing for higher quality coatings, however.

Alkyd paints	.38.0%
Alkyd varnish	.25.0
Oil-based paints	.10.0
Emulsion paints	8.0

Continued on next page.

★ 1374 ★
[Continued]
Paints and Coatings
SIC: 2851; NAICS: 32551
Paint Industry in Russia, 2004

The country consumes nearly 1,000 kiltons of paint annually. The most popular types of paint are cheap, mid and lower quality coating materials in both the industrial and decorative sectors. Demand is increasing for higher quality coatings, however.

NC paints 8.0%
Other 21.0

Source: *Polymers Paint Colour Journal*, December 2005, p. 15, from Russian statistics.

★ 1375 ★
Paints and Coatings
SIC: 2851; NAICS: 32551
Paint Industry in Thailand, 2005

The industry is valued at 415,000 tons in 2005 and is expected to grow to 557,300 tons in 2010.

Decorative professional 52.0%
Heavy duty 15.0
Automotive OEM 7.0
Decorative retail 6.0
Industrial wood finishes 6.0
Can coatings 4.0
Other 10.0

Source: *Asia Pacific Coatings Journal*, December 2005, p. 36, from Information Research.

★ 1376 ★
Paints and Coatings
SIC: 2851; NAICS: 32551
Popular Car Colors Worldwide, 2005

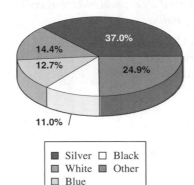

Data show share of vehicles produced. Silver has been the top color for the last six years, althought it is being challenged by gray and striking shades of blue.

Silver 37.0%
White 14.4
Blue 12.7
Black 11.0
Other 24.9

Source: *Indianapolis Star*, October 31, 2005, p. NA.

★ 1377 ★
Paints and Coatings
SIC: 2851; NAICS: 32551
Top Auto Paint Suppliers in France

There were about 30 million passenger vehicles on the road in 2004. The average vehicle was 8 years old. There are 11 manufacturers which represent 17,000 tons of paint consumption per year.

Ixell 13.0%
R-M- 12.0
Nexa Autocolor 11.5
PPG Refinish 10.5
Sikkens 10.0
DuPont Refinish 9.0
Other 34.0

Source: "French Collision Repair Market." [online] from http://www.stat-usa.gov [Published September 2005] from *Journal de l'Automobile*.

★ 1378 ★
Paints and Coatings
SIC: 2851; NAICS: 32551

Top Coatings Makers Worldwide, 2004

Firms are ranked by estimated global coatings sales in millions of dollars.

Akzo Nobel Coatings	$ 6,336
PPG Industries	5,275
Sherwin Williams	4,830
DuPont Coatings	3,980
ICI Paints	3,917
BASF Coatings	2,438
Valspar Corp.	2,215
SigmaKalon Group	2,050
Nippon Paint	1,880
Kansai Paint	1,647
RPM International	1,600

Source: *Paint & Coatings Industry*, July 2005, p. 4.

★ 1379 ★
Paints and Coatings
SIC: 2851; NAICS: 32551

Top Paint Firms, 2003

The industry has seen a number of mergers and consolidations. In 1990 the top five firms controlled 37% of sales. In 2003, the top five firms took 51% of sales. Companies are ranked by paint sales in millions of dollars.

	($ mil.)	Share
Sherwin Williams	$ 2,500	15.51%
PPG Industries	2,175	13.49
Valspar	1,300	8.06
ICI Paints	1,250	7.75
DuPont	1,000	6.20
Benjamin Moore	900	5.58
Akzo Nobel Coatings	825	5.12
Masco (Behr)	750	4.65
BASF	550	3.41
Other	4,873	30.22

Source: *Paints & Coatings Industry*, May 1, 2005, p. NA, from Impact Marketing Consultants.

★ 1380 ★
Paints and Coatings
SIC: 2851; NAICS: 32551

Wood Coatings Demand

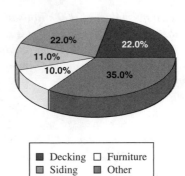

Decking ☐ Furniture
Siding ☐ Other
Cabinets

Demand for wood protection coatings and preservatives is estimated to climb to $3 billion by 2009. Manufacturers are forecast to focus on cabinets and floorings as weakness in the siding market continues. The industry is valued at $2.99 billion.

Decking	.22.0%
Siding	.22.0
Cabinets	.11.0
Furniture	.10.0
Other	.35.0

Source: *Chemical Week*, January 25, 2006, p. 23, from Freedonia Group.

★ 1381 ★
Organic Chemicals
SIC: 2865; NAICS: 32511

Ethanol Demand, 2004

Distribution is shown based on 113 million gallons.

Ethyl acrylate	.27.0%
Vinegar	.26.0
Ethylamines	.16.0
Ethyle acetate	.10.0
Other	.21.0

Source: *Chemical Market Reporter*, June 27, 2005, p. 19, from Chemical Strategies.

★ 1382 ★
Organic Chemicals
SIC: 2865; NAICS: 32511

Ethanol Production by State

States are ranked by ethanol capacity in millions of gallons per year.

Iowa	1,699.0
Illinois	881.0

Continued on next page.

★ 1382 ★

[Continued]
Organic Chemicals
SIC: 2865; NAICS: 32511

Ethanol Production by State

States are ranked by ethanol capacity in millions of gallons per year.

Nebraska	771.5
South Dakota	603.0
Minnesota	593.6

Source: *Site Selection*, January 2006, p. 92, from Renewable Fuels Association.

★ 1383 ★

Organic Chemicals
SIC: 2865; NAICS: 32511

Ethanol Production Worldwide

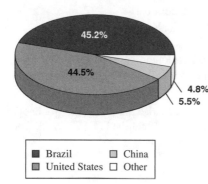

45.2%

44.5%

4.8%
5.5%

■ Brazil   ▢ China
■ United States   ▢ Other

Production of ethanol for fuel is shown by country.

Brazil	.45.2%
United States	.44.5
China	5.5
Other	4.8

Source: *St. Petersburg Times*, April 30, 2006, p. 3D, from *F.O. Licht World Ethanol & Biofuels Report*.

★ 1384 ★

Organic Chemicals
SIC: 2865; NAICS: 32511

Ethylene Market Worldwide, 2004 and 2010

Data show millions of tons by year.

	2004	2010	Share
Americas	38.469	41.415	27.62%
Asia Pacific	31.090	43.890	29.27
Europe	21.803	31.990	21.33%
Middle East/Africa	12.180	32.670	21.79

Source: *Asian Chemical News*, April 25, 2005, p. 12, from Chemical Marketing Associates Inc.

★ 1385 ★

Organic Chemicals
SIC: 2865; NAICS: 32511

Largest Ethanol Suppliers

Ethanol is a grain alcohol that can be made from a variety of products. In the United States it is mainly produced from corn. Some see ethanol-based fuels as a solution to the country's reliance on foreign oil. But some critics point out that so much energy is used in producing corn and harvesting the ethanol that it offsets any gains that might be achieved. Market shares are shown based on current capacity.

Archer Daniels Midland	.24.0%
VeraSun	5.0
Aventine Renewable Energy	4.0
Cargill	3.0
Abenogoa Bioenergy	2.0
Hawkeye Renewables	2.0
MGP Ingredients	2.0
Midwest Grain Processors	2.0
New Energy	2.0
Other	.54.0

Source: *New York Times*, June 25, 2006, p. 19, from Renewable Fuels Association and U.S. Department of Agriculture.

★ 1386 ★

Organic Chemicals
SIC: 2865; NAICS: 32511

Largest Ethylene Suppliers Worldwide

Market shares are shown based on 113 million tons annually.

Dow Chemical	8.7%
ExxonMobil Chemical	7.2
Royal Dutch/Shell Group	6.2
Saudia Arabia/Basic Industries Group	6.0
Lyondell (Equistar)	4.7
Innovene	3.4
Chevron Phillips Chemical Company	3.3
Toal	3.1

Continued on next page.

★ 1386 ★

[Continued]
Organic Chemicals
SIC: 2865; NAICS: 32511

Largest Ethylene Suppliers Worldwide

Market shares are shown based on 113 million tons annually.

SINOPEC	2.9%
Fomosa Plastics Corporation	2.8
Other	.51.7

Source: *Basic Materials*, Morgan Stanley Equity Research, December 14, 2005, p. 7, from Morgan Stanley Research.

★ 1387 ★

Organic Chemicals
SIC: 2865; NAICS: 32511

Largest Styrene Suppliers Worldwide

Market shares are shown based on 26.1 million tons annually.

Dow Chemical	8.4%
Royal Dutch/Shell Group	8.4
BASF	7.8
Lyondell	5.5
ATOFINA	5.0
NOVA Chemicals	4.5
Chevron Phillips Chemical Company . . .	3.6
Sterling Chemical Company	3.1
Innovene/Ineos	3.1
Idemitsu Kosan CL	2.8
Other	.47.9

Source: *Basic Materials*, Morgan Stanley Equity Research, December 14, 2005, p. 7, from Morgan Stanley Research and Chemical Marketing Associates Inc.

★ 1388 ★

Organic Chemicals
SIC: 2865; NAICS: 32511

Top Ethylene Firms in Japan, 2004

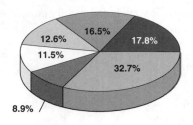

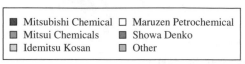

Market shares are shown based on domestic production of 7.56 million tons.

Mitsubishi Chemical	.17.8%
Mitsui Chemicals	.16.5
Idemitsu Kosan	.12.6
Maruzen Petrochemical	.11.5
Showa Denko	8.9
Other	.32.7

Source: "2004 Market Share Report." [online] from http://www.nikkei.co.jp [Published July 27, 2005] from Japan Iron and Steel Federation.

★ 1389 ★

Inorganic Chemicals
SIC: 2869; NAICS: 325199

Construction Chemical Demand

Demand is slowing in the residential sector, but the decline has been offset by increases in the nonresidential categories. Sales are shown in millions of dollars.

	2003	2008	Share
Protective coatings & sealers .	$ 2,390	$ 2,940	39.62%
Caulks & adhesives	1,465	1,950	26.28
Cement & asphalt additives .	666	850	11.46
Grouts & mortars	666	850	11.46
Other	661	830	11.19

Source: *Adhesives & Sealants Industry*, October 2005, p. 22, from Freedonia Group.

★ 1390 ★
Inorganic Chemicals
SIC: 2869; NAICS: 325188

Fine Chemicals Industry in Europe

Fine chemicals are pure, single chemical substances that are produced by chemical reactions. Examples of fine chemicals are intermediates for drug production and bulk active pharmaceutical ingredients ready to be compounded with inert pigments. The industry is valued at 54 billion euros.

Pharma	60.0%
Agrichemicals	10.0
Feed additives	10.0
Dyestuffs	5.0
Other	15.0

Source: *Specialty Chemicals*, May 2005, p. 18, from Arthur D. Little.

★ 1391 ★
Inorganic Chemicals
SIC: 2869; NAICS: 325188

Glycerine Market by End Use

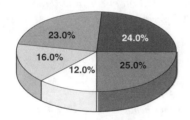

Market shares are shown in percent.

Personal care products	24.0%
Food and beverages	23.0
Oral care	16.0
Tobacco	12.0
Other	25.0

Source: *Chemical Market Reporter*, January 31, 2005, p. 31.

★ 1392 ★
Inorganic Chemicals
SIC: 2869; NAICS: 325188

Largest Caprolactam Makers in China

Companies are ranked by production in thousands of metric tons.

	(000)	Share
DSM Nanjing Chemical	140	35.0%
Sinopec Baling Company	140	35.0
Nanjing Dongfang Company	50	12.5
Shijiazhunag Chemical	50	12.5
Other	20	5.0

Source: *Chemical Week*, September 21, 2005, p. 45.

★ 1393 ★
Inorganic Chemicals
SIC: 2869; NAICS: 325199

Leading Formaldehyde Makers in China

Producers are ranked by capacity in thousands of tons annually.

Jiangsu Taicang Kingboard Chemical Co.	200
Hebei Wenan Kaly ue Chemical Co.	160
Shandong Muhua Group Co.	140
Suzhou Fine Chemical Group Co.	128
Shanghai Solvent Plant	82
Guangdong Kingboard Panyu Chemical Co.	80
Guangzhou Solvent Plant	72
Yuntianhua Group Co.	66

Source: *China Chemical Reporter*, November 16, 2005, p. 18.

★ 1394 ★
Inorganic Chemicals
SIC: 2869; NAICS: 325188

Methanol End Markets

Current installed capacity is 725 million. Industry leaders include Clear Lake Methanol and Millennium Chemicals.

Methyl tert-butyl ether	28.0%
Formaldehyde	26.0
Acetic acid	15.0
Chloromethanes	8.0
Other	8.0

Source: *Chemical Market Reporter*, October 3, 2005, p. 42, from SRI.

★ 1395 ★
Inorganic Chemicals
SIC: 2869; NAICS: 325188

Silicone Demand, 2003 and 2008

Demand is forecast to increase 6% annually to reach $3.7 billion in 2008. Gains in the market will come in part from the increase in production of durable goods such as aerospace equipment, electronic components and industrial machinery. The industry also benefits from a favorable environmental profile.

	2003	2008	Share
Fluids	$ 1,145	$ 1,490	40.38%
Resins	800	1,090	29.54
Elastomers	670	900	24.39
Gels	78	124	3.36
Other	62	86	2.33

Source: *Adhesives & Sealants Industry*, June 2005, p. 15, from Freedonia Group.

★ 1396 ★
Fertilizers
SIC: 2875; NAICS: 325314

Top Ammonia Fertilizer Makers in Canada, 2005

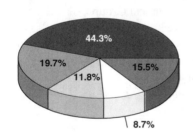

Market shares are shown in percent.

Agrium Inc.	.44.3%
Canadian Fertilizer Ltd.	.19.7
Saskferco Products Inc.	.11.8
Terra International (Canada Inc.)	.8.7
Other	.15.5

Source: "Market Share Matrix Project." [online] from http://www.marketsharematrix.org [Published May 2005].

★ 1397 ★
Fertilizers
SIC: 2875; NAICS: 325314

Top Fertilizer Makers in Germany

The fertilizer industry in the country has been stagnant for the last fifteen years. The industry suffers from a bad economy and oversupply. Firms are ranked by sales in millions of euros.

Norsk Hydro	€ 3.2
K+S (incl. Fertiva GmbH)	1.6
Kemira	1.0
DSM	0.6
Frand Paroisse	0.6
Fertiberia	0.3

Source: "Germany's Fertilizer Market.: [online] from http://www.export.gov [Published September 2005].

★ 1398 ★
Agrichemicals
SIC: 2879; NAICS: 32532

Crop Protection Industry in France, 2004

Sales rose to 1.8 billion euros in 2004. Sales have slid from the 1997 period.

Herbicides	.48.0%
Insecticides	.25.0
Fungicides	.24.0
Other	3.0

Source: *European Chemical News*, July 4, 2005, p. 9, from UIPP.

★ 1399 ★
Agrichemicals
SIC: 2879; NAICS: 32532

Global Agrichemical Market, 2004

Sales are in billions of dollars.

	($ bil.)	Share
Crop protection	$ 31	56.0%
Conventional seeds	14	26.0
Genetically modified seeds	5	9.0
Professional products	5	9.0

Source: *Syngenta AG*, Henry Fund Research, April 7, 2006, p. 6.

★ 1400 ★
Agrichemicals
SIC: 2879; NAICS: 32532

Largest Agrichemical Firms Worldwide, 2004

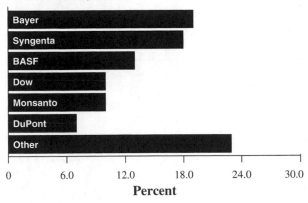

Percent

Firms are ranked by sales in millions of dollars. Total sales were $32.66 billion.

Bayer	.19.0%
Syngenta	.18.0
BASF	.13.0
Dow	.10.0
Monsanto	.10.0
DuPont	. 7.0
Other	.23.0

Source: *Tracking the Trend Towards Market Concentration*, United Nations Conference on Trade and Development, April 20, 2006 from UNCTAD Secretariat based on company records.

★ 1401 ★
Agrichemicals
SIC: 2879; NAICS: 32532

Leading Fungicide Makers Worldwide, 2004

Fungicide sales stood at $7.37 billion in 2004. They represented nearly a quarter of the crop protection market.

Bayer	.23.0%
Syngenta	.17.0
BASE	.13.0
Dow	. 6.0
DuPont	. 5.0
Other	.36.0

Source: *Chemical Market Reporter*, January 23, 2006, p. 20, from Phillips Douglas and Citigroup Investment.

★ 1402 ★
Agrichemicals
SIC: 2879; NAICS: 32532

Monsanto and the Nursery Market

Monsanto has 85-90% of the nursery market after the purchase of Seminis in January 2005. Monsanto has been buying up its competitors and holds over 11,000 seed patents. Figures include pesticides, herbicides and fertilizers.

Monsanto	.90.0%
Other	.10.0

Source: *Countryside & Small Stock Journal*, March - April 2006, p. 60.

★ 1403 ★
Herbicides
SIC: 2879; NAICS: 32532

Leading Herbicide Makers Worldwide, 2004

Herbicide sales stood at $14 billion in 2004. The world's leading herbicide is Monsanto's Roundup glyphosate (which has 15% of the herbicide market). It is a generic, however, so others have begun to market it.

	($ bil.)	Share
Monsanto	$ 2.80	20.0%
Syngenta	2.38	17.0
Bayer	1.82	13.0
Dow	1.68	12.0
BASE	1.54	11.0
DuPont	1.26	9.0

Source: *Chemical Market Reporter*, January 23, 2006, p. 20, from Phillips Douglas and Citigroup Investment.

★ 1404 ★

Insecticides

SIC: 2879; NAICS: 32532

Leading Insecticide Makers Worldwide, 2004

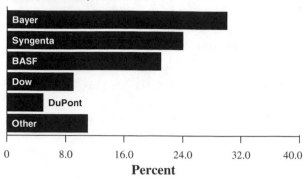

Insecticide sales stood at $14 billion in 2004. Sales were up 16% from 2003, the first year of increase since 1997. The market is going to be pressured by the increase of genetically modified crop acreage.

Bayer	30.0%
Syngenta	24.0
BASF	21.0
Dow	9.0
DuPont	5.0
Other	11.0

Source: *Chemical Market Reporter*, January 23, 2006, p. 20, from Phillips Douglas and Citigroup Investment.

★ 1405 ★

Insecticides

SIC: 2879; NAICS: 32532

Top Insecticide Makers, 2005

Market shares are shown in percent. Figures exclude Wal-Mart and other large format mass retailers.

S.C. Johnson Inc.	47.4%
Spectrum Brands	15.8
Henkel	5.6
Reckitt Benckiser	4.8
Scotts Miracle Gro	3.5
Private label	2.9
Other	20.0

Source: *U.S. Personal Care and Household Products Digest*, Citigroup Equity Research, February 24, 2006, p. 220, from ACNielsen.

★ 1406 ★

Insecticides

SIC: 2879; NAICS: 32532

Top Sun Screen/Insect Repellants, 2006

Brands are ranked by supermarket and drug store sales in millions of dollars.

	($ mil.)	Share
Coppertone Bug & Sun	$ 1.7	53.13%
Off Skintastic	1.2	37.50
Sun & Bug Stuff	0.2	6.25
Other	0.1	3.13

Source: *MMR*, April 24, 2006, p. 30, from Information Resources Inc.

★ 1407 ★

Pesticides

SIC: 2879; NAICS: 32532

Leading Pesticide Firms Worldwide, 2004

Firms are ranked by agrichemical sales in millions of dollars.

	($ mil.)	Share
Bayer	$ 6,120	17.0%
Syngenta	6,030	17.0
BASF	4,141	12.0
Dow	3,368	10.0
Dupont	2,211	6.0
Koor	1,358	4.0
Sumitomo	1,308	4.0
Nufarm	1,060	3.0
Arysta	790	2.0

Source: *ETC Communique*, November/December 2005, p. 4, from *Agrow World Crop Protection News*.

★ 1408 ★
Pesticides
SIC: 2879; NAICS: 32532

Pesticide Industry in China, 2000 and 2004

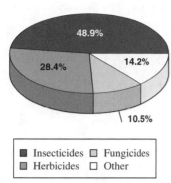

Sales increased from 25.84 billion rembini in 2000 to 46.89 billion rembini in 2004.

	2000	2004
Insecticides	61.3%	48.9%
Herbicides	18.0	28.4
Fungicides	10.6	10.5
Other	10.1	14.2

Source: *China Chemical Reporter*, October 26, 2005, p. 37, from CNCIC Chemdata.

★ 1409 ★
Adhesives & Sealants
SIC: 2891; NAICS: 32552

Adhesives Market in North America, 2004

The industry was valued at $14.4 billion.

Packaging	28.0%
Construction	17.0
Transportation	17.0
Non-rigid bonding	11.0
Rigid bonding	10.0
Tapes	9.0
Consumer	8.0

Source: *Chemical Week*, April 6, 2005, p. 19, from ChemQuest Group.

★ 1410 ★
Adhesives & Sealants
SIC: 2891; NAICS: 32552

Global Adhesives Market, 2005

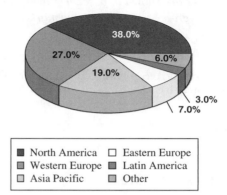

The industry was valued at $25.4 billion.

North America	38.0%
Western Europe	27.0
Asia Pacific	19.0
Eastern Europe	7.0
Latin America	3.0
Other	6.0

Source: *Chemical Week*, April 5, 2006, p. 24, from Chemark Consulting Group.

★ 1411 ★
Adhesives & Sealants
SIC: 2891; NAICS: 32552

Top Adhesive Makers, 2003

Firms are ranked by adhesive/sealant sales in millions of dollars. Total sales are forecast to increase from $11 billion in 2003 to $12.31 billion in 2008. Packaging, construction and wood are the top markets.

Henkel	$ 770
National Starch	575
H.B. Fuller	525
3M	310
Bostik Findley	285
Illinois Tool Works	255
General Electric	250
Chemicals-a	225
Rohm and Haas	220
Borden	180

Source: *Adhesives & Sealants Industry*, October 2005, p. 46, from Impact Marketing Consultants.

★ 1412 ★
Glue
SIC: 2891; NAICS: 32552

Back-to-School Glue Market, 2004

Market shares are shown in percent. Elmer's held 51% of the overall $101 million glue market in 2004.

Elmer's School Glue 80.0%
Other 20.0

Source: *Advertising Age*, August 1, 2005, p. 8, from Information Resources Inc.

★ 1413 ★
Glue
SIC: 2891; NAICS: 32552

Glue Market in Brazil

Market shares are shown in percent.

Super Bonder 80.0%
Other 20.0

Source: *Advertising Age*, April 10, 2006, p. 6.

★ 1414 ★
Glue
SIC: 2891; NAICS: 32552

Top Glue Brands, 2005

Brands are ranked by sales in millions of dollars at supermarkets, drug stores and discount stores (excluding Wal-Mart) for the 52 weeks ended August 7, 2005.

	($ mil.)	Share
Krazy Glue	$ 23.5	23.08%
Elmer's	21.8	21.41
Elmer's Glue	5.1	5.01
Loctite Quicktite	3.8	3.73
Avery	3.6	3.54
Ross	3.3	3.24
Scotch	2.9	2.85
Crayola	2.8	2.75
Duro	2.3	2.26
Faucet Queen Helping Hand	2.1	2.06
Private label	5.5	5.40
Other	25.1	24.66

Source: *MMR*, September 19, 2005, p. 1, from Information Resources Inc.

★ 1415 ★
Explosives
SIC: 2892; NAICS: 32592

Leading Explosives Makers in North America

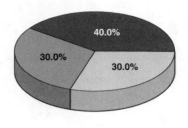

Dynco was recently sold to Orica. Worldwide, Dyno and Orica have 19% and 21% of the market respectively.

Dyno 40.0%
Orica 30.0
Other 30.0

Source: *The Australian*, December 5, 2005, p. NA.

★ 1416 ★
Ink
SIC: 2893; NAICS: 32591

Largest Ink Firms in North America

Firms are ranked by sales in millions of dollars.

Sun Chemical	$ 3,000
Flint Ink	1,450
INX International Ink Co.	300
Siegwerk Packaging Ink	185
CR/T	175
DuPont	150
Sensient Technologies Corp.	109
Hostmann-Steinberg	100
Wikoff Color	95
Toyo Ink	90

Source: *Ink Maker*, November 17, 2005, p. 4.

★ 1417 ★
Ink
SIC: 2893; NAICS: 32591

Leading Ink Makers in India

The ink industry is valued at Rs 1,200 crore.

Dainippon 23.0%
Sakata 6.0
Incowax 4.0

Continued on next page.

★ 1417 ★
[Continued]
Ink
SIC: 2893; NAICS: 32591

Leading Ink Makers in India

The ink industry is valued at Rs 1,200 crore.

Sicpa India	3.0%
Other	64.0

Source: *Financial Express*, October 29, 2005, p. NA.

★ 1418 ★
Ink
SIC: 2893; NAICS: 32591

Top Ink Producers in China

Companies are ranked by output in thousands of tons.

	(000)	Share
Tianjin Toyo Ink	20.5	7.32%
Taiyuan Coates Ink	18.2	6.50
Hangzhou Toka	16.8	6.00
Yip Shi Ink	13.3	4.75
Shanghai Silian Printing Ink	10.6	3.79
Shanghai Peony Ink	8.4	3.00
Shandhai Dainippon Ink	8.0	2.86
Gaungdong Zhaoqing Tianlong Ink	6.8	2.43
Zhejiang New East Ink	6.4	2.29
Shenzhen Dainippon Ink	6.3	2.25
Other	164.7	58.82

Source: *Asia Pacific Coatings Journal*, December 2005, p. 42, from *Report of Printing Technology*.

★ 1419 ★
Carbon Black
SIC: 2895; NAICS: 325182

Carbon Black Demand Worldwide, 2004 and 2009

Tires represent more than two-thirds of the demand for carbon black. Figures are shown in thousands of metric tons.

	2004	2009	Share
Asia/Pacific	3,323	4,320	45.71%
North America	1,725	1,950	20.63
Western Europe	1,485	1,655	17.51
Other	1,217	1,525	16.14

Source: *Rubber World*, June 2005, p. 11, from Freedonia Group.

★ 1420 ★
Air Fresheners
SIC: 2899; NAICS: 325998

Top Air Freshener Makers, 2005

Market shares are shown in percent. Figures exclude Wal-Mart and other large format mass retailers.

S.C. Johnson Son Inc.	43.0%
Reckitt Benckiser	21.4
Procter & Gamble	14.3
Henkel	8.6
Royal Dutch Petroleum Company	2.5
Private label	1.8
Other	8.4

Source: *U.S. Personal Care and Household Products Digest*, Citigroup Equity Research, February 24, 2006, p. 214, from ACNielsen.

★ 1421 ★
Air Fresheners
SIC: 2899; NAICS: 325998

Top Rug/Room Deodorizer Brands, 2005

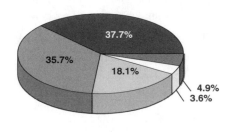

Market shares are shown in percent. Figures exclude Wal-Mart and other large format mass retailers.

Arm & Hammer	37.7%
Glade	35.7
Carpet Fresh	18.1
Rug Doctor	3.6
Other	4.9

Source: *U.S. Personal Care and Household Products Digest*, Citigroup Equity Research, February 24, 2006, p. 218, from ACNielsen.

★ 1422 ★
Air Fresheners
SIC: 2899; NAICS: 325998

Top Rug/Room Deodorizer Makers, 2005

Market shares are shown in percent. Figures exclude Wal-Mart and other large format mass retailers.

Church & Dwight 37.7%
S.C. Johnson Son 35.7
WD 40 Company 18.1
Rug Doctor Inc. 3.6
Personal Care Products Inc. 1.3
Private label 0.8
Other 2.8

Source: *U.S. Personal Care and Household Products Digest,* Citigroup Equity Research, February 24, 2006, p. 65, from ACNielsen.

★ 1423 ★
Charcoal
SIC: 2899; NAICS: 325998

Top Charcoal Brands, 2005

Market shares are shown in percent. Figures exclude Wal-Mart and other large format mass retailers.

Kingsford 73.0%
Royal Oak 1.3
Best of the West 0.7
Match Light 0.4
Steakhouse 0.4
Private label 21.2

Source: *U.S. Personal Care and Household Products Digest,* Citigroup Equity Research, February 24, 2006, p. 220, from ACNielsen.

★ 1424 ★
Charcoal
SIC: 2899; NAICS: 325998

Top Charcoal Makers, 2005

Total sales were $407 million. Figures exclude Wal-Mart and other large format mass retailers.

Clorox 73.3%
Royal Oak Enterprises 1.5
Two Trees Corporation 0.7
Imperial Products Corporation 0.5
Private label 21.2

Source: *U.S. Personal Care and Household Products Digest,* Citigroup Equity Research, February 24, 2006, p. 220, from ACNielsen.

★ 1425 ★
Firelogs
SIC: 2899; NAICS: 325998

Top Firelog Makers, 2005

Market shares are shown based on supermarket, drug store and mass merchandiser sales (excluding Wal-Mart) for the 52 weeks ended June 12, 2005.

Duraflame Inc. 37.5%
Conros Corporation 28.4
Joseph Enterprises Inc. 3.1
Robust International 0.4
Private label 30.1

Source: *Grocery Headquarters*, August 2005, p. S6, from Information Resources Inc.

★ 1426 ★
Firestarters
SIC: 2899; NAICS: 325998

Top Firestarter Brands, 2005

Market shares are shown based on supermarket, drug store and mass merchandiser sales (excluding Wal-Mart) for the 52 weeks ended June 12, 2005.

Starter Logg 32.3%
Quick Start 20.3
Duraflame Firestart 7.3
Diamond Strike A Fire 6.6
Pine Mountain 6.1
Coleman 1.2
Fatwood 1.2
Lightning Nugget 1.2
Village Candle 0.4
Other 23.4

Source: *Grocery Headquarters*, August 2005, p. S6, from Information Resources Inc.

★ 1427 ★
Firestarters
SIC: 2899; NAICS: 325998

Top Firestarter Makers, 2005

Market shares are shown based on supermarket, drug store and mass merchandiser sales (excluding Wal-Mart) for the 52 weeks ended June 12, 2005.

Conros Corporation 38.5%
Duraflame Inc. 27.6
Jarden Home Brands 6.6
Washington Lightning 1.4

Continued on next page.

★ 1427 ★
[Continued]
Firestarters
SIC: 2899; NAICS: 325998

Top Firestarter Makers, 2005

Market shares are shown based on supermarket, drug store and mass merchandiser sales (excluding Wal-Mart) for the 52 weeks ended June 12, 2005.

Private label	21.4%
Other	4.5

Source: *Grocery Headquarters*, August 2005, p. S6, from Information Resources Inc.

★ 1428 ★
Water Chemicals
SIC: 2899; NAICS: 325998

Leading Specialty Water Chemical Firms

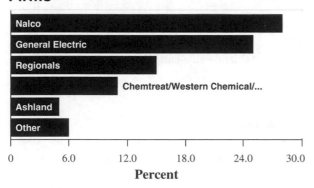

Demand for water treatment chemical products and services is estimated at $5.6 billion in 2005. Most firms are wholly or largely water treatment service oriented.

Nalco	28.0%
General Electric	25.0
Regionals	15.0
Chemtreat/Western Chemical/Garratt-Callahan	11.0
Ashland (Drew)	5.0
Other	6.0

Source: *Chemical Market Reporter*, February 21, 2005, p. 6, from Lake View Associates.

★ 1429 ★
Water Chemicals
SIC: 2899; NAICS: 325998

Water Treatment Chemicals, 2003

Data are in millions of dollars.

	($ mil.)	Share
Coagulants & flocculants	$ 1,637.5	38.22%
Corrosion & scale inhibitors . . .	875.0	20.42
Biocides & disinfectants	615.0	14.35
Activated carbon	436.2	10.18
Anti-foaming agents & defoamers . .	270.0	6.30
pH adjusters, water softeners & other inorganic commodities . . .	450.6	10.52

Source: *Chemical Market Reporter*, September 12, 2005, p. 20, from Frost & Sullivan.

★ 1430 ★
Watermarks and ID Cards
SIC: 2899; NAICS: 325998

Driver's License Watermarking Solutions Industry

Digimarc's technology produces digital-based driver's licenses for 32 states, as well as government IDs for the United States and other countries. Market shares are shown in percent.

Digimarc	60.0%
Other	40.0

Source: "Brian W. Ruttenbur." [online] from http://www.securitysstockwatch.com.investmenttrendsMK.html [Accessed November 16, 2005].

SIC 29 - Petroleum and Coal Products

★ 1431 ★
Fuel
SIC: 2911; NAICS: 32411

Heavy-Duty Fuel Industry, 2020

Major concerns for the industry include emissions, oil supplies and costs.

Traditional diesel fuel	.65.0%
Biodiesel/gas-to-liquids	.20.0
Hybrid vehicles	.18.0
Natural gas	.11.0

Source: *Mobile Emissions Today*, March 22, 2005, p. NA, from WestStart-CALSTART.

★ 1432 ★
Fuel
SIC: 2911; NAICS: 32411

Refined Petroleum Products, 2003 and 2005

Data are in thousands of billions of barrels.

	2003	2005	Share
Gasoline	208,167	210,456	29.80%
Distillate	136,542	122,518	17.35
Natural gas liquids	100,889	130,260	18.44
Unfinished oils	75,904	90,361	12.80
Kerosine jet fuel	38,767	49,439	7.00
Residual	37,800	37,042	5.25
Special naphthas	2,006	1,526	0.22
Other refined	55,364	64,619	9.15

Source: *Oil & Gas Journal*, January 16, 2006, p. 35.

★ 1433 ★
Gasoline
SIC: 2911; NAICS: 32411

Top Gasoline Firms, 2004

ConocoPhillips slipped 0.1 percent in total gasoline sales in the United States in 2004. It sold 20,787 billion gallons. Shares are shown ranked by gross sales of 140.1 billion gallons.

ConocoPhillips	.14.84%
ExxonMobil	.13.64
BP	.11.96
Shell	.11.13
CITGO	.10.13
MarathonAshland Petroleum	8.83
ChevronTexaco	7.67
Valero	4.93
Sunoco	4.84
Amerada Hess	2.12
Other	9.91

Source: *National Petroleum News*, July 15, 2005, p. 106, from company reports.

★ 1434 ★
Gasoline
SIC: 2911; NAICS: 32411

Top Gasoline Firms in Japan, 2004

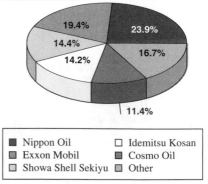

■ Nippon Oil ☐ Idemitsu Kosan
■ Exxon Mobil ■ Cosmo Oil
☐ Showa Shell Sekiyu ■ Other

Market shares are shown based on domestic sales of 61.46 million kiloliters.

Nippon Oil	.23.9%
Exxon Mobil	.19.4

Continued on next page.

★ 1434 ★

[Continued]
Gasoline
SIC: 2911; NAICS: 32411

Top Gasoline Firms in Japan, 2004

Market shares are shown based on domestic sales of 61.46 million kiloliters.

Showa Shell Sekiyu	.14.4%
Idemitsu Kosan	.14.2
Cosmo Oil	.11.4
Other	.16.7

Source: "2004 Market Share Report." [online] from http://www.nikkei.co.jp [Published July 27, 2005] from Petroleum Association of Japan.

★ 1435 ★

Petroleum Refining
SIC: 2911; NAICS: 32411

Largest Refiners, 2005

Companies are ranked by barrels per day as of January 1, 2005.

ExxonMobil Refining & Supply (Baytown)	557,000
ExxonMobil Refining & Supply Co. (Baton Rouge)	493,500
BP Products (Texas City)	437,000
BP Products (Whiting)	410,000
ExxonMobil Refining & Supply Co. (Beaumont)	348,500
Sunoco Inc. (Philadelphia)	335,000
Deer Park Refining (Deer Park)	333,700
Chevron USA (Pascagoula)	325,000
Citgo Petroleum Corp. (Lake Charles)	324,300
ConocoPhillips (Wood River)	306,000

Source: "Top U.S. Refineries." [online] from http://www.eia.doe.gov [Accessed July 5, 2006] from U.S. Department of Energy.

★ 1436 ★

Petroleum Refining
SIC: 2911; NAICS: 32411

Leading Oil Firms in the Philippines

Chevron Philippines was formerly known as Caltex Philippines.

Petron Corp.	.38.18%
Pilpinas Shell Petroleum Corp.	.32.15
Chevron Philippines Inc.	.15.80
Other	.13.87

Source: *BusinessWorld* (Philippines), March 7, 2006, p. NA, from U.S. Department of Energy.

★ 1437 ★

Petroleum Refining
SIC: 2911; NAICS: 32411

Top Refiners in Canada, 2004

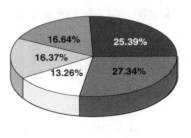

Market shares are shown in percent.

Imperial Oil (Esso)	.25.39%
Petro Canada	.16.64
Shell Canada	.16.37
Irving Oil	.13.26
Other	.27.34

Source: "Market Share Matrix Project." [online] from http://www.marketsharematrix.org [Published August 2005] from *Globe & Mail* and Competition Bureau.

★ 1438 ★
Asphalt
SIC: 2951; NAICS: 324121

Asphalt Demand in China

Demand is forecast to rise 6.8 percent each year through 2008 to 15 million metric tons. Figures are in thousands of metric tons.

	2003	2008	Share
Paving	7,660	11,300	75.33%
Roofing	3,040	3,590	23.93
Other	100	110	0.73

Source: *Roofing Contractor*, July 2005, p. 10, from Freedonia Group.

★ 1439 ★
Asphalt
SIC: 2951; NAICS: 324121

Leading Asphalt Paving/Roofing/ Saturated Material Makers, 2005

Market shares are shown in percent.

Lafarge North America	5.0%
Berkshire Hathaway	4.0
Compagnie de Saint-Gobain	2.8
Other	88.2

Source: "US Aphalt Paving, Roofing & Saturated Materials." [online] from http://www.ibisworld.com [Accessed May 1, 2006] from IBISWorld.

★ 1440 ★
Lubricants
SIC: 2992; NAICS: 324191

Lubricants Market in Sri Lanka

Market shares are shown in percent.

Caltex	88.0%
Other	12.0

Source: *Lanka Business Online*, May 15, 2005, p. NA.

★ 1441 ★
Lubricants
SIC: 2992; NAICS: 324191

Top Motor Oil Brands in South America

Lubricant demand is forecast to exceed 2.5 million tons annually by 2007. Demand in Brazil was at 1.2 millions tons in 2004, more than the rest of the countries in the region combined. Argentina follows Brazil with 260,000 tons per year. Shell makes the Pennzoil and Quaker State brands.

Shell	18.6%
ChevronTexaco	18.0
ExxonMobil	14.0
Petrobras	8.2
Castol	4.2
Other	37.0

Source: *Lube Report*, March 16, 2006, p. 1.

SIC 30 - Rubber and Misc. Plastics Products

★ 1442 ★
Rubber Track
SIC: 3011; NAICS: 326211

Rubber Track Market

The industry is worth $600 million.

ASV 65.0%
Other 35.0

Source: *Fortune*, July 1, 2005, p. NA.

★ 1443 ★
Tires
SIC: 3011; NAICS: 326211

Highway Truck Tire Market, 2005

Shares are for the replacement market.

Goodyear 17.5%
Michelin 17.0
Bridgestone 15.5
Firestone 6.0
General 4.5
Yokohama 4.5
Other 35.0

Source: *Tire Business*, February 13, 2006, p. 9, from *Tire Business Market Data Book*.

★ 1444 ★
Tires
SIC: 3011; NAICS: 326211

Leading Tire Makers in Europe (Passenger, Light Truck), 2005

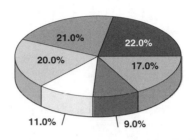

- ■ Michelin
- □ Bridgestone/Firestone
- ■ Continental
- ■ Pirelli
- ▨ Goodyear/Sumitomo
- ▨ Other

Data refer to replacement and OE markets for passenger vehicles and light trucks. Shares are shown based on volume.

Michelin 22.0%
Continental 21.0
Goodyear/Sumitomo 20.0
Bridgestone/Firestone 11.0
Pirelli 9.0
Other 17.0

Source: "Continental Visual Fact Book Full Year 2005." [online] from http://www.conti-online.com [Accessed April 20, 2006].

★ 1445 ★
Tires
SIC: 3011; NAICS: 326211

Replacement Passenger Tire Market, 2005

Market shares are shown based on 205.8 million units shipped.

Goodyear 15.5%
Michelin 8.0
Firestone 7.5

Continued on next page.

★ 1445 ★
[Continued]
Tires
SIC: 3011; NAICS: 326211

Replacement Passenger Tire Market, 2005

Market shares are shown based on 205.8 million units shipped.

Bridgestone	7.0%
BFGoodrich	5.0
Cooper	5.0
General	3.0
Kumho	3.0
Uniroyal	3.0
Dayton	2.5
Hankook	2.5
Multi-Mile	2.5
Sears	2.5
Toyo	2.5
Other	32.5

Source: *Modern Tire Dealer*, January 2006, p. 52, from *Modern Tire Dealer* estimates.

★ 1446 ★
Tires
SIC: 3011; NAICS: 326211

Replacement Passenger Tire Market in Canada, 2005

Market shares are shown based on 17.8 million units shipped.

Motomaster	17.5%
Goodyear	15.5
Michelin	10.0
Bridgestone	7.0
BFGoodrich	5.5
Hankook	5.0
Dayton	3.5
Firestone	3.5
President	3.5
Toyo	3.5
Uniroyal	3.5
Other	23.5

Source: *Modern Tire Dealer*, January 2006, p. 52, from *Modern Tire Dealer* estimates.

★ 1447 ★
Tires
SIC: 3011; NAICS: 326211

Replacement Tire Market (Light Truck), 2005

Market shares are shown based on 36.1 million units shipped.

Goodyear	12.5%
BFGoodrich	9.5
Bridgestone	7.5
Cooper	6.5
Michelin	6.5
Firestone	5.5
Multi-Mile	5.5
General	4.0
Toyo	4.0
Uniroyal	3.0
Other	35.5

Source: *Modern Tire Dealer*, January 2006, p. 52, from *Modern Tire Dealer* estimates.

★ 1448 ★
Tires
SIC: 3011; NAICS: 326211

Tire Sales, 2005

Aftermarket tire shipments are set to grow 3.2% in 2005, a record. Medium truck tire sales were up 10.4% from the previous year. Replacement light truck tires fell 1.4%, the largest decline in the group.

	(mil.)	Share
Replacement passenger	205	63.08%
OE passenger	53	16.31
Replacement light truck	36	11.08
Replacement med truck	17	5.23
OE light truck	8	2.46
OE med truck	6	1.85

Source: *Rubber & Plastics News*, December 12, 2005, p. 4, from Rubber Manufacturers Association.

★ 1449 ★

Tires

SIC: 3011; NAICS: 326211

Tire Shipments, 2005

Shipments are shown in thousands of units for year to date August 2005.

	Units	Share
Passenger	188,415.0	79.68%
Light truck	30,819.0	13.03
Medium truck	16,954.0	7.17
Heavy truck	264.9	0.11

Source: *Rubber & Plastics News*, January 9, 2006, p. 19.

★ 1450 ★

Tires

SIC: 3011; NAICS: 326211

Top Retread Tire Brands, 2005

Market shares are shown in percent.

Bandag	45.0%
Goodyear	26.5
Michelin	12.0
Oliver	9.0
Marangoni	1.5
Other	6.0

Source: *Modern Tire Dealer*, January 2006, p. 52, from *Modern Tire Dealer* estimates.

★ 1451 ★

Tires

SIC: 3011; NAICS: 326211

Top Tire Brands in Mexico, 2005

Market shares are shown based on 13.1 million units shipped for passenger cars.

Goodyear	20.0%
Firestone	16.0
Tornel	13.0
Euzkadi	11.5
Uniroyal	7.0
BFGoodrich	6.0
Bridgestone	6.0
General	3.5
Hankook	2.0
Michelin	2.0
Multi-Mile	2.0
Yokohama	2.0
Other	11.5

Source: *Modern Tire Dealer*, January 2006, p. 52, from *Modern Tire Dealer* estimates.

★ 1452 ★

Tires

SIC: 3011; NAICS: 326211

Top Tire Makers in Japan, 2004

Market shares are shown based on domestic production of 1.28 million tons.

Bridgestone	48.3%
Sumitomo Rubber Ind.	22.6
Yokohama Rubber	16.1
Toyo Tire & Rubber	11.6
Other	1.4

Source: "2004 Market Share Report." [online] from http://www.nikkei.co.jp [Published July 27, 2005] from Japan Automobile Tire Manufacturers Association and Nikkei estimates.

★ 1453 ★

Tires

SIC: 3011; NAICS: 326211

Top Tire Makers in North America, 2005

Market shares are shown in percent.

Goodyear/Dunlop	26.3%
Michelin/Uniroyal/Goodrich	23.6
Bridgestone/Firestone	17.8
Cooper	7.1
Continental Tire	6.2
Other	19.0

Source: *Tire Business*, February 13, 2006, p. 9, from *Tire Business Market Data Book*.

★ 1454 ★

Tires

SIC: 3011; NAICS: 326211

Top Tire Producing Nations, 2004

Data show passenger and commercial (light truck, truck and bus) tires.

United States	233,106
Japan	173,093
China	120,650
Germany	78,488
South Korea	76,596

Source: *Tire Business*, February 13, 2006, p. 9, from *Tire Business Market Data Book*.

★ 1455 ★
Footwear
SIC: 3021; NAICS: 316211

Athletic Shoe Market in Germany

Market shares are shown in percent.

Running/jogging	29.0%
Leisure	24.0
Outdoor	14.0
Football	10.0
Indoor	5.0
Basketball	3.0
Tennis	2.0
Aerobic/fitness	1.0
Other	12.0

Source: *Wirtschaftwoche*, April 21, 2005, p. 72.

★ 1456 ★
Footwear
SIC: 3021; NAICS: 316211

Footwear Sales by Segment, 2005

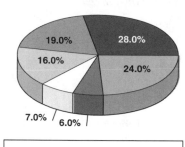

Legend:
- ■ Running/jogging □ Cross trainer
- ■ Low performance ■ Walking
- ■ Basketball ■ Other

The athletic footwear market was placed at $$18.1 billion.

Running/jogging	28.0%
Low performance	19.0
Basketball	16.0
Cross trainer	7.0
Walking	6.0
Other	24.0

Source: "U.S. Athletic Footwear Sales Grew 9% in 2005." [online] from http://www.nsga.org [Published February 20, 2006] from NPD Group.

★ 1457 ★
Footwear
SIC: 3021; NAICS: 316211

Global Sports Shoe Market, 2004

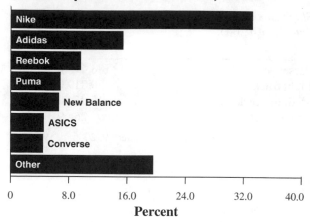

Market shares are shown in percent.

Nike	33.2%
Adidas	15.4
Reebok	9.6
Puma	6.8
New Balance	6.6
ASICS	4.5
Converse	4.4
Other	19.5

Source: *Financial Times*, January 24, 2006, p. 15, from Sporting Goods Intelligence and Banc of America Securities.

★ 1458 ★
Footwear
SIC: 3021; NAICS: 316211

High-Priced Basketball Shoe Market

Shares refer to basketball shoes costing more than $100. In the $75 and up category, Nike's business is 20 times larger than Adidas and Reebok combined. In the overall basketball shoe category, Nike's business is three times larger than Adidas and Reebok combined.

Nike	98.0%
Other	2.0

Source: *Sporting Goods Business*, June 29, 2005, p. NA, from NPD Group.

★ 1459 ★
Footwear
SIC: 3021; NAICS: 316211
Soccer Footwear Market

Market shares are shown in percent.

Adidas 52.0%
Nike 35.0
Other 13.0

Source: *Baltimore Sun*, November 29, 2004, p. NA, from SportScanInfo.

★ 1460 ★
Footwear
SIC: 3021; NAICS: 316211
Sports Shoe Market, 2004

Shares are shown for the wholesale market.

Nike 36.3%
Reebok 12.2
New Balance 11.5
Adidas 8.9
Puma 2.4
ASICS 2.2
Other 26.5

Source: *Der Spiegel*, August 8, 2005, p. 66, from Sporting Goods Intelligence.

★ 1461 ★
Gaskets
SIC: 3053; NAICS: 339991
Leading Gasket Makers in India

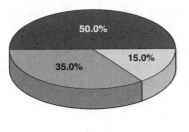

The total market is valued at Rs 350 crore. The organized sector is worth Rs 200 crore with the balance held by the unorganized sector. Shaes are for the orgnized sector.

TACL 50.0%
Banco Products 35.0
Other 15.0

Source: "Talbros Automotive Components." [online] from http://www.moneypore.com/Spec/Tal010905.htm [Accessed November 7, 2005].

★ 1462 ★
Condoms
SIC: 3069; NAICS: 326299
Top Condom Brands, 2005

Market shares are shown based on sales at supermarkets, drug stores and discount stores (excluding Wal-Mart) for the 52 weeks ended June 12, 2005.

Trojan 24.1%
Trojan Enz 15.5
Lifestyles 9.1
Trojan Magnum 7.8
Durex Extra Sensitive 5.3
Trojan Her Pleasure 4.4
Durex 3.8
Trojan Ultra Pleasure 3.7
Other 26.3

Source: *Grocery Headquarters*, September 21, 2005, p. S14, from Information Resources Inc.

★ 1463 ★
Condoms
SIC: 3069; NAICS: 326299
Top Condom Makers, 2005

Market shares are shown based on sales at supermarkets, drug stores and discount stores (excluding Wal-Mart) for the 52 weeks ended June 12, 2005.

Church & Dwight Co. Inc.	.70.5%
Durex Consumer Products	.14.9
Ansell Amer	.11.9
Medtech Products Limited	. 0.6
Global Protection Inc.	. 0.5
Other	. 1.6

Source: *Grocery Headquarters*, September 21, 2005, p. S14, from Information Resources Inc.

★ 1464 ★
Cosmetics Bags
SIC: 3069; NAICS: 326299
Top Cosmetics Storage Bags, 2006

Brands are ranked by sales in millions of dollars at supermarkets, drug stores and discount stores (excluding Wal-Mart) for the 52 weeks ended January 22, 2006.

	($ mil.)	Share
Allegro Pacific	$ 8.3	15.63%
Caboodles	8.1	15.25
Living Things	5.6	10.55
Studio Collection	4.6	8.66
Modella	4.1	7.72
Studio Basics	2.2	4.14
Basics	1.5	2.82
Worldwide Dreams	1.5	2.82
RGA	1.3	2.45
Revlon	1.0	1.88
Other	14.9	28.06

Source: *MMR*, March 20, 2006, p. 29, from Information Resources Inc.

★ 1465 ★
Sponges
SIC: 3069; NAICS: 326299
Top Sponge/Cloth Brands, 2005

Market shares are shown in percent. Figures exclude Wal-Mart and other large format mass retailers.

Swiffer	.41.4%
Mr. Clean	. 7.7

Toilet Wand	. 6.2%
Scrubbing Bubbles Fresh Brush	. 5.3
Grab It	. 4.3
Scotch Brite	. 2.6
Glass Wizard	. 0.6
Private label	. 7.7
Other	.24.2

Source: *U.S. Personal Care and Household Products Digest*, Citigroup Equity Research, February 24, 2006, p. 180, from ACNielsen.

★ 1466 ★
Surgical Gloves
SIC: 3069; NAICS: 339113
Leading Surgical Glove Makers

Annual spending on surgical gloves (excluding exam gloves) is $206 million.

Regent	.34.0%
Allegiance/Cardinal	.31.0
Ansell/J&J	.30.0
Maxxim/Medline	. 3.0
Other	. 2.0

Source: *Hospital Materials Management*, March 2006, p. 1, from industry estimates.

★ 1467 ★
Plastic Wrap
SIC: 3083; NAICS: 32613
Top Plastic Wrap Brands, 2005

Market shares are shown in percent. Figures exclude Wal-Mart and other large format mass retailers.

Glad Cling Wrap	.24.1%
Glad Press 'N Seal	.19.8
Reynolds	.16.6
Saran Classic	.10.3
Saran Cling Plus	. 5.7
Food Saver	. 4.3
Stretch-Tite	. 1.1
Private label	.17.7
Other	. 0.4

Source: *U.S. Personal Care and Household Products Digest*, Citigroup Equity Research, February 24, 2006, p. 65, from ACNielsen.

★ 1468 ★
Plastic Foam
SIC: 3086; NAICS: 32614, 32615
Plastic Foam Demand, 2004 and 2009

Plastic foam demand is set to increase from $1,013 million in 2004 to $1,325 million in 2009.

	2004	2009	Share
Polyurethane	$ 336	$ 442	33.36%
Engineered plastic	237	295	22.26
Non-plastic foam	118	173	13.06
Other plastic	322	415	31.32

Source: *Urethanes Technology*, October/November 2005, p. 41, from Freedonia Group.

★ 1469 ★
Surfboard Cores
SIC: 3086; NAICS: 32614, 32615
Global Surfboard Core Market

Clark Foam shut its doors in November 2005. It was the main supplier of foam cores for the $1 billion surfboard industry.

Clark Foam	.60.0%
Other	.40.0

Source: *Orange County Register*, December 14, 2005, p. NA.

★ 1470 ★
Surfboard Cores
SIC: 3086; NAICS: 32614, 32615
Surfboard Core Market

The company made at least 80% of the cores used in surfboards. The company abruptly closed its doors in November 2005 in response to scrutiny by EPA and reported violations of pollution and fire codes in California. The move has thrown confusion into the surfboard industry.

Clark Foam	.80.0%
Other	.20.0

Source: *Wall Street Journal*, November 8, 2005, p. B1, from comScore Media Metrix.

★ 1471 ★
Water Management Systems
SIC: 3088; NAICS: 326191
Sewer/Storm Water Management Market Worldwide

The company is the leader in the manufacturing of plastic waste-water management systems for sewer and storm water drain systems.

Infiltrator Systems	.80.0%
Other	.20.0

Source: *Standard-Examiner*, October 6, 2005, p. NA.

★ 1472 ★
Plastic Containers
SIC: 3089; NAICS: 326199
Top Food/Beverage Storage Containers, 2005

Market shares are shown in percent. Figures exclude Wal-Mart and other large format mass retailers.

Rubbermaid	.24.2%
Ziploc	.11.9
Glad Ware	.10.8
Thermos	3.1
Saran	0.5
Dixie	0.4
Private label	.12.8
Other	.36.7

Source: *U.S. Personal Care and Household Products Digest*, Citigroup Equity Research, February 24, 2006, p. 188, from ACNielsen.

★ 1473 ★
Plastic Containers
SIC: 3089; NAICS: 326199
Top Plastic Bucket/Bins/Pail Brands, 2005

Market shares are shown in percent. Figures exclude Wal-Mart and other large format mass retailers.

Sterilite	.25.0%
Rubbermaid	.11.7
Homz	2.8
Tamor	2.3
Cornerstone	2.1
Iris	2.0

Continued on next page.

★ 1473 ★
[Continued]
Plastic Containers
SIC: 3089; NAICS: 326199

Top Plastic Bucket/Bins/Pail Brands, 2005

Market shares are shown in percent. Figures exclude Wal-Mart and other large format mass retailers.

Private label	.25.7%
Other	.28.4

Source: *U.S. Personal Care and Household Products Digest*, Citigroup Equity Research, February 24, 2006, p. 188, from ACNielsen.

★ 1474 ★
Plastic Packaging
SIC: 3089; NAICS: 326199

Leading Beauty Product Packaging Makers in North America

Market shares are shown in percent.

Aptar	.10.0%
Alcan	. 9.0
Yoshino	. 7.0
Rexam	. 6.0
Crown	. 5.0
Other	.63.0

Source: *Packaging Unplugged*, Wachovia Securites, September 29, 2005, p. 23, from Wachovia Capital Markets, LLC estimates and company reports.

★ 1475 ★
Plastic Packaging
SIC: 3089; NAICS: 326199

Leading Flexible Packaging Makers in North America

Market shares are shown in percent. Top flexible packaging markets: meat/poultry 41%, commercial bakery 16%, sweet snacks 16%.

Sealed Air	.15.0%
Bemis	.10.0
Pactiv	. 9.0
DuPont	. 6.0
Alcan	. 5.0
Printpack	. 5.0
Tyco	. 5.0
AEA Investors	. 4.0
Pliant	. 4.0
Sigma	. 4.0

Alcoa	. 3.0%
Glad	. 3.0
Spartech	. 3.0
Other	.23.0

Source: *Global Packaging 101v.3*, Credit Suisse First Boston, September 12, 2005, p. 3, from *Plastics News* and CS First Boston.

★ 1476 ★
Plastic Packaging
SIC: 3089; NAICS: 326199

Leading Specialty Plastic Closure Makers

The industry is valued at $2.5 billion.

Owens-Illinois	.17.0%
Barry Plastics (Kerr)	.12.0
Rexam	.11.0
PAI Partners (Crown)	. 2.0
Other	.58.0

Source: *Global Packaging 101v.3*, Credit Suisse First Boston, September 12, 2005, p. 3, from Rexam and CS First Boston.

★ 1477 ★
Plastic Packaging
SIC: 3089; NAICS: 326199

Top Plastic Packaging Firms in North America

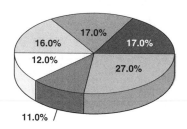

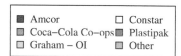

Shares are shown based on 4 billion pounds of PET resin.

Amcor	.17.0%
Coca-Cola Co-ops	.17.0
Graham - OI	.16.0
Constar	.12.0

Continued on next page.

★ 1477 ★

[Continued]
Plastic Packaging
SIC: 3089; NAICS: 326199

Top Plastic Packaging Firms in North America

Shares are shown based on 4 billion pounds of PET resin.

Plastipak	.11.0%
Other	.27.0

Source: ''First Quarter 2005 Review and Management Briefing.'' [online] from http://library. corporate-ir.net/./FINAL-1st%20Qtr%202005%20Earnings%20Release%20EN-TIRE%20SCRIPT%20(4-28-05).pdf [Published April 28, 2005] from Packaging Strategies.

★ 1478 ★

Siding
SIC: 3089; NAICS: 326199

Top Vinyl Siding Makers

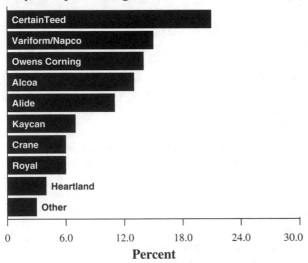

Percent

Market shares are shown in percent. Vinyl takes 30% of new residential construction (brick and stucco follow with 21% each). Vinyl takes 63% of residential repair/remodeling markets, and 59% of manufactured housing.

CertainTeed	.21.0%
Variform/Napco	.15.0
Owens Corning	.14.0
Alcoa	.13.0
Alide	.11.0
Kaycan	. 7.0
Crane	. 6.0%
Royal	. 6.0
Heartland	. 4.0
Other	. 3.0

Source: *EDGAR Online 8-K Glimpse*, May 18, 2006, p. NA, from Pure Strategy, management estimates.

SIC 31 - Leather and Leather Products

★ 1479 ★
Footwear
SIC: 3140; NAICS: 316213, 316214

Leading Fashion Footwear Makers, 2003

Market shares are shown based on $1,872 million in wholesale sales.

Skechers	.36.3%
Steven Madden	.17.1
Lugz	6.7
Diesel Footwear	5.3
Dockers	4.2
Harley-Davidson	2.4
Ugg	2.0
Panama Jack	0.5
Other	.25.5

Source: *Apparel & Footwear Yearbook*, JPMorgan North American Equity Research, January 8, 2005, p. 28, from Sporting Goods Intelligence.

★ 1480 ★
Footwear
SIC: 3140; NAICS: 316213, 316214

Leading Fashion Footwear Makers Worldwide, 2003

Market shares are shown based on $3,151 million in wholesale sales.

Skechers	.26.5%
Steven Madden	.10.3
Diesel Footwear	7.0
Dockers	5.0
Camper	4.5
Lugz	4.3
Kickers	4.0
KangaROOS	2.4
Pikolinis	2.0
Harley-Davidson	1.7
Other	.32.3

Source: *Apparel & Footwear Yearbook*, JPMorgan North American Equity Research, January 8, 2005, p. 28, from Sporting Goods Intelligence.

★ 1481 ★
Footwear
SIC: 3140; NAICS: 316213, 316214

Leading Lifestyle Casual Footwear Makers, 2003

Market shares are shown based on $1,748 million in wholesale sales.

Clarks	.21.5%
Bass	.15.2
Rockport	.15.2
Doc Martens	7.3
ECCO	6.6
Birkenstock	4.6
Dansko	4.1
Mephisto	3.1
Sperry	3.0
Josef Seibel	2.0
Caterpillar	1.7
Sebago	0.9
Other	.14.8

Source: *Apparel & Footwear Yearbook*, JPMorgan North American Equity Research, January 8, 2005, p. 28, from Sporting Goods Intelligence.

★ 1482 ★
Footwear
SIC: 3140; NAICS: 316213, 316214

Leading Lifestyle Casual Footwear Makers Worldwide, 2003

Market shares are shown based on $5,187 million in wholesale sales.

Clarks	.29.6%
ECCO	.11.4
Rockport	7.0
Geox	6.3
Birkenstock	5.8
Bass	5.5
Caterpillar	4.0
Doc Martens	3.8
Mephisto	3.5
Josef Seibel	2.3

Continued on next page.

★ 1482 ★

[Continued]
Footwear
SIC: 3140; NAICS: 316213, 316214

Leading Lifestyle Casual Footwear Makers Worldwide, 2003

Market shares are shown based on $5,187 million in wholesale sales.

Stonefly	2.3%
Other	20.9

Source: *Apparel & Footwear Yearbook*, JPMorgan North American Equity Research, January 8, 2005, p. 28, from Sporting Goods Intelligence.

★ 1483 ★

Footwear
SIC: 3140; NAICS: 316213, 316214

Leading Rugged Footwear Makers, 2003

Market shares are shown based on $1,537 million in wholesale sales.

Timberland	46.4%
Merrell	10.4
Wolverine	10.4
Columbia	4.0
Teva	3.6
LaCrosse	3.4
Hi-Tec Sports	3.3
Rocky	3.1
Other	15.3

Source: *Apparel & Footwear Yearbook*, JPMorgan North American Equity Research, January 8, 2005, p. 37, from Sporting Goods Intelligence.

★ 1484 ★

Footwear
SIC: 3140; NAICS: 316213, 316214

Leading Rugged Footwear Makers Worldwide, 2003

Market shares are shown based on $2,825 million in wholesale sales.

Timberland	36.0%
Merrell	10.3
Hi-Tec Sports	6.5
Wolverine	6.2
Columbia	4.2
Salomon	3.6
Genfoot/Kamik	3.3

Grisport	3.3%
Other	26.6

Source: *Apparel & Footwear Yearbook*, JPMorgan North American Equity Research, January 8, 2005, p. 37, from Sporting Goods Intelligence.

★ 1485 ★

Slippers
SIC: 3142; NAICS: 316212

Slipper Shipments by Year, 1999-2001

Shipments are shown in millions of dollars. Top brands in the early 2000s: Dearfoams and Isotoners.

1999	$ 152.6
2000	152.3
2001	130.2

Source: "House Slippers." [online] from http://www.reference forbusiness.com/industries/Slippers [Accessed November 14, 2005] from U.S. Bureau of the Census.

★ 1486 ★

Footwear
SIC: 3144; NAICS: 316214

China and Women's Shoe Market, 2005

Data show China's share of the shoe market in the United States. There are 15 million shoes made each year in the United States.

Synthetic shoes	95.0%
Athletic shoes	85.0
Women's leather shoes	45.0

Source: *Pacific Shipper*, May 5, 2006, p. NA, from American Apparel and Footwear Association.

★ 1487 ★
Leather Goods
SIC: 3161; NAICS: 316991
Travel Goods Sales

Figures are in thousands of dollars. Cases include brief cases and computer cases.

	2002	2003	2004
Travel/sports bags	$ 5,437,325	$ 5,344,426	$ 5,958,020
Handbags . . .	4,037,660	4,618,469	5,890,451
Luggage & cases	2,164,824	2,041,880	2,356,893
Flatgoods . . .	2,104,114	2,172,313	2,445,327
Backpacks . .	909,965	965,110	1,047,650

Source: "State of the Travel Goods Market." [online] from http://www.travel-goods.org [Accessed November 1, 2005] from Travel Goods Association and U.S. Bureau of the Census.

★ 1488 ★
Luggage
SIC: 3161; NAICS: 316991
Luggage Market in India

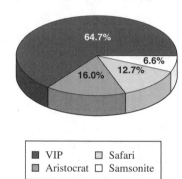

VIP   Safari
Aristocrat   Samsonite

Market shares are for the Rs 500 crore branded market. The entire industry is worth Rs 1,200 crore.

VIP	.64.7%
Aristocrat	.16.0
Safari	.12.7
Samsonite	6.6

Source: "Rule of Three in India." [online] from http://www.bitsaa.org/sandpaper/research/research.htm [Accessed May 15, 2006].

★ 1489 ★
Handbags
SIC: 3171; NAICS: 316992
Handbag Sales, 2005

Handbag sales reached $5.6 billion in 2005, up 10% from 2000. Most of this growth came in the previous year. According to the source, one woman in ten spends more than $150 on a purse. Most women spend $40-65. Luxury brands include Coach and Louis Vuitton.

Luxury	.43.5%
Down-market ($50 and less)	.35.6
Other	.20.9

Source: *DSN Retailing Today*, February 27, 2006, p. 19, from Mintel.

SIC 32 - Stone, Clay, and Glass Products

★ 1490 ★
Glass
SIC: 3211; NAICS: 327211
Flat Glass Use in the Global Building Industry

Figures are in millions of euros.

	(mil.)	Share
New building . . . .€	14,000	41.7%
Refurbishment	14,000	41.7
Interior	5,575	16.6

Source: "Pilkington and the Flat Glass Industry 2004." [online] from http://www.pilkington.com/resources/ section104.pdf [Accessed November 25, 2005].

★ 1491 ★
Glass
SIC: 3211; NAICS: 327211
Top Flat Glass Makers in Europe, 2003

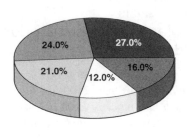

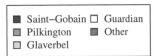
- Saint–Gobain □ Guardian
- Pilkington ■ Other
- Glaverbel

Data show percentage of flat/sheet capacity. The market size was 8 million tons.

Saint-Gobain	.27.0%
Pilkington	.24.0
Glaverbel	.21.0
Guardian	.12.0
Other	.16.0

Source: "Pilkington and the Flat Glass Industry 2004." [online] from http://www.pilkington.com/resources/ section104.pdf [Accessed November 25, 2005].

★ 1492 ★
Glass
SIC: 3211; NAICS: 327211
Top Flat Glass Makers in North America, 2003

Data show percentage of flat/sheet capacity. North America includes the United States, Canada, Mexico and the Caribbean.

Asahi (AFG)	.21.0%
PPG	.21.0
Guardian Industries	.20.0
Pilkington (not VVP)	.14.0
Vitro	. 8.0
Visteon	. 6.0
Other	. 2.0

Source: "Pilkington and the Flat Glass Industry 2004." [online] from http://www.pilkington.com/resources/ section104.pdf [Accessed November 25, 2005].

★ 1493 ★
Glass
SIC: 3211; NAICS: 327211
Top Flat Glass Makers Worldwide

The top four firms supply 60% of the market. The top three in the auto industry supply 74% of the market. Data show percentage of world capacity.

Asahi	.22.0%
Pilkington	.15.0
Saint-Gobain	.13.0
Guardian Industries	.12.0
Other	.38.0

Source: "Pilkington and the Flat Glass Industry 2004." [online] from http://www.pilkington.com/resources/ section104.pdf [Accessed November 25, 2005].

★ 1494 ★

Glass

SIC: 3211; NAICS: 327211

Top Glass Makers in Northern Europe, 2004

The industry was valued at 1.6 billion pounds.

OI	.30.0%
Rexam	.27.0
Saint-Gobain	.12.0
Ardagh	.11.0
Other	.20.0

Source: "Rexam Investors." [online] from http://www.rex-am.com/index.asp?pageid523 [Published January 17, 2006] from Rexam estimates.

★ 1495 ★

Glass

SIC: 3211; NAICS: 327211

Top Sheet Glass Makers in Japan, 2004

Market shares are shown based on domestic shipments of 334.1 million square meters.

Asahi Glass	.41.2%
Nippon Sheet Glass	.30.9
Central Glass	.18.0
PPG-CI	1.8
Guardian Industries	1.7
Other	6.4

Source: "2004 Market Share Report." [online] from http://www.nikkei.co.jp [Published July 27, 2005] from Nikkei estimates.

★ 1496 ★

Glass Containers

SIC: 3221; NAICS: 327213

Glass Consumer Packaging Industry Worldwide

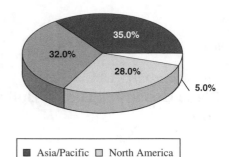

The industry is valued at $350 billion.

Asia/Pacific	.35.0%
Europe	.32.0
North America	.28.0
Latin America	5.0

Source: "Glass Executive Summary." [online] from http://www.packagingdigest.com/pdf/sim_rigidFlex.pdf [Accessed January 30, 2006].

★ 1497 ★

Glass Containers

SIC: 3221; NAICS: 327213

Largest Glass Container Producers Worldwide, 2000 and 2005

Glass container production worldwide is forecast to grow to 53 million tons from 2000 to 2005. Much of this growth will take place in Eastern Europe. Production in North America is expected to continue to fall.

	2000	2005
United States	9,348,040	8,260,000
China	7,300,000	7,700,000
South Korea	4,250,000	4,450,000
Germany	4,256,815	4,040,000
France	3,826,545	3,835,000
Italy	3,248,000	3,150,000
Spain	1,967,000	2,010,000
Mexico	2,085,000	1,950,000

Source: *International Glass Review*, Summer 2005, p. 4, from ITC and DMG.

★ 1498 ★
Barware
SIC: 3229; NAICS: 327212

Home Barware Sales, 2004

Total sales were $1,426.41 million in 2004, up from $1,314.18 milllion in 2003. "Other" includes corkscrews, ice buckets and similar bar tools.

Glass & crystal drinkware 40.0%
Glass & crystal sets, decanters and related
  items 33.0
Other 27.0

Source: *HFN*, July 11, 2005, p. 24.

★ 1499 ★
Glass Containers
SIC: 3229; NAICS: 327212

Leading Glass Container Makers in North America

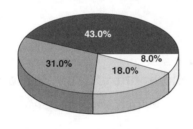

| ■ Owens–Illinois | □ Anchor Glass Container |
| ■ Saint–Gobain | □ Other |

The market is estimated to be worth $4.2 billion and 35 billion units. The end markets for glass containers: beer 52%, food 24% and soft drinks 12%.

Owens-Illinois 43.0%
Saint-Gobain 31.0
Anchor Glass Container 18.0
Other 8.0

Source: *Packaging Unplugged*, Wachovia Securites, September 29, 2005, p. 23, from Wachovia Capital Markets, LLC estimates and company reports.

★ 1500 ★
Glass Containers
SIC: 3229; NAICS: 327212

Leading Glass Containers in Europe, 2005

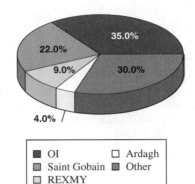

■ OI	□ Ardagh
■ Saint Gobain	■ Other
□ REXMY	

Market shares by segment: beer 37%, food 23%, wine 19%, spirits 11% and tea & juice 10%.

OI 35.0%
Saint Gobain 22.0
REXMY 9.0
Ardagh 4.0
Other 30.0

Source: *Packaging Industry*, North American Equity Research, October 8, 2005, p. 5, from JPMorgan estimates and company reports.

★ 1501 ★
Auto Mirrors
SIC: 3231; NAICS: 327215

Automatic Dimming Mirror Market Worldwide, 2005

Gentex estimates that auto-dimming mirrors have 50% market penetration of the 59 million vehicles produced annually worldwide. Murakami Kaimeido has less than 0.1% of the market.

Gentex 80.0%
Magna Donnelly 17.0
Tokai Rika 2.9
Murakami Kaimeido 0.1

Source: "The Gentex Edge." [online] from http://library.corporate-ir.net/library/72/721/72190/items/188728/Summary-IRpresentationMarch2006.pdf.

★ 1502 ★
Auto Mirrors
SIC: 3231; NAICS: 327215

Exterior Mirror Market in India

Market shares are shown based on volume.

Schefenacker	.50.0%
KTL	.20.0
Ficosa	.18.0
Sandahar	.3.0
Other	.9.0

Source: "Third Quarter Results 2005." [online] http://www.schefenacker-ir.com/pdf/Presentation_Conference_Call_10_November_2005.pdf [Published Nov. 10, 2005] from Schefenacker estimates.

★ 1503 ★
Auto Mirrors
SIC: 3231; NAICS: 327215

Exterior Mirror Market in Western Europe

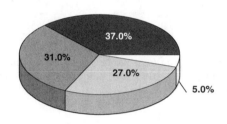

Legend: ■ Schefenacker ▨ Ficosa □ Magna Donnelly □ Other

Market shares are shown based on volume.

Schefenacker	.37.0%
Ficosa	.31.0
Magna Donnelly	.27.0
Other	.5.0

Source: "Third Quarter Results 2005." [online] http://www.schefenacker-ir.com/pdf/Presentation_Conference_Call_10_November_2005.pdf [Published Nov. 10, 2005] from Schefenacker estimates.

★ 1504 ★
Auto Mirrors
SIC: 3231; NAICS: 327215

Exterior Mirror Market Worldwide

Market shares are shown based on volume.

Schefenacker	.27.0%
Magna Donnelly	.26.0
Ficosa	.12.0

Murakami	.10.0%
Ichikoh	.6.0
Other	.19.0

Source: "Third Quarter Results 2005." [online] http://www.schefenacker-ir.com/pdf/Presentation_Conference_Call_10_November_2005.pdf [Published Nov. 10, 2005] from JD Power, Schefenacker estimates and CSM Worldwide.

★ 1505 ★
Auto Mirrors
SIC: 3231; NAICS: 327215

Global Auto Mirror Market

Market shares are shown in percent.

Gentex	.77.0%
Other	.23.0

Source: "Preparing for the Future." [online] from http://www.oesa.org/pdf/presentations/110804_Bauer_Gentex.pdf [Published November 8, 2004], p. NA.

★ 1506 ★
Skylights
SIC: 3231; NAICS: 327215

Tubular Skylight Industry Worldwide

Nearly 1 million Solatubes have been sold worldwide.

Solatube	.85.0%
Other	.15.0

Source: "Becoming a Solatube Dealer." [online] from http://www.solatube.com/dealer_opportunities.php [Accessed April 4, 2006].

★ 1507 ★
Cement
SIC: 3241; NAICS: 32731
Largest Cement Firms in West Bengal, India

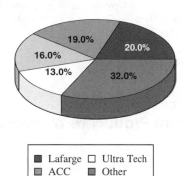

Market shares are shown in percent.

Lafarge	.20.0%
ACC	.19.0
ACEL	.16.0
Ultra Tech	.13.0
Other	.32.0

Source: "Ambuja Cement to Invest Rs 115 cr in Farakka Unit." [online] from http://cities.expressindia.com/full-story.php?newsid159379 [Accessed July 1, 2006].

★ 1508 ★
Cement
SIC: 3241; NAICS: 32731
Largest Cement Makers in Japan, 2004

Market shares are shown based on domestic shipments of 57.56 million tons.

Taiheiyo Cement	.36.0%
Ube-Mitsubishi Cement	.24.4
Sumitomo Osaka Cement	.19.1
Tokuyama	. 7.7
Aso Lafarge Cement	. 3.6
Other	. 9.2

Source: "2004 Market Share Report." [online] from http://www.nikkei.co.jp [Published July 27, 2005] from Nikkei estimates and Japan Cement Association.

★ 1509 ★
Cement
SIC: 3241; NAICS: 32731
Portland Cement Consumption by State

Data are in thousands of tons.

	(000)	Share
California	14,222	12.40%
Texas	13,096	11.42
Florida	9,698	8.45
Arizona	4,118	3.59
Georgia	4,109	3.58
Ohio	3,999	3.49
Illinois	3,939	3.43
Pennsylvania	3,396	2.96
New York	3,227	2.81
Michigan	3,175	2.77
Other	51,737	45.10

Source: *North American Cement Industry Yearbook*, Annual 2005, p. 27, from Portland Cement Association and Canadian Portland Cement Industry.

★ 1510 ★
Cement
SIC: 3241; NAICS: 32731
Top Cement Firms in Canada, 2002

Companies are ranked by clinker capacity in thousands of metric tons.

	(000)	Share
Lafarge Canada Inc.	5,564	34.8%
St. Lawrence Cement Inc.	2,783	17.4
St. Marys Cement Inc.	2,619	16.4
Essroc Canada	1,116	7.0
Lehigh Northwest Cement	1,116	7.0

Source: *North American Cement Industry Yearbook*, Annual 2005, p. 27, from Portland Cement Association and Canadian Portland Cement Industry.

★ 1511 ★
Cement
SIC: 3241; NAICS: 32731

Top Cement Firms in Eastern India

The region consumes 18.5 million tons each year. Market shares are shown in percent.

Lafarge India 20.0%
ACC 19.0
Ultra Tech Cement 13.0
Ambuja Cement Eastern 9.0
Other 39.0

Source: *Asia Africa Intelligence Wire*, September 2, 2005, p. NA.

★ 1512 ★
Cement
SIC: 3241; NAICS: 32731

Top Cement Firms in India

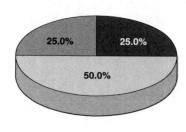

■ Aditya Birla Group □ Other
■ Holcim

Market shares are shown in percent.

Aditya Birla Group 25.0%
Holcim 25.0
Other 50.0

Source: *India Business Insight*, April 30, 2006, p. NA.

★ 1513 ★
Cement
SIC: 3241; NAICS: 32731

Top Cement Makers, 2003

Companies are ranked by clinker capacity in thousands of tons as of December 31, 2003.

	(000)	Share
Cemex	12,771	13.8%
Lafarge North America Inc.	12,731	13.7
Holcim	11,960	12.9
Buzzi Unicem	7,253	7.8
Ash Grove Cement Company	6,334	6.8
Lehigh Cement Company	5,613	6.1

	(000)	Share
Texas Industries	4,536	4.9%
Essroc Cement	4,442	4.8
California Portland Cement Co. . . .	3,301	3.6
Eagle Materials	1,651	1.8

Source: *North American Cement Industry Yearbook*, Annual 2005, p. 27, from Portland Cement Association and Canadian Portland Cement Industry.

★ 1514 ★
Cement
SIC: 3241; NAICS: 32731

Top Cement Producers Worldwide, 2005

Data show mine production in thousands of metric tons. Cement went to ready-mixed concrete 75%, 14% went to concrete production and 6% went to contractors (mainly road paving) and 5% went to other uses.

	(000)	Share
China	1,000,000	45.05%
India	130,000	5.86
United States	99,100	4.46
Japan	66,000	2.97
Korea, Rep. Of	50,000	2.25
Spain	48,000	2.16
Russia	45,000	2.03
Thailand	40,000	1.80
Brazil	39,000	1.76
Other	702,900	31.66

Source: *Mineral Commodities Summaries 2006*, Annual, p. 21, from U.S. Geological Survey, U.S. Department of the Interior.

★ 1515 ★
Ceramics
SIC: 3250; NAICS: 327121, 327122, 327331

Advanced Ceramic Components, 2004 and 2009

Sales are shown in millions of dollars. Structural ceramics had an average annual growth rate of 15%, chemical coatings grew 7.6%, electronic ceramics grew 7.5%, chemical processing and environmental related grew 7%.

	2004	2009	Share
Electronic ceramics	$ 6,060	$ 8,700	62.46%
Chemical processing and environmental related . . .	1,660	2,330	16.73
Ceramic coatings	1,108	1,600	11.49
Structural ceramics	650	1,300	9.33

Source: *Ceramic Industry*, June 2005, p. 15, from BCC Inc.

★ 1516 ★
Bricks
SIC: 3251; NAICS: 327121, 327331

Brick Market in Slovakia

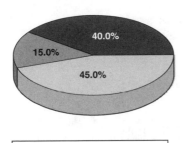

Market shares are shown in percent.

Bramac	.40.0%
Tondach Slovensko	.15.0
Other	.45.0

Source: *Europe Intelligence Wire*, January 31, 2006, p. NA.

★ 1517 ★
Bricks
SIC: 3251; NAICS: 327121, 327331

Leading Brick Makers in North America, 2003

The top six firms are Vulcan, Martin Marietta, Hanson, Lafarge, CRH, and Rinker.

Top six	.34.0%
Other	.66.0

Source: "Hanson PLC A World Leader." [online] from http://www.hanson.com [Accessed January 30, 2006] from JPMorgan.

★ 1518 ★
Tiles
SIC: 3251; NAICS: 327121

Roof Tile Market in the Philippines

Market shares are shown in percent.

CMPI	.64.0%
Other	.36.0

Source: *BusinessWorld*, August 31, 2005, p. NA.

★ 1519 ★
Tiles
SIC: 3253; NAICS: 327122

Ceramic Floor Tile Sales in the U.K., 2007 amd 2010

The industry was split almost evenly between the retail and contract categories in 2005 (33 million square meters retail, 34 million square meters contract). By 2010, the gap will increase slightly, with retail taking 35.1 million and contract taking 40.6 million square meters. The contracting category will benefit from government spending on new buildings and leisure facilities, particularly those related to the Olympics. MRI believes the ceramic tile industry is affected by many factors such as hygiene demands, cost, wider product selection and number of retail outlets.

	2007	2010	Share
Porcelain	21.2	25.9	61.67%
Natural stone	7.4	10.1	24.05
Unglazed tiles	2.4	3.2	7.62
Terracotta	0.7	0.6	1.43
Other	2.1	2.2	5.24

Source: *Contract Flooring Journal*, May 2006, p. 38, from Trade and Marketing Research for Industry forecasts.

★ 1520 ★
Tiles
SIC: 3253; NAICS: 327122

Leading Ceramic Floor Tile Makers, 2002

Market shares are shown in percent.

Mohawk	.53.0%
ITW	. 6.0
Marazzi	. 6.0
Roca	. 6.0
Other	.29.0

Source: "U.S. Market for Floor Coverings." [online] from http://www.osec.ch [Published December 2004].

★ 1521 ★
Plumbing Fixtures
SIC: 3261; NAICS: 327111

Leading Pottery/Ceramic/Plumbing Fixture Makers, 2005

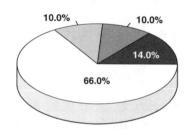

10.0%   10.0%

14.0%

66.0%

■ AVX Corporation □ ARC International
■ American Standard □ Other

AVX Corporation had 12.0%-14.0% of the market while American Standard and ARC International each took 8.0%-10.0% of the market.

AVX Corporation	.14.0%
American Standard	.10.0
ARC International	.10.0
Other	.66.0

Source: "Pottery, Ceramics and Plumbing Fixture Manufacturing." [online] from http://www.ibisworld.com [Accessed May 2, 2006] from IBISWorld.

★ 1522 ★
Plumbing Fixtures
SIC: 3261; NAICS: 327111

Leading Toilet Makers in China

Market shares are shown for fiscal year 2001.

Toto	.35.0%
American Standard	.32.0

Kohler	.17.0%
HCG	.16.0

Source: "Toto Annual Report 2001." [online] from http://www.toto.co.jp [Accessed November 1, 2005] from Toto.

★ 1523 ★
Plumbing Fixtures
SIC: 3261; NAICS: 327111

Top Sanitary Ceramic Makers in Japan, 2004

Market shares are shown based on domestic shipments of 8.18 million units.

Toto	.61.9%
Inax	.29.0
Janis	. 4.0
Asahi Eito	. 3.9
Other	. 1.2

Source: "2004 Market Share Report." [online] from http://www.nikkei.co.jp [Published July 27, 2005] from Nikkei estimates and Ministry of Economy, Trade and Industry.

★ 1524 ★
Spas
SIC: 3261; NAICS: 327111

Leading Spa Makers

Shares are shown based on 400,680 units.

Jacuzzi (Sundance)	.16.0%
Hot Springs	.14.0
Other	.70.0

Source: "Jacuzzi Brands Investor Presentation." [online] from http://www.jacuzzibrands.com [Published October 27, 2005] from Aristech LLC.

★ 1525 ★
Whirlpools
SIC: 3261; NAICS: 327111

Leading Whirlpool Bath Makers

Shares are shown based on 600,000 units.

Jacuzzi	.31.0%
American Standard	.23.0
Kohler	.14.0
MAAX	. 9.0
Other	.22.0

Source: "Jacuzzi Brands Investor Presentation." [online] from http://www.jacuzzibrands.com [Published October 27, 2005] from company estimates and U.S. Bureau of the Census.

★ 1526 ★
Whirlpools
SIC: 3261; NAICS: 327111

Leading Whirlpool Bath Makers in Europe, 2004

Shares are shown based on 547,000 units. Figures are based on 30 countries.

Jacuzzi Europe	.10.0%
Roca	. 6.7
Spa Tech	. 5.9
Sanitec	. 4.7
Teuco	. 4.2
V&B	. 3.2
Other	.65.3

Source: ''Jacuzzi Brands Investor Presentation.'' [online] from http://www.jacuzzibrands.com [Published October 27, 2005] from GB Consult.

★ 1527 ★
Dinnerware
SIC: 3262; NAICS: 327112

Fine China Unit Sales, 2005

Sales are shown by accent. Data are from June 2004 - May 2005. There were 3.762 billion units sold worth $153.4 billion.

Platinum	.49.8%
Gold	.27.0
None	.22.9
Gold & platinum	. 0.2
Silver	. 0.1

Source: *DSN Retailing Today*, August 8, 2005, p. 15, from NPD Group/NPD Houseworld/POS.

★ 1528 ★
Concrete
SIC: 3272; NAICS: 32739

Concrete Paver Market in North America

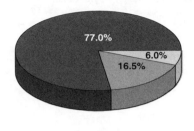

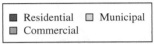

The North American concrete paver market has more than doubled since 1999. The market was placed at 630 million square feet in the United States and 80 million square feet in Canada.

Residential	.77.0%
Commercial	.16.5
Municipal	. 6.0

Source: *Concrete Products*, November 1, 2005, p. NA, from Industry Insights.

★ 1529 ★
Concrete
SIC: 3272; NAICS: 32739

How Concrete is Used, 2004

Figures are in millions of cubic yards.

	(mil.)	Share
Residential	199	41.12%
Pavement	145	29.96
Commercial	32	6.61
Other	108	22.31

Source: *Concrete Construction*, November 2005, p. 33.

★ 1530 ★
Plasterboard
SIC: 3275; NAICS: 32742

Leading Plasterboard Makers in Japan, 2003

Market shares are shown in percent.

Yoshino Group 78.0%
Other 22.0

Source: "Yoshino Gypsum." [online] from http://www. yoshino-gypsum.com/en/company/gaiyou.html [Accessed October 26, 2005].

★ 1531 ★
Abrasives
SIC: 3291; NAICS: 32791

Abrasives (Manufactured) Production Worldwide, 2005

Data are in metric tons based on fused aluminum oxide capacity.

	(000)	Share
China	700,000	58.82%
Germany	80,000	6.72
United States/Canada	60,400	5.08
Austria	60,000	5.04
Other	289,600	24.34

Source: *Mineral Commodities Summaries 2006*, Annual, p. 21, from U.S. Geological Survey, U.S. Department of the Interior.

★ 1532 ★
Scouring Pads
SIC: 3291; NAICS: 32791

Top Scouring Pad Brands, 2005

Total sales were $259 million. Figures exclude Wal-Mart and other large format mass retailers.

Scotch-Brite 38.6%
S.O.S. 16.4
O-Cel-O 9.7
Brillo 6.3
Chore Boy 4.6
Arden 1.3
Private label 11.1
Other 12.0

Source: *U.S. Personal Care and Household Products Digest*, Citigroup Equity Research, February 24, 2006, p. 65, from ACNielsen.

★ 1533 ★
Scouring Pads
SIC: 3291; NAICS: 32791

Top Scouring Pad Makers, 2005

Market shares are shown in percent. Figures exclude Wal-Mart and other large format mass retailers.

Minnesota Mining 48.2%
Clorox Company 16.7
Church & Dwight 6.3
GTCR Golden Rauner 4.6
Arden Corporation 1.3
Other 11.1

Source: *U.S. Personal Care and Household Products Digest*, Citigroup Equity Research, February 24, 2006, p. 65, from ACNielsen.

★ 1534 ★
Insulation
SIC: 3292; NAICS: 327993

Insulation Market in Australia, 2001 and 2005

The market grew from A$370 million in 2001 to A$445 million in 2005.

	2001	2005	Share
Glasswool	$ 149	$ 185	41.57%
Foil	62	74	16.63
Polyester	49	54	12.13
Cellulose	45	38	8.54
Rockwool	13	29	6.52
Other	52	65	14.61

Source: "Analysts Briefing." [online] from http://www. fletcherbuilding.co.nz [Published October 2005] from management estimates.

★ 1535 ★

Insulation

SIC: 3296; NAICS: 327993

Insulation Sales by Type, 2005 and 2010

Fiberglass remains the leading insulation material in use. Demand is forecast to increase from 7.7 billion in 2005 to 9.78 billion in 2010.

	2005	2010	Share
Fiberglass	3,890	4,705	48.08%
Foamed plastic	3,410	4,500	45.99
Reflective/radiant	150	265	2.71
Other	265	315	3.22

Source: *Research Studies - Freedonia Group*, June 22, 2006, p. 1, from Freedonia Group.

★ 1536 ★

Mineral Wool

SIC: 3296; NAICS: 327993

Mineral Wool Shipments by Year, 1999-2001

This industry's products include mineral wool acoustical board and tile, fiberglass insulation, glasswool, mineral wool roofing mats, and insulation. Shipments are shown in millions of dollars.

1999	$ 4.47
2000	4.53
2001	4.52

Source: ''Mineral Wool.'' [online] from http://www.referenceforbusiness.com/industries/Stone-Clay-Glass-Products [Accessed November 14, 2005] from U.S. Bureau of the Census.

SIC 33 - Primary Metal Industries

★ 1537 ★
Service Centers
SIC: 3312; NAICS: 331111

Leading Service Centers, 2005

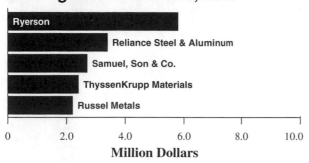

Million Dollars

Firms are ranked by revenue in millions of dollars.

Ryerson	$ 5.8
Reliance Steel & Aluminum	3.4
Samuel, Son & Co.	2.7
ThyssenKrupp Materials	2.4
Russel Metals	2.2

Source: *Investor's Business Daily*, May 31, 2006, p. A7, from *Purchasing*, International Iron and Steel Institute and Goldman Sachs.

★ 1538 ★
Steel
SIC: 3312; NAICS: 331111

Steel Industry Worldwide

Data are in millions of metric tons.

	2005	2006	2007
Asia	500.4	507.8	506.8
European Union	165.0	165.0	165.0
NAFTA	134.0	135.0	135.0
Former U.S.S.R.	118.0	122.0	125.0
South America	45.0	47.0	49.0
Africa	17.5	18.0	18.5
Middle East	15.0	16.0	16.5
Oceania	9.0	9.0	9.0

Source: *Steel Times International*, September 2005, p. 28, from International Iron and Steel Institute, MEPS and VAI.

★ 1539 ★
Steel
SIC: 3312; NAICS: 331111

Steel Production by State

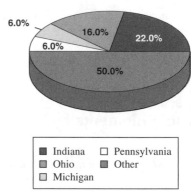

■ Indiana	□ Pennsylvania
■ Ohio	■ Other
□ Michigan	

The top four states hold % of raw steel production. Warehouses and steel service centers take 23% of shipments, followed by construction with 15%, transportation 13% and other 49%.

Indiana	22.0%
Ohio	16.0
Michigan	6.0
Pennsylvania	6.0
Other	50.0

Source: *Mineral Commodities Summaries 2006*, Annual, p. 21, from U.S. Geological Survey, U.S. Department of the Interior.

★ 1540 ★
Steel
SIC: 3312; NAICS: 331111

Top Automotive Steel Makers Worldwide

Arcelor and Severstal agreed to a merger in May 2006.

Arcelor/Severstal	22.0%
Nippon Steel	9.0
Mittal Steel	8.0
Other	61.0

Source: *Russia & CIS Business and Financial Newswire*, May 29, 2006, p. NA, from Arcelor estimates.

★ 1541 ★
Steel
SIC: 3312; NAICS: 331111

Top Finished Steel Suppliers Worldwide, 2005

Mittal Steel includes ISG production. Market shares are estimated in percent.

Mittal Steel	6.0%
Arcelor	5.0
JFE	3.0
Nippon Steel	2.0
POSCO	2.0
US Steel	2.0
Other	80.0

Source: *Basic Materials*, Morgan Stanley Equity Research, December 14, 2005, p. 38, from International Iron and Steel Institute and Morgan Stanley research.

★ 1542 ★
Steel
SIC: 3312; NAICS: 331111

Top Stainless Steel Makers in Japan, 2004

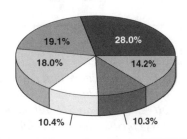

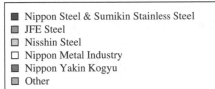

- ■ Nippon Steel & Sumikin Stainless Steel
- ■ JFE Steel
- ▨ Nisshin Steel
- ☐ Nippon Metal Industry
- ▨ Nippon Yakin Kogyu
- ▨ Other

Market shares are shown based on domestic production of 3.43 million tons.

Nippon Steel & Sumikin Stainless Steel	28.0%
JFE Steel	19.1
Nisshin Steel	18.0
Nippon Metal Industry	10.4
Nippon Yakin Kogyu	10.3
Other	14.2

Source: "2004 Market Share Report." [online] from http://www.nikkei.co.jp [Published July 27, 2005] from Nikkei estimates.

★ 1543 ★
Steel
SIC: 3312; NAICS: 331111

Top Steel Firms in Japan, 2004

Market shares are shown based on domestic output of 112.89 million tons.

Nippon Steel	29.0%
JFE Steel	27.7
Sumitomo Metal Industries	11.4
Kobe Steel	6.8
Nisshin Steel	3.6
Other	21.5

Source: "2004 Market Share Report." [online] from http://www.nikkei.co.jp [Published July 27, 2005] from Japan Iron and Steel Federation.

★ 1544 ★
Steel
SIC: 3312; NAICS: 331111

Top Steel Firms in Russia

Roughly 86% of the country's total steel output is concentrated among the top ten companies.

Severstal/MMK/NLMK	47.0%
EvrazGroup	38.0
Other	15.0

Source: *Steel Times International*, May - June 2005, p. 60.

★ 1545 ★
Steel
SIC: 3312; NAICS: 331111

Top Steel Firms Worldwide

Companies are ranked by production in millions of tons.

Mittal	57.0
Arcelor	42.8
Nippon Steel	31.3
JFE	30.2
POSCO	28.9
Corus, Netherlands	19.1
Shanghai Baosteel	9.9

Source: *India Abroad*, April 1, 2005, p. 1.

★ 1546 ★
Cable and Coils
SIC: 3315; NAICS: 331222, 332618
Structure Cable Industry Worldwide

Data are based on a study of 20 countries. The industry is forecast to grow 2.8% between 2004 and 2007.

United States	.43.7%
Germany	.10.0
United Kingdom	9.4
China	6.0
France	5.3
Other	.25.6

Source: *Cabling Installation & Maintenance*, June 2005, p. 20, from Building Services Research Industry Association.

★ 1547 ★
Cable and Coils
SIC: 3315; NAICS: 331222, 332618
Top Hot-Rolled Coil Firms in Japan, 2004

Market shares are shown based on domestic production of 43.29 million tons.

Nippon Steel	.36.0%
JFE Holdings	.35.1
Sumitomo Metal Indsutries	.12.5
Nisshin Steel	6.7
Kobe Steel	6.1
Other	3.6

Source: "2004 Market Share Report." [online] from http://www.nikkei.co.jp [Published July 27, 2005] from Nikkei estimates.

★ 1548 ★
Minimills
SIC: 3317; NAICS: 33121
Largest Minimill Makers in North America

Firms are ranked by production in thousands of tons. The top three firms take 53% of the market, 18% imports and with other players taking 29% of the market. Market size was 34 million tons.

Nucor	9.4
GNA	6.4
Commercial Metals	2.4

Source: "Investor Presentation." [online] from http://www.gerdauameristeel.com/documents/Investor-PresentationSep05.pdf [Published Sep. 2005].

★ 1549 ★
Tubing
SIC: 3317; NAICS: 33121
Radiant Heating Tubing

Total hydronic radiant tubing was over 331 million linear feet.

Half-inch	.70.5%
Five-eighths	.10.8
Three-eighths	9.6

Source: *Supply House Times*, July 2005, p. 29, from Radiant Panel Association.

★ 1550 ★
Waterworks
SIC: 3317; NAICS: 33121
Waterworks Market Shares

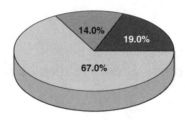

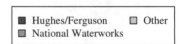

The waterworks industry includes pipes, fittings, valves, meters and other products used in the transportation of water. It represents an $11 billion piece of the $120 pro/heavy construction/industrial channel.

Hughes/Ferguson	.19.0%
National Waterworks	.14.0
Other	.67.0

Source: *Home Channel News*, August 8, 2005, p. 1.

★ 1551 ★
Foundries
SIC: 3321; NAICS: 331511

Fabless Semiconductor Foundry Market Worldwide

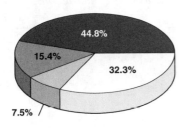

- ■ Taiwan Semiconductor Manufacturing
- ■ United Microelectronics
- ■ Semiconductor Manufacturing International...
- □ Other

According to Wikipedia, "A fabless semiconductor company specializes in the design and sale of hardware devices implemented on semiconductor chips. It achieves an advantage by outsourcing the fabrication of the devices to a specialized semiconductor manufacturer called a semiconductor foundry." Market shares are shown in percent.

Taiwan Semiconductor Manufacturing	.44.8%
United Microelectronics	.15.4
Semiconductor Manufacturing International Corp. of China	7.5
Other	.32.3

Source: *Electronic Engineering Times*, May 22, 2006, p. 46, from Gartner Dataquest.

★ 1552 ★
Foundries
SIC: 3321; NAICS: 331511

Largest Foundries Worldwide

Foundries are ranked by revenues in millions of dollars. TSMC - Taiwan Semiconductor Manufacturing; UMC - United Microelectronics; SMIC stands for Semiconductor Manufacturing International Corp. of China.

TSMC	$ 8,128
UMC	4,082
SMIC	975
Chartered	932

Source: *Electronic Business*, December 2005, p. 24, from Hoovers.

★ 1553 ★
Foundries
SIC: 3321; NAICS: 331511

Specialty Foundry Sales Worldwide

Sales are in millions of dollars. TSMC and UMC represent about 70% of the $16.4 billion foundry industry. Smaller firms are doing well, however.

Jazz	$ 223
X-Fab	177
ASMC	141
Tower	126
Episil	106
1st Silicon	87

Source: *Electronic Business*, August 2005, p. 22, from iSuppli.

★ 1554 ★
Foundries
SIC: 3321; NAICS: 331511

Top Foundries in China, 2004

Total foundry revenue were $2.31 billion in 2004. Forecast revenue were $2.61 billion in 2006 and $2.92 billion in 2007.

	($ mil.)	Share
SMIC	$ 975	42.0%
HHNBC	254	11.0
Hejian Tech	239	10.0
GSMC	148	6.0
ASMC	141	6.0
CSMC	64	3.0
Other	489	21.0

Source: *Electronic News*, June 20, 2005, p. NA, from iSuppli.

★ 1555 ★
Copper
SIC: 3331; NAICS: 331411

How Copper is Used

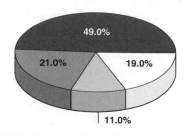

Building construction **Transportation equipment**
Electronics **Other**

Domestic mine production was 1.15 million tons and valued at $4.3 billion.

Building construction	.49.0%
Electronics	.21.0
Transportation equipment	.11.0
Other	.19.0

Source: *Mineral Commodities Summaries 2006*, Annual, p. 21, from U.S. Geological Survey, U.S. Department of the Interior.

★ 1556 ★
Copper
SIC: 3331; NAICS: 331411

Largest Copper Suppliers Worldwide

Firms are ranked by production in thousands of tons.

	(000)	Share
Codelco	1,885	12.5%
BHP Billiton	1,203	8.0
Phelps Dodge	1,150	7.6
Southern Copper/Grupo Mexico . . .	780	5.2
Rio Tinto	731	4.9
Anglo American	728	4.8
Freeport Copper	667	4.4
KGHM Polska Miedz	499	3.3
Falconbridge	480	3.2
Antofagasta plc	457	3.0

Source: *Basic Materials*, Morgan Stanley Equity Research, December 14, 2005, p. 38, from Morgan Stanley Research and Chemical Marketing Associates Inc.

★ 1557 ★
Aluminum
SIC: 3334; NAICS: 331312

Aluminum Production by Country, 2005

Figures are in thousands of metric tons.

	(000)	Share
China	7,200	24.13%
Russia	3,650	12.23
Canada	2,800	9.38
United States	2,500	8.38
Australia	1,920	6.43
Brazil	1,470	4.93
South Africa	830	2.78
Other	9,470	31.74

Source: *Mineral Commodities Summaries 2006*, Annual, p. 21, from U.S. Geological Survey, U.S. Department of the Interior.

★ 1558 ★
Aluminum
SIC: 3334; NAICS: 331312

How Aluminum is Used, 2005

In 2005, primary aluminum production was valued at $4.8 billion. It was centered in the Eastern United States.

Transportation	.39.0%
Packaging	.28.0
Building	.14.0
Consumer durables	. 6.0
Electrical	. 6.0
Other	. 7.0

Source: *Mineral Commodities Summaries 2006*, Annual, p. 21, from U.S. Geological Survey, U.S. Department of the Interior.

★ 1559 ★
Aluminum
SIC: 3334; NAICS: 331312

Largest Aluminum Firms in India

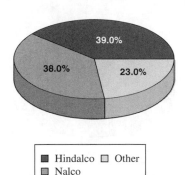

The industry is valued at Rs 15,000 crore.

Hindalco	.39.0%
Nalco	.38.0
Other	.23.0

Source: *Financial Express*, January 8, 2006, p. NA.

★ 1560 ★
Aluminum
SIC: 3334; NAICS: 331312

Largest Aluminum Suppliers Worldwide

Firms are ranked by production in millions of tons. The top 10 firms take 55% of the market. Transportation is the top end market for aluminum in the Western World, followed by building & construction needs (31% and 18% respectively). In China, the building & construction market leads with electrical in second place (29% and 16%).

Alcoa	3.5
Alcan	3.4
Rusal	2.7
Hydro	1.8
BHP Billiton	1.3
Chalco	1.1
Sual	1.0
Alba	0.8
Comalco	0.8
Dubai	0.7

Source: *Basic Materials*, Morgan Stanley Equity Research, December 14, 2005, p. 7, from Morgan Stanley Research and Chemical Marketing Associates Inc.

★ 1561 ★
Cadmium
SIC: 3339; NAICS: 331419

How Cadmium is Used, 2005

Data show mine production in thousands of metric tons. China is the top producer worldwide with a 17.6% share followed by Japan with a 13.3% share.

Batteries	.81.0%
Pigments	.10.0
Coatings and plating	. 7.0
Stabilizers for plastics	. 1.5
Other	. 0.5

Source: *Mineral Commodities Summaries 2006*, Annual, p. 21, from U.S. Geological Survey, U.S. Department of the Interior.

★ 1562 ★
Germanium
SIC: 3339; NAICS: 331419

How Germanium is Used Worldwide

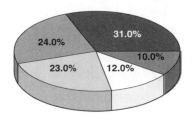

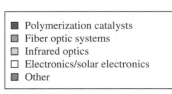

Market shares are shown in percent.

Polymerization catalysts	.31.0%
Fiber optic systems	.24.0
Infrared optics	.23.0
Electronics/solar electronics	.12.0
Other	.10.0

Source: *Mineral Commodities Summaries 2006*, Annual, p. 21, from U.S. Geological Survey, U.S. Department of the Interior.

★ 1563 ★
Aluminum
SIC: 3355; NAICS: 331319

Top Rolled Aluminum Makers in Japan, 2004

Market shares are shown based on domestic production of 2.45 million tons.

Furukawa-Sky Aluminum	18.9%
Sumitomo Light Metal	15.9
Kobe Steel	15.3
Mitsubishi Aluminum	7.3
Showa Denko	3.9
Other	33.7

Source: ''2004 Market Share Report.'' [online] from http://www.nikkei.co.jp [Published July 27, 2005] from Nikkei estimates.

★ 1564 ★
Magnet Wire
SIC: 3357; NAICS: 331422

Leading Magnet Wire Makers in Europe

Market shares are shown in percent.

Essex Nexans	27.0%
Elektro-Koppar	11.0
IRCE	11.0
Invex	10.0
Schwering	9.0
Other	32.0

Source: ''Superior Essex SunTrust Robinson Humphrey.'' [online] from http://www.shareholder.com/superior/downloads/IRpresentation2006.PPT [Published April 12, 2006] from internal estimates.

★ 1565 ★
Magnet Wire
SIC: 3357; NAICS: 331422

Leading Magnet Wire Makers in North America

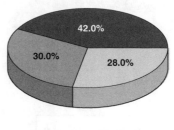

Market shares are shown in percent.

Rea	42.0%
Superior Essex	30.0
Other	28.0

Source: ''Superior Essex SunTrust Robinson Humphrey.'' [online] from http://www.shareholder.com/superior/downloads/IRpresentation2006.PPT [Published April 12, 2006] from internal estimates.

★ 1566 ★
Castings
SIC: 3369; NAICS: 331528

Global Castings Production

Countries are ranked by production in metric tons.

	(mt)	Share
China	22,420,452	28.12%
United States	12,314,121	15.44
Japan	6,386,449	8.01
Russia	6,300,000	7.90
Germany	4,984,473	6.25
India	4,623,000	5.80
Brazil	2,829,916	3.55
France	2,465,617	3.09
Italy	2,441,282	3.06
Mexico	2,185,200	2.74
Korea	1,857,300	2.33
Taiwan	1,451,768	1.82
Other	9,485,889	11.90

Source: *Modern Casting*, December 2005, p. 27, from *Modern Casting's 39th Annual Census of World Casting Production.*

SIC 34 - Fabricated Metal Products

★ 1567 ★
Metal Cans
SIC: 3411; NAICS: 332431

Leading Aerosol Can Makers in North America

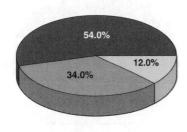

Market shares are shown in percent.

U.S. Can	.54.0%
Crown, Cork & Seal	.34.0
Bway	.12.0

Source: *Global Packaging 101v.3*, Credit Suisse First Boston, September 12, 2005, p. 3, from Can Manufacturers Institute and CS First Boston.

★ 1568 ★
Metal Cans
SIC: 3411; NAICS: 332431

Leading Beverage Can Firms in North America

Shares are shown based on 100 billion units.

Ball	.32.0%
Metal Container	.22.0
Rexam	.22.0
Crown	.20.0
RMMC	. 4.0

Source: "First Quarter 2005 Review and Management Briefing." [online] from http://library. corporate-ir.net/./FINAL-1st%20Qtr%202005%20Earnings%20Release%20ENTIRE%20SCRIPT%20(4-28-05).pdf [Published April 28, 2005].

★ 1569 ★
Metal Cans
SIC: 3411; NAICS: 332431

Leading Beverage Can Makers in Europe, 2005

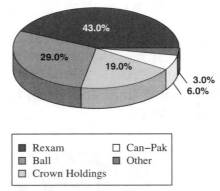

The market is estimated to be worth 40 billion metal beverage cans.

Rexam	.43.0%
Ball	.29.0
Crown Holdings	.19.0
Can-Pak	. 6.0
Other	. 3.0

Source: *Packaging Unplugged*, Wachovia Securites, September 29, 2005, p. 23, from Wachovia Capital Markets, LLC estimates and company reports.

★ 1570 ★
Metal Cans
SIC: 3411; NAICS: 332431

Leading Can Makers in Europe/Middle East/North Africa, 2006

Shares are estimated based on $54 billion market.

Rexam	.33.0%
Crown Holdings	.27.0
Ball	.24.0
Cpack	. 6.0
Other	.10.0

Source: *Packaging Industry*, North American Equity Research, October 8, 2005, p. 5, from JPMorgan estimates and company reports.

★ 1571 ★
Metal Cans
SIC: 3411; NAICS: 332431

Leading Food Can Makers in Europe, 2005

The market is estimated to be worth $2.6 billion.

Crown Holdings	.46.0%
Impress Packaging	.28.0
Mivisa	7.0
LMC	4.0
US Can	4.0
Other	.11.0

Source: *Packaging Unplugged*, Wachovia Securites, September 29, 2005, p. 23, from Wachovia Capital Markets, LLC estimates and company reports.

★ 1572 ★
Metal Cans
SIC: 3411; NAICS: 332431

Leading Food Can Makers in North America, 2005

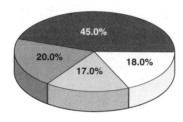

The market is estimated to be worth $3 billion and 33 billion metal food cans.

Silgan	.45.0%
Ball	.20.0
Crown Holdings	.17.0
Other	.18.0

Source: *Packaging Unplugged*, Wachovia Securites, September 29, 2005, p. 23, from Wachovia Capital Markets, LLC estimates and company reports.

★ 1573 ★
Metal Cans
SIC: 3411; NAICS: 332431

Metal Can Market in North America

Market shares are shown based on unit production.

Vegetables/vegetable juice	.34.0%
Pet food	.23.0

Dairy	7.0%
Meat/poultry	7.0
Fruit/fruit juice	6.0
Other	.23.0

Source: *Global Packaging 101v.3*, Credit Suisse First Boston, September 12, 2005, p. 3, from Can Manufacturers Institute and CS First Boston.

★ 1574 ★
Shipping Containers
SIC: 3412; NAICS: 332439

Leading Container Makers Worldwide

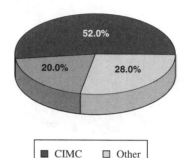

Market shares are shown in percent. CIMC stands for China International Marine Containers.

CIMC	.52.0%
Singamas	.20.0
Other	.28.0

Source: *South China Morning Post*, February 28, 2006, p. NA, from Singamas executive estimates.

★ 1575 ★
Hardware
SIC: 3420; NAICS: 33251

Leading Hardware Firms, 2005

Market shares are estimated in percent. ASSA ABLOY's share is 5.0%-10.0%, Stanley Works 5.5%-6.0%, Strattec Security Corporation 1.5%-2.0% and The Eastern Company 0.50%-1.0%.

ASSA ABLOY	.10.0%
Stanley Works	6.0
Strattec Security	2.0
The Eastern Company	1.0
Other	.81.0

Source: "US Hardware Manufacturing Industry Research." [online] from http://www.ibisworld.com [Accessed May 2, 2006] from IBISWorld.

★ 1576 ★
Cutlery
SIC: 3421; NAICS: 332211
Cutlery Sales, 2005

Industry sales were placed at about $200 million for July 2004 - June 2005. Carbon stainless steel took 62.8%, stainless steel took 33.7% and ceramic took 1.2%.

Sets 68.3%
Cutting boards 10.3
Specialty knives 9.7
Other 11.7

Source: *Gourmet Retailer*, October 2005, p. 82, from NPD Group.

★ 1577 ★
Cutlery
SIC: 3421; NAICS: 332211
Cutlery Sales by Metal, 2005

Sales were just over $200 million from July 2004 - July 2005. Knife sets were 68.3% of sales, specialty knives 9.7% and cutting boards 10.3%.

Carbon stainless steel 62.8%
Stainless steel 33.7
Ceramic 1.2

Source: *Gourmet Retailer*, October 2005, p. 82, from NPD Group.

★ 1578 ★
Cutlery
SIC: 3421; NAICS: 332211
Multi-Tool Market

Victorinex manufactures Swiss Army Knives.

Victorinex 85.0%
Other 15.0

Source: *Incentive*, October 2005, p. 96.

★ 1579 ★
Razor Blades
SIC: 3421; NAICS: 332211
Leading Razor Blade Brands in Germany, 2003

Market shares are shown in percent.

Wilkinson Sword 42.5%
Gillette Mach3 . . . . .27.0

Gillette Sensor 23.1%
Private label 4.3
Other 3.1

Source: "Germany's Men's Cosmetic Market." [online] from http://www.export.gov [Published October 2005] from Euromonitor.

★ 1580 ★
Razor Blades
SIC: 3421; NAICS: 332211
Razor Blade Market Worldwide

Gillette has more than 70% of the razor and blade market.

Gillette 70.0%
Schick 20.0
Other 10.0

Source: *Boston Globe*, February 17, 2006, p. NA, from analysts.

★ 1581 ★
Razor Blades
SIC: 3421; NAICS: 332211
Top Razor Blade/Cartridge Brands, 2005

Brands are ranked by sales in millions of dollars at supermarkets, drug stores and discount stores (excluding Wal-Mart) for the 52 weeks ended October 2, 2005.

	($ mil.)	Share
Gillette Mach 3	$ 171.9	12.54%
Gillette Mach 3 Turbo	126.3	9.22
Gillette M3 Power	68.2	4.98
Gillette Venus	61.0	4.45
Gillette Sensor Excel	47.4	3.46
Schick Intuition	42.5	3.10
Schick Quattro	39.7	2.90
Gillette Venus Divine	33.7	2.46
Gillette Sensor	26.4	1.93

Continued on next page.

★ 1581 ★
[Continued]
Razor Blades
SIC: 3421; NAICS: 332211

Top Razor Blade/Cartridge Brands, 2005

Brands are ranked by sales in millions of dollars at supermarkets, drug stores and discount stores (excluding Wal-Mart) for the 52 weeks ended October 2, 2005.

	($ mil.)	Share
Gillette Sensor 3	$ 18.3	1.34%
Other	735.0	53.63

Source: *MMR*, November 14, 2005, p. 1, from Information Resources Inc.

★ 1582 ★
Razor Blades
SIC: 3421; NAICS: 332211

Top Razor Blade Makers, 2005

Market shares are shown in percent. Sales exclude Wal-Mart and other large-format mass retailers.

Procter & Gamble	.68.0%
Energizer	.18.0
Bic	6.0
Private label	5.0
Other	3.0

Source: *U.S. Personal Care and Household Products Digest*, Citigroup Equity Research, February 24, 2006, p. 84, from ACNielsen.

★ 1583 ★
Razor Blades
SIC: 3421; NAICS: 332211

Top Razor Blade Makers (Disposable), 2006

Market shares are shown for the first quarter ended January 22, 2006.

Gillette	.44.0%
Schick	.23.0
Other	.33.0

Source: *Household & Personal Care*, Morgan Stanley Equity Research, February 2, 2006, p. 7, from Information Resources Inc. and Morgan Stanley.

★ 1584 ★
Razor Blades
SIC: 3421; NAICS: 332211

Top Razor Blade Makers (Refill), 2005

Market shares are shown based on sales at supermarkets, drug stores and discount stores (excluding Wal-Mart) for the 52 weeks ended June 12, 2005.

The Gillette Co.	.83.0%
Energizer Holdings	.13.6
American Safety Razor	0.5
Universal Razor Industries	0.1
Private label	2.9

Source: *Grocery Headquarters*, September 21, 2005, p. S14, from Information Resources Inc.

★ 1585 ★
Razor Blades
SIC: 3421; NAICS: 332211

Top Razor Blades (Disposable), 2006

Brands are ranked by supermarket and drug store sales in millions of dollars.

	($ mil.)	Share
Schick Xtreme3	$ 54.1	12.64%
Gillette Custom Plus	40.4	9.44
Schick Slim Twin	36.4	8.51
Gillette Sensor 3	33.8	7.90
Gillette Good News	25.0	5.84
Gillette Daisy Plus	23.2	5.42
Gillette Good News Plus	21.4	5.00
Bic Comfort 3	17.5	4.09
Gillette Venus	16.7	3.90
Private label	45.2	10.56
Other	114.2	26.69

Source: *MMR*, April 24, 2006, p. 30, from Information Resources Inc.

★ 1586 ★
Hand Tools
SIC: 3423; NAICS: 332212

Hand Tool Industry in the U.K.

The hand tool industry was worth $365 million in 2004. By 2008, the industry is projected to be worth $412 million.

Saws	.18.0%
Screwdrivers	.11.0
Other	.71.0

Source: "UK Do-It-Yourself Market." [online] from http://www.export.gov [Published September 2005].

★ 1587 ★
Hand Tools
SIC: 3423; NAICS: 332212

Leading Hand Tool Makers, 2005

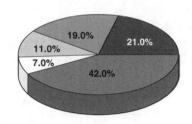

■ Stanley Works □ Cooper Industries
■ Danaher   ■ Other
□ Snap–On

Hand tool sales are estimated to increase from $8.1 billion in 2005 to $8.3 billion in 2006.

Stanley Works	.21.0%
Danaher	.19.0
Snap-On	.11.0
Cooper Industries	. 7.0
Other	.42.0

Source: *Homebuilding June 2006 Monthly*, Credit Suisse, June 2006 from Census Bureau, company reports and Credit Suisse analysis and estimates.

★ 1588 ★
Sawblades
SIC: 3425; NAICS: 332213

Saw Blade and Handsaw Shipments by Year, 1998-2001

Shipments are in millions of dollars.

1998	$ 1.32
1999	1.27

2000	$ 1.23
2001	1.07

Source: "Sawblade and Handsaws." [online] from http://www.referenceforbusiness.com/industries/Fabricated-Metal [Accessed November 14, 2005] from U.S. Bureau of the Census.

★ 1589 ★
Faucets
SIC: 3432; NAICS: 327111

Faucet Market Leaders

Market shares are shown in percent.

Delta	.25.0%
Moen	.25.0
Other	.50.0

Source: *Indianapolis Star*, May 1, 2005, p. NA, from Bear Stearns & Co. Inc.

★ 1590 ★
Faucets
SIC: 3432; NAICS: 332913

Leading Faucet Makers, 2005

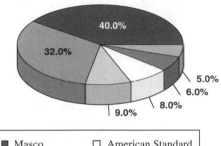

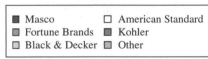

■ Masco   □ American Standard
■ Fortune Brands ■ Kohler
□ Black & Decker ■ Other

Faucet sales are estimated to increase from $3.1 billion in 2005 to $3.2 billion in 2006. In 1995, the industry was valued at $1.9 billion.

Masco	.40.0%
Fortune Brands	.32.0
Black & Decker	. 9.0
American Standard	. 8.0
Kohler	. 6.0
Other	. 5.0

Source: *Homebuilding June 2006 Monthly*, Credit Suisse, June 2006 from Census Bureau, company reports and Credit Suisse analysis and estimates.

★ 1591 ★
Plumbing Fixtures
SIC: 3432; NAICS: 332913, 332919

Plumbing Supplies Sales, 2003-2006

Residential sales of plumbing supplies for existing homes from all outlets are shown in billions of dollars. The industry benefited from an active housing market and Baby Boomers making upgrades to their homes.

2003	$ 20.14
2004	23.48
2005	25.02
2006	26.13

Source: *Contractor*, July 2005, p. 1, from Home Improvement Research Institute.

★ 1592 ★
Solar Equipment
SIC: 3433; NAICS: 333414

Solar Equipment Industry Worldwide

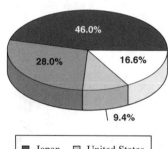

Japan	46.0%
Europe	28.0
United States	9.4
Other	16.6

Solar cell production reached 1,656 Megawatts in 2005. Solarbuzz predicts limited growth rates because of a shortage of polysilicon. Demand forecasts show worldwide industry revenues will reach $18.6-$23.1 billion.

Source: *PR Newswire*, March 15, 2006, p. NA, from Solarbuzz LLC.

★ 1593 ★
Solar Equipment
SIC: 3433; NAICS: 333414

Top Solar Equipment Makers in Japan, 2004

Market shares are shown based on domestic production of 272.6 megawatts.

Sharp	.47.5%
Kyocera	.19.3
Sanyo Electric	.19.1
Mitsubishi Electric	.11.0
Kaneka	1.0
Other	2.1

Source: "2004 Market Share Report." [online] from http://www.nikkei.co.jp [Published July 27, 2005] from Nikkei estimates.

★ 1594 ★
Solar Equipment
SIC: 3433; NAICS: 333414

Top Solar Panel Makers Worldwide, 2004

Companies are ranked by production in mega watts.

	MW	Share
Sharp	324,000	27.1%
Kyocera	105,000	8.8
BP Solar Group	85,000	7.1
Mitsubishi	75,000	6.3
Shell Solar	72,000	6.0
Q Cells	65,000	5.4

Source: "Japanese Green Building Products Market." [online] from http://www.export.gov [Published July 2005] from Kalllos Publishing.

★ 1595 ★
H-Beams
SIC: 3441; NAICS: 332312

Top H-Beam Firms in Japan, 2004

An H-beams is a structural steel member shaped like an H in section. Market shares are shown based on domestic shipments of 4.51 million tons.

Tokyo Steel Manufacturing	.34.2%
Nippon Steel	.18.2
JFE Steel	.12.8
Sumikin Steel & Shapes	.12.2

Continued on next page.

★ 1595 ★

[Continued]
H-Beams
SIC: 3441; NAICS: 332312

Top H-Beam Firms in Japan, 2004

An H-beams is a structural steel member shaped like an H in section. Market shares are shown based on domestic shipments of 4.51 million tons.

Yamato Steel	.11.2%
Other	.11.4

Source: "2004 Market Share Report." [online] from http://www.nikkei.co.jp [Published July 27, 2005] from Japan Iron and Steel Federation.

★ 1596 ★

Doors and Trim
SIC: 3442; NAICS: 332321

Cold Storage Rigid Door Market

The company has more than 60% of the market. It also makes doors for grocery store distribution centers, sliding doors, bi-folding doors, and swing doors.

Jamison Door	.60.0%
Other	.40.0

Source: *Frozen Food Digest*, October 2005, p. 24.

★ 1597 ★

Doors and Trim
SIC: 3442; NAICS: 332321

Leading Door Module Makers Worldwide, 2003

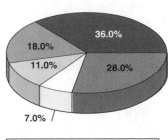

■ Brose   □ Faurecia
■ ArvinMeritor   ■ Other
□ Antolin/Kuester

Market shares are shown in percent.

Brose	.36.0%
ArvinMeritor	.18.0
Antolin/Kuester	.11.0
Faurecia	.7.0
Other	.28.0

Source: *SupplierBusiness.com*, August 12, 2004, p. 1, from Brose.

★ 1598 ★

Doors and Trim
SIC: 3442; NAICS: 332321

Top Aluminum Sash/Doors Makers in Japan, 2004

Market shares are shown based on domestic shipments of 219,568 metric units. Data are for wooden homes.

Tostem	.36.8%
YKK AP	.29.4
Sankyo Aluminum	.14.7
Shin Nikkei	.13.4
Tateyama Aluminum	.4.9
Other	.0.8

Source: "2004 Market Share Report." [online] from http://www.nikkei.co.jp [Published July 27, 2005] from Nikkei estimates and Ministry of Economy, Trade and Industry.

★ 1599 ★

Boilers
SIC: 3443; NAICS: 33241

Boiler Market in Eastern Europe, 2004

The total market is 30,700 units. By type, gas atmospheric took 46% of sales, pressure jet boilers took 39%, while boilers sold without burners and solid fuel burners took 15%.

Poland	.25.0%
Russia	.24.0
Romania	.19.0
Czech Republic	.13.0
Hungary	.7.0
Ukraine	.7.0
Slovakia	.5.0

Source: "Eastern European Commercial Boilers." [online] from http://bsria.co.uk/press/?press220 [Accessed November 3, 2005] from Building Services Research and Information Association.

★ 1600 ★

Gas Cylinders
SIC: 3443; NAICS: 33242

Gas Cylinder Market in India

Market shares are shown in percent.

Everest Kanto Clinders	.80.0%
Other	.20.0

Source: *India Business Insight*, November 21, 2005, p. NA.

★ 1601 ★
Access Equipment
SIC: 3446; NAICS: 332323

Access Equipment Market in the U.K.

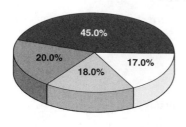

■ Mobile elevating work platforms ☐ Scaffolding
■ Ladders   ☐ Other

There was growth from 1996-1999 but the industry was flat until 2003. Market demand is driven by outsourcing, privatization and construction. The industry was valued at 247 million pounds in 2004.

Mobile elevating work platforms	.45.0%
Ladders	.20.0
Scaffolding	.18.0
Other	.17.0

Source: "Access Equipment Market - UK 2004." [online] from http://www.gii.co.jp [Published July 2004].

★ 1602 ★
Architectural Metal Work
SIC: 3446; NAICS: 332323

Ornamental/Architectural Metal Industry

The market includes the manufacturing of metal framed windows, metal doors, canopies, concrete forms, ducts, gutters, railings, flooring and many other products. Griffon's share is estimated to be 1.7%-4.2%. Industry revenue was $34.2 billion.

Griffon Corporation	4.2%
Quanex	2.5
Other	.93.3

Source: "US Ornamental & Architectural Metal Products." [online] from http://www.ibisworld.com [Accessed March 15, 2006] from IBISWorld.

★ 1603 ★
Metal Buildings
SIC: 3448; NAICS: 332311

Metal Buildings by Market

About 40% of non-residential low-rise buildings in the United States were comprised of metal building systems. "Community buildings" include recreation, education, hospitals, churches, transportation terminals. "Other" includes parking garages, commercial labs, and greenhouses.

Commercial	.43.7%
Manufacturing	.30.6
Community	.16.9
Other	.9.8

Source: *Construction News*, June 20, 2005, p. 50, from Metal Building Manufacturers Association.

★ 1604 ★
Car Rails
SIC: 3462; NAICS: 332111

Car Rail Market

The market was valued at 270 million euros.

AAS	.60.0%
JAC	.38.0
Other	2.0

Source: "Thule First in Sports Utility Transportation." [online] from http://www.corporate.thule.com/eng/filearchive/getfile.asp?type1&objectid167 [Published Feb. 2005].

★ 1605 ★
Car Rails
SIC: 3462; NAICS: 332111

Car Rail Market in Europe

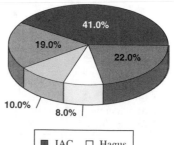

■ JAC   ☐ Hagus
■ Thule ■ Other
☐ AAS

The market was valued at 150 million euros.

JAC	.41.0%
Thule	.19.0
AAS	.10.0

Continued on next page.

★ 1605 ★

[Continued]
Car Rails
SIC: 3462; NAICS: 332111

Car Rail Market in Europe

The market was valued at 150 million euros.

Hagus 8.0%
Other .22.0

Source: "Thule First in Sports Utility Transportation." [online] from http://www.corporate.thule.com/eng/filearchive/getfile.asp?type1&objectid167 [Published Feb. 2005].

★ 1606 ★

Snow Chains
SIC: 3462; NAICS: 332111

Snow Chain Market Worldwide

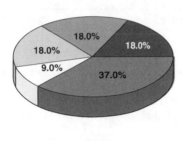

■ Chinese	□ RUD
■ Pewag	■ Other
□ Thule	

The market was valued at 5.4 million pairs worth SEK 1,420 million. Automotive chains take 79% of the market, with heavy and light transport chains making up the balance.

Chinese 18.0%
Pewag 18.0
Thule .18.0
RUD 9.0
Other .37.0

Source: "Thule First in Sports Utility Transportation." [online] from http://www.corporate.thule.com/eng/filearchive/getfile.asp?type1&objectid167 [Published Feb. 2005].

★ 1607 ★

Automotive Stampings
SIC: 3465; NAICS: 33637

Largest Auto Metal Firms in North/South America

Companies are ranked by millions of tons.

	(mil.)	Share
Mittal Steel	6.0	26.09%
US Steel	4.5	19.57
AK Steel	2.0	8.70
Dofasco	1.0	4.35
Other	9.5	41.30

Source: *Financial Times*, January 30, 2006, p. 18.

★ 1608 ★

Automotive Stampings
SIC: 3465; NAICS: 33637

Leading Stampers in Europe

Market shares are shown in percent.

Tower Automotive 25.0%
ThyssenKrupp Automotive 15.0
August Lapelle 10.0
Stadco 7.5
Other 42.5

Source: *Automotive News*, August 1, 2005, p. 243, from Stadco and companies.

★ 1609 ★

Caps & Closures
SIC: 3466; NAICS: 332115

Caps and Closures in Western Europe, 2004 and 2009

The market is estimated to be worth 415.8 billion units in 2009.

	2004	2009
Metal	57.8%	48.1%
Plastic	40.4	49.8

Source: *Modern Plastics Worldwide*, October 2005, p. 82, from AMI Consulting.

★ 1610 ★
Fuel Tank Caps
SIC: 3466; NAICS: 332115
Fuel Tank Filler Cap Industry Worldwide

Market shares are shown for the commercial segment.

Reutter	80.0%
Other	20.0

Source: *SupplierBusiness.com*, March 28, 2006, p. NA.

★ 1611 ★
Cookware
SIC: 3469; NAICS: 332116, 332214
Cookware Sales, 2005

Total sales were $695 million and 20.4 million units.

Aluminum	38.9%
Stainless steel	31.5
Anodized aluminum	18.9
Steel	6.8
Cast iron	3.2
Copper	0.5
Other	0.2

Source: *Do-It-Yourself Retailing*, March 2006, p. 33, from NPD Group/Point-of-sale information.

★ 1612 ★
Ammunition
SIC: 3482; NAICS: 332992
Ammunition Sales, 2005

Data are in millions of dollars.

Shotshell (lead)	$ 49,036,220
Centerfire rifle	28,290,576
Airgun/paintball	18,558,468
Handguns	17,005,957
Rimfire	13,905,664
Slugs	12,789,068
Shotshell (Non-toxic)	6,826,591
Black powder	4,982,391
Ammo. Components	3,131,210

Source: "Ammunition Market Indicator Report." [online] from http://www.nssf.org/IndustryResearch/pdf/ammunitiontrends.pdf [Accessed June 6, 2006] from SportscanInfo.

★ 1613 ★
Guns
SIC: 3484; NAICS: 332994
Non-Military Gun Market, 2004

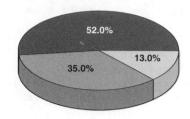

Sales are in millions of dollars.

	($ mil.)	Share
Bolt action rifles	$ 510	52.0%
Shotguns	346	35.0
Tactical rifles	132	13.0

Source: "Smith & Wesson." [online] from http://media. corporate-ir.net/media_files/irol/90/90977/presentations/swb_March2006.pdf [Published March 2006] from *BATF 2004 Excise Tax Study* and Smith & Wesson Management estimates.

★ 1614 ★
Guns
SIC: 3484; NAICS: 332994
Police Firearm Sales

GLOCK pistols are used by 65% of law enforcement agencies, according to their web site.

GLOCK	65.0%
Other	35.0

Source: "Market Position." [online] from http://www.glock.com/body_market_position1.htm [April 6, 2005].

★ 1615 ★
Guns
SIC: 3484; NAICS: 332994
Revolver Market, 2004

Market shares are shown in percent.

Smith & Wesson/Sturm Ruger	80.0%
Other	20.0

Source: "Gun Manufacturing Industry Profile Excerpt." [online] from http://www.firstresearch.com [Published January 16, 2006] from *BATF 2004 Excise Tax Study* and Smith & Wesson Management estimates.

★ 1616 ★
Springs and Wires
SIC: 3490; NAICS: 332611, 332612

Leading Springs/Wire Makers, 2004

MMI Products had 5.0%-5.5% of the market and Insteel Industries had 3.0%-3.5% of the market.

MMI Products	5.5%
Insteel Industries	3.5
Other	91.0

Source: "Fuel Dealers in the U.S." [online] from http://www.ibisworld.com [Published March 31, 2006] from IBISWorld.

★ 1617 ★
Valves
SIC: 3491; NAICS: 332911

Industrial Valve Demand

Demand is forecast to increase 4.6% each year until reaching $14.8 billion in 2009. Public utilities demand will grow 6.5% from 2004 to 2009, the largest increase.

	2004	2009	Share
Process manufacturing	$ 4,240	$ 4,770	32.34%
Public utilities	3,655	5,010	33.97
Resources industry	2,050	2,750	18.64
Construction	1,435	1,730	11.73
Other	420	490	3.32

Source: *Supply House Times*, August 2005, p. 22, from Freedonia Group.

★ 1618 ★
Valves
SIC: 3491; NAICS: 332911

Leading Metal Valve Makers, 2005

Market shares are shown based on $23.9 billion in revenue.

Tyco Valves	5.0%
Meggitt	1.5
Numatics Incorporated	0.5
Sun Hydraulics	0.5
Other	92.5

Source: "Metal Valve Manufacturing in the US." [online] from http://www.ibisworld.com [Published December 14, 2005] from IBISWorld.

★ 1619 ★
Valves
SIC: 3491; NAICS: 332911

Top Valve Makers Worldwide

The top five firms take 12% of the market, while the top 10 firms take 16%. Control valves take 24% of the market while ball valves follow with 22% of the market.

Tyco Valves	$ 2,000
Flowserve	1,200
Emersson	930
Dresser Inc.	550

Source: "Targeting the Pump & Valve Industry." [online] from http://www.indek.kth.se/./modules.php?opmodload&nameUpDownload&fileindex&reqgetit&lid355 [Accessed June 1, 2006] from McIlvaine Co.

★ 1620 ★
Valves
SIC: 3491; NAICS: 332911

Valve Market Worldwide, 2003

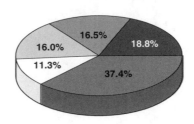

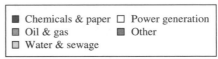

The industry is valued at $20.25 billion.

Chemicals & paper	18.8%
Oil & gas	16.5
Water & sewage	16.0
Power generation	11.3
Other	37.4

Source: "Metso Automation Metso Capital Markets Day 2005." [online] from http://www.metso.com [Accessed May 15, 2005].

★ 1621 ★
Hangers
SIC: 3496; NAICS: 332618

Wire Hanger Market in North America

Laidlaw is North America's largest manufacturer and distributor of wire hangers and other products to U.S. dry cleaning and commercial uniform industries. The company has sold more than 1 billion hanger products in North America in the past year.

Laidlaw 33.0%
Other 67.0

Source: *Paducah Sun*, May 31, 2006, p. NA.

SIC 35 - Industry Machinery and Equipment

★ 1622 ★
Turbines
SIC: 3511; NAICS: 333611

Global Wind Turbine Market, 2005

Market shares are shown in percent.

Vestas	34.0%
Gamesa	17.0
Enercon	15.0
GE Wind	11.0
Siemens	6.0
Suzlon	4.0
RePower	3.0
Other	10.0

Source: "1st Quarter Information 2005." [online] from http://www.vestas.com/pdf/2005/VesInvPresQ12005_UK.pdf [Published May 26, 2005] from BTM Consult.

★ 1623 ★
Turbines
SIC: 3511; NAICS: 333611

Leading Wind Turbine Makers, 2005

Companies are ranked by thousands of megawatts newly installed during the year. New megawatt installations totaled 2,348. Total wind energy equipment sales were $11 billion and have been growing 27% over the past five years.

	(000)	Share
GE Energy	1,433	37.11%
Vestas	700	18.13
Mitsubishi	190	4.92
Suzlon	55	1.42
Gamesa	50	1.30
Other	1,433	37.11

Source: *Forbes*, June 19, 2006, p. 126, from American Wind Energy Association.

★ 1624 ★
Turbines
SIC: 3511; NAICS: 333611

Top Wind Generator Makers in Japan, 2004

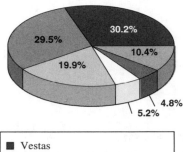

- ■ Vestas
- ■ Mitsubishi Heavy Industries
- ▨ General Electric
- ☐ Siemens
- ■ Repower Systems AG
- ▨ Other

Market shares are shown based on domestic power output of 249,300 kilowatts.

Vestas	30.2%
Mitsubishi Heavy Industries	29.5
General Electric	19.9
Siemens	5.2
Repower Systems AG	4.8
Other	10.4

Source: "2004 Market Share Report." [online] from http://www.nikkei.co.jp [Published July 27, 2005] from New Energy Industrial Technology Development Organization.

★ 1625 ★
Turbines
SIC: 3511; NAICS: 333611

Top Wind Power Firms in Germany, 2004

Germany is the largest single market for wind energy in the world. Germany has an installed capacity of 16,629 MW (megawatts).

Enercon	42.0%
Vestas	30.0

Continued on next page.

★ 1625 ★
[Continued]
Turbines
SIC: 3511; NAICS: 333611

Top Wind Power Firms in Germany, 2004

Germany is the largest single market for wind energy in the world. Germany has an installed capacity of 16,629 MW (megawatts).

RE-power systems	9.0%
GE Wind Energy	8.0
AN Windenergie	4.0
Nordex	4.0
DeWind	1.0
Fuhrlaender	1.0
Gamesa	1.0

Source: "Market Overview: Wind Energy in Germany." [online] from http://www.export.gov [Published July 2005] from Danish Energy Authority.

★ 1626 ★
Turbines
SIC: 3511; NAICS: 333611

Wind Turbine Market in Austria, 2004

Shares are shown based on percent of new capacity installed during 2004.

Enercon	66.5%
Vestas	19.7
De Wind	7.6
Other	6.2

Source: *Wind Directions*, March/April 2005, p. 23, from IG Windkraft.

★ 1627 ★
Turbines
SIC: 3511; NAICS: 333611

Wind Turbine Market in Greece, 2004

Shares are shown based on percent of capacity during 2004.

Rokas	40.3%
Neg Micon	22.2
Vestas	10.8
Enercon	9.9
Nordex	5.3
Other	11.6

Source: *Wind Directions*, March/April 2005, p. 23, from Helenic Wind Energy Association.

★ 1628 ★
Turbines
SIC: 3511; NAICS: 333611

Wind Turbine Market in Italy, 2004

Shares are shown based on percent of capacity during 2004.

Vestas	59.0%
Enercon	16.0
Gamesa	12.0
GE Energy	2.6
Bonus	2.3
RWT	2.3
Repower	1.6
West	1.6

Source: *Wind Directions*, March/April 2005, p. 23, from Helenic Wind Energy Association.

★ 1629 ★
Turbines
SIC: 3511; NAICS: 333611

Wind Turbine Market in Spain, 2004

Market shares are shown in percent.

Gamesa Eolica	51.63%
Made (Gamesa Eolica)	12.23
Neg Micon (Vestas)	8.68
Ecotecnia	7.79
Izar-Bonus (Siemens)	3.26
Other	16.41

Source: *Technology Review*, December 2005, p. S1, from 2004 Asociación Empresarial Eólica.

★ 1630 ★
Engines
SIC: 3519; NAICS: 333618

Engines for Ocean-Going Vessels

The company is the leading supplier of large-bore diesel engines for marine propulsion and power stations. Market shares are for two-stroke and four-stroke engines for large ocean-going vessels.

MAN B&W Diesel	50.0%
Other	50.0

Source: *International Cruise & Ferry Review*, Autumn - Winter 2005, p. 68.

★ 1631 ★
Engines
SIC: 3519; NAICS: 333618

Leading Engine Families Worldwide, 2004

Production is shown in units.

Volkswagen EAO 86/153/188	1,970,435
General Motors GEN3/GEN4	1,754,505
Volkswagen EA827/113	1,661,848
Adams Opel I	1,550,138
Ford Motor MOD I V8	1,446,968
Toyota ZZ	1,289,050
Renault K	1,252,068
Toyota AZ	1,201,595

Source: *just-auto.com (Management Briefing)*, February 2006, p. 2.

★ 1632 ★
Engines
SIC: 3519; NAICS: 333618

Leading Marine Diesel Engine Makers in North America

Shares include total repower and new construction market.

Caterpillar	23.0%
CMD	18.5
John Deere	15.0
Volvo Penta	11.0
Yanmar	8.5
Other	24.0

Source: *Diesel Progress North American Edition*, October 2005, p. NA, from Power Products Marketing.

★ 1633 ★
Engines
SIC: 3519; NAICS: 333618

Leading Medium Truck/School Bus Engine Makers, 2005

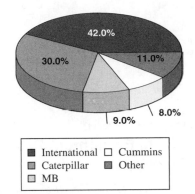

■ International □ Cummins
■ Caterpillar ■ Other
□ MB

Market shares are shown in percent.

International	42.0%
Caterpillar	30.0
MB	9.0
Cummins	8.0
Other	11.0

Source: "Navistar International Corp. Investor Presentation." http://www.shareholder.com/nav/downloads/creditsuissemar06.pdf [Published March 2006].

★ 1634 ★
Engines
SIC: 3519; NAICS: 333618

Leading Tug Boat Engine Makers

Market shares are shown in percent.

Caterpillar	17.0%
GM	12.0
EMD	11.0
Cummins	8.0
Deutz	4.0
Niigata	4.0
Yanmar	4.0
Other	40.0

Source: "Tug Market Report." [online] from http://www.marcon.com [Published April 2005] from Marcon International.

★ 1635 ★
Engines
SIC: 3519; NAICS: 333618
Small Engine Market Worldwide

The company has 60-65% of the market.

Briggs & Stratton	.65.0%
Other	.35.0

Source: *Briggs & Stratton Corp.*, Henry Fund Research,
April 3, 2006, p. 1.

★ 1636 ★
Industrial Machinery
SIC: 3520; NAICS: 33312, 333111
Industrial OEM Equipment Production in North America

*Total production was 21,818,558 units, and is forecast
to increase 4.1% in 2006. Production orders will then
slip as inventories grow and imports gain share.*

Lawn & garden	17,410,312
Recreation products	1,971,300
General industrial	1,413,062
Marine	510,699
Construction	298,280
Agricultural	155,192
Mining	59,693

Source: *OEM Off-Highway*, October 2005, p. 8, from Power Systems Research.

★ 1637 ★
Farm Equipment
SIC: 3523; NAICS: 333111
Automatic Tractor Steering Equipment in Europe

Market shares are shown in percent.

AutoTrac	.75.0%
Other	.25.0

Source: *Farmers Guardian*, June 2, 2006, p. NA, from John
Deere.

★ 1638 ★
Farm Equipment
SIC: 3523; NAICS: 333111
Compact Tractor Market Worldwide

Market shares are shown in percent.

Kubota	.70.0%
Other	.30.0

Source: *The Daily Mail*, November 29, 2005, p. 26.

★ 1639 ★
Farm Equipment
SIC: 3523; NAICS: 333111
Farm Machinery Sales in Germany

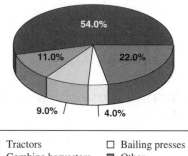

■ Tractors   □ Bailing presses
■ Combine harvesters   ■ Other
□ Harvesting machinery

Domestic demand has been stagnant. In the market abroad, German agricultural equipment sales were up15% in 2004.

Tractors	.54.0%
Combine harvesters	.11.0
Harvesting machinery	9.0
Bailing presses	4.0
Other	.22.0

Source: "Agricultural Machinery in Germany." [online]
from http://www. buyusainfo.net [Published January 2006].

★ 1640 ★
Farm Equipment
SIC: 3523; NAICS: 333111
Leading Tractor Makers in Brazil, 2005

Market shares are shown in percent for the first quarter of 2005.

AGCO (Massey Ferguson)	.36.0%
Valtra	.29.0
New Holland	.18.0
John Deere	7.5
Other	9.5

Source: *Farm Industry News*, July 2005, p. NA.

★ 1641 ★

Farm Equipment

SIC: 3523; NAICS: 333111

Leading Tractor Makers in France, 2003-2004

In 2004, the market for farm tractors increased in volume by over 5% to reach 40,279 units.

	2003	2004
John Deere	17.80%	18.6%
New Holland	16.13	14.8
Renault	15.42	13.8
Massey Ferguson	8.04	10.9
Other	42.60	41.9

Source: ''Agricultural Machinery in France.'' [online] from http://www.export.gov [Published September 2005].

★ 1642 ★

Farm Equipment

SIC: 3523; NAICS: 333111

Leading Tractor Makers in India, 2005

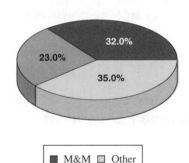

Legend: ■ M&M ☐ Other ■ TAFE

Market shares are shown for April - August 2005.

M&M	32.0%
TAFE	23.0
Other	35.0

Source: *Financial Express*, October 29, 2005, p. NA.

★ 1643 ★

Farm Equipment

SIC: 3523; NAICS: 333111

Leading Tractor Makers in the U.K.

Tractor sales climbed to 19,715 units, a record high. This is nearly double the level sold in 1990.

	Units	Share
Daf	5,458	27.7%
Mercedes-Benz	3,458	17.5

	Units	Share
Volvo	3,290	16.7%
Scania	3,242	16.4
MAN	1,596	8.1
Iveco	967	4.9
Renault	911	4.6
Other	790	4.0

Source: *Motor Transport*, January 12, 2006, p. p1.

★ 1644 ★

Farm Equipment

SIC: 3523; NAICS: 333111

Top Tractor Makers in Uruguay, 2004

Agriculture plays a major role in the country. There is a strong demand for used and refurbished machinery. The number of tractors sold in 2004 was double the number in 2003. Data show number of units.

	Units	Share
Valmet	134	25.33%
New Holland	131	24.76
John Deere	125	23.63
Massey	124	23.44
Case	15	2.84

Source: ''Agricultural Machinery in Uruguay.'' [online] from http://www.export.gov [Published September 2005].

★ 1645 ★

Lawn & Garden Equipment

SIC: 3524; NAICS: 333112

Electric Gardening Tool Market In Europe, 2003

The industry was placed at 10.7 million power tool units worth 740 million euros. Industry sales were down 8% from the previous year due to a depressed economy in Germany and the delayed start of the gardening season from poor weather.

United Kingdom	24.0%
Germany	24.0
France	13.0
Eastern Europe	12.0
Other Western Europe	27.0

Source: ''German Market for Lawn & Garden Products.'' [online] from http://www.usatrade.gov [Published July 2005] from Bosch.

★ 1646 ★
Lawn & Garden Equipment
SIC: 3524; NAICS: 333112

Gasoline-Powered Outdoor Equipment

Pole pruners grew 27.9% over 2004, the highest increase on the list (130,282 units in 2004). Handheld blowers fell 4.8%, the biggest fall from 2004 (2.08 million units).

Trimmers/brushcutters	6,460,115
Chain saws	3,123,106
Handheld blowers	1,989,211
Backpack blowers	503,744
Hedge clippers	377,925
Handheld tillers	305,308
Cut off saws	167,707
Pole pruners	166,613
Stick edgers	89,251
Engine drills	9,673
Earth/ice augers	5,488

Source: *Landscape & Irrigation*, February 2006, p. 11, from Outdoor Power Equipment Institute.

★ 1647 ★
Lawn & Garden Equipment
SIC: 3524; NAICS: 333112

Lawn & Garden Equipment Market

In 2004, Deere & Co., Toro, MTD Products, Electrolux and Murray supplied more than 60% of the market. Total shipments in millions of dollars: $9,550 in 2004, $11,050 in 2009 to $12,900 in 2014. Lawnmowers will represent 37% of shipments in 2014.

	2004	2009	2014
Lawnmowers	$ 3,490	$ 4,060	$ 4,760
Turf & grounds equipment	1,500	2,310	2,790
Parts, accessories	1,120	1,320	1,550
Tractors & rotary tillers	885	1,050	1,235
Trimmers & edgers	710	820	960
Snow blowers	405	360	380
Blowers, sweepers, chippers, shredders	360	420	480

Source: *Modern Plastics Worldwide*, September 2005, p. 38, from Freedonia Group.

★ 1648 ★
Lawn & Garden Equipment
SIC: 3524; NAICS: 333112

Lawn & Garden Equipment Sales, 2003 and 2004

In 2004, roughly 80 million households purchased one or more types of lawn and garden products. This was a decline of 2 million households from the previous year. Retail sales are shown in millions of dollars.

	2003	2004
Landscaping	$ 10,507	$ 11,346
Lawn care	10,413	8,887
Flower gardening	3,025	2,735
Tree care	2,359	3,067
Insect control	2,053	1,823
Indoor houseplants	1,571	1,495
Water gardening	1,565	1,128
Vegetable gardening	1,408	1,058
Container gardening	1,219	1,196
Shrub care	1,042	1,027

Source: *Do-It-Yourself Retailing*, August 2005, p. 64, from *2004 National Gardening Survey* and National Gardening Association.

★ 1649 ★
Lawn & Garden Equipment
SIC: 3524; NAICS: 333112

Lawn & Garden Equipment Sales, 2005-2009

Retail sales are shown in millions of dollars. Equipment took 58% of the total, supplies took 23% and services took 19%. The service sector refers to the professional lawn care services specializing in treatment. It has been growing the fastest, up 34.77% from 2000 to 2004.

2005	$ 24,850
2006	25,800
2007	26,730
2008	27,625
2009	28,545

Source: *ECRM Focus*, July 2005, p. 24, from Packaged Facts.

★ 1650 ★
Lawn & Garden Equipment
SIC: 3524; NAICS: 333112

Lawn & Garden Industry in Germany, 2004

The industry is valued at 8.53 million euros.

Lawnmowers	.55.0%
Chainsaws	.17.0
Lawn trimmers	.10.0
Hedge trimmers	.5.0
Hoes	.5.0
Other	.8.0

Source: *Wirtschaftswoche*, March 31, 2005, p. 56, from GfK.

★ 1651 ★
Lawn & Garden Equipment
SIC: 3524; NAICS: 333112

Lawn & Garden Industry in Germany, 2004

Total lawn and garden product shipments totaled an estimated 8.43 billion in 2004.

Herbaceous & potted plants	.39.8%
Garden furniture	.14.6
Fruit trees & ornamental trees	.12.8
Garden tools	.10.2
Bio-chemical products	.7.0
Garden accessories, decoration	.5.8
Water technology, water decoration	.4.6
Other	.5.2

Source: "German Market for Lawn & Garden Products." [online] from http://www.export.gov [Published September 2005] from Dahne Publishing.

★ 1652 ★
Lawn & Garden Equipment
SIC: 3524; NAICS: 333112

Leading Leaf Blower (Hand-held Electric) Makers, 2004

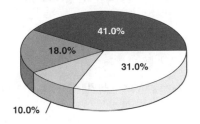

- ■ Black & Decker
- ■ Toro
- ■ Electrolux Home Products
- □ Other

Market shares are shown based on shipments.

Black & Decker	.41.0%
Toro	.18.0
Electrolux Home Products	.10.0
Other	.31.0

Source: *Appliance*, September 2005, p. P-2, from *Appliance* estimates and various surveys.

★ 1653 ★
Lawn & Garden Equipment
SIC: 3524; NAICS: 333112

Leading Mower (Riding, Gas) Makers, 2004

Market shares are shown based on shipments.

John Deere	.24.0%
American Yard Products	.21.0
Murray	.12.0
Briggs & Stratton (Simplicity/Snapper)	.5.0
Toro	.2.0
Other	.36.0

Source: *Appliance*, September 2005, p. P-2, from *Appliance* estimates and various surveys.

★ 1654 ★
Lawn & Garden Equipment
SIC: 3524; NAICS: 333112

Popular Types of Grills

Users may have more than one type of grill. An average cost of grill $237. A charcoal grill typically costs $96.

Gas	.61.0%
Charcoal	.51.0
Electric	. 9.0

Source: *Casual Living*, March 1, 2006, p. 18, from Hearth, Patio and Barbeque Association.

★ 1655 ★
Construction Equipment
SIC: 3531; NAICS: 33312

Construction Equipment Sales in North America, 2005-2006

Unit sales are forecasts.

	2005	2006
Skid steer loaders	72,420	75,317
Backhoe loaders	31,659	32,292
Crawler excavators	26,950	28,837
Mini excavators	24,973	26,971
Wheeled loaders	21,192	23,509
Wheeled loaders > 80 Hp	18,816	21,074
Crawler dozers	14,820	15,709
RTLTs - telescopic	12,507	13,508
Graders	4,100	4,387
Articulated dump trucks	2,904	3,195

Source: *Global Construction Equipment Dealer Survey*, Citigroup Equity Research, January 25, 2006, p. 10, from Citigroup Investment Research.

★ 1656 ★
Construction Equipment
SIC: 3531; NAICS: 33312

Earth Moving Equipment Market in Europe, 2004

The United Kingdom took 22% of the market followed by Italy with 20% of the market.

Mini-excavators	.38.0%
Crawler excavators	.20.0
Wheel loaders	.15.0
Backhoe loaders	.10.0

Skid steer loaders	. 9.0%
Wheel excavators	. 8.0

Source: *Construction Machinery Markets in Europe, Asia*, Morgan Stanley Equity Research, April 25, 2006, p. 4, from Construction Division of the Canadian Society for Civil Engineering and Morgan Stanley Research.

★ 1657 ★
Construction Equipment
SIC: 3531; NAICS: 33312

Forklift Side Shifter Market

Market shares are shown in percent.

Cascade	.90.0%
Other	.10.0

Source: *Investor's Business Daily*, October 14, 2005, p. A8.

★ 1658 ★
Construction Equipment
SIC: 3531; NAICS: 33312

Front Discharge Ready-Mix Truck Market

Market shares are shown in percent.

Terex	.50.0%
Other	.50.0

Source: "Terex Conexpo '05." [online] from http://library.corporate-ir.net/library/78/787/78780/items/142094/AEM_Morgan.pdf [Accessed April 20, 2006].

★ 1659 ★
Construction Equipment
SIC: 3531; NAICS: 33312

Largest Construction Equipment Firms Worldwide, 2003

Market shares are shown in percent.

Caterpillar	.31.0%
CNH Global	.15.0
Komatsu	.15.0
Volvo	. 6.0
John Deere	. 5.0
Terex Corporation	. 5.0
Hitachi	. 4.0
Ingersoll-Rand	. 4.0
JCB	. 3.0

Continued on next page.

★ 1659 ★

[Continued]

Construction Equipment

SIC: 3531; NAICS: 33312

Largest Construction Equipment Firms Worldwide, 2003

Market shares are shown in percent.

Liebherr	3.0%
Other	18.0

Source: *Middle East Economic Digest*, July 15, 2005, p. 40, from Volvo CE.

★ 1660 ★

Construction Equipment

SIC: 3531; NAICS: 33312

Leading Construction Equipment Firms in China (foreign-based)

The industry was valued at $15.7 billion in 2003 and is forecast to increase to $16.7 billion in 2004. Market shares are shown for foreign-based companies.

Zhonglian Holding Co.	2.27%
Chengdu Shengong Construction Machinery	2.17
Fujian Longgong Co.	2.15
Guangxi Liugong Machinery Limited Stock Co.	2.07
Xiamen Construction Machinery Limited Stock Co.	1.95
Xugong Group Zuzhou Heavy Machinery Factory	1.78
Sanyao Heavy Industry Limited Stock Co.	1.68
Shandong Linyi Construction Machinery Limited Stock Co.	1.45
Other	15.52

Source: "China Construction Machinery Market." [online] from http://www.stat-usa.gov [Published September 2005] from *China Construction Machinery Industry Yearbook 2004*.

★ 1661 ★

Construction Equipment

SIC: 3531; NAICS: 33312

Leading Construction Equipment Firms in Europe

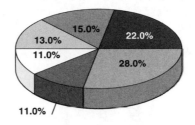

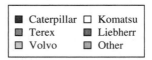

The industry is valued at $15 billion, with Germany and the United Kingdom leading the market with 18% shares.

Caterpillar	22.0%
Terex	15.0
Volvo	13.0
Komatsu	11.0
Liebherr	11.0
Other	28.0

Source: *Global Construction Equipment Dealer Survey*, Citigroup Equity Research, January 25, 2006 from Citigroup Investment Research.

★ 1662 ★

Construction Equipment

SIC: 3531; NAICS: 33312

Leading Construction Equipment Firms in Latin America

The industry is valued at $3 billion, with Brazil taking 42% of the market followed by Mexico with 29%.

Caterpillar	54.0%
Komatsu	13.0
CNH Global	6.0
Volvo	5.0
Deere	2.0
Other	20.0

Source: *Global Construction Equipment Dealer Survey*, Citigroup Equity Research, January 25, 2006 from Citigroup Investment Research.

★ 1663 ★
Construction Equipment
SIC: 3531; NAICS: 33312

Leading Construction Equipment Firms in North America

The industry is valued at $24 billion, with the United States and Canada taking 90% and 10% of the market.

Caterpillar	.42.0%
Deere	.14.0
Komatsu	.11.0
Terex	. 8.0
CNH Global	. 6.0
Volvo	. 5.0
Other	.14.0

Source: *Global Construction Equipment Dealer Survey*, Citigroup Equity Research, January 25, 2006 from Citigroup Investment Research.

★ 1664 ★
Construction Equipment
SIC: 3531; NAICS: 33312

Leading Hydraulic Excavator Makers in China, 2004

Market shares are shown based on unit volume.

Hyundai	.20.0%
Doosan	.16.0
Hitachi	.15.0
Komatsu	.14.0
Other	.35.0

Source: *Chinese Construction Equipment*, Bear Stearns Equity Research, November 11, 2005, p. 14, from Bear Stearns & Co. Inc.

★ 1665 ★
Construction Equipment
SIC: 3531; NAICS: 33312

Leading Wheel Loaders in China, 2004

Market shares are shown based on unit volume.

Liugong	.14.0%
XEMC	.14.0
Longgong	.12.0
XuGong	. 9.0
Changlin	. 7.0
Other	.44.0

Source: *Chinese Construction Equipment*, Bear Stearns Equity Research, November 11, 2005, p. 14.

★ 1666 ★
Construction Equipment
SIC: 3531; NAICS: 33312

Plant Construction Equipment Market in the U.K.

The industry is placed at 126,000 units and 1.5 billion pounds sterling.

Mini excavators	.51.0%
Crawler excavators	.28.0
Backhoe loaders	.11.0
Wheel loaders	. 6.0
Skid steers	. 3.0
Wheeled excavators	. 3.0

Source: *Plant Manager's Journal*, July 2005, p. 8, from Committee for the European Construction Equipment.

★ 1667 ★
Construction Equipment
SIC: 3531; NAICS: 33312

Top Concrete Placement Makers, 2004

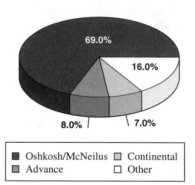

Market shares are estimated in percent. Drivers in the market include price increases, changes in engine and emission standards and concrete being used in place of other building materials.

Oshkosh/McNeilus	.69.0%
Advance	. 8.0
Continental	. 7.0
Other	.16.0

Source: "Oshkosh Full Throttle." [online] from http://media. corporate-ir.net/media_files/irol/93/93403/presentations/ 04_%20Nov_%20Baird_%20Conf_%20Presentation.pdf [Accessed June 1, 2006].

★ 1668 ★
Construction Equipment
SIC: 3531; NAICS: 33312

Top Construction Compactor Makers in North America

Market shares are shown in percent.

Ingersoll-Rand/Caterpillar/Bomag-Hypac/
  Dynapac 65.0%
Other 35.0

Source: *Diesel Progress North American Edition*, October 2005, p. 10.

★ 1669 ★
Construction Equipment
SIC: 3531; NAICS: 33312

Top Forklift Makers in Japan, 2004

Market shares are shown based on domestic shipments of 75,445 units.

Toyota Industries 42.6%
Komatsu Forklift 19.7
Nippon Yusoki 11.1
TCM 8.2
Nissan Motor 7.7
Other 10.7

Source: "2004 Market Share Report." [online] from http://www.nikkei.co.jp [Published July 27, 2005] from Japan Industrial Vehicles Association.

★ 1670 ★
Construction Equipment
SIC: 3531; NAICS: 33312

Top Hydraulic Shovel Makers in Japan, 2004

Market shares are shown based on domestic shipments of 25,321 units.

Komatsu 28.7%
Shin Caterpillar Mitsubishi 22.2
Hitachi Construction Machinery 22.1
Kobelco Construction Machinery 14.5
Sumitomo Construction Machinery 8.0
Other 6.5

Source: "2004 Market Share Report." [online] from http://www.nikkei.co.jp [Published July 27, 2005] from Japan Construction Equipment Manufacturers Association.

★ 1671 ★
Mining Equipment
SIC: 3532; NAICS: 333131

Coal Mining Monitoring in the Western United States

The company manufactures equipment that monitor gases in mines and also radio equipment.

Conspec 80.0%
Other 20.0

Source: *Canadian Business*, January 30, 2006, p. NA.

★ 1672 ★
Mining Equipment
SIC: 3532; NAICS: 333131

Roof Bolting Machine Market Worldwide

The company has manufactured 4,500 machines since 1960. The United States, South Africa and Poland are its top markets.

Fletcher 90.0%
Other 10.0

Source: *Mining Review*, no 4, 2005, p. 45.

★ 1673 ★
Oil & Gas Equipment
SIC: 3533; NAICS: 333132

Drill Stem Products Market Worldwide

Drill stem products include drill pipe, drill collars and heavy weight drill pipe.

	($ mil.)	Share
Grant	$ 299.0	49.01%
OMSCO	61.0	10.00
IDPA	57.0	9.34
SMFI	49.0	8.03
Daido	24.0	3.93
Sinarsky	24.0	3.93
Tagenrok	24.0	3.93
Texas Steel	19.0	3.11
Drilco	16.0	2.62
BHNKK Republica	14.0	2.29
Other	23.1	3.79

Source: "Grant Prideco." [online] from http://sec.edgar-online.com [Published February 2, 2005] from Grant Prideco.

★ 1674 ★
Oil & Gas Equipment
SIC: 3533; NAICS: 333132

Leading Oil/Gas Field Machinery Makers, 2004

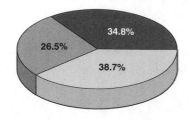

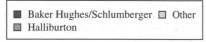

The market was valued at $4.6 billion in 2004. Drilling equipment was the leading sector with a 38.7% share.

Baker Hughes/Schlumberger 34.8%
Halliburton 26.5
Other 38.7

Source: "Oil and Gas Field Machinery in the USA." [online] from http://www.bharatbook.com [Accessed May 1, 2006].

★ 1675 ★
Oil & Gas Equipment
SIC: 3533; NAICS: 333132

Offshore Engineering Equipment Market Worldwide

The market for offshore engineering, construction and equipment is hard to quantify. It includes platform construction, subsea installation construction and subsea production equipment. It excludes maintenance services or the leasing of floating installations. Tecnip, Saipem and AkerKvaerner took 12-13% of the market each.

Aker Kvaerner 13.0%
Saipem 13.0
Technip 13.0
Halliburton-KBR 6.0
McDermott 6.0
Stolt Offshore 6.0
Other 43.0

Source: "Exploration & Production Activites and Markets." [online] from http://www.ifp.fr/IFP/en/events/panorama/IFP-Panorama06_01-ActiviteExploProd-VA.pdf [Accessed May 1, 2006].

★ 1676 ★
Oil & Gas Equipment
SIC: 3533; NAICS: 333132

Seamless OCTG Production Worldwide, 2005

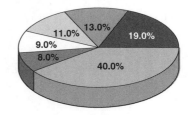

Oil country tubular goods (OCTG) are oilwell casing, production tubing and drill pipe used in oil and natural gas drilling and production operations. The market has been driven in part by repairs needed to infrastructure in the Gulf of Mexico after Hurricanes Rita, Katrina and Wilma. Large diameter pipe bookings are expected to be running at full capacity through 2006.

Tenaris 19.0%
V&M 13.0
TMK 11.0
TPCO 9.0
US Steel 8.0
Other 40.0

Source: "Tenaris Investor Day." [online] from http://www.tenaris.com/en/Investors/files/ID_2006.pdf [Published April 6, 2006] from company estimates.

★ 1677 ★
Oil & Gas Equipment
SIC: 3533; NAICS: 333132

Subsea Tree Market Shares Worldwide

The function of a subsea tree is to both prevent the release of oil or gas from an oil well into the environment and also to direct and control the flow of fluids. Market shares are for year to date June 2005.

FMC Technologies 37.0%
Cooper Cameron 31.0
Vetco 16.0
Aker Kvaerner 15.0
Dril-Quip 1.0

Source: "FMC Technologies." [online] from http://www.secinfo.com/d14D5a.z5H475.d.htm [Published Sept. 9, 2005] from Quest Offshore Resources Inc.

★ 1678 ★
Elevators
SIC: 3534; NAICS: 333921
Elevator Market Worldwide, 2004

Total elevators in operation were 7.4 million. The new elevator market: Europe 29%, China 26%, Americas 12%, Japan 10% and other 23%.

Europe	.51.0%
Americas	.17.0
China	8.0
Japan	8.0
Korea	3.0
Other	.13.0

Source: "Elevator Market." [online] from http://www.kone.com/en/main/0,content4808.00html [Accessed November 7, 2005].

★ 1679 ★
Elevators
SIC: 3534; NAICS: 333921
Global Elevator Market, 2009

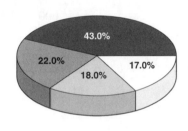

■ Asia/Pacific □ North America
▨ Western Europe □ Other

The world market for elevator and escalator products and services is forecast to increase 7% annually through 2009. It is expected to reach $609 billion. The industry will benefit from an improved nonresidential building sector. There will also a slowdown in residential buildiing construction according to the source, which is an important elevator market in Europe and Asia.

Asia/Pacific	.43.0%
Western Europe	.22.0
North America	.18.0
Other	.17.0

Source: *World Elevators - Freedonia New World Industry Study*, January 2006, p. 1, from Freedonia Group.

★ 1680 ★
Elevators
SIC: 3534; NAICS: 333921
Largest Elevator/Escalator Makers Worldwide

The industry is valued at 30 billion euros.

Otis	.27.0%
Schindler	.18.0
ThyssenKrupp	.13.0
Mitsubishi	.10.0
Kone	9.0
Hitachi	7.0
Toshiba	4.0
Fujitec	2.0
Other	.10.0

Source: "The Fifth Annual CERT CEO Roundtable." [online] from http://www.canada-europe.org/en/pdf/Elliott_Berlin_CERT_Segment_Presentation_En_Okt05.ppt from ThyssenKrupp.

★ 1681 ★
Elevators
SIC: 3534; NAICS: 333921
Leading Elevator Firms in France, 2003

France is the third largest elevator market in Europe after Italy and Germany. It has 430,000 existing elevators. Housing takes 54% of the market, offices 15% and industries, hotels and hospitals another 15%.

Otis	.34.0%
Schindler	.19.0
Kone	.14.0
ThyssenKrupp	.10.5
CG2A	5.8
CFA	4.7
Soulier	1.8
Other	.10.2

Source: "French Elevator Market." http://www.buyusainfo.net [Published January 2006] from CECI.

★ 1682 ★
Escalators
SIC: 3534; NAICS: 333921

Escalator Market Worldwide, 2004

Total escalators in operation were 328,000 units. The 28,000 new escalator market: China 51%, Europe 13%, Japan 9%, Americas 7% and other 20%.

China	.24.0%
Europe	.23.0
Americas	.18.0
Japan	.17.0
Other	.18.0

Source: "Elevator Market." [online] from http://www.kone.com/en/main/0,content4808.00html [Accessed November 7, 2005].

★ 1683 ★
Escalators
SIC: 3534; NAICS: 333921

World Escalator Railing Market

The two companies have the lion's share of the market for rubber and plastic railing for escalators.

Escalator Handrail Co./Semperit AG	.80.0%
Other	.20.0

Source: "Getting a Grip on the Market." [online] from http://www.transobj.workopolis.com/servlet/content/qprinter [Published October 29, 2005].

★ 1684 ★
Cranes
SIC: 3536; NAICS: 333923

Crane Production in Japan

Japan's mobile crane market peaked in the 1990s. Production hit its peak with 7,244 units in 1996 but fell 68% to 2,033 units in 2002. At the end of Japan's recession the mobile crane makers were still left standing. The source points out that many American and European crane makers closed their doors in the 1970s and 1980s during similar economic hardships.

	2001	2002	Share
Rough terrain	1,252	1,003	49.34%
Crawler crane	458	467	22.97
Trucks	242	307	15.10
Tower crane	236	256	12.59

Source: *Cranes Today*, January 2006, p. 28.

★ 1685 ★
Cranes
SIC: 3536; NAICS: 333923

Global RT Crane Sales, 2004-2005

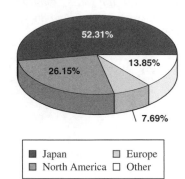

Japan	Europe
North America	Other

RT stands for rough terrain. Japan is number one in the marekt. RT cranes once sold in thousands in the United States but lost ground to the versatile telescopic handlers that took over the low-end of the capacity scale.

	2004	2005	Share
Japan	1,100	1,700	52.31%
North America	600	850	26.15
Europe	275	250	7.69
Other	385	450	13.85

Source: *Cranes Today*, February 2006, p. 12.

★ 1686 ★
Cranes
SIC: 3536; NAICS: 333923

Leading Mobile Crane Makers in China, 2004

Market shares are shown based on unit volume.

XCMC	.43.0%
Puyuan	.18.0
Changjiang	.12.0
Tai'an Crane	.9.0
Bengbu	.5.0
Other	.13.0

Source: *Chinese Construction Equipment*, Bear Stearns Equity Research, November 11, 2005, p. 14.

★ 1687 ★

Cranes

SIC: 3536; NAICS: 333923

Ship-to-Shore Container Crane Market Worldwide

The company has about half of the ship-to-shore container crane market.

ZPMC 50.0%
Other 50.0

Source: *Cranes Today*, June 2005, p. 55.

★ 1688 ★

Hoists

SIC: 3536; NAICS: 333923

Hoist Sales by Type

In 1987 the industry was valued at $350 million. Currently it is placed at about $600 million. Current products are still similar: electric, air and manual-powered chain and wire rope hoists. Electric chain hoists were the most popular type of hoist between 1998 and 2002. They represent about 15% of the industry.

Components, parts 18.9%
Electric chain 15.1
Electric wire rope 11.4
Hand chain 6.0
Wire pullers 5.1
Air chain 4.4
Ratchet lever 3.4
Other 64.3

Source: *Hoist*, July - August 2005, p. 17, from Material Handling Industry of America.

★ 1689 ★

Travel Towers

SIC: 3536; NAICS: 333923

Travel Tower Market in Australia

Market shares are estimated in percent.

Sherrin Hire 80.0%
Other 20.0

Source: "Investor Presentation." [online] from http://www.boomlogistics.com.au/images/boom—-ohboh.pdf [Published June 2005].

★ 1690 ★

Lift Trucks

SIC: 3537; NAICS: 333924

Largest Lift Truck Makers Worldwide, 2004

Lift truck orders soared globally, posting a 17% jump over 2003. Firms are ranked by worldwide revenue in millions of dollars.

Toyota . . . . $ 4,890
Linde 4,490
Jungheinrich 2,070
NACCO Industries 1,900
Mitsubishi/Caterpillar 1,300
Crown 1,230
Komatsu 1,030
Nissan 828
TCM 759
Nichiyu 357
Daewoo 321
Manitou 300

Source: *Modern Materials Handling*, August 2005, p. 43.

★ 1691 ★

Machine Tools

SIC: 3541; NAICS: 333512

Largest Drilling Machine Makers Worldwide, 2005

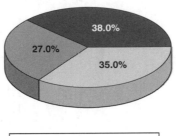

Total demand was 2,500 machines.

Hitachi 38.0%
Schmoll/Posalux 27.0
Other 35.0

Source: *EIPC Speednews*, January 2006, p. 7.

★ 1692 ★
Machine Tools
SIC: 3541; NAICS: 333512

Largest Drilling Tool Firms Worldwide

Firms are ranked by millions of pieces annually.

Union Tool	240
TCT	120
HPTec	72
Toshiba	72
Kemmer	40
Kyocera Tycom	35
Tera	28
Jinzhou	26
Mitsubishi	25
HAN	20

Source: *CircuiTree*, November 2005, p. 66, from Union Tool.

★ 1693 ★
Machine Tools
SIC: 3541; NAICS: 333512

Largest Machine Tool Consumers Worldwide, 2005

Countries are ranked by machine-tool consumption (cutting and forming types) in millions of dollars. Shares are shown based on the top 25 countries.

	($ mil.)	Share
China	$ 10,900.0	21.94%
Japan	7,527.8	15.15
United States	5,822.6	11.72
Germany	5,307.6	10.68
Korea, Rep. Of	3,665.6	7.38
Italy	3,293.8	6.63
Taiwan	2,192.6	4.41
Canada	1,428.9	2.88
France	1,423.2	2.86
Spain	1,087.4	2.19
Brazil	1,082.3	2.18
India	999.7	2.01
Other	4,948.9	9.96

Source: "2006 World Machine Tool Output & Consumption Survey." [online] from http://www.gardnerweb.com [Accessed March 15, 2006] from *2006 World Machine Tool Output & Consumption Survey*.

★ 1694 ★
Machine Tools
SIC: 3541; NAICS: 333512

Largest Machine Tool Producers Worldwide, 2005

Countries are ranked by machine-tool production (cutting and forming types) in millions of dollars.

	($ mil.)	Share
Japan	$ 13,258.6	25.55%
Germany	9,508.7	18.33
China	5,000.0	9.64
Italy	4,878.6	9.40
Taiwan	3,295.1	6.35
United States	3,169.4	6.11
Korea, Rep. Of	2,815.6	5.43
Switzerland	2,635.1	5.08
Spain	1,141.4	2.20
Canada	949.1	1.83
France	907.4	1.75
Brazil	689.2	1.33
Other	3,639.0	7.01

Source: "2006 World Machine Tool Output & Consumption Survey." [online] from http://www.gardnerweb.com [Accessed March 15, 2006] from *2006 World Machine Tool Output & Consumption Survey*.

★ 1695 ★
Machine Tools
SIC: 3541; NAICS: 333512

Machine Tool Industry

The industry consists of 7,000 firms with annual revenues of $25 billion. A typical company's revenue was under $10 million. Industry revenue shares are shown by segment.

Dies and molds	50.0%
Cutting tools	20.0
Machining centers	15.0
Other	15.0

Source: *Business Wire*, November 29, 2005, p. NA, from Research and Markets.

★ 1696 ★
Machine Tools
SIC: 3541; NAICS: 333512

Top Machining Center Makers in Japan, 2004

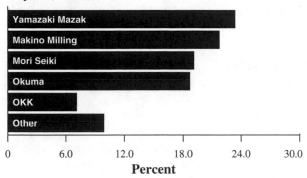

Market shares are shown based on domestic shipments of 267.4 billion yen.

Yamazaki Mazak	.23.4%
Makino Milling	.21.8
Mori Seiki	.19.1
Okuma	.18.7
OKK	7.1
Other	9.9

Source: "2004 Market Share Report." [online] from http://www.nikkei.co.jp [Published July 27, 2005] from Ministry of Economy, Trade and Industry.

★ 1697 ★
Machine Tools
SIC: 3541; NAICS: 333512

Top NC Lathe Makers in Japan, 2004

Market shares are shown based on domestic shipments of 207.6 billion yen. NC stands for numerically controlled.

Yamazaki Mazak	.29.9%
Mori Seiki	.22.8
Okuma	.21.1
Citizen Watch	.11.2
Star Micronics	5.8
Other	9.2

Source: "2004 Market Share Report." [online] from http://www.nikkei.co.jp [Published July 27, 2005] from Ministry of Economy, Trade and Industry.

★ 1698 ★
Machine Tools
SIC: 3541; NAICS: 333512

Top Super-Hard Tool Makers in Japan, 2004

Market shares are shown based on domestic sales of 243.8 billion yen.

Mitsubishi Materials	.14.8%
Sumitomo Electric Hardmetal	.12.1
Tungaloy	.11.8
OSG	5.8
Hitachi Tool Engineering	4.8
Other	.50.7

Source: "2004 Market Share Report." [online] from http://www.nikkei.co.jp [Published July 27, 2005] from Japan Cemented Carbide Tool Manufacturers Association.

★ 1699 ★
Metalworking Machinery
SIC: 3541; NAICS: 333512

Leading Metalcutting Tool Makers Worldwide

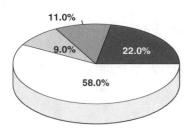

Market shares are shown in percent.

Sandvik	.22.0%
Kennametal	.11.0
Iscar	9.0
Other	.58.0

Source: *Israel Business Arena*, May 10, 2006, p. NA, from Goldman Sachs.

★ 1700 ★
Metalworking Machinery
SIC: 3541; NAICS: 333512

Leading Metalworking Machinery Firms, 2005

Market shares are estimated: Kennametal Inc's share is 5.0%-5.8%, Milacron Inc.'s share is 4.0%- 4.5% and Lincoln Electric Holding Inc's share is 3.0%-3.5%.

Kennametal Inc.	5.8%
Milacron Inc.	4.5
Lincoln Electric Holdings Inc.	3.5
Other	86.2

Source: "US Metalworking Machinery Industry Research." [online] from http://www.ibisworld.com [Accessed May 2, 2006] from IBISWorld.

★ 1701 ★
Metalworking Machinery
SIC: 3541; NAICS: 333512

Metal-Cutting Tool Sales Worldwide

The world market was valued at 100 SEK.

Cemented-carbide tools	75.0%
High-speed steel tools	25.0

Source: "The Sandvik World." [online] from http://www.sanvik.com [Accessed May 30, 2006].

★ 1702 ★
Power Tools
SIC: 3546; NAICS: 333991

Global Market for Chainsaw Parts

The company has half the market for saw chains and guide bars.

Blount International	50.0%
Other	50.0

Source: "Ariel Small Cap Value." [online] from www.arieladvisor.com [Published September 30, 2005].

★ 1703 ★
Power Tools
SIC: 3546; NAICS: 333991

Leading Power Tool Makers, 2005

Power tool sales are estimated to increase have from $3.5 billion in 1995 to $4.9 billion in 2005. The source forecasts industry sales of $5.1 billion in 2006.

BDK	42.0%
TTI/Milwaukee	27.0
Bosch	17.0
Makita	7.0
Craftsman	6.0
Other	1.0

Source: *Homebuilding June 2006 Monthly*, Credit Suisse, June 2006 from Census Bureau, company reports and Credit Suisse analysis and estimates.

★ 1704 ★
Welding Equipment
SIC: 3548; NAICS: 333992

Top Welding Equipment Makers

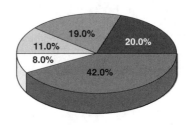

Market shares are shown in percent.

Lincoln Electric	20.0%
Miller (ITW)	19.0
ESAB	11.0
Thermadyne	8.0
Other	42.0

Source: "An Introduction to Thermadyne." [online] from http://www.thermadyne.com/pdf/financials/Thermadyne-Intro.pdf [Published Feb. 1, 2006] from Thermadyne estimates.

★ 1705 ★
Welding Equipment
SIC: 3548; NAICS: 333992

Top Welding Equipment Makers Worldwide

Shares are shown based on a $9 billion market.

Lincoln Electric	14.0%
ESAB	12.0
Miller/Hobart (ITW)	9.0
Thermadyne	5.0
Other	60.0

Source: "An Introduction to Thermadyne." [online] from http://www.thermadyne.com/pdf/financials/Thermadyne-Intro.pdf [Published Feb. 1, 2006] from Thermadyne estimates.

★ 1706 ★
Welding Equipment
SIC: 3548; NAICS: 333992

Top Welding Equipment Markets

Market shares are shown in percent. Figures are based on welding expenditures in 2000 reported to the Bureau of Export Administration.

Automotive	35.0%
Construction	19.0
Light manufacturing	17.0
Capitalized repair & maintenance	15.0
Other	14.0

Source: "An Introduction to Thermadyne." [online] from http://www.thermadyne.com/pdf/financials/Thermadyne-Intro.pdf [Published Feb. 1, 2006] from U.S. Department of Commerce.

★ 1707 ★
Woodworking Machinery
SIC: 3553; NAICS: 33321

Leading Sawmill/Woodworking Machinery Firms, 2005

Market shares are estimated in percent.

Stanley Works	10.0%
Pioneer Machinery	8.0
Greenlee Textron	6.0
Wood-Mizer Products Inc.	5.0
Other	71.0

Source: "US Sawmill & Woodworking Industry Research." [online] from http://www.ibisworld.com [Accessed May 2, 2006] from IBISWorld.

★ 1708 ★
Woodworking Machinery
SIC: 3553; NAICS: 33321

Stranding Technology Market Worldwide

Market shares are shown in percent.

Carmanah	80.0%
Other	20.0

Source: "Saddle Up for Tuscon." [online] from http://www.apawood.org [Accessed November 1, 2005].

★ 1709 ★
Plotters
SIC: 3555; NAICS: 333293

Popular Brands of Plotters

Data show the most owned types of plotters, based on a survey.

Gerber Scientific Products	29.0%
Graphtec USA	25.0
Roland DGA Corporation	23.0
Summa	10.0
Ioiline	6.0

Source: *Signs of the Times*, February 2006, p. 98, from *Signs of the Times 2005 Vinyl Survey*.

★ 1710 ★
Printing Equipment
SIC: 3555; NAICS: 333293

Commercial Digital Production Industry

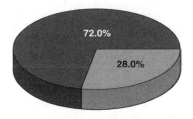

Strategies on Demand forecast that demand for digital color publication and commercial production printing would rise from $3.9 billion in 2000 to $7.3 billion in 2005.

Xerox	72.0%
HP/Kodak	28.0

Source: *Forbes*, July 4, 2005, p. 91.

★ 1711 ★
Printing Equipment
SIC: 3555; NAICS: 333293
Roll-Fed Printer Placements, 2005

Oce has been the leader in monochrome and spot color production since the source began tracking the market in 2003.

Oce .41.0%
Other .59.0

Source: *PR Newswire*, May 10, 2006, p. NA, from *2004-2005 U.S. Production Copying & Printing Placements: Summary and Trends*, Infotrends.

★ 1712 ★
Printing Equipment
SIC: 3555; NAICS: 333293
Top Printing Equipment Makers in Gemany

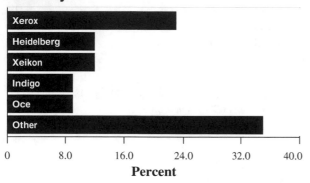

Percent

The market for digital printing systems was valued at $197 million in 2004. Market shares are shown in percent.

Xerox .23.0%
Heidelberg 12.0
Xeikon .12.0
Indigo 9.0
Oce 9.0
Other .35.0

Source: "German Market for Digital Printing Systems." [online] from http://www.stat-usa.gov [Published September 2005].

★ 1713 ★
Beverage Equipment
SIC: 3556; NAICS: 333294
Global Hand-Held Beverage Dispenser Market

Automatic Bar Controls is the largest producer of hand-held beverager dispensers for restaurants, bars and taverns worldwide.

Automatic Bar Controls 90.0%
Other .10.0

Source: *Buyouts*, July 18, 2005, p. NA.

★ 1714 ★
Food Equipment
SIC: 3556; NAICS: 333294
Commercial Pie Baking Equipment

Market shares are shown in percent.

Colborner 90.0%
Other .10.0

Source: "Colborne Corporation." [online] from http://www.careermag.com/JS/General/Job.asp?id6288561 [Published November 18, 2005].

★ 1715 ★
Food Equipment
SIC: 3556; NAICS: 333294
Leading Foodservice Equipment Providers

Firms are ranked by estimated equipment and supply sales in millions of dollars.

Edward Don & Co. . . . . $ 482.0
The Wasserstrom Co. 383.0
Strategic Equipment & Supply 275.0
TriMark USA 231.9
Franke Contract Group 227.0
QualServ Corp. 201.0
The Boetler Companies 138.0
Hubert Co. 120.0
Bargreen-Ellingson 105.0

Source: *Foodservice Equipment & Supplies*, April 2006, p. 32.

★ 1716 ★
Food Equipment
SIC: 3556; NAICS: 333294

Leading Poultry Processing Equipment Makers

Market shares are shown in percent.

Stork	.50.0%
Other	.50.0

Source: "U.S. Acquisition Beefs Up." [online] from http://www.foodproductiondaily.com/news/printNewsBis.asp?id63298 [Published October 18, 2005].

★ 1717 ★
Food Equipment
SIC: 3556; NAICS: 333294

Milking Machine Market Worldwide

Lely has now sold 3,000 machines worldwide.

Lely	.69.0%
Other	.31.0

Source: *Farmers Guardian*, December 2, 2005, p. 81.

★ 1718 ★
Food Machinery
SIC: 3556; NAICS: 333294

Meat Packaging Industry in the U.K.

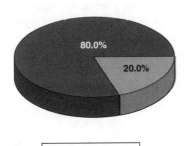

■ Busch ■ Other

Market shares are shown in percent.

Busch	.80.0%
Other	.20.0

Source: *Shropshire Star*, July 25, 2005, p. NA.

★ 1719 ★
Auto Painting Equipment
SIC: 3559; NAICS: 333298

Auto Paint Robotics Market

The company has 80% of the robotics market for items produced by automakers.

ABB	.80.0%
Other	.20.0

Source: *Crain's Detroit Business*, April 10, 2006, p. 3.

★ 1720 ★
Building Maintenance Units
SIC: 3559; NAICS: 333319

BMU Industry in Australia

E.W. Cox is the leader in the manufacturing of building maintenance units, used for window cleaning and façade repairs.

E.W. Cox	.80.0%
Other	.20.0

Source: "Alumni Profiles." [online] from http://www.alumni.rmit.edu.au/fame/profiles/profile/asp?id264 [Accessed April 27, 2006].

★ 1721 ★
Plastics Machinery
SIC: 3559; NAICS: 333298

Largest PU Machinery Makers

Companies are ranked by sales in thousands of dollars.

Canon Group	$ 142,000
Henneck GmbH	118,000
Krauss Maffei	105,000
Klockner	30,000
Pecken-Kirfel GmbH	24,500
Impianti OMS	16,500
EDF Polymer	10,200
Nortec-Cannon	10,000
Wintech International	8,750
Baule	7,500

Source: *Urethanes Technology*, April/May 2005, p. 22.

★ 1722 ★
Plastics Machinery
SIC: 3559; NAICS: 33322

Top Plastic Injection Molding Machine Makers in Japan, 2004

Market shares are shown based on domestic production of 18,093 units.

Sumitomo Heavy Industries	.22.8%
Fanuc	.19.2
Nissei Plastic Industrial	.18.4
Japan Steel Works	.13.3
Toshiba Machine	.10.3
Other	.16.0

Source: "2004 Market Share Report." [online] from http://www.nikkei.co.jp [Published July 27, 2005] from Nikkei estimates and Ministry of Economy, Trade and Industry.

★ 1723 ★
Semiconductor Equipment
SIC: 3559; NAICS: 333295

CDMA Test Equipment Market Worldwide, 2004

Distribution is shown based on revenue. CDMA stands for code division multiple access.

North America	.56.3%
Asia-Pacific	.33.6
Europe	. 2.6
Other	. 7.5

Source: *Telecommunications America*, June 2005, p. 36, from Frost & Sullivan.

★ 1724 ★
Semiconductor Equipment
SIC: 3559; NAICS: 333295

Chemical Mechanical Planarization Industry Worldwide

Market shares are shown in percent.

Applied Materials	.73.8%
Ebara	.20.6

Source: "Chemical Mechanical Planarization Polisher Market." [online] from http://blogs.zdnet.com/ITFacts?p8037 [Published June 16, 2005] from Information Network.

★ 1725 ★
Semiconductor Equipment
SIC: 3559; NAICS: 333295

Largest Mask Blank Makers Worldwide

Market shares are shown in percent.

Hoya	.80.0%
Other	.20.0

Source: *Business Week Online*, September 15, 2005, p. NA.

★ 1726 ★
Semiconductor Equipment
SIC: 3559; NAICS: 333295

Pad and Slurry Industry

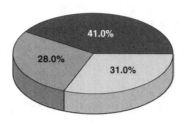

■ Rohm and Hass Electronics Materials   □ Other
■ Cabot Microelectronics

The CMP (chemical mechanical planarization) consumables market climbed to a record $1.1 billion in 2005 according to a recently completed industry analysis report from Linx Consulting. The report establishes that the global market in 2005 for CMP slurries and pads was $975 million combined, with the balance being cleaners and conditioners.

Rohm and Hass Electronics Materials	.41.0%
Cabot Microelectronics	.28.0
Other	.31.0

Source: *PR Newswire*, April 20, 2006, p. NA, from Linx Consulting.

★ 1727 ★
Semiconductor Equipment
SIC: 3559; NAICS: 333295

Physical Vapor Deposition Industry Worldwide

The industry is valued at $1.6 billion.

Applied Materials	.78.0%
Other	.22.0

Source: *Electronic Chemicals News*, June 15, 2005, p. NA, from VLSI Research.

★ 1728 ★
Semiconductor Equipment
SIC: 3559; NAICS: 333295

Top Semiconductor Equipment Makers Worldwide, 2005

Firms are ranked by sales in millions of dollars.

	($ mil.)	Share
Applied Materials	$ 4,738.0	13.7%
Tokyo Electron	3,851.7	11.2
ASML	2,732.6	7.9
Advantest	2,089.3	6.1
KLA-Tencor	1,654.9	4.8
Nikon	1,507.8	4.4
LAM Research	1,147.0	3.3
Novellus Systems	1,130.1	3.3
Dainippon Screen	991.5	2.9
Hitachi High-Technologies	837.5	2.4
Other	13,793.7	40.0

Source: *Electronic Business*, May 1, 2006, p. NA, from Gartner Dataquest.

★ 1729 ★
Wastewater Equipment
SIC: 3559; NAICS: 333298

Wastewater Sludge Equipment Market

The wastewater sludge equipment market reached $338.6 million.

Dewatering	72.1%
Digestion	17.5
Incineration	6.1
Drying	4.3

Source: *Water World*, September 2005, p. 82, from Frost & Sullivan.

★ 1730 ★
Bearings
SIC: 3562; NAICS: 332991

Top Bearings Makers in Japan, 2004

Market shares are shown based on domestic sales of 434.1 billion yen.

NSK	34.1%
Koyo Seiko	28.0
NTN	27.2
Nachi-Fujikoshi	6.2
Minebea	3.8
Other	20.7

Source: "2004 Market Share Report." [online] from http://www.nikkei.co.jp [Published July 27, 2005] from Nikkei estimates and Japan Bearing Industrial Association.

★ 1731 ★
Compressors
SIC: 3563; NAICS: 333912

Largest Gas Compression Operators

Firms are ranked by sales in millions of dollars. After the top two firms there are 100 more operators.

Hanover Compressor	$ 1,300
Universal Compression Holdings	785

Source: *Investor's Business Daily*, October 13, 2005, p. A8.

★ 1732 ★
Packaging Equipment
SIC: 3565; NAICS: 333993

Packaging Equipment Industry in Germany

Packaging machinery was placed at $4.65 billion in 2004.

Packaging machinery for beverages	27.0%
Meat processing machinery	13.0
Coffee, tea and tobacco processing machinery	12.0
Beverage processing machinery	8.0
Bakery machinery	7.0
Confectionery machinery	6.0
Other	27.0

Source: "Packaging Machinery and Equipment." [online] from http://www.export.gov [Published September 2005].

★ 1733 ★
Incinerators
SIC: 3567; NAICS: 333994

Top Garbage Incincerator Makers in Japan, 2004

Market shares are shown based on domestic orders of 2,200 tons each day.

Kawasaki Heavy Industries	24.5%
Nippon Steel	20.5
Hitachi Zosen	19.0
JFE Engineering	15.1
Ebara	8.2
Other	12.7

Source: "2004 Market Share Report." [online] from http://www.nikkei.co.jp [Published July 27, 2005] from Nikkei estimates.

★ 1734 ★
Centrifuges
SIC: 3568; NAICS: 333613
Uranium Enrichment Market Worldwide, 2004

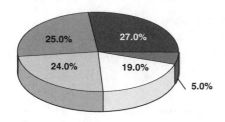

Market shares are shown in percent.

USEC	.27.0%
EURODIF/AREVA	.25.0
Tenex	.24.0
Urenco	.19.0
Other	5.0

Source: "Urenco Eurobond Issue." [online] from http:// www.urenco.com/im/uploaded/1136981670.pdf [Published November 2005] from Urenco.

★ 1735 ★
Filters
SIC: 3569; NAICS: 333999
Air Filter Market Worldwide, 2008

Companies are ranked by air filter sales in millions of dollars.

United States	$ 1,397
China	298
Japan	250
Germany	121
United Kingdom	108
India	94
South Korea	89
France	84
Brazil	82
Italy	76
Russia	71

Source: "U.S. Continues to Dominate the Medium Efficiency Air Filter Market." [online] from http:// www.mcilvainecompany.com [Published May 2005] from McIlvaine Company.

★ 1736 ★
Filters
SIC: 3569; NAICS: 333999
New Filter and Pre-filter Sales Worldwide, 2008

Sales are shown in millions of dollars.

United States	$ 47.62
Japan	43.93
Taiwan	26.68
South Korea	21.98
China	13.14
Thailand	9.53
Malaysia	9.18
United Kingdom	7.78
Germany	6.98
France	6.90
Singapore	5.63
Philippines	5.15

Source: *CleanRooms*, June 2005, p. 14, from McIlvaine Company.

★ 1737 ★
Water Filters
SIC: 3569; NAICS: 333999
Top Water Filter Brands, 2005

Market shares are shown in percent. Figures exclude Wal-Mart and other large format mass retailers.

Brita (Clorox)	.70.7%
Pur (Procter & Gamble)	.28.0
Culligan (United States Filter)	0.8
Sunbeam (Prestige Home Products)	0.1
Private label	0.1
Other	0.4

Source: *U.S. Personal Care and Household Products Digest*, Citigroup Equity Research, February 24, 2006, p. 223, from ACNielsen.

★ 1738 ★
Water Filters
SIC: 3569; NAICS: 333999

Ultrapure Water Market Worldwide

The major application of the ultrapure water market is for the power industry. Water is heated and used to turn turbines. The industry sees about $2 billion in revenues. Hardware represents 65% of the revenues, with the balance held by consumables.

	($ mil.)	Share
Semiconductor	$ 1,300	40.63%
Non-cleanroom	1,247	38.97
Pharmaceuticals	231	7.22
Flat panel	222	6.94
Other cleanroom	200	6.25

Source: *CleanRooms*, July 2005, p. 14, from McIlvaine Company.

★ 1739 ★
Water Filters
SIC: 3569; NAICS: 333999

Water Purification Industry in India

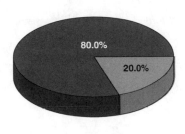

The industry is valued at Rs 500 crore. The company's share exceeds 80%.

Eureka Forbes	.80.0%
Other	.20.0

Source: *Economic Times*, November 21, 2005, p. NA.

★ 1740 ★
Computers
SIC: 3571; NAICS: 334111

Computer Shipments by Region, 2004-2005

Total shipments increased from 189.53 million units in 2004 to 218.53 million in 2005.

	2004	2005
United States	32.9%	30.7%
EMEA	32.7	33.2
Asia/Pacific	17.9	19.6
Japan	7.2	6.7
Latin America	6.2	6.7
Canada	3.1	3.0

Source: *Business Communications Review*, March 2006, p. 6, from Gartner.

★ 1741 ★
Computers
SIC: 3571; NAICS: 334111

Leading Commercial Desktop PC Makers, 2006

Market shares are shown based on unit sales for February 2006.

Hewlett-Packard	.52.0%
IBM	.24.0
Apple	6.0
Compaq	1.0
Sony	1.0
Other	.16.0

Source: *Systems and PC Hardware*, Morgan Stanley, March 16, 2006, p. 20, from Morgan Stanley Research and NPD Techworld.

★ 1742 ★
Computers
SIC: 3571; NAICS: 334111

Leading Notebook PC Makers, 2006

Market shares are shown based on unit sales for February 2006.

IBM	.44.0%
HP	.24.0
Sony	6.0
Apple	4.0
Toshiba	4.0
Compaq	1.0
Other	.17.0

Source: *Systems and PC Hardware*, Morgan Stanley, March 16, 2006, p. 20, from Morgan Stanley Research.

★ 1743 ★
Computers
SIC: 3571; NAICS: 334111

PC Sales by Year

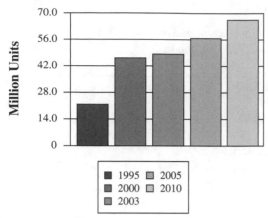

Data are in millions of units. Dell's market share is
forecast to grow from 37.86% in 2005 and 49.19% in
2010.

1995	21.4
2000	46.0
2003	48.3
2005	56.6
2010	66.7

Source: "eTForecasts - Worldwide PC Forecast." [online]
from http://www.eforecasts.com/products/ES_pcww1203.
htm [Accessed Feb 9, 2006].

★ 1744 ★
Computers
SIC: 3571; NAICS: 334111

Rugged Computer Market

*Panasonic Corp. manufactures the Toughbook line, a
line of extra-durable laptop and notebook computers.
Department of Defense workers used to buy regular
notebooks, which are less expensive than rugged computers. However, a new dilemna has now presented it-
self — how to dispose of damaged notebooks (damaged by sun, sand, etc.) with sensitive information on
them.*

Pansonic	70.0%
Other	30.0

Source: *Military & Aerospace Electronics*, March 2006,
p. 28.

★ 1745 ★
Computers
SIC: 3571; NAICS: 334111

Top Computer Makers, 2005

Vendors are ranked by preliminary unit shipments.

	(000)	Share
Dell	21,466	33.5%
Hewlett-Packard	12,452	19.4
Gateway	3,924	6.1
Apple	2,554	4.0
Toshiba	2,260	3.5
Lenovo	2,075	3.2
Other	19,357	30.2

Source: "PC Market Continues Rapid Growth in Fourth
Quarter." [online] from http://www.idc.com [Press release
January 18, 2006] from International Data Corp's World-
wide Quarterly PC Tracker.

★ 1746 ★
Computers
SIC: 3571; NAICS: 334111

Top Computer Makers in Asia/Pacific, 2004-2005

*Shares are estimated for 2005. Figures exclude
Japann.*

	2004	2005
Lenovo	12.0	18.0%
Hewlett-Packard	10.1	11.6
Dell	7.0	8.3
Founder	5.3	5.7
Acer	4.3	5.4
Other	61.3	51.0

Source: "IDC Reports that 2005 Marked the Strongest
Growth." [online] from http://www.idc.com [Press release
January 18, 2006] from International Data Corp's World-
wide Quarterly PC Tracker.

★ 1747 ★
Computers
SIC: 3571; NAICS: 334111

Top Computer Makers in China, 2005

Market shares are shown based on units shipped.

Lenovo	32.5%
Founder	12.3
Dell	8.8
HP	7.1
Tsinghua Tongfang	6.5
Other	32.5

Source: *Wall Street Journal*, April 6, 2006, p. B5, from International Data Corp.

★ 1748 ★
Computers
SIC: 3571; NAICS: 334111

Top Computer Makers in Israel, 2005

Israel's PC market was placed at $507 million in 2005. Lenovo led the $209.1 million laptop market with a 27.6% share.

Hewlett-Packard	17.3%
IBM/Lenovo	13.8
Dell Computer	9.1
Other	59.8

Source: *Israel Business Arena*, February 28, 2006, p. NA, from International Data Corp. Israel.

★ 1749 ★
Computers
SIC: 3571; NAICS: 334111

Top Computer Makers in Japan, 2005

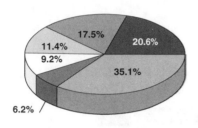

17.5% | 20.6% | 11.4% | 9.2% | 35.1% | 6.2%

- ■ NEC   □ Toshiba
- ■ Fujitsu ■ Sony
- □ Dell   ■ Other

Personal computer sales stood at 14.15 million units in 2005.

NEC	20.6%
Fujitsu	17.5
Dell	11.4
Toshiba	9.2
Sony	6.2
Other	35.1

Source: *Japan Computer Industry Scan*, February 6, 2006, p. NA, from Gartner Japan.

★ 1750 ★
Computers
SIC: 3571; NAICS: 334111

Top Computer Makers in the U.K., 2005

Market shares are shown for the third quarter of 2005.

Dell	26.0%
Hewlett-Packard	18.0

NEC	8.0%
Acer	6.0
Toshiba	6.0
Other	37.0

Source: *Computer Trade Shopper*, November 9, 2005, p. 10, from Gartner.

★ 1751 ★
Computers
SIC: 3571; NAICS: 334111

Top Computer Makers Worldwide, 2005

Vendors are ranked by preliminary unit shipments.

	(000)	Share
Dell	37,732	18.1%
Hewlett-Packard	32,525	15.6
Lenovo	12,995	6.2
Acer	9,803	4.7
Fujitsu/Fujitsu Siemens	8,489	4.1
Other	107,041	51.3

Source: "PC Market Continues Rapid Growth in Fourth Quarter." [online] from http://www.idc.com [Press release January 18, 2006] from International Data Corp's Worldwide Quarterly PC Tracker.

★ 1752 ★
Computers
SIC: 3571; NAICS: 334111

Top Electronic Dictionary Makers in Japan, 2004

Market shares are shown based on domestic shipments of 2.58 million units.

Casio Computer	51.0%
Sharp	26.5
Seiko Instruments	13.8
Canon Sales	6.7
Sony	2.0

Source: "2004 Market Share Report." [online] from http://www.nikkei.co.jp [Published July 27, 2005] from Nikkei estimates.

★ 1753 ★
Computers
SIC: 3571; NAICS: 334111

Top Handheld Device Makers in Western Europe, 2005

Market shares are estimated for the first quarter of 2005. The market grew 55% over the same quarter in 2004. Converged devices (voice-enabled PDAs and smart phones) continue to drive the industry.

Nokia	.45.0%
Hewlett-Packard	8.0
palmOne	6.0
RIM	6.0
Sony Ericsson	5.0
Other	.30.0

Source: ''GPS Drives European Handheld Growth.'' [online] from http://www.idc.com [Published May 5, 2005] from International Data Corp.

★ 1754 ★
Computers
SIC: 3571; NAICS: 334111

Top Notebook Makers in Spain

Shares are from July - September 2005.

Acer	.22.6%
Hewlett-Packard	.20.6
Other	.56.8

Source: *Expansion*, October 26, 2005, p. NA.

★ 1755 ★
Computers
SIC: 3571; NAICS: 334111

Top Notebook Makers in the Asia/ Pacific Region

Market shares are shown for the third quarter of 2005. Figures exclude Japan.

Lenovo	.20.4%
Hewlett-Packard	.12.4
Dell	7.8
Founder	6.2
Acer	5.5
Other	.47.7

Source: *Taiwan Economic News*, October 26, 2005, p. NA, from International Data Corp.

★ 1756 ★
Computers
SIC: 3571; NAICS: 334111

Top Notebook Makers in the U.K., 2005

Market shares are shown for the second quarter of 2005.

	Units	Share
Toshiba	983,401	33.16%
Dell	592,190	19.97
Sony	592,190	19.97
HP	347,242	11.71
Acer	127,662	4.30
NEC CI	109,887	3.71
Fujitsu Siemens	101,692	3.43
Lenovo	98,550	3.32
IBM	8,250	0.28
Maxdata	2,423	0.08
Other	2,331	0.08

Source: *Computer Trade Shopper*, August 17, 2005, p. 30, from Context.

★ 1757 ★
Computers
SIC: 3571; NAICS: 334111

Top PDA Makers Worldwide

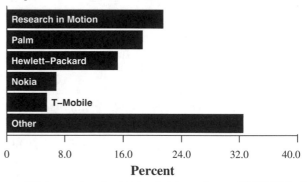

Companies are ranked by estimated shipments. Totals do not include smartphones, such as Treo 650 and Blackberry 7100 but include wireless PDAs, such as IPAQ 65xx and Blackberry 8700.

	Units	Share
Research in Motion	3,193,000	21.4%
Palm	2,773,025	18.6
Hewlett-Packard	2,264,666	15.2
Nokia	1,010,000	6.8
T-Mobile	812,600	5.5
Other	4,839,701	32.5

Source: ''Gartner Says Worldwide Server Shipments Experience Double-Digit Growth.'' [online] from http://www.gartner.com [Press release March 7, 2006] from Gartner Dataquest.

★ 1758 ★
Mobile Devices
SIC: 3571; NAICS: 334111

Leading Mobile Smart Device Makers, 2005

Market shares are shown for the third quarter.

Nokia	.54.8%
Palm	8.1
Research in Motion	7.5
Motorola	5.3
Hewlett-Packard	4.2
Other	.20.0

Source: *Computer Reseller News*, November 7, 2005, p. NA, from Canalys.

★ 1759 ★
Computer Disk Drives
SIC: 3572; NAICS: 334112

Leading 2.5-inch Drive Makers Worldwide, 2005

Volume shares are shown for July - September 2005.

HGST	.27.0%
Toshiba	.24.0
Fujitsu	.23.0
Seagate	.13.0
Samsung	8.0
WD	5.0

Source: *Electronic Component Industry*, JPMorgan Asia Pacific Equity Research, January 24, 2006, p. 4, from Techno Systems Research.

★ 1760 ★
Computer Disk Drives
SIC: 3572; NAICS: 334112

Leading Storage System Makers Worldwide

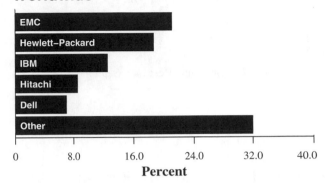

Market shares are shown in percent.

EMC	.21.1%
Hewlett-Packard	.18.7
IBM	.12.6
Hitachi	8.6
Dell	7.0
Other	.32.0

Source: *Technology (Computer Storage Devices)*, Henry Fund Research, April 23, 2006, p. 2, from International Data Corp.

★ 1761 ★
Computer Disk Drives
SIC: 3572; NAICS: 334112

Top External Disk Storage Makers in Asia/Pacific, 2005

Market shares are estimated for the first half of 2005.

Hewlett-Packard	.24.5%
EMC	.23.1
IBM	.18.9
Dell	8.5
HDS	7.6
Sun	7.4
Other	.10.0

Source: "According to IDC's Recent Study, Asia/Pacific External Disk Storage Systems Market." [online] from http://www.idc.com [Published Sep. 5, 2005] from International Data Corp. Asia Pacific Quarterly Disk Storage System Tracker.

★ 1762 ★
Computer Mice
SIC: 3577; NAICS: 334119

Computer Mice Market

Market shares are shown in percent.

Microsoft	.31.1%
Logitech	.24.8
Other	.44.1

Source: *Logitech*, Henry Fund Research, September 18, 2005, p. 3.

★ 1763 ★
Computer Monitors
SIC: 3577; NAICS: 334119

Leading LCD Monitor Makers in North America, 2005

Market shares are shown based on unit sales.

Dell	.37.1%
Hewlett-Packard	.12.6
Acer	. 6.0
Gateway	. 4.9
Samsung	. 4.6
Other	.34.8

Source: "DisplaySearch Indicates Q4'05 LCD Desktop Monitors Rise 11%." [online] from http://www.displaysearch.com/press?id638 [Press release March 20, 2006] from DisplaySearch.

★ 1764 ★
Computer Monitors
SIC: 3577; NAICS: 334119

Leading LCD Monitor Makers Worldwide, 2005

Market shares are shown based on unit sales.

Dell	.19.2%
Samsung	.11.3
Hewlett-Packard	. 9.7
Acer	. 8.6
LGE	. 5.4
Other	.46.7

Source: "DisplaySearch Indicates Q4'05 LCD Desktop Monitors Rise 11%." [online] from http://www.displaysearch.com/press?id638 [Press release March 20, 2006] from DisplaySearch.

★ 1765 ★
Computer Printer Cartridges
SIC: 3577; NAICS: 334119

Leading Printer Cartridge Makers, 2006

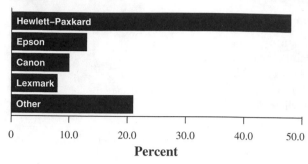

Market shares are shown based on unit sales for February 2006.

Hewlett-Packard	.48.0%
Epson	.13.0
Canon	.10.0
Lexmark	. 8.0
Other	.21.0

Source: *Systems and PC Hardware*, Morgan Stanley, March 16, 2006 from Morgan Stanley Research and NPD Techworld.

★ 1766 ★
Computer Printers
SIC: 3577; NAICS: 334119

Leading Printer Makers (Color), 2005

Market shares are shown for the first quarter of 2005.

Ricoh	.28.0%
Xerox	.28.0
Canon	.26.0
Konica Minolta	.18.0
Toshiba	. 6.0
Other	. 9.0

Source: *Purchasing*, September 15, 2005, p. 47, from Gartner.

★ 1767 ★
Computer Printers
SIC: 3577; NAICS: 334119

Leading Printer Makers in Europe/ Middle East/Africa, 2005

Market shares are shown for the second quarter of the year.

Hewlett-Packard	.37.0%
Canon	.18.0
Epson	.13.0
Lexmark	.10.0
Other	.22.0

Source: *Investor's Business Daily*, September 12, 2005, p. A8, from Gartner Dataquest.

★ 1768 ★
Computer Printers
SIC: 3577; NAICS: 334119

Leading Printer Makers in the U.K.

Hewlett–Packard ■   Samsung ▨
Brother ▨   Other □

Unit sales fell from 61,286 in 2004 to 42,809 in 2005.

Hewlett-Packard	.56.1%
Brother	.10.3
Samsung	7.8
Other	.25.8

Source: *MicroScope*, January 16, 2006, p. 10, from Context.

★ 1769 ★
Computer Printers
SIC: 3577; NAICS: 334119

Leading Printer Makers (Serial Dot Matrix), 2004

Market shares are shown based on shipments.

Oki Data	.50.0%
Epson	.22.0
Lexmark	.11.0
Panasonic	6.0

Genicom (Tally)	5.0%
Citizen	3.0
Other	3.0

Source: *Appliance*, September 2005, p. P-2, from International Data Corp.

★ 1770 ★
Computer Printers
SIC: 3577; NAICS: 334119

Top Inkjet Printer Makers in Japan, 2004

Market shares are shown based on 6.46 million units.

Canon	.43.6%
Seiko Epson	.40.9
HP Japan	6.1
Lexmark	3.2
Other	3.4
Brother Industries	2.8

Source: "2004 Market Share Report." [online] from http://www.nikkei.co.jp [Published July 27, 2005] from Gartner Dataquest.

★ 1771 ★
Computer Printers
SIC: 3577; NAICS: 334119

Top Inkjet Printer Makers Worldwide, 2004

Market shares are shown in percent.

Hewlett-Packard	.40.0%
Canon	.20.0
Other	.40.0

Source: *Fortune*, February 6, 2006, p. 98.

★ 1772 ★
Computer Printers
SIC: 3577; NAICS: 334119

Top Laser Printer Makers in India

The overall market was worth 15,343 units. Roughly 60-70% of new unit sales come from small business customers.

Hewlett-Packard India	.89.0%
Other	.11.0

Source: *Hindu*, February 23, 2006, p. NA, from company.

★ 1773 ★
Computer Printers
SIC: 3577; NAICS: 334119

Top Printer Makers, 2006

Market shares are estimated based on revenue.

Hewlett-Packard	.23.0%
Canon	.16.0
Epson	. 7.0
Xerox	. 6.0
Lexmark	. 4.0
Dell	. 2.0
Other	.42.0

Source: *Printer Hardware*, Credit Suisse, February 7, 2006, p. 12, from company data and Credit Suisse estimates.

★ 1774 ★
Computer Printers
SIC: 3577; NAICS: 334119

Top Printer Makers Worldwide, 2005

Companies are ranked by estimated shipments in millions of units. Global page printer shipments exceeded 21.4 million units in 2005, a 18.6% increase over 2004.

	(mil.)	Share
Hewlett-Packard	10.52	49.0%
Samsung	1.87	8.7
Lexmark	1.26	5.9
Brother	1.17	5.5
Canon	1.15	5.4
Other	5.46	25.5

Source: "Gartner Says Color Printers Drive Worldwide Page Printer Market." [online] from http://www.gartner.com [Press release March 7, 2006] from Gartner Dataquest.

★ 1775 ★
Automated Teller Machines
SIC: 3578; NAICS: 334119

ATM Distribution in Thailand

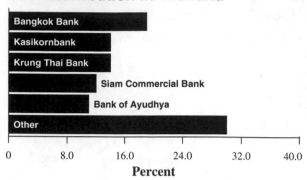

The top firms have 70% of ATM distribution.

Bangkok Bank	.19.0%
Kasikornbank	.14.0
Krung Thai Bank	.14.0
Siam Commercial Bank	.12.0
Bank of Ayudhya	.11.0
Other	.30.0

Source: *Retail Banker International*, December 20, 2005, p. 10, from banks.

★ 1776 ★
Automated Teller Machines
SIC: 3578; NAICS: 334119

Leading ATM Makers, 2005

The growth in shipments has been driven in recent years by banks replacing old ATMs with new ones that meet current encryption standards. The total increased from 65,296 million in 2004 to 71,866 million in 2005.

	Units	Share
Diebold	17,180	23.82%
NCR	15,860	21.99
Triton	14,782	20.49
Tranax	13,500	18.71
Wincor	3,427	4.75
NexTran	3,270	4.53
Tidel	3,135	4.35
Greenlink	857	1.19
Fujitsu	125	0.17

Source: *ATM & Debit News*, April 6, 2006, p. 1.

★ 1777 ★
Automated Teller Machines
SIC: 3578; NAICS: 334119
Leading ATM Makers in Latin America

Market shares are shown based on hardware, terminal software and traditional services for the bank segment.

Diebold	.56.0%
NCR	.17.0
Wincor	7.0
Other	.20.0

Source: "Diebold Investment Community Conference." [online] from http://http://www2.nicewebcast.net/DBDICC-2005/dbd_icc_2005.pdf [Published May 18, 2005].

★ 1778 ★
Automated Teller Machines
SIC: 3578; NAICS: 334119
Leading ATM Makers in the Asia Pacific Region

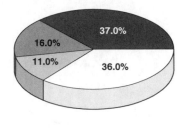

Market shares are shown based on hardware, terminal software and traditional services for the bank segment.

NCR	.37.0%
Diebold	.16.0
Wincor	.11.0
Other	.36.0

Source: "Diebold Investment Community Conference." [online] from http://http://www2.nicewebcast.net/DBDICC-2005/dbd_icc_2005.pdf [Published May 18, 2005].

★ 1779 ★
Automated Teller Machines
SIC: 3578; NAICS: 334119
Leading ATM Makers in the EMEA

Market shares are shown based on hardware, terminal software and traditional services for the bank segment. EMEA stands for Europe, Middle East and Africa.

NCR	.47.0%
Wincor	.34.0
Diebold	.16.0
Other	3.0

Source: "Diebold Investment Community Conference." [online] from http://http://www2.nicewebcast.net/DBDICC-2005/dbd_icc_2005.pdf [Published May 18, 2005].

★ 1780 ★
POS Terminals
SIC: 3578; NAICS: 334119
Largest POS Terminal Makers Worldwide

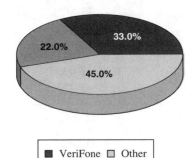

Market shares are shown in percent. POS stands for point of service.

VeriFone	.33.0%
Ingenico	.22.0
Other	.45.0

Source: *Cardline*, March 31, 2006, p. 1, from JP Morgan Securities.

★ 1781 ★
POS Terminals
SIC: 3578; NAICS: 334119
Leading POS Terminal Makers, 2004

Market shares are shown in percent. POS stands for point of service.

Ingenico	.23.0%
VeriFone	.21.8

Continued on next page.

★ 1781 ★

[Continued]
POS Terminals
SIC: 3578; NAICS: 334119

Leading POS Terminal Makers, 2004

Market shares are shown in percent. POS stands for point of service.

Hypercom	.15.2%
Lipman	9.7
Thales	5.7
Sagem	4.4
Axalto	3.0
Other	.13.2

Source: *American Banker*, March 14, 2006, p. 11.

★ 1782 ★

POS Terminals
SIC: 3578; NAICS: 334119

POS Installations in Europe

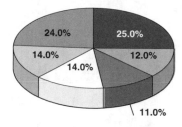

Market shares are shown in percent. POS stands for point of service.

Food and drug	.25.0%
Hypermarkets	.24.0
Department stores	.14.0
Hospitality	.14.0
Specialty stores	.11.0
Other	.12.0

Source: *Stores*, October 2005, p. 16, from IHL Consulting Group.

★ 1783 ★

Postal Metering
SIC: 3579; NAICS: 333313

Mail Metering Market

Pitney also has 60% of the world market.

Pitney Bowes	.80.0%
Other	.20.0

Source: *Smart Money*, January 3, 2006, p. NA.

★ 1784 ★

Scanners
SIC: 3579; NAICS: 333313

Bar Code Scanner Hardware Market Worldwide

Figures are in millions of dollars.

	2007	2008	Share
Hand-held	$ 958	$ 1,027	44.12%
Industrial	520	563	24.18
Stationary	425	451	19.37
Scanner engines	265	287	12.33

Source: "Raymond James Conference." [online] from http://www.metrologic.com/corporate/presentations/raymond_ james [Published March 8, 2006] from Venture Development Corp.

★ 1785 ★

Scanners
SIC: 3579; NAICS: 333313

Leading Bar Code Scanner Hardware Makers Worldwide, 2004

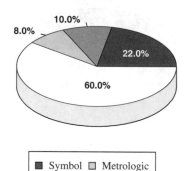

Market shares are shown in percent.

Symbol	.22.0%
PSC	.10.0
Metrologic	8.0
Other	.60.0

Source: "Raymond James Conference." [online] from http://www.metrologic.com/corporate/presentations/raymond_ james [Published March 8, 2006] from Venture Development Corp.

★ 1786 ★
Thermal Printers
SIC: 3579; NAICS: 333313

Leading Thermal Receipt Printer Makers in North America, 2004

Market shares are shown based on shipments.

Epson	.42.0%
Citizen	.16.0
Star	.13.0
TPG	.13.0
Samsung	.4.0
Transact/Ithaca	.4.0
Other	.8.0

Source: *Stores*, January 2006, p. 15, from IHL Consulting Group and *2005 North American Retail Point-of-Sale Printers: Market Study*.

★ 1787 ★
Compressors
SIC: 3585; NAICS: 333415

Air Conditioning Compressor Market Worldwide

World production totaled 75.5 million units valued at $6.5 billion. China represents 43% and East Asia 28% of production. Small hermetic compressors dominate both air conditioning and refrigeration.

	Units	Share
Rotary 1 cycle	64,280,894	74.54%
Scroll	10,850,324	12.58
Reciprocating	7,732,716	8.97
Rotary 2 cycle	3,293,277	3.82
Screw	75,399	0.09
Centrifugal	5,950	0.01

Source: "World ACR Compressors Market." [online] from http://www.bsria.co.uuk/press/press170 [Accessed October 6, 2005] from Building Services Research and Information Association.

★ 1788 ★
Compressors
SIC: 3585; NAICS: 333415

Refrigerator Compressor Market in Thailand

The company also has 40% of the local air conditioning compressor market.

Kulthorn Group	.80.0%
Other	.20.0

Source: *Bangkok Post*, September 20, 2005, p. NA.

★ 1789 ★
Heating and Cooling
SIC: 3585; NAICS: 333415

Air Conditioning Market in South Korea

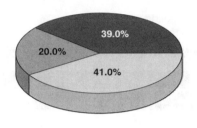

The industry produces around 1.2 million units.

LG	.39.0%
Samsung	.20.0
Other	.41.0

Source: *Financial Express*, March 13, 2006, p. NA, from ORG-MARG.

★ 1790 ★
Heating and Cooling
SIC: 3585; NAICS: 333415

Leading Air Conditioner Brands in China, 2005

Market shares are shown for the first six months of the year.

Haier	.19.32%
Midea	.13.71
Gree	.11.85
Other	.55.12

Source: *Asia Pulse*, July 22, 2005, p. NA.

★ 1791 ★
Heating and Cooling
SIC: 3585; NAICS: 333415

Leading Air Conditioner (Room) Makers, 2004

Market shares are shown based on shipments.

LG Electronics	29.0%
Fedders	22.0
Electrolux (Frigidaire)	11.0
Whirlpool	11.0
Haier	6.0
Samsung	6.0
Sharp	4.0
Other	11.0

Source: *Appliance*, September 2005, p. P-2, from *Appliance* estimates and various surveys.

★ 1792 ★
Heating and Cooling
SIC: 3585; NAICS: 333415

Leading Dehumidifer Makers, 2004

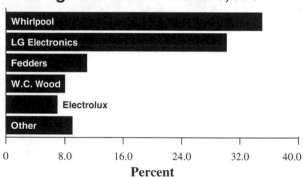

Market shares are shown based on shipments.

Whirlpool	35.0%
LG Electronics	30.0
Fedders	11.0
W.C. Wood	8.0
Electrolux (Frigidaire)	7.0
Other	9.0

Source: *Appliance*, September 2005, p. P-2, from *Appliance* estimates and various surveys.

★ 1793 ★
Heating and Cooling
SIC: 3585; NAICS: 333415

Leading Gas Water Heater (Commercial) Makers, 2004

Market shares are shown based on shipments.

A.O. Smith/State Industries	47.0%
Rheem	25.0
Bradford White	16.0
American Water Heater Co.	7.0
Other	5.0

Source: *Appliance*, September 2005, p. P-2, from *Appliance* estimates and various surveys.

★ 1794 ★
Heating and Cooling
SIC: 3585; NAICS: 333415

Leading Ice Machine Makers, 2004

Market shares are shown based on shipments.

Manitowc	45.0%
Enodis	31.0
Hoshizaki	20.0
Cornelius	4.0

Source: *Appliance*, September 2005, p. P-2, from *Appliance* estimates and various surveys.

★ 1795 ★
Heating and Cooling
SIC: 3585; NAICS: 333415

Leading Refrigerated Display Case Makers, 2004

Market shares are shown based on shipments.

Hussmann	48.0%
Tyler Refrigeration	16.0
Hill Phoenix	15.0
Kysor/Warren	6.0
Other	15.0

Source: *Appliance*, September 2005, p. P-2, from *Appliance* estimates and various surveys.

★ **1796** ★

Heating and Cooling

SIC: 3585; NAICS: 333415

Leading Unitary AC/Heat Pump Makers, 2004

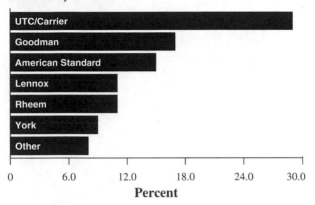

Percent

Market shares are shown based on shipments.

UTC/Carrier	.29.0%
Goodman (Amana)	.17.0
American Standard (Trane)	.15.0
Lennox	.11.0
Rheem	.11.0
York	9.0
Other	8.0

Source: *Appliance*, September 2005, p. P-2, from *Appliance* estimates and various surveys.

★ **1797** ★

Heating and Cooling

SIC: 3585; NAICS: 333415

Top Home Air Conditioner Makers in Japan, 2004

Market shares are shown based on domestic shipments of 7.03 million units.

Daikin Industries	.17.7%
Matsushita Electric Industrial	.16.5
Mitsubishi Electric	.15.0
Toshiba Carrier	.13.0
Hitachi Home & Life Solutions	.10.7
Other	.27.1

Source: "2004 Market Share Report." [online] from http://www.nikkei.co.jp [Published July 27, 2005] from Japan Refrigeration and Air Conditioning Industry Association.

★ **1798** ★

Gas Nozzles

SIC: 3586; NAICS: 332913

Gas Refueling Nozzles

Dover Corp's OPW division makes 80% of gasoline station nozzles.

OPW	.80.0%
Other	.20.0

Source: *Hydraulics & Pneumatics*, June 2005, p. 46.

★ **1799** ★

Paint Dispensing Pumps

SIC: 3586; NAICS: 333913

Pumps in the Paint/Coating Industry Worldwide

The company is the world leader in automatic and manually operated dispensing, metering and mixing equipment for the paints and coatings market, paint mixers and shakers, car refinish products and point-of-purchase dispensers for personal care products.

Idex	.50.0%
Other	.50.0

Source: "About Idex." [online] from http://www.idexcorp.com/aboutleadership.asp [Accessed November 1, 2005] from Idex Corp.

★ **1800** ★

Injection Systems

SIC: 3592; NAICS: 336311

Diesel Injection Systems Market in Europe

Diesels make up about 25% of the passenger car market in Europe, and the penetration is expected to reach 30% within four years and 35% by about 2010. Market shares are shown in percent.

Bosch	.68.4%
Delphi	.14.9
Siemens	6.4
Magnetti Marelli	3.6
Denso	2.6
Other	4.1

Source: *Automotive News Europe*, August 22, 2005, p. 8, from Robert Bosch.

★ 1801 ★
Pumps
SIC: 3594; NAICS: 333996

Top Pump Makers Worldwide, 2005

Market shares are shown in percent. Centrifugal pumps take 80% of the market, while rotary and reciprocating pumps took 7% each and diaphragm with a 5% share.

ITT Industries	6.3%
Flowserve	3.9
Grundfos	3.8
Ebara	3.7
KSB	3.4
Other	78.9

Source: "Targeting the Pump & Valve Industry." [online] from http://www.indek.kth.se/./modules.php?opmodload& nameUpDownload&fileindex&reqgetit&lid355 [Accessed June 1, 2006] from company web sites.

★ 1802 ★
Robots
SIC: 3599; NAICS: 333999

Top Industrial Robot Makers in Japan, 2004

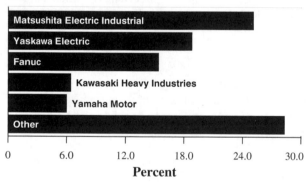

Percent

Market shares are shown based on domestic shipments of 272.21 billion yen.

Matsushita Electric Industrial	25.1%
Yaskawa Electric	18.8
Fanuc	15.4
Kawasaki Heavy Industries	6.4
Yamaha Motor	6.0
Other	28.3

Source: "2004 Market Share Report." [online] from http://www.nikkei.co.jp [Published July 27, 2005] from Japan Robot Association.

SIC 36 - Electronic and Other Electric Equipment

★ 1803 ★

Electronics

SIC: 3600; NAICS: 334111, 33422

China and Electronics Production

China is taking a growing share of electronics production. International electronics firms have turned to local suppliers in China for lower costs and speedier delivery to bypass import delays.

	1999	2002	2005
China	5.2%	11.4%	15.7%
Other	94.8	88.6	84.3

Source: *Electronic Business*, February 2006, p. 36, from *Yearbook of World Electronics* data and Reed Electronics Research.

★ 1804 ★

Electronics

SIC: 3600; NAICS: 334111, 33422

Global Electronics Production, 2004

According to the source electronics recently surpassed the automotive market as the world's largest single industry. Asia's share is close to two-thirds, up from 53% in 2001. Production is shown in billions of dollars.

	($ bil.)	Share
Southeast Asia	$ 515	41.63%
Japan	266	21.50
Europe	229	18.51
America	227	18.35

Source: *CircuiTree*, March 2006, p. 58, from Semiconductor Industry Association and Wait Custer.

★ 1805 ★

Electronics

SIC: 3600; NAICS: 334111, 33422

Largest Electronics Firms

Firms are ranked by electronics revenue in billions of dollars.

IBM	$ 96.29
Hewlett-Packard	81.48
Matsushita Electric Industrial	80.43
Siemens	56.60
Samsung Electronics	56.19
Dell	49.20
Hitachi	47.02
NEC	46.70
Fujitsu	45.12
Sony	43.91

Source: *Electronic Business*, August 2005, p. 40, from Reed Research Group.

★ 1806 ★

Power Products

SIC: 3612; NAICS: 335311

Leading Grid System Makers, 2005

The market size was placed at $2.9 billion.

ABB	26.0%
Siemens	16.0
Areva	7.0
GE	3.0
Other	48.0

Source: "ABB Products Power Division." [online] from http://wwww.abb.com [Accessed May 15, 2006] from Goulden Reports, ARC, ABS Reports, NEMA, ZVEI, CORTEZ and ABB estimates.

★ 1807 ★
Power Products
SIC: 3612; NAICS: 335311

Leading Medium Voltage Product Makers, 2005

The market size was placed at $10.5 billion.

ABB .20.0%
Schneider 12.0
Siemens 10.0
Areva 7.0
Other 51.0

Source: "ABB Products Power Division." [online] from http://www.abb.com [Accessed May 15, 2006] from Goulden Reports, ARC, ABS Reports, NEMA, ZVEI, CORTEZ and ABB estimates.

★ 1808 ★
Power Products
SIC: 3612; NAICS: 335311

Leading Power Generation Makers, 2005

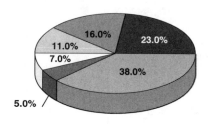

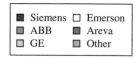

■ Siemens	□ Emerson
■ ABB	■ Areva
□ GE	■ Other

The market size was placed at $5.4 billion.

Siemens 23.0%
ABB 16.0
GE 11.0
Emerson 7.0
Areva 5.0
Other 38.0

Source: "ABB Products Power Division." [online] from http://www.abb.com [Accessed May 15, 2006] from Goulden Reports, ARC, ABS Reports, NEMA, ZVEI, CORTEZ and ABB estimates.

★ 1809 ★
Power Products
SIC: 3612; NAICS: 335311

Leading Power Supply Makers Worldwide, 2005

Delta gained about 2% of its share from 2004 to 2005. This growth came largely from its involvement in consumer electronics and notebooks.

Delta 11.9%
Emerson/Artesyn 9.4
Other 78.7

Source: *Power Electronics Technology (Online Executive)*, March 20, 2006, p. NA, from IMS Research.

★ 1810 ★
Power Products
SIC: 3612; NAICS: 335311

Leading Substation Makers, 2005

The market size was placed at $14 billion.

ABB 20.0%
Siemens/VA Tech 20.0
Areva 10.0
Other 50.0

Source: "ABB Products Power Division." [online] from http://www.abb.com [Accessed May 15, 2006] from Goulden Reports, ARC, ABS Reports, NEMA, ZVEI, CORTEZ and ABB estimates.

★ 1811 ★
Power Products
SIC: 3612; NAICS: 335311

Leading Transformer Makers, 2005

The market size was placed at $14.5 billion.

ABB 21.0%
Siemens 9.0
Areva 5.0
Schneider 3.0
Other 62.0

Source: "ABB Products Power Division." [online] from http://www.abb.com [Accessed May 15, 2006] from Goulden Reports, ARC, ABS Reports, NEMA, ZVEI, CORTEZ and ABB estimates.

★ 1812 ★
Generators
SIC: 3621; NAICS: 335312

Portable Generator Market, 2002

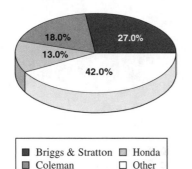

Briggs & Stratton ■ **Honda** □
Coleman ■ **Other** □

Market shares are shown in percent. Data are for under 15kW, the kind used by most consumers.

Briggs & Stratton	.27.0%
Coleman	.18.0
Honda	.13.0
Other	.42.0

Source: ''Portable Generators U.S. Consumer Product Safety Commission Memorandum.'' [online] from http://http://www.cpsc.gov/volstd/engine/econpg.pdf [Published August 22, 2005].

★ 1813 ★
Injection Systems
SIC: 3621; NAICS: 335312

Diesel Injection Market in Western Europe, 2004 and 2009

Diesel engines represent about half of the global market in 2004. Magneti Marelli and Siemens VDO have announced plans to develop a new diesel injection system for medium sized passenger cars, which could reduce Bosch's market share in 2009.

	2004	2009
Bosch	70.0%	62.0%
Other	30.0	38.0

Source: *just-auto.com*, December 2005, p. NA.

★ 1814 ★
Swimming Pool Covers
SIC: 3621; NAICS: 335312

Automatic Swimming Pool Cover Sales

Coverstar is the leading producer in the market.

Coverstar Inc.	.40.0%
Other	.60.0

Source: *Salt Lake Tribune*, February 24, 2006, p. NA.

★ 1815 ★
Appliances
SIC: 3630; NAICS: 335221, 335222, 335224

Appliance Demand Worldwide

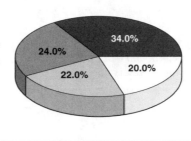

Asia/Pacific ■ **Western Europe** □
North America ■ **Other** □

Top sales were 325 million units in 2004. Freedonia projects microwave ovens to be the fastest growing category through 2009.

Asia/Pacific	.34.0%
North America	.24.0
Western Europe	.22.0
Other	.20.0

Source: *World Major Household Appliances*, Freedonia Group, January 2006, p. 1, from Freedonia Group.

★ 1816 ★
Appliances
SIC: 3630; NAICS: 335221, 335222, 335224

Appliance Market in Europe, 2004

The industry is shown by country. Emerging markets such as Turkey and the Commonwealth of Independent States are showing double-digit growth rates. Much of the growth comes from rising penetration rates. Penetration rates are lower in Eastern Europe than in Western Europe, where penetration rates are close to rates in North America.

U.K.	.16.0%
France	.12.0

Continued on next page.

★ 1816 ★

[Continued]

Appliances

SIC: 3630; NAICS: 335221, 335222, 335224

Appliance Market in Europe, 2004

The industry is shown by country. Emerging markets such as Turkey and the Commonwealth of Independent States are showing double-digit growth rates. Much of the growth comes from rising penetration rates. Penetration rates are lower in Eastern Europe than in Western Europe, where penetration rates are close to rates in North America.

Nordic Europe	9.0%
Italy	8.0
Spain	8.0
Russia	7.0
Turkey	7.0
Other	36.0

Source: *Airing Out of the Laundry*, Citigroup Equity Research, December 15, 2005, p. 29, from Indesit, Arcelik and Citigroup Investment Research.

★ 1817 ★

Appliances

SIC: 3630; NAICS: 335221, 335222, 335224

Leading Appliance Firms in Europe

Market shares are shown based on unit sales of white goods (ovens, cookers, dishwashers, dryers, freezers, refrigerators, hobs and washers). Countries are the Czech Republic, France, Germany, Hungary, Italy, Poland, Russia, Spain, Sweden, Turkey and the United Kingdom.

AB Electrolux	16.9%
BSH Bosch und Siemens Hausgerate	15.1
Indesit Elettrodomesticic Spa	14.2
Whirlpool Corporation	9.4
Koc Group	5.7
Candy Elettrodomestici srl	3.4
Other	35.3

Source: *Appliance*, November 2005, p. 71, from *Appliance Magazine's Portrait of the European Appliance Industry*.

★ 1818 ★

Appliances

SIC: 3631; NAICS: 335221

Top Appliance Makers

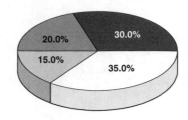

Whirlpool   General Electric   Maytag   Other

Market shares are shown in percent.

Whirlpool	30.0%
General Electric	20.0
Maytag	15.0
Other	35.0

Source: "Maytag Will Consider Whirlpool's Sweetened Bid of $18 a Share." [online] from http://www.bloomberg.com [Published July 25, 2005] from Morgan Keegan.

★ 1819 ★

Cooking Equipment

SIC: 3631; NAICS: 335221

Leading Built-In Oven Makers in France

Market shares are shown based on unit sales.

Elco Brandt	25.4%
Electrolux	18.4
Indesit (formerly Merloni)	17.4
BSH	14.1
Candy	9.8
Other	14.9

Source: *Appliance*, November 2005, p. 71, from *Appliance Magazine's Portrait of the European Appliance Industry*.

★ 1820 ★
Cooking Equipment
SIC: 3631; NAICS: 335221

Leading Built-In Oven Makers in Germany

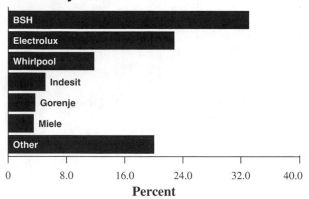

Market shares are shown based on unit sales.

BSH 33.1%
Electrolux 22.8
Whirlpool 11.8
Indesit (formerly Merloni) 5.1
Gorenje 3.7
Miele 3.5
Other 20.0

Source: *Appliance*, November 2005, p. 71, from *Appliance Magazine's Portrait of the European Appliance Industry.*

★ 1821 ★
Cooking Equipment
SIC: 3631; NAICS: 335221

Leading Cooking Appliance Makers Worldwide, 2002

Market shares are shown based on a $20 billion industry.

Bosch-Siemens-Hausgerate GmbH 6.3%
General Electric 5.1
Electrolux 5.0
Rinnai Corp. 4.8
Zheijang Shuaikang Co. 4.2
GD Midea Holding 3.5
Whirlpool 3.3
Nortek Inc. 2.7
Zhongshan Vantage Holdings 2.7
Other 63.4

Source: "Invensys Appliance Controls." [online] from http://www.invensys-investor.com [Accessed January 20, 2005].

★ 1822 ★
Cooking Equipment
SIC: 3631; NAICS: 335221

Leading Microwave Makers, 2004

Market shares are shown based on shipments. Data exclude combination ranges.

LG Electronics 38.0%
Sharp 23.0
Daewoo 11.0
Samsung 10.0
Other 18.0

Source: *Appliance*, September 2005, p. P-2, from *Appliance* estimates and various surveys.

★ 1823 ★
Cooking Equipment
SIC: 3631; NAICS: 335221

Leading Microwave Makers in Latin America

Market shares are shown based on unit sales.

Panasonic 24.0%
Brastemp 10.4
LG 9.0
Consul 5.3
Sharp 4.8
Other 46.5

Source: *Appliance*, December 2005, p. 71, from *Appliance Magazine's Portrait of the Latin American Appliance Industry.*

★ 1824 ★
Freezers
SIC: 3632; NAICS: 335222

Leading Freezer Makers in France

Market shares are shown based on unit sales.

Whirlpool 23.9%
Electrolux 11.9
Elco Brandt 9.2
Indesit (formerly Merloni) 7.3
BSH 6.9
Liebherr 6.5
Other 34.3

Source: *Appliance*, November 2005, p. 71, from *Appliance Magazine's Portrait of the European Appliance Industry.*

★ 1825 ★

Freezers

SIC: 3632; NAICS: 335222

Leading Freezer Makers in the U.K.

Market shares are shown based on unit sales.

Electrolux	.26.0%
Indesit (formerly Merloni)	.13.7
Whirlpool	9.7
Arcelik	9.3
BSH	5.0
Other	.36.3

Source: *Appliance*, November 2005, p. 71, from *Appliance Magazine's Portrait of the European Appliance Industry*.

★ 1826 ★

Refrigerators

SIC: 3632; NAICS: 335222

Leading Refrigeration Appliance Makers Worldwide, 2002

Market shares are shown based on a $32.4 billion industry.

Electrolux	.12.0%
Whirlpool	.10.8
Bosch-Siemens-Hausgerate GmbH	5.6
Haier Group	5.6
General Electric	4.6
Maytag Corp.	3.0
Guangdong Kelong	2.9
Merloni Elettrodomestici	2.8
Matsushita Electric Industrial	2.7
Other	.50.0

Source: "Invensys Appliance Controls." [online] from http://www.invensys-investor.com [Accessed January 20, 2005].

★ 1827 ★

Refrigerators

SIC: 3632; NAICS: 335222

Leading Refrigerator (Built-in, Undercounter) Makers, 2004

Market shares are shown based on shipments.

U-Line	.67.0%
Marvel Industries	.22.0
Sub-Zero	7.0
Other	4.0

Source: *Appliance*, September 2005, p. P-2, from *Appliance* estimates and various surveys.

★ 1828 ★

Refrigerators

SIC: 3632; NAICS: 335222

Leading Refrigerator Makers, 2004

Market shares are shown based on shipments.

GE	.29.0%
Electrolux (Frigidaire)	.25.0
Whirlpool	.25.0
Maytag	.11.0
Other	.10.0

Source: *Appliance*, September 2005, p. P-2, from *Appliance* estimates and various surveys.

★ 1829 ★

Refrigerators

SIC: 3632; NAICS: 335222

Leading Refrigerator Makers in France

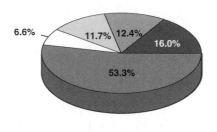

Market shares are shown based on unit sales.

Whirlpool	.16.0%
Indesit (formerly Merloni)	.12.4
Electrolux	.11.7
BSH	6.6
Other	.53.3

Source: *Appliance*, November 2005, p. 71, from *Appliance Magazine's Portrait of the European Appliance Industry*.

★ 1830 ★

Refrigerators

SIC: 3632; NAICS: 335222

Leading Refrigerator Makers in Germany

Market shares are shown based on unit sales.

BSH	.27.8%
Electrolux	.14.1
Liebherr	8.8

Continued on next page.

★ 1830 ★

[Continued]
Refrigerators
SIC: 3632; NAICS: 335222

Leading Refrigerator Makers in Germany

Market shares are shown based on unit sales.

Whirlpool 7.4%
Other 41.9

Source: *Appliance*, November 2005, p. 71, from *Appliance Magazine's Portrait of the European Appliance Industry.*

★ 1831 ★

Refrigerators
SIC: 3632; NAICS: 335222

Leading Refrigerator Makers in Latin America

Market shares are shown based on unit sales.

Consul 18.7%
Electrolux 17.2
Continental 16.1
Whirlpool 11.7
Other 36.3

Source: *Appliance*, December 2005, p. 71, from *Appliance Magazine's Portrait of the Latin American Appliance Industry.*

★ 1832 ★

Refrigerators
SIC: 3632; NAICS: 335222

Leading Refrigerator Makers in Spain

Market shares are shown based on unit sales.

BSH 20.8%
Fagor 19.8
Electrolux 12.0
LG 7.7
Other 39.7

Source: *Appliance*, November 2005, p. 71, from *Appliance Magazine's Portrait of the European Appliance Industry.*

★ 1833 ★

Refrigerators
SIC: 3632; NAICS: 335222

Leading Refrigerator Makers in the U.K.

Market shares are shown based on unit sales.

Electrolux 17.4%
Indesit (formerly Merloni) 17.1
Arcelik 13.6
BSH 10.4
Other 41.5

Source: *Appliance*, November 2005, p. 71, from *Appliance Magazine's Portrait of the European Appliance Industry.*

★ 1834 ★

Refrigerators
SIC: 3632; NAICS: 335222

Leading Wine Cellar/Beverage Refrigeration Makers, 2004

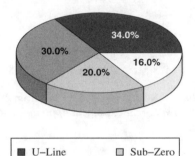

- ■ U–Line
- ■ Marvel Industries
- ◻ Sub–Zero
- ◻ Other

Market shares are shown based on shipments.

U-Line 34.0%
Marvel Industries 30.0
Sub-Zero 20.0
Other 16.0

Source: *Appliance*, September 2005, p. P-2, from *Appliance* estimates and various surveys.

★ 1835 ★

Refrigerators
SIC: 3632; NAICS: 335222

Top Refrigerator Makers in Japan, 2004

Market shares are shown based on domestic shipments of 4.43 million units.

Matsushita Electric Industrial 22.8%
Mitsubishi Electric 16.2
Toshiba Consumer Marketing 15.8

Continued on next page.

★ 1835 ★
[Continued]
Refrigerators
SIC: 3632; NAICS: 335222

Top Refrigerator Makers in Japan, 2004

Market shares are shown based on domestic shipments of 4.43 million units.

Sanyo Electric 15.6%
Sharp 15.5
Other 14.1

Source: "2004 Market Share Report." [online] from http://www.nikkei.co.jp [Published July 27, 2005] from Japan Electrical Manufacturers Association.

★ 1836 ★
Laundry Equipment
SIC: 3633; NAICS: 335224

Leading Dryer Makers in Germany

Market shares are shown based on unit sales.

BSH 27.1%
Electrolux 14.4
Whirlpool 13.8
Miele 10.1
Other 34.6

Source: *Appliance*, November 2005, p. 71, from *Appliance Magazine's Portrait of the European Appliance Industry.*

★ 1837 ★
Laundry Equipment
SIC: 3633; NAICS: 335224

Leading Laundry Appliance Makers Worldwide, 2002

Market shares are shown based on a $26.1 billion industry.

Whirlpool 12.0%
Wuxi Little Swan Co. 8.0
Electrolux AB 7.9
Haier Group 6.5
Bosch-Siemens Hausergerate 5.9
Maytag 5.4
General Electric 5.2
Matsushita Electric Industrial 3.6
Merloni Elettrodomestici 3.2
Other 42.3

Source: "Invensys Appliance Controls." [online] from http://www.invensys-investor.com [Accessed January 20, 2005].

★ 1838 ★
Laundry Equipment
SIC: 3633; NAICS: 335224

Leading Washer Makers, 2004

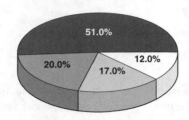

Market shares are shown based on shipments.

Whirlpool 51.0%
Maytag 20.0
GE .17.0
Other 12.0

Source: *Appliance*, September 2005, p. P-2, from *Appliance* estimates and various surveys.

★ 1839 ★
Laundry Equipment
SIC: 3633; NAICS: 335224

Leading Washer Makers in France

Market shares are shown based on unit sales.

Elco Brandt 19.5%
Whirlpool 18.4
Electrolux 15.1
Indesit (formerly Merloni) 12.6
Other 34.4

Source: *Appliance*, November 2005, p. 71, from *Appliance Magazine's Portrait of the European Appliance Industry.*

★ 1840 ★
Laundry Equipment
SIC: 3633; NAICS: 335224

Leading Washer Makers in Japan, 2004

Market shares are shown based on domestic shipments.

Matsushita 24.3%
Hitachi Home & Life 21.4
Toshiba Consumer Marketing 20.3
Sharp 13.9

Continued on next page.

★ 1840 ★

[Continued]
Laundry Equipment
SIC: 3633; NAICS: 335224

Leading Washer Makers in Japan, 2004

Market shares are shown based on domestic shipments.

Sanyo	.13.5%
Other	6.6

Source: "2004 Market Share Report." [online] from http://www.nikkei.co.jp [Published July 27, 2005] from Japan Electrical Manufacturers Association.

★ 1841 ★

Laundry Equipment
SIC: 3633; NAICS: 335224

Leading Washer Makers in the U.K.

Market shares are shown based on unit sales.

Indesit (formerly Merloni)	.40.9%
Electrolux	.15.6
BSH	.14.0
Candy	8.1
Other	.21.4

Source: *Appliance*, November 2005, p. 71, from *Appliance Magazine's Portrait of the European Appliance Industry.*

★ 1842 ★

Personal Care Appliances
SIC: 3634; NAICS: 335211

Leading Beard/Mustache Trimmer Makers, 2004

Market shares are shown based on shipments.

Conair	.30.0%
Micro Touch	.30.0
Remington	.20.0
Wahl	.10.0
Norelco Consumer Products	5.0
Other	5.0

Source: *Appliance*, September 2005, p. P-2, from *Appliance* estimates and various surveys.

★ 1843 ★

Personal Care Appliances
SIC: 3634; NAICS: 335211

Leading Hair Dryer (Hand-Held) Makers, 2004

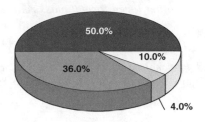

Market shares are shown based on shipments.

Conair	.50.0%
Helen of Troy	.36.0
Rayovac (Remington)	4.0
Other	.10.0

Source: *Appliance*, September 2005, p. P-2, from *Appliance* estimates and various surveys.

★ 1844 ★

Personal Care Appliances
SIC: 3634; NAICS: 335211

Leading Hair Setter Makers, 2004

Market shares are shown based on shipments.

Conair	.51.0%
Rayovac (Remington)	.30.0
Helen of Troy	5.0
Other	.14.0

Source: *Appliance*, September 2005, p. P-2, from *Appliance* estimates and various surveys.

★ 1845 ★

Personal Care Appliances
SIC: 3634; NAICS: 335211

Top Razor Trimmer Brands, 2005

Market shares are shown in percent. Sales exclude Wal-Mart and other large-format mass retailers.

Norelco	.26.9%
Remington	.23.1
Braun	.15.2
Conair	.13.2
Wahl	8.8

Continued on next page.

★ 1845 ★

[Continued]
Personal Care Appliances
SIC: 3634; NAICS: 335211

Top Razor Trimmer Brands, 2005

Market shares are shown in percent. Sales exclude Wal-Mart and other large-format mass retailers.

Micro Touch 1.5%
Other 11.3

Source: *U.S. Personal Care and Household Products Digest,* Citigroup Equity Research, February 24, 2006, p. 86, from ACNielsen.

★ 1846 ★

Personal Care Appliances
SIC: 3634; NAICS: 335211

Top Toothbrush Brands (Power), 2005

Market shares are shown based on drug store sales for the 52 weeks ended October 30, 2005.

Sonicare Elite 12.0%
Sonicare Advance 11.7
Braun Oral B 10.6
Oral B Professional Care 6.8
Braun Oral B Crossaction 5.8
Oral B Crossaction Power Max 5.4
Crest Spinbrush Pro 5.1
Braun Oral B Sonic Complete 4.8
Crest Spinbrush Multiangle 3.6
Other 34.2

Source: *Chain Drug Review,* January 2, 2006, p. 94.

★ 1847 ★

Small Appliances
SIC: 3634; NAICS: 335211

Coffee Maker Sales, 2004

Electric drip coffee makers are used by 79% of American households. Coffee grinders are used by 23%. Pod sales could make up 20% of retail coffee sales. Data show unit sales.

	(000)	Share
Drip	18,800	92.22%
Expresso makers	1,300	6.38
Pod	285	1.40

Source: *US Food Industry,* North American Equity Research, March 29, 2005, p. 3, from *Home World Business* and JPMorgan estimates.

★ 1848 ★

Small Appliances
SIC: 3634; NAICS: 335211

Coffee Maker Unit Shares

Market shares are shown in percent.

White 45.0%
Black 44.0
Other 11.0

Source: *Gourmet Retailer,* July 2005, p. 103, from NPD Houseworld.

★ 1849 ★

Small Appliances
SIC: 3634; NAICS: 335211

Crock Pot Market, 2005

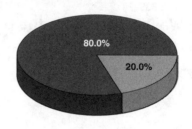

■ Rival ■ Other

Rival expects to produce five million crock pots this year.

Rival 80.0%
Other 20.0

Source: *Brandweek,* August 8, 2005, p. 16.

★ 1850 ★

Small Appliances
SIC: 3634; NAICS: 335211

Kitchen Appliance Sales

Sales are in thousands of dollars.

Coffee/espresso makers . . . . $ 941,148
Blenders 464,477
Mixers 444,683
Toasters 295,237
Electric grills/griddles 278,190

Source: *DSN Retailing Today,* March 27, 2006, p. 25, from NPD Group.

★ 1851 ★
Small Appliances
SIC: 3634; NAICS: 335211

Leading Breadmaker Producers, 2004

Market shares are shown based on shipments.

Oster/Sunbeam	.38.0%
Salton/Toastmaster/Welbilt/Breadman	.36.0
West Bend	.4.0
Other	.22.0

Source: *Appliance*, September 2005, p. P-2, from *Appliance* estimates and various surveys.

★ 1852 ★
Small Appliances
SIC: 3634; NAICS: 335211

Leading Food Processor Makers, 2004

Market shares are shown based on shipments.

Cuisinart	.27.0%
Applica (Windmere/Black & Decker)	.21.0
Hamilton Beach/Proctor-Silex	.12.0
Other	.40.0

Source: *Appliance*, September 2005, p. P-2, from *Appliance* estimates and various surveys.

★ 1853 ★
Small Appliances
SIC: 3634; NAICS: 335211

Leading Iron Makers, 2004

Market shares are shown based on shipments. Figures exclude travel irons.

Applica (Windmere/Black & Decker)	.26.0%
Hamilton Beach/Proctor-Silex	.16.0
Oster/Sunbeam	.16.0
Rowenta	.12.0
The Holmes Group (Rival)	.7.0
Other	.23.0

Source: *Appliance*, September 2005, p. P-2, from *Appliance* estimates and various surveys.

★ 1854 ★
Small Appliances
SIC: 3634; NAICS: 335211

Leading Toaster Oven Makers, 2004

Market shares are shown based on shipments.

Applica (Windmere/Black & Decker)	.37.0%
Salton (Toastmaster)	.17.0
Oster/Sunbeam	.14.0
De'Longhi	.10.0
Other	.22.0

Source: *Appliance*, September 2005, p. P-2, from *Appliance* estimates and various surveys.

★ 1855 ★
Small Appliances
SIC: 3634; NAICS: 335211

Leading Waffle Iron Makers, 2004

Market shares are shown based on shipments.

Salton (Toastmaster)	.32.0%
Applica (Windmere/Black & Decker)	.14.0
Cuisinart	.10.0
Hamilton Beach/Proctor-Silex	.4.0
Oster/Sunbeam	.4.0
Other	.36.0

Source: *Appliance*, September 2005, p. P-2, from *Appliance* estimates and various surveys.

★ 1856 ★
Vacuum Cleaners
SIC: 3635; NAICS: 335212

Leading Vacuum Cleaner Makers (Canister), 2004

Market shares are shown based on shipments.

Panasonic (includes Kenmore)	.33.0%
Electrolux (Eureka)	.9.0
Euro Pro/Fantom	.9.0
Maytag (Hoover)	.7.0
Royal (Dirt Devil)	.7.0
Bissell	.6.0
Other	.29.0

Source: *Appliance*, September 2005, p. P-2, from *Appliance* estimates and various surveys.

★ 1857 ★
Vacuum Cleaners
SIC: 3635; NAICS: 335212

Leading Vacuum Cleaner Makers (Stick), 2004

Market shares are shown based on shipments.

Euro Pro/Fantom 24.0%
Electrolux (Eureka) 20.0
Royal (Dirt Devil) 19.0
Bissell 16.0
Other 21.0

Source: *Appliance*, September 2005, p. P-2, from International Data Corp.

★ 1858 ★
Vacuum Cleaners
SIC: 3635; NAICS: 335212

Vacuum Cleaner Sales by Type

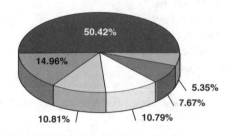

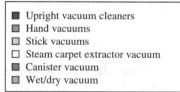

- ■ Upright vacuum cleaners
- ▨ Hand vacuums
- □ Stick vacuums
- □ Steam carpet extractor vacuum
- ▨ Canister vacuum
- ▨ Wet/dry vacuum

Shares are shown based on unit shipments.

	Units	Share
Upright vacuum cleaners	17,815	50.42%
Hand vacuums	5,287	14.96
Stick vacuums	3,821	10.81
Steam carpet extractor vacuum . . .	3,812	10.79
Canister vacuum	2,711	7.67
Wet/dry vacuum	1,890	5.35

Source: *DSN Retailing Today*, May 23, 2005, p. 38, from NPD Group.

★ 1859 ★
Dishwashers
SIC: 3639; NAICS: 335228

Leading Dishwasher/Dryer Makers in Japan, 2004

Market shares are shown based on domestic shipments of 935,000 units.

Matsushita Electric Industrial 69.8%
Toshiba CM 10.1
Toto 6.9
Sanyo Electric 6.1
Hitachi Home & Life Solutions 4.5
Other 2.6

Source: "2004 Market Share Report." [online] from http://www.nikkei.co.jp [Published July 27, 2005] from Japan Electrical Manufacturers Association.

★ 1860 ★
Dishwashers
SIC: 3639; NAICS: 335228

Leading Dishwasher Makers in France

Market shares are shown based on unit sales.

BSH 23.9%
Whirlpool 18.6
Indesit (formerly Merloni) 13.4
Electrolux 12.5
Other 31.6

Source: *Appliance*, November 2005, p. 71, from *Appliance Magazine's Portrait of the European Appliance Industry.*

★ 1861 ★
Dishwashers
SIC: 3639; NAICS: 335228

Leading Dishwasher Makers in Germany

Market shares are shown based on unit sales.

BSH 44.4%
Electrolux 19.2
Whirlpool 9.0
Miele 6.6
Other 20.8

Source: *Appliance*, November 2005, p. 71, from *Appliance Magazine's Portrait of the European Appliance Industry.*

★ **1862** ★
Dishwashers
SIC: 3639; NAICS: 335228

Leading Dishwasher Makers in Latin America

Market shares are shown based on unit sales.

Whirlpool 31.5%
GE 21.8
Brastemp 8.1
IEM 7.6
Other 31.0

Source: *Appliance*, December 2005, p. 71, from *Appliance Magazine's Portrait of the Latin American Appliance Industry.*

★ **1863** ★
Light Bulbs
SIC: 3643; NAICS: 335931

Top Light Bulb Brands, 2006

Market shares are shown based on drug store stores for the 52 weeks March 19, 2006.

General Electric 40.9%
Reveal 6.2
Feit Electric 3.3
GE Long Life 2.7
GE Miser 2.5
Sylvania 1.9
First Alert 1.5
Airwick by Wizard Scent Night Light 1.4
Feit 1.0
Other 38.6

Source: *Snack Food & Wholesale Bakery*, April 2006, p. 11, from Information Resources Inc.

★ **1864** ★
Lighting
SIC: 3643; NAICS: 335931

Common Light Market in Ho Chi Minh City, Vietnam

Common lighting market includes lighting bulbs, fluorescent tubes, compact lamps and lighting accessories. Market shares are shown in percent.

Dien Quang Lamps Company 90.0%
Other 10.0

Source: *Asia Africa Intelligence Wire*, August 18, 2005, p. NA.

★ **1865** ★
Lighting
SIC: 3645; NAICS: 335121

Lamp Sales by Price Range

About 8 million households purchase a lamp each year.

$50-99 . . . . .23.0%
$100-$149 . . . . .18.0
$200 or more 17.0
$30-49 . . . . .15.0
Under $20 . . . . .10.0
$20-29 . . . . 9.0
$150-199 . . . . 8.0

Source: *Home Accents Today*, March 2005, p. 78, from *Home Accents Today Consumer Buying Trends Survey.*

★ **1866** ★
Automotive Lighting
SIC: 3647; NAICS: 336321

Auto Lamp Market in Thailand

The company has more than 80% of the market.

Ta Yih Industrial Co. 80.0%
Other 20.0

Source: *Asia Africa Intelligence Wire*, September 15, 2005, p. NA.

★ **1867** ★
Automotive Lighting
SIC: 3647; NAICS: 336321

Leading Tail Light Makers in Japan/ Korea, 2004

Market shares are shown based on volume.

Koito 27.0%
Ichikoh 22.0
Stanley 20.0

Continued on next page.

★ 1867 ★

[Continued]
Automotive Lighting
SIC: 3647; NAICS: 336321

Leading Tail Light Makers in Japan/ Korea, 2004

Market shares are shown based on volume.

Inhee	.10.0%
Other	.21.0

Source: "Third Quarter Results 2005." [online] http:// www.schefenacker-ir.com/pdf/Presentation_Conference_ Call_10_November_2005.pdf [Published Nov. 10, 2005] from Schefenacker estimates.

★ 1868 ★

Automotive Lighting
SIC: 3647; NAICS: 336321

Leading Tail Light Makers (NAFTA), 2004

Market shares are shown based on volume.

Guide	.27.0%
Visteon	.23.0
N.A.L.	.18.0
Stanley	.11.0
Hella	4.0
Other	.14.0

Source: "Third Quarter Results 2005." [online] http:// www.schefenacker-ir.com/pdf/Presentation_Conference_ Call_10_November_2005.pdf [Published Nov. 10, 2005] from Schefenacker estimates.

★ 1869 ★

Flashlights
SIC: 3648; NAICS: 335129

Top Flashlight Brands, 2006

Market shares are shown based on drug store stores for the 52 weeks March 19, 2006.

Garrity	.27.6%
Energizer	6.4
Garrity G-Tech	5.7
Eveready	5.6
Garrity Life Lite	4.4
Garrity Tuff Lite	4.3
Duracell	4.1
Rayovac	4.0
Garrity I Beam	3.2
LED Club	2.9
Other	.31.8

Source: *Chain Drug Review*, May 23, 2006, p. 79, from Information Resources Inc.

★ 1870 ★

Flashlights
SIC: 3648; NAICS: 335129

Top Flashlight Makers, 2005

Market shares are shown in percent. Figures exclude Wal-Mart and other large format mass retailers.

Energizer	.16.7%
Garrity Industries	.13.8
Spectrum Brands	.12.6
Mag Instrument	9.9
Jarden Corporation	9.3
Private label	7.0
Other	.10.7

Source: *U.S. Personal Care and Household Products Digest*, Citigroup Equity Research, February 24, 2006, p. 212, from ACNielsen.

★ 1871 ★

UV Curing Equipment
SIC: 3648; NAICS: 335129

UC Curing Equipment Market Worldwide

Market shares are shown in percent.

Ushio	.70.0%
Other	.30.0

Source: *Ushio Annual Report*, 2005, p. 12.

★ 1872 ★

Audio Equipment
SIC: 3651; NAICS: 33431

Leading Car Stereo Speaker Brands, 2005

Dollar shares are shown based on point-of-sale data for January - October 2005 collected by NPD from selected retailers.

Pioneer/Infinity/Alpine/Rockford Fosgate/JL

Audio	.84.5%
Other	.15.5

Source: *Twice*, January 5, 2006, p. NA, from NPD Group.

★ 1873 ★
Audio Equipment
SIC: 3651; NAICS: 33431
Leading Cassette Deck Brands, 2005

Dollar shares are shown based on point-of-sale data for January - October 2005 collected by NPD from selected retailers.

Sony/Onkyo/JVC/Denon/Yamaha 96.7%
Other 3.3

Source: *Twice*, January 5, 2006, p. NA, from NPD Group.

★ 1874 ★
Audio Equipment
SIC: 3651; NAICS: 33431
Leading CD Boombox Brands, 2005

Dollar shares are shown based on point-of-sale data for January - October 2005 collected by NPD from selected retailers.

Sony/RCA/Memorex/Emerson/Audiovox . . .79.5%
Other 20.5

Source: *Twice*, January 5, 2006, p. NA, from NPD Group.

★ 1875 ★
Audio Equipment
SIC: 3651; NAICS: 33431
Leading CD Player Brands, 2005

Dollar shares are shown based on point-of-sale data for January - October 2005 collected by NPD from selected retailers.

Sony/RCA/Yamaha/Denon/Onkyo 84.1%
Other 15.9

Source: *Twice*, January 5, 2006, p. NA, from NPD Group.

★ 1876 ★
Audio Equipment
SIC: 3651; NAICS: 33431
Leading Cellular Headset Brands, 2005

Dollar shares are shown based on point-of-sale data for January - October 2005 collected by NPD from selected retailers.

Motorola/Plantronics/Jabra/Fellowes/GE . . .84.6%
Other 15.4

Source: *Twice*, January 5, 2006, p. NA, from NPD Group.

★ 1877 ★
Audio Equipment
SIC: 3651; NAICS: 33431
Leading Home Audio Brands, 2005

Dollar shares are shown based on point-of-sale data for January - October 2005 collected by NPD from selected retailers.

Sony/Bose/Yamaha/Panasonic/Onkyo 52.4%
Other 48.0

Source: *Twice*, January 5, 2006, p. NA, from NPD Group.

★ 1878 ★
Audio Equipment
SIC: 3651; NAICS: 33431
Leading Home Speaker Brands, 2005

Dollar shares are shown based on point-of-sale data for January - October 2005 collected by NPD from selected retailers.

Klipsch/Bose/Polk/Infinity/JBL 54.7%
Other 45.3

Source: *Twice*, January 5, 2006, p. NA, from NPD Group.

★ 1879 ★
Audio Equipment
SIC: 3651; NAICS: 33431
Leading In-Dash CD-Player Brands, 2005

Dollar shares are shown based on point-of-sale data for January - October 2005 collected by NPD from selected retailers.

Pioneer/Alpine/Kenwood/JVC/Sony 83.2%
Other 16.8

Source: *Twice*, January 5, 2006, p. NA, from NPD Group.

★ 1880 ★

Audio Equipment

SIC: 3651; NAICS: 33431

Leading PC Headset/Microphone Brands, 2005

Dollar shares are shown based on point-of-sale data for January - October 2005 collected by NPD from selected retailers.

Logitech/Altec/Plantronics/Cyber Acoustics/
   Labtec 93.9%
Other 6.1

Source: *Twice*, January 5, 2006, p. NA, from NPD Group.

★ 1881 ★

Audio Equipment

SIC: 3651; NAICS: 33431

Leading Portable Radio Brands (No Cassette), 2005

Dollar shares are shown based on point-of-sale data for January - October 2005 collected by NPD from selected retailers.

Sony/Emerson/Tivoli Audio/Curtis
   International/Grundig 56.4%
Other 43.6

Source: *Twice*, January 5, 2006, p. NA, from NPD Group.

★ 1882 ★

Audio Equipment

SIC: 3651; NAICS: 33431

Leading Shelf System Brands, 2005

Dollar shares are shown based on point-of-sale data for January - October 2005 collected by NPD from selected retailers.

Sony/Panasonic/JVC/RCA/Sharp 77.1%
Other 22.9

Source: *Twice*, January 5, 2006, p. NA, from NPD Group.

★ 1883 ★

Audio Equipment

SIC: 3651; NAICS: 33431

Leading Stereo Headphone Brands, 2005

Dollar shares are shown based on point-of-sale data for January - October 2005 collected by NPD from selected retailers.

Sony/Philips/Koss/Bose/Apple 69.0%
Other 31.0

Source: *Twice*, January 5, 2006, p. NA, from NPD Group.

★ 1884 ★

Consumer Electronics

SIC: 3651; NAICS: 33431

Consumer Electronics Industry, 2005

Factory sales were $125.9 billion, up 11% in 2004. Audio was the fastest-growing segment, up 28% to $7.3 billion. MP-3 players were responsible for this growth.

Home information products 35.8%
Home video 17.9
Mobile electronics 17.8
Electronic gaming 9.2
Audio 5.8
Other 13.5

Source: *Screen Digest*, January 2006, p. 13, from *Screen Digest*.

★ 1885 ★
Consumer Electronics
SIC: 3651; NAICS: 33431

Infotainment Electronics Sales Worldwide, 2004-2006

According to Telematics Research Group Inc., in 2004, 66 percent of automotive brands offered some form of in-car infotainment system in one or more of their models. Consumers are interested in navigation devices but also equipment to play digital music. According to a survey conducted by Strategy One on behalf of Microsoft Corp.'s Automotive Business Unit if consumers could give their high-tech car a voice, their top choice would be former 007 Sean Connery's famous Scottish brogue. Their second choice would be that of actor James Earl Jones' Darth Vader. Data are in millions of units.

	2004	2005	2006
Navigation/GPS systems	6.20	9.40	30.0
DVD entertainment systems	4.00	8.40	21.9
Voice recognition system	3.00	5.80	30.0
Satellite radios	0.35	2.20	15.1
Bluetooth devices	0.10	0.46	11.4

Source: *Electronic Business*, September 2005, p. S3, from Telematics Research Group.

★ 1886 ★
Consumer Electronics
SIC: 3651; NAICS: 33431

Leading Answering Device Brands (Stand Alone), 2005

Dollar shares are shown based on point-of-sale data for January - October 2005 collected by NPD from selected retailers.

AT&T/GE/Conair/Southwestern Bell/
  Panasonic 77.6%
Other 22.4

Source: *Twice*, January 5, 2006, p. NA, from NPD Group.

★ 1887 ★
Consumer Electronics
SIC: 3651; NAICS: 33431

Leading Camcorder DV Producers

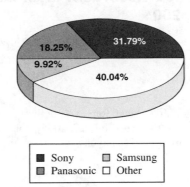

Market shares are shown in percent.

Sony 31.79%
Panasonic 18.25
Samsung 9.92
Other 40.04

Source: "Sony Revises Downward Sales Numbers." [online] from http://www.camcorderinfo.com [Press release January 20, 2005] from NPD Intelect.

★ 1888 ★
Consumer Electronics
SIC: 3651; NAICS: 33431

Leading DVD Recorder/Player Makers in Japan, 2004

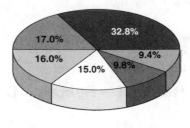

Market shares are shown based on domestic shipments of 4.7 million units.

Matsushita Electric Industrial 32.8%
Sony 17.0
Toshiba 16.0
Pioneer 15.0

Continued on next page.

★ 1888 ★

[Continued]
Consumer Electronics
SIC: 3651; NAICS: 33431

Leading DVD Recorder/Player Makers in Japan, 2004

Market shares are shown based on domestic shipments of 4.7 million units.

Sharp	9.8%
Other	9.4

Source: "2004 Market Share Report." [online] from http://www.nikkei.co.jp [Published July 27, 2005] from Japan Electronics and Information Technology Industries Association.

★ 1889 ★

Consumer Electronics
SIC: 3651; NAICS: 33431

Leading DVR Brands

Unit sales forecast by year: 16.3 million in 2005, 23.5 million in 2006 and 30.9 million in 2007. Market shares are as of May 2, 2005.

RCA High Definition Digital Video Recorder	52.2%
TiVo Series 2 40-hour recorder	32.0
TiVo Series 2 80-hour recorder	9.2
Humax T800 Digital Video Recorder with Tivo	2.7
TiVo Series 2 140-hour Digital Video Recorder	2.3
Other	1.6

Source: "DVR Sales are Expected to Rocket." [online] from http://www.businessweek.com/technology/tech_stats/dvrsales050303.htm [Accessed June 29, 2005] from NPD Group and NPD Techworld.

★ 1890 ★

Consumer Electronics
SIC: 3651; NAICS: 33431

Leading Hard Drive Recorder Brands, 2005

Dollar shares are shown based on point-of-sale data for January - October 2005 collected by NPD from selected retailers.

Tivo/RCA/Humax Corp./Replay Networks/ Sony	96.8%
Other	3.2

Source: *Twice*, January 5, 2006, p. NA, from NPD Group.

★ 1891 ★

Consumer Electronics
SIC: 3651; NAICS: 33431

Leading Remote Controller Brands, 2005

Dollar shares are shown based on point-of-sale data for January - October 2005 collected by NPD from selected retailers.

RCA/Logitech/Sony/Philips/Universal	70.5%
Other	29.5

Source: *Twice*, January 5, 2006, p. NA, from NPD Group.

★ 1892 ★

Consumer Electronics
SIC: 3651; NAICS: 33431

Leading VCR Makers in the U.K., 2004

Total shipments decreased from 3.7 million in 2000 to 2 million in 2004.

	(000)	Share
Alba	380	19.0%
Sony	260	13.0
Panasonic	240	12.0
Philips	140	7.0
Samsung	100	5.0
Other	880	44.0

Source: *Marketing*, July 20, 2005, p. 34, from Mintel.

★ 1893 ★

Consumer Electronics
SIC: 3651; NAICS: 33431

Leading Video Camera Makers in Japan, 2004

Market shares are shown based on domestic shipments of 1,587,000 units.

Sony	38.0%
Matsushita Electric	26.6
Canon	13.0
Victor	12.0
Sharp	9.1
Other	1.3

Source: "2004 Market Share Report." [online] from http://www.nikkei.co.jp [Published July 27, 2005] from Japan Electronics and Information Technology Industries Association.

★ **1894** ★
Consumer Electronics
SIC: 3651; NAICS: 33431

Portable Digital Player Accessory Sales, 2005

Sales of $412 million were made for the first nine months of the year. Sales are up 370% over the same period in 2004. Accessories include power cords, dockers, cases and similar items.

Speaker systems	.26.5%
Portable digital player cases/bags	.18.0
FM transmitters	.16.0
Car kits	7.0
FM modulators/car chargers	7.0

Source: "NPD Group Reports on Sales for Portable Digital Accessories." [online] from http://www.npd.com [Published November 14, 2005] from NPD Group.

★ **1895** ★
Consumer Electronics
SIC: 3651; NAICS: 33431

Top DVD Players in the U.K., 2004

An estimated 57% of households at the end of 2004.

	(000)	Share
Own label	3,417	50.0%
Alba	752	11.0
Philips	684	10.0
Sony	615	9.0
Bush	479	7.0
Panasonic	410	6.0
LG	137	2.0
Others	342	5.0

Source: *Marketing*, July 20, 2005, p. 34, from Mintel.

★ **1896** ★
Music Players
SIC: 3651; NAICS: 33431

Digital Music Player Market

Market shares are shown for flash-based and hard-drive devices.

Apple	.69.0%
SanDisk	7.8
Other	.23.2

Source: *TMCnet*, January 6, 2006, p. NA, from NPD Group.

★ **1897** ★
Music Players
SIC: 3651; NAICS: 33431

Leading Digital Music Player Makers in Japan

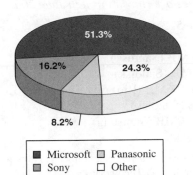

Market shares are shown in percent.

Microsoft	.51.3%
Sony	.16.2
Panasonic	8.2
Other	.24.3

Source: *Business Week Online*, February 24, 2006, p. NA, from BCN.

★ **1898** ★
Music Players
SIC: 3651; NAICS: 33431

MP3 and Portable Media Player Sales, 2003 - 2007

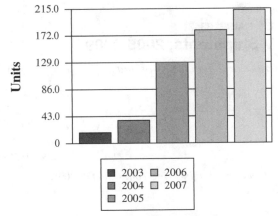

Factory shipments are in millions of units.

2003	17.0
2004	36.5
2005	128.7
2006	181.4
2007	212.7

Source: *Electronic Business*, April 2006, p. 18, from iSuppli.

★ 1899 ★

Music Players

SIC: 3651; NAICS: 33431

Top Digital Music Players (Flash Memory)

Market shares are shown through June 2005.

iPod Shuffle 512MB (Apple)	.34.4%
iPod Shuffle 1GB (Apple)	.11.9
SDMX 256 MB (Sandisk)	4.9
SDMX 512MB (Sandisk)	4.0
Forge Sport 256MB (Rio)	2.9
SDMX 1GB (Sandisk)	1.9
YPMT6X 512MB (Samsung)	1.9
Other	.38.1

Source: *Wall Street Journal*, September 1, 2005, p. B3, from NPD Group and NOD Techworld.

★ 1900 ★

Music Players

SIC: 3651; NAICS: 33431

Top Portable Music Players in Japan

Market shares are shown for August 2005.

Apple	.39.4%
Sony	.16.1
Other	.44.5

Source: *New York Times*, September 15, 2005, p. C6, from BCN.

★ 1901 ★

Televisions

SIC: 3651; NAICS: 33431

HDTV Shipments, 2005-2009

Shipments are in thousands of units.

2005	26,114
2006	39,984
2007	57,175
2008	78,597
2009	101,388

Source: *Electronic Engineering Times*, July 4, 2005, p. 26, from iSuppli.

★ 1902 ★

Televisions

SIC: 3651; NAICS: 33431

High-Definition TV Households

In-Stat estimates that about 21% of all households will have at least one widescreen HDTV by the end of 2006. This could double by the end of 2009. Data show millions of households.

2005	16.4
2006	26.3
2007	36.7
2008	46.1
2009	55.4

Source: *Video Business*, December 19, 2005, p. 1, from In-Stat.

★ 1903 ★

Televisions

SIC: 3651; NAICS: 33431

Leading FPD TV Makers in China

Market shares are shown in percent. FPD stands for flat panel display.

Changhong	.14.23%
Skyworth	.10.42
Philips	9.92
Haier	8.98
Hisense	8.52
Other	.47.93

Source: *Asia Pulse*, April 12, 2006, p. NA, from State Press and Publication Administration.

★ 1904 ★

Televisions

SIC: 3651; NAICS: 33431

Leading TV Makers in India

The top three companies take 80% of the market.

LG/Videocon/Samsung	.60.0%
Other	.40.0

Source: *Economic Times*, February 14, 2006, p. NA.

★ 1905 ★
Televisions
SIC: 3651; NAICS: 33431

Leading TV Makers in Thailand

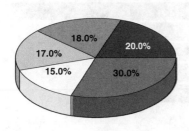

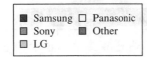

Market shares are shown based on unit sales.

Samsung	.20.0%
Sony	.18.0
LG	.17.0
Panasonic	.15.0
Other	.30.0

Source: *Business Daily Update*, January 13, 2006, p. NA.

★ 1906 ★
Televisions
SIC: 3651; NAICS: 33431

Leading TV Makers Worldwide, 2005

Market shares are shown for the fourth quarter.

LG Electronics	.11.0%
Samsung	.10.3
TTE	.9.7
Philips	.6.8
Sony	.6.1
Panasonic	.5.8
Sanyo	.5.3
Other	.45.0

Source: *USA TODAY*, March 20, 2006, p. B1, from iSuppli.

★ 1907 ★
Televisions
SIC: 3651; NAICS: 33431

LPD Television Market in China

Market shares are shown in percent. LPD stands for liquid panel displays.

Changhong	.14.23%
Skyworth	.10.42
Philips	.9.92

Haier	.8.98%
Other	.56.45

Source: *Asia Pulse*, April 12, 2006, p. NA.

★ 1908 ★
Televisions
SIC: 3651; NAICS: 33431

Television Sales Worldwide (Unit Sales), 2005

Market shares are shown based on fourth quarter unit sales.

Cathode ray tube	.78.9%
Liquid crystal display	.14.7
Plasma display panel	.3.9
Microdisplay rear projection	.1.6
CRT rear projection	.0.9

Source: "Global TV Revenues Rise 13% in Q4'05 ." [online] from http://www.displaysearch. com/press?id638 [Press release March 7, 2006] from DisplaySearch.

★ 1909 ★
Televisions
SIC: 3651; NAICS: 33431

Top CRT TV Makers in Japan, 2004

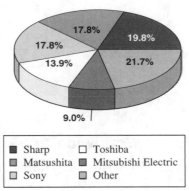

Market shares are shown based on domestic shipments of 5.7 million units. CRT stands for cathode ray tube.

Sharp	.19.8%
Matsushita	.17.8
Sony	.17.8
Toshiba	.13.9
Mitsubishi Electric	.9.0
Other	.21.7

Source: "2004 Market Share Report." [online] from http://www.nikkei.co.jp [Published July 27, 2005] from Japan Electronics and Information Technology Industries Association.

★ 1910 ★
Televisions
SIC: 3651; NAICS: 33431

Top LCD Television Makers in Japan, 2004

Market shares are shown based on domestic shipments of 2.4 million units.

Sharp	.50.1%
Sony	.18.6
Matsushita Electric Industrial	.17.7
Toshiba	8.0
Victor Co. of Japan	3.6
Other	2.0

Source: "2004 Market Share Report." [online] from http://www.nikkei.co.jp [Published July 27, 2005] from Japan Electronics and Information Technology Industries Association.

★ 1911 ★
Televisions
SIC: 3651; NAICS: 33431

Top LCD TV Firms Worldwide, 2005

Market shares are shown through November 2005.

Sharp	.65.0%
Magnavox	.13.0
Samsung	.11.0
Sony	.10.0
Westinghouse	8.0

Source: *Sound & Video Contractor*, January 3, 2006, p. NA, from *Consumer Electronics Daily*.

★ 1912 ★
Televisions
SIC: 3651; NAICS: 33431

Top MD RPTV Worldwide, 2005

Market shares are shown based on fourth quarter unit sales. MD RPTV stands for microdisplay rear projection television.

Sony	.53.8%
Samsung	.13.6
Toshiba	6.8
JVC	6.3
Mitsubishi	5.5
Other	.14.0

Source: "Sony Dominates Q4'05 Microdisplay Rear Projection TV Market." [online] from http://www.displaysearch.com/press?id638 [Press release March 2, 2006] from DisplaySearch.

★ 1913 ★
Televisions
SIC: 3651; NAICS: 33431

Top Plasma TV Brands, 2005

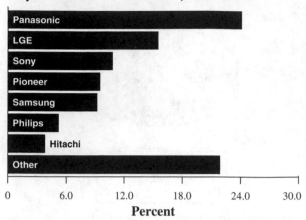

Market shares are shown for the first quarter of 2005.

Panasonic	.24.1%
LGE	.15.5
Sony	.10.8
Pioneer	9.5
Samsung	9.2
Philips	5.2
Hitachi	3.8
Other	.21.9

Source: *Dealerscope*, August 2005, p. 48, from DisplaySearch.

★ 1914 ★
Televisions
SIC: 3651; NAICS: 33431

Top Plasma TV Makers in Japan, 2004

Market shares are shown based on domestic shipments of 34,000 units.

Matsushita Electric	.42.1%
Hitachi	.27.0
Sony	.15.0
Pioneer	8.8
JVC	5.0
Other	2.1

Source: "2004 Market Share Report." [online] from http://www.nikkei.co.jp [Published July 27, 2005] from Japan Electronics and Information Technology Industries Association.

★ 1915 ★

Audio Books

SIC: 3652; NAICS: 334612

Leading Audio Book Publishers in Germany, 2003

The audio book market saw sales of $68 million in 2003. Audio books are enjoying increasing popularity with those 25-34 years of age. The overall book trade (including audiovisual media, and specialist/academic journals) is worth $11.5 billion. English-language tapes are in high demand and increasing in sales (roughly 35% of the population speak English).

Horverlag	$ 14.9
Random House Audio	5.4
Deutsche Grammophon	3.9
Lubbe Audio	2.9
Patmos	2.4
Steinbach Sprechende	2.4
Ullstein Horverlag	2.3
Der Audioverlag	2.1

Source: "German Audio Book Market." [online] from http://www.usatrade.gov [Published August 2005] from Borsenblatt, Das Horbuch Geht Online and Deutsche Borsenverein.

★ 1916 ★

Music

SIC: 3652; NAICS: 334612, 51222

Album Sales by Year, 2000-2005

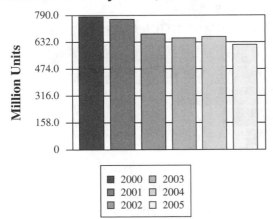

Sales slid 21% since 2000 as the industry struggles with iPods and music downloading. The top five albums sold 35 million copies in 2000. In 2005, the top five companies sold 19.7 million.

2000	$ 785.1
2001	762.8
2002	681.4
2003	656.3

2004	$ 666.7
2005	618.7

Source: *Rolling Stone*, January 26, 2006, p. 9, from Nielsen SoundScan.

★ 1917 ★

Music

SIC: 3652; NAICS: 334612, 51222

Best-Selling Albums, 2005

Data show sales in millions of units for the year.

The Emancipation of Mimi, Mariah Carey	4.97
The Massacre, 50 Cent	4.97
Breakaway, Kelly Clarkson	3.50
American Idiot, Green Day	3.36
Monkey Business, Black Eyed Peas	3.04
X&Y, Coldplay	2.62
Feels Like Today, Rascal Flatts	2.51
Love Angel Music Baby, Gwen Stafani	2.51
Late Registration, Kanye West	2.41
Documentary, The Game	2.28
Now 20, various	2.06
Hot Fuss, The Killers	2.04

Source: *USA TODAY*, January 5, 2006, p. 6D, from Nielsen SoundScan.

★ 1918 ★

Music

SIC: 3652; NAICS: 334612, 51222

Best-Selling Christian Albums, 2005

Data show unit sales for January 3, 2005 - January 1, 2006.

Nothing is Sound, Switchfoot	449,102
Lifesong, Casting Crowns	430,227
MMHMM, Relient K	421,291
Beautiful Letdown, Switchfoot	407,482
Hero, Kirk Franklin	377,123
Wow Hits 2005, various	368,940
Casting Crowns, Casting Crowns	360,274
Wow Hits 2006, various	360,146
Mary Mary, Mary Mary	347,952
Wow Gospel 2005, various	341,749

Source: *Tennessean*, January 5, 2006, p. NA, from Nielsen SoundScan.

★ 1919 ★

Music

SIC: 3652; NAICS: 334612, 51222

Best-Selling Country Albums, 2005

Data show millions of unit sales for January 3, 2005 - January 1, 2006.

Feels Like Today, Rascal Flatts	2.51
Road & the Radio, Kenny Chesney	1.81
Be Here, Keith Urban	1.71
Some Hearts, Carrie Underwood	1.63
Fireflies, Faith Hill	1.53
Twice the Speed of Life, Sugarland	1.51
Honky Tonk University, Toby Keith	1.44
Here for the Party, Gretchen Wilson	1.21
Be as You Are, Kenny Chesney	1.07
Vol 2 Greatest Hits, Toby Keith	1.02

Source: *Tennessean*, January 5, 2006, p. NA, from Nielsen SoundScan.

★ 1920 ★

Music

SIC: 3652; NAICS: 334612, 51222

Best-Selling Digital Artists, 2006

Data show millions of track sales for January 3, 2005 - January 1, 2006.

Green Day	3.49
Black Eyed Peas	3.40
50 Cent	3.24
Kelly Clarkson	3.02
Eminem	2.59
Gwen Stefani	2.53
Mariah Carey	2.39
Kanye West	2.13
U2	1.89
Killers	1.76

Source: "Overall Music Sales." [online] from http://www.fmqb.com/article.asp?tp&id-161421 [Published January 9, 2006] from Nielsen SoundScan.

★ 1921 ★

Music

SIC: 3652; NAICS: 334612, 51222

Best-Selling Musicians in the U.K., 2005

Data show million of albums sold.

Coldplay	2.36
James Blunt	2.36
Robbie Williams	1.85
Green Day	1.63
Eminem	1.32
Kaiser Chiefs	1.31
Westlife	1.31
Gorillaz	1.30
Oasis	1.24
Il Divo	1.20

Source: *Music Week*, January 14, 2006, p. 15.

★ 1922 ★

Music

SIC: 3652; NAICS: 334612, 51222

CD and Digital Music Sales, 2003-2005

Total album sales fell 7.2% from 666.7 million in 2004 to 618.9 million in 2005. CD sales fell 8% from 651.1 million to 598.9 million. Digital track sales increased 150% to 352.7 million downloads. NielsenSoundScan only started tracking digital downloads in the second half of 2003, which accounts for the low figure.

	2003	2004
CDs	635.8	651.1
Digital tracks	19.2	140.9

Source: *USA TODAY*, January 5, 2006, p. D1, from Nielsen SoundScan.

★ 1923 ★

Music

SIC: 3652; NAICS: 334612, 51222

Leading Music Firms (Country), 2005

Market shares are shown in percent.

Sony BMG	35.7%
UMG	30.3
Warner Music	16.7
EMI	10.3
Indies	7.1

Source: *Billboard*, January 21, 2006, p. 20, from Nielsen SoundScan.

★ 1924 ★

Music

SIC: 3652; NAICS: 334612, 51222

Leading Music Firms (Latin), 2005

Market shares are shown in percent.

UMG	.50.0%
Sony BMG	.23.5
Indies	.13.5
EMI	8.2
Warner Music	4.8

Source: *Billboard*, January 21, 2006, p. 20, from Nielsen SoundScan.

★ 1925 ★

Music

SIC: 3652; NAICS: 334612, 51222

Leading Music Firms (R&B), 2005

Market shares are shown in percent.

UMG	.43.4%
Sony BMG	.26.2
Warner Music	.13.8
Indies	8.6
EMI	8.0

Source: *Billboard*, January 21, 2006, p. 20, from Nielsen SoundScan.

★ 1926 ★

Music

SIC: 3652; NAICS: 334612, 51222

Leading Music Firms (Rap), 2005

Market shares are shown in percent.

UMG	.52.5%
Warner Music	.17.0
Indies	.14.7
Sony	.10.9
EMI	4.9

Source: *Billboard*, January 21, 2006, p. 20, from Nielsen SoundScan.

★ 1927 ★

Music

SIC: 3652; NAICS: 334612, 51222

Leading Music Markets Worldwide, 2005

Shares are shown based on sales of the top 20 countries.

	($ mil.)	Share
United States	$ 4,783.2	36.36%
Japan	2,258.2	17.17
United Kingdom	1,248.2	9.49
Germany	887.7	6.75
France	861.1	6.55
Italy	278.0	2.11
Canada	262.9	2.00
Australia	259.6	1.97
Other	2,314.7	17.60

Source: "World Music Market." [online] from http://en.wikipedia.org/wiki/major_record_labels [Accessed June 5, 2006] from International Federation of the Phonographic Industry.

★ 1928 ★

Music

SIC: 3652; NAICS: 334612, 51222

Music Industry in Japan, 2003-2004

A total of 312.7 million audio recordings were produced in 2004, down 4.8% over 2003. The continuing decline in music CD sales was offset by music downloads such as ring tones, which increased 56%.

	2003	2004
Music CD sales	¥ 458	¥ 448
Mobile phone music downloads	90	110
Music CD rentals	59	60
Internet music downlaods	3	5

Source: *JETRO Japan Economic Monthly*, December 2005, p. NA, from *Digital Contents White Paper 2005*, Digital Content Association of Japan.

★ 1929 ★

Music

SIC: 3652; NAICS: 334612, 51222

Music Sales by Format, 2001 and 2005

"Other" for 2005 includes downloaded singles with a 2.9% share, downloaded albums with a 1.1% share, subscription services with 1.2% and mobile with 3.4%. The industry was valued at $12.3 billion.

	2001	2005
CDs	94.5%	85.80%
Cassette	2.6	0.10
Music video	2.4	4.90
Vinyl	0.4	0.22
Other	0.1	8.98

Source: *Billboard*, April 15, 2006, p. 28, from Recording Industry Association of America.

★ 1930 ★

Music

SIC: 3652; NAICS: 334612, 51222

Music Sales by Genre, 2004-2005

Album sales fell from 667.4 million in 2004 to 618.9 million in 2005. Data show unit sales.

	2004 (000)	2005 (000)	Share
R&B	162,234	143,392	23.17%
Alternative	132,487	120,797	19.52
Rap	81,418	75,062	12.13
Country	77,912	75,327	12.17
Metal	75,278	64,473	10.42
Christian/gospel	42,653	39,211	6.34
Latin	31,903	35,907	5.80
Soundtracks	27,367	22,849	3.69
Jazz	18,794	17,139	2.77
Classical	18,686	15,875	2.57
New Age	4,794	4,412	0.71

Source: "Overall Music Sales." [online] from http://www.fmqb.com/article.asp?tp&id-161421 [Published January 9, 2006] from Nielsen SoundScan.

★ 1931 ★

Music

SIC: 3652; NAICS: 334612, 51222

Specialty Music Market in North America

Somerset is the leading producer and distributor of specialty music sold internationally through retailers using interactive displays.

Somerset	.85.0%
Other	.15.0

Source: "Somerset 2005 Year-End Result." [online] from http://www.somersetent.com [Accessed April 20, 2006].

★ 1932 ★

Music

SIC: 3652; NAICS: 334612, 51222

Top Music Firms, 2005

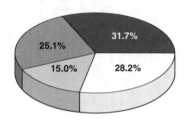

Market shares are shown based on album sales.

Universal	.31.7%
Sony BMG	.25.1
Warner	.15.0
Other	.28.2

Source: *Los Angeles Times*, January 5, 2006, p. NA, from Soundscan.

★ 1933 ★

Music

SIC: 3652; NAICS: 334612, 51222

Top Music Firms (Album) in Denmark, 2005

Market shares are shown for the 12 months ended May 31, 2005.

Universal	.22.9%
Sony	.19.2
EMI	.17.3
MBO	.17.2

Continued on next page.

★ 1933 ★

[Continued]

Music

SIC: 3652; NAICS: 334612, 51222

Top Music Firms (Album) in Denmark, 2005

Market shares are shown for the 12 months ended May 31, 2005.

Warner	.11.2%
Other	.12.2

Source: *Billboard*, August 6, 2005, p. 12, from International Federation of the Phonographic Industry.

★ 1934 ★

Music

SIC: 3652; NAICS: 334612, 51222

Top Music Firms (Current Album)

Market shares are shown for January 3, 2005 - January 1, 2006.

UMVD	.34.82%
WEA	.16.02
Sony	.14.55
BMG	.13.16
EMD	.9.21
Other	.12.24

Source: "Overall Music Sales." [online] from http://www.fmqb.com/article.asp?tp&id-161421 [Published January 9, 2006] from Nielsen SoundScan.

★ 1935 ★

Music

SIC: 3652; NAICS: 334612, 51222

Top Music Firms (Digital Track)

Market shares are shown for January 3, 2005 - January 1, 2006.

UMVD	.33.27%
WEA	.18.26
Sony	.13.39
BMG	.13.22
EMI	.7.84
Other	.14.02

Source: "Overall Music Sales." [online] from http://www.fmqb.com/article.asp?tp&id-161421 [Published January 9, 2006] from Nielsen SoundScan.

★ 1936 ★

Music

SIC: 3652; NAICS: 334612, 51222

Top Music Firms in France, 2005

France's recorded music market was valued at $1.17 billion.

Universal Music	.35.3%
Sony BMG	.27.6
EMI	.18.6
Warner	.14.2
Other	.4.3

Source: *Billboard*, February 11, 2006, p. NA, from Syndicat Nationale de l'Edition Phonographique (SNEP).

★ 1937 ★

Music

SIC: 3652; NAICS: 334612, 51222

Top Music Firms in Germany, 2004

Market shares are shown in percent.

Independents	.27.9%
Sony/BMG	.26.3
Universal	.24.7
EMI	.12.1
Warner	.9.0

Source: "Universal Presentation." http://finance.vivendi-universal.com/finance/download/pdf/UMGInvestor-Meeting_061005.pdf [Oct. 2005] from International Federation of the Phonographic Industry.

★ 1938 ★

Music

SIC: 3652; NAICS: 334612, 51222

Top Music Firms in Japan, 2004

Market shares are shown based on domestic shipments of 377.3 billion yen.

Sony Music Entertainment (Japan)	.18.5%
Toshiba-EMI	.13.7
Universal Music	.13.5
Avex Group Holdings	.10.5
Victor Entertainment	.7.3
Other	.36.5

Source: "2004 Market Share Report." [online] from http://www.nikkei.co.jp [Published July 27, 2005] from Recording Industry Association of Japan.

★ 1939 ★
Music
SIC: 3652; NAICS: 334612, 51222

Top Music Firms in the U.K.

*Shares are shown for the top 100. By genre, hip hop/
R&B took 38%, pop 25%, rock 26%, dance 9%.*

	2004	2005
Sony BMG	32.0%	26.0%
Universal	32.0	39.0
EMI	15.0	14.0
Indies	11.0	10.0
Warner	10.0	11.0

Source: *Music Week*, January 14, 2006, p. 12.

★ 1940 ★
Music
SIC: 3652; NAICS: 334612, 51222

Top Music Firms Worldwide, 2006

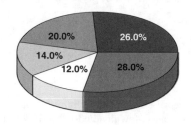

*EMI Group and Warner Music Group each offered to
buy the other during June 2006. Each rejected the over-
ture of the other. There have been merger talks between these two companies for some time.*

Universal	26.0%
Sony BMG	20.0
EMI	14.0
Warner Music	12.0
Other	28.0

Source: *USA TODAY*, June 29, 2006, p. 3B, from Credit
Suisse.

★ 1941 ★
Music
SIC: 3652; NAICS: 334612, 51222

Top Singles Publishers in the U.K.

Market shares are shown for the first three quarters.

EMI	23.9%
Universal	18.0
BMG	12.7
Warner/Chappell	12.7
Sony/ATV	9.4
Chrysalis	2.7
Other	20.6

Source: *Music Week*, November 19, 2005, p. 12.

★ 1942 ★
Ring Tones
SIC: 3652; NAICS: 51222

Ring Tone Sales Worldwide

*Global mobile phone ring tone sales were $4 billion in
2004. Telephia reports that 70% of downloads come
from women.*

	($ bil.)	Share
Western Europe	$ 1.5	37.5%
Japan	1.0	25.0
Korea	0.5	12.5
United States	0.3	7.5
Other	0.7	17.5

Source: *Investor's Business Daily*, May 13, 2005, p. A4,
from Consect.

★ 1943 ★
Camera Phones
SIC: 3661; NAICS: 33421

Camera Phone Sales Worldwide, 2005 and 2009

The developing markets will see the largest growth rates during this period. The camera phone market in Latin America is forecast to grow 56.8% in this period, followed by Africa with 47.5% and the Middle East with 41.7%. Japan and North America will see growth rates of 3.4% and 14% respectively in comparison. The source points out that these markets also see higher quality phones.

	2005	2009	Share
Western Europe . . .	$ 84,896.0	$ 143,199.8	19.17%
North America . . .	70,862.3	146,115.8	19.56
Asia/Pacific	66,387.6	278,396.6	37.27
Japan	39,991.9	45,784.6	6.13
Eastern Europe . . .	13,927.2	40,942.8	5.48
Latin America . . .	8,750.8	52,832.9	7.07
Africa	4,595.4	21,771.0	2.91
Middle East	4,437.7	17,915.1	2.40

Source: "Gartner Says Sales of Camera Phones Will Reach Nearly 300 Million." [online] from http://www.gartner.com [Press release December 9, 2005] from Gartner.

★ 1944 ★
Cellular Phones
SIC: 3661; NAICS: 33421

Cellular Phone Sales in Russia, 2003-2005

Sales are shown in millions of units.

2003	15.1
2004	24.3
2005	33.2

Source: *Wall Street Journal*, June 8/, 206, p. B1, from Mobile Research Group.

★ 1945 ★
Cellular Phones
SIC: 3661; NAICS: 33421

Cellular Phone Shipments Worldwide

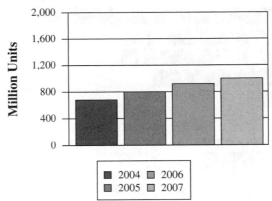

Sales are in millions of units.

2004	681
2005	810
2006	930
2007	1,000

Source: *Investor's Business Daily*, January 27, 2006, p. A5, from Strategy Analytics.

★ 1946 ★
Cellular Phones
SIC: 3661; NAICS: 33421

Leading EMS/ODM Phone Makers Worldwide

EMS stands for electronic manufacturing services. ODM stands for original design manufacturer.

Flextronics	.24.0%
Elcoteq	.14.0
Foxcomm International	.14.0
Arima	. 5.0
BenQ	. 3.0
Other	.42.0

Source: *Financial Times*, June 21, 2005, p. 20, from Merrill Lynch.

★ 1947 ★
Cellular Phones
SIC: 3661; NAICS: 33421

Top Cellular Phone Makers, 2006

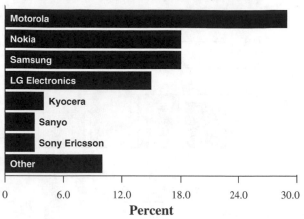

Market shares are shown for the first quarter of 2006.

Motorola 29.0%
Nokia 18.0
Samsung 18.0
LG Electronics 15.0
Kyocera 4.0
Sanyo 3.0
Sony Ericsson 3.0
Other 10.0

Source: *RCR Wireless News*, May 22, 2006, p. 30, from NPD Group.

★ 1948 ★
Cellular Phones
SIC: 3661; NAICS: 33421

Top Cellular Phone Makers in China, 2005

Market shares include GSM handsets and CDMA handsets.

Nokia 23.8%
Motorola 13.3
Samsung 9.6
Bird 6.1
Amoi 4.2
Leovo 4.1
Sony-Ericsson 4.1
TCL 3.7
Konka 2.8
Haier 2.5
Other 25.8

Source: *Asia Pulse*, March 9, 2006, p. NA, from Norson Consulting.

★ 1949 ★
Cellular Phones
SIC: 3661; NAICS: 33421

Top Cellular Phone Makers in India, 2005

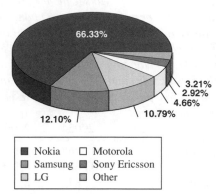

Companies are ranked by shipments in thousands of units for the third quarter of 2005.

	(000)	Share
Nokia	4,550	66.33%
Samsung	830	12.10
LG	740	10.79
Motorola	320	4.66
Sony Ericsson	200	2.92
Other	220	3.21

Source: *Wall Street Journal*, January 3, 2006, p. A18, from International Data Corp.

★ 1950 ★
Cellular Phones
SIC: 3661; NAICS: 33421

Top Cellular Phone Makers in Japan, 2005

Shares are for April - June 2005.

Sharp 18.2%
NEC Corp. 15.9
Toshiba 14.8
Panasonic Mobile 14.6
Other 36.5

Source: *Asia Pulse*, November 30, 2005, p. NA, from International Data Corp. Japan.

★ 1951 ★
Cellular Phones
SIC: 3661; NAICS: 33421

Top Cellular Phone Makers in Saigon, 2005

Market shares are shown for the first six months of the year.

Nokia	51.0%
Samsung	25.0
Sony Ericsson	6.0
Other	18.0

Source: *Saigon Times Magazine*, December 10, 2005, p. NA, from GfK.

★ 1952 ★
Cellular Phones
SIC: 3661; NAICS: 33421

Top Cellular Phone Makers Worldwide, 2006

Market shares are shown based on shipments for the first quarter of the year. Motorola has cut Nokia's lead with the RAZR and low-end models.

Nokia	34.1%
Motorola	21.0
Samsung	13.2
LG Electronics	7.1
Sony Ericsson	6.0
BenQ-Siemens	3.2
Other	15.4

Source: *Financial Times*, June 28, 2006, p. 21, from iSuppli.

★ 1953 ★
Cellular Phones
SIC: 3661; NAICS: 33421

Top Cellular Phone Models in Europe, 2006

Market shares are shown for pan-Europe for the first quarter of 2006. Pan-Europe includes the United Kingdom, Germany, Sweden, France, Italy and Spain.

Motorola RAZR series (V3, V3x)	6.2%
Nokia 6230 (6230, 6230i)	3.4
Nokia 6101	2.6
Nokia 6630	2.0
Samsung SGH-D600	2.0

Sony Ericsson K750 series (K750, K750i)	2.0%
Other	81.8

Source: "Motorola Razr Doubles Market Share." [online] from http://www.telephia.com [Press release March 29, 2006] from *Telephia European Subscriber and Device Report.*

★ 1954 ★
Converged Devices
SIC: 3661; NAICS: 33421

Leading Converged Device Makers Worldwide, 2006

Worldwide converged mobile device shipments totaled 18.9 million units in Q1 2006, an increase of 7.5% from the fourth quarter of 2005 and 67.8% compared to the same quarter one year ago.

	Units	Share
Nokia	8.16	43.2%
Panasonic	1.89	10.0
NEC	1.79	9.5
Research in Motion	1.45	7.7
Sharp	1.07	5.7
Other	4.52	23.9

Source: *Business Wire*, June 8, 2006, p. NA, from International Data Corp's Worldwide Quarterly Mobile Phone Tracker.

★ 1955 ★
Fiber Optics
SIC: 3661; NAICS: 334418

Leading Fiber Optic Cable Makers Worldwide

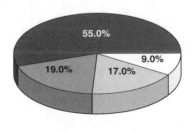

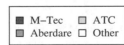

Market shares are shown in percent.

M-Tec	55.0%
Aberdare	19.0

Continued on next page.

★ 1955 ★
[Continued]
Fiber Optics
SIC: 3661; NAICS: 334418

Leading Fiber Optic Cable Makers Worldwide

Market shares are shown in percent.

ATC 17.0%
Other 9.0

Source: "Competition Tribunal Republic of South Africa." [online] from http://www.comptrib.co.za/decidedcases/doc/23LMMar05.doc [Published March 2005] from Competition Tribunal Republic of South Africa.

★ 1956 ★

Fiber Optics
SIC: 3661; NAICS: 334418

Top Fiber Optic Telecom Firms (Household) in Japan, 2004

Market shares are shown based on 2.77 million subscribers.

NTT East 31.9%
NTT West 28.1
Usen 10.1
K-Opticom 7.9
Tokyo Electric Power 4.7
KDDI 3.3
Other 14.0

Source: "2004 Market Share Report." [online] from http://www.nikkei.co.jp [Published July 27, 2005] from Yano Research Institute.

★ 1957 ★

Headsets
SIC: 3661; NAICS: 33421

Ear Monitoring Industry

In-ear monitors are small bi-amplified multi-armature speakers that reduce external noise and preserve the entire frequency range of audio input.

Ultimate Ears 75.0%
Other 25.0

Source: "Ultimate UESc Ear Monitors for Ultimate Music." [online] from http://www.gismag.com/go/3387 [Published Janaury 16, 2006].

★ 1958 ★

Headsets
SIC: 3661; NAICS: 33421

Leading Call Center/Office Headset Makers

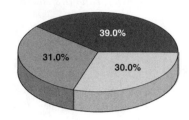

Legend: ■ Plantronics □ Other ■ GN Netcom

The industry is valued at $900 million.

Plantronics 39.0%
GN Netcom 31.0
Other 30.0

Source: *Business 2.0*, October 2005, p. 64, from RW Baird.

★ 1959 ★

Telephones
SIC: 3661; NAICS: 33421

Audio Speaker Phone Market

The company also has 56% of the global video conferencing market.

Polycom 75.0%
Other 25.0

Source: "ShoreTel Names Industry Veteran Joe Vitalone." [online] from http://www.businesswire.com [Published October 25, 2005].

★ 1960 ★

Telephones
SIC: 3661; NAICS: 33421

Leading Cordless Telephone Brands, 2005

Dollar shares are shown based on point-of-sale data for January - October 2005 collected by NPD from selected retailers.

AT&T/General Electric/RCA/Conair/
  Southwestern Bell 72.9%
Other 27.1

Source: *Twice*, January 5, 2006, p. NA, from NPD Group.

★ 1961 ★
Aircraft Electronics
SIC: 3663; NAICS: 33422
Airline Entertainment Spending

The industry suffered immediately after September 11. Spending dropped by 25% in 2001 and further 11.4% in 2002. According to Frost & Sullivan estimates, the industry is seeing double digit growth. Spending is shown in billions of dollars.

2004	$ 1.81
2005	2.19
2006	2.87
2007	3.30
2008	4.08
2009	4.95

Source: *Air Transport World*, October 2005, p. 26, from Frost & Sullivan.

★ 1962 ★
Broadcasting Equipment
SIC: 3663; NAICS: 33422
Leading Direct Broadcast Satellite Brands, 2005

Dollar shares are shown based on point-of-sale data for January - October 2005 collected by NPD from selected retailers.

Hughes/Samsung/RCA/JVC/Pro Brand	95.4%
Other	4.6

Source: *Twice*, January 5, 2006, p. NA, from NPD Group.

★ 1963 ★
Broadcasting Equipment
SIC: 3663; NAICS: 33422
TV Card and Box Industry in China

Market shares are shown in percent.

10moons	31.29%
Gadmei	16.66
Leadtek	8.39
Compro	7.05
LifeView	6.38
Other	30.23

Source: *Asia Pulse*, April 18, 2006, p. NA, from Chinese State Press and Publications Adminisitration.

★ 1964 ★
Radios
SIC: 3663; NAICS: 33422
Leading Portable Two-Radio Brands, 2005

Dollar shares are shown based on point-of-sale data for January - October 2005 collected by NPD from selected retailers.

Motorola/Cobra/Uniden/Midland/Audiovox	95.6%
Other	4.4

Source: *Twice*, January 5, 2006, p. NA, from NPD Group.

★ 1965 ★
Radios
SIC: 3663; NAICS: 33422
Multiband Tactical Radio Market, 2005

The total multiband radio market was worth $470 million in 2005. Harris has 53% of the HF tactical radio market followed by Thales with a 12% share.

Harris	38.0%
Thales	32.0
Raytheon	13.0
General Dynamics	7.0
Other	10.0

Source: "Lehman Brothers Industrial Select Conference." [online] from http://www.harris.com/webcast/lance/2-14-2006/2-14-06-presentation.pdf [Published Feb. 14, 2006] from Lehman Brothers.

★ 1966 ★
Satellites
SIC: 3663; NAICS: 33422
Global Satellite Industry

The industry generated $7 billion in revenues in 2004.

SES Global SA	20.0%
Eutelsat	13.0
Other	67.0

Source: *Via Satellite*, January 2, 2006, p. NA.

★ 1967 ★

Satellites

SIC: 3663; NAICS: 33422

Leading Satellite Makers Worldwide, 2006-2010

Communication satellites have become more powerful and are having longer lives. The source points out that despite this development, demand for satellites is increasing. Advances in data compression technology could also drive down production. Market shares are shown based on five-year production of 373 units.

Boeing Satellite System	6.7%
EADS Atrium	6.4
Alcatel Alenia Space	5.6
Indian Space Research	5.4
Surrey Satellite Tech	4.6
Other	71.3

Source: *Aviation Week & Space Technology*, January 16, 2006, p. 83, from Forecast International.

★ 1968 ★

Networking Equipment

SIC: 3669; NAICS: 33429

Handheld xDSL Test Tool Market

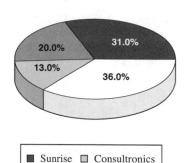

■ Sunrise   □ Consultronics
■ Acterna   □ Other

xDSL refers to the different varieties of DSL technologies including asymmetric DSL (ADSL), symmetric DSL (SDSL), rate adaptive DSL (RADSL), and high bit-rate DSL (HDSL). xDSL test equipment include tools and systems used to qualify the copper loops on which the xDSL service runs as well as many other applications. The market was worth $68 million in 2004.

Sunrise	31.0%
Acterna	20.0
Consultronics	13.0
Other	36.0

Source: "EXFO Buys, Ixia Plummets." [online] from http://www.lightreading.com [Published January 6, 2006] from Frost & Sullivan.

★ 1969 ★

Networking Equipment

SIC: 3669; NAICS: 33429

LAN Switch Market in EMEA, 2005

LAN stands for local area network. Shares are shown based on revenue for the fourth quarter of 2005. EMEA stands for Europe, Middle East and Africa.

Cisco	65.8%
ProCurve	10.0
Other	24.2

Source: *MicroScope*, April 24, 2006, p. NA, from International Data Corp.

★ 1970 ★

Networking Equipment

SIC: 3669; NAICS: 33429

Largest Data Converters Worldwide, 2004

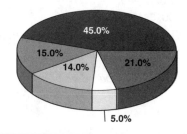

■ Analog Devices   □ Linear Technology
■ Maxim Integrated Products   ■ Other
□ Texas Instruments

Data converter companies were once concerned with balancing resolution and conversion speed. Manufacturers are now focusing on concepts such as spurious free dynamic range and paying only for the effective number of bits they need for a particular application. The industry is valued at $2.4 billion.

Analog Devices	45.0%
Maxim Integrated Products	15.0
Texas Instruments	14.0
Linear Technology	5.0
Other	21.0

Source: *Electronic Engineering Times*, August 12, 2005, p. 36, from Gartner Dataquest.

★ 1971 ★

Networking Equipment

SIC: 3669; NAICS: 33429

Leading 10G Long-Haul Firms Worldwide

Infinera is in the lead in the shipments of 10 Gigabit per second (Gb/s) long-haul wavelengths.

Infinera	.20.0%
Nortel	.16.6
Alcatel	. 9.4
Other	.54.0

Source: *Internet Wire*, February 28, 2006, p. NA, from Dell'Oro Group.

★ 1972 ★

Networking Equipment

SIC: 3669; NAICS: 33429

Leading Business Data Networking Firms Worldwide, 2005

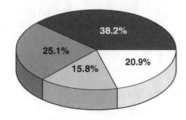

Nortel ■   Lucent □
Alcatel ■   Other □

Market shares are shown in percent.

Nortel	.38.2%
Alcatel	.25.1
Lucent	.15.8
Other	.20.9

Source: *New York Times*, March 25, 2006, p. B4, from Dell'Oro Group.

★ 1973 ★

Networking Equipment

SIC: 3669; NAICS: 33429

Leading BWA Firms Worldwide, 2005

Alvarion is the leader in broadband wireless access. Market shares are shown for the last four quarters (Q4 2004 - Q3 2005), worth $505 million.

Alvarion	.50.0%
Airspan	. 7.0
NextNet	. 6.0

Proxim (Terebeam)	. 5.0%
Other	.52.0

Source: "Alvarion Ltd." [online] from http://www.alvarion. com/upload/images/investor%20docs/Q4%2005%20In- vestor%20presentation%20FINAL.ppt [Accessed July 1, 2006].

★ 1974 ★

Networking Equipment

SIC: 3669; NAICS: 33429

Leading DSL Signal Aggregator Firms Worldwide, 2005

An aggregator takes two separate Internet connec- tions and then pools bandwidth to make a connection e- qual to the size of the aggregate of the two inde- pendent connections. Market shares are shown in per- cent.

Alcatel	.33.2%
Siemens	. 8.7
Lucent	. 7.0
Other	.51.1

Source: *New York Times*, March 25, 2006, p. B4, from Dell'Oro Group.

★ 1975 ★

Networking Equipment

SIC: 3669; NAICS: 33429

Leading E-Commerce Firms (B2C) in Argentina

Argentina has the third largest number of Internet users in Latin America. Firms are ranked by e-com- merce annual earnings. B2C stands for business to con- sumer. Mercado Libre is an online auction site. Disco Virtual handles groceries, Desepegar handles travel bookings. Officenet handles office products. Leshop handles groceries.

Mercado Libre	$ 140.0
DeRemate.com	100.0
Disco Virtual	24.0
Despegar	15.0
Officenet	10.0
Leshop	5.5

Source: "E-Commerce Overview 2005." [online] from http://www.stat-usa.gov [Published September 2005] from Convergencia Research.

★ 1976 ★
Networking Equipment
SIC: 3669; NAICS: 33429

Leading IP Telephony Firms for Small/ Medium Businesses, 2005

Internet Protocol telephony is, according to Wikipedia, "the routing of voice conversations over the Internet or through any other IP-based network. Protocols used to carry voice signals over the IP network are commonly referred to as Voice over IP or VoIP protocols."

Mitel	.12.6%
Cisco	.11.7
Other	.75.7

Source: *TelecomWeb News Digest*, March 14, 2006, p. NA, from InfoTech.

★ 1977 ★
Networking Equipment
SIC: 3669; NAICS: 33429

Leading Media Gateway/Softswitch VoIP Port Suppliers in China, 2004

The global market for media gateways and Class 4 and 5 softswitches will jump from $2.7 bln in 2005 to $8.4 bln in 2010, according to In-Stat. Media gatways and softswitches are attractive to some companies because they are less expensive than traditional equipment. VoIP stands for Voice Over Internet Protocol.

Huawei	.24.80%
Nortel	.18.21
Sonus	.11.36
UTStarcom	7.63
Siemens	7.25
Other	.30.75

Source: *IT Wire*, April 18, 2006, p. NA, from *2005 Wireline Telecom Equipment Market Perception Study.*

★ 1978 ★
Networking Equipment
SIC: 3669; NAICS: 33429

Leading Network/Telecom Firms Worldwide, 2004

Sales of networking and telecommunications equipment reached $117.7 billion worldwide.

Cisco	.16.3%
Ericsson	.10.9
Alcatel	9.6

Nortel	8.5%
Other	.54.7

Source: *Computer Reseller News*, June 8, 2005, p. 33, from Synergy Research Group.

★ 1979 ★
Networking Equipment
SIC: 3669; NAICS: 33429

Leading Security Appliances Makers Worldwide, 2005

Market shares are shown for the second quarter of 2005. Security appliances include virtual private networks, firewalls and similar equipment.

Cisco	.29.5%
Juniper	.11.8
Nokia	6.6
Sonicwall	4.5
ISS	3.7
Other	.44.0

Source: "Worldwide Security Appliance Market Grows 16.6%." [online] from http://www.idc.com [Published September 19, 2005] from IDC Worldwide Quarterly Security Appliance Tracker.

★ 1980 ★
Networking Equipment
SIC: 3669; NAICS: 33429

Leading Wi-Fi Equipment Firms in Argentina

Wi-Fi is a wireless system where a user can connect to the Internet through an access point using a computer, phone or mobile device. Argentina is projected to have about 900,000 broadband subscribers at the end of 2005. The number of Wi-Fi spots in Buenos Aires has increased 274% from October 2004 - June 2005.

Lucent	.34.0%
Cisco	.20.0
Amigo	7.0
D-Link	6.0
Motorola	5.0
Micronet	4.0
Other	.24.0

Source: "Wi-Fi Market in Argentina." [online] from http://www.stat-usa.gov [Published September 2005] from Convergencia Research.

★ 1981 ★
Networking Equipment
SIC: 3669; NAICS: 33429

Leading Wireless Infrastructure Firms Worldwide, 2005

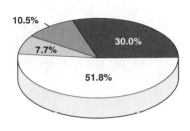

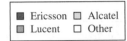

Market shares are shown in percent.

Ericsson 30.0%
Lucent 10.5
Alcatel 7.7
Other 51.8

Source: *New York Times*, March 25, 2006, p. B4, from Dell'Oro Group.

★ 1982 ★
Networking Equipment
SIC: 3669; NAICS: 33429

ROADM Market Worldwide

ROADMs (Reconfigurable optical add/drop multi-plexers) are used to remotely reconfigure, add and drop capacity at each node, which allows for network upgrades without affecting in-service traffic. Market shares are shown in percent.

Fujitsu 75.0%
Hitachi 8.0
Cisco 6.0
Marconi 5.0
Other 6.0

Source: *Telecommunications Americas*, June 2005, p. 32, from RHK Inc.

★ 1983 ★
Networking Equipment
SIC: 3669; NAICS: 33429

Top DSL Port Vendors Worldwide, 2005

Market shares are shown base on shipments for the first quarter of the year.

Alcatel 25.8%
Huawei 18.1
Siemens 9.4
Lucent 8.0
ECI Telecom 6.1
Other 32.6

Source: *Telephony*, May 23, 2005, p. 13, from Broadbandtrends.com.

★ 1984 ★
Networking Equipment
SIC: 3669; NAICS: 33429

World Softswitch Market, 2004

Global revenues from the softswitch and media gateways markets are expected to increase from $1.35 billion in 2004 to $9.27 billion in 2009. Softswitches are forecast to replace TDM equipment as they move to multimedia IP networks.

Huawei 24.5%
Nortel 18.2
Sonus Networks 11.4
Other 46.9

Source: *Total Telecom Magazine*, June 1, 2005, p. NA, from Dittberner.

★ 1985 ★
Radio Frequency ID Tags
SIC: 3669; NAICS: 33429

RFID Shipments Worldwide, 2004 and 2008

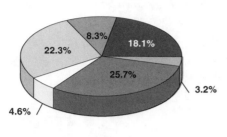

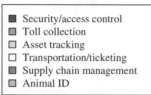

- ■ Security/access control
- ■ Toll collection
- □ Asset tracking
- □ Transportation/ticketing
- ■ Supply chain management
- □ Animal ID

According to Gartner, a market research firm, "RFID is an automated data collection technology that uses radio frequency waves to transfer data between a reader and an RFID tag to identify, track or locate that item. RFID does not, specifically, require physical sight or contact between the reader/scanner and the tagged item." Data show percent of total revenue.

	2004	2008
Security/access control	33.4%	18.1%
Toll collection	20.4	8.3
Asset tracking	17.8	22.3
Transportation/ticketing	4.4	4.6
Supply chain management	4.0	25.7
Animal ID	2.9	3.2

Source: "UK RFID Networking Forum." [online] from http://www.comitproject.org.uk/downloads/events/TheRFIDLandscape1.pdf [Published May 5, 2005] from Venture Development Corp.

★ 1986 ★
Security Equipment
SIC: 3669; NAICS: 33429

Airport Security Equipment Market

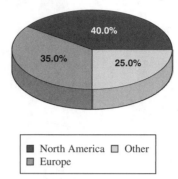

- ■ North America □ Other
- ■ Europe

The airport security market is worth about 75% of the $69 billion aviation security market worldwide.

North America	.40.0%
Europe	.35.0
Other	.25.0

Source: *Airport Security Report*, December 28, 2005, p. NA, from Frost & Sullivan.

★ 1987 ★
Security Equipment
SIC: 3669; NAICS: 33429

Alarm Sales by Type, 2005-2006

Industry revenue grew from $27 billion in 2005 to $29.5 billion in 2006.

	2005	2006
Burglar alarms	38.0%	37.0%
Fire alarms	18.0	15.0
Video surveillance	16.0	17.0
Access control	12.0	11.0
Integrated security systems	6.0	9.0
Home systems (other burger/fire)	6.0	7.0
Other	4.0	4.0

Source: *Security Distributing & Marketing*, January 2006, p. 52, from *SDM 2006 Industry Forecast*.

★ 1988 ★
Security Equipment
SIC: 3669; NAICS: 335999

Anti-Burglary Smoke Industry Worldwide

The PROTECT Smoke Cannon was introduced in the United States during the spring of 2005. It is already used in Europe to protect banks, jewelry stores, drug stores and warehouses.

PROTECT Smoke Cannon 85.0%
Other 15.0

Source: "California Police Get Look at Anti-Theft Smoke Screen." [online] from http://www.securityinfowatch.com [Published October 26, 2005].

★ 1989 ★
Security Equipment
SIC: 3669; NAICS: 335999

CCDs and Digital Camera Industry Worldwide

CCDs stands for charge-coupled devices. The source describes them as the digital equivalent of photographic film. Sony has nearly 70% of the CCD market for still digital cameras.

Sony 70.0%
Other 30.0

Source: *Chief Executive*, November 2005, p. 34.

★ 1990 ★
Security Equipment
SIC: 3669; NAICS: 33429

Cockpit Door/Cabin/Cargo Pit Surveillance Market in Germany

Market shares are shown in percent.

GEPT 88.0%
Other 12.0

Source: "GEPT Investor Presentation." [online] from http://www.globalepoint.com/website/investor/pdf/GEPT%20presentation.pdf [Accessed May 1, 2006].

★ 1991 ★
Security Equipment
SIC: 3669; NAICS: 33429

Home Automation Market in North America, 2005

The market has increased by 26% in the last three years.

Integrated & entertainment controls 30.2%
Lighting controls 26.0
Security controls 23.5
HVAC controls 20.3

Source: *Security Dealer*, March 2006, p. 74, from Frost & Sullivan.

★ 1992 ★
Security Equipment
SIC: 3669; NAICS: 33429

Security Sales Worldwide, 2003, 2008 and 2013

Demand for alarms, fire extinguishers and similar products have benefited from the current healthy construction market. In 2008, total sales are forecast to be $73.8 billion, with Western Europe representing $23.2 billion, North America $20.9 billion and Asia/Pacific $17 billion. Access controls and alarms will each take about 44% of the market in 2013.

	2003	2008	2013
Alarms	$ 15,150	$ 22,290	$ 32,360
Access controls	11,300	19,400	32,415
Other	3,150	5,430	8,750

Source: *Electronic Business*, May 2005, p. 30, from Freedonia Group.

★ 1993 ★
Security Equipment
SIC: 3669; NAICS: 33429

Top Smoke Detector Makers in EMEA

Market shares are estimated in percent. EMEA stands for Europe, Middle East and Africa.

Honeywell 18.9%
Siemens 13.2
Other 67.8

Source: "IMS Research Recognizes Honeywell." [online] from http://www.imsresearch.com [Press release April 7, 2006] from IMS Research.

★ 1994 ★
Telecommunications Equipment
SIC: 3669; NAICS: 33429

Antenna Market in India

Market shares are shown in percent.

Kathrein Werke KG	.75.0%
Other	.25.0

Source: "News." [online] from http://
www.kathreindochina.com/news3.html [Accessed January
19, 2006].

★ 1995 ★
Telecommunications Equipment
SIC: 3669; NAICS: 33429

Leading Infrastructure Hardware Makers Worldwide

Market shares are shown in percent.

Siemens	.51.0%
Alcatel	.10.0
Ericsson	.10.0
Plessey	.9.0
Andrew Satcom	.6.0
Webb Industries	.3.5
Kathrein	.2.6
Radio Frequency Systems	.2.6
Sectional Poles	.2.6
Dartcom	.0.2

Source: "Competition Tribunal Republic of South Africa."
[online] from http://www.comptrib.co.za/decidedcases/doc/
23LMMar05.doc [Published March 2005] from Competition
Tribunal Republic of South Africa.

★ 1996 ★
Telecommunications Equipment
SIC: 3669; NAICS: 33429

Top Telecom Equipment Firms Worldwide, 2005

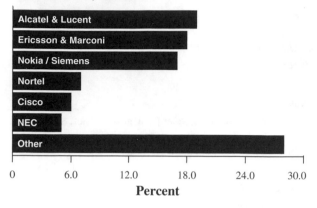

Market shares are shown based on sales to carriers.

Alcatel & Lucent	.19.0%
Ericsson & Marconi	.18.0
Nokia / Siemens	.17.0
Nortel	.7.0
Cisco	.6.0
NEC	.5.0
Other	.28.0

Source: *Financial Times*, June 20, 2006, p. 16, from Nokia
and Siemens.

★ 1997 ★
Telecommunications Equipment
SIC: 3669; NAICS: 33429

Wireless Phone Antenna and Booster Industry

*Powerwave is the leader in the market for wireless pho-
ne networks. The company manufactures amplifiers,
antennas, combiners, filters, radio frequency, power
amplifiers, repeaters and similar equipment. The other
large company in the field is Andrew Corp. Smaller
firms include Filtronic PLC, Fujitsu Ltd. And Hitachi
Kokusai Electric Ltd.*

Powerwave	.60.0%
Other	.40.0

Source: *San Diego Business Journal*, December 5, 2005,
p. 29.

★ 1998 ★
Traffic Signals
SIC: 3669; NAICS: 33429

LED Traffic Signal Market in Europe

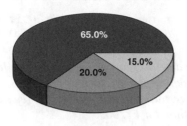

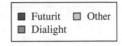

Market shares are shown in percent.

Futurit	.65.0%
Dialight	.20.0
Other	.15.0

Source: "Exploring the Lighting Revolution." [online] from http://production.investis.com/financial/presentations/investorsdec05/investorsdec05.ppt [Accessed May 1, 2006].

★ 1999 ★
Vehicle Communication Systems
SIC: 3669; NAICS: 33429

Vehicle Communication/Information Market

Onstar has about two million subscribers.

OnStar	.80.0%
Other	.20.0

Source: "GM Corporate Responsibility Report." [online] from http://www.gm.com/company/gmability/sustainability/reports/03/pdfs/sus03pdf_100.pdf.

★ 2000 ★
Circuit Boards
SIC: 3672; NAICS: 334412

Global Fax Board Market

The market saw a 9.5% growth rate, up from $95 million in 2003 to $105 million in 2004.

Brooktrout	.70.0%
Other	.30.0

Source: *PR Newswire*, July 28, 2005, p. NA.

★ 2001 ★
Circuit Boards
SIC: 3672; NAICS: 334412

Global Flex-Rigid Printed Circuit Boards

Flex circuiting is a form of electronic interconnection and 3D-structure that is a rival to rigid board cables and connectors. The industry is valued at $546 million.

	($ mil.)	Share
Military and aerospace	$ 188	34.43%
Mobile phones and digital cameras .	183	33.52
Industrial and instrumentation . . .	41	7.51
Telecom/datacom infrastructure . . .	40	7.33
Medical	32	5.86
Computer/business retail	31	5.68
Automotive	18	3.30
Consumer	13	2.38

Source: *CircuiTree*, October 2005, p. 12, from BPA Consulting.

★ 2002 ★
Circuit Boards
SIC: 3672; NAICS: 334412

Largest Flexible Circuit Producers, 2005

Firms are ranked by sales in millions of dollars for mid 2005. Flexible circuits are gaining in popularity over traditional circuit boards. They are smaller, lighter and feature stronger signal integrity. The North American market is valued at roughly $858 million.

	($ mil.)	Share
Hutchinson	$ 150	17.48%
3M	78	9.09
Parlex	75	8.74
Multek Flex	64	7.46
M-Flex	50	5.83
Innovex	40	4.66
Tyco	40	4.66
Minco	28	3.26
Amphenol	24	2.80
Teledyne	22	2.56
Other	287	33.45

Source: *CircuiTree*, July 2005, p. 26, from FabFile Online.

★ 2003 ★
Fuel Cells
SIC: 3674; NAICS: 334413

Fuel Cell Demand Worldwide

Demand is shown in millions of dollars. Proton-exchange membrane is the best-selling type of fuel cell. In 2014 the United States is forecast to take 29% of the market with Japan in second place with a 13% share.

	2004	2009	2014
United States	$ 67	$ 545	$ 2,025
Japan	50	230	910
Germany	20	140	495
Other Western Europe	37	270	1,245
Other Asia/Pacific	25	165	1,050
Other	21	190	1,275

Source: *Power Engineering*, November 2005, p. 130, from Freedonia Group, *World Fuel Cells*.

★ 2004 ★
Lasers
SIC: 3674; NAICS: 334413

Diode Laser Sales Worldwide

The diode-laser market was basically flat in 2005, inching up from $3.2 billion in 2004 to $3.23 billion in 2005. Revenue climbed in the telecom and high-power markets but fell in the optical storage category, which represents 54% of revenue. Optical storage has driven the diode-laser market since it bottomed out in 2002. Unit sales increased from 778.14 million in 2005 to 806.82 million in 2006.

	2005	2006
Optical storage	691,300,000	715,700,000
Entertainment	32,950,000	32,800,000
Inspection, measurement, control .	16,740,000	16,710,000
Image recording	9,607,000	10,315,000
Barcode scanning . . .	6,600,000	7,000,000
Telecom	4,385,000	5,095,000
Sensing	3,510,000	3,510,000
Medical therapeutics . .	283,350	299,350
Solid state pumping . . .	213,130	261,530
Basic research	1,050	1,050
Instrumentation	1,200	1,200
Materials processing . .	3,610	4,385
Other	12,549,875	15,652,251

Source: *Laser Focus World*, February 2006, p. 69, from *Laser Focus World 2006 Annual Review and Forecast of the Laser Marketplace*.

★ 2005 ★
Lasers
SIC: 3674; NAICS: 334413

Global Nondiode Laser Sales by Application, 2005-2006

Unit sales increased from 119,001 in 2005 to 120,278 in 2006. Nondiode laser sales have taken 41% of the laser market (based on dollar sales) for 2004-2006. The source discusses how some fields in the laser industry are becoming mature, such as photonics. Coherent, the largest laser maker worldwide, reported sales of $516 million for FY2005.

	2005	2006
Materials processing	41,752	42,997
Instrumentation	39,815	40,195
Medical therapeutics	13,385	14,735
Inspection, measurement & control .	5,815	5,900
Image recording	4,965	4,825
Basic research	3,795	3,795
Barcode scanning	5,500	3,500
Entertainment	1,710	1,505
Sensing	760	825
Optical storage	50	50
Other	1,455	1,972

Source: *Optoelectronics Report*, January 1, 2006, p. 1, from Strategies Unlimited and *Laser Focus World 2006 World Review*.

★ 2006 ★
Lasers
SIC: 3674; NAICS: 334413

Semiconductor Laser Market Worldwide

Cymer has 80% of the laser market in semiconductor production. Lasers create patterns on silicone chips which control the flow of electricity on a chip.

Cymer	.80.0%
Other	.20.0

Source: *San Diego Union-Tribune*, April 19, 2006, p. NA.

★ 2007 ★

Microprocessors
SIC: 3674; NAICS: 334413

802.11G Chip Industry Worldwide, 2004

Total shipments forecasted in units: 3.6 million in 2005, 28.9 million in 2007 and 113.0 million in 2009.

	(mil.)	Share
Broadcom	230.5	37.66%
Intel	122.0	19.93
Atheros	102.0	16.67
Conexant	88.0	14.38
Marvell	29.0	4.74
Texas Instruments	21.0	3.43
Other	19.5	3.19

Source: *Electronic Business*, February 2006, p. 42, from *IDC Worldwide WEAN Semiconductor 2005-2009*.

★ 2008 ★

Microprocessors
SIC: 3674; NAICS: 334413

Desktop Graphics Market

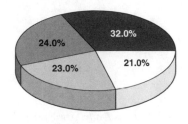

■ Intel □ Nvidia
■ ATI □ Other

The graphics industry is valued at $1.6 billion.

Intel	32.0%
ATI	24.0
Nvidia	23.0
Other	21.0

Source: *ExtremeTech.com*, February 8, 2006, p. NA.

★ 2009 ★

Microprocessors
SIC: 3674; NAICS: 334413

DSP Industry Worldwide

DSP stands for digital signal processor.

Europe	20.8%
Japan	15.0
Americas	10.9%
Other	53.3

Source: *Electronic News*, November 28, 2005, p. NA, from IC Insights.

★ 2010 ★

Microprocessors
SIC: 3674; NAICS: 334413

GPS Chip Sales, 2005

GPS (global positioning system) chips are appearing in more consumer products as prices decline. The chips can help them navigate in unfamiliar areas or locate coworkers, children or pets. Figures are for the noncellular market and show percent of units shipped.

Vehicle tracking	31.1%
Vehicle navigation	28.6
Recreation	19.7
Maritime	11.5
Timing	2.4
Surveying	0.8
Other	5.9

Source: *Electronic Business*, February 2006, p. 24, from Forward Concepts.

★ 2011 ★

Microprocessors
SIC: 3674; NAICS: 334413

Leading PC Graphics Firms, 2005

Market shares are shown in percent.

	1Q	2Q
Intel	43.1%	43.7%
ATI Technologies	26.1	26.8
Nvidia	17.9	15.9
VIA Technologies	6.9	8.1
Silicon Integrated Systems	5.4	5.0
Matrox Graphics	0.3	0.3
Other	0.3	0.2

Source: "PC Graphics Shipments up Sequentially." [online] from http://www.jonpeddie.com [Press release July 27, 2005] from Jon Peddie.

★ 2012 ★

Microprocessors

SIC: 3674; NAICS: 334413

Leading Wi-Fi Chip Makers Worldwide, 2005

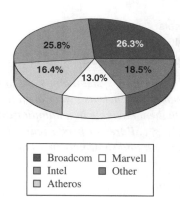

Broadcom	□ Marvell
Intel	Other
Atheros	

Market shares are shown for the second quarter of the year.

Broadcom	.26.3%
Intel	.25.8
Atheros	.16.4
Marvell	.13.0
Other	.18.5

Source: *Wall Street Journal*, October 11, 2005, p. B3, from ABI Research.

★ 2013 ★

Microprocessors

SIC: 3674; NAICS: 334413

Memory Industry Worldwide

Market shares are shown in percent.

	2004	2009	Share
DRAM	$ 26.5	$ 33.5	54.03%
NOR flash	8.3	7.9	12.74
NAND flash	6.6	15.9	25.65
SRAM	3.2	2.7	4.35
Other	2.2	2.0	3.23

Source: *Electronic Business*, December 2005, p. 22, from iSuppli.

★ 2014 ★

Microprocessors

SIC: 3674; NAICS: 334413

NOR Market Worldwide, 2004

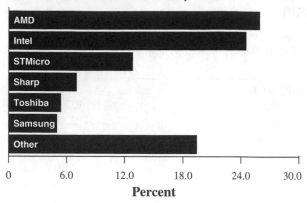

Worldwide high-density NOR flash memory revenue will decline to $5.2 billion in 2005, down 7.4 percent from $5.6 billion in 2004, according to iSuppli. Average Selling Prices (ASPs) for high-density NOR will decline to an average of $4.85 in 2005, down 24 percent from $6.40 in 2004. Market shares are estimated in percent.

AMD	.25.9%
Intel	.24.5
STMicro	.12.8
Sharp	7.0
Toshiba	5.4
Samsung	5.0
Other	.19.4

Source: *Investor's Business Daily*, April 13, 2005, p. A6, from iSuppli.

★ 2015 ★

Microprocessors

SIC: 3674; NAICS: 334413

Programmable DSP Market Worldwide

The global market grew 27% to $7.9 billion.

TI	.50.0%
Freescale	.13.0
Agere	.10.0
Analog Devices	8.0
Philips	7.0
Other	.13.0

Source: *Electronic Business*, May 2005, p. 46, from *IC Insights' Strategic Review Database*.

★ **2016** ★
Microprocessors
SIC: 3674; NAICS: 334413

RF EDA Market Shares Worldwide

RF EDA has been around for a long time, in the form of microwave component PCB and monolithic microwave integrated circuit (MMIC) tools. Drivers for this market include aerospace, satellite communications, high-speed optical, wireless infrastructure, and power amplifiers products. These products are largely used in compound semiconductor technologies such as gallium arsenide, indium phosphide, and silicon germanium.

Agilent	71.0%
Ansoft	11.0
Cadence	9.0
AWR	8.0
Other	1.0

Source: *Electronic Engineering Times*, June 13, 2005, p. 8, from Gartner Dataquest.

★ **2017** ★
Microprocessors
SIC: 3674; NAICS: 334413

Television Graphics Chips Worldwide, 2005-2009

The market for advanced television sets is forecast to grow from 22.2 million units in 2004 to 127 million units in 2009 worldwide.

2005	$ 686
2006	995
2007	1,477
2008	1,739
2009	1,937

Source: *Electronic Business*, June 2005, p. 12, from Jon Peddie.

★ **2018** ★
Microprocessors
SIC: 3674; NAICS: 334413

Top DNA Chip Makers in Japan, 2004

Market shares are shown based on domestic sales of 5 billion yen. DNA chips, according to Wikipedia are "a collection of microscopic DNA spots attached to a solid surface, such as glass, plastic or silicon chip forming an array for the purpose of expression profiling, monitoring expression levels for thousands of genes simultaneously."

Affymetrix	42.1%
Hitachi Software Engineering/DNA Chip Research	15.2
Agilent Technologies	13.0
Takara Bio	10.2
Amersham Biosciences	8.6
Other	10.9

Source: "2004 Market Share Report." [online] from http://www.nikkei.co.jp [Published July 27, 2005] from Nikkei estimates.

★ **2019** ★
Microprocessors
SIC: 3674; NAICS: 334413

Top Memory Card Makers in Japan, 2004

Market shares are shown based on domestic shipments of 62 million units.

Matsushita Electric	24.3%
Sony	15.3
Hagiwara Sys-Com	14.9
SanDisk	13.7
Buffalo	10.6
Other	21.2

Source: "2004 Market Share Report." [online] from http://www.nikkei.co.jp [Published July 27, 2005] from Japan Recording Media Industries Association.

★ 2020 ★

Semiconductors

SIC: 3674; NAICS: 334413

Dry Etch Categories Worldwide

The dry etch market grew 89% in 2004 but is forecast to dip 10.2% in 2005 to $3.1 billion.

Dielectric etch	.58.0%
Polysilicon etch	.30.0
Other	2.0

Source: *Electronic Chemicals News*, May 15, 2005, p. NA, from Information Network.

★ 2021 ★

Semiconductors

SIC: 3674; NAICS: 334413

Largest ASIC Makers Worldwide

ASIC stands for Application Specific Integrated Circuits. An ASIC is an integrated circuit built for a specific purpose or application. Market shares are shown in percent.

Texas Instruments	.14.1%
STMicroelectronics	.11.4
IBM Electronics	9.9
Freescale Semiconductor	7.3
NEC Electronics	7.2
Fujitsu	6.5
Renesas Technology	5.6
Agree Systems	5.4
Toshiba	4.1
Sony	4.0
Other	.24.5

Source: *Electronic Engineering Times*, September 26, 2005, p. 1, from Dataquest.

★ 2022 ★

Semiconductors

SIC: 3674; NAICS: 334413

Largest DRAM Makers Worldwide, 2005

Market shares are shown in percent for the second quarter. DRAM stands for Dynamic Random Access Memory.

Samsung	.30.6%
Hynix	.16.4
Micron	.14.7
Infineon	.13.5

Elpida	6.9%
Other	.17.8

Source: *Wall Street Journal*, August 4, 2005, p. B4, from iSuppli.

★ 2023 ★

Semiconductors

SIC: 3674; NAICS: 334413

Leading NAND Chip Makers Worldwide, 2005

Sales totaled $3 billion for the three months ended September 30, 2005. NAND represents about 59% of the overall flash memory market, according to one estimate.

Samsung Electronics	.50.2%
Toshiba	.22.8
Hynix Semiconductor	.13.2
Renesas Technology	6.9
Micron Technology	3.4
Other	3.5

Source: *New York Times*, December 12, 2005, p. C6, from iSuppli.

★ 2024 ★

Semiconductors

SIC: 3674; NAICS: 334413

Top Flash Memory Suppliers Worldwide, 2005

Total sales were $18.6 billion in 2005, up 19% from $15.6 billion in 2004. The NOR segment fell 13% to $8 billion while the NAND segment grew 64% to $10.6 billion.

Samsung	.35.0%
Toshiba	.13.0
Intel	.12.0
AMD/Spansion	.10.0
Hynix	7.0
ST	7.0
Sharp	5.0
Renesas	4.0
SST	2.0
Micron	1.0
Other	4.0

Source: *Electronic News*, April 3, 2006, p. 21, from IC Insights' *McClean Report*.

★ 2025 ★

Semiconductors

SIC: 3674; NAICS: 334413

Top Semiconductor Makers Worldwide, 2005

Firms are ranked by sales in millions of dollars. Shares are shown based on the top 50 firms.

	($ mil.)	Share
Intel	$ 35,395	16.54%
Samsung	17,830	8.33
TI	11,300	5.28
Toshiba	9,116	4.26
ST	8,870	4.15
Infineon	8,297	3.88
Renesas	8,266	3.86
TSMC	8,217	3.84
Sony	5,845	2.73
Philips	5,646	2.64
Hynix	5,599	2.62
Freescale	5,598	2.62
Other	84,004	39.26

Source: *Electronic Business*, May 1, 2006, p. NA, from IC Insights.

★ 2026 ★

Capacitors

SIC: 3675; NAICS: 334414

Leading MLCC Makers Worldwide

MLCC stands for multi-layer ceramic capacitor.

AVX	6.4%
KEMET	4.3
Vishay	4.3
Other	85.0

Source: *Electronic Components*, KGI Securities, April 11, 2006, p. 6, from KGI Securities.

★ 2027 ★

Backlight Units

SIC: 3679; NAICS: 334419

Backlight Market Worldwide, 2005

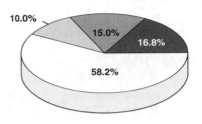

Market shares are shown for the first seven months of the year.

Coretronic	16.8%
Radiant Opto-Electronicshas	15.0
Forehouse	10.0
Other	58.2

Source: *Asia Africa Intelligence Wire*, August 19, 2005, p. NA.

★ 2028 ★

Display Screens

SIC: 3679; NAICS: 33431

Leading Video Displays for Gaming Machines

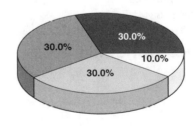

Market shares are shown in percent.

Kortek	30.0%
Plaintiff Wells-Gardner	30.0
Tovis	30.0
Other	10.0

Source: *EDGAR Online 8-K Glimpse*, May 2, 2006, p. NA.

★ 2029 ★

Electronic Components

SIC: 3679; NAICS: 334419

Leading Fastener Makers for Disk Drives Worldwide

Volume shares are shown for July - September 2005.

Unisteel	.50.0%
Textron Fastening Systems	.30.0
Other	.20.0

Source: *Electronic Component Industry*, JPMorgan Asia Pacific Equity Research, January 24, 2006, p. 4, from Techno Systems Research.

★ 2030 ★

Electronic Components

SIC: 3679; NAICS: 334419

Leading Hearing Aid Components

Market shares are shown in percent.

Sonion	.54.0%
Knowles	.14.0
RTI	.13.0
HA Manufacturers	.8.0
Other	.11.0

Source: ''Dover Bank of America Investment Conference.'' [online] http://library. corporate-ir.net/library/85/855/85517/items/166141/BofA_Conference.pdf [Published September 20, 2005] from Knowles management.

★ 2031 ★

Electronic Components

SIC: 3679; NAICS: 334419

Leading Pivot Assembly Makers for Disk Drives Worldwide, 2005

Volume shares are shown for July - September 2005.

Minebea	.68.0%
Sil	.15.0
NSK	.9.0
Nidec	.8.0

Source: *Electronic Component Industry*, JPMorgan Asia Pacific Equity Research, January 24, 2006, p. 4, from Techno Systems Research.

★ 2032 ★

Electronic Components

SIC: 3679; NAICS: 334419

Leading Suspension Makers for Disk Drives Worldwide

Volume shares are shown for July - September 2005.

Hutchinson	.55.0%
NHK Spring	.23.0
Magnecomp	.20.0
Suncall	.2.0

Source: *Electronic Component Industry*, JPMorgan Asia Pacific Equity Research, January 24, 2006, p. 4, from Techno Systems Research.

★ 2033 ★

Liquid Crystal Displays

SIC: 3679; NAICS: 33431

Largest LCD Makers Worldwide, 2005

Market shares are shown based on shipments.

LG Philips	.21.4%
Samsung Electronics	.20.9
AU Optronics Corp.	.14.5
Chi Mei Optoelectronics Corp.	.11.8
Chunghwa Picture Tube Co.	.7.3
Other	.24.1

Source: *Asia Pulse*, January 19, 2006, p. NA, from iSuppli.

★ 2034 ★

Liquid Crystal Displays

SIC: 3679; NAICS: 33431

Leading CCFL Suppliers Worldwide

Market shares are shown for the third quarter of 2005. CCFT stands for Cold Cathode Fluorescent Light.

Harrison Toshiba	.21.0%
Matsushita	.14.0
Sanken	.12.0
Kumho	.9.0
NEC	.9.0
Wellypower	.9.0
Heesung	.6.0
Stanley	.6.0
Wooree ETI	.6.0
Other	.8.0

Source: *Taiwan Economic News*, January 2, 2005, p. NA, from DisplaySearch.

★ 2035 ★
Liquid Crystal Displays
SIC: 3679; NAICS: 33431

Leading TFT LCD Suppliers, 2005

Market shares are shown for the third quarter. TFT stands for Thin Film Transistor. TFT monitors are rapidly displacing competing Cathode Ray Tube technology.

Samsung 21.8%
LG Philips LCD 21.4
AUO 13.7
CMO 11.2
Sharp 6.9
Other 25.0

Source: "LCD TV Module Shipments Catalyze Q3'05 TFT LCD Shipments." [online] from http://www.displaysearch. com [Press release December 13, 2005] from DisplaySearch.

★ 2036 ★
Nanoelectronics
SIC: 3679; NAICS: 334419

Nanoelectronic Material Sales, 2004

Nanotechnology comprises technological developments on the nanometer scale, usually 0.1 to 100 nm. One nanometer equals one thousandth of a micrometre or one millionth of a millimeter.

	($ mil.)	Share
Design molecules	$ 89.3	55.43%
Nanotubes	30.0	18.62
Coatings	28.5	17.69
Precursors	5.0	3.10
Slurries	5.0	3.10
Other	3.3	2.05

Source: *Investor's Business Daily*, November 15, 2005, p. A4, from Semiconductor Equipment and Materials International.

★ 2037 ★
OLED Screens
SIC: 3679; NAICS: 33431

Leading OLED Screen Makers Worldwide, 2005

Market shares are shown for fourth quarter 2005. OLED stands for Organic Light Emitting Diode. Wikipedia defines OLEDs as "thin-film light-emitting diode (LED) in which the emissive layer is an organic compound".

Samsung 28.4%
RITDisplay 20.5
Pioneer 13.7
Univision 11.5
Other 25.9

Source: *Financial Times*, February 6, 2006, p. 23, from DisplaySearch.

★ 2038 ★
PDP Panels
SIC: 3679; NAICS: 33431

Leading PDP Panel Makers Worldwide

Market shares are shown for the first three quarters of 2005. A Plasma Display Panel is defined by Wikipedia as "an emissive flat panel display where light is created by phosphors excited by a plasma discharge between two flat panels of glass".

Samsung SDI 31.0%
LGE 27.0
Matsushita 23.0
FHP 9.0
Pioneer 9.0
Other 1.0

Source: *Taiwan Economic News*, December 9, 2005, p. NA, from DisplaySearch.

★ 2039 ★
Batteries
SIC: 3691; NAICS: 335911

Global Battery Sales, 2004

Sales are in billions of dollars. The popularity of energy hungry electronic devices will help drive expansion in the market. Some of the strongest market growth will come from China, India, Brazil, the Czech Republic and South Korea.

	($ bil.)	Share
Lead acid auto	$ 15.8	49.69%
Alkaline	6.0	18.87
Rechargable lithium ion	5.0	15.72
Rechargable nickel	1.8	5.66
Other lead acid	3.2	10.06

Source: *Wall Street Journal*, November 2, 2005, p. B1, from Frost & Sullivan.

★ 2040 ★
Batteries
SIC: 3691; NAICS: 335911

Stationary Battery Sales in North America

Distribution is shown based on sales.

	2003	2004
Telecommunications	55.0%	52.0%
UPS	30.0	34.0
Control & switchgear	10.0	9.0
Misc. standby	5.0	5.0

Source: *Battery Man*, September 2005, p. 18, from BCI.

★ 2041 ★
Batteries
SIC: 3691; NAICS: 335911

Top Auto Battery Makers in Europe

Market shares are shown in percent.

JCI	.28.0%
Exide	.22.0
Fiamm	. 8.0
Delphi	. 4.0
Other	.38.0

Source: "Johnson Controls Acquision of Delphi Battery Business." [online] from http://www.johnsoncontrols.com [Published March 22, 2005].

★ 2042 ★
Batteries
SIC: 3691; NAICS: 335911

Top Battery Brands, 2005

Market shares are shown based on supermarket, drug store and mass merchandiser sales (excluding Wal-Mart) for the 52 weeks ended June 12, 2005.

Duracell	.43.0%
Energizer Max	.27.6
Duracell Ultra	. 3.8
Rayovac	. 3.0
Rayovac Maximum	. 2.6
Energizer E2 Titanium	. 2.2
Energizer	. 1.6
Eveready	. 1.0
Panasonic	. 0.4
Other	.18.8

Source: *Grocery Headquarters*, August 2005, p. S6, from Information Resources Inc.

★ 2043 ★
Batteries
SIC: 3691; NAICS: 335911

Top Battery Makers, 2005

Market shares are shown based on supermarket, drug store and mass merchandiser sales (excluding Wal-Mart) for the 52 weeks ended June 12, 2005.

Duracell Inc.	.47.0%
Energizer Holdings	.32.5
Rayovac	. 5.9
Panasonic	. 0.5
Private label	.13.6

Source: *Grocery Headquarters*, August 2005, p. S6, from Information Resources Inc.

★ 2044 ★
Batteries
SIC: 3691; NAICS: 335911

Top OE Battery Makers in China

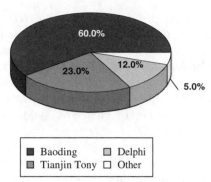

Market shares are estimated in percent. OE stands for original equipment.

Baoding 60.0%
Tianjin Tony 23.0
Delphi 12.0
Other 5.0

Source: "Johnson Controls Acquision of Delphi Battery Business." [online] from http://www.johnsoncontrols.com [Published March 22, 2005].

★ 2045 ★
Batteries

SIC: 3692; NAICS: 335912

Top Carbon Zinc Battery Makers, 2005

Market shares are shown in percent. Figures exclude Wal-Mart and other large format mass retailers.

Energizer 37.8%
Spectrum Brands 7.6
The Powerhouse Group 2.9
Matsushita 2.8
Private label 45.9
Other 3.0

Source: *U.S. Personal Care and Household Products Digest*, Citigroup Equity Research, February 24, 2006, p. 212, from ACNielsen.

★ 2046 ★
Batteries
SIC: 3692; NAICS: 335912

Top NICD/NIMD/Lithium-Ion/Lead Acid Brands, 2005

Brands are shown based on supermarket, drug store and discount store sales (excluding Wal-Mart) for the 52 weeks ended October 30, 2005.

	($ mil.)	Share
Energizer	$ 15.0	34.64%
GE	8.8	20.32
Ray O Vac	6.2	14.32
Duracell Accu	4.4	10.16
Duracell	2.3	5.31
Southwestern Bell	2.3	5.31
Panasonic	0.9	2.08
New Bright	0.7	1.62
Energizer Accu	0.5	1.15
Tyco	0.5	1.15
Other	1.7	3.93

Source: *MMR*, January 9, 2006, p. 67, from Information Resources Inc.

★ 2047 ★
Batteries
SIC: 3692; NAICS: 335912

Top Nickel Metal Hydride Makers, 2005

Sales increased 24.5% to $29.5 million. It has been up steadily since 2001. Figures exclude Wal-Mart and other large format mass retailers.

Energizer Holdings 54.6%
Procter & Gamble 23.1
Spectrum Brands 14.8
General Electric 4.7
Gemini Industries 0.4
Other 2.4

Source: *U.S. Personal Care and Household Products Digest*, Citigroup Equity Research, February 24, 2006, p. 65, from ACNielsen.

★ 2048 ★
Automotive Electronics
SIC: 3694; NAICS: 336322

Auto Electronics Market

The typical vehicle was equipped with auto electronics valued at $250 in 1980. The current value is $700. By 2010 the source estimates the value could be $1,000. Market shares are shown in percent.

Motorola Telematics	.80.0%
Other	.20.0

Source: *Global News Wire*, December 29, 2005, p. NA.

★ 2049 ★
Automotive Electronics
SIC: 3694; NAICS: 336322

Electrical Distribution Market in Europe

The industry is valued at $7 billion.

Delphi	.35.0%
Lear	.15.0
Valeo	.15.0
Other	.35.0

Source: *EDGAR Online 8-K Glimpse*, September 15, 2005, p. NA, from Lear Market Research, 2004.

★ 2050 ★
Automotive Electronics
SIC: 3694; NAICS: 336322

Electrical Distribution Market in North America

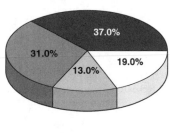

The industry is valued at $5 billion.

Delphi	.37.0%
Yazaki	.31.0
Lear	.13.0
Other	.19.0

Source: *EDGAR Online 8-K Glimpse*, September 15, 2005, p. NA, from Lear Market Research, 2004.

★ 2051 ★
Recording Media
SIC: 3695; NAICS: 334613

Leading DVD Hardware Firms, 2003 and 2005

The Blu-ray disc is competing with the HD (high definition) DVD in the DVD hardware market. According to Wikipedia, HD DVD has a single layer capacity of 15 GB and a dual-layer capacity of 30 GB. This is less than its primary competitor Blu-ray Disc, which supports 25GB for one layer, 50GB for two layers. HD DVD is promoted by Toshiba, NEC, Sanyo, Microsoft, HP, and Intel. HD DVD may be non-exclusively backed by three major studios: Paramount Pictures, Universal Studios and Warner Brothers. Market shares are shown for January - July 2005.

	2003	2005
Sony	21.9%	18.5%
Toshiba	11.1	9.4
Samsung	7.9	8.5
Panasonic/Technics	7.7	4.5
Philips/Magnavox	6.4	5.3
Cyberhome	2.1	11.5
Other	42.9	42.3

Source: *Screen Digest*, December 2005, p. 362, from *Screen Digest* analysis of NPD Techworld.

★ 2052 ★
Recording Media
SIC: 3695; NAICS: 334613

Leading DVD Hardware Firms in Western Europe, 2003 and 2005

Market shares are shown for January - July 2005.

	2003	2005
Philips	11.5%	13.5%
Sony	9.9	7.6
Samsung	7.5	5.9
Panasonic/Technics	5.7	3.4
LG	5.3	4.7
Shenzhen Electronics Group	4.8	3.2
Amstrad	0.0	3.8
Other	60.1	57.7

Source: *Screen Digest*, December 2005, p. 362, from *Screen Digest* analysis of NPD Techworld.

★ 2053 ★
Recording Media
SIC: 3695; NAICS: 334613

Top Blank Audio/Video Brands, 2006

Market shares are shown based on drug store stores for the 52 weeks March 19, 2006.

Sony V videocassette	7.3%
Maxell videocassette	7.2
Maxell CD-R	6.4
TDK Revue videocassette	5.7
Memorex CD-R	5.4
Sony videocassette	5.0
Maxell GX Silver videocassette	4.8
TDK CD-R	4.5
Fuji CD-R	4.2
Other	49.5

Source: *Chain Drug Review*, May 23, 2006, p. 79, from Information Resources Inc.

★ 2054 ★
Recording Media
SIC: 3695; NAICS: 334613

Top Blank CD-R Brands, 2005

Brands are shown based on supermarket, drug store and discount store sales (excluding Wal-Mart) for the 52 weeks ended October 30, 2005.

	($ mil.)	Share
Sony	$ 22.6	17.89%
TOK	20.8	16.47
Memorex	19.9	15.76
Maxell	12.5	9.90
Imation	12.4	9.82
Fuji	12.0	9.50
Khypermedia Egear	1.5	1.19
Napster	1.3	1.03
Hypermedia	0.4	0.32
Khypermedia	0.3	0.24
Other	22.6	17.89

Source: *MMR*, January 9, 2006, p. 67, from Information Resources Inc.

★ 2055 ★
Recording Media
SIC: 3695; NAICS: 334613

Top Blank Tape Makers, 2005

Market shares are shown based on supermarket, drug store and mass merchandiser sales (excluding Wal-Mart) for the 52 weeks ended June 12, 2005.

Sony Tape Sales	32.1%
Maxell Corp. of America	23.8
TDK Elec. Corp.	22.9
Fuji Photo Film	18.1
Other	3.1

Source: *Grocery Headquarters*, August 2005, p. S6, from Information Resources Inc.

★ 2056 ★
Recording Media
SIC: 3695; NAICS: 334613

Top Blank Video Tape Brands, 2005

Brands are shown based on supermarket, drug store and discount store sales (excluding Wal-Mart) for the 52 weeks ended October 30, 2005.

	($ mil.)	Share
Sony	$ 28.4	14.35%
Sony V	17.0	8.59
Fuji	16.3	8.24
Maxell	14.7	7.43
TDK Revue	14.5	7.33
TDK	14.4	7.28
Fuji HQ	12.1	6.11
Maxell GX Silver	10.1	5.10
Sony HMP	7.0	3.54
Maxell HGX Gold	5.6	2.83
Other	57.8	29.21

Source: *MMR*, January 9, 2006, p. 67, from Information Resources Inc.

★ 2057 ★
Access Control Devices
SIC: 3699; NAICS: 335999

Access Control Demand

Demand is forecast to increase 10 each year to $7.2 billion. Anti-terrorism measures and lower-cost systems will help drive the market.

	2009	2014	Share
Card	$ 2,350	$ 3,400	27.98%
Biometric	1,045	3,075	25.31
Software	930	1,500	12.35
Keypad/combination	880	1,200	9.88
Other	1,985	2,975	24.49

Source: *Terror Response Technology Report*, November 2, 2005, p. NA, from Freedonia Group.

★ 2058 ★
Biometrics
SIC: 3699; NAICS: 335999

Biometric Market Worldwide by Application, 2006

Spending is expected to increase from $2.1 billion to $5.8 billion by the end of the decade. One of the barriers to adopting the devices is that businesses feel the technology is unproven or untrustworthy.

Fingerprint	43.6%
Face	19.0
Middleware	11.5
Hand geometry	8.8
Iris	7.1
Voice	4.4
Other	15.6

Source: *Security Director's Report*, March 2006, p. 8, from *Biometrics Market and Industry Report 2006-2010*.

★ 2059 ★
Biometrics
SIC: 3699; NAICS: 335999

Biometrics Industry

Viisage announced plans to purchase main rival Identix. The new company will possess 80% of the market. Viisage is a leader in the field of fingerprinting and secure documents. It takes 40% of the driver's-license market and all of the passport market on its own.

Viisage	80.0%
Other	20.0

Source: *Knight-Ridder/Tribune Business News*, January 13, 2006, p. NA.

★ 2060 ★
Biometrics
SIC: 3699; NAICS: 335999

Fingerprint Technology by Application, 2008

Sales are shown in millions of dollars.

	($ mil.)	Share
Civil ID	$ 262.1	26.95%
Access control/attendants	217.7	22.39
PC/enterprise network access	200.2	20.59
Retail/ATM/POS	137.1	14.10
Device access	82.2	8.45
E-commerce/telephony	55.5	5.71
Criminal ID	17.7	1.82

Source: *Electronic Business*, September 2005, p. 26, from International Biometric Group.